X-MEN
Age of APOCALYPSE
THE COMPLETE EPIC
BOOK 1

WRITERS
Howard Mackie, John Francis Moore, Brian K. Vaughan, Scott Lobdell,
Ralph Macchio, Terry Kavanagh & Judd Winick

PENCILERS
Terry Dodson, Steve Epting, Nick Napolitano, Joe Bennett,
Ian Churchill, Roger Cruz, Alan Davis & Trevor McCarthy

INKERS
Klaus Janson, Al Milgrom, Joe Pimentel, Scott Hanna, Al Vey,
Steve Moncuse, Bob Wiacek, Bud Larosa, Wellington Diaz, Mark Farmer,
Robin Riggs, Tyson McAdoo, Rodney Ramos, Rick Ketcham & Norm Rapmund

COLORS
Matt Webb, Kevin Tinsley, Gloria Vasquez,
Mike Thomas, Tom Vincent & Liquid!

LETTERS
Richard Starkings & Comicraft

COVER ART
Joe Madureira & Tim Townsend

COVER COLORS
Avalon's Matt Milla

EDITORS: Kelly Corvese, Matt Idelson, Mark Powers & Jaye Gardner

SENIOR EDITOR, SPECIAL PROJECTS: Jeff Youngquist
ASSISTANT EDITOR: Jennifer Grünwald
DIRECTOR OF SALES: David Gabriel
PRODUCTION: Jerron Quality Color
BOOK DESIGNERS: Jeof Vita & Carrie Beadle
CREATIVE DIRECTOR: Tom Marvelli

EDITOR IN CHIEF: Joe Quesada
PUBLISHER: Dan Buckley

SPECIAL THANKS TO ERIC J. MOREELS AND POND SCUM

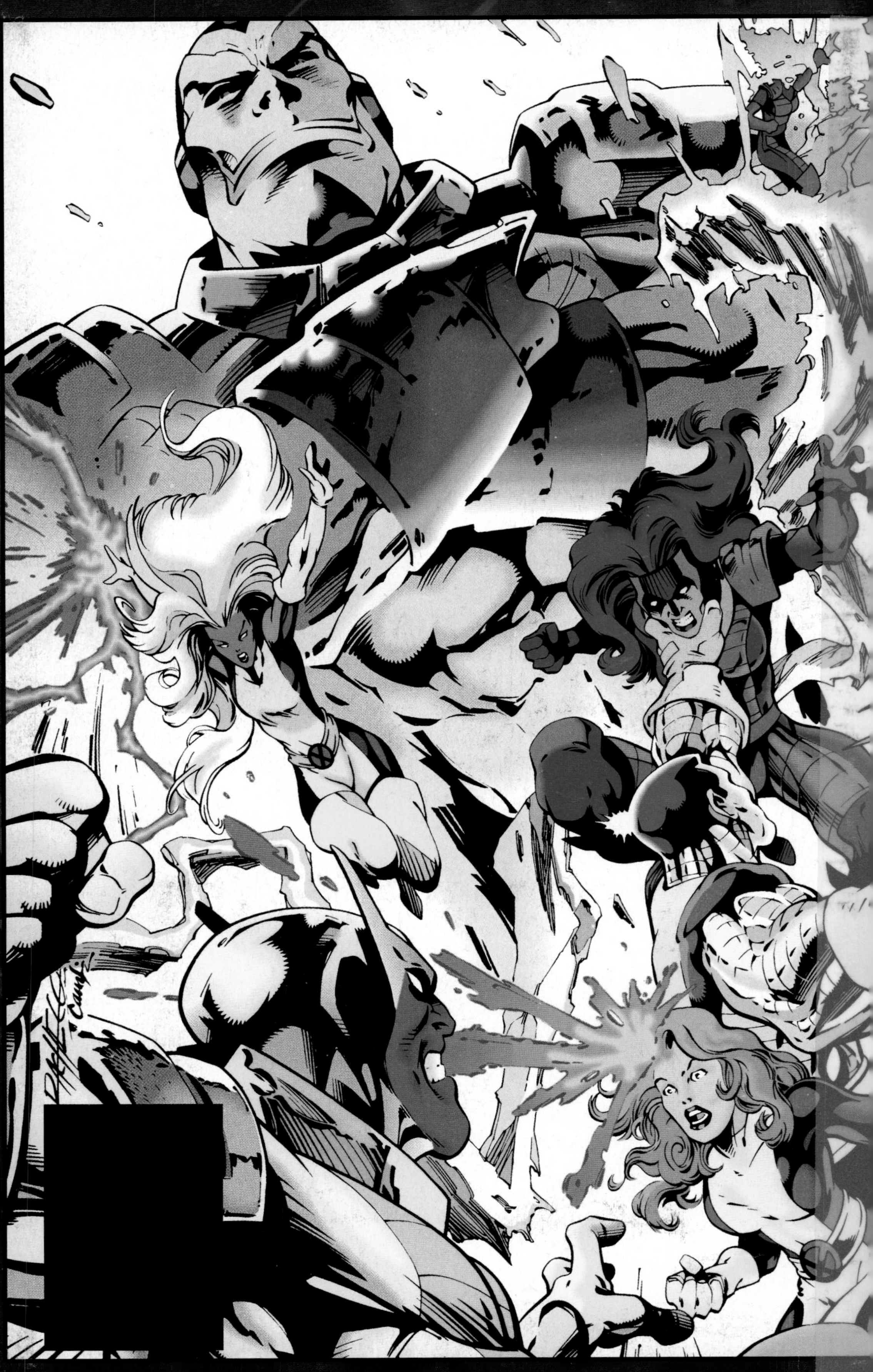

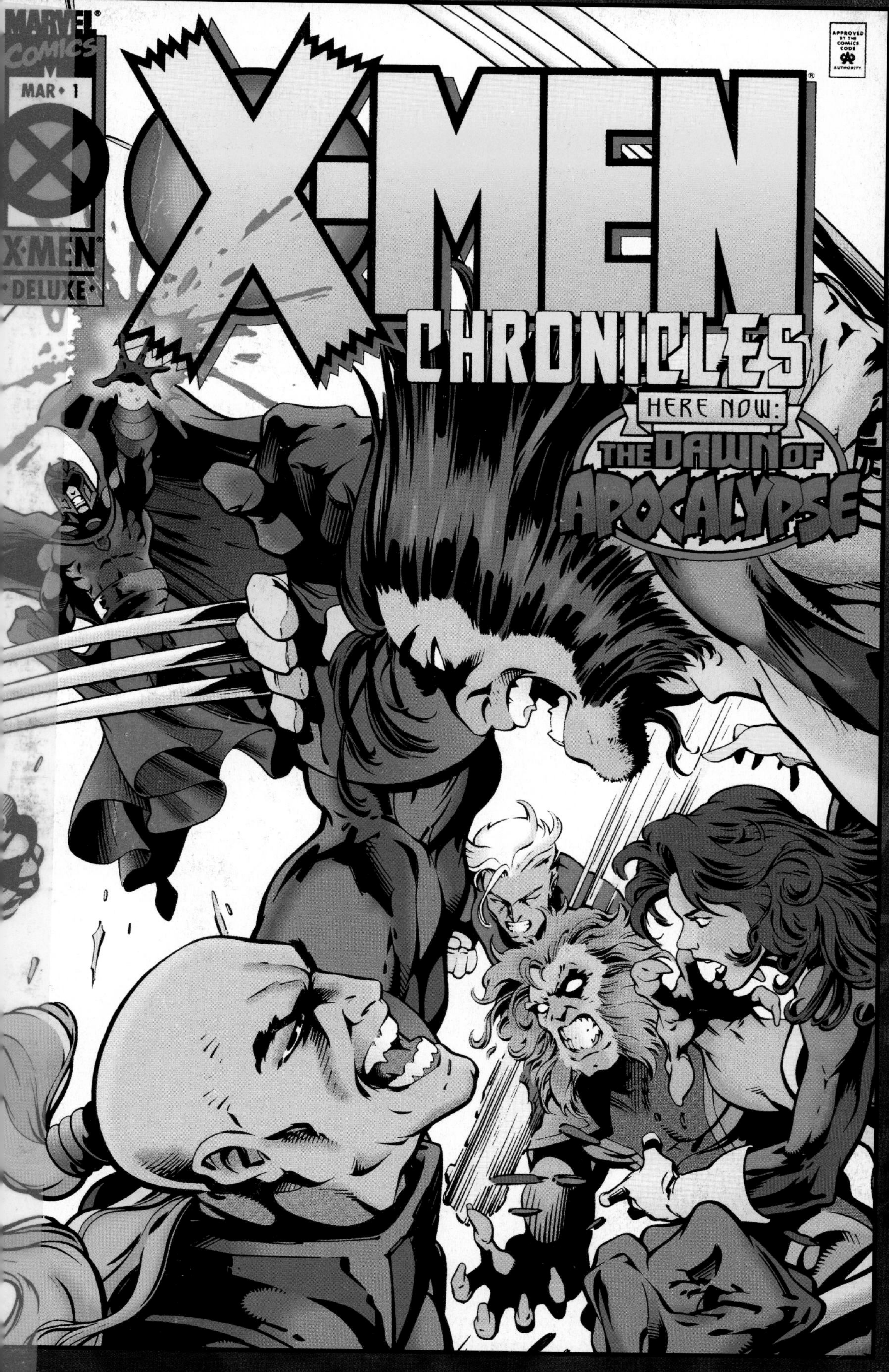

MARVEL COMICS
MAR 1
X-MEN DELUXE
APPROVED BY THE COMICS CODE AUTHORITY
X-MEN
CHRONICLES
HERE NOW:
THE DAWN OF APOCALYPSE

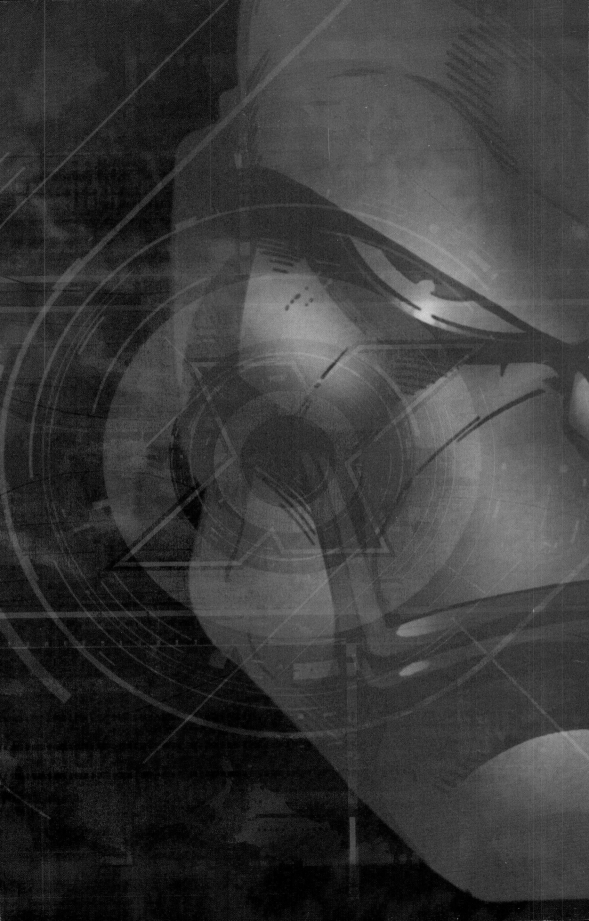

Wundagore Mountain — called the HAUNTED MOUNTAIN — in EASTERN EUROPE.

He is called MAGNETO.

An evolutionary twist of fate has given him the power to control and manipulate magnetic fields.

He and others like him, born with the genetic potential for great powers, are known as MUTANTS.

The world of humans fears them for being different...and hates them for being gifted.

And MAGNETO senses that the hatred is growing and darker times are at hand.

STAN LEE PRESENTS

THE FIRST ADVENTURE OF MAGNETO'S ASTONISHING

ORIGINS X-MEN

| HOWARD MACKIE WRITER | TERRY DODSON PENCILER | KLAUS JANSON INKER | MATT WEBB COLORIST | STARKINGS/ COMICRAFT LETTERING | KELLY CORVESE EDITOR | BOB HARRAS CHIEF |

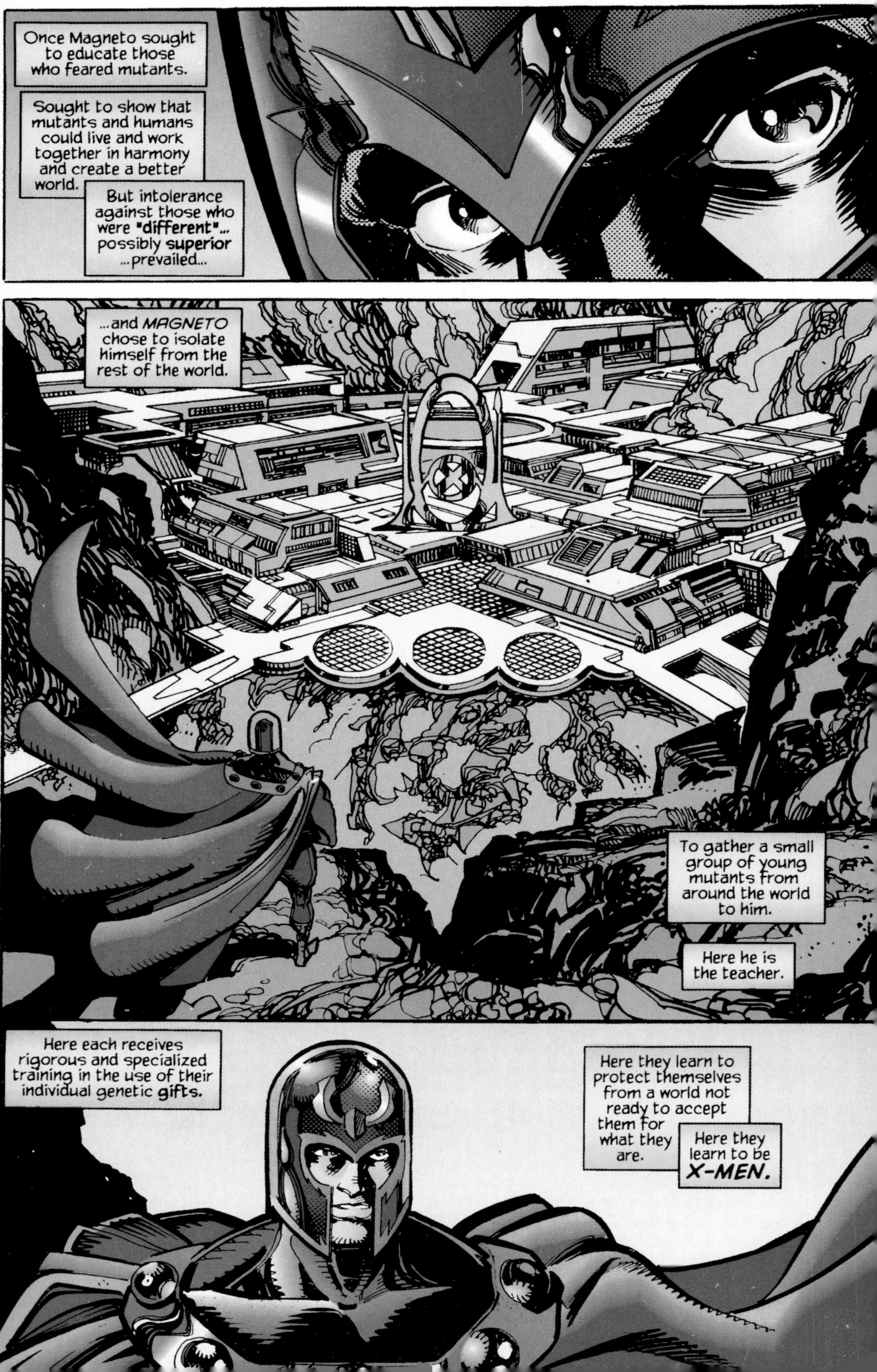
Once Magneto sought to educate those who feared mutants.
Sought to show that mutants and humans could live and work together in harmony and create a better world.
But intolerance against those who were "different"... possibly superior ...prevailed...
...and MAGNETO chose to isolate himself from the rest of the world.
To gather a small group of young mutants from around the world to him.
Here he is the teacher.
Here each receives rigorous and specialized training in the use of their individual genetic gifts.
Here they learn to protect themselves from a world not ready to accept them for what they are.
Here they learn to be X-MEN.

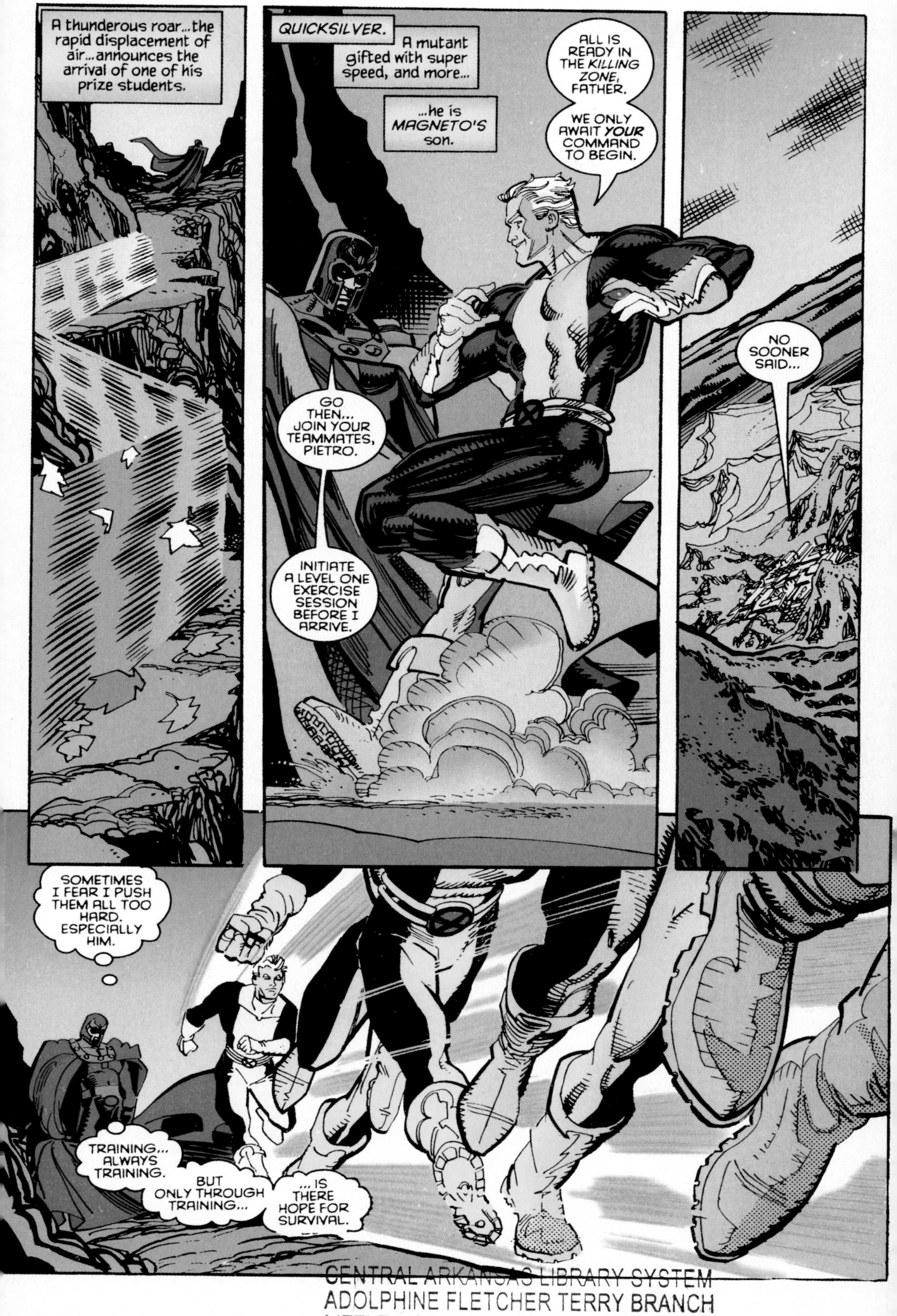
A thunderous roar...the rapid displacement of air...announces the arrival of one of his prize students.
QUICKSILVER.
A mutant gifted with super speed, and more...
...he is MAGNETO'S son.
ALL IS READY IN THE KILLING ZONE, FATHER.
WE ONLY AWAIT YOUR COMMAND TO BEGIN.
GO THEN... JOIN YOUR TEAMMATES, PIETRO.
INITIATE A LEVEL ONE EXERCISE SESSION BEFORE I ARRIVE.
NO SOONER SAID...
SOMETIMES I FEAR I PUSH THEM ALL TOO HARD. ESPECIALLY HIM.
TRAINING... ALWAYS TRAINING.
BUT ONLY THROUGH TRAINING...
...IS THERE HOPE FOR SURVIVAL.

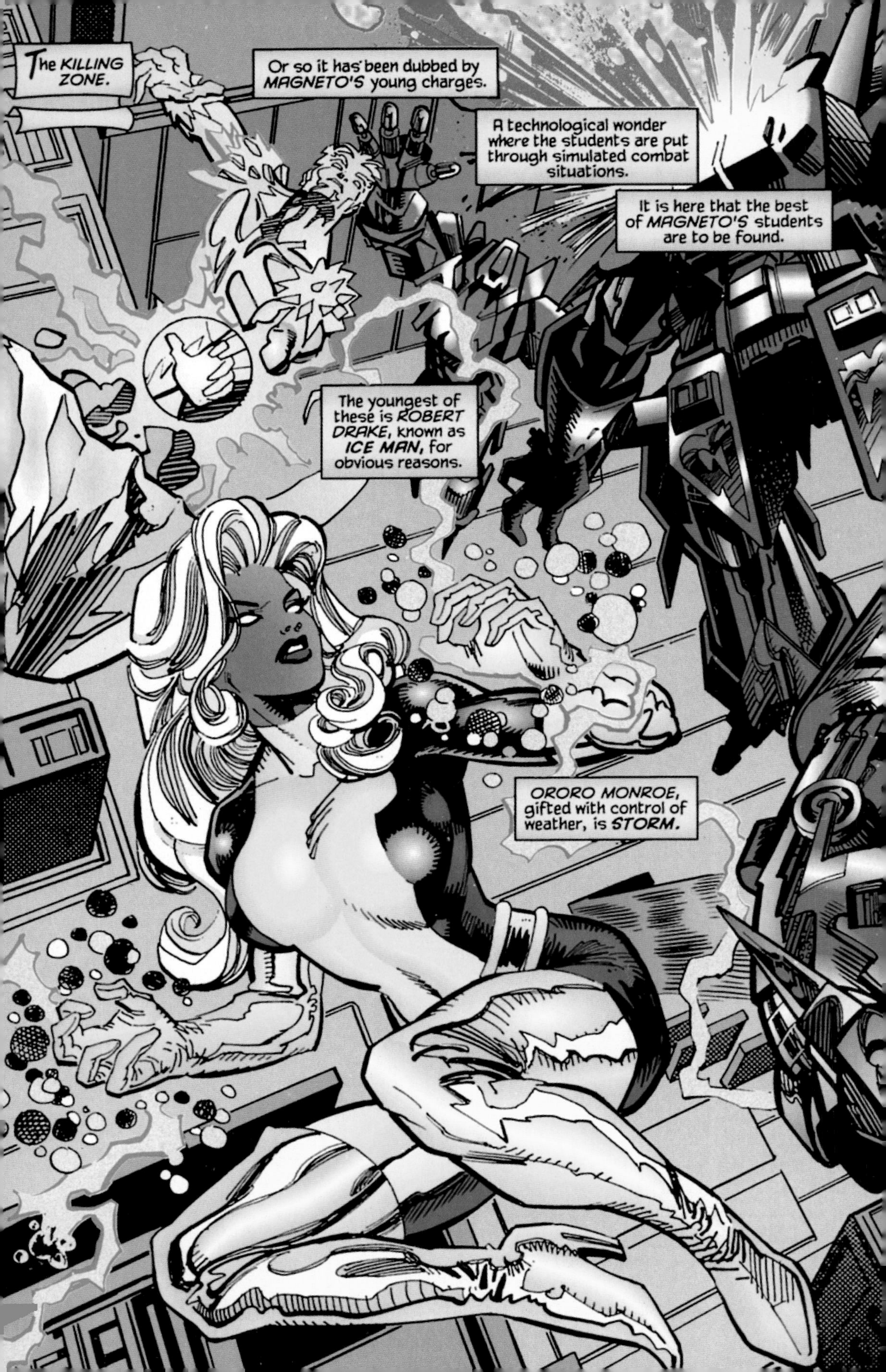
The KILLING ZONE.
Or so it has been dubbed by MAGNETO'S young charges.
A technological wonder where the students are put through simulated combat situations.
It is here that the best of MAGNETO'S students are to be found.
The youngest of these is ROBERT DRAKE, known as ICE MAN, for obvious reasons.
ORORO MONROE, gifted with control of weather, is STORM.

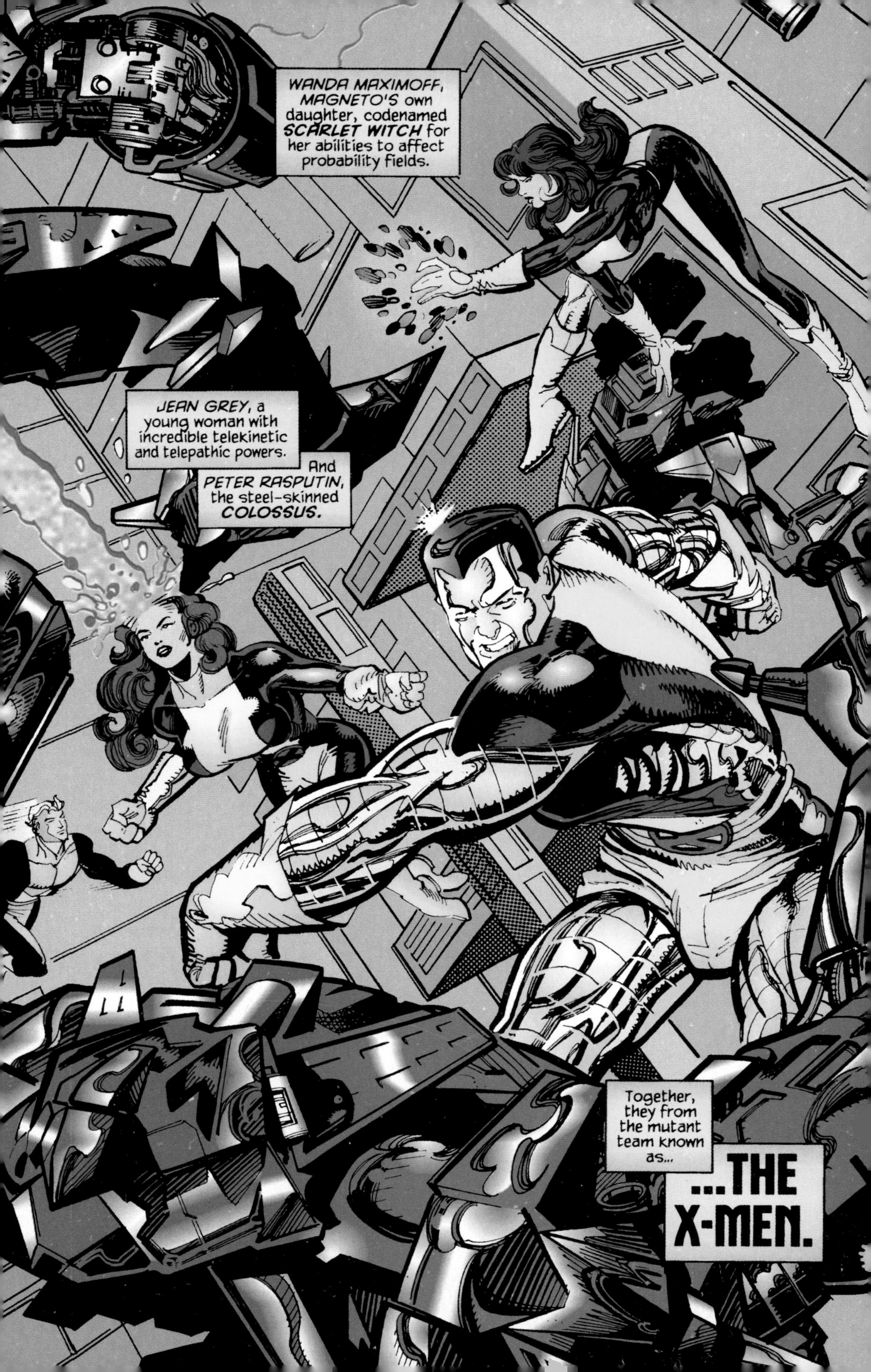
WANDA MAXIMOFF, MAGNETO'S own daughter, codenamed SCARLET WITCH for her abilities to affect probability fields.
JEAN GREY, a young woman with incredible telekinetic and telepathic powers.
And PETER RASPUTIN, the steel-skinned COLOSSUS.
Together, they from the mutant team known as...
...THE X-MEN.

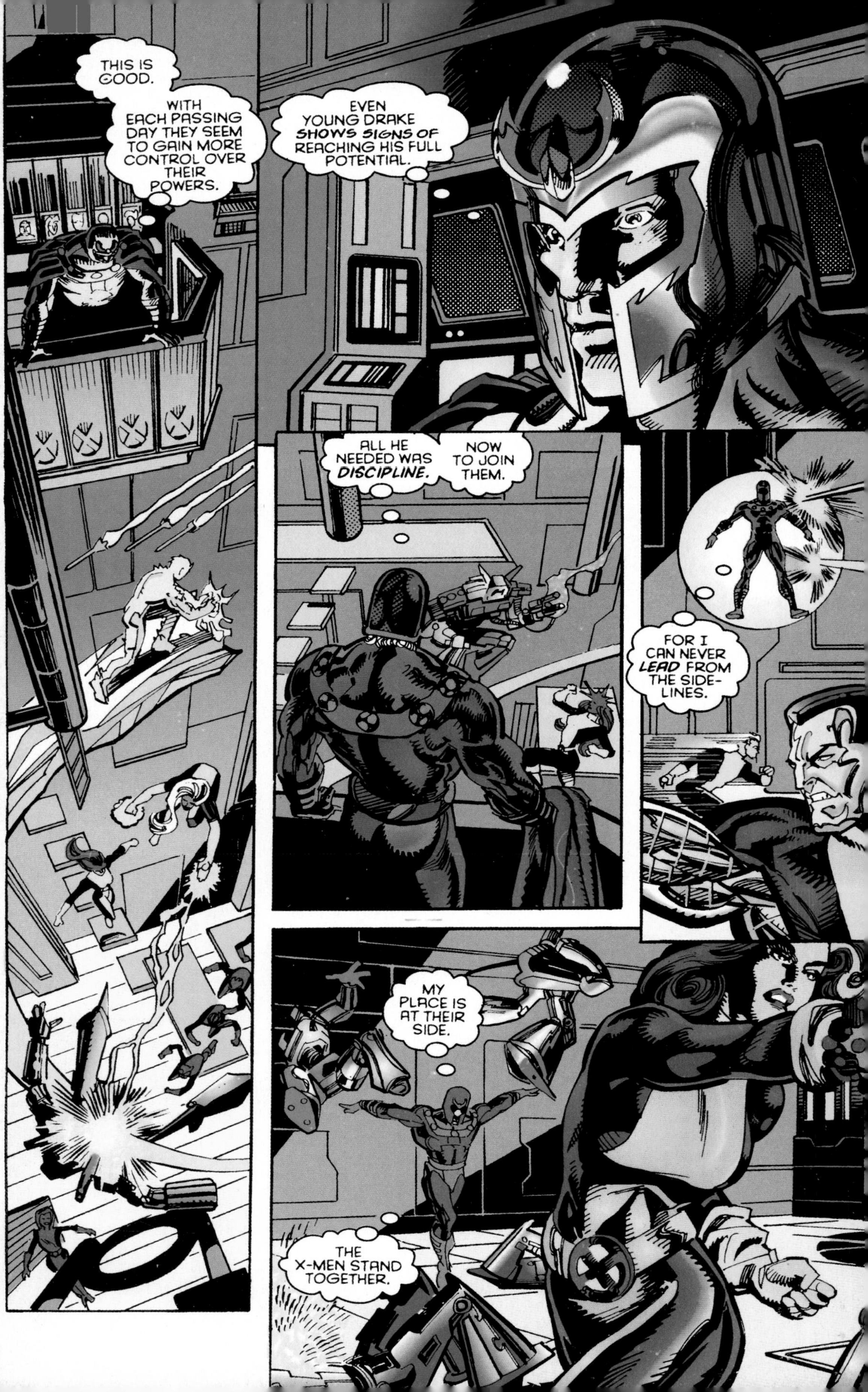

THIS IS GOOD.
WITH EACH PASSING DAY THEY SEEM TO GAIN MORE CONTROL OVER THEIR POWERS.
EVEN YOUNG DRAKE SHOWS SIGNS OF REACHING HIS FULL POTENTIAL.
ALL HE NEEDED WAS DISCIPLINE.
NOW TO JOIN THEM.
FOR I CAN NEVER LEAD FROM THE SIDE-LINES.
MY PLACE IS AT THEIR SIDE.
THE X-MEN STAND TOGETHER.

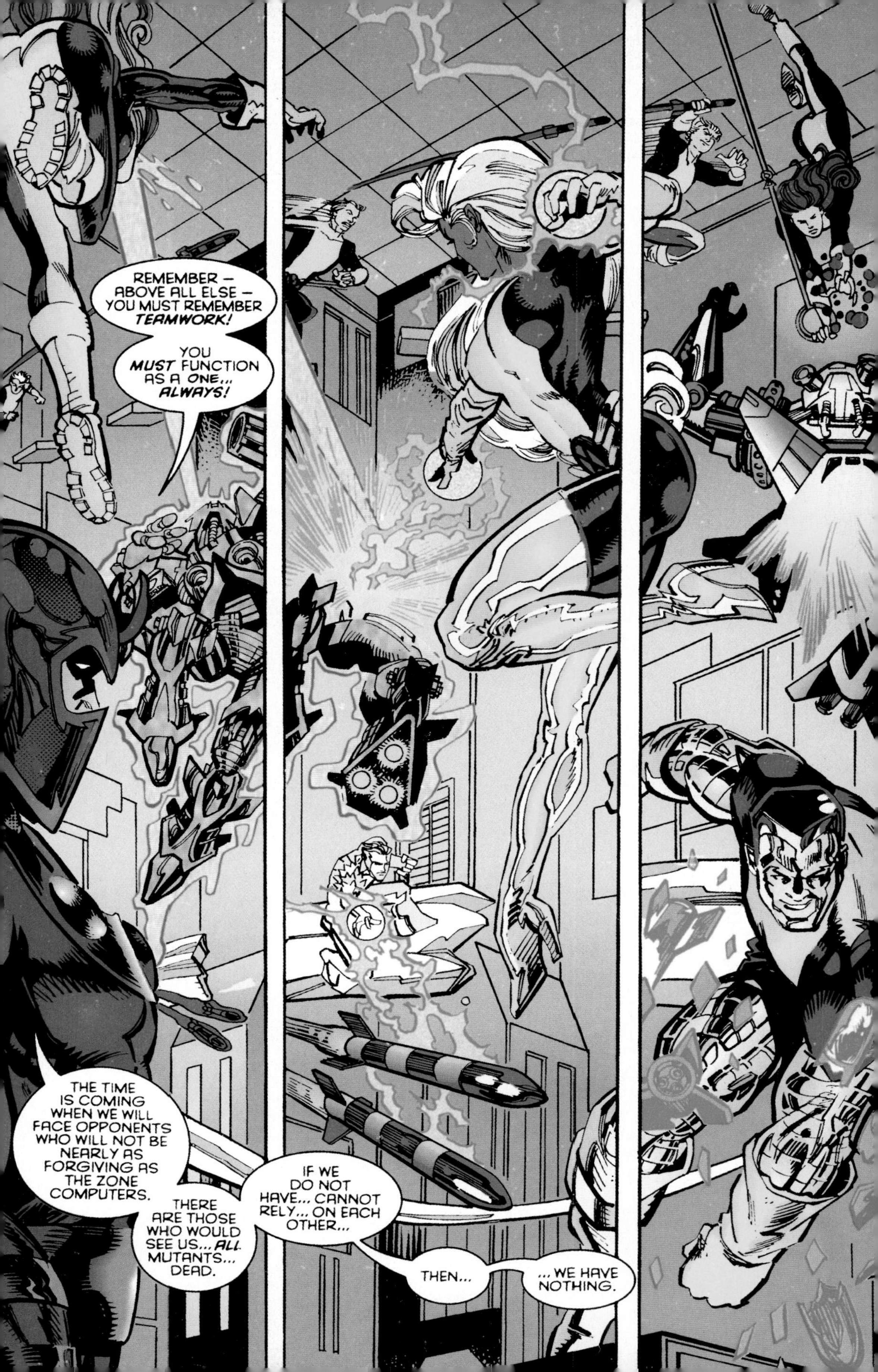
REMEMBER — ABOVE ALL ELSE — YOU MUST REMEMBER *TEAMWORK!*
YOU *MUST* FUNCTION AS A *ONE*... *ALWAYS!*
THE TIME IS COMING WHEN WE WILL FACE OPPONENTS WHO WILL NOT BE NEARLY AS FORGIVING AS THE ZONE COMPUTERS.
THERE ARE THOSE WHO WOULD SEE US... *ALL* MUTANTS... DEAD.
IF WE DO NOT HAVE... CANNOT RELY... ON EACH OTHER...
THEN...
...WE HAVE NOTHING.

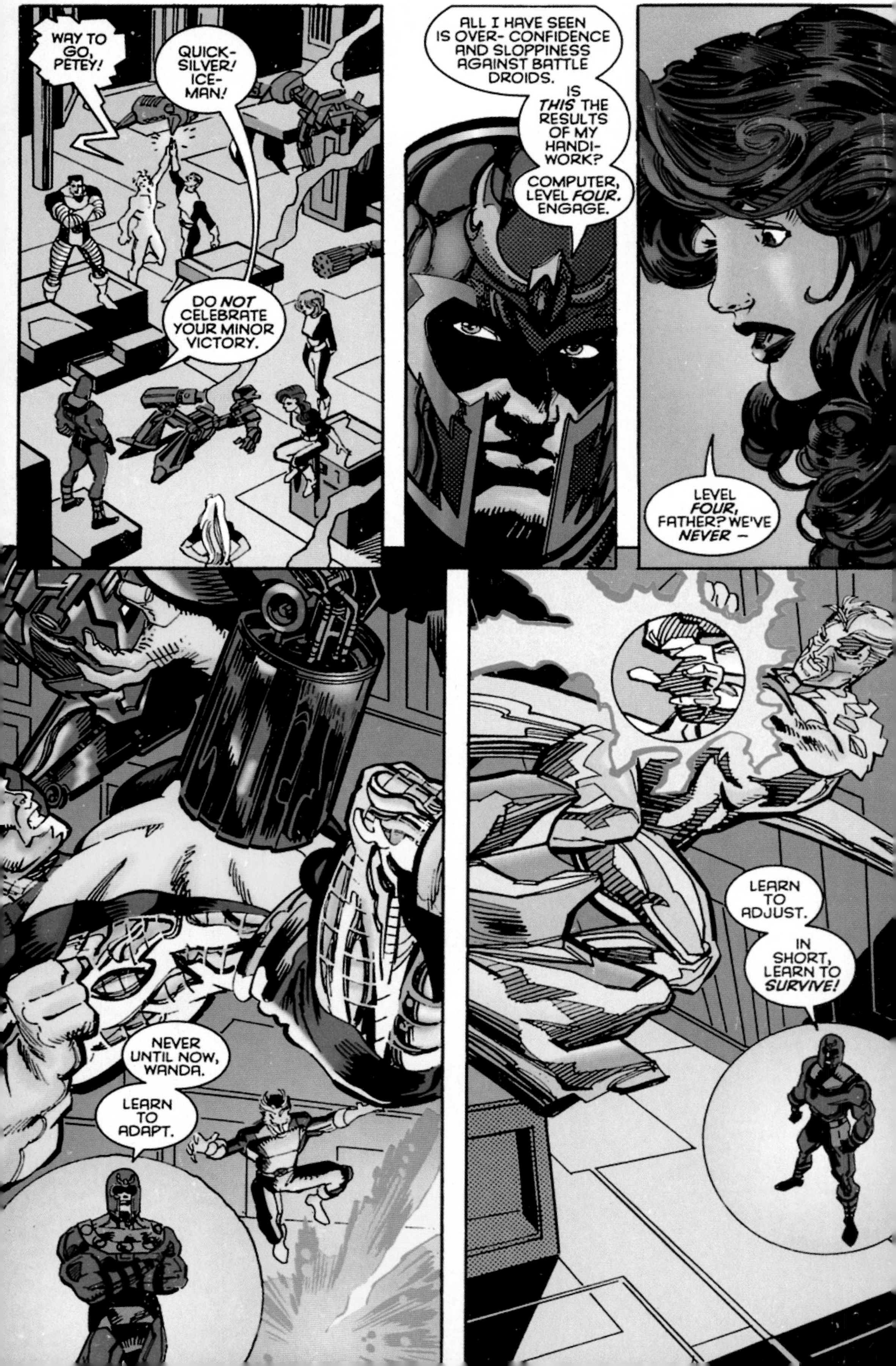

WAY TO GO, PETEY!
QUICK-SILVER! ICE-MAN!
DO NOT CELEBRATE YOUR MINOR VICTORY.
ALL I HAVE SEEN IS OVER- CONFIDENCE AND SLOPPINESS AGAINST BATTLE DROIDS.
IS THIS THE RESULTS OF MY HANDI-WORK?
COMPUTER, LEVEL FOUR. ENGAGE.
LEVEL FOUR, FATHER? WE'VE NEVER –
NEVER UNTIL NOW, WANDA.
LEARN TO ADAPT.
LEARN TO ADJUST.
IN SHORT, LEARN TO SURVIVE!

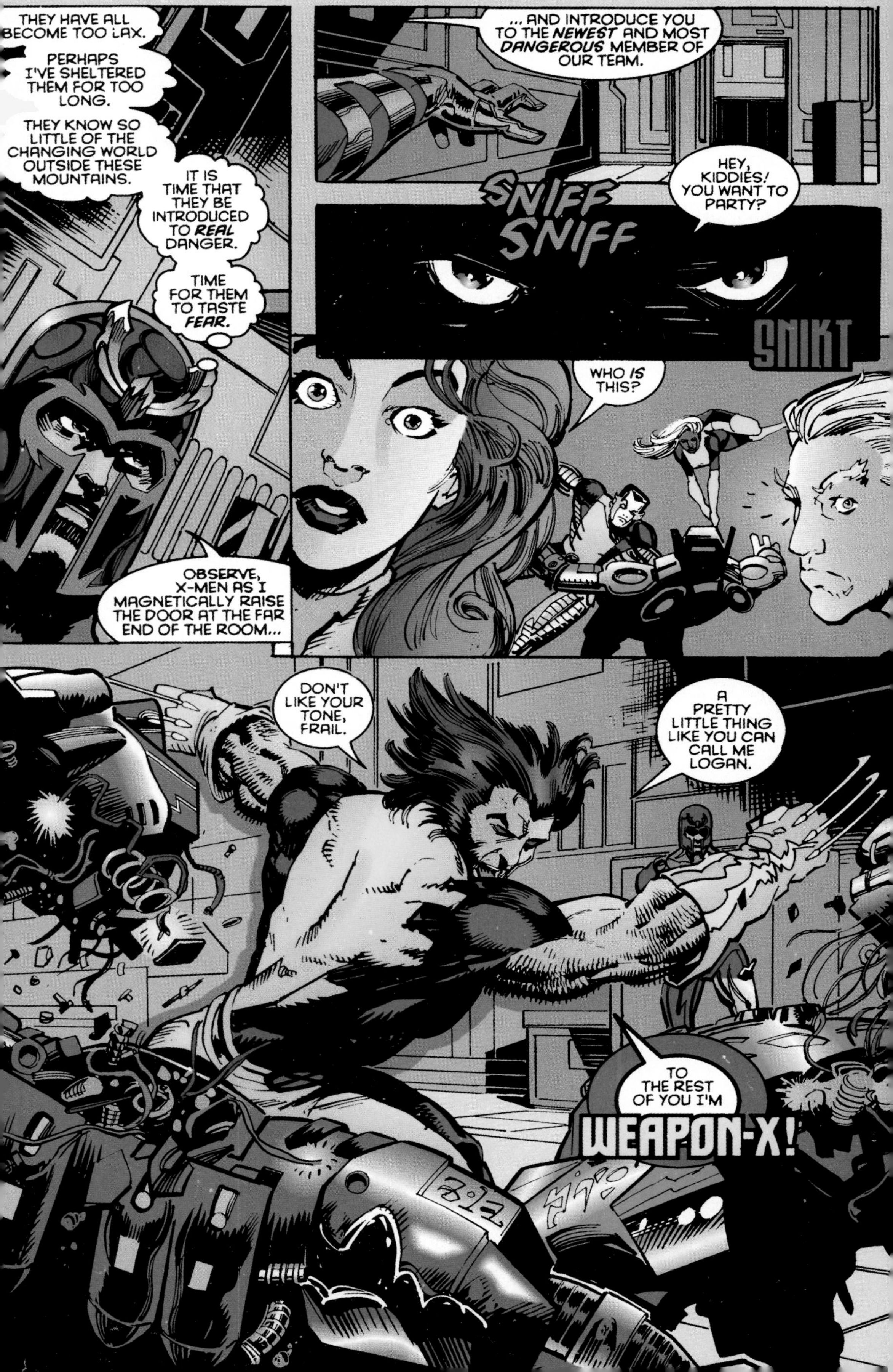
THEY HAVE ALL BECOME TOO LAX.
PERHAPS I'VE SHELTERED THEM FOR TOO LONG.
THEY KNOW SO LITTLE OF THE CHANGING WORLD OUTSIDE THESE MOUNTAINS.
IT IS TIME THAT THEY BE INTRODUCED TO REAL DANGER.
TIME FOR THEM TO TASTE FEAR.
OBSERVE, X-MEN AS I MAGNETICALLY RAISE THE DOOR AT THE FAR END OF THE ROOM...
... AND INTRODUCE YOU TO THE NEWEST AND MOST DANGEROUS MEMBER OF OUR TEAM.
SNIFF SNIFF
HEY, KIDDIES! YOU WANT TO PARTY?
SNIKT
WHO IS THIS?
DON'T LIKE YOUR TONE, FRAIL.
A PRETTY LITTLE THING LIKE YOU CAN CALL ME LOGAN.
TO THE REST OF YOU I'M
WEAPON-X!

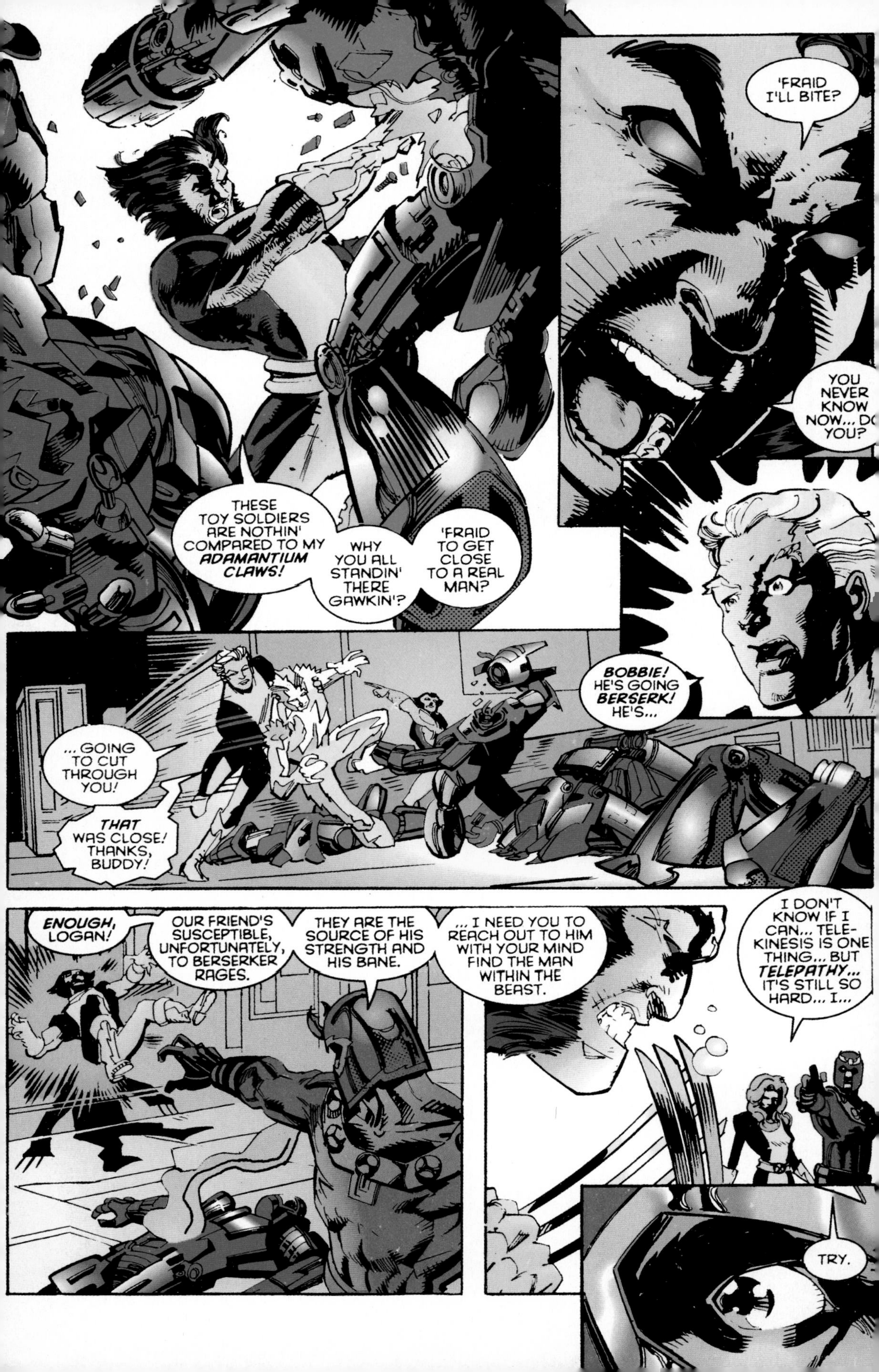
'FRAID I'LL BITE?
YOU NEVER KNOW NOW... DO YOU?
THESE TOY SOLDIERS ARE NOTHIN' COMPARED TO MY ADAMANTIUM CLAWS!
WHY YOU ALL STANDIN' THERE GAWKIN'?
'FRAID TO GET CLOSE TO A REAL MAN?
BOBBIE! HE'S GOING BERSERK! HE'S...
...GOING TO CUT THROUGH YOU!
THAT WAS CLOSE! THANKS, BUDDY!
ENOUGH, LOGAN!
OUR FRIEND'S SUSCEPTIBLE, UNFORTUNATELY, TO BERSERKER RAGES.
THEY ARE THE SOURCE OF HIS STRENGTH AND HIS BANE.
...I NEED YOU TO REACH OUT TO HIM WITH YOUR MIND FIND THE MAN WITHIN THE BEAST.
I DON'T KNOW IF I CAN... TELEKINESIS IS ONE THING... BUT TELEPATHY... IT'S STILL SO HARD... I...
TRY.

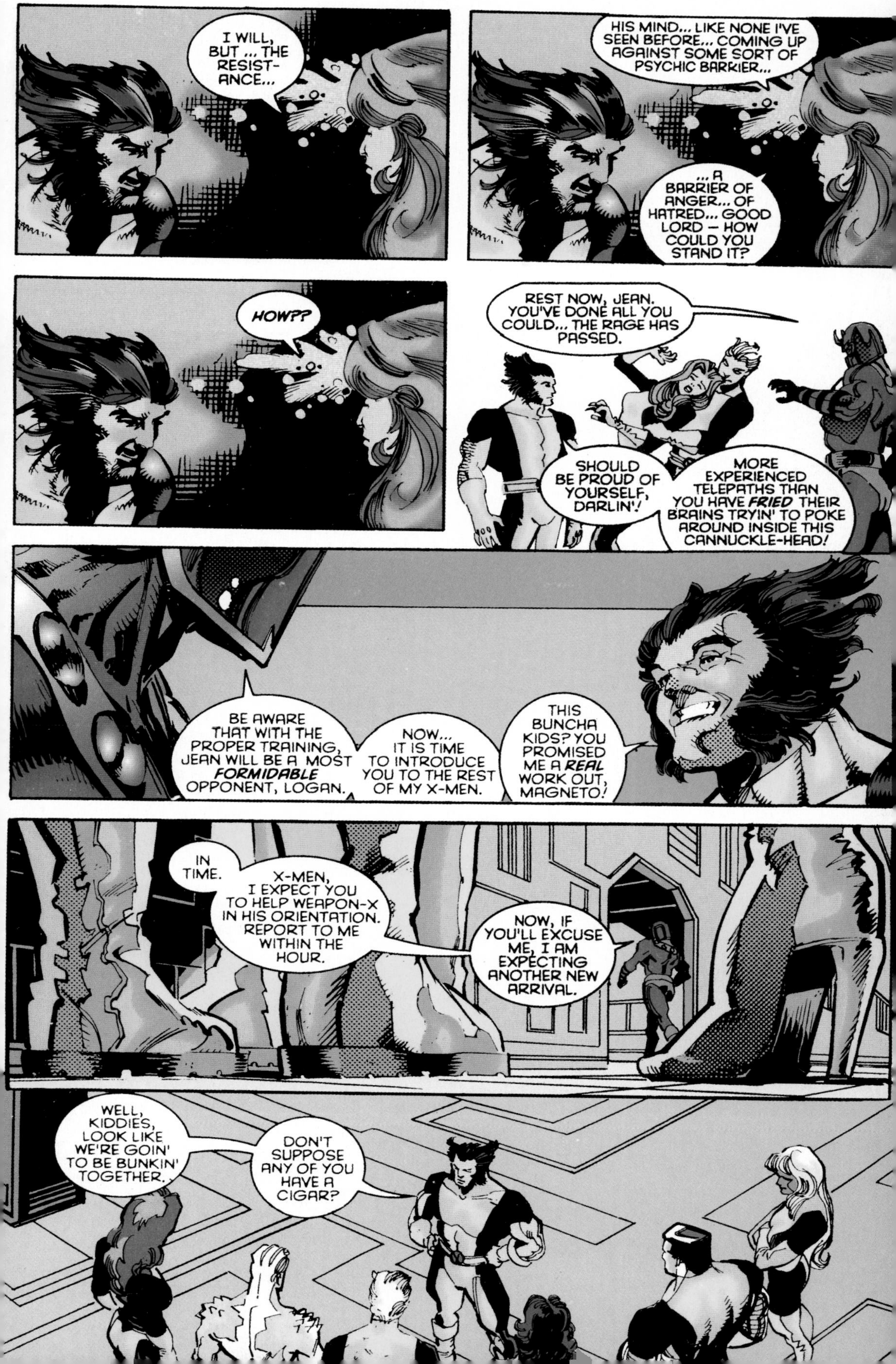
I WILL, BUT ... THE RESIST-ANCE...
HIS MIND... LIKE NONE I'VE SEEN BEFORE... COMING UP AGAINST SOME SORT OF PSYCHIC BARRIER...
... A BARRIER OF ANGER... OF HATRED... GOOD LORD — HOW COULD YOU STAND IT?
HOW??
REST NOW, JEAN. YOU'VE DONE ALL YOU COULD... THE RAGE HAS PASSED.
SHOULD BE PROUD OF YOURSELF, DARLIN'!
MORE EXPERIENCED TELEPATHS THAN YOU HAVE FRIED THEIR BRAINS TRYIN' TO POKE AROUND INSIDE THIS CANNUCKLE-HEAD!
BE AWARE THAT WITH THE PROPER TRAINING, JEAN WILL BE A MOST FORMIDABLE OPPONENT, LOGAN.
NOW... IT IS TIME TO INTRODUCE YOU TO THE REST OF MY X-MEN.
THIS BUNCHA KIDS? YOU PROMISED ME A REAL WORK OUT, MAGNETO!
IN TIME.
X-MEN, I EXPECT YOU TO HELP WEAPON-X IN HIS ORIENTATION. REPORT TO ME WITHIN THE HOUR.
NOW, IF YOU'LL EXCUSE ME, I AM EXPECTING ANOTHER NEW ARRIVAL.
WELL, KIDDIES, LOOK LIKE WE'RE GOIN' TO BE BUNKIN' TOGETHER.
DON'T SUPPOSE ANY OF YOU HAVE A CIGAR?

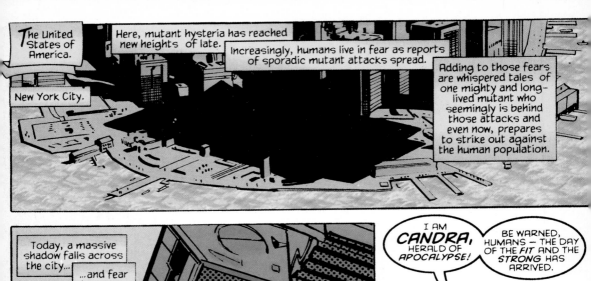

The United States of America.

New York City.

Here, mutant hysteria has reached new heights of late.

Increasingly, humans live in fear as reports of sporadic mutant attacks spread.

Adding to those fears are whispered tales of one mighty and long-lived mutant who seemingly is behind those attacks and even now, prepares to strike out against the human population.

Today, a massive shadow falls across the city...

...and fear becomes reality.

All eyes are drawn upward, and behold a tremendous floating fortress which fills the sky.

From its mammoth bow, a holographic projection issues forth, towering over the city...

...and words of doom echo through the streets.

I AM **CANDRA,** HERALD OF *APOCALYPSE!*

BE WARNED, HUMANS — THE DAY OF THE *FIT* AND THE *STRONG* HAS ARRIVED.

THE WORLD IS *YOURS* NO LONGER. SOON, IT SHALL BE DELIVERED INTO THE HANDS OF THOSE EVOLUTION HAS DEEMED ITS *INHERITORS* — *HOMO SUPERIOR.*

The word is carried forth.

The future has arrived...

...and a nation trembles.

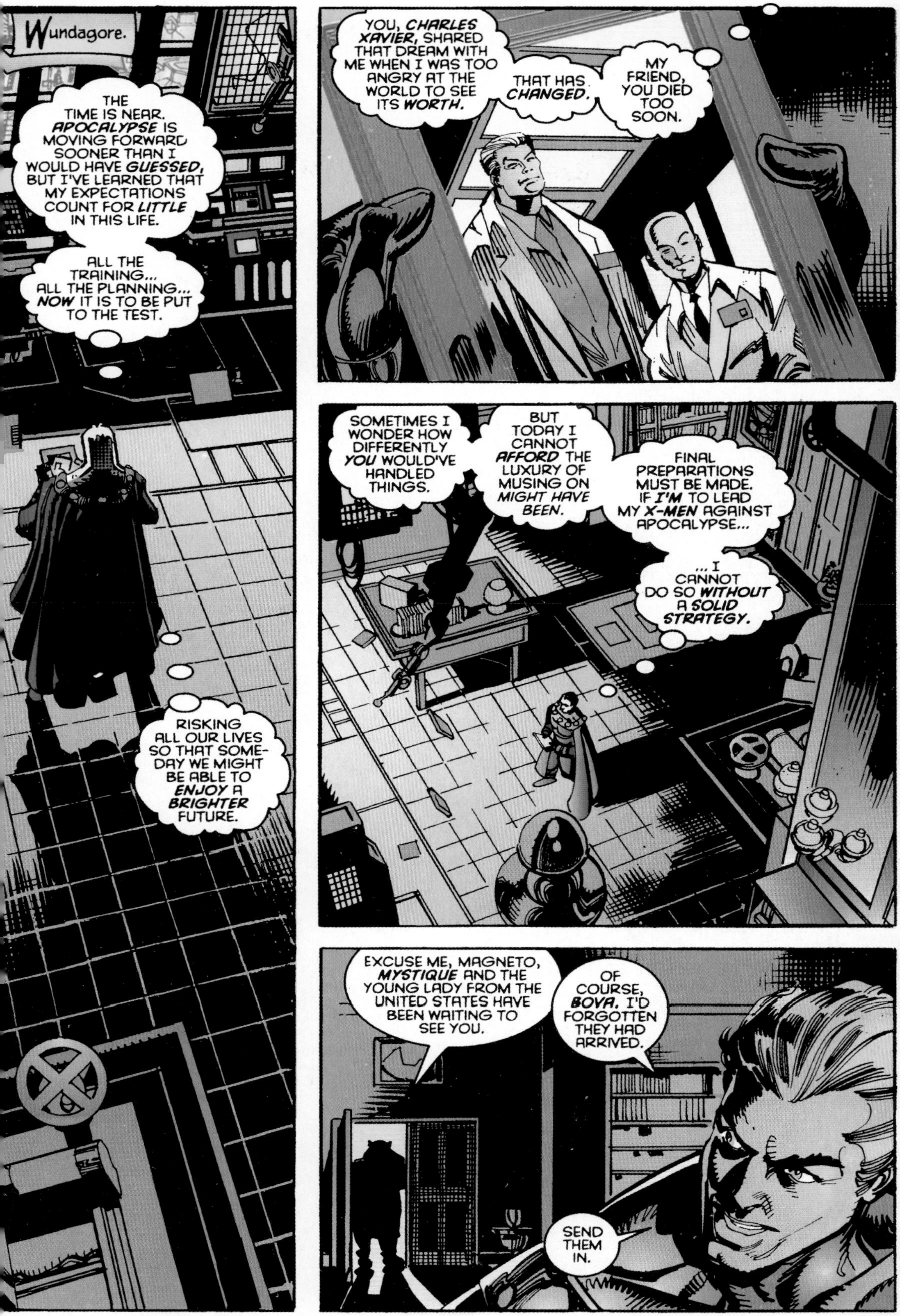
Wundagore.
THE TIME IS NEAR. APOCALYPSE IS MOVING FORWARD SOONER THAN I WOULD HAVE GUESSED, BUT I'VE LEARNED THAT MY EXPECTATIONS COUNT FOR LITTLE IN THIS LIFE.
ALL THE TRAINING... ALL THE PLANNING... NOW IT IS TO BE PUT TO THE TEST.
RISKING ALL OUR LIVES SO THAT SOME-DAY WE MIGHT BE ABLE TO ENJOY A BRIGHTER FUTURE.
YOU, CHARLES XAVIER, SHARED THAT DREAM WITH ME WHEN I WAS TOO ANGRY AT THE WORLD TO SEE ITS WORTH.
THAT HAS CHANGED.
MY FRIEND, YOU DIED TOO SOON.
SOMETIMES I WONDER HOW DIFFERENTLY YOU WOULD'VE HANDLED THINGS.
BUT TODAY I CANNOT AFFORD THE LUXURY OF MUSING ON MIGHT HAVE BEEN.
FINAL PREPARATIONS MUST BE MADE. IF I'M TO LEAD MY X-MEN AGAINST APOCALYPSE...
... I CANNOT DO SO WITHOUT A SOLID STRATEGY.
EXCUSE ME, MAGNETO, MYSTIQUE AND THE YOUNG LADY FROM THE UNITED STATES HAVE BEEN WAITING TO SEE YOU.
OF COURSE, BOVA. I'D FORGOTTEN THEY HAD ARRIVED.
SEND THEM IN.

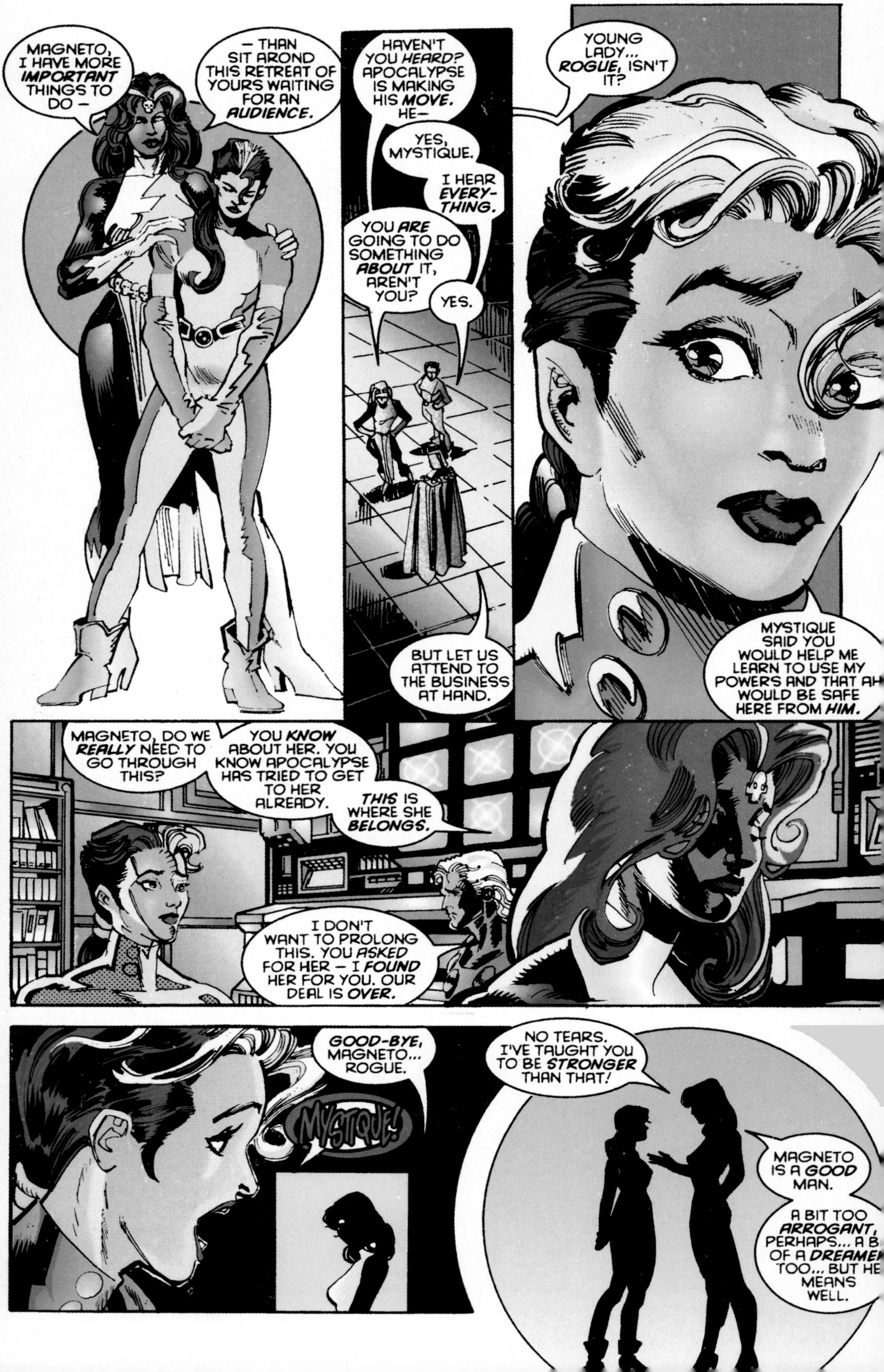
MAGNETO, I HAVE MORE IMPORTANT THINGS TO DO –
– THAN SIT AROND THIS RETREAT OF YOURS WAITING FOR AN AUDIENCE.
HAVEN'T YOU HEARD? APOCALYPSE IS MAKING HIS MOVE. HE–
YES, MYSTIQUE.
I HEAR EVERYTHING.
YOU ARE GOING TO DO SOMETHING ABOUT IT, AREN'T YOU?
YES.
BUT LET US ATTEND TO THE BUSINESS AT HAND.
YOUNG LADY... ROGUE, ISN'T IT?
MYSTIQUE SAID YOU WOULD HELP ME LEARN TO USE MY POWERS AND THAT AH WOULD BE SAFE HERE FROM HIM.
MAGNETO, DO WE REALLY NEED TO GO THROUGH THIS?
YOU KNOW ABOUT HER. YOU KNOW APOCALYPSE HAS TRIED TO GET TO HER ALREADY.
THIS IS WHERE SHE BELONGS.
I DON'T WANT TO PROLONG THIS. YOU ASKED FOR HER – I FOUND HER FOR YOU. OUR DEAL IS OVER.
GOOD-BYE, MAGNETO... ROGUE.
MYSTIQUE!
NO TEARS. I'VE TAUGHT YOU TO BE STRONGER THAN THAT!
MAGNETO IS A GOOD MAN.
A BIT TOO ARROGANT, PERHAPS... A B OF A DREAME TOO... BUT HE MEANS WELL.

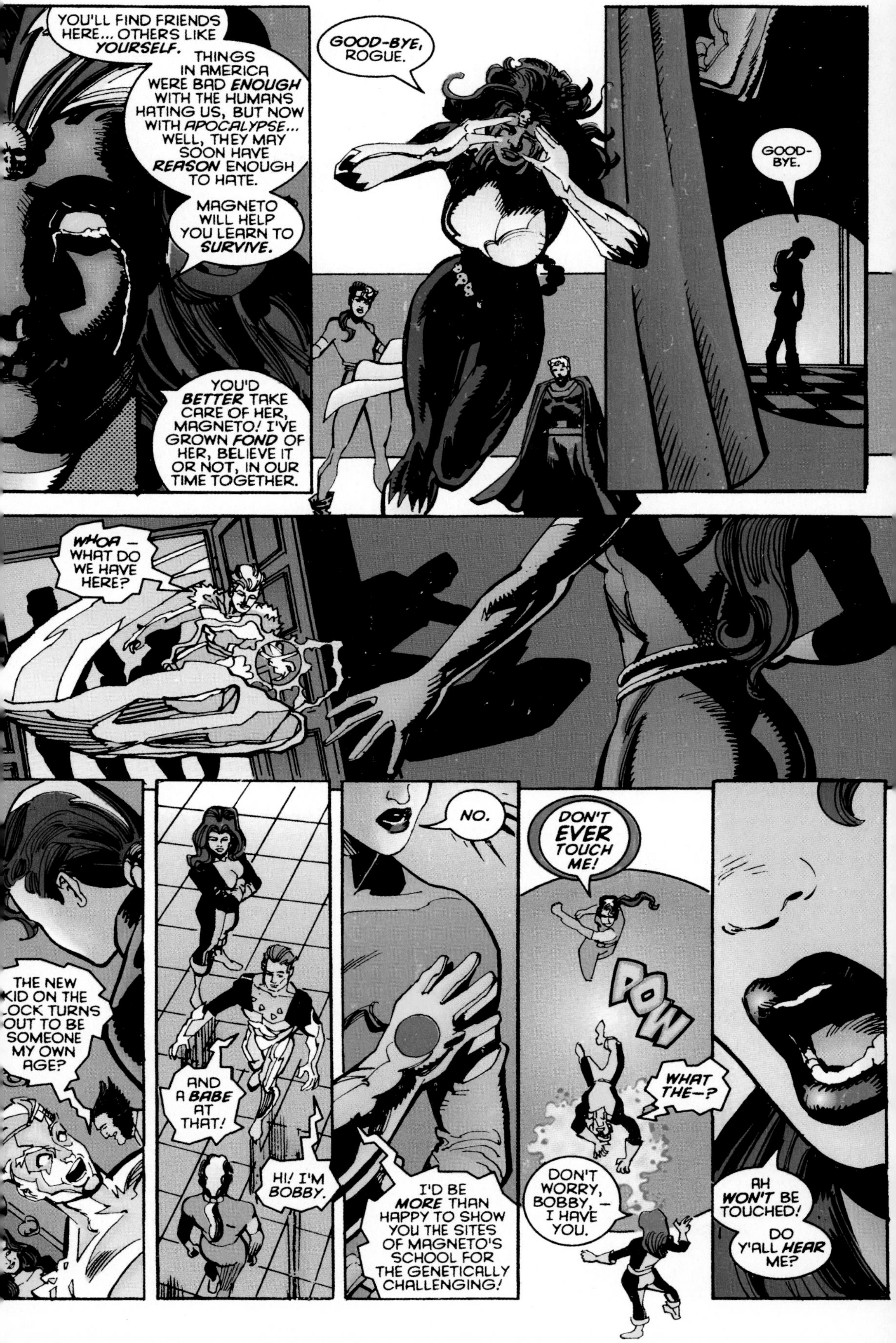

YOU'LL FIND FRIENDS HERE... OTHERS LIKE YOURSELF.
THINGS IN AMERICA WERE BAD ENOUGH WITH THE HUMANS HATING US, BUT NOW WITH APOCALYPSE... WELL, THEY MAY SOON HAVE REASON ENOUGH TO HATE.
MAGNETO WILL HELP YOU LEARN TO SURVIVE.
YOU'D BETTER TAKE CARE OF HER, MAGNETO! I'VE GROWN FOND OF HER, BELIEVE IT OR NOT, IN OUR TIME TOGETHER.
GOOD-BYE, ROGUE.
GOOD-BYE.
WHOA -- WHAT DO WE HAVE HERE?
THE NEW KID ON THE LOCK TURNS OUT TO BE SOMEONE MY OWN AGE?
AND A BABE AT THAT!
HI! I'M BOBBY.
I'D BE MORE THAN HAPPY TO SHOW YOU THE SITES OF MAGNETO'S SCHOOL FOR THE GENETICALLY CHALLENGING!
NO.
DON'T EVER TOUCH ME!
POW
WHAT THE--?
DON'T WORRY, BOBBY, -- I HAVE YOU.
AH WON'T BE TOUCHED!
DO Y'ALL HEAR ME?

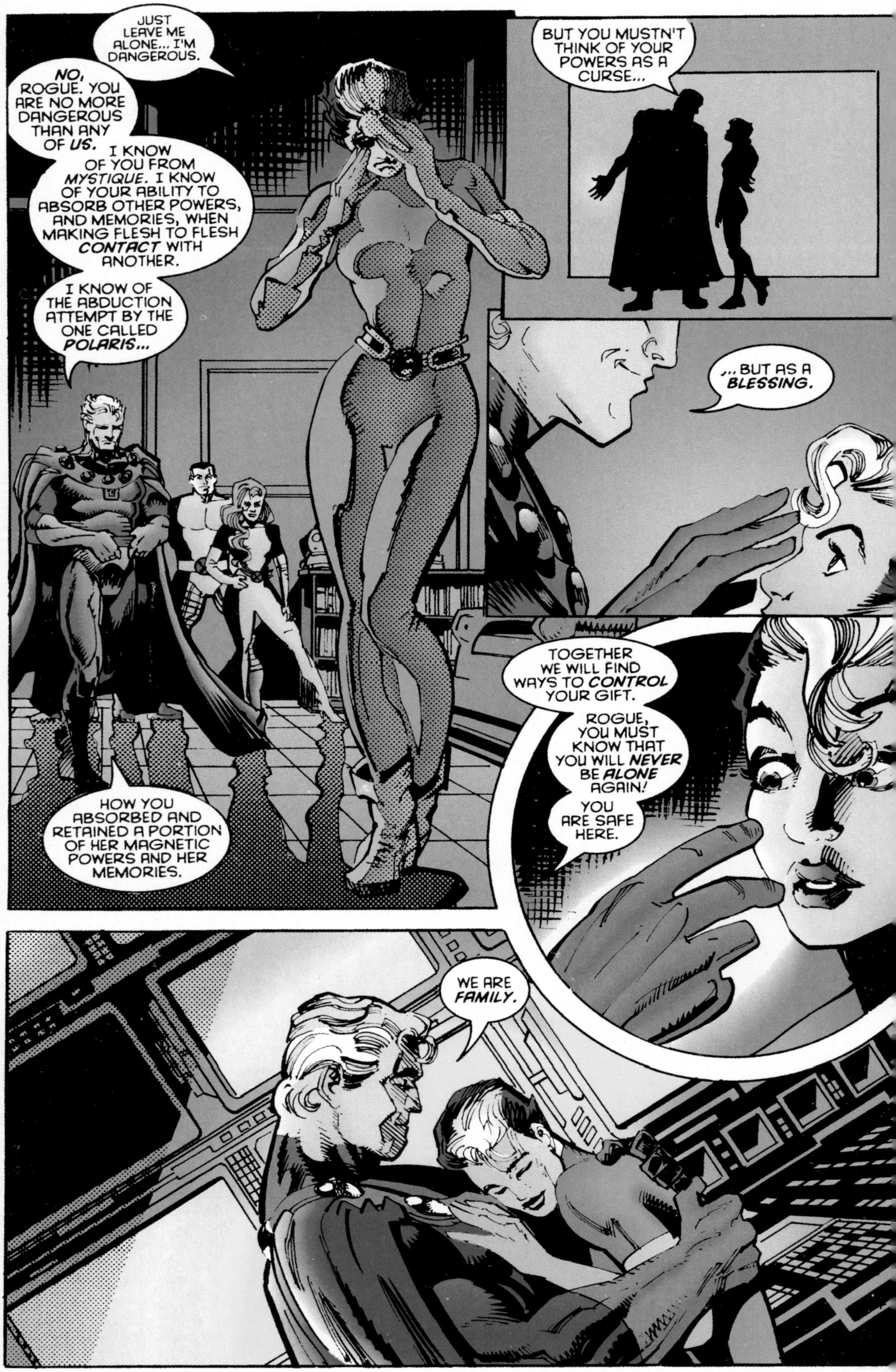
JUST LEAVE ME ALONE... I'M DANGEROUS.
NO, ROGUE. YOU ARE NO MORE DANGEROUS THAN ANY OF US. I KNOW OF YOU FROM MYSTIQUE. I KNOW OF YOUR ABILITY TO ABSORB OTHER POWERS, AND MEMORIES, WHEN MAKING FLESH TO FLESH CONTACT WITH ANOTHER.
I KNOW OF THE ABDUCTION ATTEMPT BY THE ONE CALLED POLARIS...
HOW YOU ABSORBED AND RETAINED A PORTION OF HER MAGNETIC POWERS AND HER MEMORIES.
BUT YOU MUSTN'T THINK OF YOUR POWERS AS A CURSE...
...BUT AS A BLESSING.
TOGETHER WE WILL FIND WAYS TO CONTROL YOUR GIFT.
ROGUE, YOU MUST KNOW THAT YOU WILL NEVER BE ALONE AGAIN!
YOU ARE SAFE HERE.
WE ARE FAMILY.

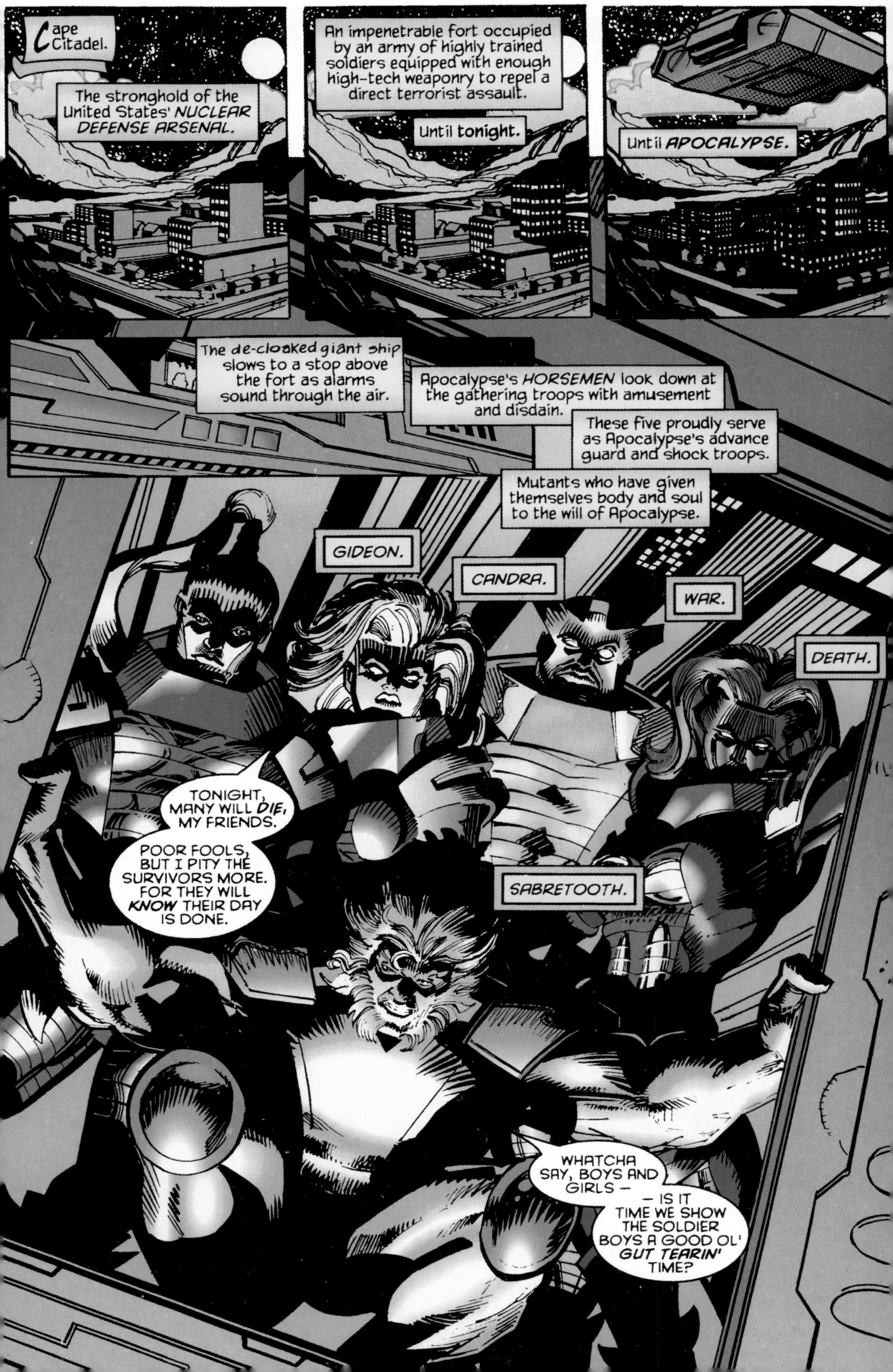
Cape Citadel.
The stronghold of the United States' NUCLEAR DEFENSE ARSENAL.
An impenetrable fort occupied by an army of highly trained soldiers equipped with enough high-tech weaponry to repel a direct terrorist assault.
Until tonight.
Until APOCALYPSE.
The de-cloaked giant ship slows to a stop above the fort as alarms sound through the air.
Apocalypse's HORSEMEN look down at the gathering troops with amusement and disdain.
These five proudly serve as Apocalypse's advance guard and shock troops.
Mutants who have given themselves body and soul to the will of Apocalypse.
GIDEON.
CANDRA.
WAR.
DEATH.
TONIGHT, MANY WILL DIE, MY FRIENDS.
POOR FOOLS, BUT I PITY THE SURVIVORS MORE. FOR THEY WILL KNOW THEIR DAY IS DONE.
SABRETOOTH.
WHATCHA SAY, BOYS AND GIRLS —
— IS IT TIME WE SHOW THE SOLDIER BOYS A GOOD OL' GUT TEARIN' TIME?

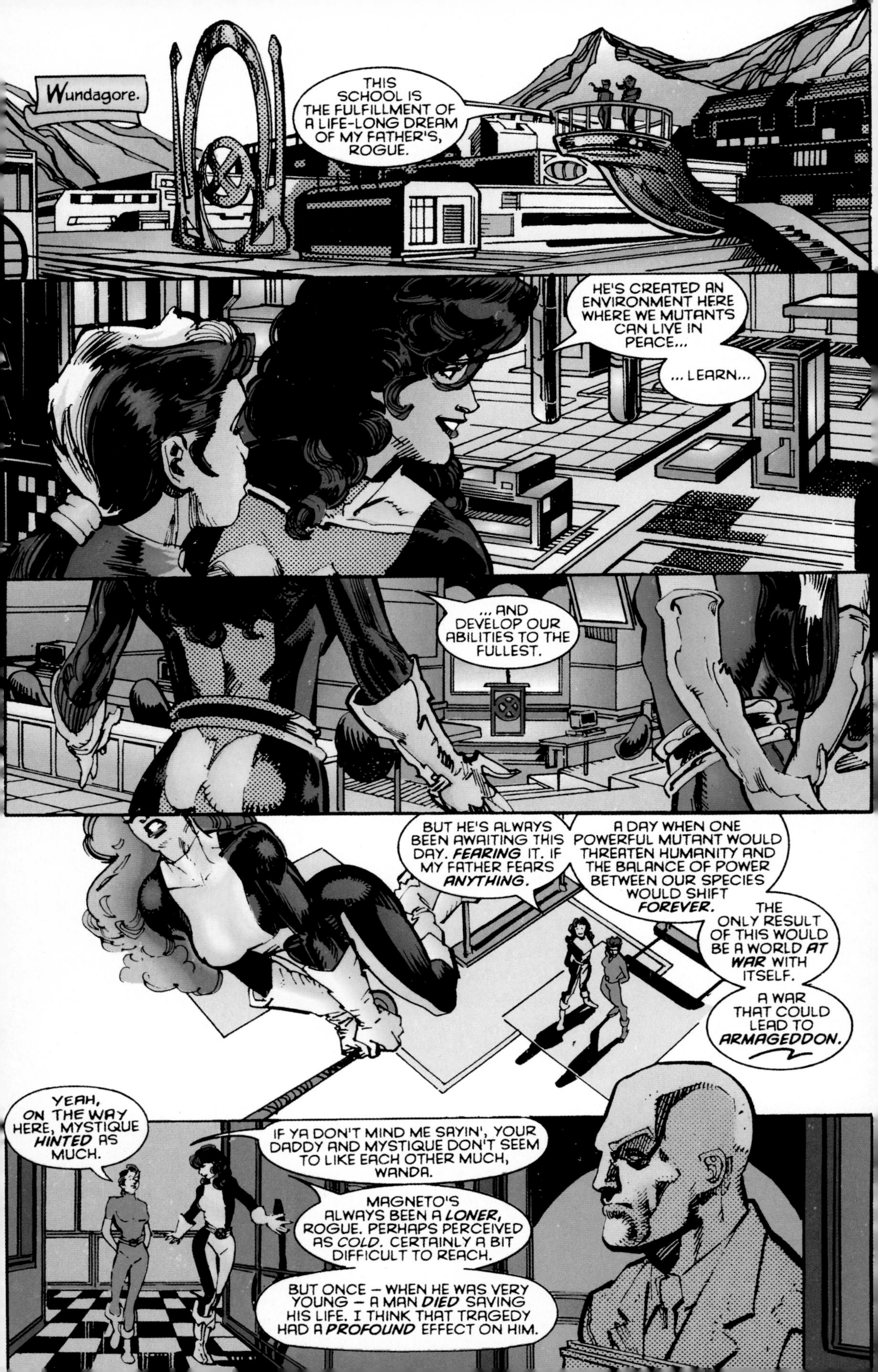
Wundagore.
THIS SCHOOL IS THE FULFILLMENT OF A LIFE-LONG DREAM OF MY FATHER'S, ROGUE.
HE'S CREATED AN ENVIRONMENT HERE WHERE WE MUTANTS CAN LIVE IN PEACE...
...LEARN...
...AND DEVELOP OUR ABILITIES TO THE FULLEST.
BUT HE'S ALWAYS BEEN AWAITING THIS DAY. FEARING IT. IF MY FATHER FEARS ANYTHING.
A DAY WHEN ONE POWERFUL MUTANT WOULD THREATEN HUMANITY AND THE BALANCE OF POWER BETWEEN OUR SPECIES WOULD SHIFT FOREVER.
THE ONLY RESULT OF THIS WOULD BE A WORLD AT WAR WITH ITSELF.
A WAR THAT COULD LEAD TO ARMAGEDDON.
YEAH, ON THE WAY HERE, MYSTIQUE HINTED AS MUCH.
IF YA DON'T MIND ME SAYIN', YOUR DADDY AND MYSTIQUE DON'T SEEM TO LIKE EACH OTHER MUCH, WANDA.
MAGNETO'S ALWAYS BEEN A LONER, ROGUE. PERHAPS PERCEIVED AS COLD. CERTAINLY A BIT DIFFICULT TO REACH.
BUT ONCE — WHEN HE WAS VERY YOUNG — A MAN DIED SAVING HIS LIFE. I THINK THAT TRAGEDY HAD A PROFOUND EFFECT ON HIM.

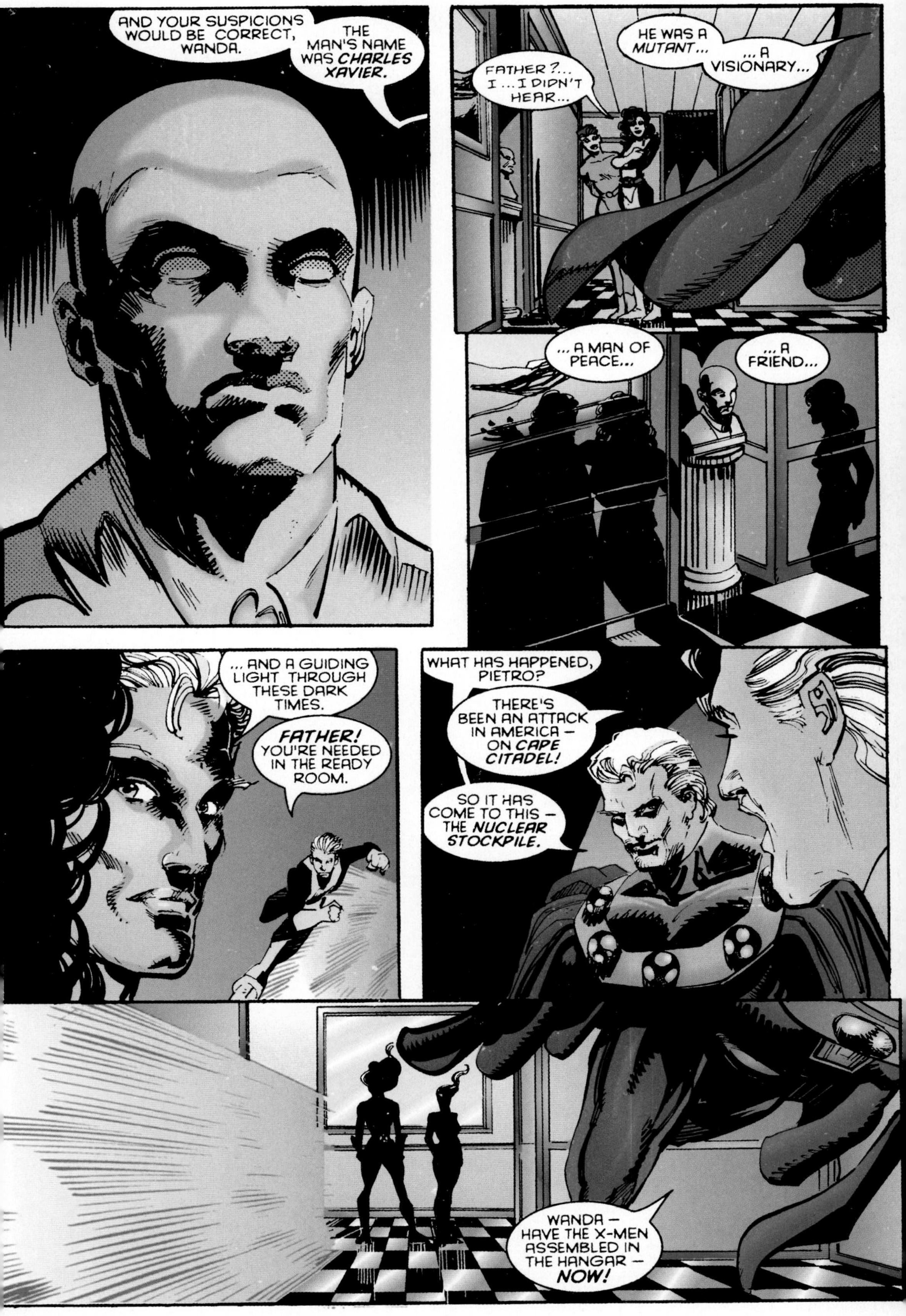
AND YOUR SUSPICIONS WOULD BE CORRECT, WANDA.
THE MAN'S NAME WAS CHARLES XAVIER.
FATHER?... I... I DIDN'T HEAR...
HE WAS A MUTANT...
... A VISIONARY...
... A MAN OF PEACE...
... A FRIEND...
... AND A GUIDING LIGHT THROUGH THESE DARK TIMES.
FATHER! YOU'RE NEEDED IN THE READY ROOM.
WHAT HAS HAPPENED, PIETRO?
THERE'S BEEN AN ATTACK IN AMERICA — ON CAPE CITADEL!
SO IT HAS COME TO THIS — THE NUCLEAR STOCKPILE.
WANDA — HAVE THE X-MEN ASSEMBLED IN THE HANGAR — NOW!

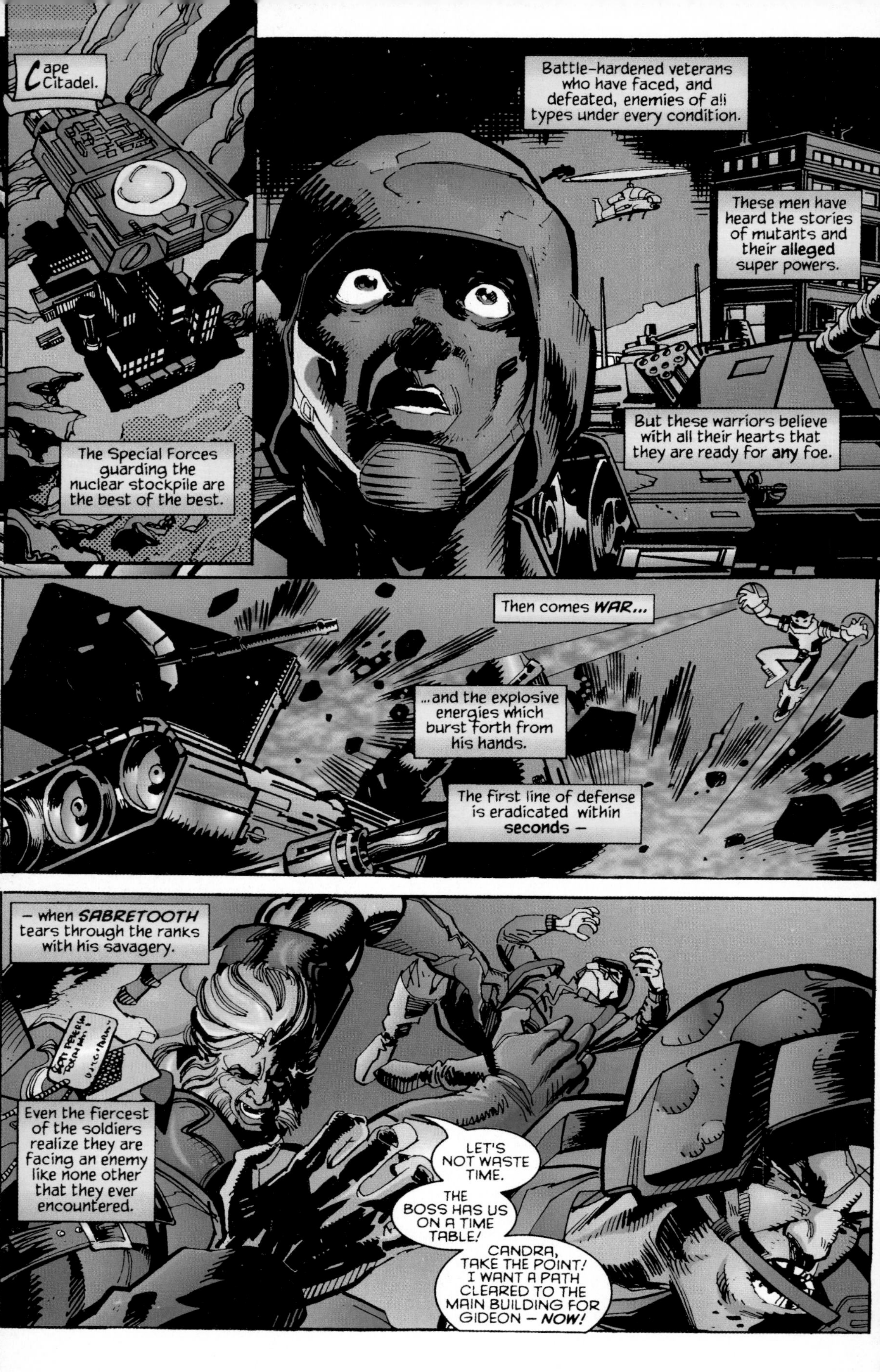
Cape Citadel.
The Special Forces guarding the nuclear stockpile are the best of the best.
Battle-hardened veterans who have faced, and defeated, enemies of all types under every condition.
These men have heard the stories of mutants and their **alleged** super powers.
But these warriors believe with all their hearts that they are ready for **any** foe.
Then comes ***WAR...***
...and the explosive energies which burst forth from his hands.
The first line of defense is eradicated within **seconds** –
– when ***SABRETOOTH*** tears through the ranks with his savagery.
Even the fiercest of the soldiers realize they are facing an enemy like none other that they ever encountered.
LET'S NOT WASTE TIME.
THE BOSS HAS US ON A TIME TABLE!
CANDRA, TAKE THE POINT! I WANT A PATH CLEARED TO THE MAIN BUILDING FOR GIDEON – ***NOW!***

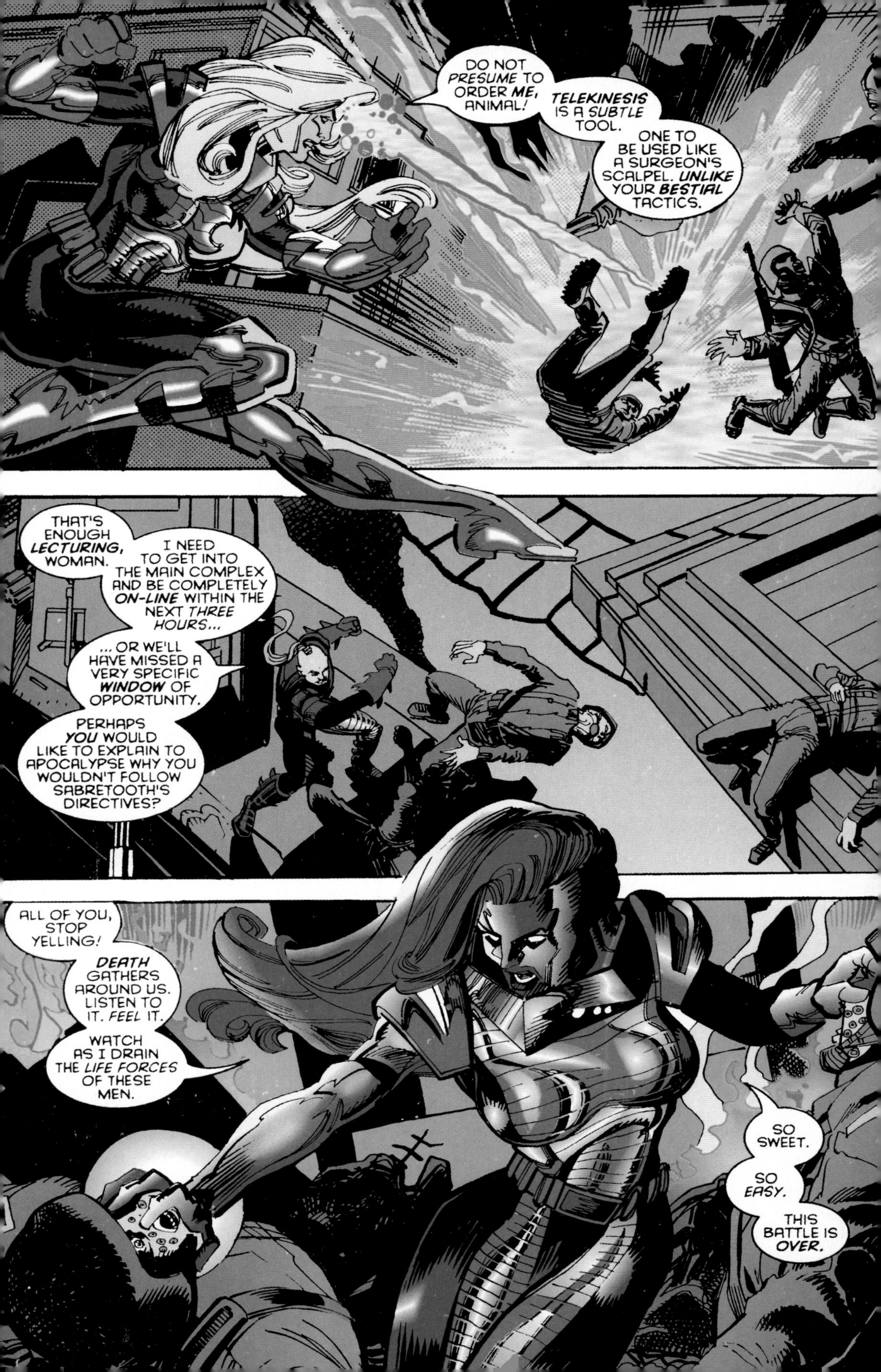

DO NOT PRESUME TO ORDER ME, ANIMAL!
TELEKINESIS IS A SUBTLE TOOL.
ONE TO BE USED LIKE A SURGEON'S SCALPEL. UNLIKE YOUR BESTIAL TACTICS.
THAT'S ENOUGH LECTURING, WOMAN.
I NEED TO GET INTO THE MAIN COMPLEX AND BE COMPLETELY ON-LINE WITHIN THE NEXT THREE HOURS...
...OR WE'LL HAVE MISSED A VERY SPECIFIC WINDOW OF OPPORTUNITY.
PERHAPS YOU WOULD LIKE TO EXPLAIN TO APOCALYPSE WHY YOU WOULDN'T FOLLOW SABRETOOTH'S DIRECTIVES?
ALL OF YOU, STOP YELLING!
DEATH GATHERS AROUND US. LISTEN TO IT. FEEL IT.
WATCH AS I DRAIN THE LIFE FORCES OF THESE MEN.
SO SWEET.
SO EASY.
THIS BATTLE IS OVER.

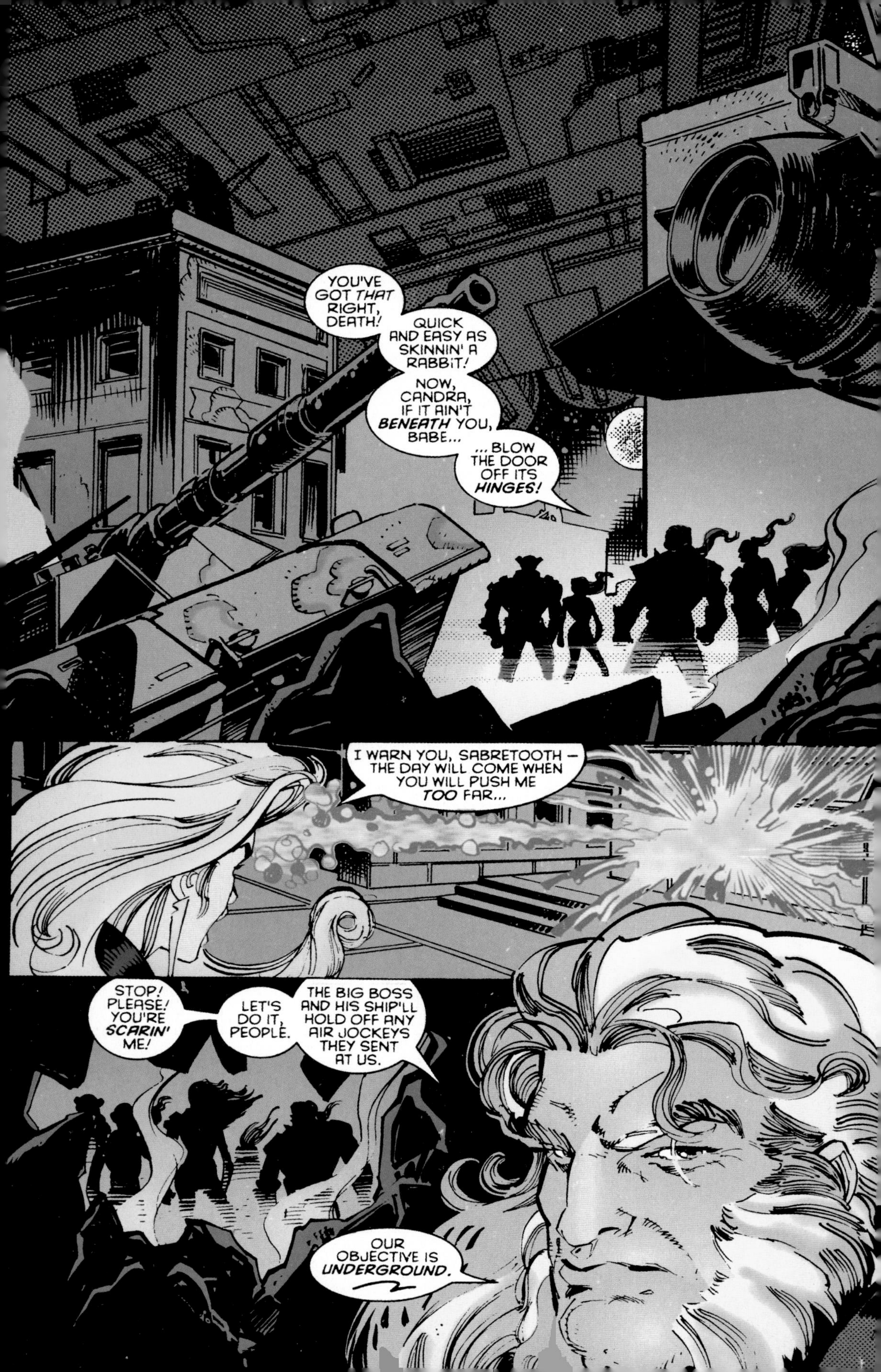

YOU'VE GOT THAT RIGHT, DEATH!
QUICK AND EASY AS SKINNIN' A RABBIT!
NOW, CANDRA, IF IT AIN'T BENEATH YOU, BABE...
...BLOW THE DOOR OFF ITS HINGES!
I WARN YOU, SABRETOOTH – THE DAY WILL COME WHEN YOU WILL PUSH ME TOO FAR...
STOP! PLEASE! YOU'RE SCARIN' ME!
LET'S DO IT, PEOPLE.
THE BIG BOSS AND HIS SHIP'LL HOLD OFF ANY AIR JOCKEYS THEY SENT AT US.
OUR OBJECTIVE IS UNDERGROUND.

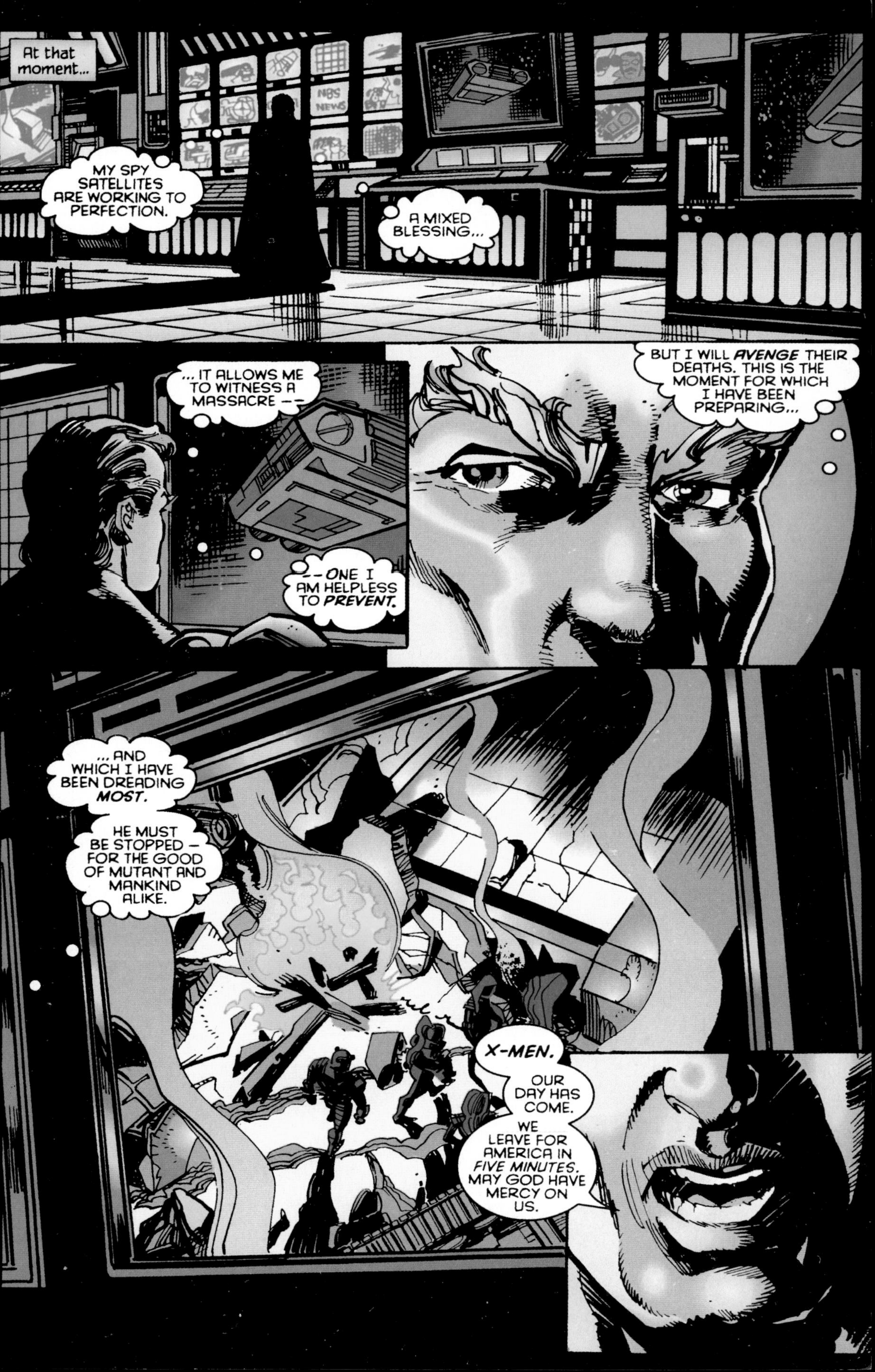
At that moment...
MY SPY SATELLITES ARE WORKING TO PERFECTION.
A MIXED BLESSING...
...IT ALLOWS ME TO WITNESS A MASSACRE --
--ONE I AM HELPLESS TO PREVENT.
BUT I WILL AVENGE THEIR DEATHS. THIS IS THE MOMENT FOR WHICH I HAVE BEEN PREPARING...
...AND WHICH I HAVE BEEN DREADING MOST.
HE MUST BE STOPPED -- FOR THE GOOD OF MUTANT AND MANKIND ALIKE.
X-MEN.
OUR DAY HAS COME.
WE LEAVE FOR AMERICA IN FIVE MINUTES. MAY GOD HAVE MERCY ON US.

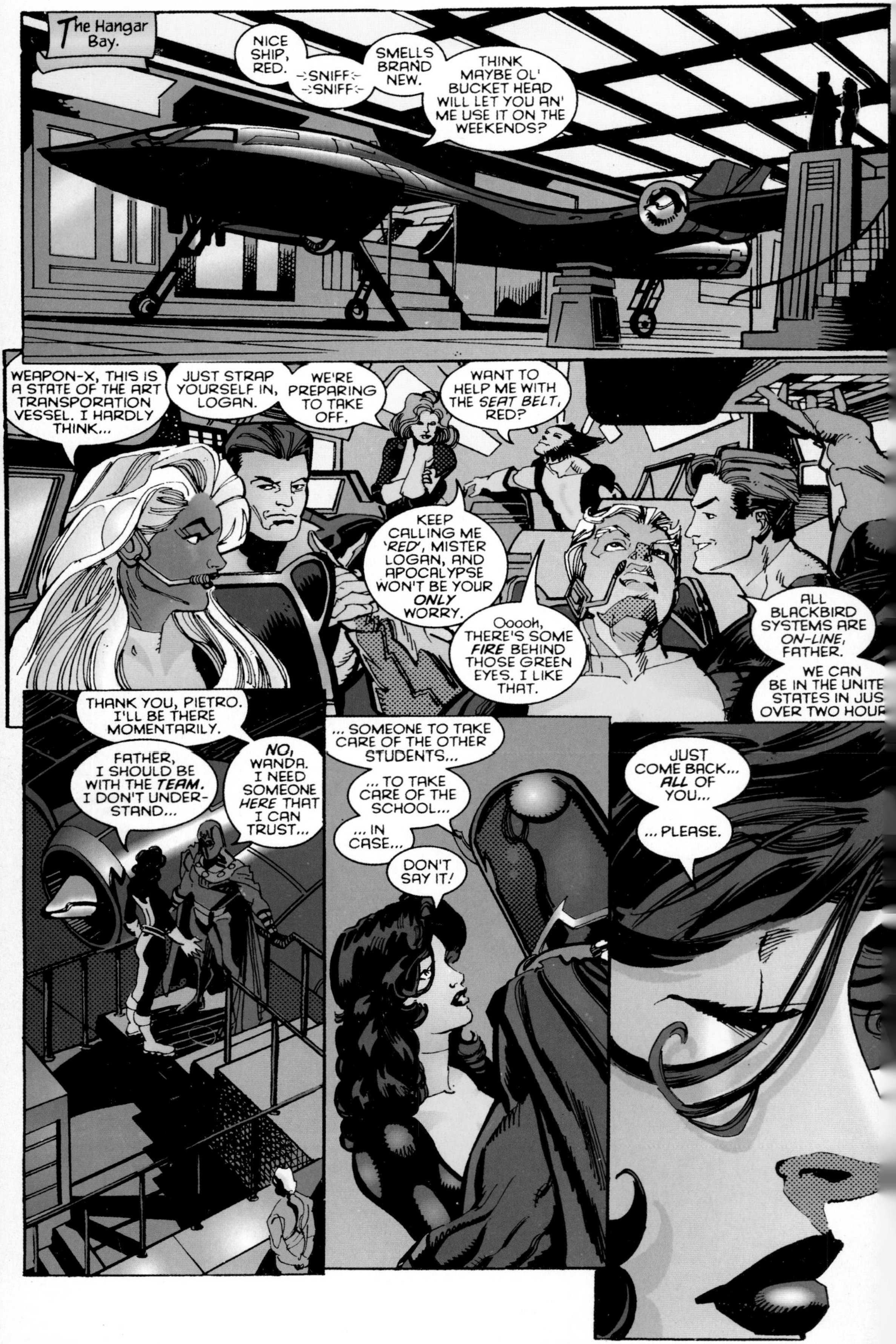
The Hangar Bay.
NICE SHIP, RED.
-SNIFF- -SNIFF-
SMELLS BRAND NEW.
THINK MAYBE OL' BUCKET HEAD WILL LET YOU AN' ME USE IT ON THE WEEKENDS?
WEAPON-X, THIS IS A STATE OF THE ART TRANSPORATION VESSEL. I HARDLY THINK...
JUST STRAP YOURSELF IN, LOGAN.
WE'RE PREPARING TO TAKE OFF.
WANT TO HELP ME WITH THE SEAT BELT, RED?
KEEP CALLING ME 'RED', MISTER LOGAN, AND APOCALYPSE WON'T BE YOUR ONLY WORRY.
Ooooh, THERE'S SOME FIRE BEHIND THOSE GREEN EYES. I LIKE THAT.
ALL BLACKBIRD SYSTEMS ARE ON-LINE, FATHER.
WE CAN BE IN THE UNITE STATES IN JUS OVER TWO HOUR
THANK YOU, PIETRO. I'LL BE THERE MOMENTARILY.
FATHER, I SHOULD BE WITH THE TEAM. I DON'T UNDER-STAND...
NO, WANDA. I NEED SOMEONE HERE THAT I CAN TRUST...
... SOMEONE TO TAKE CARE OF THE OTHER STUDENTS...
... TO TAKE CARE OF THE SCHOOL...
... IN CASE...
DON'T SAY IT!
JUST COME BACK... ALL OF YOU...
... PLEASE.

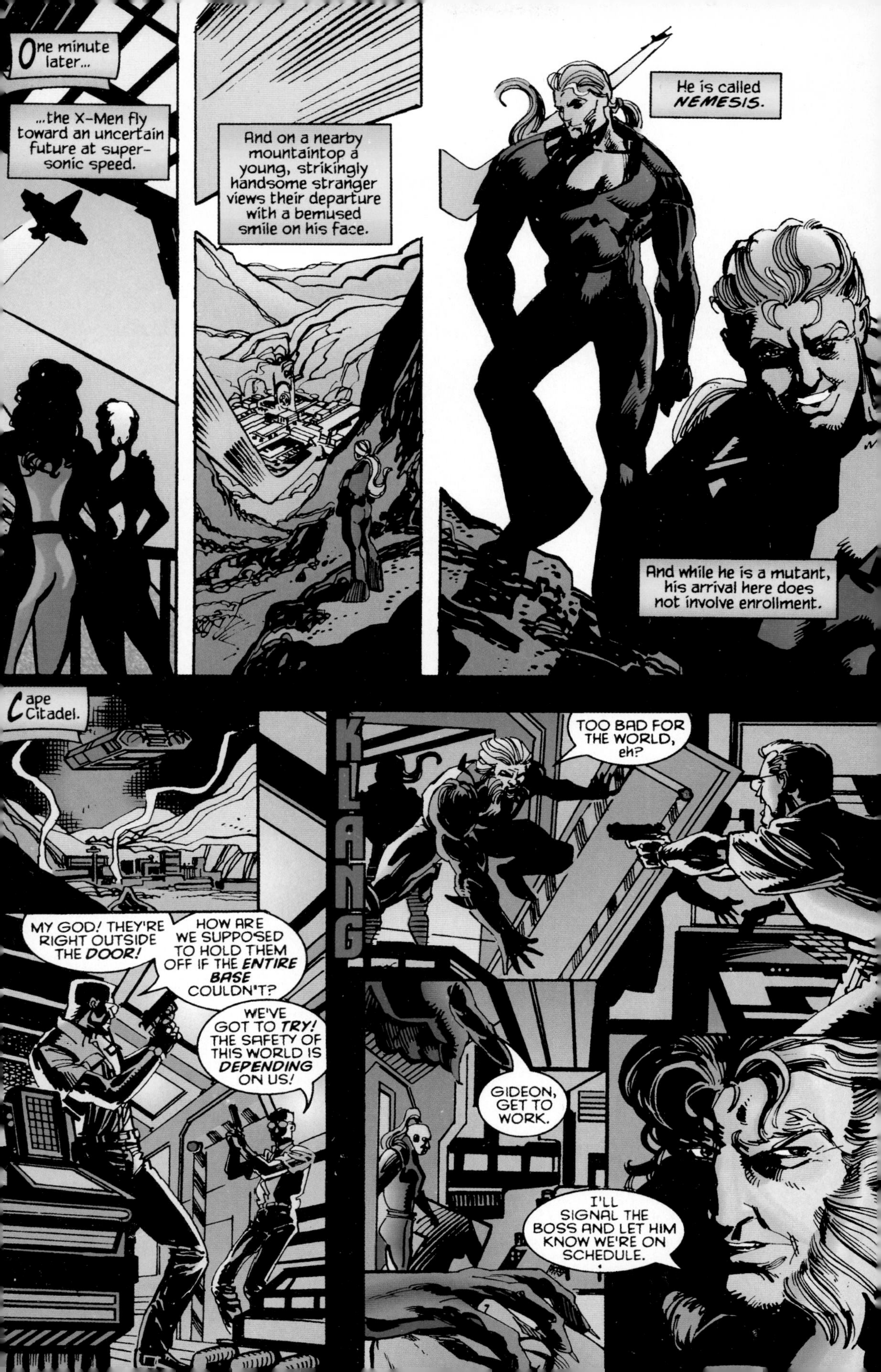
One minute later...
...the X-Men fly toward an uncertain future at super-sonic speed.
And on a nearby mountaintop a young, strikingly handsome stranger views their departure with a bemused smile on his face.
He is called NEMESIS.
And while he is a mutant, his arrival here does not involve enrollment.
Cape Citadel.
MY GOD! THEY'RE RIGHT OUTSIDE THE DOOR!
HOW ARE WE SUPPOSED TO HOLD THEM OFF IF THE ENTIRE BASE COULDN'T?
WE'VE GOT TO TRY! THE SAFETY OF THIS WORLD IS DEPENDING ON US!
KLANG
TOO BAD FOR THE WORLD, eh?
GIDEON, GET TO WORK.
I'LL SIGNAL THE BOSS AND LET HIM KNOW WE'RE ON SCHEDULE.

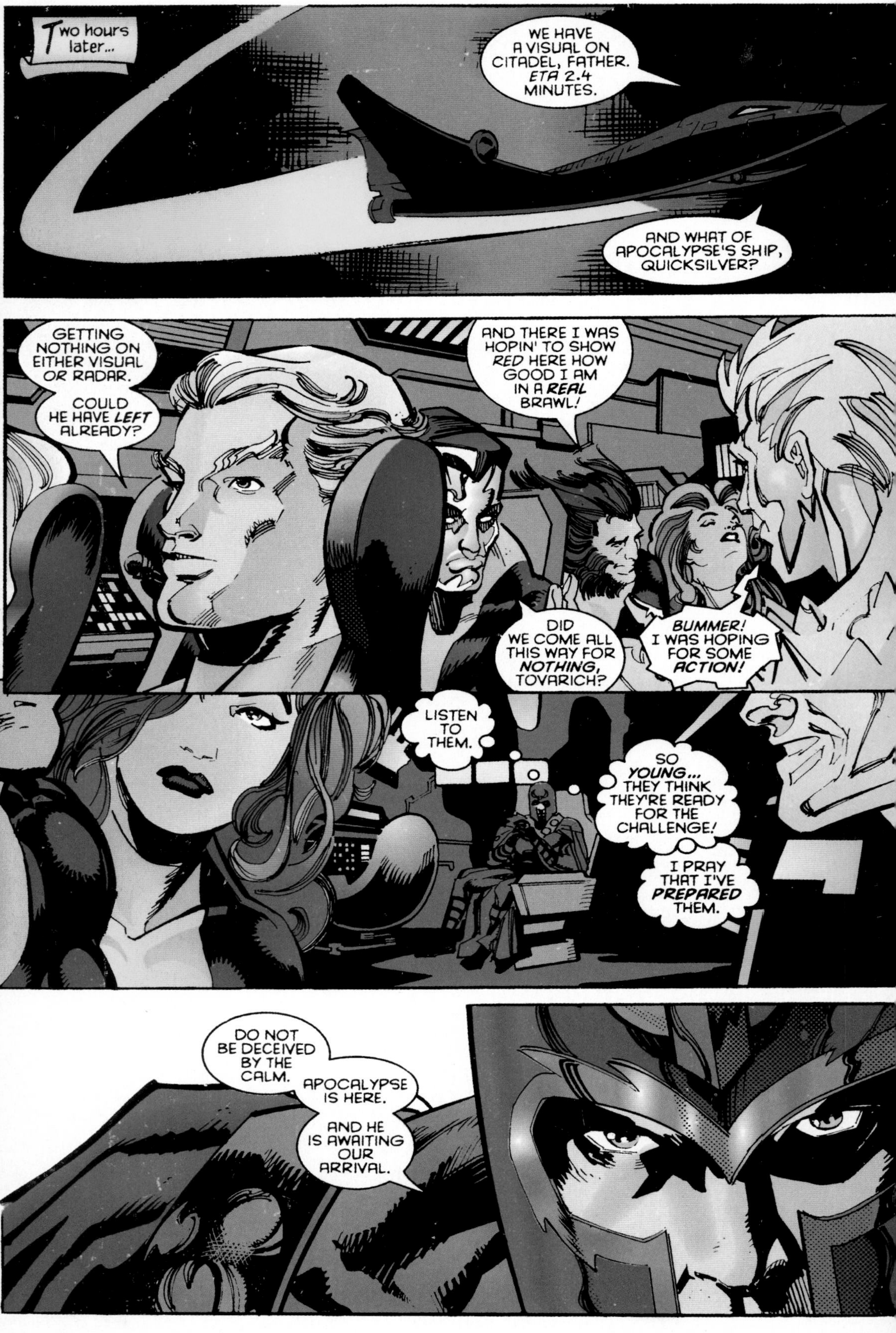
Two hours later...
WE HAVE A VISUAL ON CITADEL, FATHER. ETA 2.4 MINUTES.
AND WHAT OF APOCALYPSE'S SHIP, QUICKSILVER?
GETTING NOTHING ON EITHER VISUAL OR RADAR.
COULD HE HAVE LEFT ALREADY?
AND THERE I WAS HOPIN' TO SHOW RED HERE HOW GOOD I AM IN A REAL BRAWL!
DID WE COME ALL THIS WAY FOR NOTHING, TOVARICH?
BUMMER! I WAS HOPING FOR SOME ACTION!
LISTEN TO THEM.
SO YOUNG... THEY THINK THEY'RE READY FOR THE CHALLENGE!
I PRAY THAT I'VE PREPARED THEM.
DO NOT BE DECEIVED BY THE CALM.
APOCALYPSE IS HERE.
AND HE IS AWAITING OUR ARRIVAL.

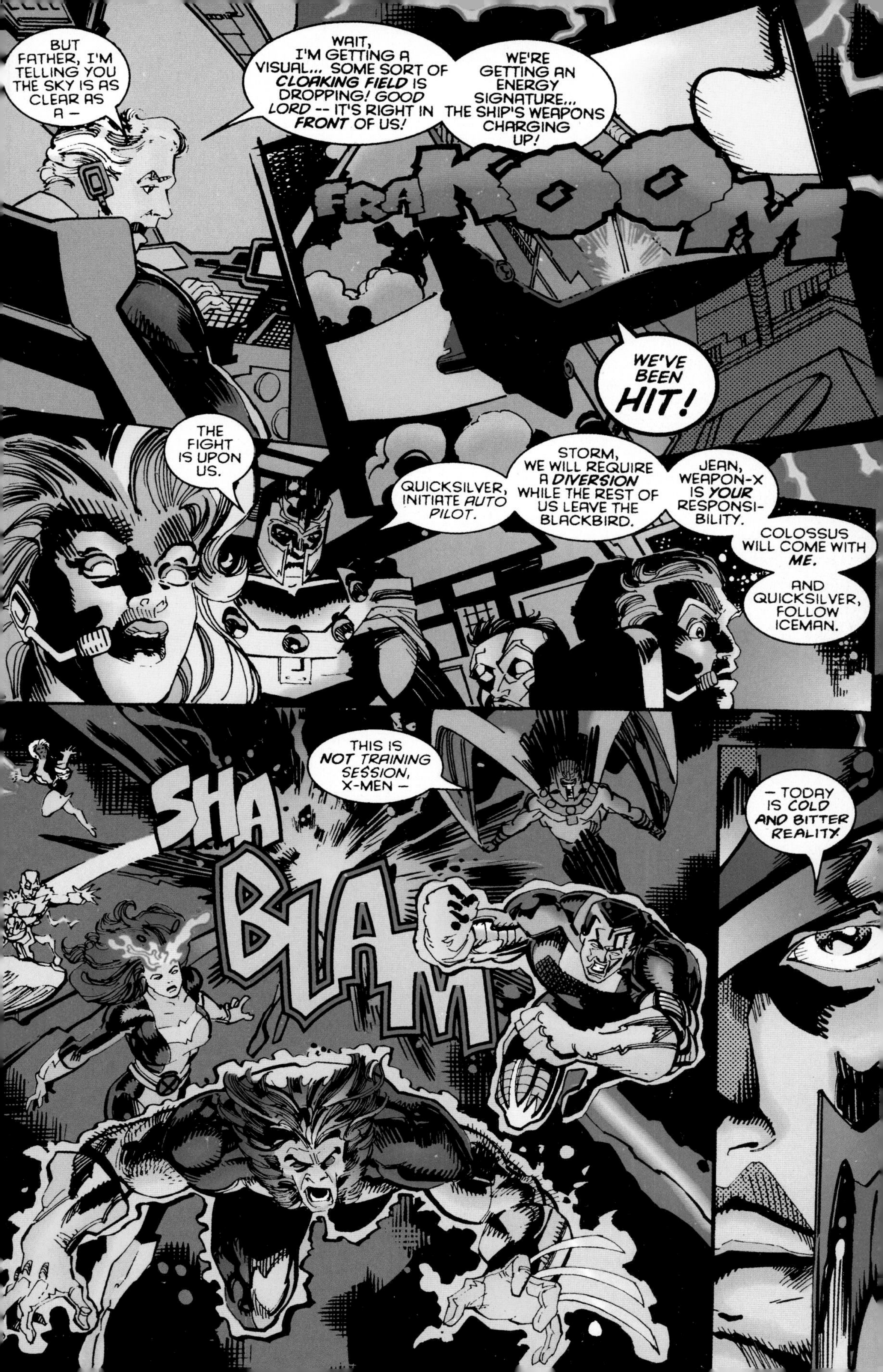
BUT FATHER, I'M TELLING YOU THE SKY IS AS CLEAR AS A –
WAIT, I'M GETTING A VISUAL... SOME SORT OF CLOAKING FIELD IS DROPPING! GOOD LORD -- IT'S RIGHT IN FRONT OF US!
WE'RE GETTING AN ENERGY SIGNATURE... THE SHIP'S WEAPONS CHARGING UP!
FRAKOOOM
WE'VE BEEN HIT!
THE FIGHT IS UPON US.
QUICKSILVER, INITIATE AUTO PILOT.
STORM, WE WILL REQUIRE A DIVERSION WHILE THE REST OF US LEAVE THE BLACKBIRD.
JEAN, WEAPON-X IS YOUR RESPONSIBILITY.
COLOSSUS WILL COME WITH ME.
AND QUICKSILVER, FOLLOW ICEMAN.
SHA
BLAM
THIS IS NOT TRAINING SESSION, X-MEN –
– TODAY IS COLD AND BITTER REALITY.

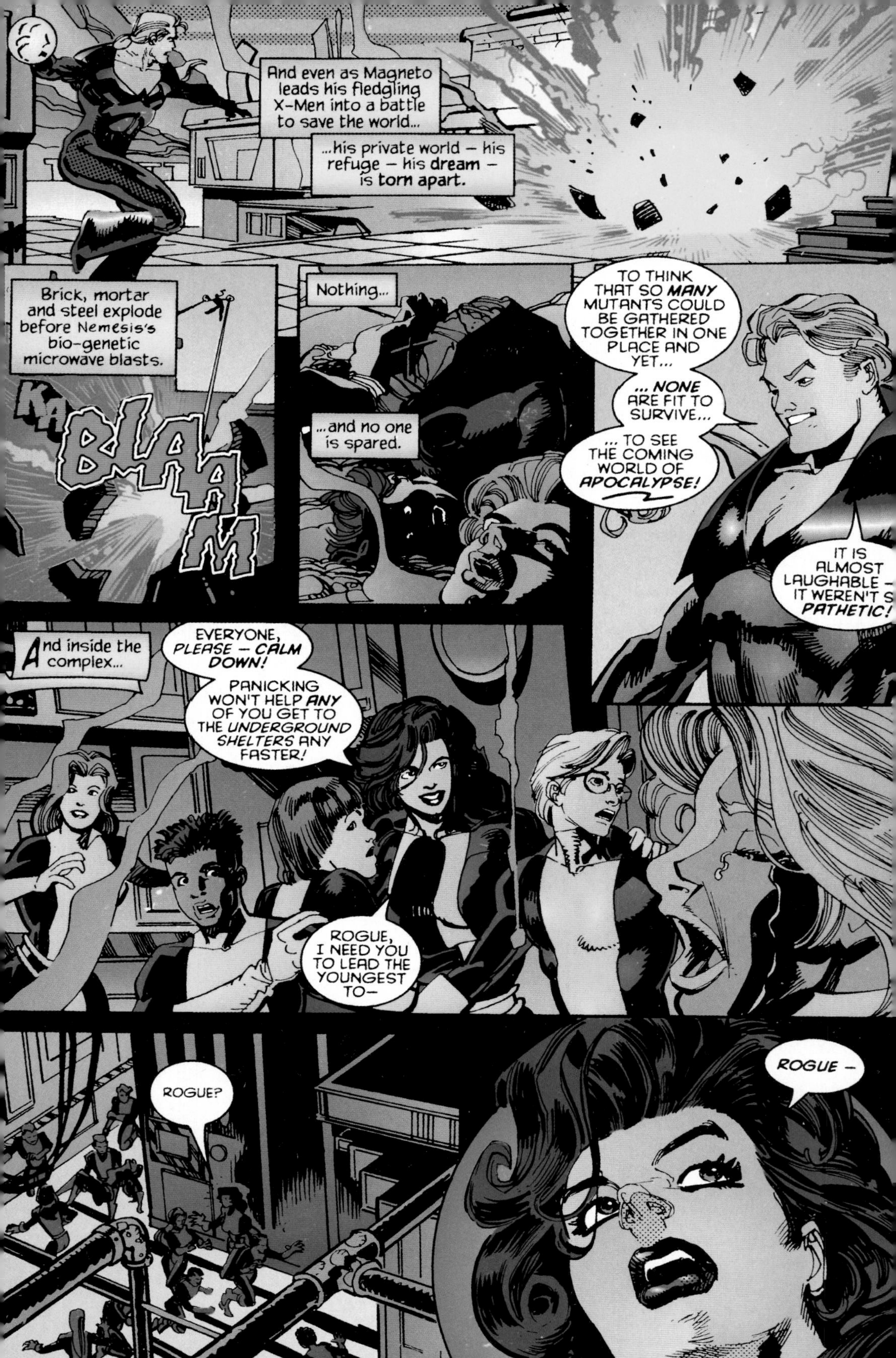
And even as Magneto leads his fledgling X-Men into a battle to save the world...
...his private world — his refuge — his dream — is torn apart.
Brick, mortar and steel explode before Nemesis's bio-genetic microwave blasts.
KA BLAAM
Nothing...
...and no one is spared.
TO THINK THAT SO MANY MUTANTS COULD BE GATHERED TOGETHER IN ONE PLACE AND YET...
...NONE ARE FIT TO SURVIVE...
...TO SEE THE COMING WORLD OF APOCALYPSE!
IT IS ALMOST LAUGHABLE — IT WEREN'T S PATHETIC!
And inside the complex...
EVERYONE, PLEASE — CALM DOWN!
PANICKING WON'T HELP ANY OF YOU GET TO THE UNDERGROUND SHELTERS ANY FASTER!
ROGUE, I NEED YOU TO LEAD THE YOUNGEST TO—
ROGUE?
ROGUE —

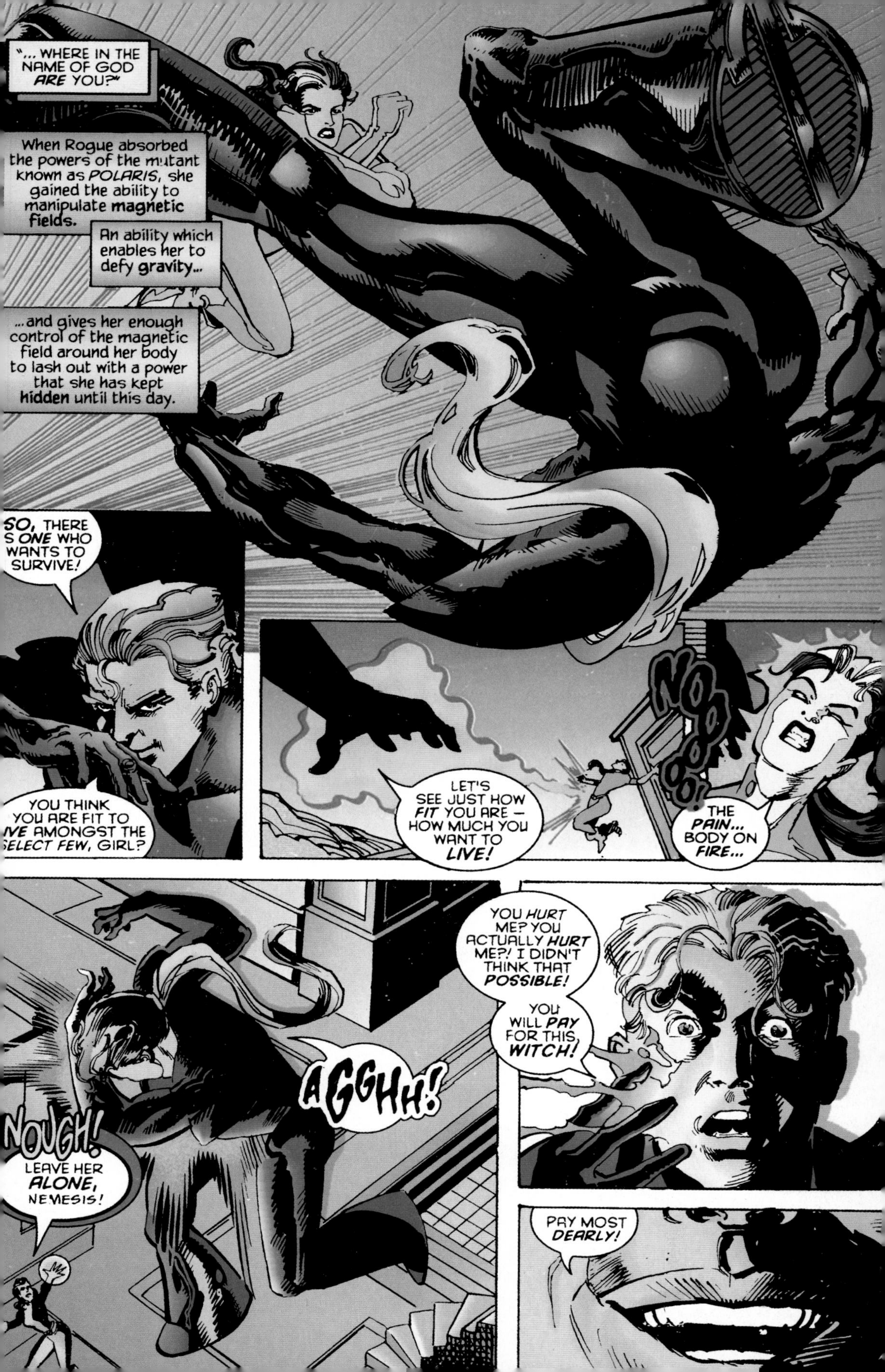
"... WHERE IN THE NAME OF GOD *ARE* YOU?"
When Rogue absorbed the powers of the mutant known as *POLARIS*, she gained the ability to manipulate **magnetic fields.**
An ability which enables her to defy **gravity**...
...and gives her enough control of the magnetic field around her body to lash out with a power that she has kept **hidden** until this day.
SO, THERE S *ONE* WHO WANTS TO SURVIVE!
YOU THINK YOU ARE FIT TO *IVE* AMONGST THE *SELECT FEW*, GIRL?
LET'S SEE JUST HOW *FIT* YOU ARE — HOW MUCH YOU WANT TO *LIVE!*
NOOOOO!
THE *PAIN...* BODY ON *FIRE...*
AGGHH!
NOUGH! LEAVE HER *ALONE,* NEMESIS!
YOU *HURT* ME? YOU ACTUALLY *HURT* ME?! I DIDN'T THINK THAT *POSSIBLE!*
YOU WILL *PAY* FOR THIS, *WITCH!*
PAY MOST *DEARLY!*

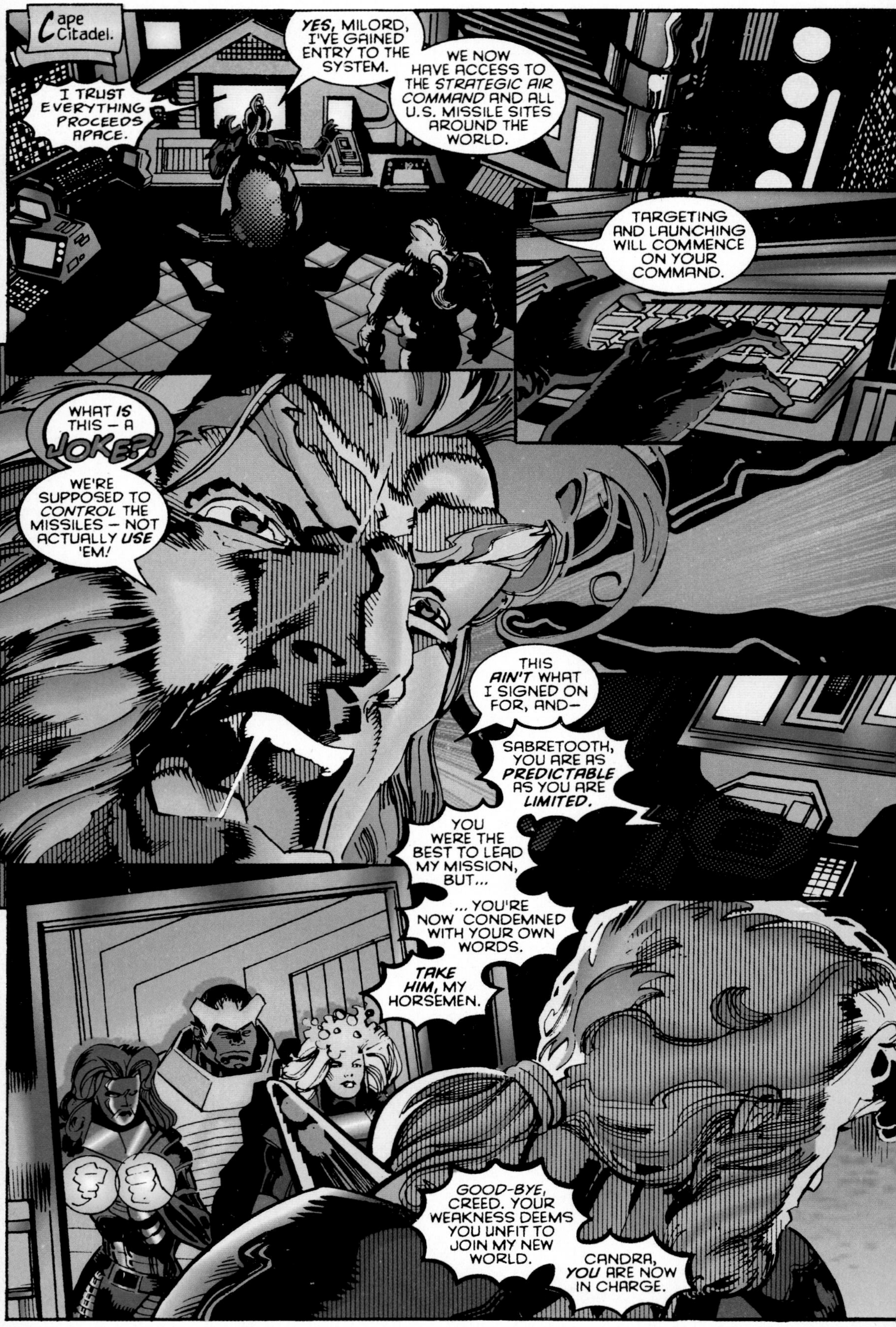
Cape Citadel.
I TRUST EVERYTHING PROCEEDS APACE.
YES, MILORD, I'VE GAINED ENTRY TO THE SYSTEM.
WE NOW HAVE ACCESS TO THE STRATEGIC AIR COMMAND AND ALL U.S. MISSILE SITES AROUND THE WORLD.
TARGETING AND LAUNCHING WILL COMMENCE ON YOUR COMMAND.
WHAT IS THIS — A JOKE?!
WE'RE SUPPOSED TO CONTROL THE MISSILES — NOT ACTUALLY USE 'EM!
THIS AIN'T WHAT I SIGNED ON FOR, AND—
SABRETOOTH, YOU ARE AS PREDICTABLE AS YOU ARE LIMITED.
YOU WERE THE BEST TO LEAD MY MISSION, BUT...
... YOU'RE NOW CONDEMNED WITH YOUR OWN WORDS.
TAKE HIM, MY HORSEMEN.
GOOD-BYE, CREED. YOUR WEAKNESS DEEMS YOU UNFIT TO JOIN MY NEW WORLD.
CANDRA, YOU ARE NOW IN CHARGE.

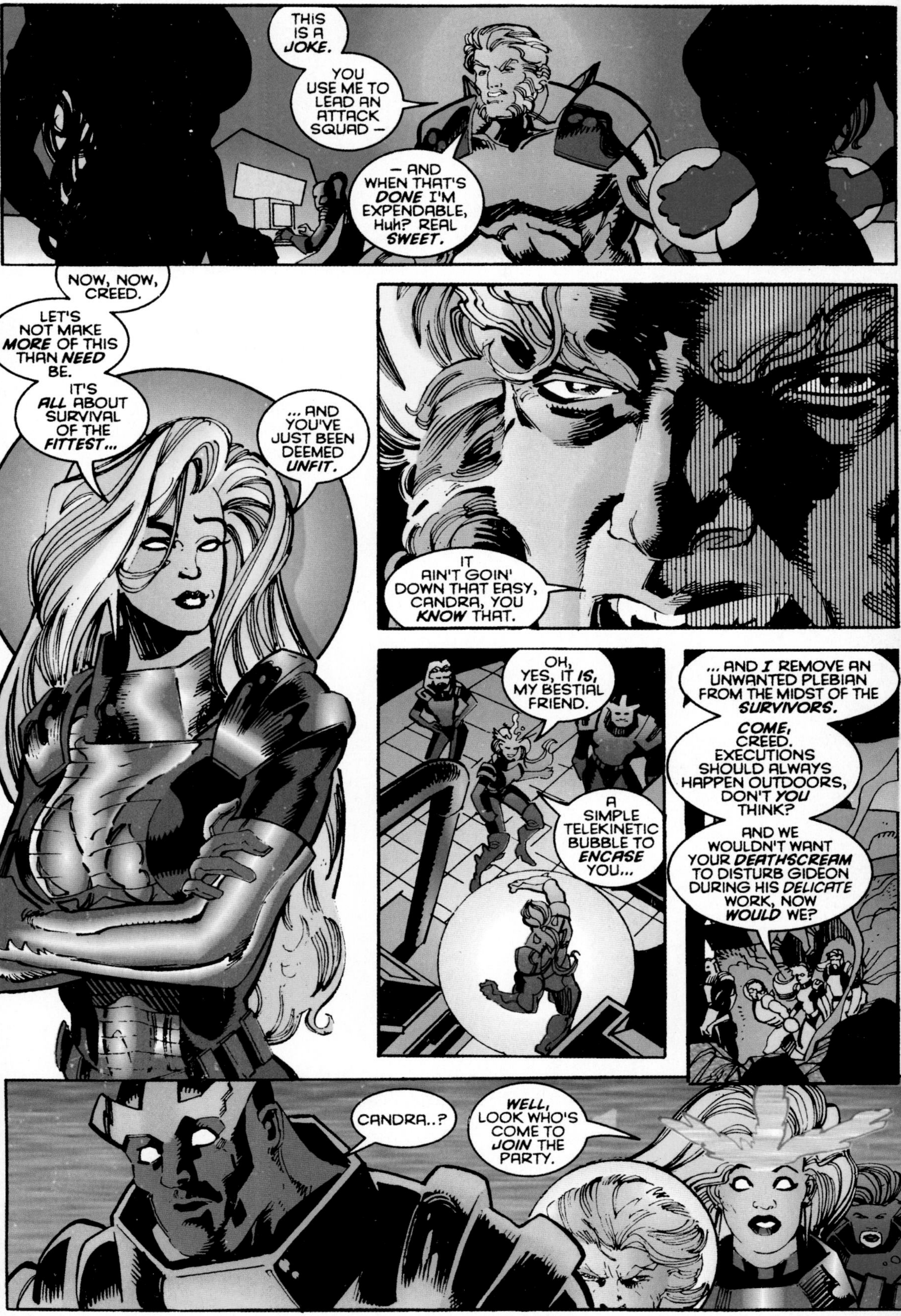

THIS IS A JOKE.
YOU USE ME TO LEAD AN ATTACK SQUAD —
— AND WHEN THAT'S DONE I'M EXPENDABLE, Huh? REAL SWEET.
NOW, NOW, CREED.
LET'S NOT MAKE MORE OF THIS THAN NEED BE.
IT'S ALL ABOUT SURVIVAL OF THE FITTEST...
...AND YOU'VE JUST BEEN DEEMED UNFIT.
IT AIN'T GOIN' DOWN THAT EASY, CANDRA, YOU KNOW THAT.
OH, YES, IT IS, MY BESTIAL FRIEND.
A SIMPLE TELEKINETIC BUBBLE TO ENCASE YOU...
...AND I REMOVE AN UNWANTED PLEBIAN FROM THE MIDST OF THE SURVIVORS.
COME, CREED. EXECUTIONS SHOULD ALWAYS HAPPEN OUTDOORS, DON'T YOU THINK?
AND WE WOULDN'T WANT YOUR DEATHSCREAM TO DISTURB GIDEON DURING HIS DELICATE WORK, NOW WOULD WE?
CANDRA..?
WELL, LOOK WHO'S COME TO JOIN THE PARTY.

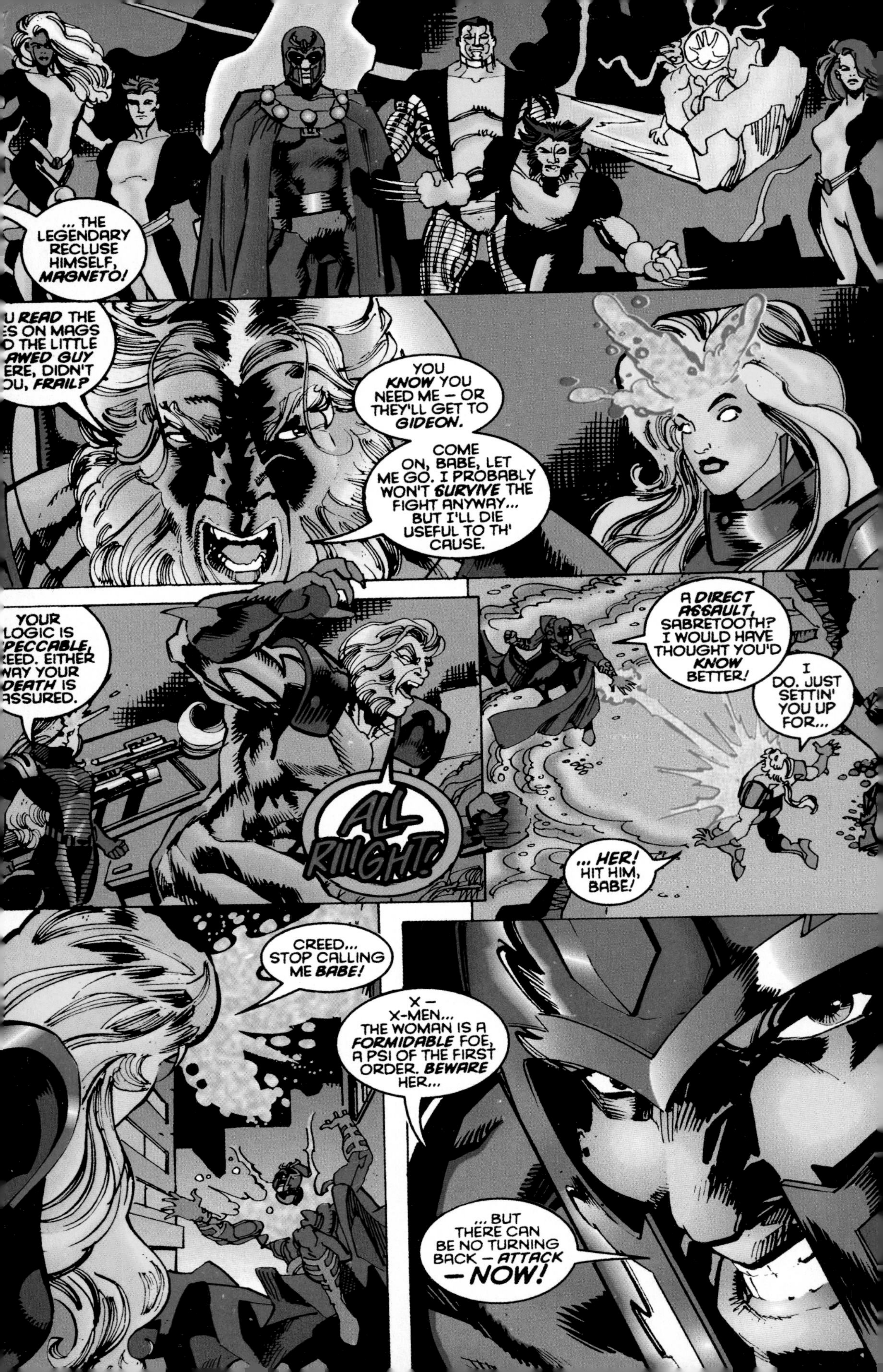

... THE LEGENDARY RECLUSE HIMSELF, MAGNETO!
U READ THE ES ON MAGS D THE LITTLE AWED GUY ERE, DIDN'T OU, FRAIL?
YOU KNOW YOU NEED ME — OR THEY'LL GET TO GIDEON.
COME ON, BABE, LET ME GO. I PROBABLY WON'T SURVIVE THE FIGHT ANYWAY... BUT I'LL DIE USEFUL TO TH' CAUSE.
YOUR LOGIC IS PECCABLE, REED. EITHER WAY YOUR DEATH IS ASSURED.
ALL RIIIGHT!
A DIRECT ASSAULT, SABRETOOTH? I WOULD HAVE THOUGHT YOU'D KNOW BETTER!
I DO. JUST SETTIN' YOU UP FOR...
... HER! HIT HIM, BABE!
CREED... STOP CALLING ME BABE!
X — X-MEN... THE WOMAN IS A FORMIDABLE FOE, A PSI OF THE FIRST ORDER. BEWARE HER...
... BUT THERE CAN BE NO TURNING BACK — ATTACK — NOW!

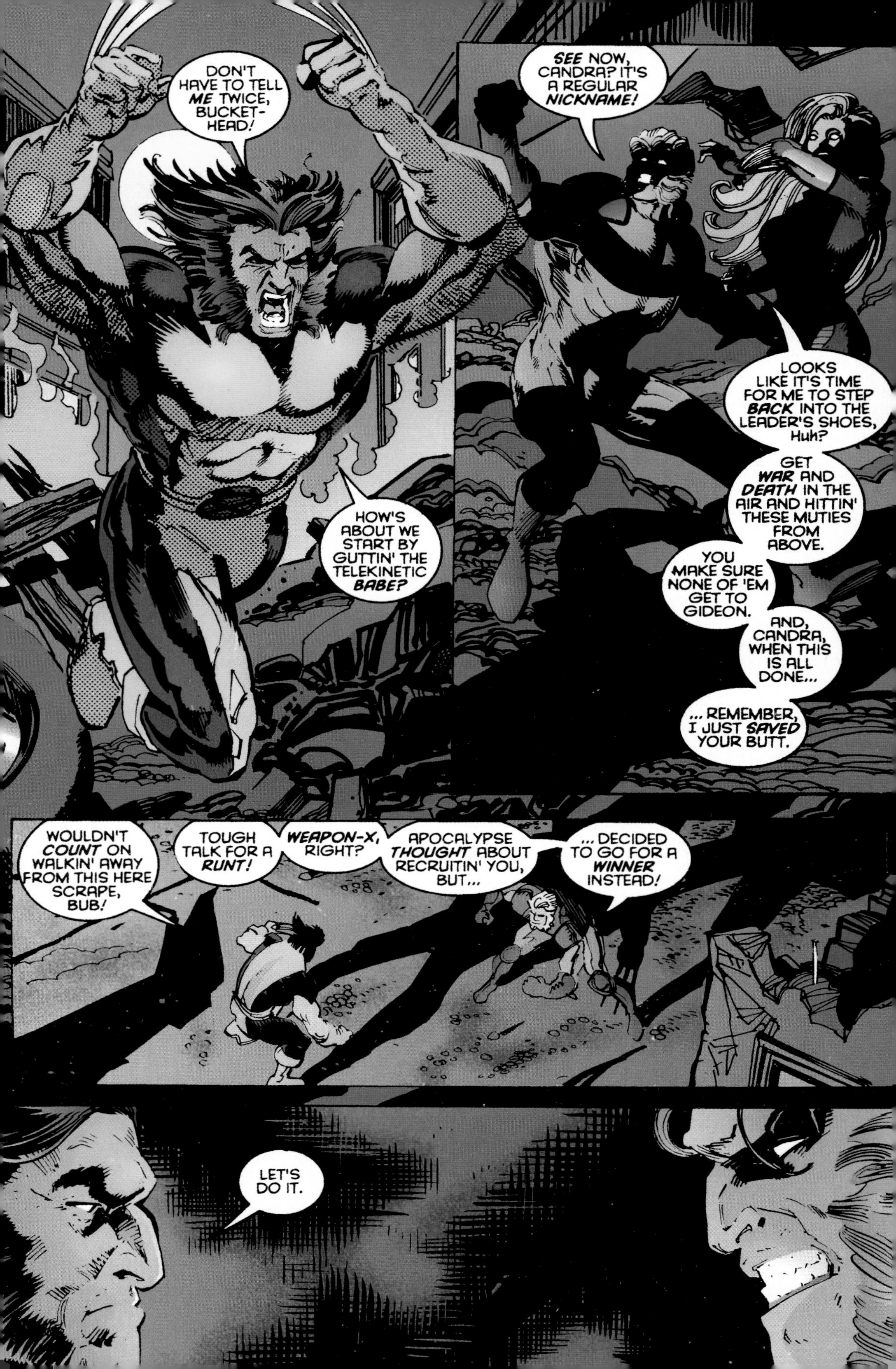
DON'T HAVE TO TELL *ME* TWICE, BUCKET-HEAD!
HOW'S ABOUT WE START BY GUTTIN' THE TELEKINETIC *BABE?*
SEE NOW, CANDRA? IT'S A REGULAR *NICKNAME!*
LOOKS LIKE IT'S TIME FOR ME TO STEP *BACK* INTO THE LEADER'S SHOES, Huh?
GET *WAR* AND *DEATH* IN THE AIR AND HITTIN' THESE MUTIES FROM ABOVE.
YOU MAKE SURE NONE OF 'EM GET TO GIDEON.
AND, CANDRA, WHEN THIS IS ALL DONE...
... REMEMBER, I JUST *SAVED* YOUR BUTT.
WOULDN'T *COUNT* ON WALKIN' AWAY FROM THIS HERE SCRAPE, BUB!
TOUGH TALK FOR A *RUNT!*
WEAPON-X, RIGHT?
APOCALYPSE *THOUGHT* ABOUT RECRUITIN' YOU, BUT...
... DECIDED TO GO FOR A *WINNER* INSTEAD!
LET'S DO IT.

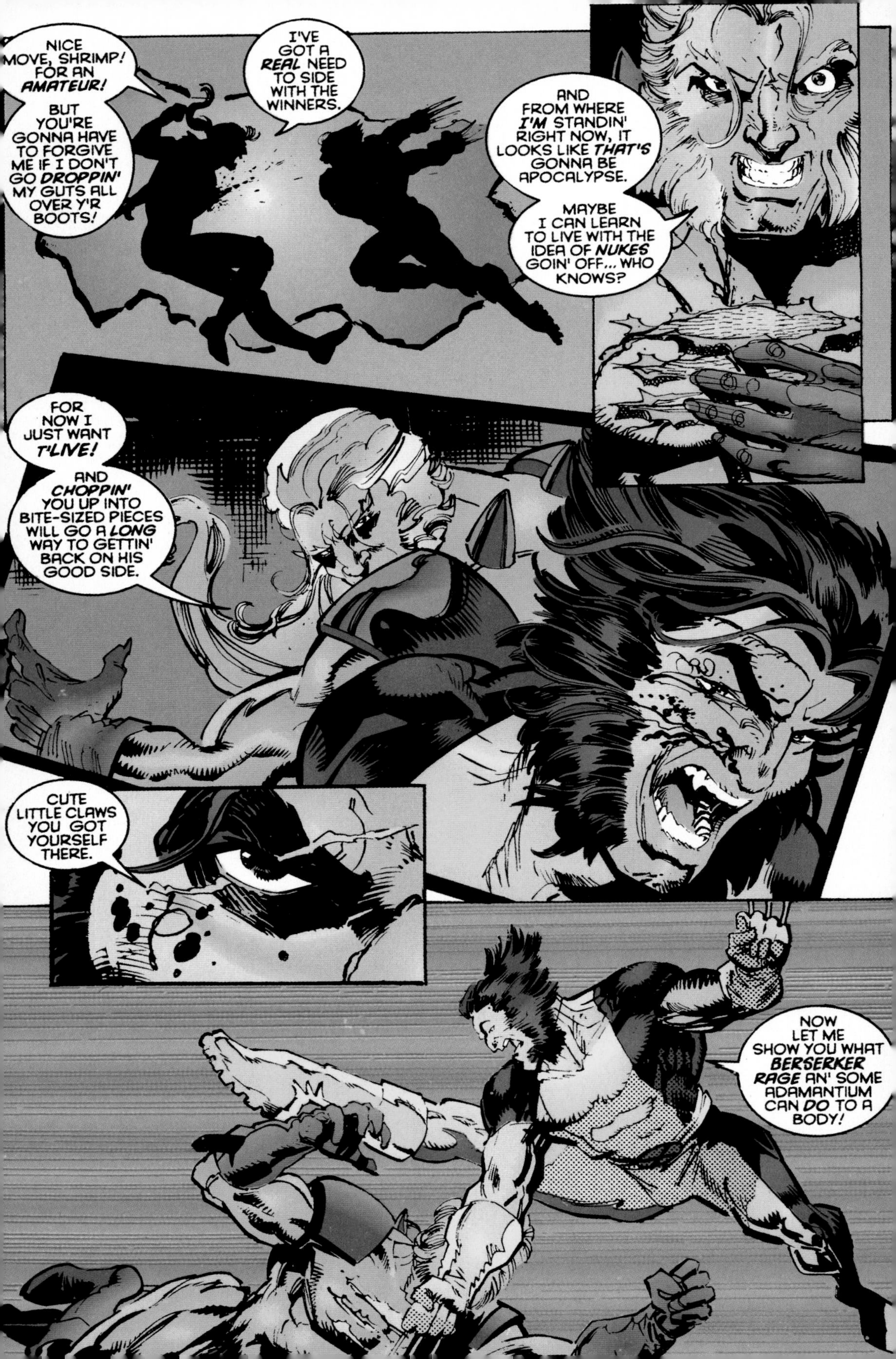
NICE MOVE, SHRIMP! FOR AN AMATEUR!
BUT YOU'RE GONNA HAVE TO FORGIVE ME IF I DON'T GO DROPPIN' MY GUTS ALL OVER Y'R BOOTS!
I'VE GOT A REAL NEED TO SIDE WITH THE WINNERS.
AND FROM WHERE I'M STANDIN' RIGHT NOW, IT LOOKS LIKE THAT'S GONNA BE APOCALYPSE.
MAYBE I CAN LEARN TO LIVE WITH THE IDEA OF NUKES GOIN' OFF... WHO KNOWS?
FOR NOW I JUST WANT T'LIVE!
AND CHOPPIN' YOU UP INTO BITE-SIZED PIECES WILL GO A LONG WAY TO GETTIN' BACK ON HIS GOOD SIDE.
CUTE LITTLE CLAWS YOU GOT YOURSELF THERE.
NOW LET ME SHOW YOU WHAT BERSERKER RAGE AN' SOME ADAMANTIUM CAN DO TO A BODY!

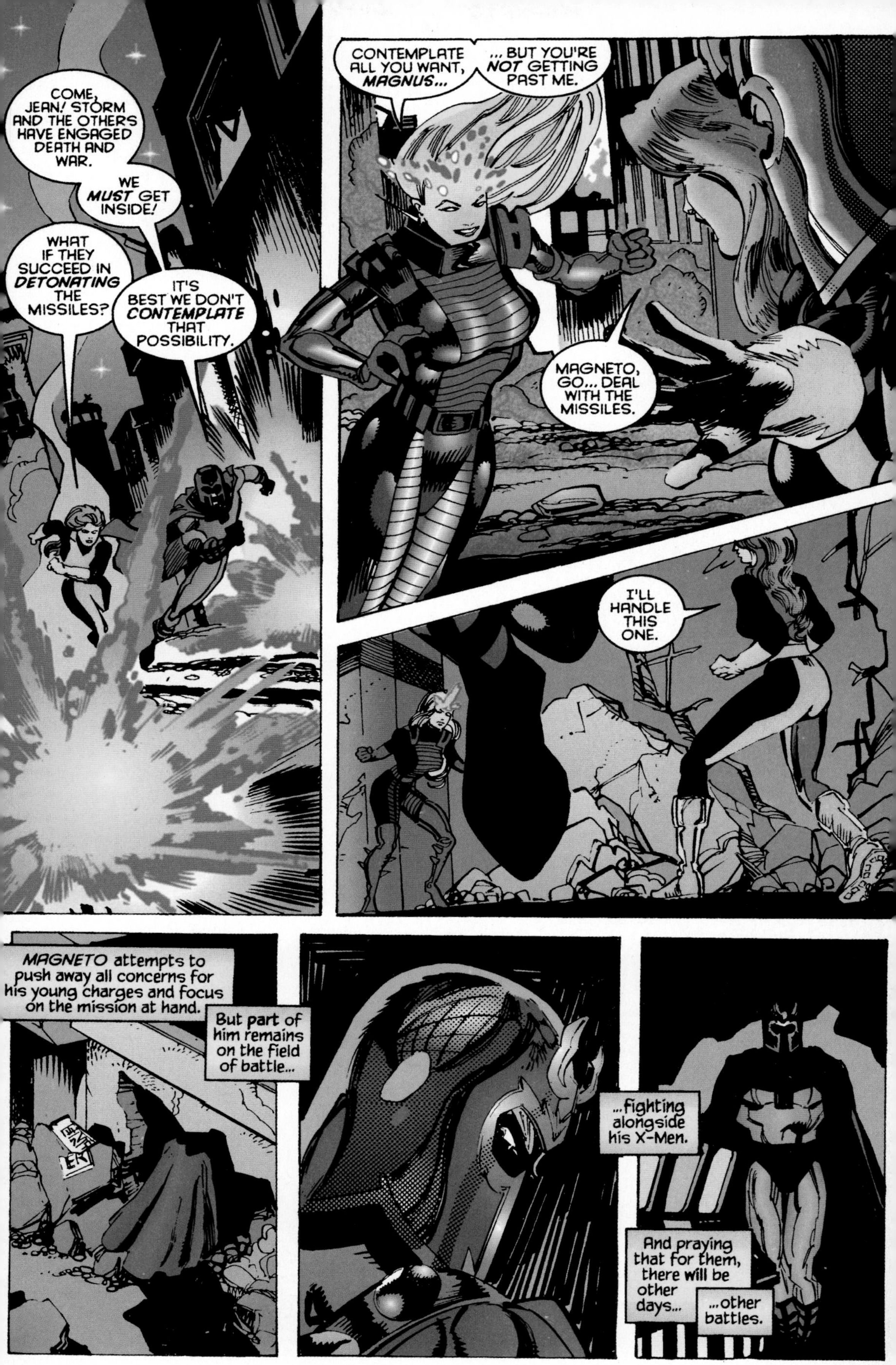
COME, JEAN! STORM AND THE OTHERS HAVE ENGAGED DEATH AND WAR.
WE MUST GET INSIDE!
WHAT IF THEY SUCCEED IN DETONATING THE MISSILES?
IT'S BEST WE DON'T CONTEMPLATE THAT POSSIBILITY.
CONTEMPLATE ALL YOU WANT, MAGNUS...
... BUT YOU'RE NOT GETTING PAST ME.
MAGNETO, GO... DEAL WITH THE MISSILES.
I'LL HANDLE THIS ONE.
MAGNETO attempts to push away all concerns for his young charges and focus on the mission at hand.
But part of him remains on the field of battle...
...fighting alongside his X-Men.
And praying that for them, there will be other days...
...other battles.

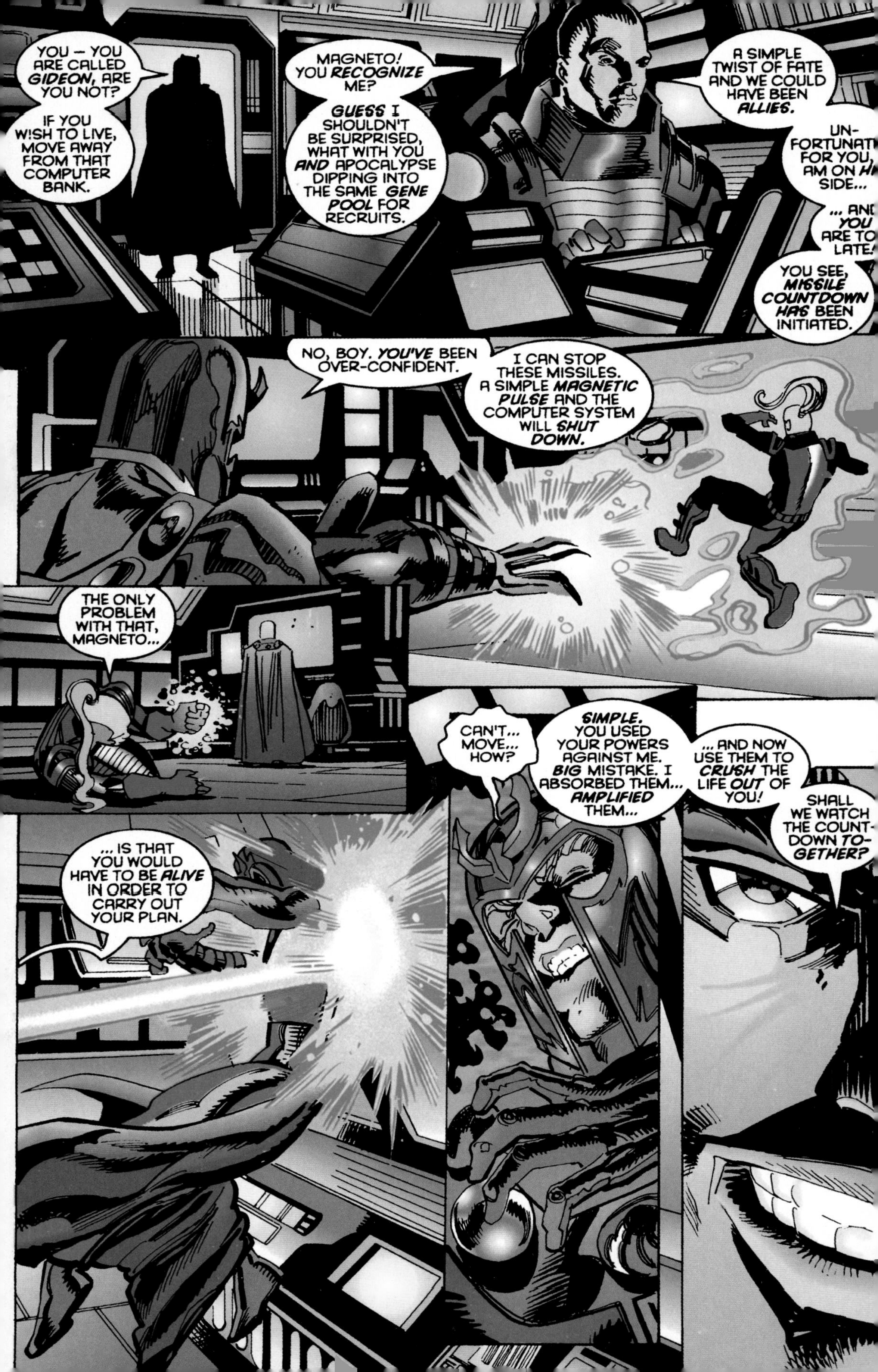
YOU — YOU ARE CALLED GIDEON, ARE YOU NOT?
IF YOU WISH TO LIVE, MOVE AWAY FROM THAT COMPUTER BANK.
MAGNETO! YOU RECOGNIZE ME?
GUESS I SHOULDN'T BE SURPRISED, WHAT WITH YOU AND APOCALYPSE DIPPING INTO THE SAME GENE POOL FOR RECRUITS.
A SIMPLE TWIST OF FATE AND WE COULD HAVE BEEN ALLIES.
UN-FORTUNAT FOR YOU, AM ON HI SIDE...
... AND YOU ARE TO LATE!
YOU SEE, MISSILE COUNTDOWN HAS BEEN INITIATED.
NO, BOY. YOU'VE BEEN OVER-CONFIDENT.
I CAN STOP THESE MISSILES. A SIMPLE MAGNETIC PULSE AND THE COMPUTER SYSTEM WILL SHUT DOWN.
THE ONLY PROBLEM WITH THAT, MAGNETO...
... IS THAT YOU WOULD HAVE TO BE ALIVE IN ORDER TO CARRY OUT YOUR PLAN.
CAN'T... MOVE... HOW?
SIMPLE. YOU USED YOUR POWERS AGAINST ME. BIG MISTAKE. I ABSORBED THEM... AMPLIFIED THEM...
... AND NOW USE THEM TO CRUSH THE LIFE OUT OF YOU!
SHALL WE WATCH THE COUNT-DOWN TO-GETHER?

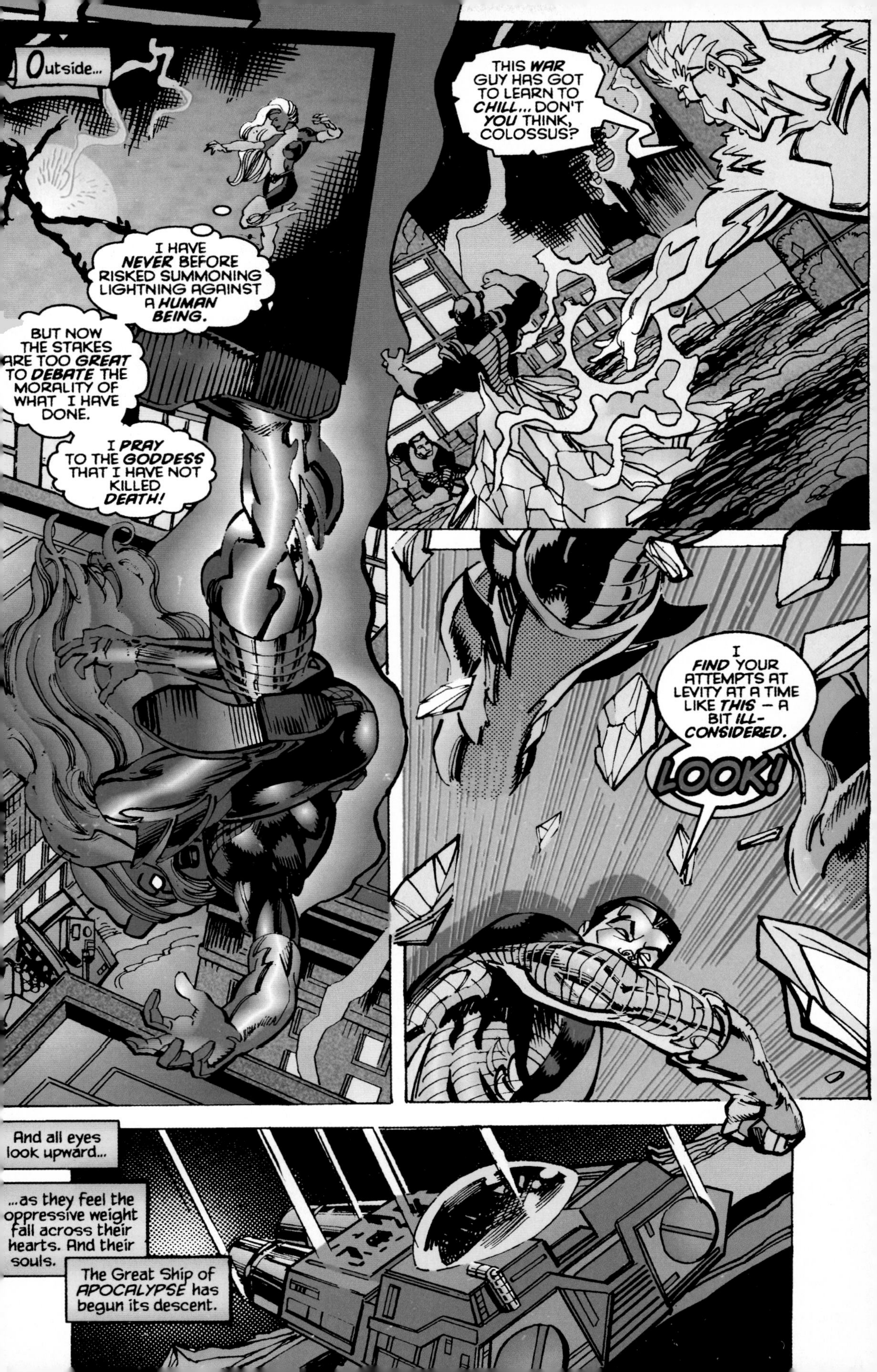
Outside...
I HAVE NEVER BEFORE RISKED SUMMONING LIGHTNING AGAINST A HUMAN BEING.
BUT NOW THE STAKES ARE TOO GREAT TO DEBATE THE MORALITY OF WHAT I HAVE DONE.
I PRAY TO THE GODDESS THAT I HAVE NOT KILLED DEATH!
THIS WAR GUY HAS GOT TO LEARN TO CHILL... DON'T YOU THINK, COLOSSUS?
I FIND YOUR ATTEMPTS AT LEVITY AT A TIME LIKE THIS — A BIT ILL-CONSIDERED.
LOOK!
And all eyes look upward...
...as they feel the oppressive weight fall across their hearts. And their souls.
The Great Ship of APOCALYPSE has begun its descent.

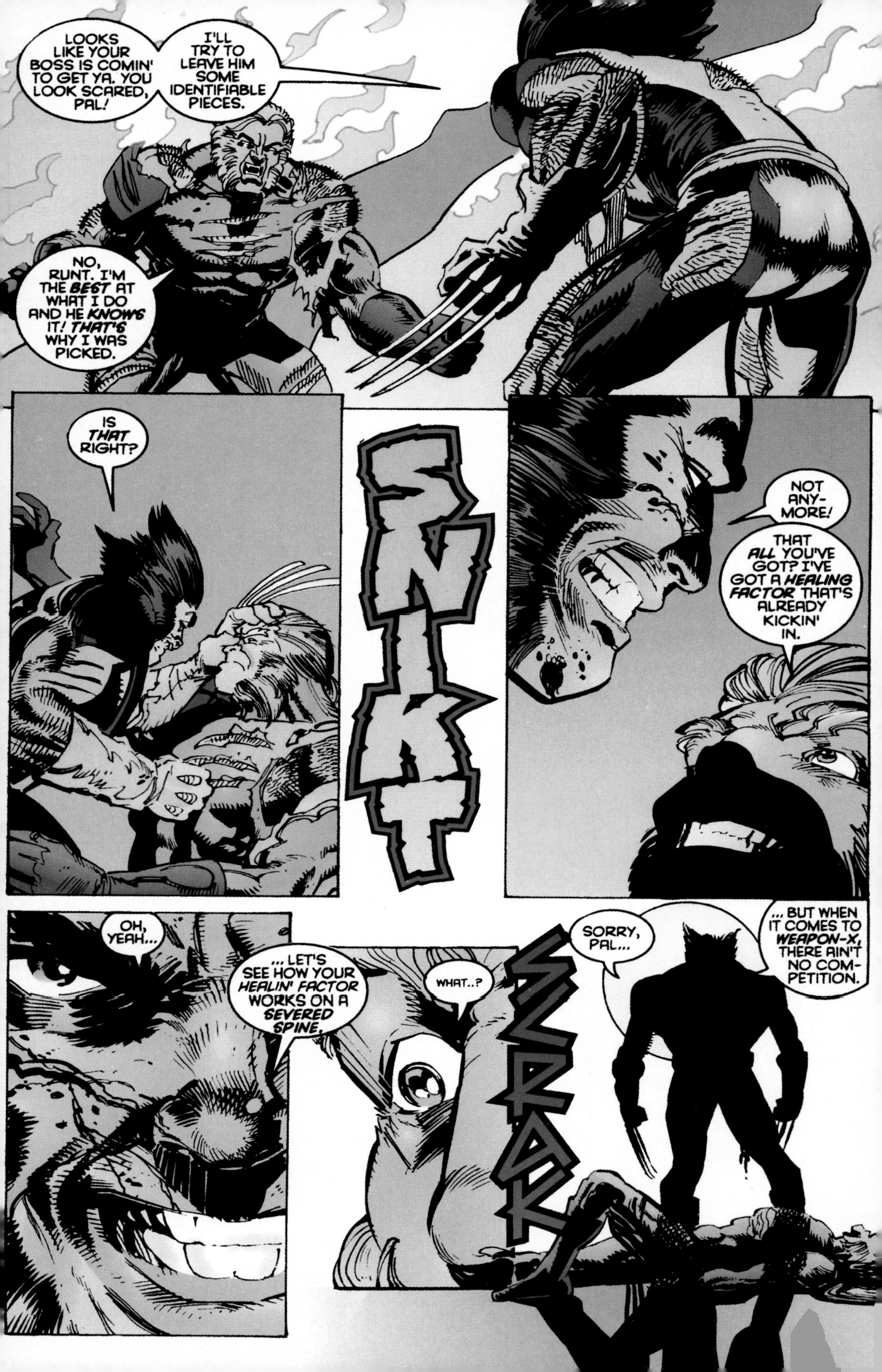
LOOKS LIKE YOUR BOSS IS COMIN' TO GET YA. YOU LOOK SCARED, PAL!
I'LL TRY TO LEAVE HIM SOME IDENTIFIABLE PIECES.
NO, RUNT. I'M THE BEST AT WHAT I DO AND HE KNOWS IT! THAT'S WHY I WAS PICKED.
IS THAT RIGHT?
SNIKT
NOT ANY-MORE!
THAT ALL YOU'VE GOT? I'VE GOT A HEALING FACTOR THAT'S ALREADY KICKIN' IN.
OH, YEAH...
... LET'S SEE HOW YOUR HEALIN' FACTOR WORKS ON A SEVERED SPINE.
WHAT..?
SKRAK
SORRY, PAL...
... BUT WHEN IT COMES TO WEAPON-X, THERE AIN'T NO COM-PETITION.

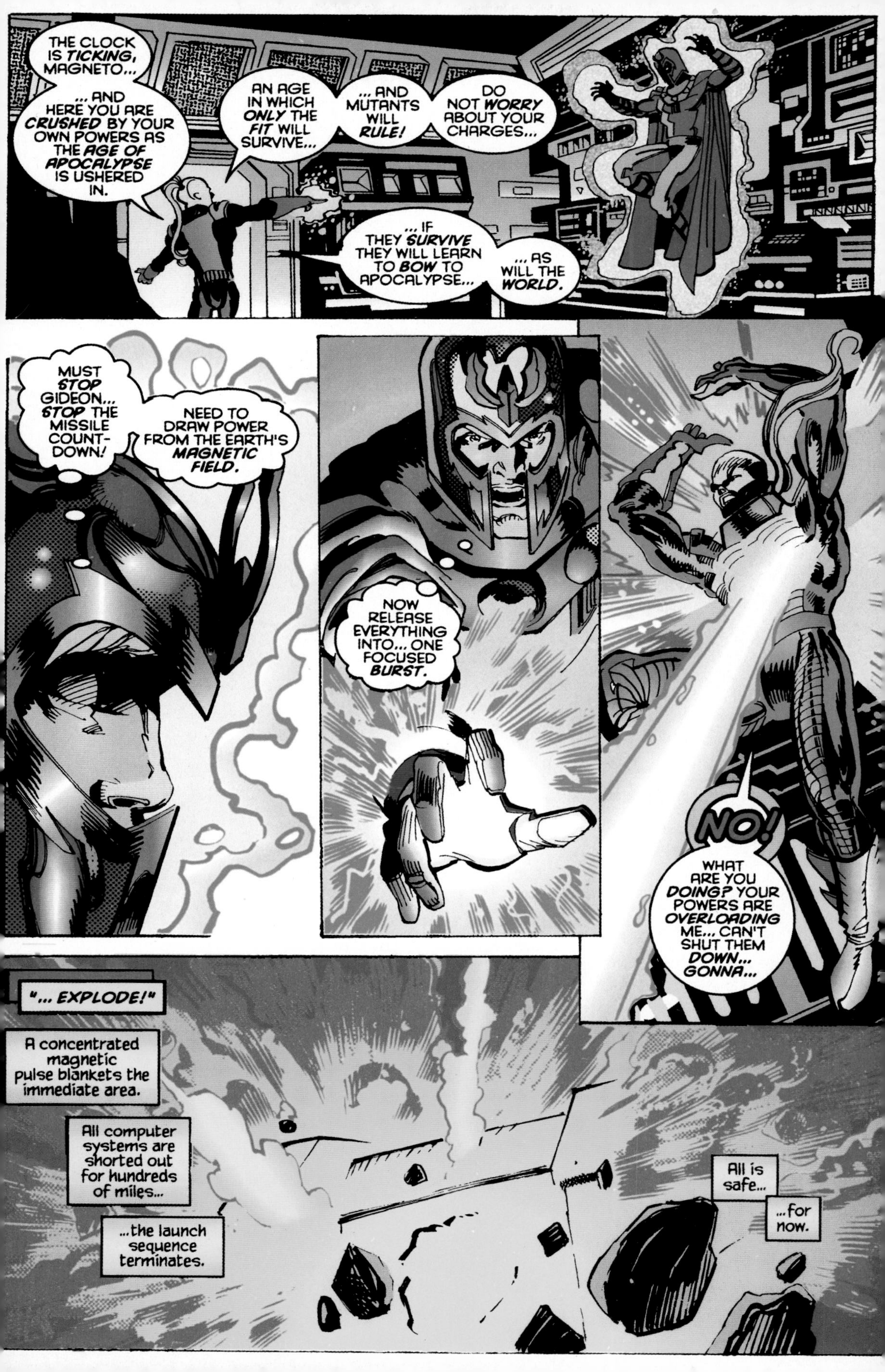

THE CLOCK IS TICKING, MAGNETO...
... AND HERE YOU ARE CRUSHED BY YOUR OWN POWERS AS THE AGE OF APOCALYPSE IS USHERED IN.
AN AGE IN WHICH ONLY THE FIT WILL SURVIVE...
... AND MUTANTS WILL RULE!
DO NOT WORRY ABOUT YOUR CHARGES...
... IF THEY SURVIVE THEY WILL LEARN TO BOW TO APOCALYPSE...
... AS WILL THE WORLD.
MUST STOP GIDEON... STOP THE MISSILE COUNT-DOWN!
NEED TO DRAW POWER FROM THE EARTH'S MAGNETIC FIELD.
NOW RELEASE EVERYTHING INTO... ONE FOCUSED BURST.
NO!
WHAT ARE YOU DOING? YOUR POWERS ARE OVERLOADING ME... CAN'T SHUT THEM DOWN... GONNA...
"... EXPLODE!"
A concentrated magnetic pulse blankets the immediate area.
All computer systems are shorted out for hundreds of miles...
...the launch sequence terminates.
All is safe...
...for now.

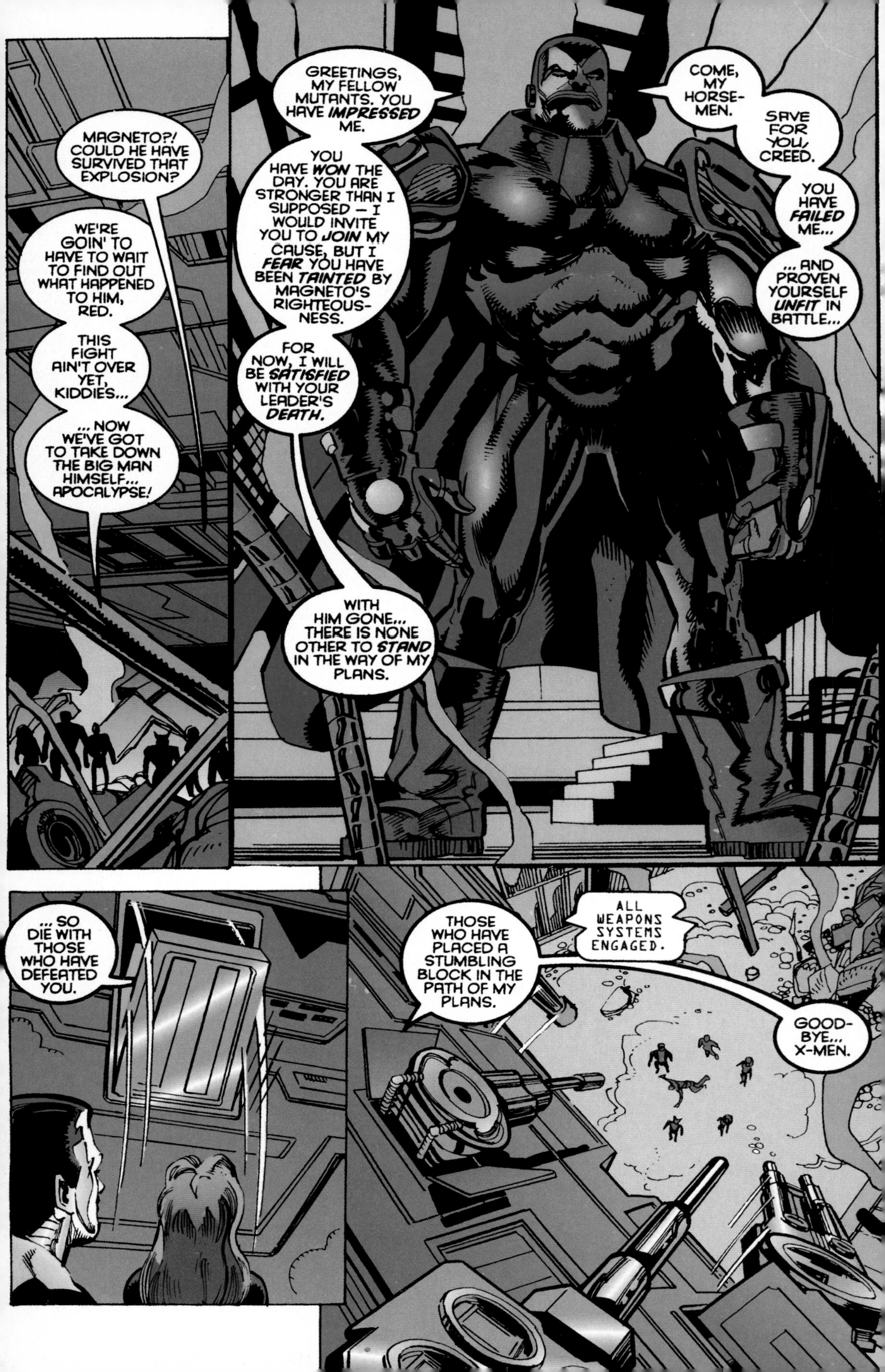
MAGNETO?! COULD HE HAVE SURVIVED THAT EXPLOSION?
WE'RE GOIN' TO HAVE TO WAIT TO FIND OUT WHAT HAPPENED TO HIM, RED.
THIS FIGHT AIN'T OVER YET, KIDDIES...
... NOW WE'VE GOT TO TAKE DOWN THE BIG MAN HIMSELF... APOCALYPSE!
GREETINGS, MY FELLOW MUTANTS. YOU HAVE IMPRESSED ME.
YOU HAVE WON THE DAY. YOU ARE STRONGER THAN I SUPPOSED — I WOULD INVITE YOU TO JOIN MY CAUSE, BUT I FEAR YOU HAVE BEEN TAINTED BY MAGNETO'S RIGHTEOUSNESS.
FOR NOW, I WILL BE SATISFIED WITH YOUR LEADER'S DEATH.
WITH HIM GONE... THERE IS NONE OTHER TO STAND IN THE WAY OF MY PLANS.
COME, MY HORSEMEN.
SAVE FOR YOU, CREED.
YOU HAVE FAILED ME...
... AND PROVEN YOURSELF UNFIT IN BATTLE...
... SO DIE WITH THOSE WHO HAVE DEFEATED YOU.
THOSE WHO HAVE PLACED A STUMBLING BLOCK IN THE PATH OF MY PLANS.
ALL WEAPONS SYSTEMS ENGAGED.
GOOD-BYE... X-MEN.

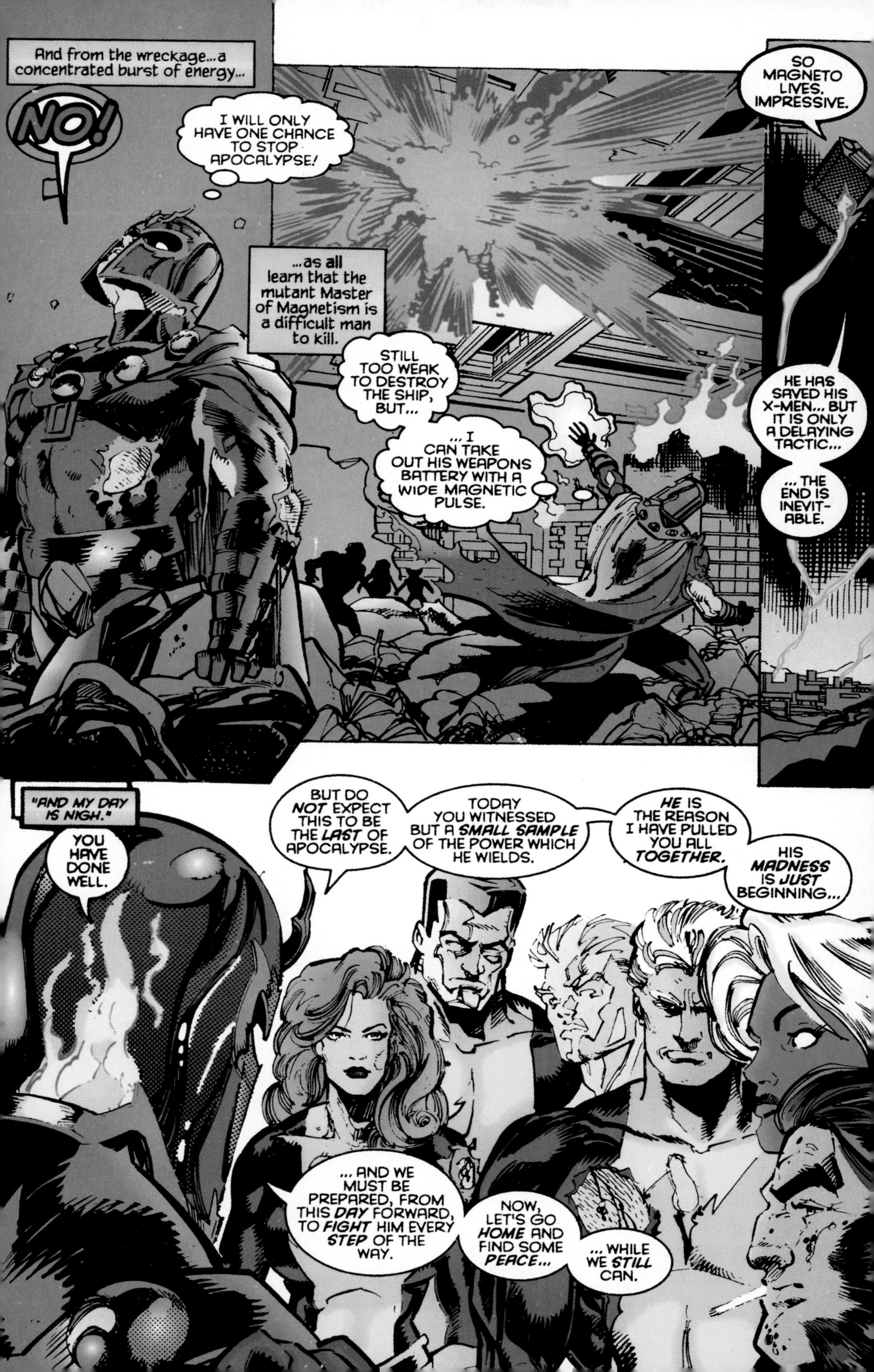

And from the wreckage...a concentrated burst of energy...
NO!
I WILL ONLY HAVE ONE CHANCE TO STOP APOCALYPSE!
...as all learn that the mutant Master of Magnetism is a difficult man to kill.
STILL TOO WEAK TO DESTROY THE SHIP, BUT...
...I CAN TAKE OUT HIS WEAPONS BATTERY WITH A WIDE MAGNETIC PULSE.
SO MAGNETO LIVES. IMPRESSIVE.
HE HAS SAVED HIS X-MEN... BUT IT IS ONLY A DELAYING TACTIC...
...THE END IS INEVIT-ABLE.
"AND MY DAY IS NIGH."
YOU HAVE DONE WELL.
BUT DO NOT EXPECT THIS TO BE THE LAST OF APOCALYPSE.
TODAY YOU WITNESSED BUT A SMALL SAMPLE OF THE POWER WHICH HE WIELDS.
HE IS THE REASON I HAVE PULLED YOU ALL TOGETHER.
HIS MADNESS IS JUST BEGINNING...
...AND WE MUST BE PREPARED, FROM THIS DAY FORWARD, TO FIGHT HIM EVERY STEP OF THE WAY.
NOW, LET'S GO HOME AND FIND SOME PEACE...
...WHILE WE STILL CAN.

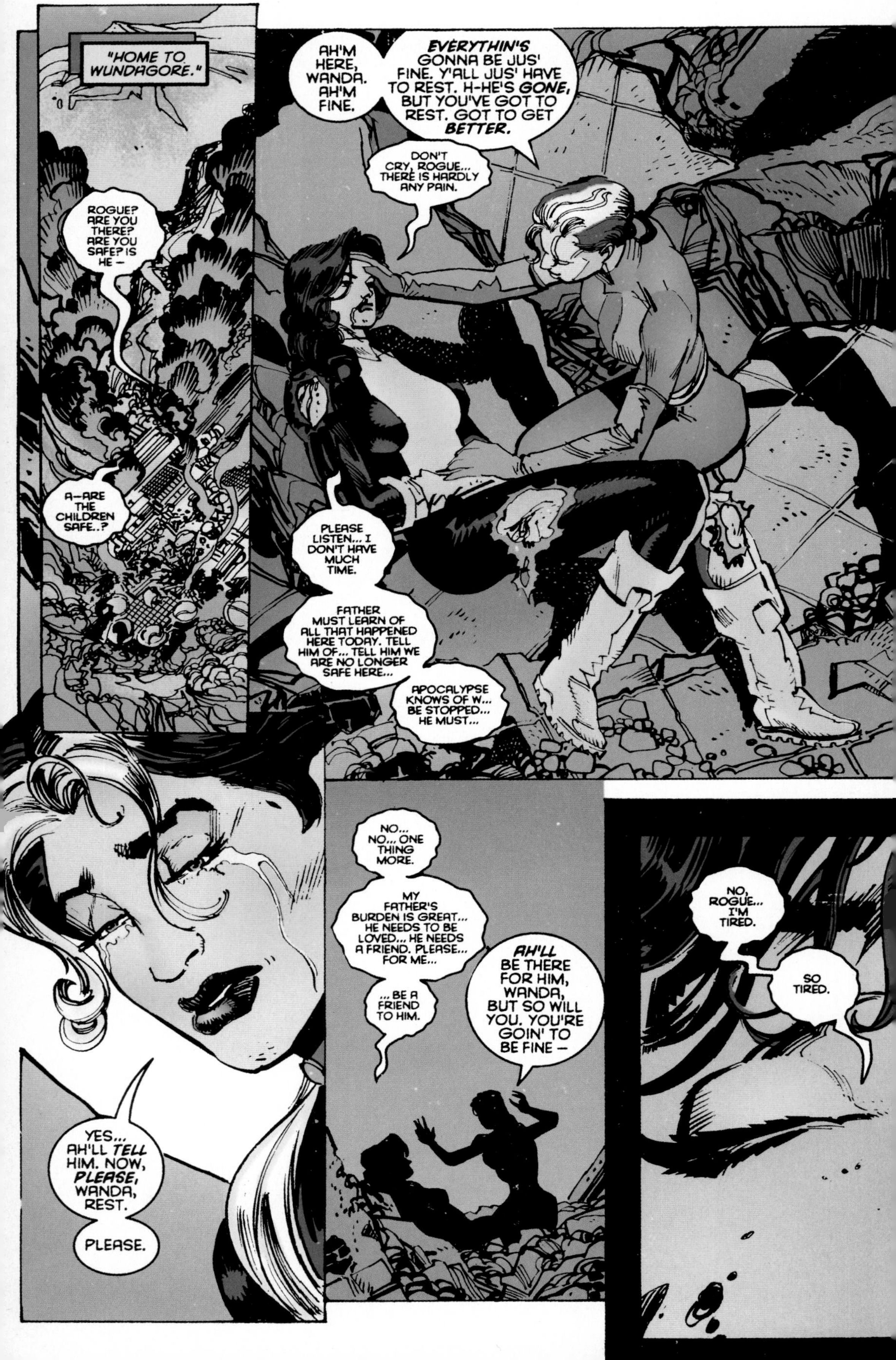

"HOME TO WUNDAGORE."
ROGUE? ARE YOU THERE? ARE YOU SAFE? IS HE –
A–ARE THE CHILDREN SAFE..?
AH'M HERE, WANDA. AH'M FINE.
EVERYTHIN'S GONNA BE JUS' FINE. Y'ALL JUS' HAVE TO REST. H-HE'S GONE, BUT YOU'VE GOT TO REST. GOT TO GET BETTER.
DON'T CRY, ROGUE... THERE IS HARDLY ANY PAIN.
PLEASE LISTEN... I DON'T HAVE MUCH TIME.
FATHER MUST LEARN OF ALL THAT HAPPENED HERE TODAY. TELL HIM OF... TELL HIM WE ARE NO LONGER SAFE HERE...
APOCALYPSE KNOWS OF W... BE STOPPED... HE MUST...
YES... AH'LL TELL HIM. NOW, PLEASE, WANDA, REST.
PLEASE.
NO... NO... ONE THING MORE.
MY FATHER'S BURDEN IS GREAT... HE NEEDS TO BE LOVED... HE NEEDS A FRIEND. PLEASE... FOR ME...
...BE A FRIEND TO HIM.
AH'LL BE THERE FOR HIM, WANDA, BUT SO WILL YOU. YOU'RE GOIN' TO BE FINE –
NO, ROGUE... I'M TIRED.
SO TIRED.

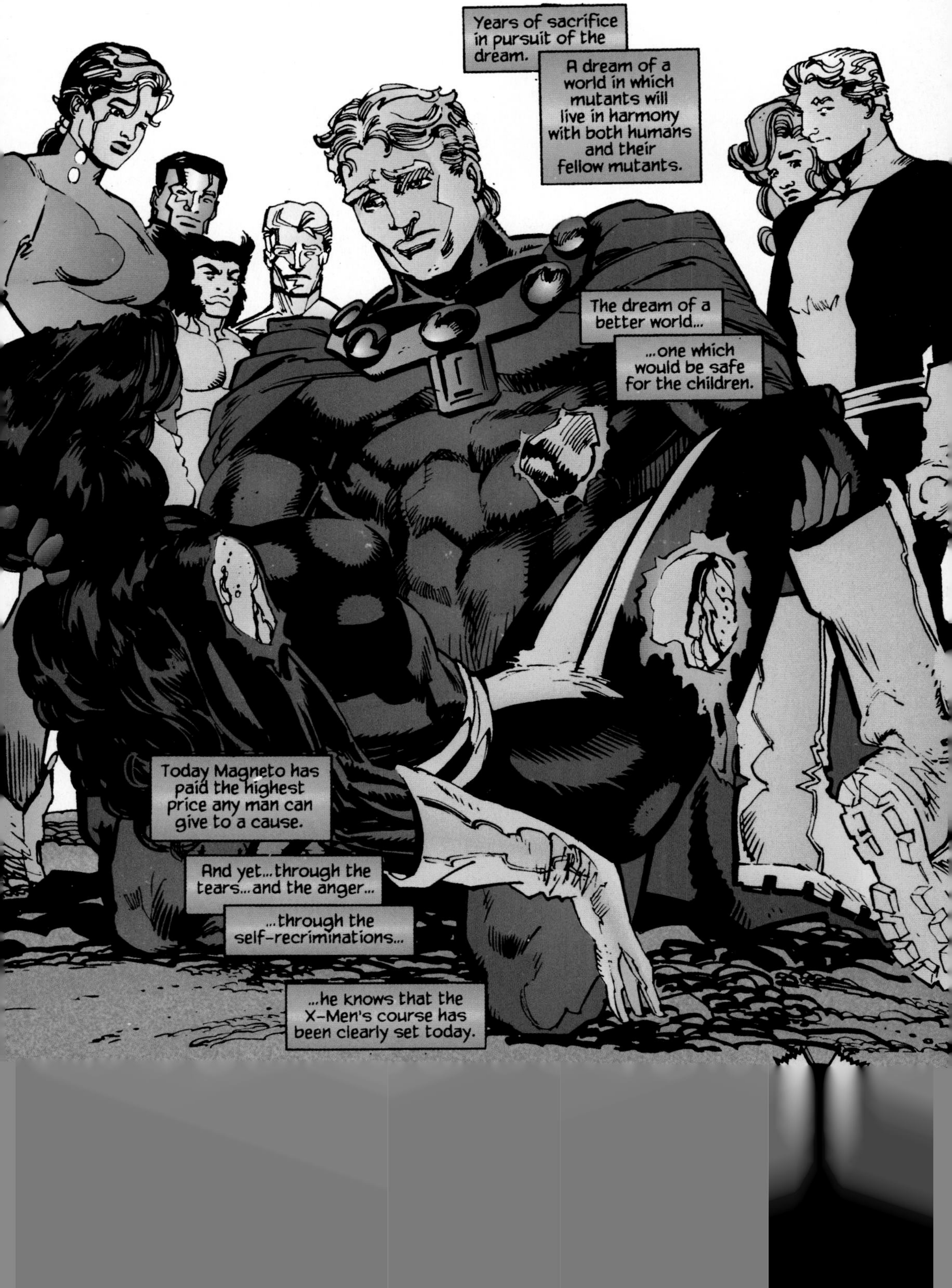
Years of sacrifice in pursuit of the dream.
A dream of a world in which mutants will live in harmony with both humans and their fellow mutants.
The dream of a better world...
...one which would be safe for the children.
Today Magneto has paid the highest price any man can give to a cause.
And yet...through the tears...and the anger...
...through the self-recriminations...
...he knows that the X-Men's course has been clearly set today.

MARVEL COMICS
TALES FROM THE AGE OF
APOCALYPSE™
STARRING
FACTOR X
MOORE
VAUGHAN
EPTING
NAPOLITANO

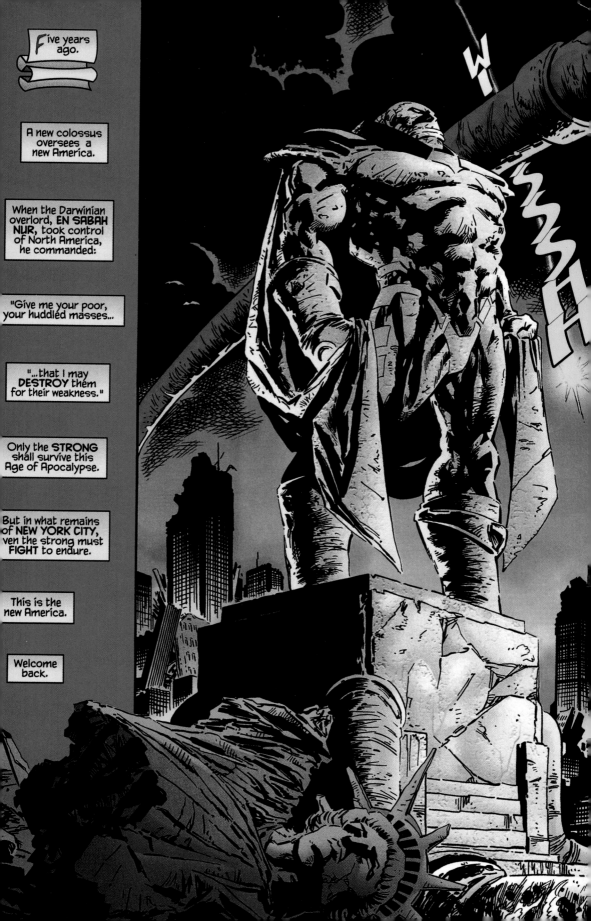

Five years ago.

A new colossus oversees a new America.

When the Darwinian overlord, **EN SABAH NUR**, took control of North America, he commanded:

"Give me your poor, your huddled masses...

"...that I may **DESTROY** them for their weakness."

Only the **STRONG** shall survive this Age of Apocalypse.

But in what remains of **NEW YORK CITY**, ven the strong must **FIGHT** to endure.

This is the new America.

Welcome back.

Had CHARLES XAVIER and his dream of humans and mutants living in harmony SURVIVED --

-- perhaps the old America would have as WELL.

Perhaps the country would still open her arms to all "tempest-tossed" OUTSIDERS.

THAT, however, is senseless fantasy and pointless conjecture.

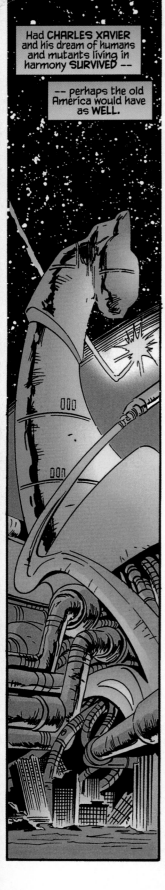

THIS... is reality.

SCARAB NINE IN PURSUIT OF AN UN-IDENTIFIED AND WOUNDED BOGEY.

SCARAB FOUR SCANNING FOR LIFE-SIGNS. CAN'T GET A CLEAR READ.

MIGHT BE EMPTY. MIGHT BE A FLATSCAN.

LONG LIVE THE DARK LORD.

DOESN'T MATTER. YOU KNOW THE DRILL. "THE WEAK SHALL PERISH." SCARAB SEVEN LOCKING ON.

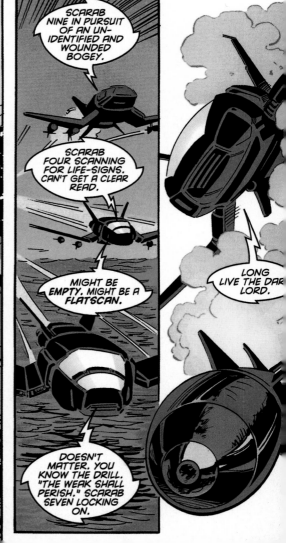

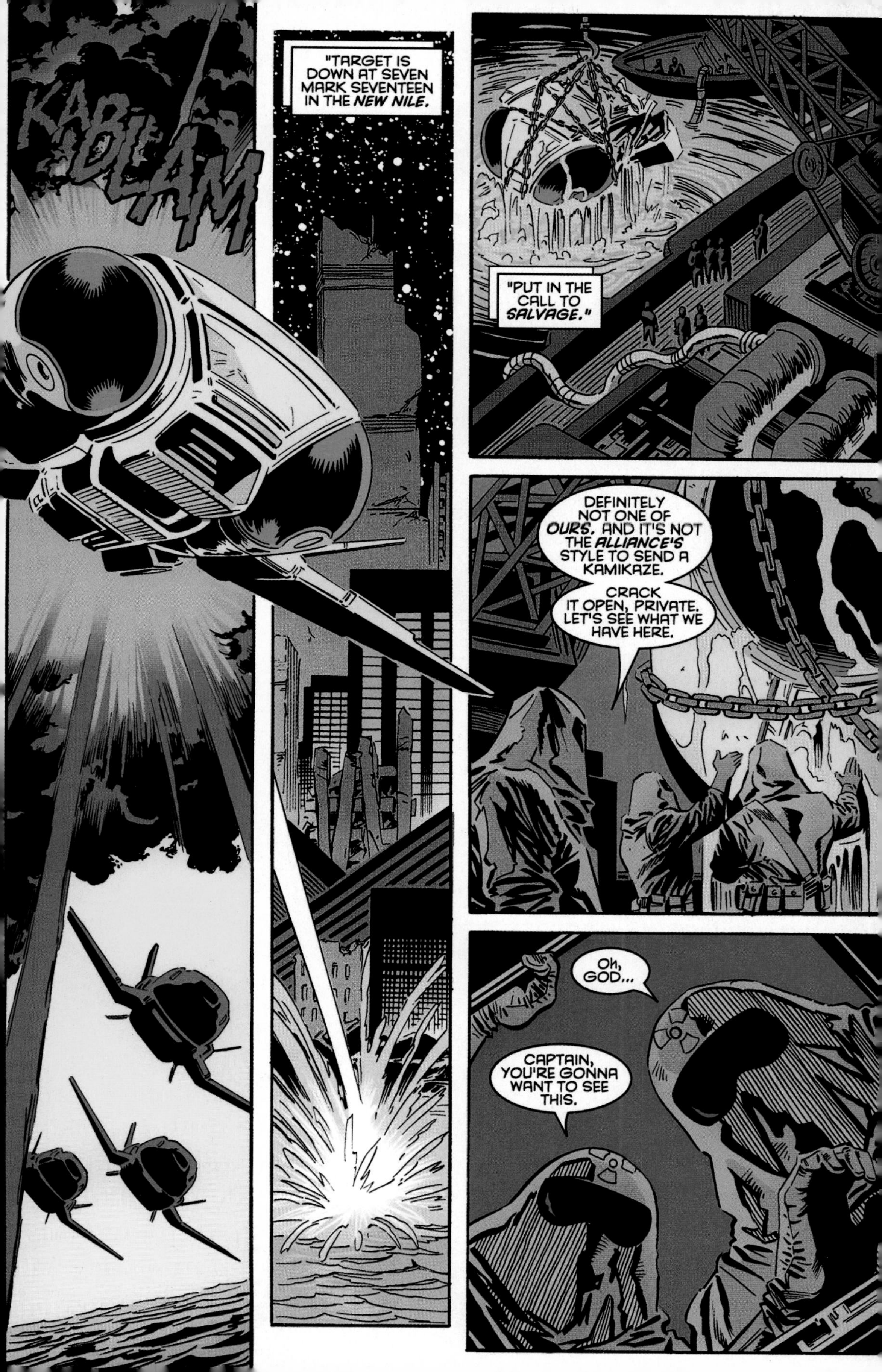
KABLAM
"TARGET IS DOWN AT SEVEN MARK SEVENTEEN IN THE NEW NILE.
"PUT IN THE CALL TO SALVAGE."
DEFINITELY NOT ONE OF OURS. AND IT'S NOT THE ALLIANCE'S STYLE TO SEND A KAMIKAZE.
CRACK IT OPEN, PRIVATE. LET'S SEE WHAT WE HAVE HERE.
Oh, GOD...
CAPTAIN, YOU'RE GONNA WANT TO SEE THIS.

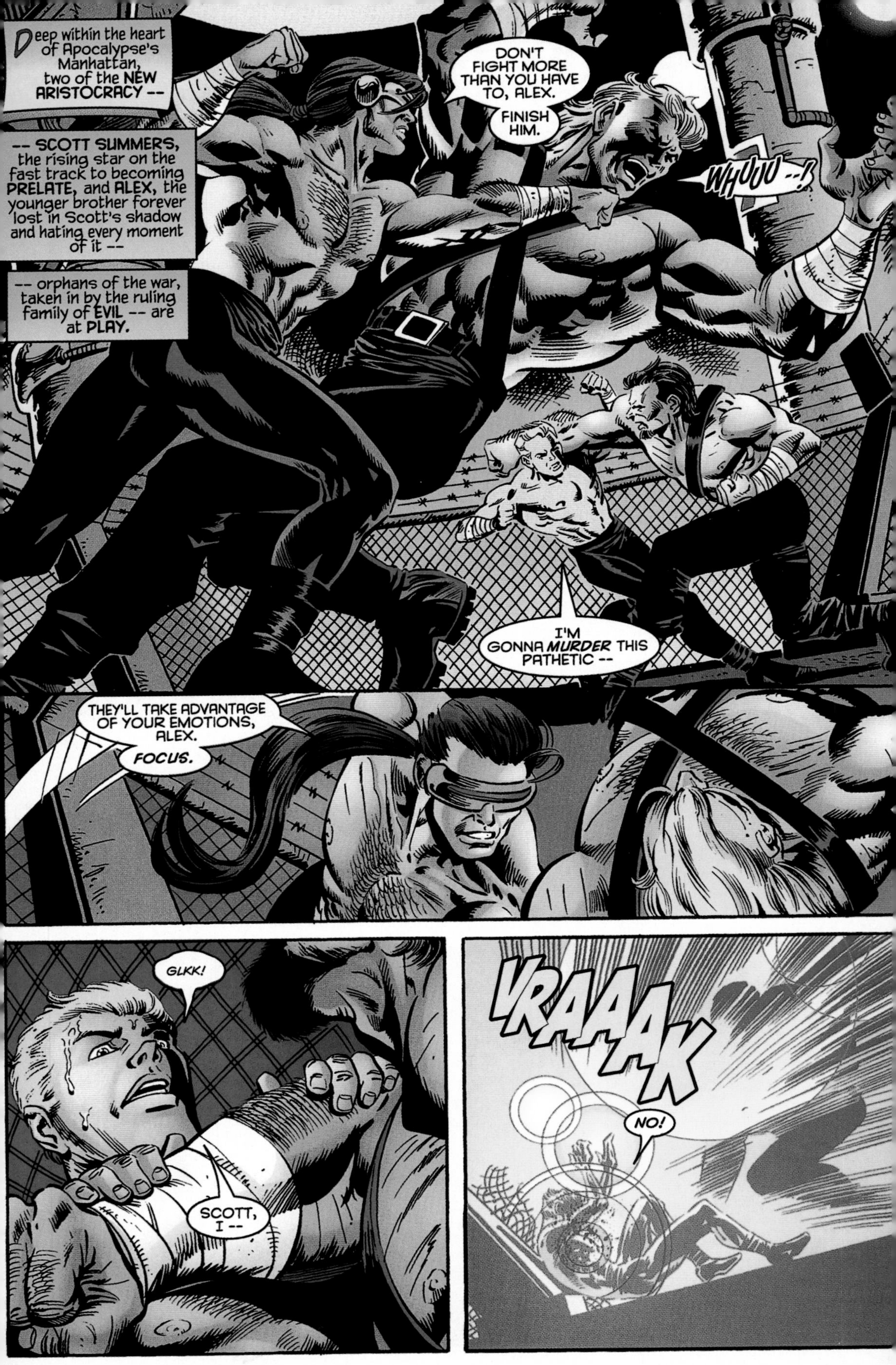
Deep within the heart of Apocalypse's Manhattan, two of the NEW ARISTOCRACY --
DON'T FIGHT MORE THAN YOU HAVE TO, ALEX.
FINISH HIM.
-- SCOTT SUMMERS, the rising star on the fast track to becoming PRELATE, and ALEX, the younger brother forever lost in Scott's shadow and hating every moment of it --
WHUUU --!
-- orphans of the war, taken in by the ruling family of EVIL -- are at PLAY.
I'M GONNA MURDER THIS PATHETIC --
THEY'LL TAKE ADVANTAGE OF YOUR EMOTIONS, ALEX.
FOCUS.
GLKK!
SCOTT, I --
VRAAAK
NO!

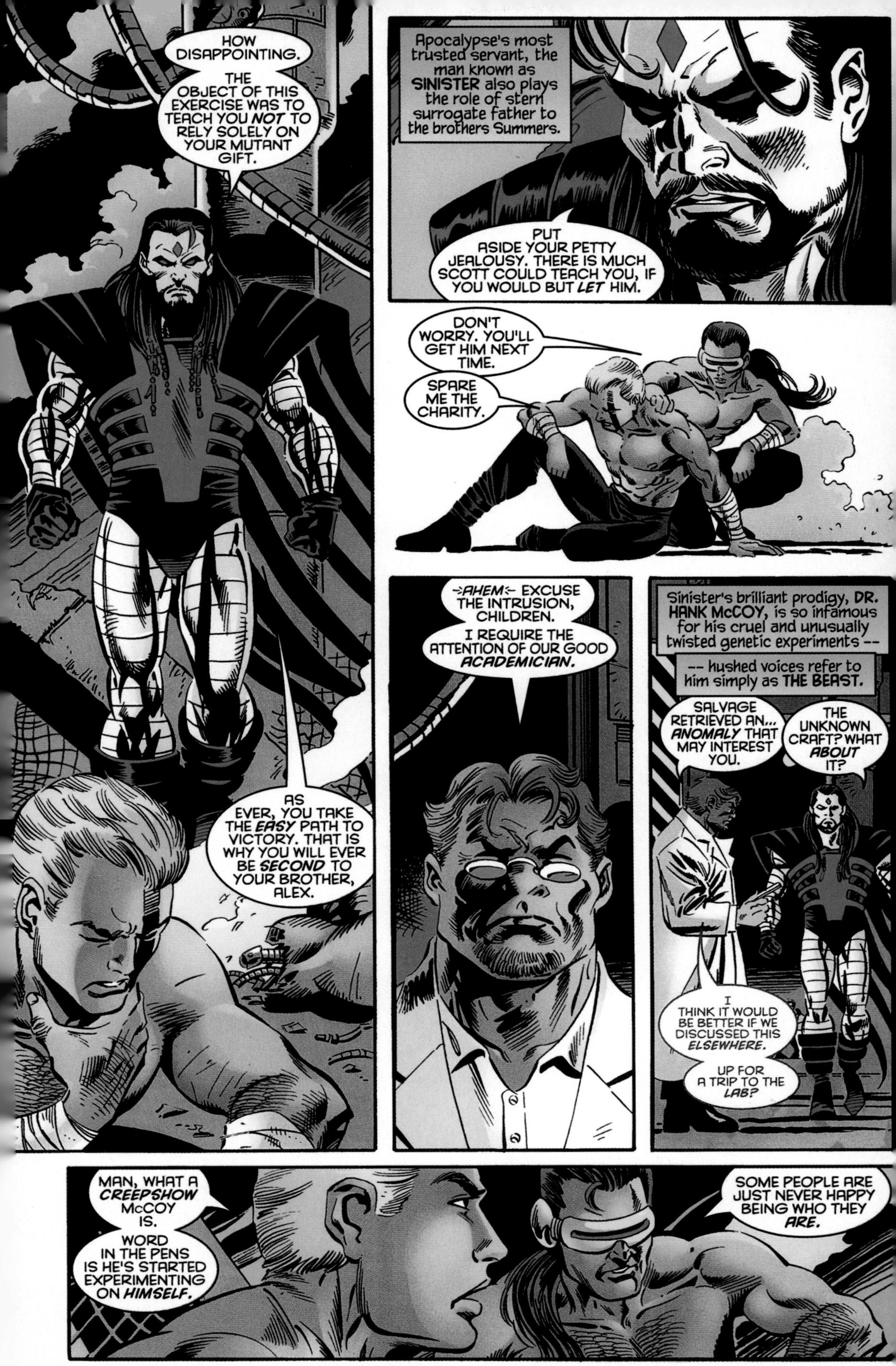
HOW DISAPPOINTING.
THE OBJECT OF THIS EXERCISE WAS TO TEACH YOU NOT TO RELY SOLELY ON YOUR MUTANT GIFT.
AS EVER, YOU TAKE THE EASY PATH TO VICTORY. THAT IS WHY YOU WILL EVER BE SECOND TO YOUR BROTHER, ALEX.
Apocalypse's most trusted servant, the man known as SINISTER also plays the role of stern surrogate father to the brothers Summers.
PUT ASIDE YOUR PETTY JEALOUSY. THERE IS MUCH SCOTT COULD TEACH YOU, IF YOU WOULD BUT LET HIM.
DON'T WORRY. YOU'LL GET HIM NEXT TIME.
SPARE ME THE CHARITY.
-AHEM- EXCUSE THE INTRUSION, CHILDREN.
I REQUIRE THE ATTENTION OF OUR GOOD ACADEMICIAN.
Sinister's brilliant prodigy, DR. HANK McCOY, is so infamous for his cruel and unusually twisted genetic experiments --
-- hushed voices refer to him simply as THE BEAST.
SALVAGE RETRIEVED AN... ANOMALY THAT MAY INTEREST YOU.
THE UNKNOWN CRAFT? WHAT ABOUT IT?
I THINK IT WOULD BE BETTER IF WE DISCUSSED THIS ELSEWHERE.
UP FOR A TRIP TO THE LAB?
MAN, WHAT A CREEPSHOW McCOY IS.
WORD IN THE PENS IS HE'S STARTED EXPERIMENTING ON HIMSELF.
SOME PEOPLE ARE JUST NEVER HAPPY BEING WHO THEY ARE.

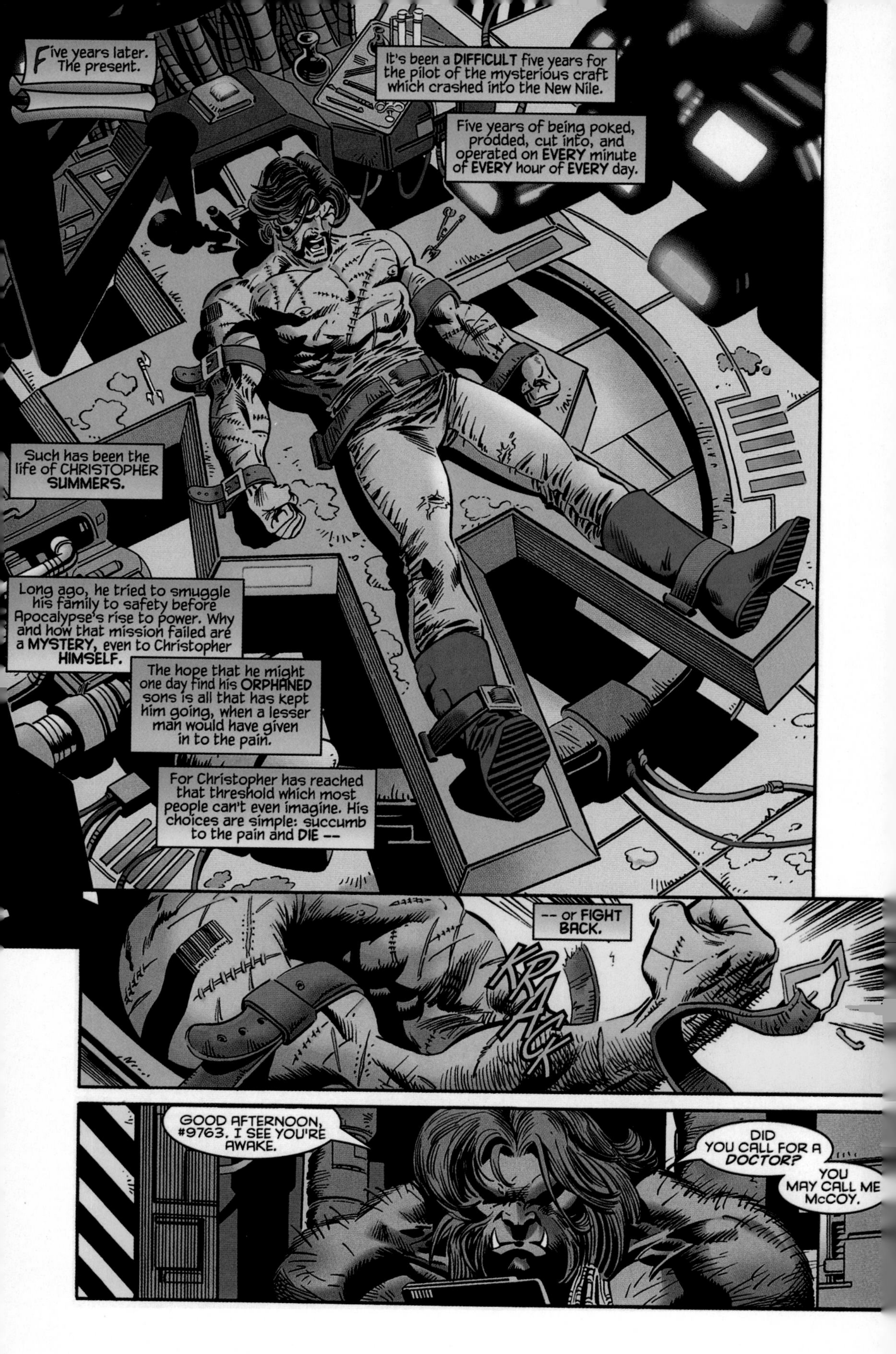
Five years later. The present.
It's been a DIFFICULT five years for the pilot of the mysterious craft which crashed into the New Nile.
Five years of being poked, prodded, cut into, and operated on EVERY minute of EVERY hour of EVERY day.
Such has been the life of CHRISTOPHER SUMMERS.
Long ago, he tried to smuggle his family to safety before Apocalypse's rise to power. Why and how that mission failed are a MYSTERY, even to Christopher HIMSELF.
The hope that he might one day find his ORPHANED sons is all that has kept him going, when a lesser man would have given in to the pain.
For Christopher has reached that threshold which most people can't even imagine. His choices are simple: succumb to the pain and DIE --
-- or FIGHT BACK.
KRAACK
GOOD AFTERNOON, #9763. I SEE YOU'RE AWAKE.
DID YOU CALL FOR A DOCTOR?
YOU MAY CALL ME McCOY.

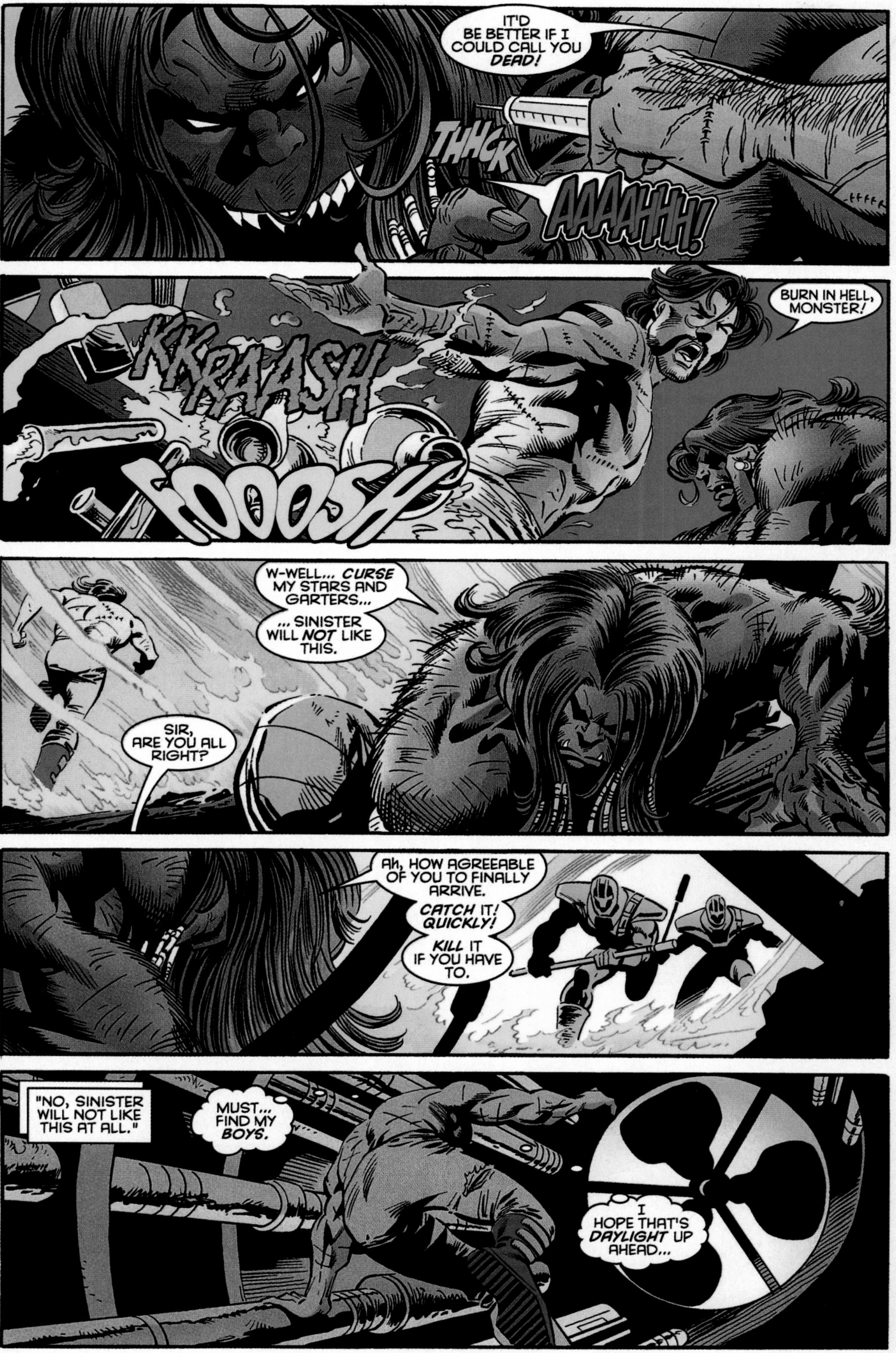

IT'D BE BETTER IF I COULD CALL YOU DEAD!
THHCK
AAAAHHH!
KKRAASH
BURN IN HELL, MONSTER!
FOOOSH
W-WELL... CURSE MY STARS AND GARTERS...
... SINISTER WILL NOT LIKE THIS.
SIR, ARE YOU ALL RIGHT?
Ah, HOW AGREEABLE OF YOU TO FINALLY ARRIVE.
CATCH IT! QUICKLY!
KILL IT IF YOU HAVE TO.
"NO, SINISTER WILL NOT LIKE THIS AT ALL."
MUST... FIND MY BOYS.
I HOPE THAT'S DAYLIGHT UP AHEAD...

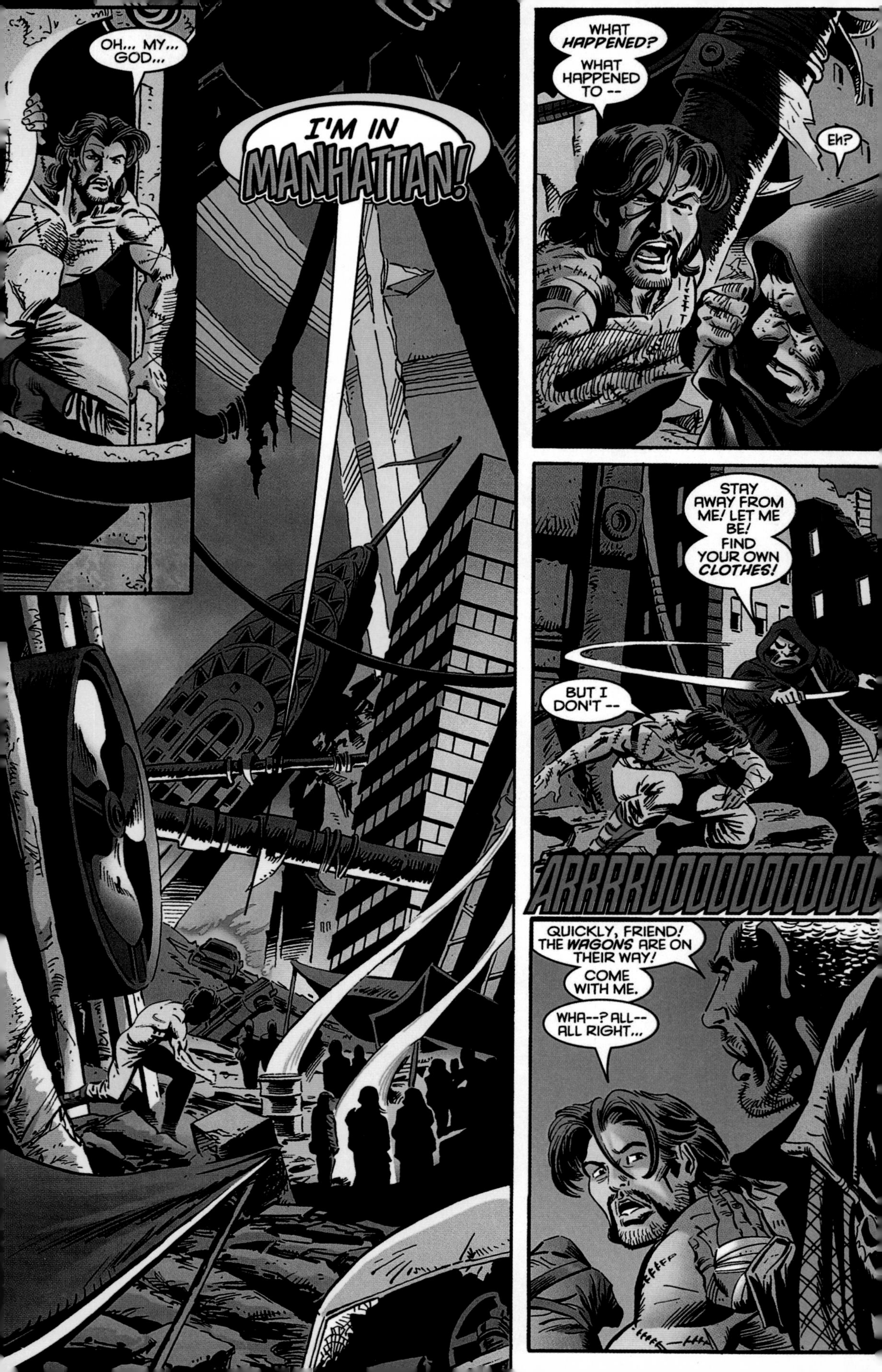
OH... MY... GOD...
I'M IN MANHATTAN!
WHAT *HAPPENED?*
WHAT HAPPENED TO --
Eh?
STAY AWAY FROM ME! LET ME BE! FIND YOUR OWN *CLOTHES!*
BUT I DON'T --
ARRRROOOOOOOOOOO
QUICKLY, FRIEND! THE *WAGONS* ARE ON THEIR WAY!
COME WITH ME.
WHA--? ALL-- ALL RIGHT...

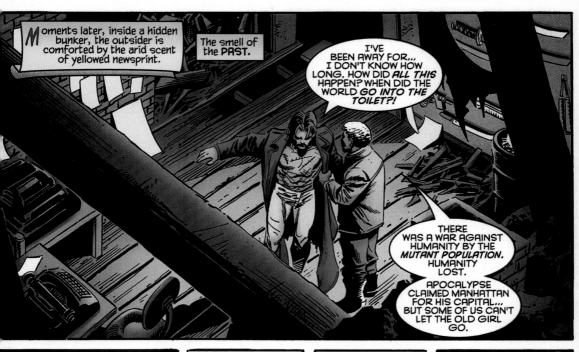

Moments later, inside a hidden bunker, the outsider is comforted by the arid scent of yellowed newsprint.

The smell of the **PAST.**

I'VE BEEN AWAY FOR... I DON'T KNOW HOW LONG. HOW DID *ALL THIS* HAPPEN? WHEN DID THE WORLD *GO INTO THE TOILET?!*

THERE WAS A WAR AGAINST HUMANITY BY THE *MUTANT POPULATION.* HUMANITY LOST. APOCALYPSE CLAIMED MANHATTAN FOR HIS CAPITAL... BUT SOME OF US CAN'T LET THE OLD GIRL GO.

I TRY TO KEEP THE *FLATSCANS* LIKE MYSELF INFORMED OF THE NEWS APOCALYPSE WON'T TELL THEM. I --

SORRY. TOO MUCH TIME WITH THE MIMEOGRAPH AND A MAN LOSES HIS SOCIAL SKILLS. *JOE ROBERTSON.*

FRIENDS I HAVE LEFT CALL ME *ROBBIE.*

WISH IT WERE UNDER BETTER CIRCUMSTANCES, ROBBIE. I'M *CHRIS. CHRIS SUMMERS.*

I REMEMBER... FLEEING THE COMING WAR WITH MY WIFE AND CHILDREN... ...WE *CRASHED...* I THINK..? I REMEMBER WAKING UP IN A STRANGE SHIP... AND THEN THIS GREY MONSTER WAS CONDUCTING *TESTS* --

CHRIS... SUMMERS..?

-- BUT THAT COULDN'T HAVE BEEN THAT LONG AGO. EVERYTHING'S SO *DIFFERENT...* SO *HORRIBLE.* IS MY FAMILY EVEN *ALIVE?*

...

SUMMERS?! NOT... ALEX AND --

SCOTT! YES! THANK GOD! YOU *KNOW MY BOYS?*

AFRAID I DO. I'M SO SORRY, FRIEND.

THEY'RE ALIVE, BUT I DON'T KNOW IF THEY'LL BE AS ANXIOUS TO SEE YOU, CONSIDERING YOU'RE HUMAN --

-- AND *THEY AREN'T.* I THINK IT'S TIME YOU HAD A *HISTORY LESSON.*

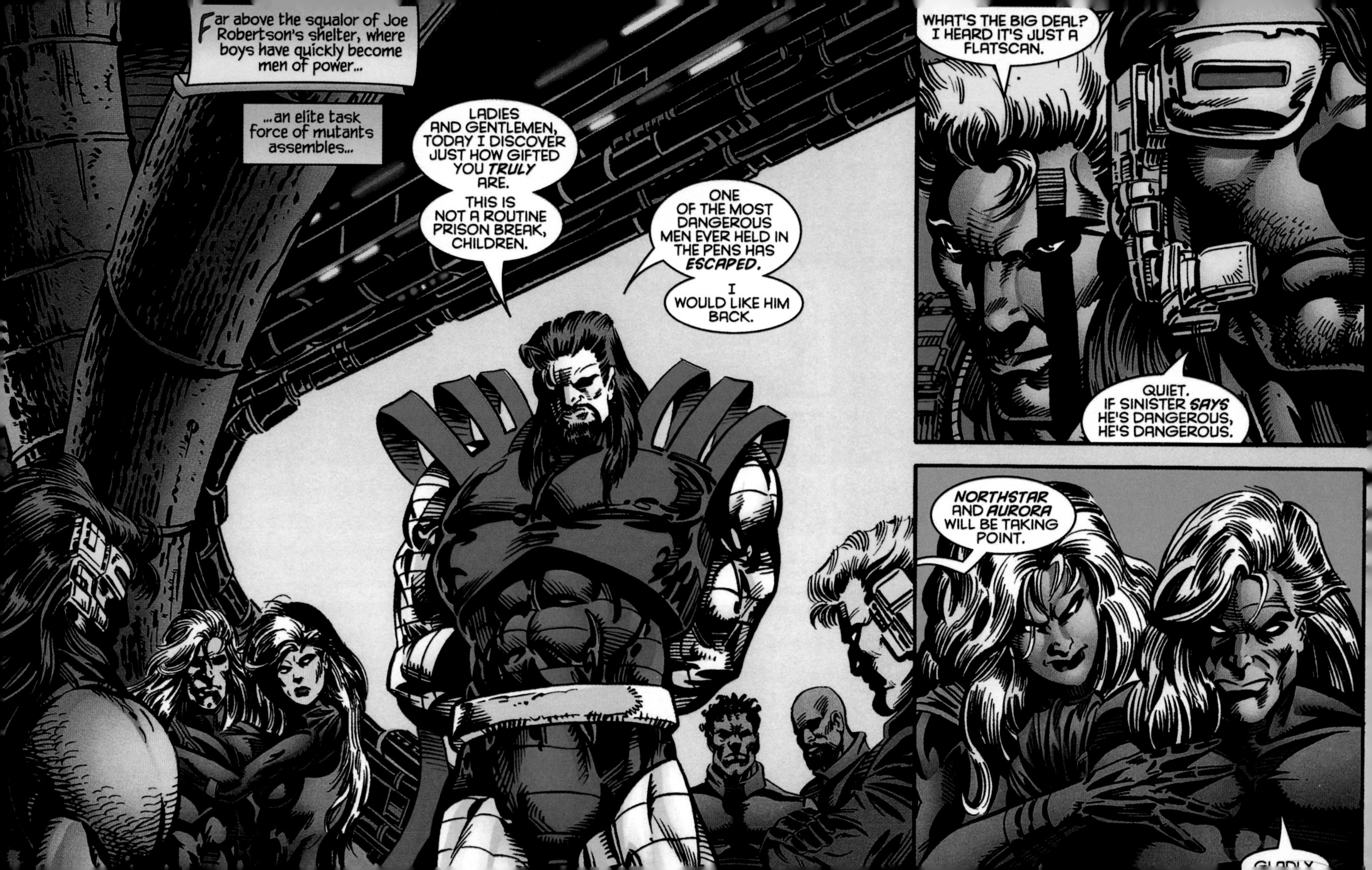
Far above the squalor of Joe Robertson's shelter, where boys have quickly become men of power...
...an elite task force of mutants assembles...
LADIES AND GENTLEMEN, TODAY I DISCOVER JUST HOW GIFTED YOU TRULY ARE.
THIS IS NOT A ROUTINE PRISON BREAK, CHILDREN.
ONE OF THE MOST DANGEROUS MEN EVER HELD IN THE PENS HAS ESCAPED.
I WOULD LIKE HIM BACK.
WHAT'S THE BIG DEAL? I HEARD IT'S JUST A FLATSCAN.
QUIET. IF SINISTER SAYS HE'S DANGEROUS, HE'S DANGEROUS.
NORTHSTAR AND AURORA WILL BE TAKING POINT.

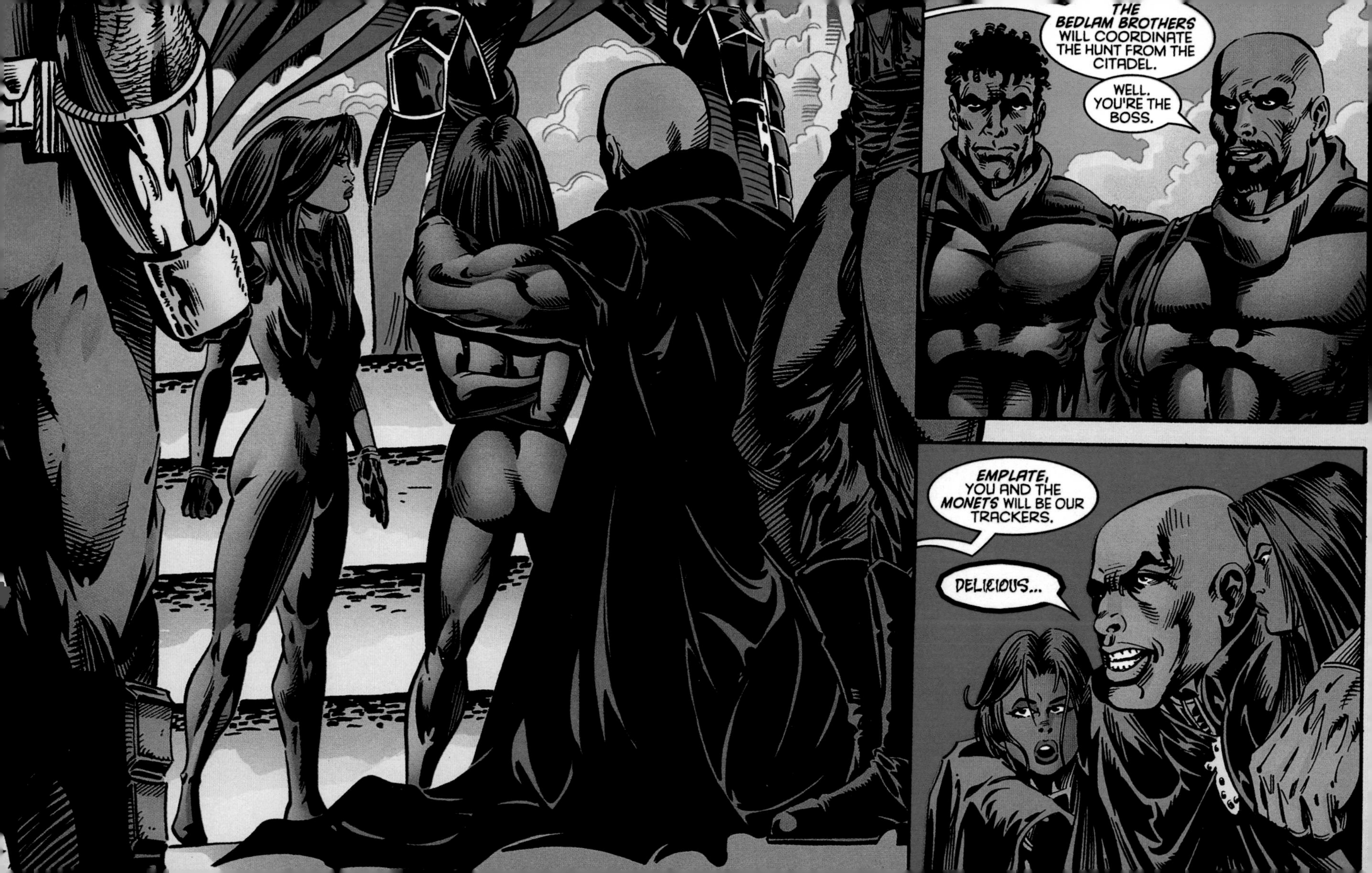
THE BEDLAM BROTHERS WILL COORDINATE THE HUNT FROM THE CITADEL.
WELL. YOU'RE THE BOSS.
EMPLATE, YOU AND THE MONETS WILL BE OUR TRACKERS.
DELICIOUS...

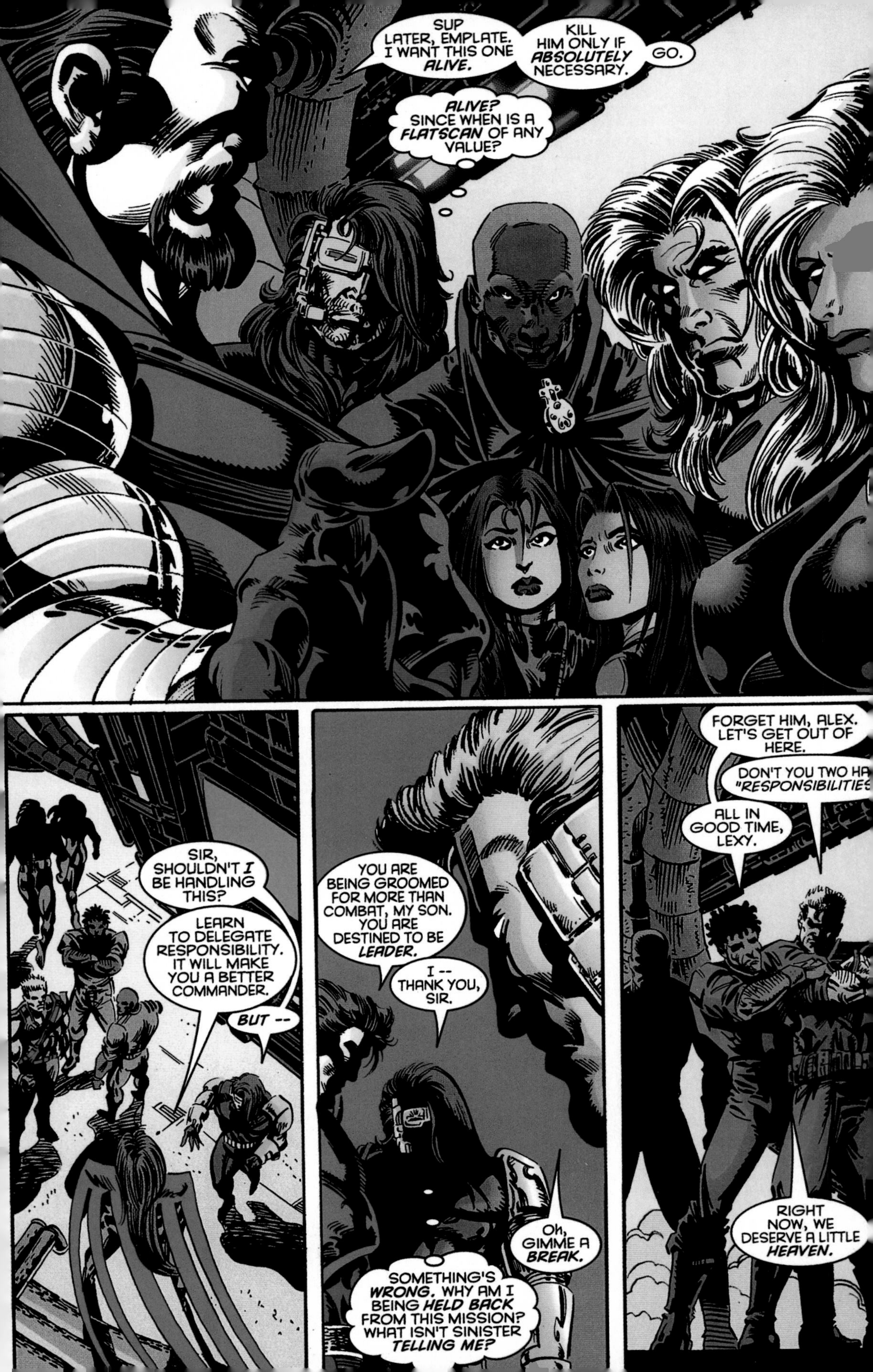
SUP LATER, EMPLATE. I WANT THIS ONE *ALIVE.*
KILL HIM ONLY IF *ABSOLUTELY* NECESSARY.
GO.
ALIVE? SINCE WHEN IS A *FLATSCAN* OF ANY VALUE?
SIR, SHOULDN'T *I* BE HANDLING THIS?
LEARN TO DELEGATE RESPONSIBILITY. IT WILL MAKE YOU A BETTER COMMANDER.
BUT --
YOU ARE BEING GROOMED FOR MORE THAN COMBAT, MY SON. YOU ARE DESTINED TO BE *LEADER.*
I -- THANK YOU, SIR.
Oh, GIMME A *BREAK.*
SOMETHING'S *WRONG.* WHY AM I BEING *HELD BACK* FROM THIS MISSION? WHAT ISN'T SINISTER *TELLING ME?*
FORGET HIM, ALEX. LET'S GET OUT OF HERE.
DON'T YOU TWO HA *"RESPONSIBILITIES*
ALL IN GOOD TIME, LEXY.
RIGHT NOW, WE DESERVE A LITTLE *HEAVEN.*

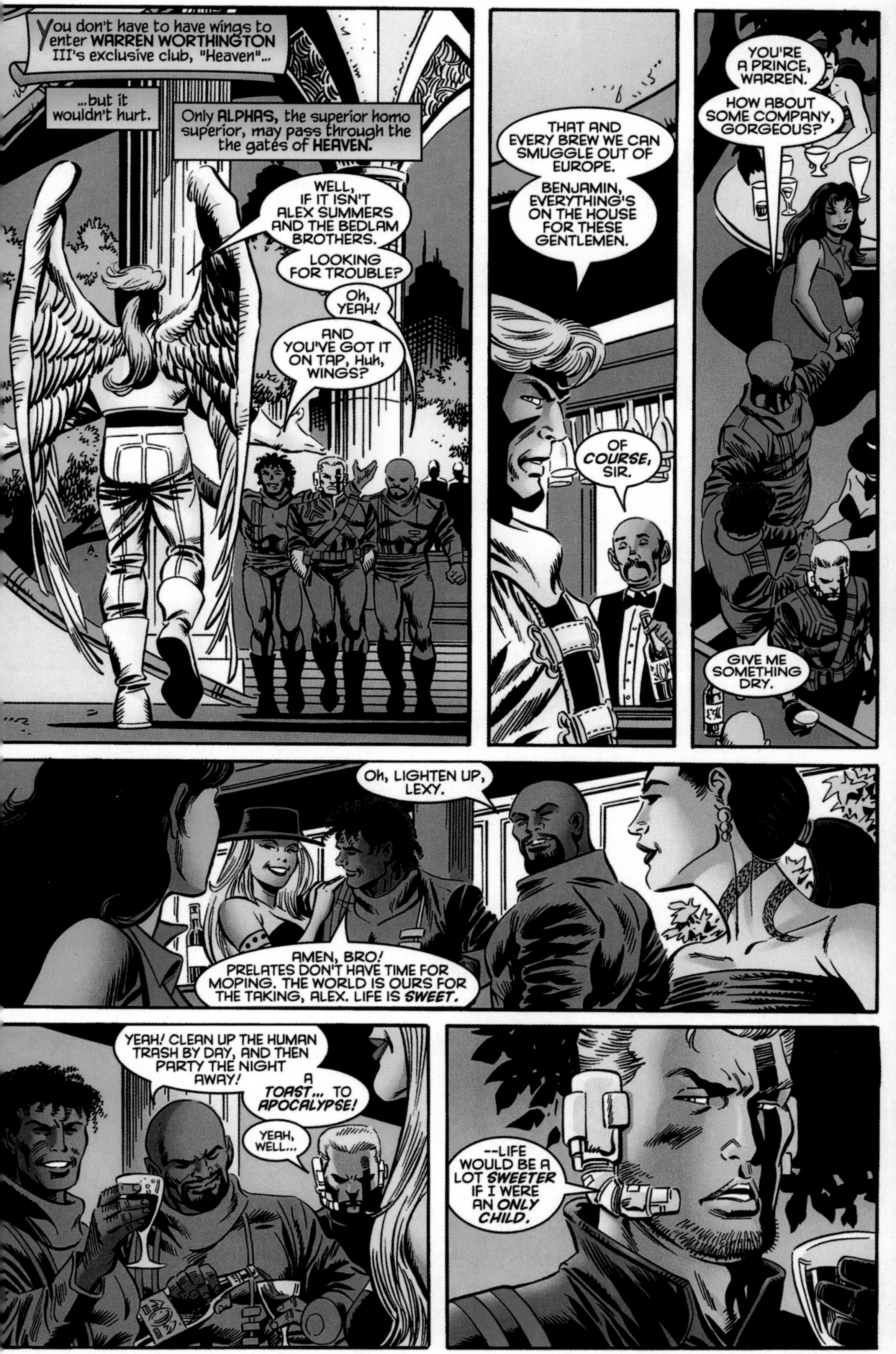
You don't have to have wings to enter WARREN WORTHINGTON III's exclusive club, "Heaven"...
...but it wouldn't hurt.
Only ALPHAS, the superior homo superior, may pass through the the gates of HEAVEN.
WELL, IF IT ISN'T ALEX SUMMERS AND THE BEDLAM BROTHERS.
LOOKING FOR TROUBLE?
Oh, YEAH!
AND YOU'VE GOT IT ON TAP, Huh, WINGS?
THAT AND EVERY BREW WE CAN SMUGGLE OUT OF EUROPE.
BENJAMIN, EVERYTHING'S ON THE HOUSE FOR THESE GENTLEMEN.
OF COURSE, SIR.
YOU'RE A PRINCE, WARREN.
HOW ABOUT SOME COMPANY, GORGEOUS?
GIVE ME SOMETHING DRY.
Oh, LIGHTEN UP, LEXY.
AMEN, BRO! PRELATES DON'T HAVE TIME FOR MOPING. THE WORLD IS OURS FOR THE TAKING, ALEX. LIFE IS SWEET.
YEAH! CLEAN UP THE HUMAN TRASH BY DAY, AND THEN PARTY THE NIGHT AWAY!
A TOAST... TO APOCALYPSE!
YEAH, WELL...
--LIFE WOULD BE A LOT SWEETER IF I WERE AN ONLY CHILD.

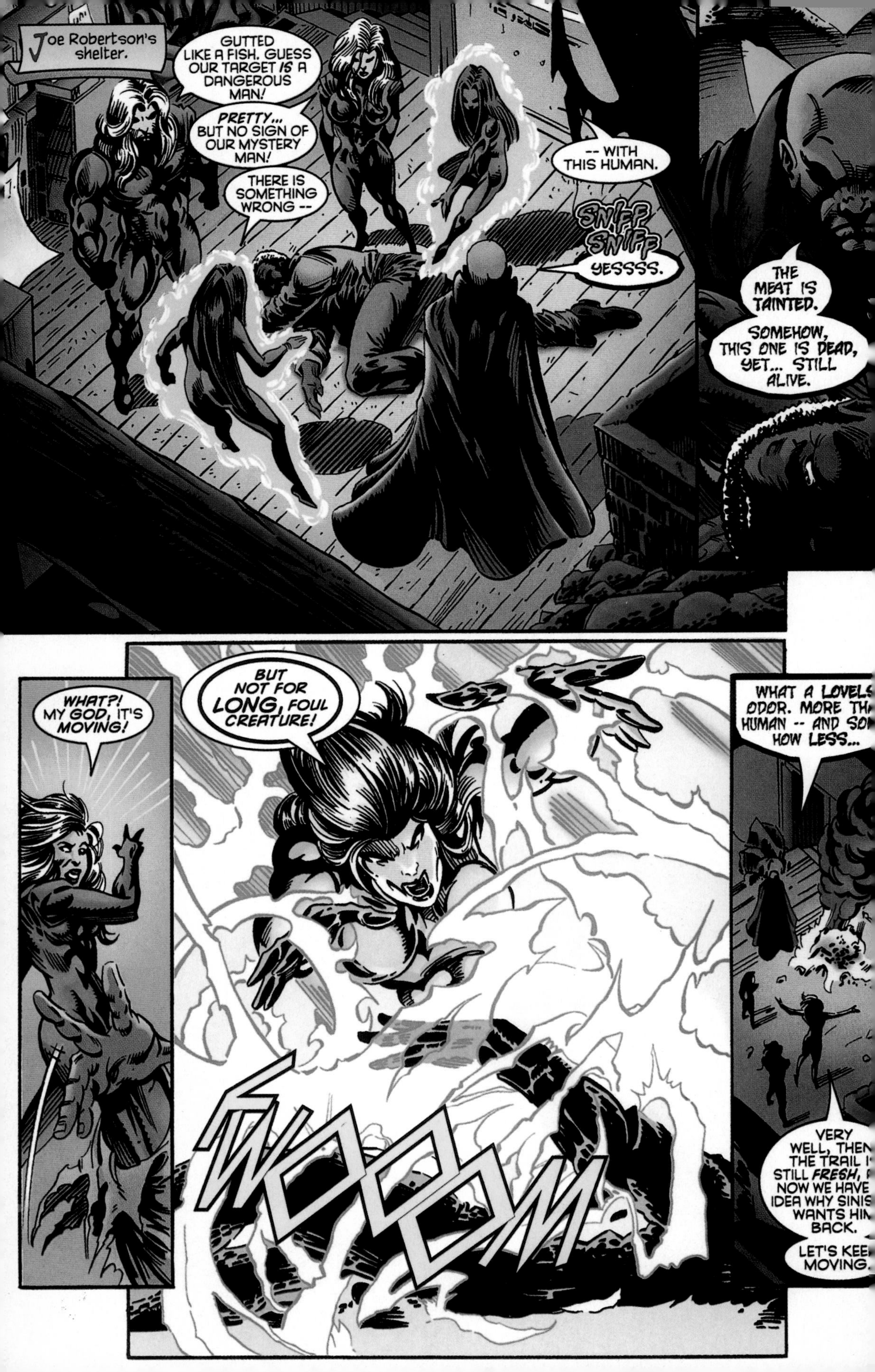
Joe Robertson's shelter.
GUTTED LIKE A FISH. GUESS OUR TARGET IS A DANGEROUS MAN!
PRETTY... BUT NO SIGN OF OUR MYSTERY MAN!
THERE IS SOMETHING WRONG --
-- WITH THIS HUMAN.
SNIFF SNIFF
YESSSS.
THE MEAT IS TAINTED.
SOMEHOW, THIS ONE IS DEAD, YET... STILL ALIVE.
WHAT?! MY GOD, IT'S MOVING!
BUT NOT FOR LONG, FOUL CREATURE!
WOOOM
WHAT A LOVELS ODOR. MORE THA HUMAN -- AND SOM HOW LESS...
VERY WELL, THEN THE TRAIL I STILL FRESH, NOW WE HAVE IDEA WHY SINIS WANTS HIM BACK.
LET'S KEE MOVING.

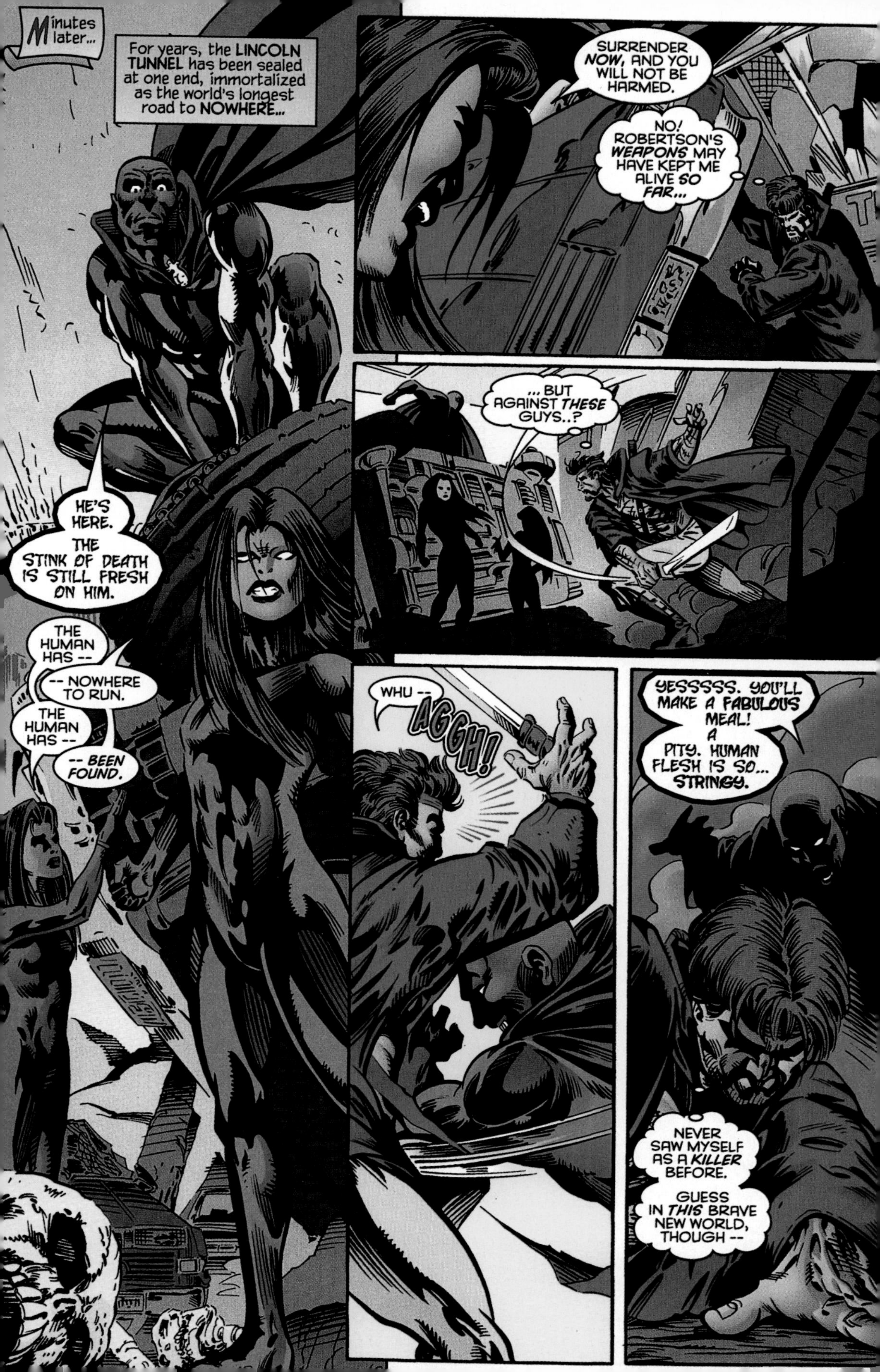
Minutes later...
For years, the LINCOLN TUNNEL has been sealed at one end, immortalized as the world's longest road to NOWHERE...
HE'S HERE.
THE STINK OF DEATH IS STILL FRESH ON HIM.
THE HUMAN HAS --
-- NOWHERE TO RUN.
THE HUMAN HAS --
-- BEEN FOUND.
SURRENDER NOW, AND YOU WILL NOT BE HARMED.
NO! ROBERTSON'S WEAPONS MAY HAVE KEPT ME ALIVE SO FAR...
... BUT AGAINST THESE GUYS..?
WHU --
AGGH!
YESSSSS. YOU'LL MAKE A FABULOUS MEAL!
A PITY. HUMAN FLESH IS SO... STRINGY.
NEVER SAW MYSELF AS A KILLER BEFORE.
GUESS IN THIS BRAVE NEW WORLD, THOUGH --

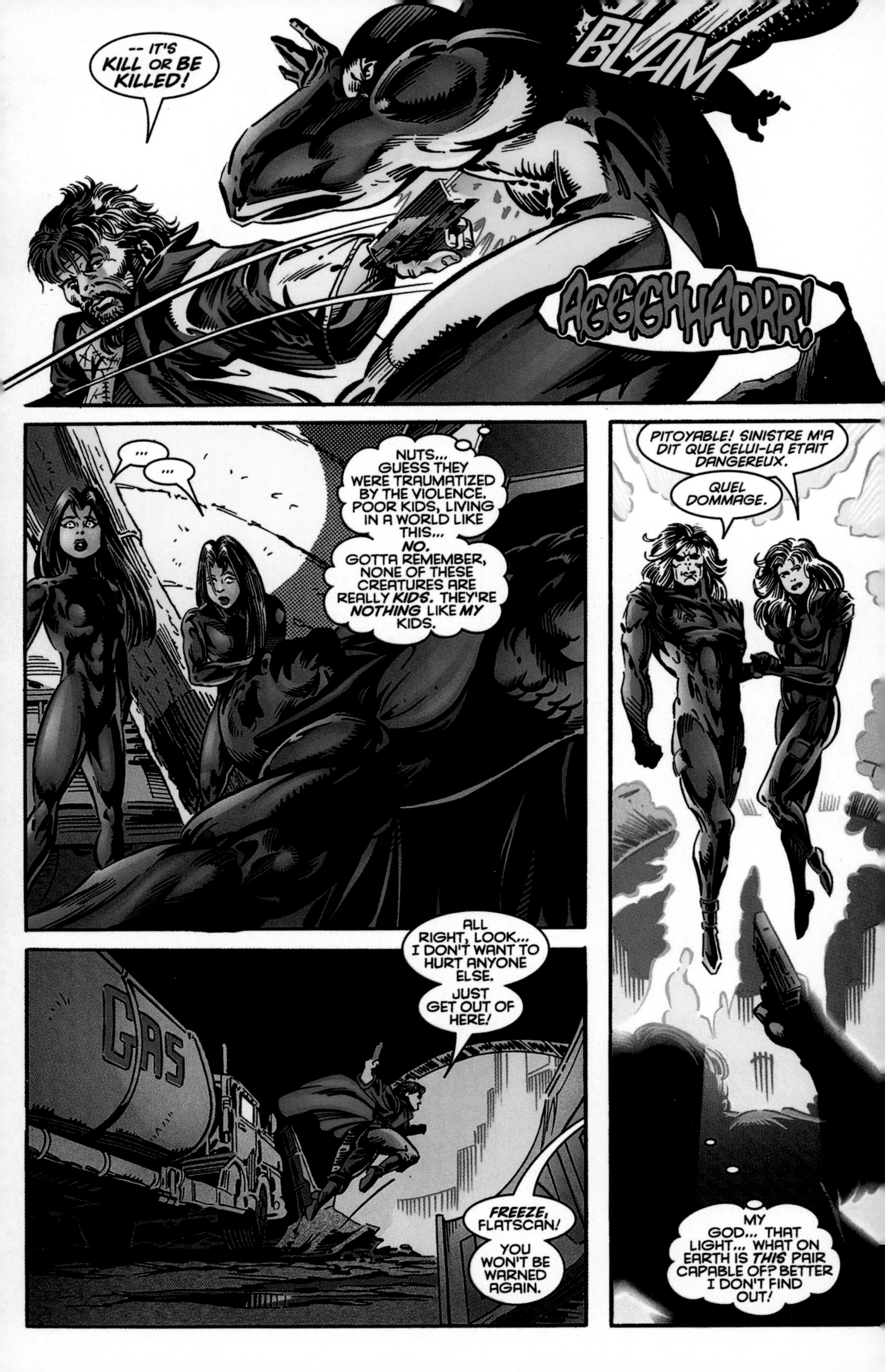
-- IT'S KILL OR BE KILLED!
BLAM
AGGGHHARRR!
...
...
NUTS... GUESS THEY WERE TRAUMATIZED BY THE VIOLENCE. POOR KIDS, LIVING IN A WORLD LIKE THIS... NO. GOTTA REMEMBER, NONE OF THESE CREATURES ARE REALLY KIDS. THEY'RE NOTHING LIKE MY KIDS.
PITOYABLE! SINISTRE M'A DIT QUE CELUI-LA ETAIT DANGEREUX.
QUEL DOMMAGE.
ALL RIGHT, LOOK... I DON'T WANT TO HURT ANYONE ELSE.
JUST GET OUT OF HERE!
GAS
FREEZE, FLATSCAN!
YOU WON'T BE WARNED AGAIN.
MY GOD... THAT LIGHT... WHAT ON EARTH IS THIS PAIR CAPABLE OF? BETTER I DON'T FIND OUT!

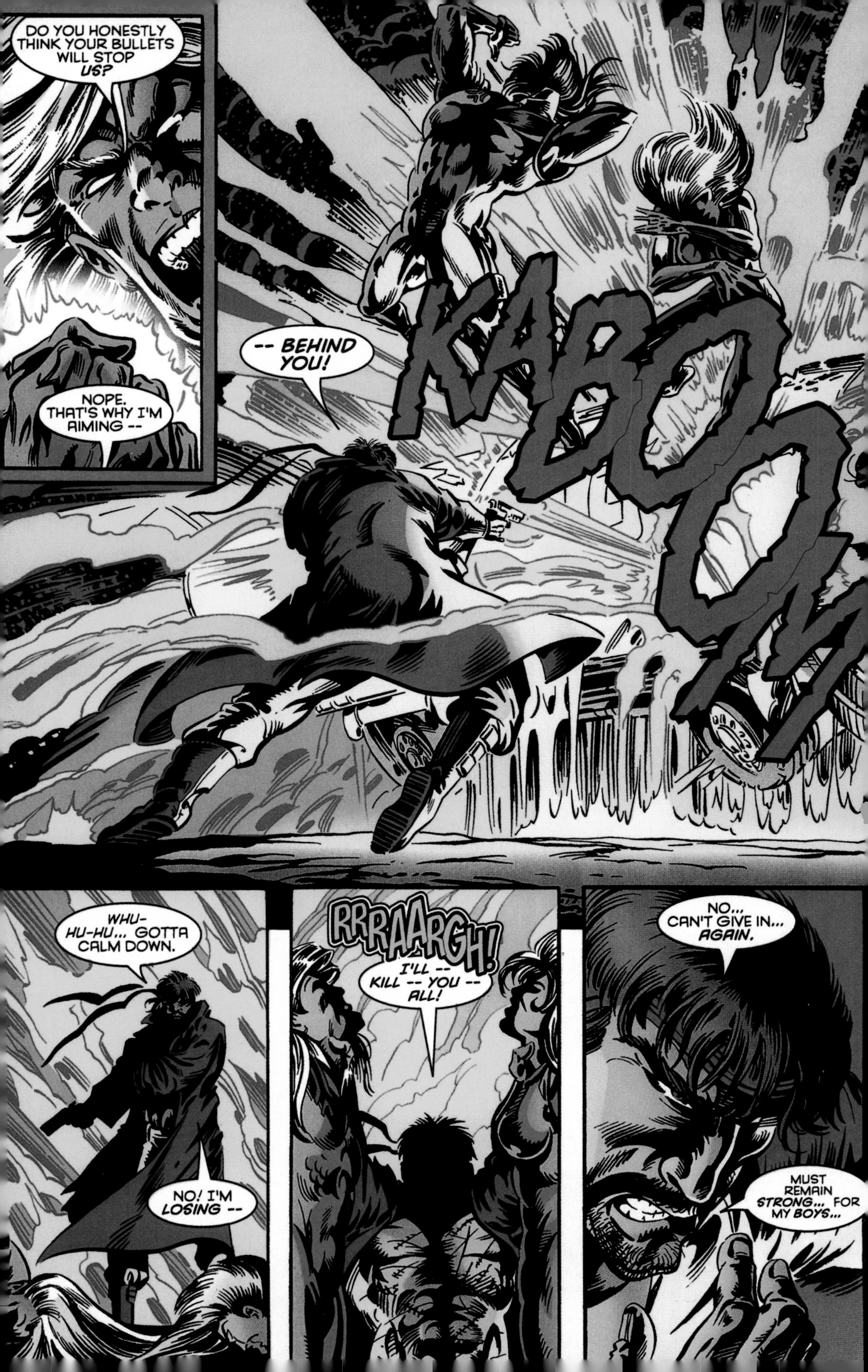
DO YOU HONESTLY THINK YOUR BULLETS WILL STOP *US?*
NOPE. THAT'S WHY I'M AIMING --
-- *BEHIND YOU!*
KABOOM
WHU-HU-HU... GOTTA CALM DOWN.
NO! I'M *LOSING* --
RRRAARGH!
I'LL -- KILL -- YOU -- ALL!
NO... CAN'T GIVE IN... *AGAIN.*
MUST REMAIN *STRONG*... FOR MY *BOYS*...

Laughter, the rarest commodity of this age, echoes softly through the high walls of Heaven.

LIGHTEN UP, ALEX. YOU'RE ALMOST AS FUN AS YOUR *BROTHER* TONIGHT. THIS --

-- ISN'T ABOUT FUN, TERRY. WHY WEREN'T YOU TWO AT YOUR POSTS?

-- SO I USE MY *PSIONICS* TO REROUTE ALEX'S COMM TO THE LOUD-SPEAKERS, AND TERRY USES HIS *MIND-SCRAMBLE* ON HIM -- -- AND THE ENTIRE PARADE HEARD *THE* ALEX SUMMERS SCREAM, *"JAMBOREE MONKEY UVULA CRUNCH!"*

HAHAHAHA HAHA

HA HA.

IT'S CALLED *"LIVING IT UP,"* DEAR BROTHER. REMIND ME TO INTRODUCE YOU TO *WOMEN* SOMETIME.

WE PICKED UP THE SEARCH-TEAM'S *EMERGENCY BEACON.* SOMETHING'S GONE *WRONG.*

WE'RE GOING AFTER THEM.

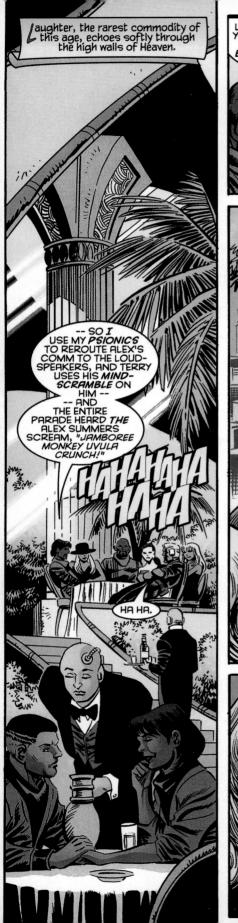

SORRY, BRO. YOU CAUGHT ME ON MY NIGHT OFF.

NOW.

AND THEN MAYBE I'LL FIGURE OUT WHY THIS WHOLE MISSION HAS FELT *WRONG* FROM THE BEGINNING.

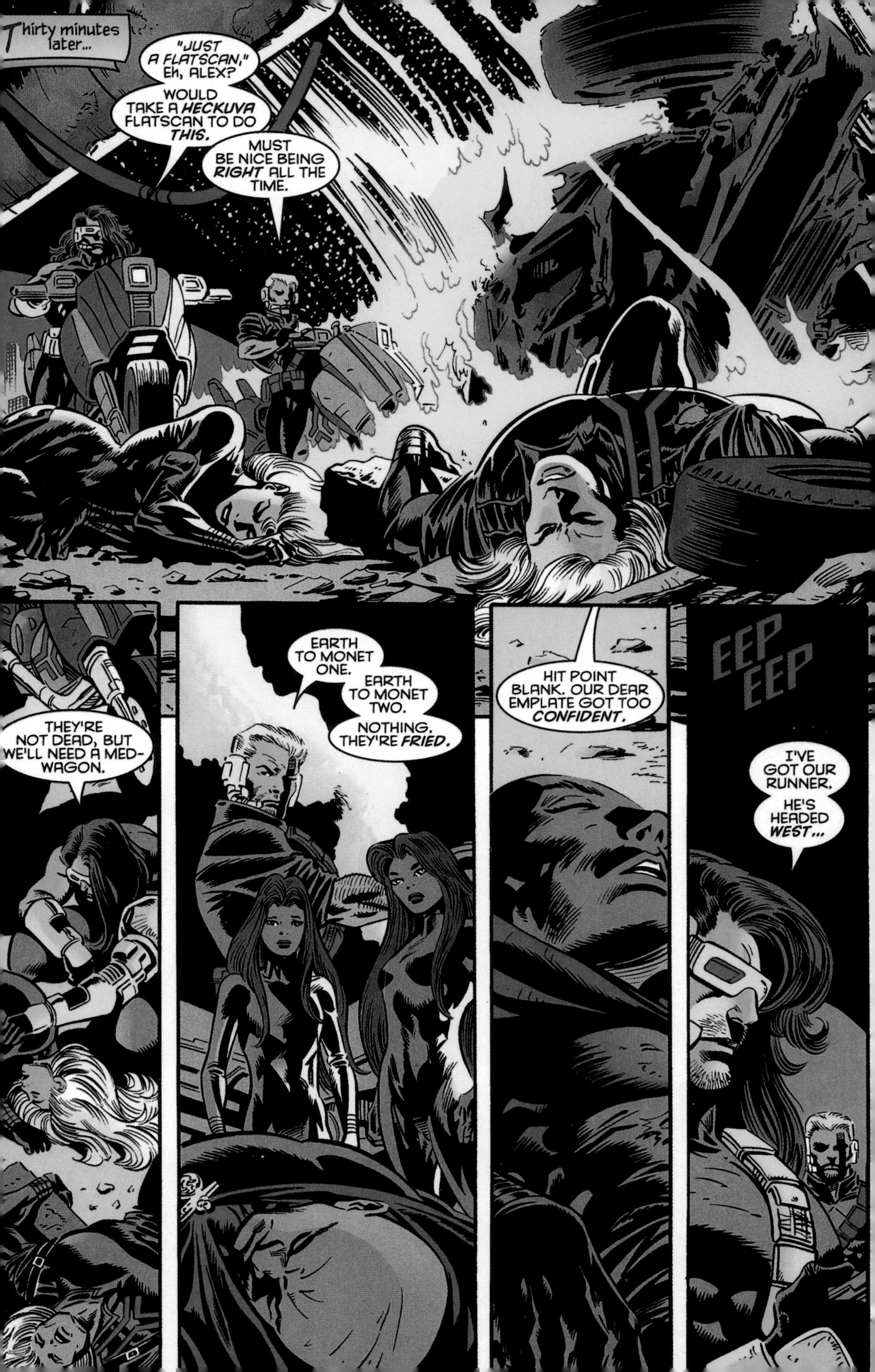
Thirty minutes later...
"JUST A FLATSCAN," Eh, ALEX? WOULD TAKE A HECKUVA FLATSCAN TO DO THIS.
MUST BE NICE BEING RIGHT ALL THE TIME.
THEY'RE NOT DEAD, BUT WE'LL NEED A MED-WAGON.
EARTH TO MONET ONE. EARTH TO MONET TWO.
NOTHING. THEY'RE FRIED.
HIT POINT BLANK. OUR DEAR EMPLATE GOT TOO CONFIDENT.
EEP EEP
I'VE GOT OUR RUNNER. HE'S HEADED WEST...

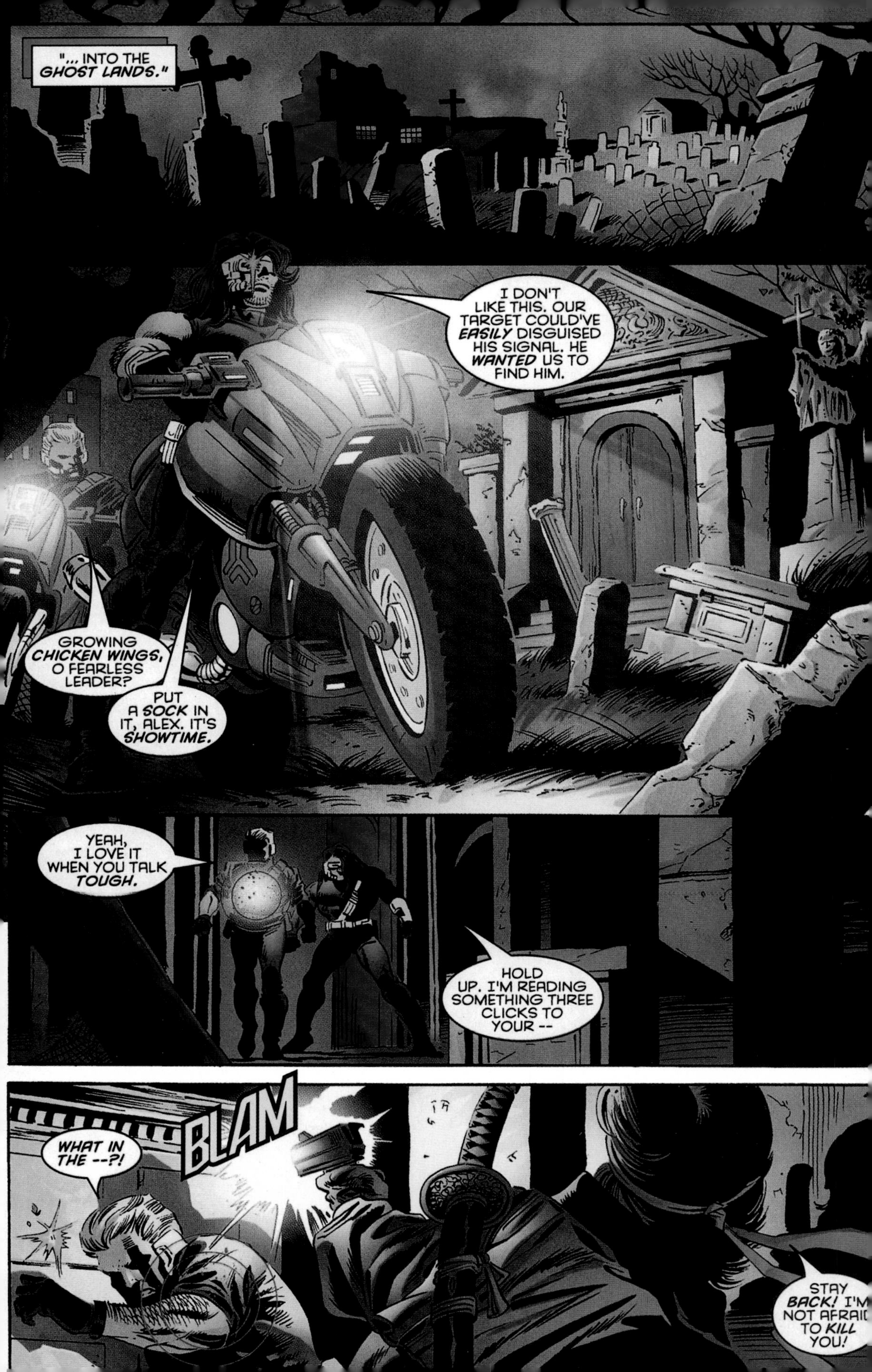
"... INTO THE GHOST LANDS."
I DON'T LIKE THIS. OUR TARGET COULD'VE EASILY DISGUISED HIS SIGNAL. HE WANTED US TO FIND HIM.
GROWING CHICKEN WINGS, O FEARLESS LEADER?
PUT A SOCK IN IT, ALEX. IT'S SHOWTIME.
YEAH, I LOVE IT WHEN YOU TALK TOUGH.
HOLD UP. I'M READING SOMETHING THREE CLICKS TO YOUR --
BLAM
WHAT IN THE --?!
STAY BACK! I'M NOT AFRAID TO KILL YOU!

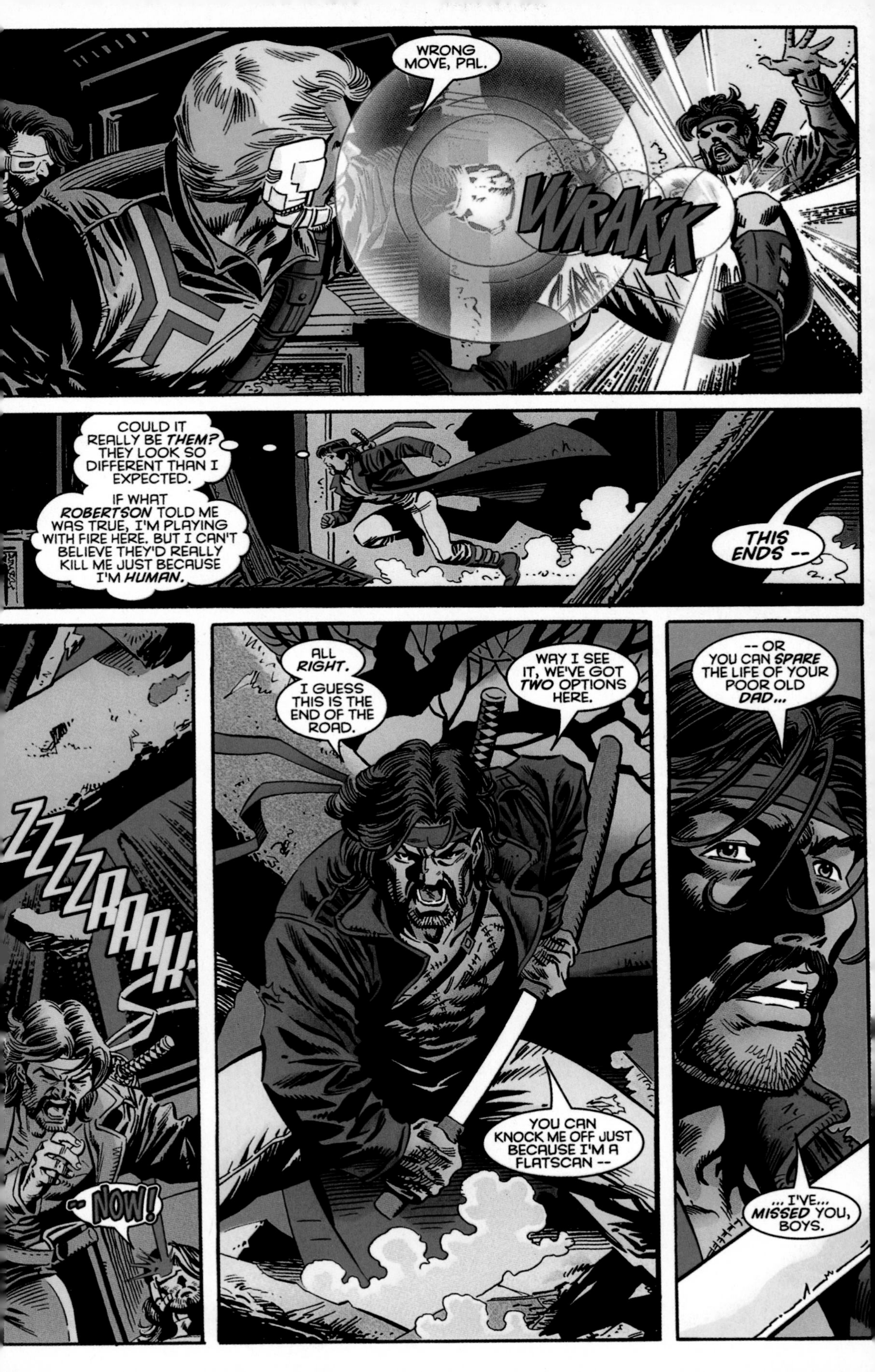

WRONG MOVE, PAL.
VVRAKK
COULD IT REALLY BE THEM? THEY LOOK SO DIFFERENT THAN I EXPECTED.
IF WHAT ROBERTSON TOLD ME WAS TRUE, I'M PLAYING WITH FIRE HERE, BUT I CAN'T BELIEVE THEY'D REALLY KILL ME JUST BECAUSE I'M HUMAN.
THIS ENDS --
ZZZZRAAAK!
-- NOW!
ALL RIGHT.
I GUESS THIS IS THE END OF THE ROAD.
WAY I SEE IT, WE'VE GOT TWO OPTIONS HERE.
YOU CAN KNOCK ME OFF JUST BECAUSE I'M A FLATSCAN --
-- OR YOU CAN SPARE THE LIFE OF YOUR POOR OLD DAD...
... I'VE... MISSED YOU, BOYS.

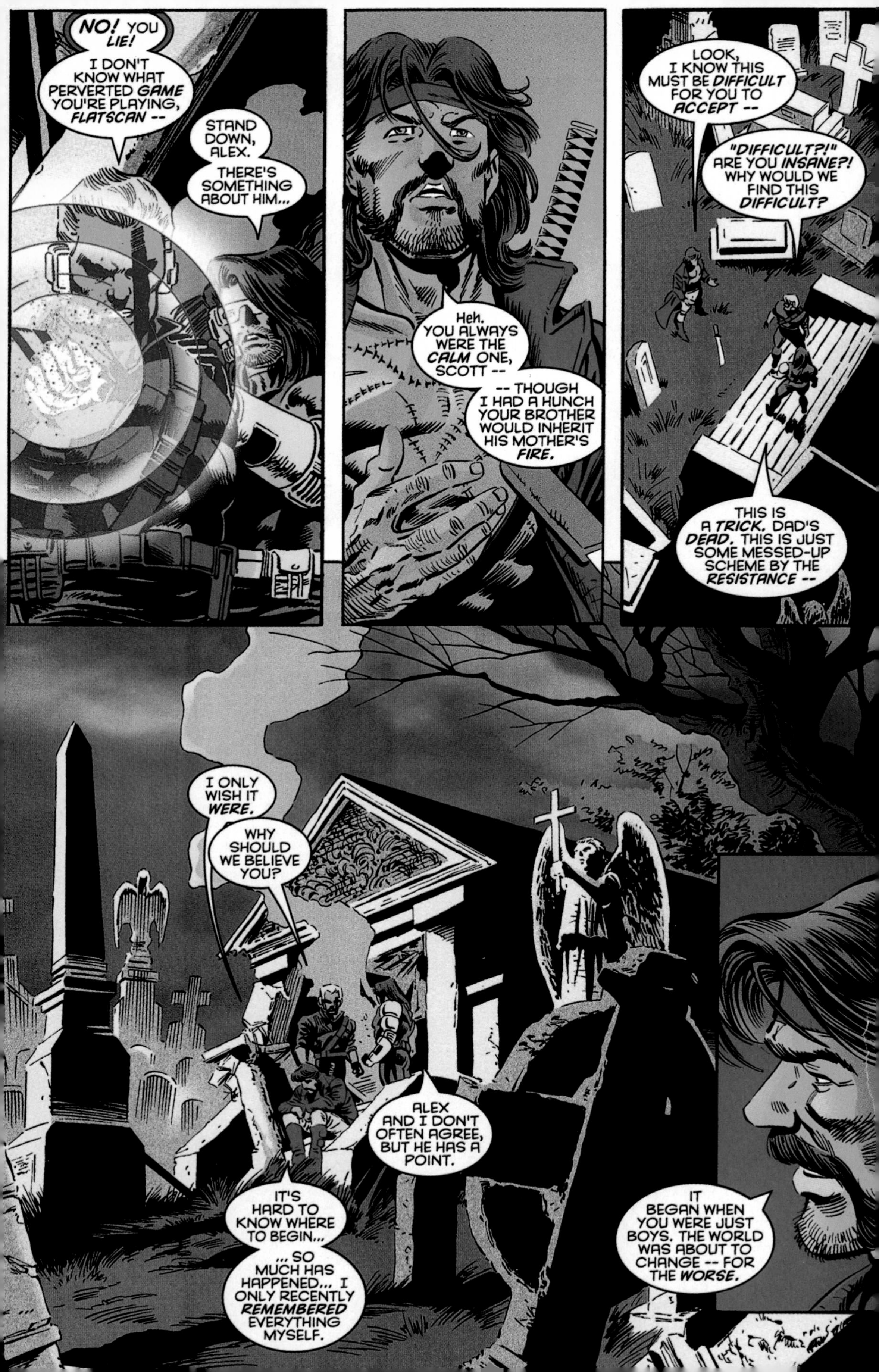
NO! YOU LIE!
I DON'T KNOW WHAT PERVERTED GAME YOU'RE PLAYING, FLATSCAN --
STAND DOWN, ALEX.
THERE'S SOMETHING ABOUT HIM...
Heh. YOU ALWAYS WERE THE CALM ONE, SCOTT --
-- THOUGH I HAD A HUNCH YOUR BROTHER WOULD INHERIT HIS MOTHER'S FIRE.
LOOK, I KNOW THIS MUST BE DIFFICULT FOR YOU TO ACCEPT --
"DIFFICULT?!" ARE YOU INSANE?! WHY WOULD WE FIND THIS DIFFICULT?
THIS IS A TRICK. DAD'S DEAD. THIS IS JUST SOME MESSED-UP SCHEME BY THE RESISTANCE --
I ONLY WISH IT WERE.
WHY SHOULD WE BELIEVE YOU?
ALEX AND I DON'T OFTEN AGREE, BUT HE HAS A POINT.
IT'S HARD TO KNOW WHERE TO BEGIN...
... SO MUCH HAS HAPPENED... I ONLY RECENTLY REMEMBERED EVERYTHING MYSELF.
IT BEGAN WHEN YOU WERE JUST BOYS. THE WORLD WAS ABOUT TO CHANGE -- FOR THE WORSE.

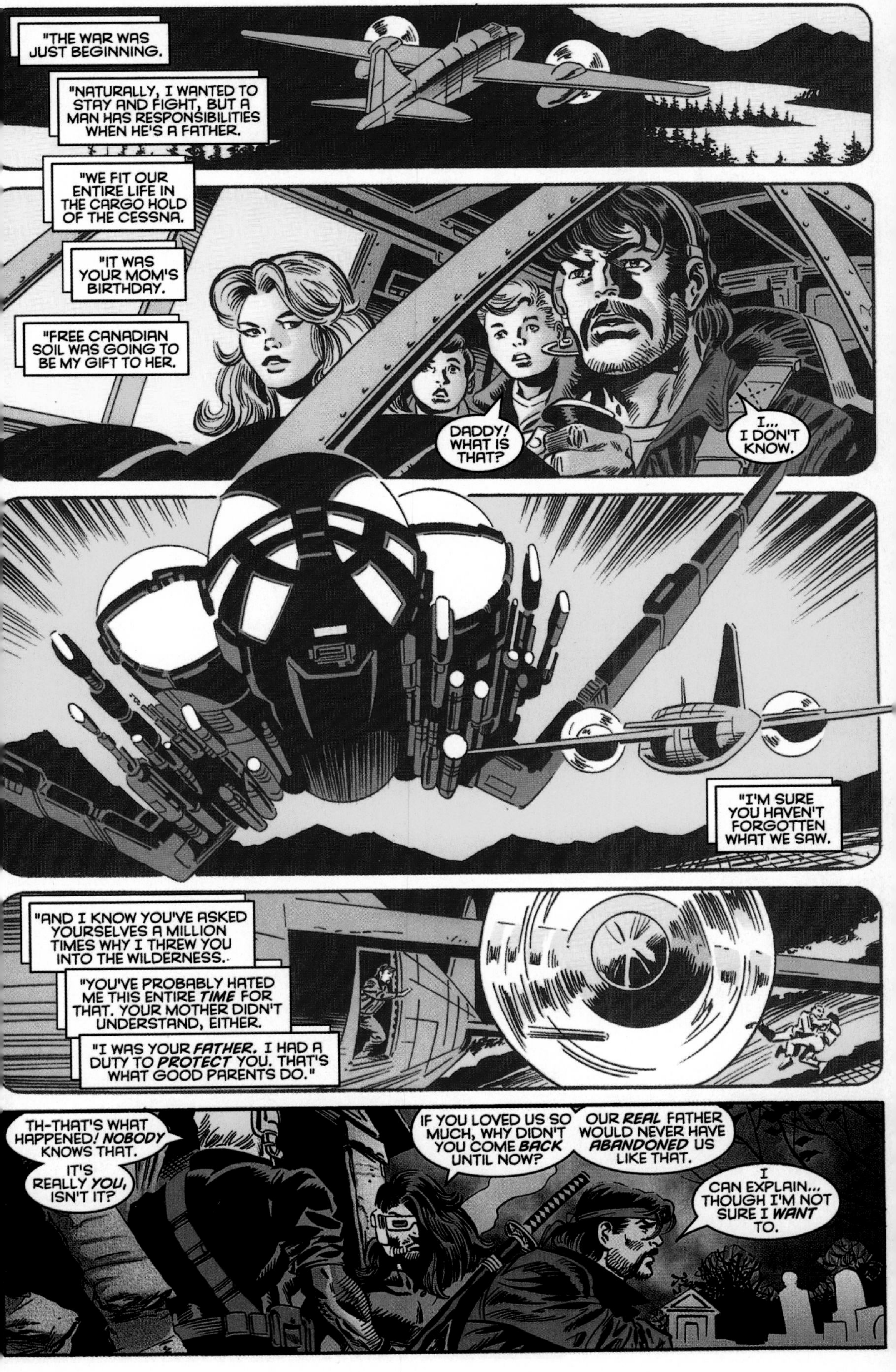
"THE WAR WAS JUST BEGINNING.
"NATURALLY, I WANTED TO STAY AND FIGHT, BUT A MAN HAS RESPONSIBILITIES WHEN HE'S A FATHER.
"WE FIT OUR ENTIRE LIFE IN THE CARGO HOLD OF THE CESSNA.
"IT WAS YOUR MOM'S BIRTHDAY.
"FREE CANADIAN SOIL WAS GOING TO BE MY GIFT TO HER.
DADDY! WHAT IS THAT?
I... I DON'T KNOW.
"I'M SURE YOU HAVEN'T FORGOTTEN WHAT WE SAW.
"AND I KNOW YOU'VE ASKED YOURSELVES A MILLION TIMES WHY I THREW YOU INTO THE WILDERNESS.
"YOU'VE PROBABLY HATED ME THIS ENTIRE TIME FOR THAT. YOUR MOTHER DIDN'T UNDERSTAND, EITHER.
"I WAS YOUR FATHER. I HAD A DUTY TO PROTECT YOU. THAT'S WHAT GOOD PARENTS DO."
TH-THAT'S WHAT HAPPENED! NOBODY KNOWS THAT.
IT'S REALLY YOU, ISN'T IT?
IF YOU LOVED US SO MUCH, WHY DIDN'T YOU COME BACK UNTIL NOW?
OUR REAL FATHER WOULD NEVER HAVE ABANDONED US LIKE THAT.
I CAN EXPLAIN... THOUGH I'M NOT SURE I WANT TO.

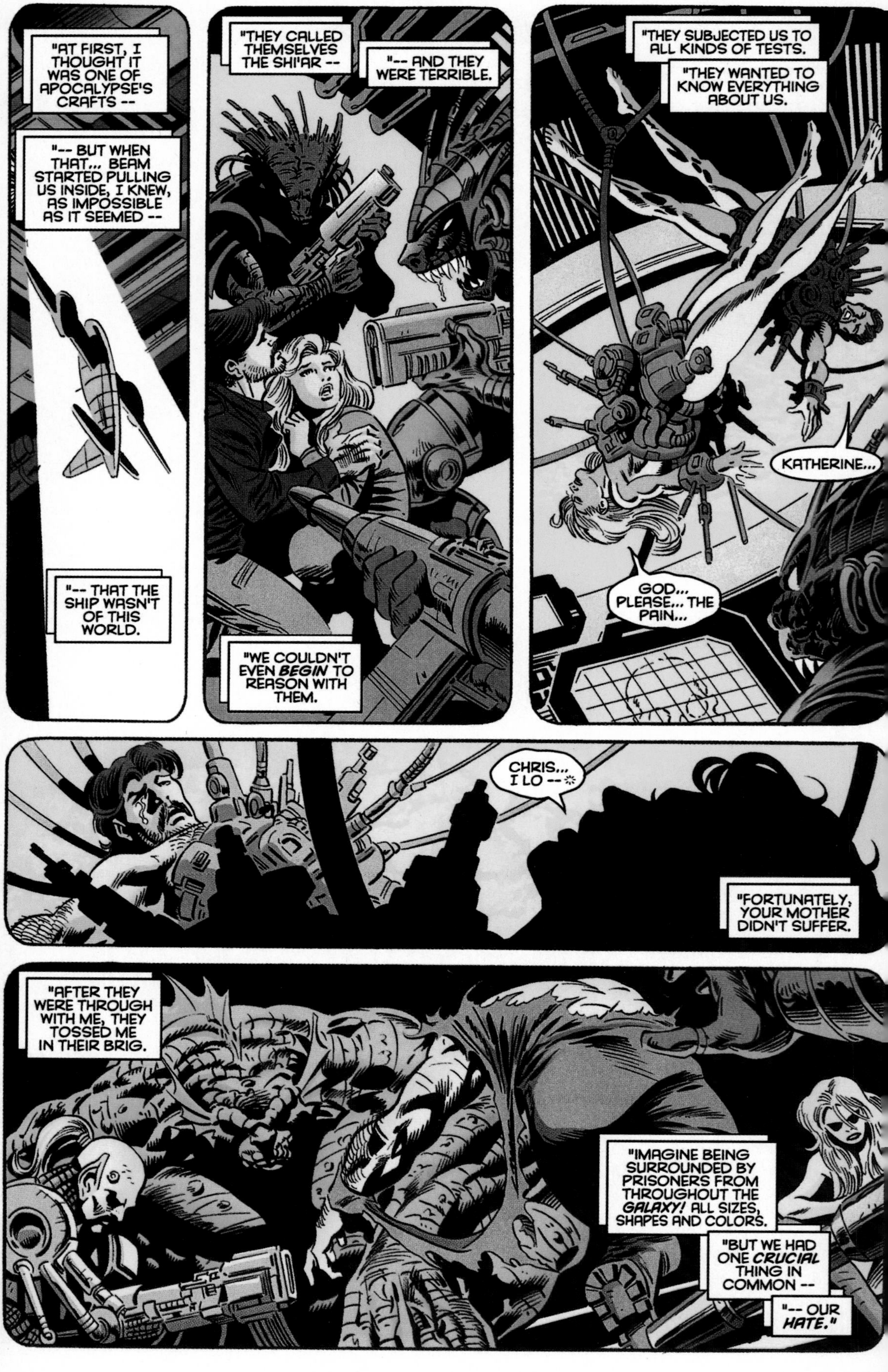
"AT FIRST, I THOUGHT IT WAS ONE OF APOCALYPSE'S CRAFTS --
"-- BUT WHEN THAT... BEAM STARTED PULLING US INSIDE, I KNEW, AS IMPOSSIBLE AS IT SEEMED --
"-- THAT THE SHIP WASN'T OF THIS WORLD.
"THEY CALLED THEMSELVES THE SHI'AR --
"-- AND THEY WERE TERRIBLE.
"WE COULDN'T EVEN *BEGIN* TO REASON WITH THEM.
"THEY SUBJECTED US TO ALL KINDS OF TESTS.
"THEY WANTED TO KNOW EVERYTHING ABOUT US.
KATHERINE...
GOD... PLEASE... THE PAIN...
CHRIS... I LO --
"FORTUNATELY, YOUR MOTHER DIDN'T SUFFER.
"AFTER THEY WERE THROUGH WITH ME, THEY TOSSED ME IN THEIR BRIG.
"IMAGINE BEING SURROUNDED BY PRISONERS FROM THROUGHOUT THE *GALAXY!* ALL SIZES, SHAPES AND COLORS.
"BUT WE HAD ONE *CRUCIAL* THING IN COMMON --
"-- OUR *HATE.*"

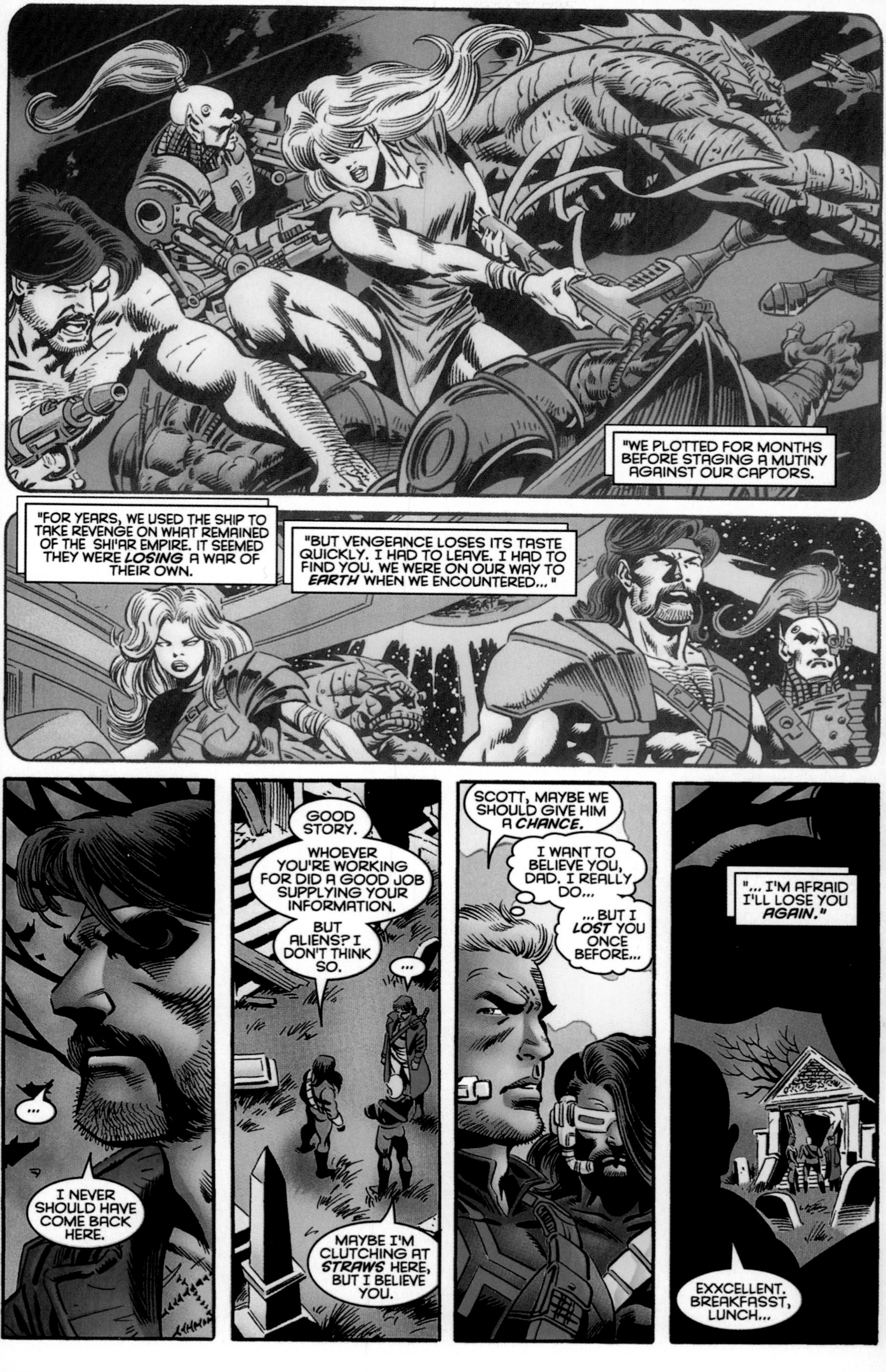
"WE PLOTTED FOR MONTHS BEFORE STAGING A MUTINY AGAINST OUR CAPTORS.
"FOR YEARS, WE USED THE SHIP TO TAKE REVENGE ON WHAT REMAINED OF THE SHI'AR EMPIRE. IT SEEMED THEY WERE *LOSING* A WAR OF THEIR OWN.
"BUT VENGEANCE LOSES ITS TASTE QUICKLY. I HAD TO LEAVE. I HAD TO FIND YOU. WE WERE ON OUR WAY TO *EARTH* WHEN WE ENCOUNTERED..."
...
I NEVER SHOULD HAVE COME BACK HERE.
GOOD STORY.
WHOEVER YOU'RE WORKING FOR DID A GOOD JOB SUPPLYING YOUR INFORMATION.
BUT ALIENS? I DON'T THINK SO.
...
MAYBE I'M CLUTCHING AT *STRAWS* HERE, BUT I BELIEVE YOU.
SCOTT, MAYBE WE SHOULD GIVE HIM A *CHANCE*.
I WANT TO BELIEVE YOU, DAD. I REALLY DO...
...BUT I *LOST* YOU ONCE BEFORE...
"...I'M AFRAID I'LL LOSE YOU *AGAIN*."
EXXCELLENT. BREAKFASST, LUNCH...

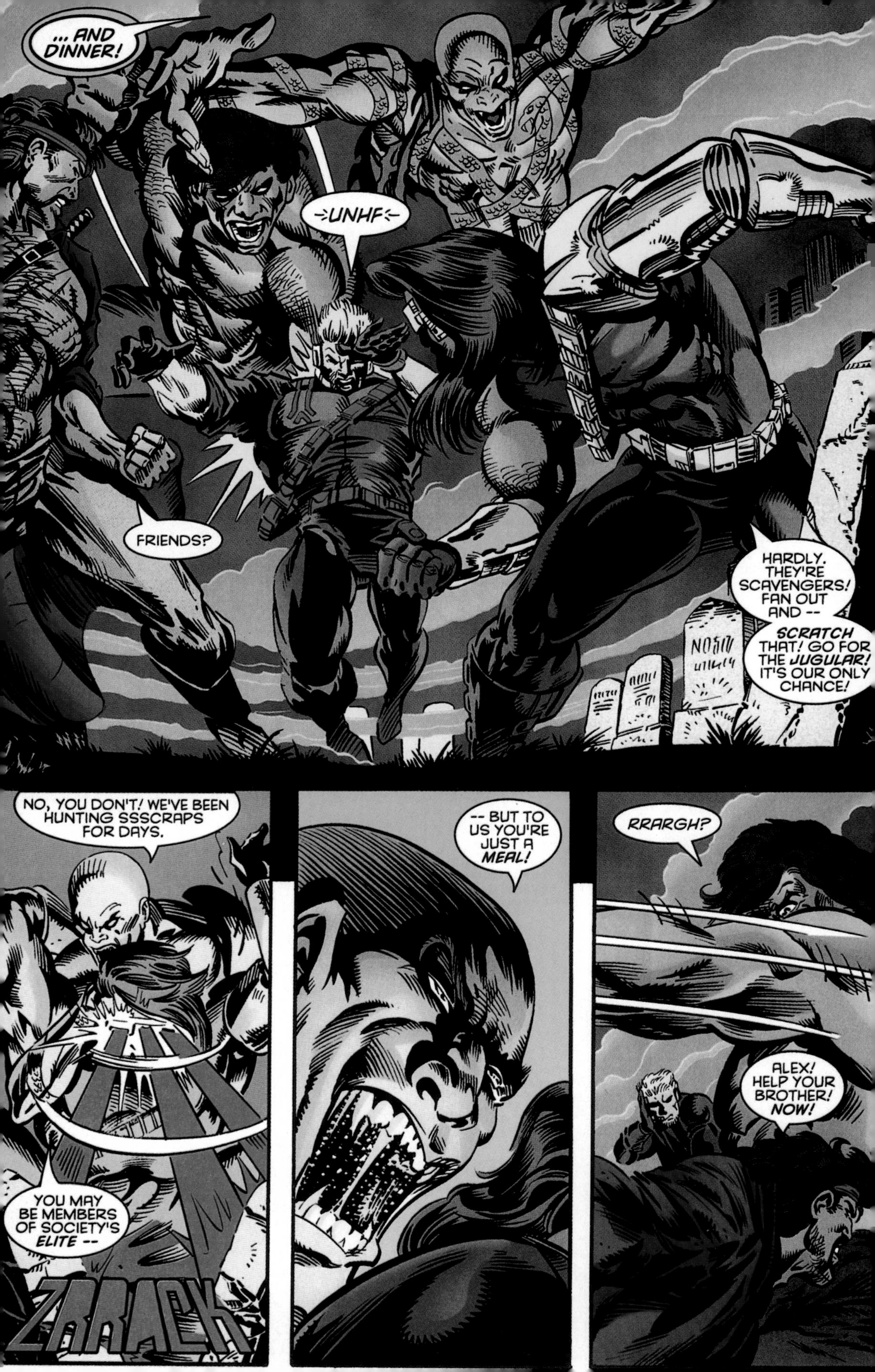

...AND DINNER!
-UNHF-
FRIENDS?
HARDLY. THEY'RE SCAVENGERS! FAN OUT AND --
SCRATCH THAT! GO FOR THE JUGULAR! IT'S OUR ONLY CHANCE!
NO, YOU DON'T! WE'VE BEEN HUNTING SSSCRAPS FOR DAYS.
YOU MAY BE MEMBERS OF SOCIETY'S ELITE --
ZARACK
-- BUT TO US YOU'RE JUST A MEAL!
RRARGH?
ALEX! HELP YOUR BROTHER! NOW!

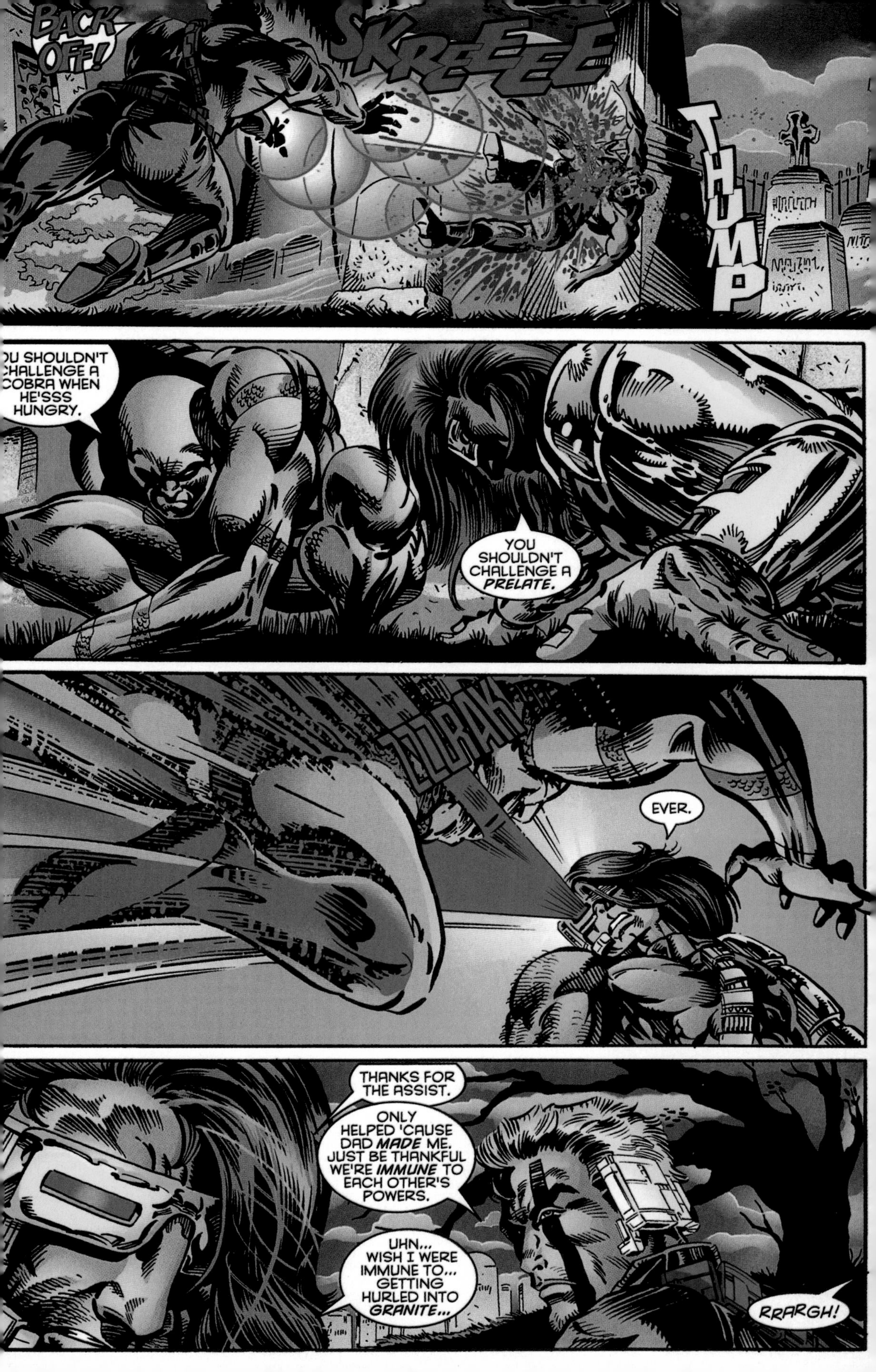
BACK OFF!
SKREEEEE
THUMP
OU SHOULDN'T CHALLENGE A COBRA WHEN HE'SSS HUNGRY.
YOU SHOULDN'T CHALLENGE A *PRELATE*.
ZZRAK
EVER.
THANKS FOR THE ASSIST.
ONLY HELPED 'CAUSE DAD *MADE* ME. JUST BE THANKFUL WE'RE *IMMUNE* TO EACH OTHER'S POWERS.
UHN... WISH I WERE IMMUNE TO... GETTING HURLED INTO *GRANITE*...
RRARGH!

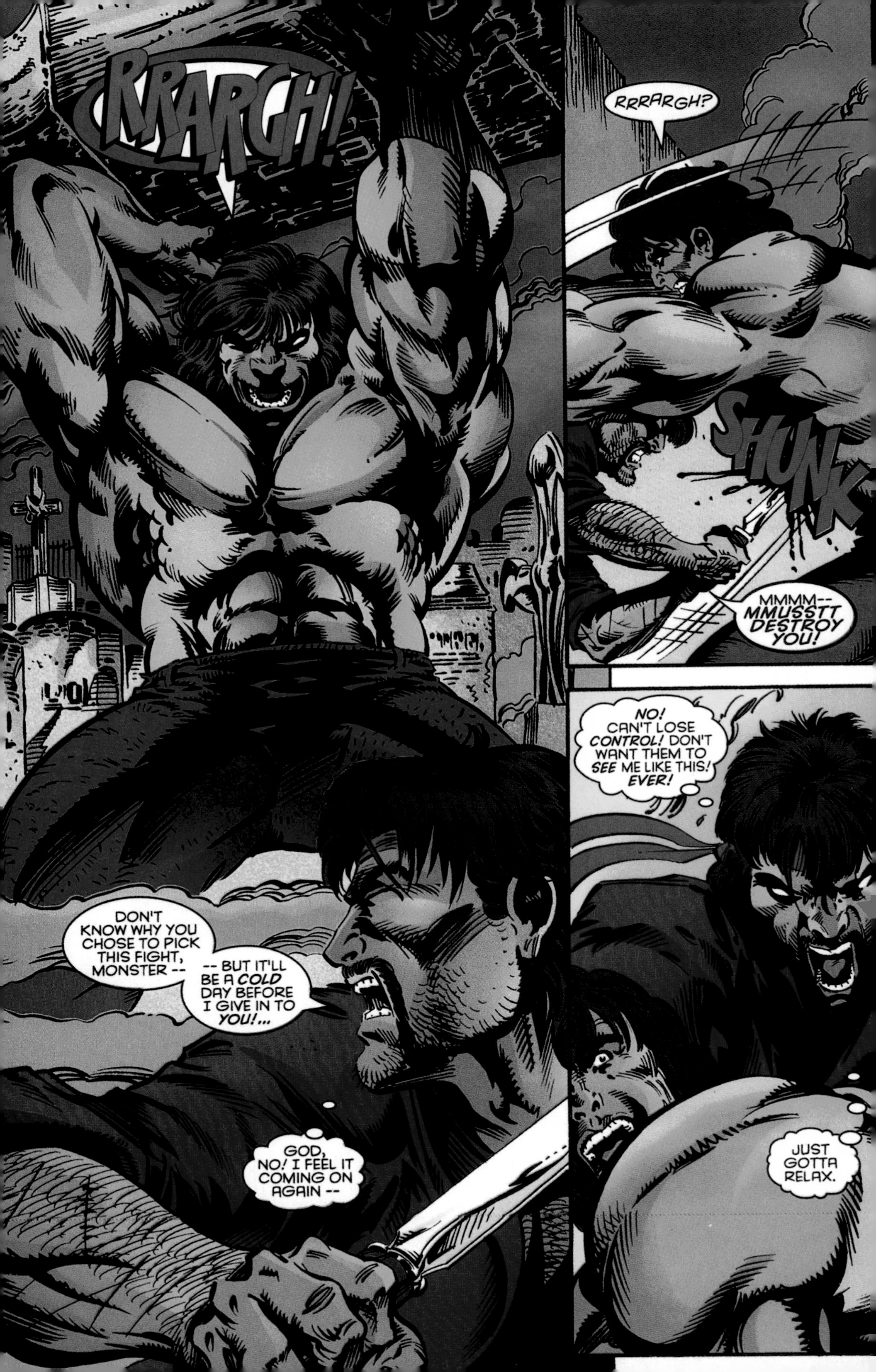
RRARGH!
DON'T KNOW WHY YOU CHOSE TO PICK THIS FIGHT, MONSTER --
-- BUT IT'LL BE A COLD DAY BEFORE I GIVE IN TO YOU!...
GOD, NO! I FEEL IT COMING ON AGAIN --
RRRARGH?
SHUNK
MMMM-- MMUSSTT DESTROY YOU!
NO! CAN'T LOSE CONTROL! DON'T WANT THEM TO SEE ME LIKE THIS! EVER!
JUST GOTTA RELAX.

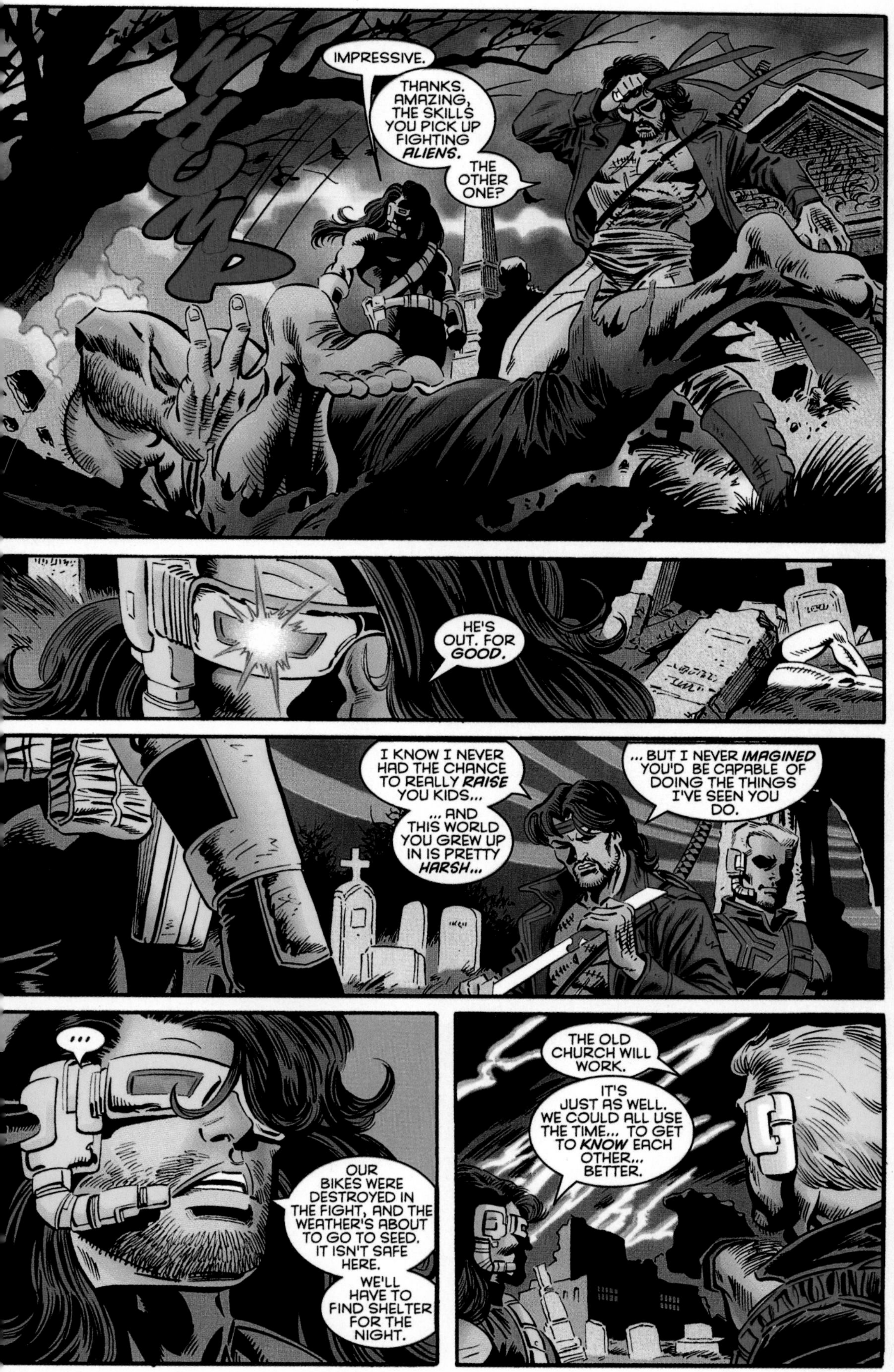
WHOMP
IMPRESSIVE.
THANKS. AMAZING, THE SKILLS YOU PICK UP FIGHTING *ALIENS*.
THE OTHER ONE?
HE'S OUT. FOR *GOOD*.
I KNOW I NEVER HAD THE CHANCE TO REALLY *RAISE* YOU KIDS...
...AND THIS WORLD YOU GREW UP IN IS PRETTY *HARSH*...
...BUT I NEVER *IMAGINED* YOU'D BE CAPABLE OF DOING THE THINGS I'VE SEEN YOU DO.
...
OUR BIKES WERE DESTROYED IN THE FIGHT, AND THE WEATHER'S ABOUT TO GO TO SEED. IT ISN'T SAFE HERE.
WE'LL HAVE TO FIND SHELTER FOR THE NIGHT.
THE OLD CHURCH WILL WORK.
IT'S JUST AS WELL. WE COULD ALL USE THE TIME... TO GET TO *KNOW* EACH OTHER... BETTER.

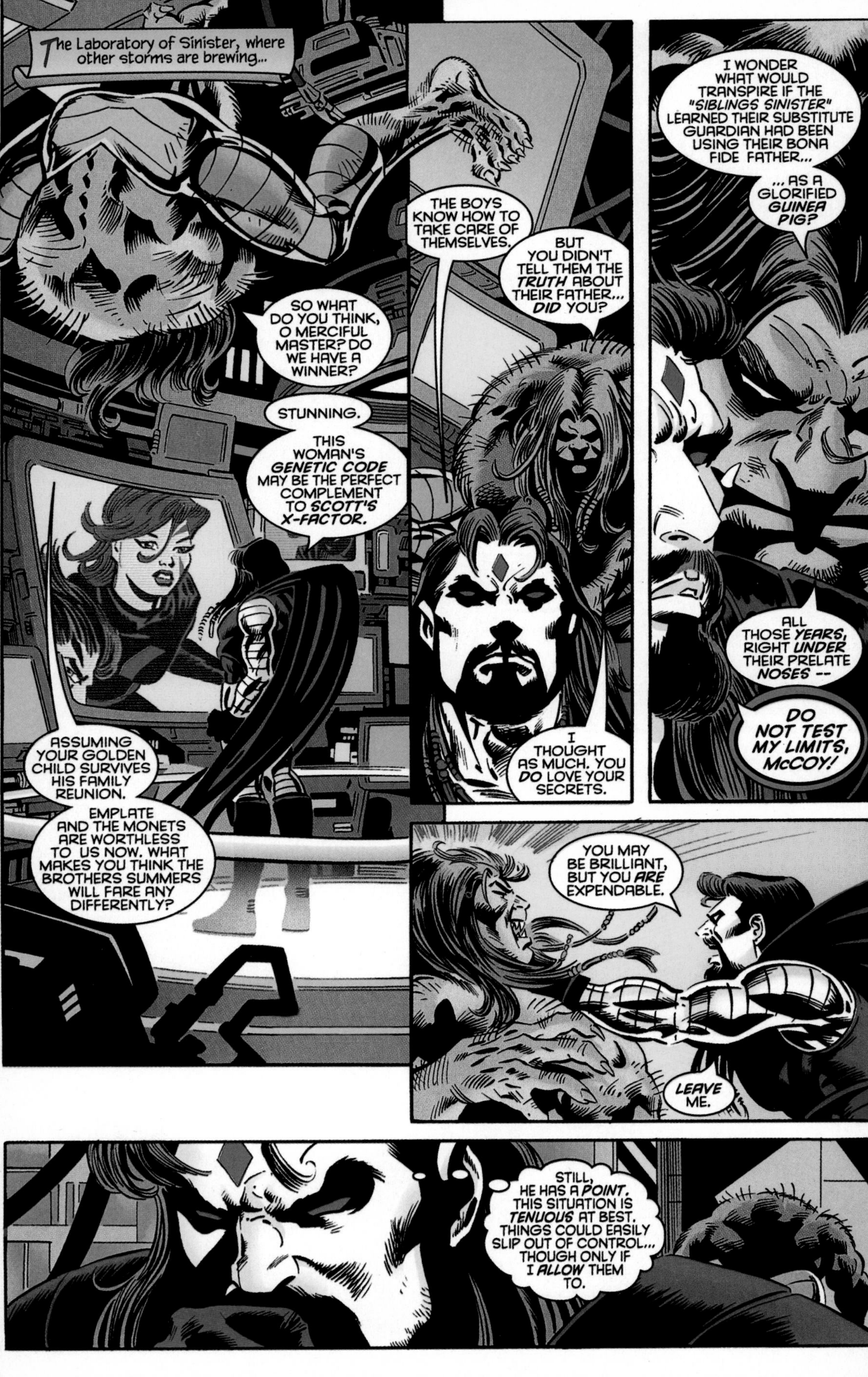
The Laboratory of Sinister, where other storms are brewing...
SO WHAT DO YOU THINK, O MERCIFUL MASTER? DO WE HAVE A WINNER?
STUNNING.
THIS WOMAN'S GENETIC CODE MAY BE THE PERFECT COMPLEMENT TO SCOTT'S X-FACTOR.
ASSUMING YOUR GOLDEN CHILD SURVIVES HIS FAMILY REUNION.
EMPLATE AND THE MONETS ARE WORTHLESS TO US NOW. WHAT MAKES YOU THINK THE BROTHERS SUMMERS WILL FARE ANY DIFFERENTLY?
THE BOYS KNOW HOW TO TAKE CARE OF THEMSELVES.
BUT YOU DIDN'T TELL THEM THE TRUTH ABOUT THEIR FATHER... DID YOU?
I THOUGHT AS MUCH. YOU DO LOVE YOUR SECRETS.
I WONDER WHAT WOULD TRANSPIRE IF THE "SIBLINGS SINISTER" LEARNED THEIR SUBSTITUTE GUARDIAN HAD BEEN USING THEIR BONA FIDE FATHER...
...AS A GLORIFIED GUINEA PIG?
ALL THOSE YEARS, RIGHT UNDER THEIR PRELATE NOSES --
DO NOT TEST MY LIMITS, McCOY!
YOU MAY BE BRILLIANT, BUT YOU ARE EXPENDABLE.
LEAVE ME.
STILL, HE HAS A POINT. THIS SITUATION IS TENUOUS AT BEST. THINGS COULD EASILY SLIP OUT OF CONTROL... THOUGH ONLY IF I ALLOW THEM TO.

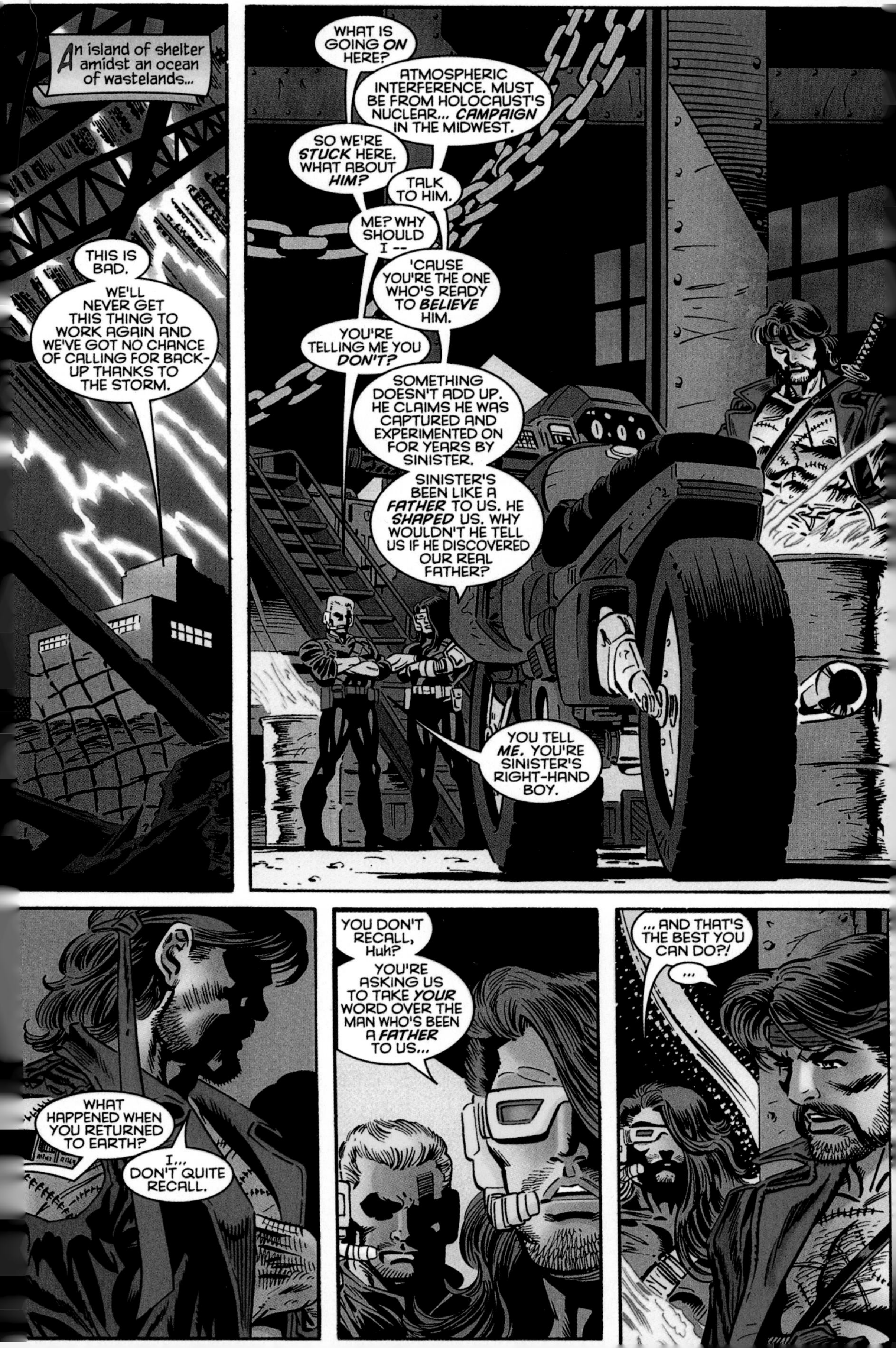
An island of shelter amidst an ocean of wastelands...
THIS IS BAD.
WE'LL NEVER GET THIS THING TO WORK AGAIN AND WE'VE GOT NO CHANCE OF CALLING FOR BACK-UP THANKS TO THE STORM.
WHAT IS GOING ON HERE?
ATMOSPHERIC INTERFERENCE. MUST BE FROM HOLOCAUST'S NUCLEAR... CAMPAIGN IN THE MIDWEST.
SO WE'RE STUCK HERE. WHAT ABOUT HIM?
TALK TO HIM.
ME? WHY SHOULD I --
'CAUSE YOU'RE THE ONE WHO'S READY TO BELIEVE HIM.
YOU'RE TELLING ME YOU DON'T?
SOMETHING DOESN'T ADD UP. HE CLAIMS HE WAS CAPTURED AND EXPERIMENTED ON FOR YEARS BY SINISTER.
SINISTER'S BEEN LIKE A FATHER TO US. HE SHAPED US. WHY WOULDN'T HE TELL US IF HE DISCOVERED OUR REAL FATHER?
YOU TELL ME. YOU'RE SINISTER'S RIGHT-HAND BOY.
WHAT HAPPENED WHEN YOU RETURNED TO EARTH?
I... DON'T QUITE RECALL.
YOU DON'T RECALL, Huh?
YOU'RE ASKING US TO TAKE YOUR WORD OVER THE MAN WHO'S BEEN A FATHER TO US...
... AND THAT'S THE BEST YOU CAN DO?!
...

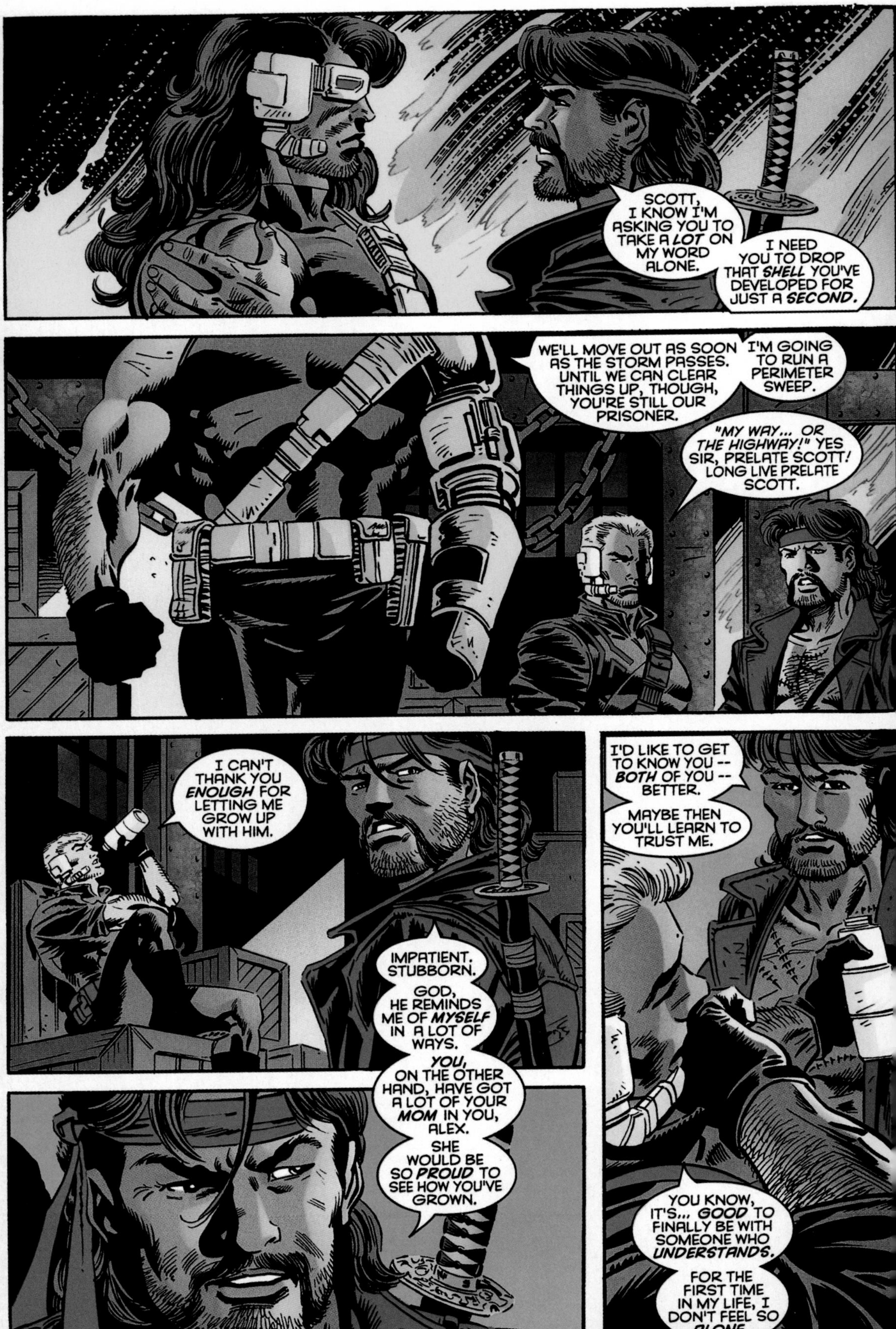
SCOTT, I KNOW I'M ASKING YOU TO TAKE A *LOT* ON MY WORD ALONE.
I NEED YOU TO DROP THAT *SHELL* YOU'VE DEVELOPED FOR JUST A *SECOND*.
WE'LL MOVE OUT AS SOON AS THE STORM PASSES. UNTIL WE CAN CLEAR THINGS UP, THOUGH, YOU'RE STILL OUR PRISONER.
I'M GOING TO RUN A PERIMETER SWEEP.
"MY WAY... OR THE HIGHWAY!" YES SIR, PRELATE SCOTT! LONG LIVE PRELATE SCOTT.
I CAN'T THANK YOU *ENOUGH* FOR LETTING ME GROW UP WITH HIM.
IMPATIENT. STUBBORN.
GOD, HE REMINDS ME OF *MYSELF* IN A LOT OF WAYS.
YOU, ON THE OTHER HAND, HAVE GOT A LOT OF YOUR *MOM* IN YOU, ALEX.
SHE WOULD BE SO *PROUD* TO SEE HOW YOU'VE GROWN.
I'D LIKE TO GET TO KNOW YOU -- *BOTH* OF YOU -- BETTER.
MAYBE THEN YOU'LL LEARN TO TRUST ME.
YOU KNOW, IT'S... *GOOD* TO FINALLY BE WITH SOMEONE WHO *UNDERSTANDS*.
FOR THE FIRST TIME IN MY LIFE, I DON'T FEEL SO *ALONE*.

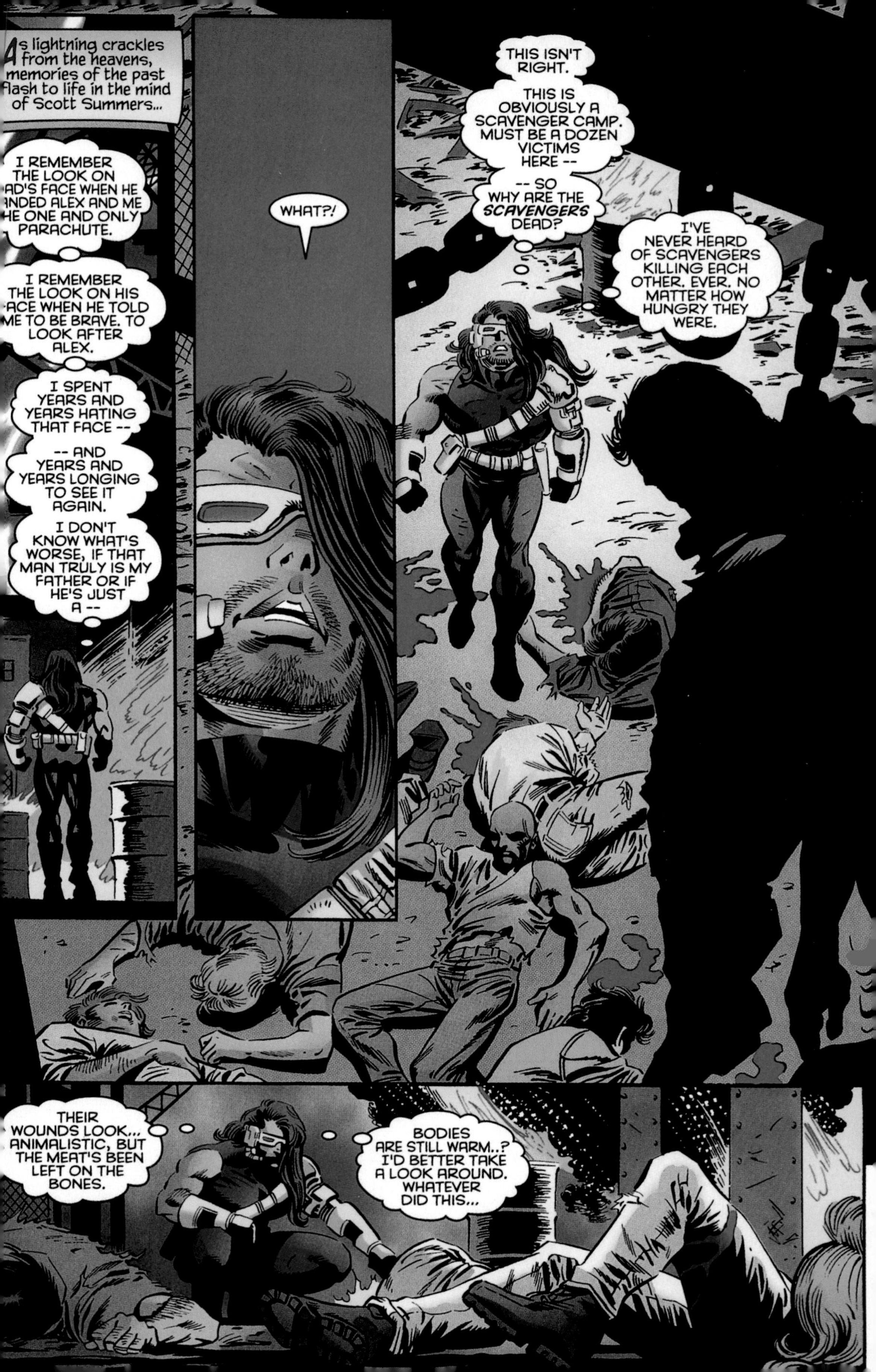
As lightning crackles from the heavens, memories of the past flash to life in the mind of Scott Summers...
I REMEMBER THE LOOK ON AD'S FACE WHEN HE ANDED ALEX AND ME HE ONE AND ONLY PARACHUTE.
I REMEMBER THE LOOK ON HIS ACE WHEN HE TOLD ME TO BE BRAVE. TO LOOK AFTER ALEX.
I SPENT YEARS AND YEARS HATING THAT FACE --
-- AND YEARS AND YEARS LONGING TO SEE IT AGAIN.
I DON'T KNOW WHAT'S WORSE, IF THAT MAN TRULY IS MY FATHER OR IF HE'S JUST A --
WHAT?!
THIS ISN'T RIGHT.
THIS IS OBVIOUSLY A SCAVENGER CAMP. MUST BE A DOZEN VICTIMS HERE --
-- SO WHY ARE THE SCAVENGERS DEAD?
I'VE NEVER HEARD OF SCAVENGERS KILLING EACH OTHER. EVER. NO MATTER HOW HUNGRY THEY WERE.
THEIR WOUNDS LOOK... ANIMALISTIC, BUT THE MEAT'S BEEN LEFT ON THE BONES.
BODIES ARE STILL WARM..? I'D BETTER TAKE A LOOK AROUND. WHATEVER DID THIS...

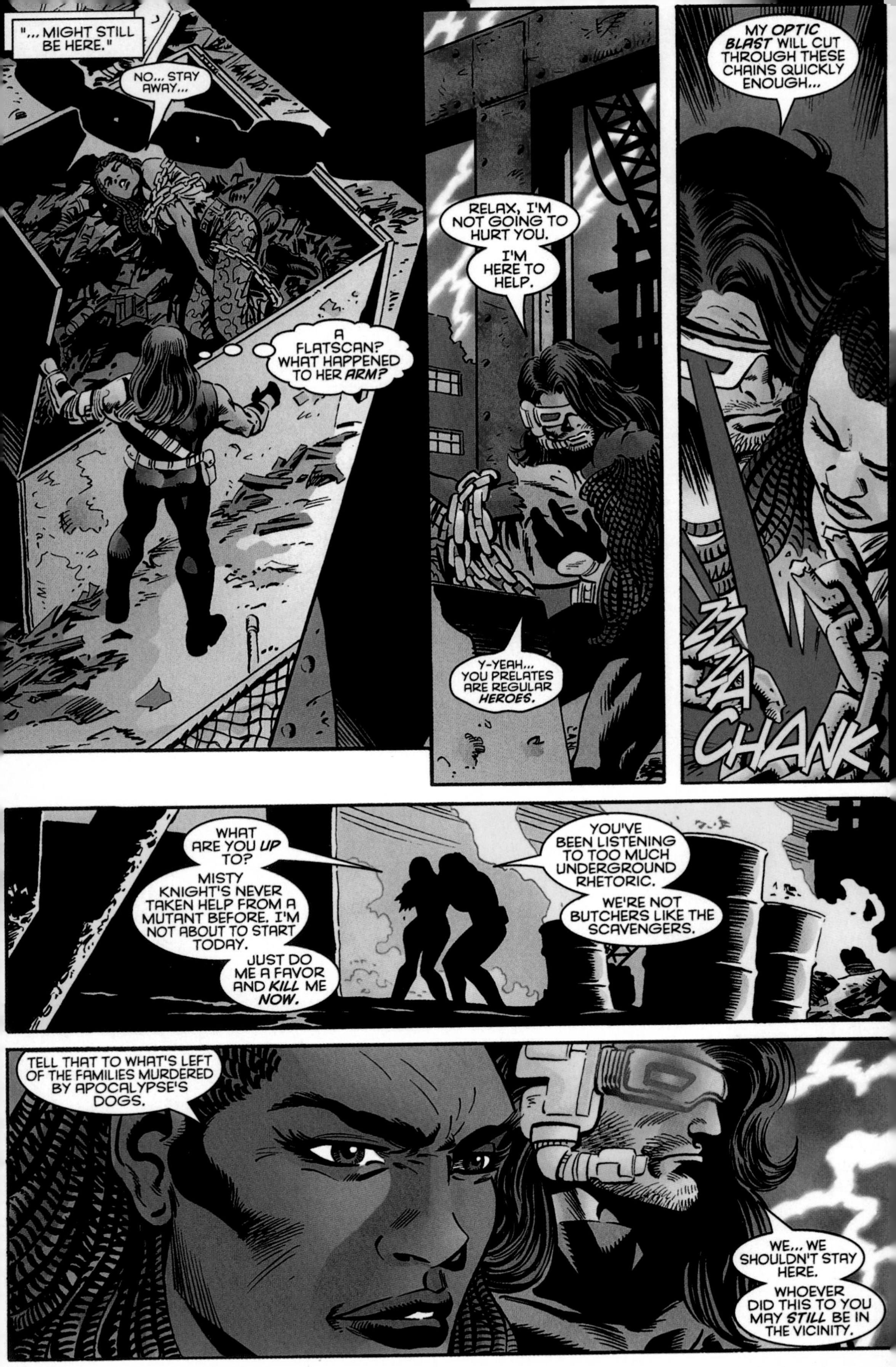
"... MIGHT STILL BE HERE."
NO... STAY AWAY...
A FLATSCAN? WHAT HAPPENED TO HER ARM?
RELAX, I'M NOT GOING TO HURT YOU.
I'M HERE TO HELP.
Y-YEAH... YOU PRELATES ARE REGULAR HEROES.
MY OPTIC BLAST WILL CUT THROUGH THESE CHAINS QUICKLY ENOUGH...
ZZZAA
CHANK
WHAT ARE YOU UP TO?
MISTY KNIGHT'S NEVER TAKEN HELP FROM A MUTANT BEFORE. I'M NOT ABOUT TO START TODAY.
JUST DO ME A FAVOR AND KILL ME NOW.
YOU'VE BEEN LISTENING TO TOO MUCH UNDERGROUND RHETORIC.
WE'RE NOT BUTCHERS LIKE THE SCAVENGERS.
TELL THAT TO WHAT'S LEFT OF THE FAMILIES MURDERED BY APOCALYPSE'S DOGS.
WE... WE SHOULDN'T STAY HERE.
WHOEVER DID THIS TO YOU MAY STILL BE IN THE VICINITY.

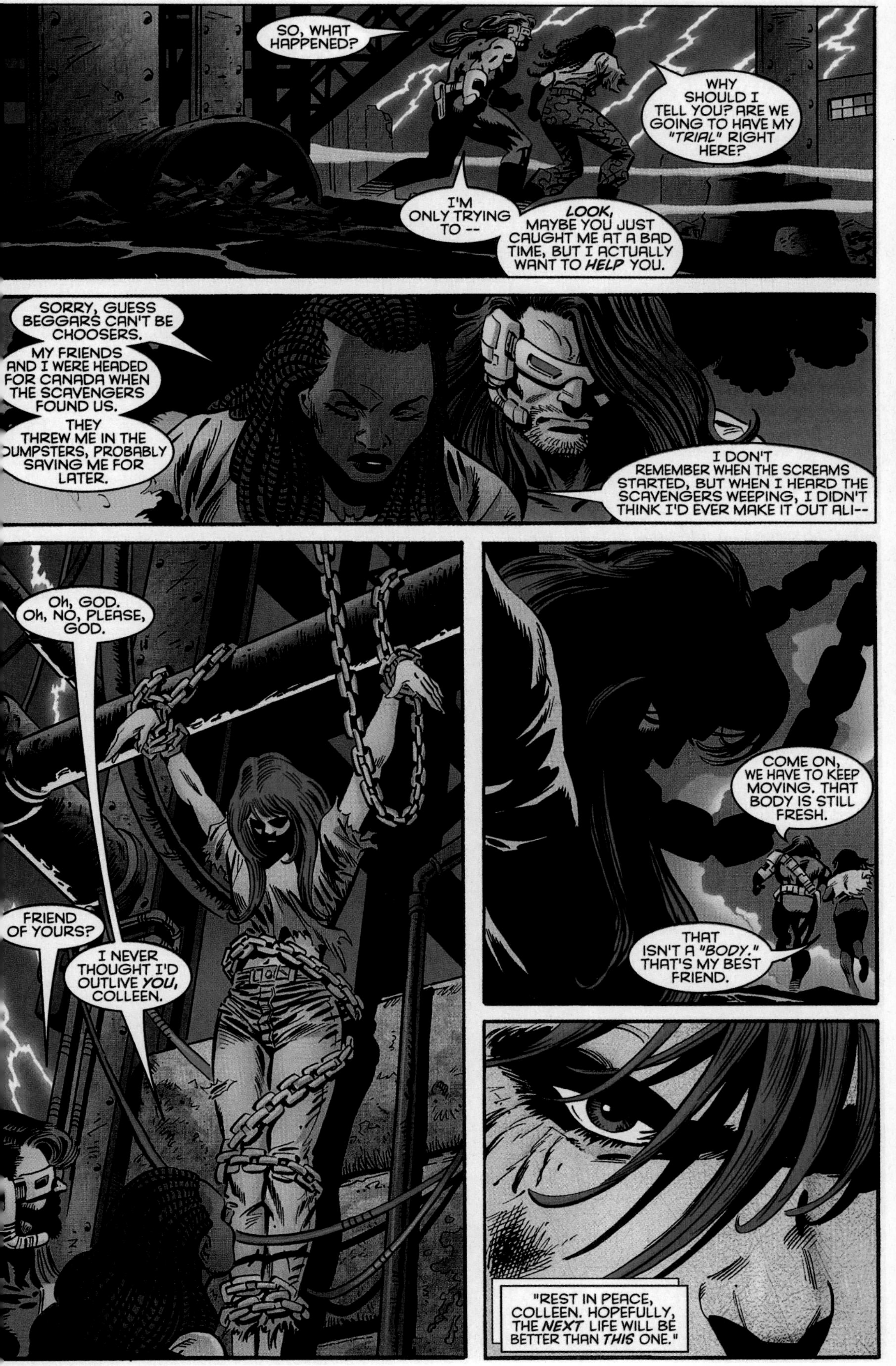
SO, WHAT HAPPENED?
WHY SHOULD I TELL YOU? ARE WE GOING TO HAVE MY "TRIAL" RIGHT HERE?
I'M ONLY TRYING TO --
LOOK, MAYBE YOU JUST CAUGHT ME AT A BAD TIME, BUT I ACTUALLY WANT TO HELP YOU.
SORRY, GUESS BEGGARS CAN'T BE CHOOSERS.
MY FRIENDS AND I WERE HEADED FOR CANADA WHEN THE SCAVENGERS FOUND US.
THEY THREW ME IN THE DUMPSTERS, PROBABLY SAVING ME FOR LATER.
I DON'T REMEMBER WHEN THE SCREAMS STARTED, BUT WHEN I HEARD THE SCAVENGERS WEEPING, I DIDN'T THINK I'D EVER MAKE IT OUT ALI--
Oh, GOD. Oh, NO, PLEASE, GOD.
FRIEND OF YOURS?
I NEVER THOUGHT I'D OUTLIVE YOU, COLLEEN.
COME ON, WE HAVE TO KEEP MOVING. THAT BODY IS STILL FRESH.
THAT ISN'T A "BODY." THAT'S MY BEST FRIEND.
"REST IN PEACE, COLLEEN. HOPEFULLY, THE NEXT LIFE WILL BE BETTER THAN THIS ONE."

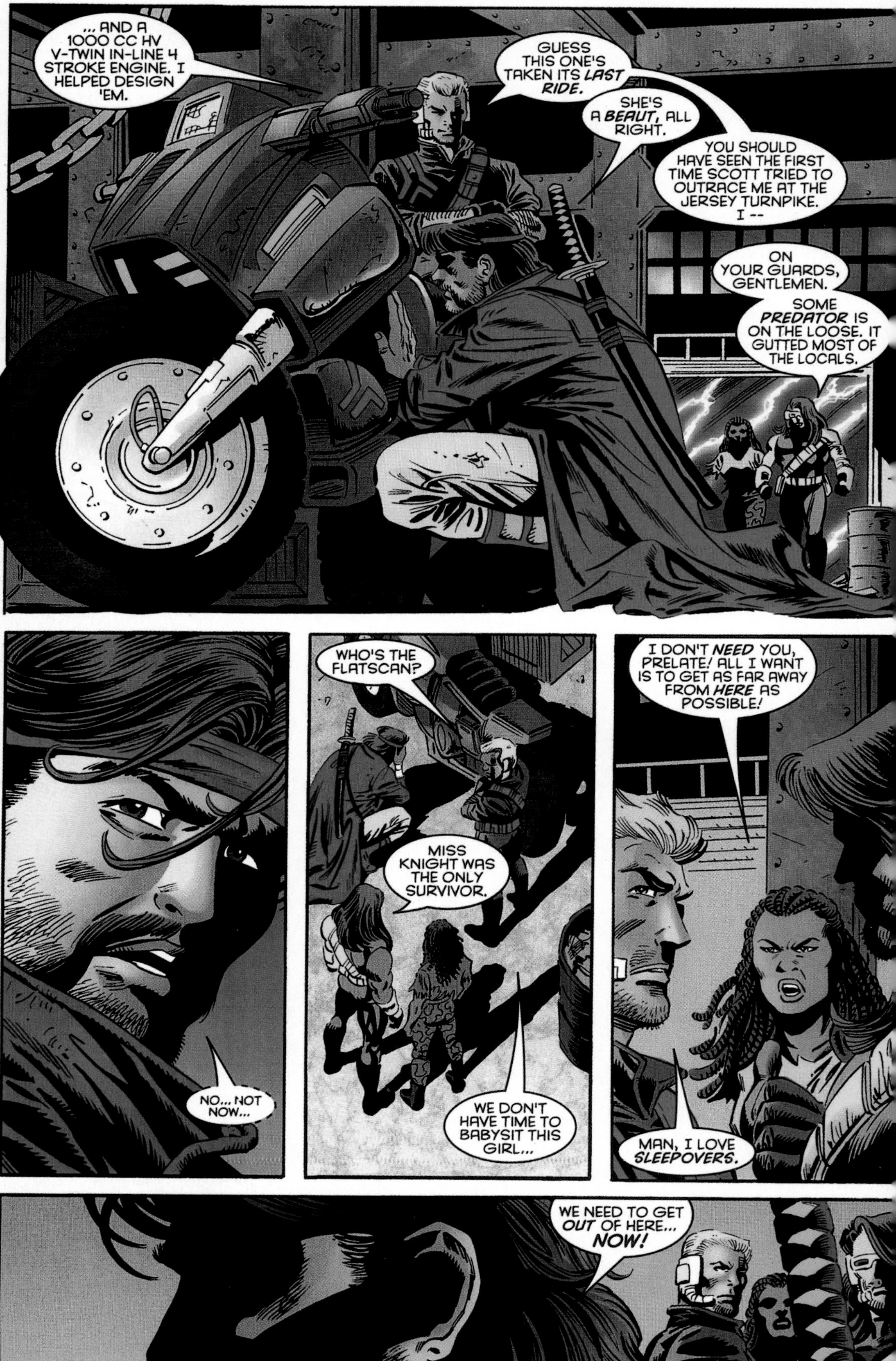
... AND A 1000 CC HV V-TWIN IN-LINE 4 STROKE ENGINE. I HELPED DESIGN 'EM.
GUESS THIS ONE'S TAKEN ITS LAST RIDE.
SHE'S A BEAUT, ALL RIGHT.
YOU SHOULD HAVE SEEN THE FIRST TIME SCOTT TRIED TO OUTRACE ME AT THE JERSEY TURNPIKE. I --
ON YOUR GUARDS, GENTLEMEN.
SOME PREDATOR IS ON THE LOOSE. IT GUTTED MOST OF THE LOCALS.
NO... NOT NOW...
WHO'S THE FLATSCAN?
MISS KNIGHT WAS THE ONLY SURVIVOR.
WE DON'T HAVE TIME TO BABYSIT THIS GIRL...
I DON'T NEED YOU, PRELATE! ALL I WANT IS TO GET AS FAR AWAY FROM HERE AS POSSIBLE!
MAN, I LOVE SLEEPOVERS.
WE NEED TO GET OUT OF HERE... NOW!

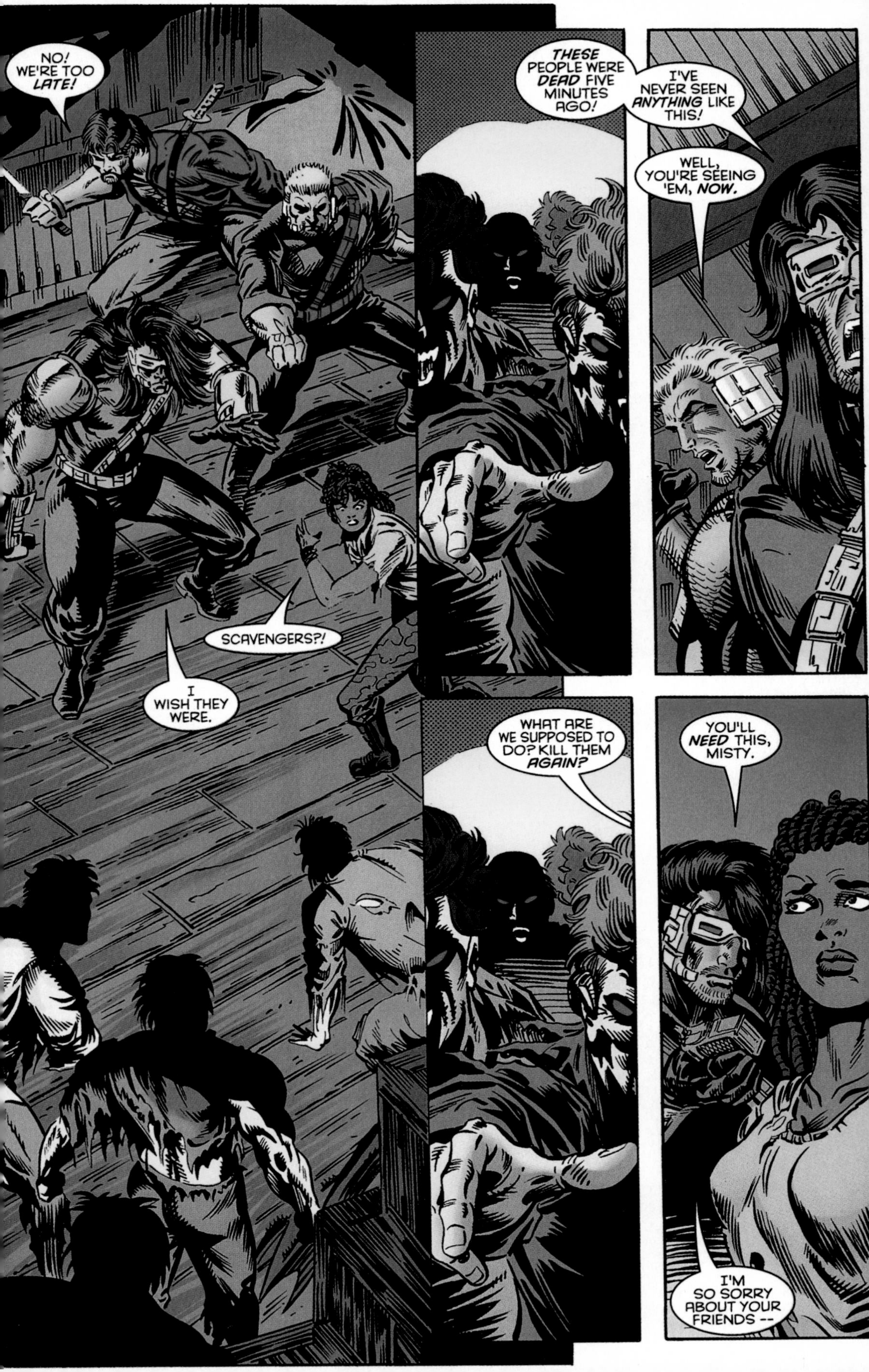
NO! WE'RE TOO LATE!
SCAVENGERS?!
I WISH THEY WERE.
THESE PEOPLE WERE DEAD FIVE MINUTES AGO!
I'VE NEVER SEEN ANYTHING LIKE THIS!
WELL, YOU'RE SEEING 'EM, NOW.
WHAT ARE WE SUPPOSED TO DO? KILL THEM AGAIN?
YOU'LL NEED THIS, MISTY.
I'M SO SORRY ABOUT YOUR FRIENDS --

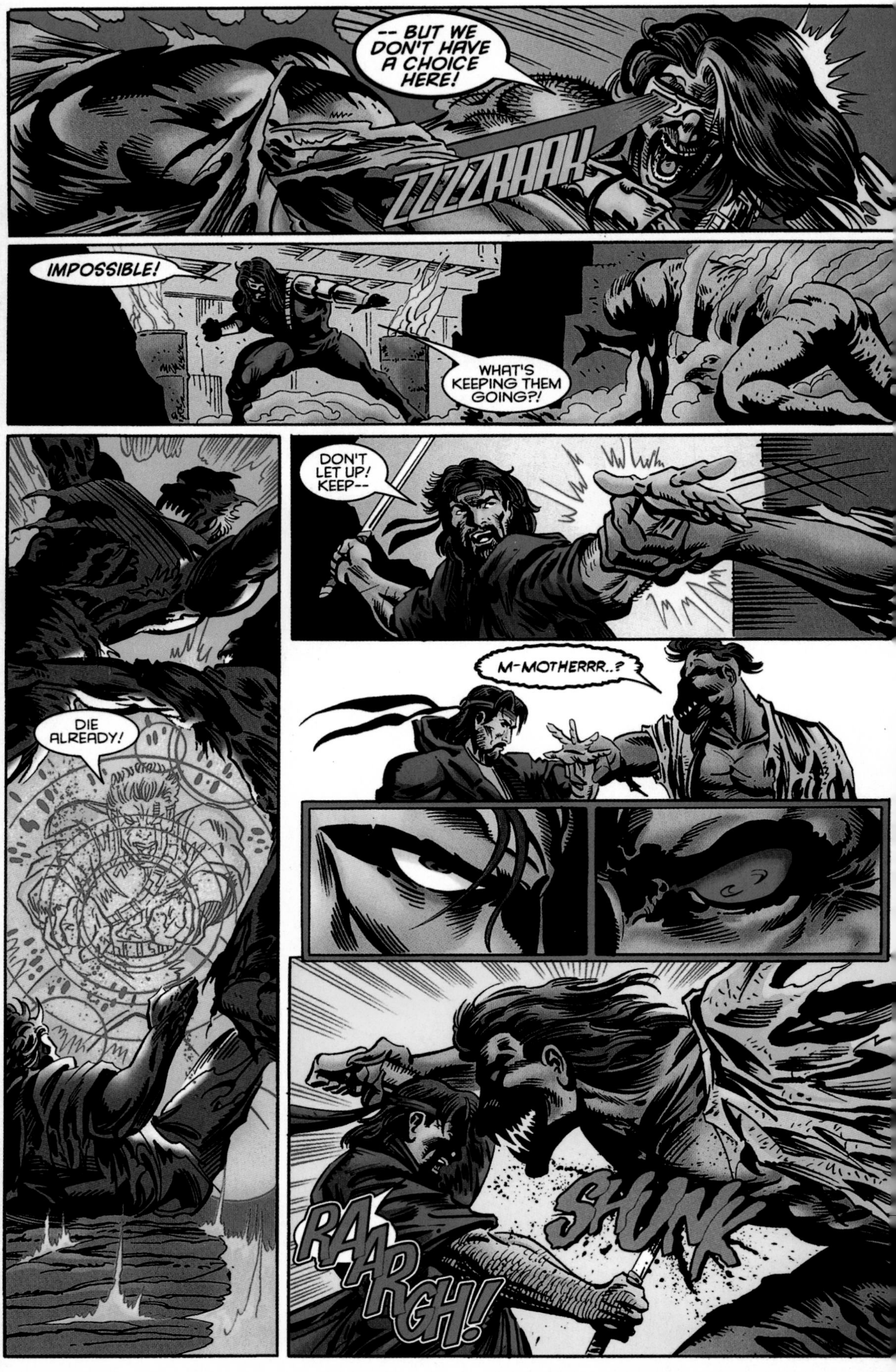
-- BUT WE DON'T HAVE A CHOICE HERE!
ZZZZRAAK
IMPOSSIBLE!
WHAT'S KEEPING THEM GOING?!
DIE ALREADY!
DON'T LET UP! KEEP--
M-MOTHERRR..?
SHUNK
RAAARGH!

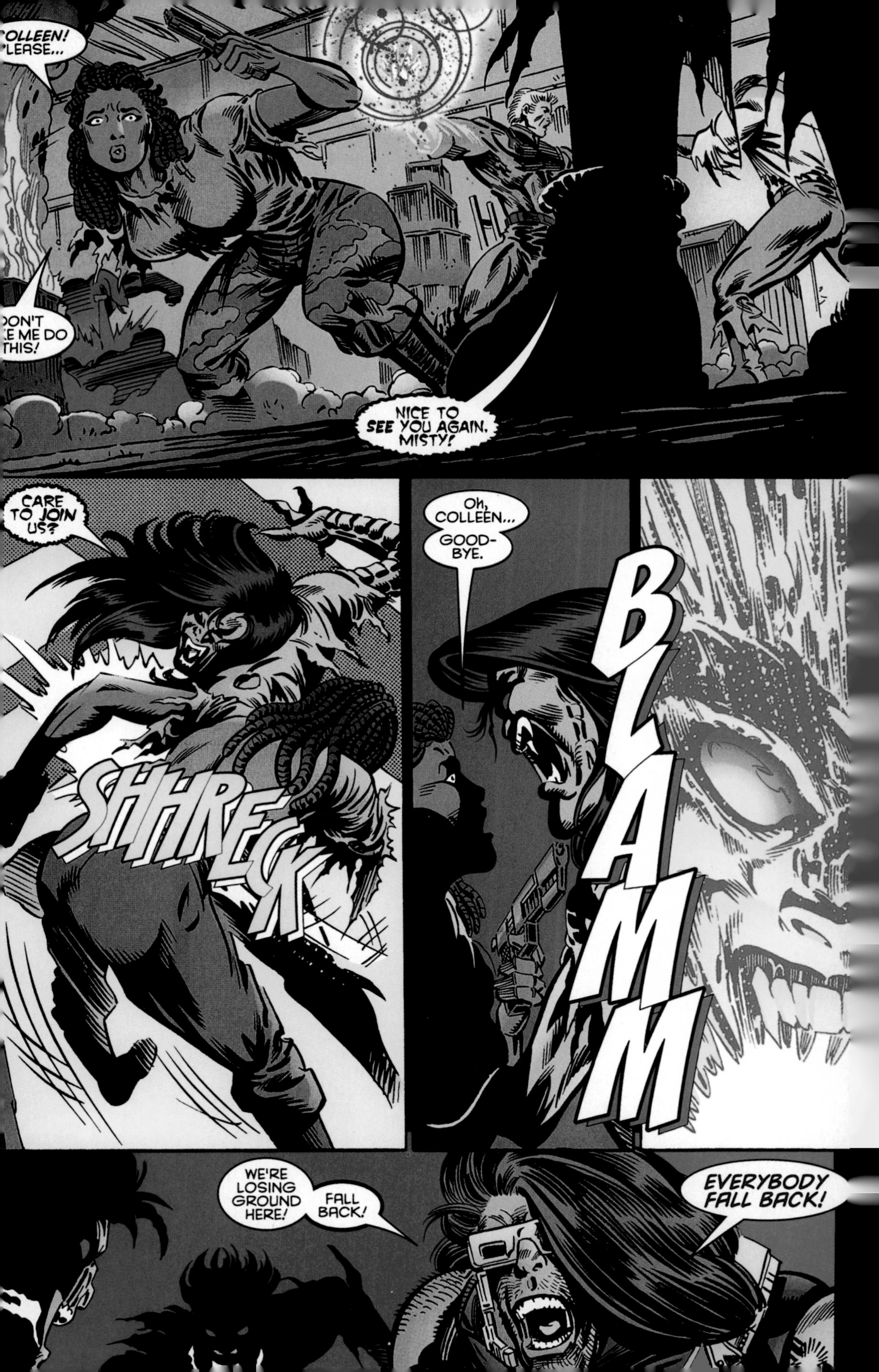
COLLEEN! PLEASE...
DON'T ...E ME DO THIS!
NICE TO SEE YOU AGAIN, MISTY!
CARE TO JOIN US?
SHHRECK
Oh, COLLEEN...
GOOD-BYE.
BLAMM
WE'RE LOSING GROUND HERE!
FALL BACK!
EVERYBODY FALL BACK!

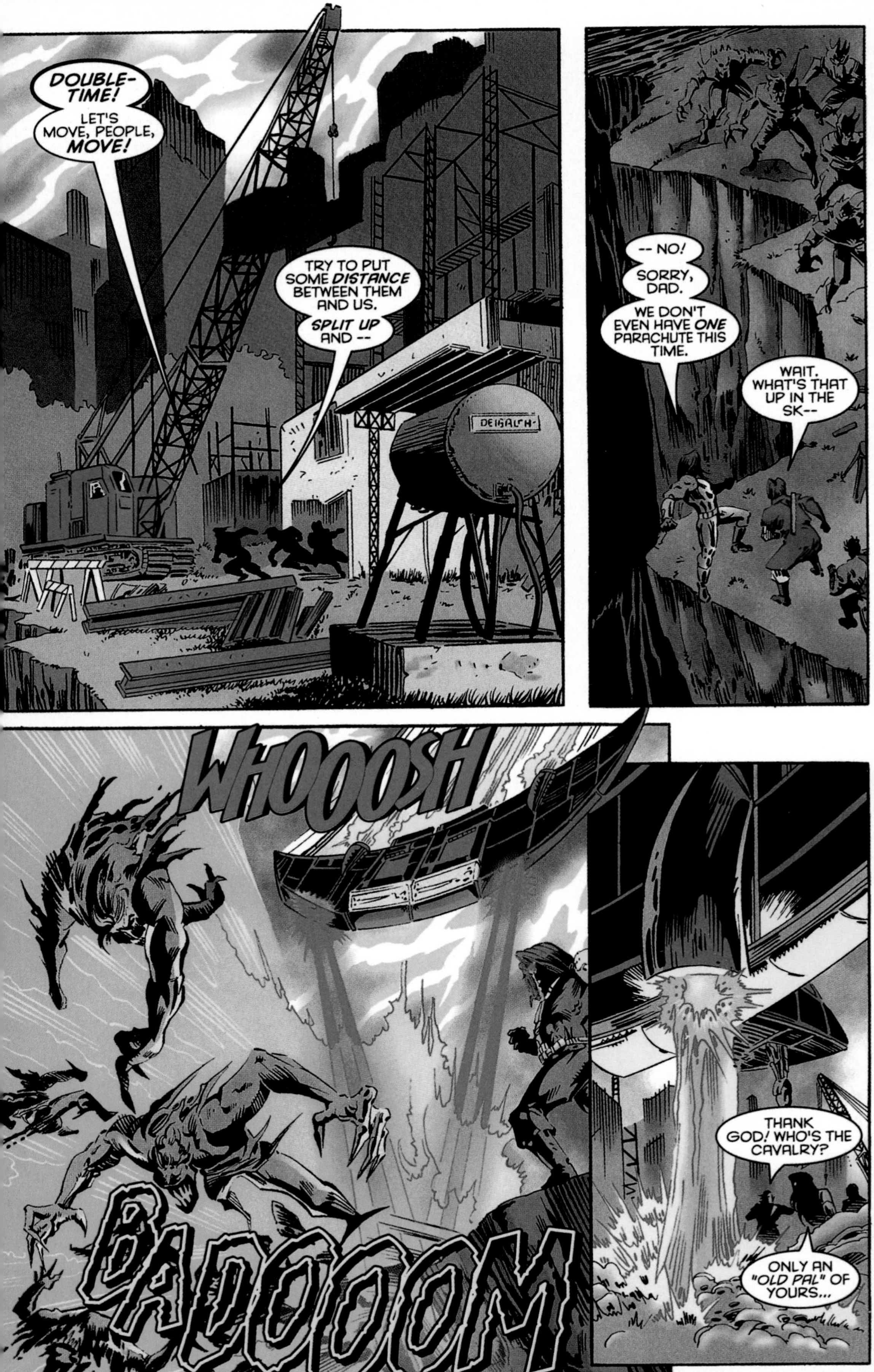
DOUBLE-TIME! LET'S MOVE, PEOPLE, MOVE!
TRY TO PUT SOME DISTANCE BETWEEN THEM AND US.
SPLIT UP AND --
DEIGALCH
-- NO!
SORRY, DAD.
WE DON'T EVEN HAVE ONE PARACHUTE THIS TIME.
WAIT. WHAT'S THAT UP IN THE SK--
WHOOOSH
BADOOOOM
THANK GOD! WHO'S THE CAVALRY?
ONLY AN "OLD PAL" OF YOURS...

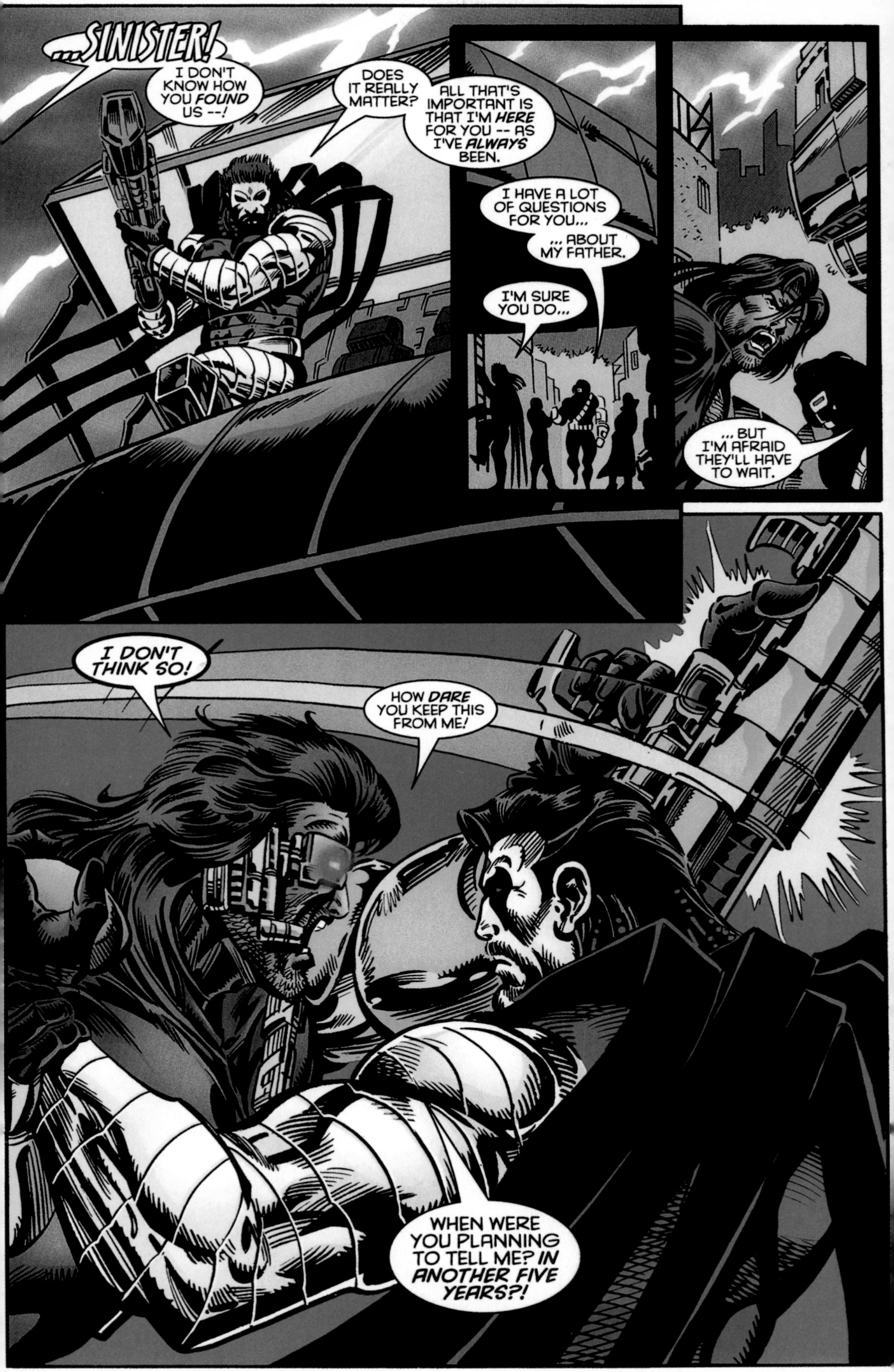
...SINISTER!
I DON'T KNOW HOW YOU FOUND US --!
DOES IT REALLY MATTER?
ALL THAT'S IMPORTANT IS THAT I'M HERE FOR YOU -- AS I'VE ALWAYS BEEN.
I HAVE A LOT OF QUESTIONS FOR YOU...
... ABOUT MY FATHER.
I'M SURE YOU DO...
... BUT I'M AFRAID THEY'LL HAVE TO WAIT.
I DON'T THINK SO!
HOW DARE YOU KEEP THIS FROM ME!
WHEN WERE YOU PLANNING TO TELL ME? IN ANOTHER FIVE YEARS?!

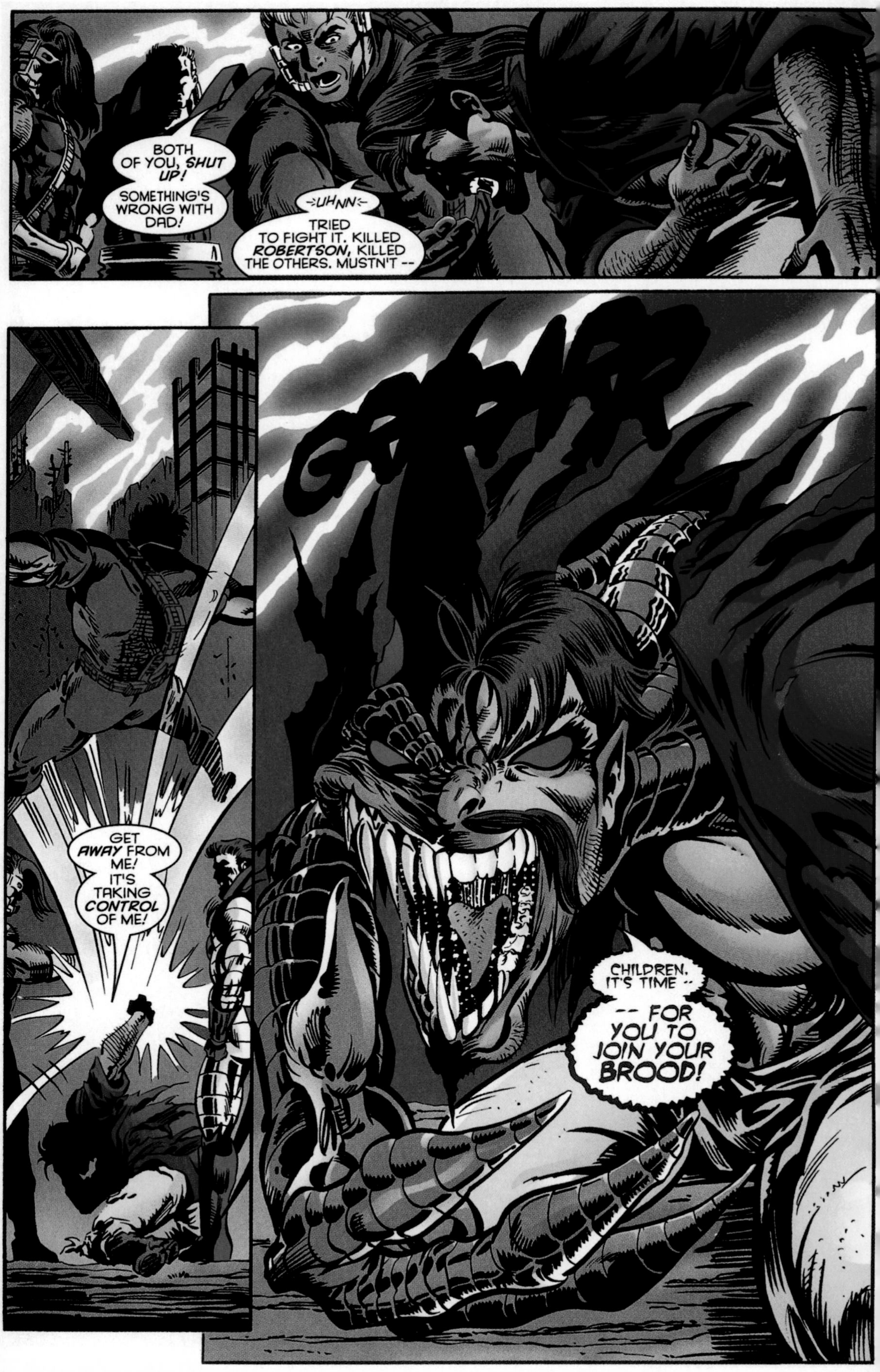

BOTH OF YOU, SHUT UP! SOMETHING'S WRONG WITH DAD!
-UHNN- TRIED TO FIGHT IT. KILLED ROBERTSON, KILLED THE OTHERS. MUSTN'T --
GET AWAY FROM ME! IT'S TAKING CONTROL OF ME!
GRRAHRR
CHILDREN. IT'S TIME --
-- FOR YOU TO JOIN YOUR BROOD!

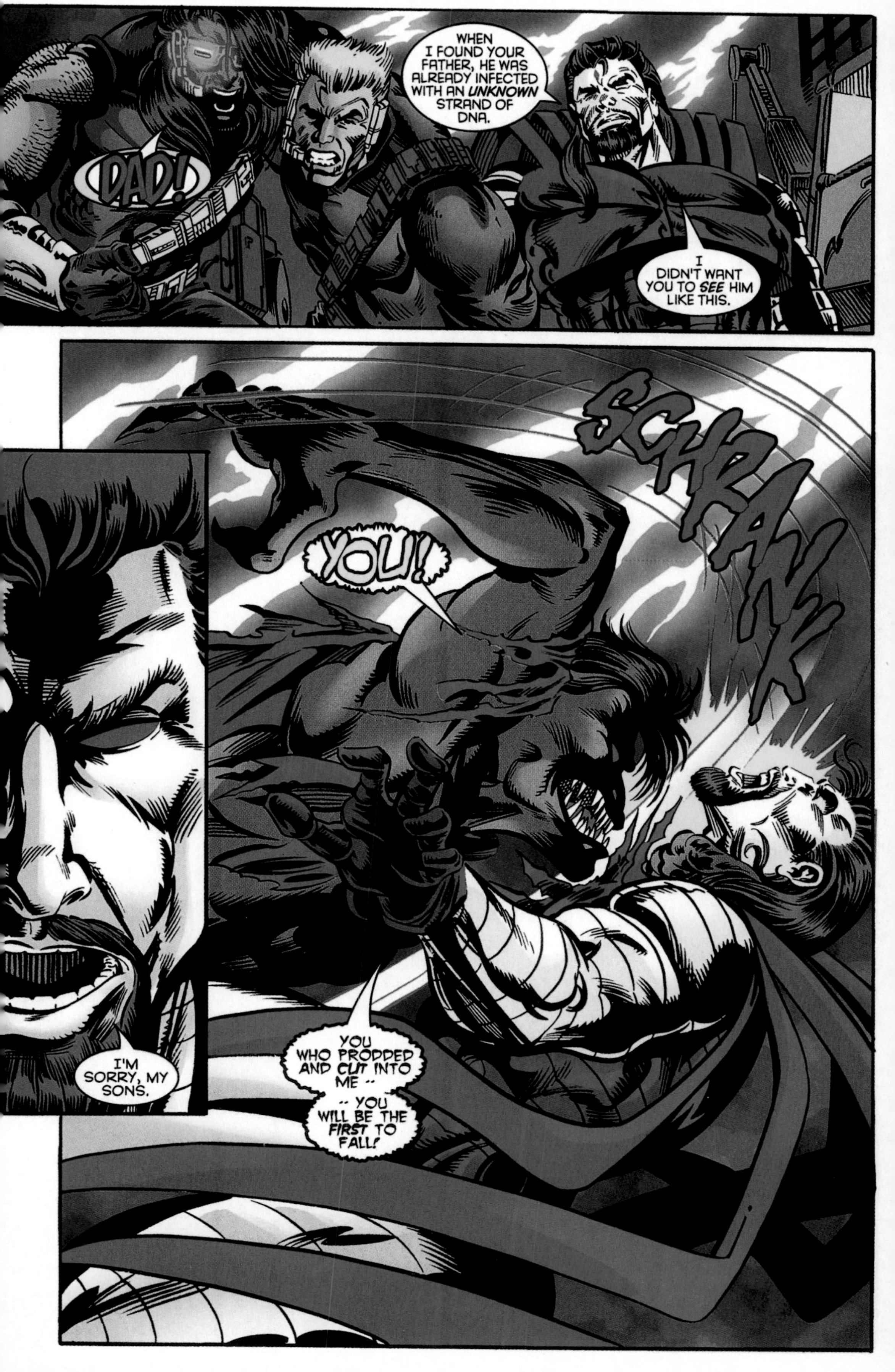
DAD!
WHEN I FOUND YOUR FATHER, HE WAS ALREADY INFECTED WITH AN UNKNOWN STRAND OF DNA.
I DIDN'T WANT YOU TO SEE HIM LIKE THIS.
SCHRANK
YOU!
YOU WHO PRODDED AND CUT INTO ME --
-- YOU WILL BE THE FIRST TO FALL!
I'M SORRY, MY SONS.

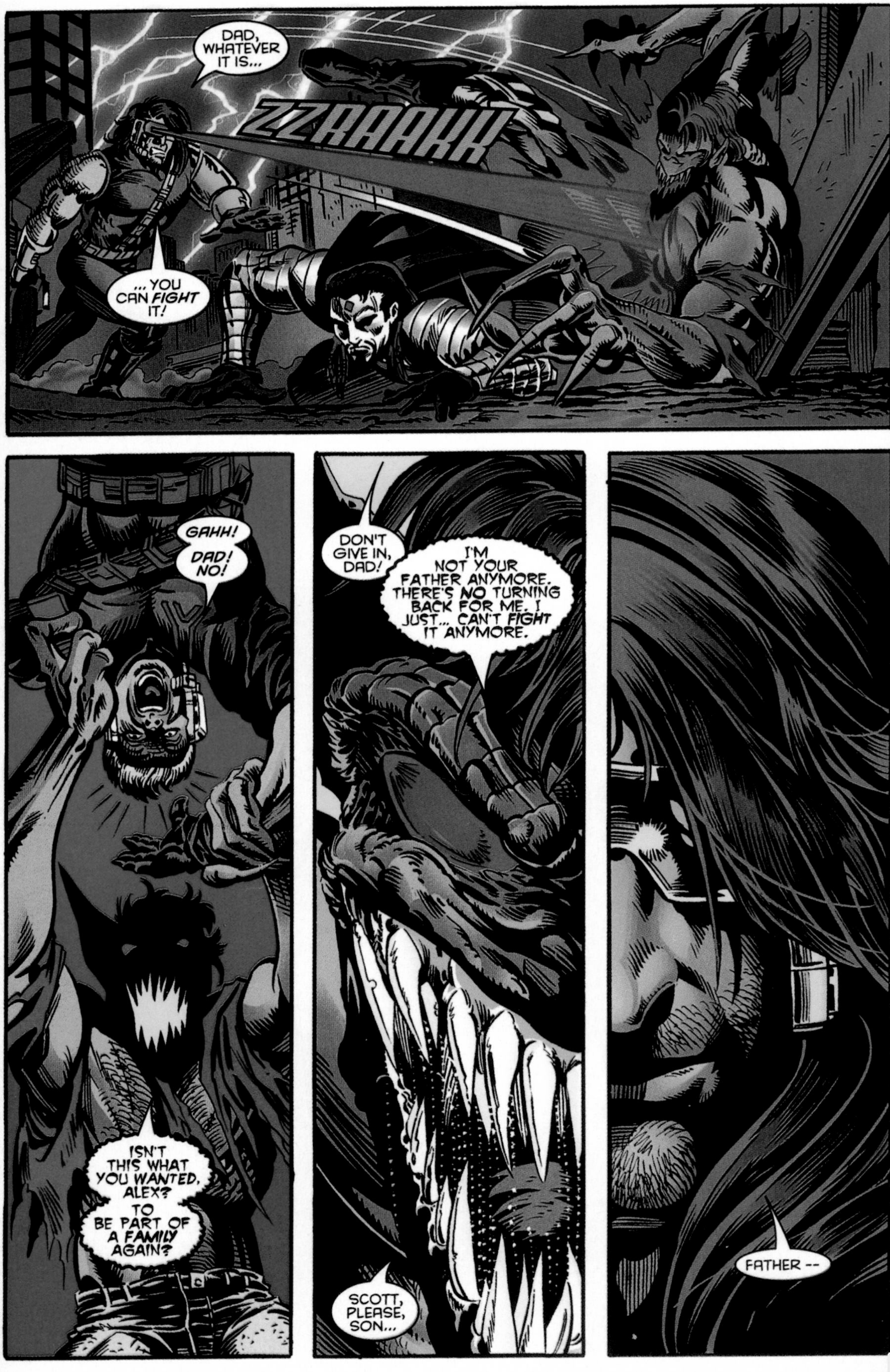
DAD, WHATEVER IT IS...
ZZRAAAKK
...YOU CAN FIGHT IT!
GAHH!
DAD! NO!
ISN'T THIS WHAT YOU WANTED, ALEX?
TO BE PART OF A FAMILY AGAIN?
DON'T GIVE IN, DAD!
I'M NOT YOUR FATHER ANYMORE. THERE'S NO TURNING BACK FOR ME. I JUST... CAN'T FIGHT IT ANYMORE.
SCOTT, PLEASE, SON...
FATHER --

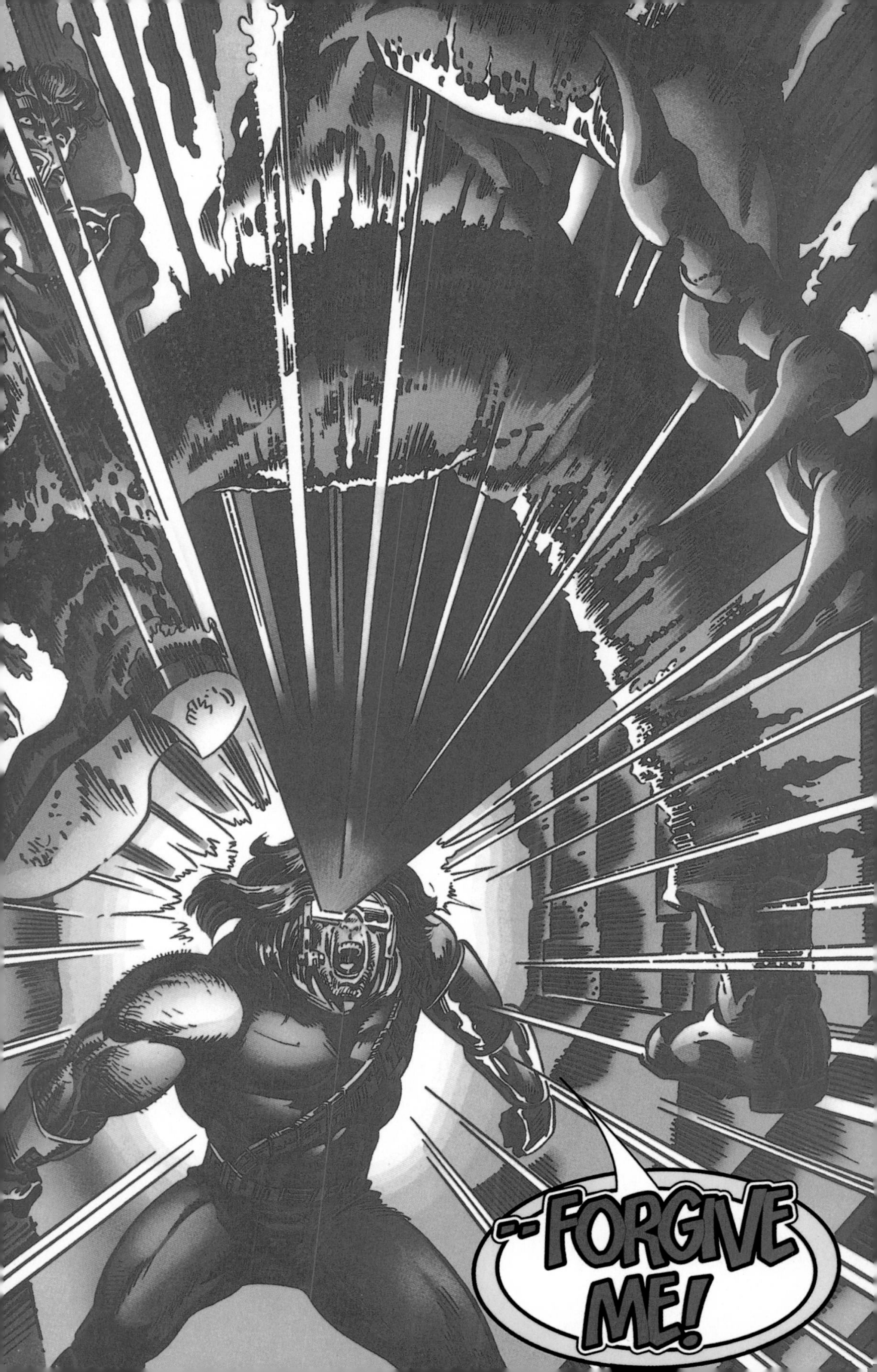
--FORGIVE ME!

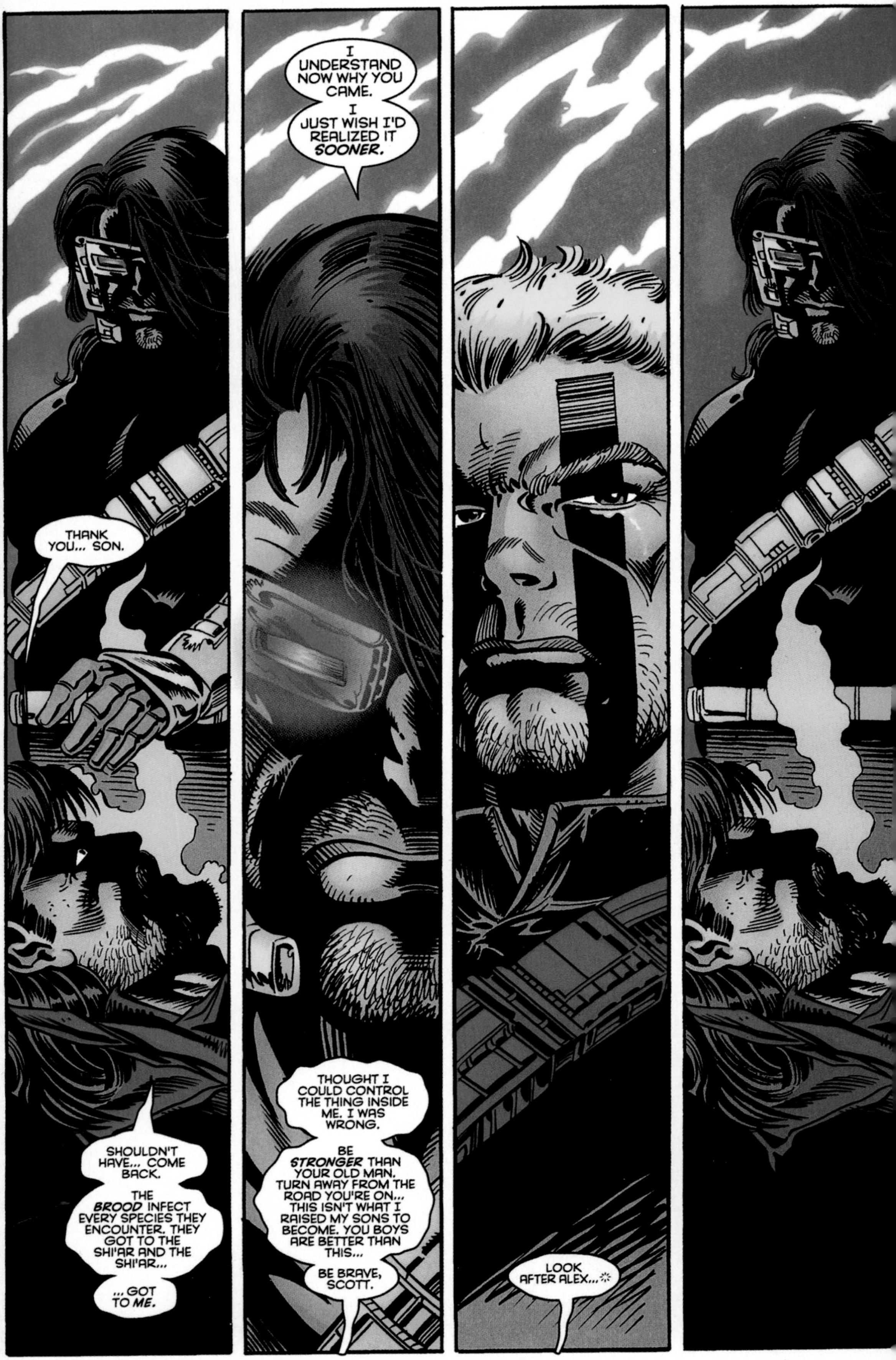
THANK YOU... SON.
SHOULDN'T HAVE... COME BACK.
THE *BROOD* INFECT EVERY SPECIES THEY ENCOUNTER. THEY GOT TO THE SHI'AR AND THE SHI'AR...
...GOT TO *ME.*
I UNDERSTAND NOW WHY YOU CAME.
I JUST WISH I'D REALIZED IT *SOONER.*
THOUGHT I COULD CONTROL THE THING INSIDE ME. I WAS WRONG.
BE *STRONGER* THAN YOUR OLD MAN. TURN AWAY FROM THE ROAD YOU'RE ON... THIS ISN'T WHAT I RAISED MY SONS TO BECOME. YOU BOYS ARE BETTER THAN THIS...
BE BRAVE, SCOTT.
LOOK AFTER ALEX...

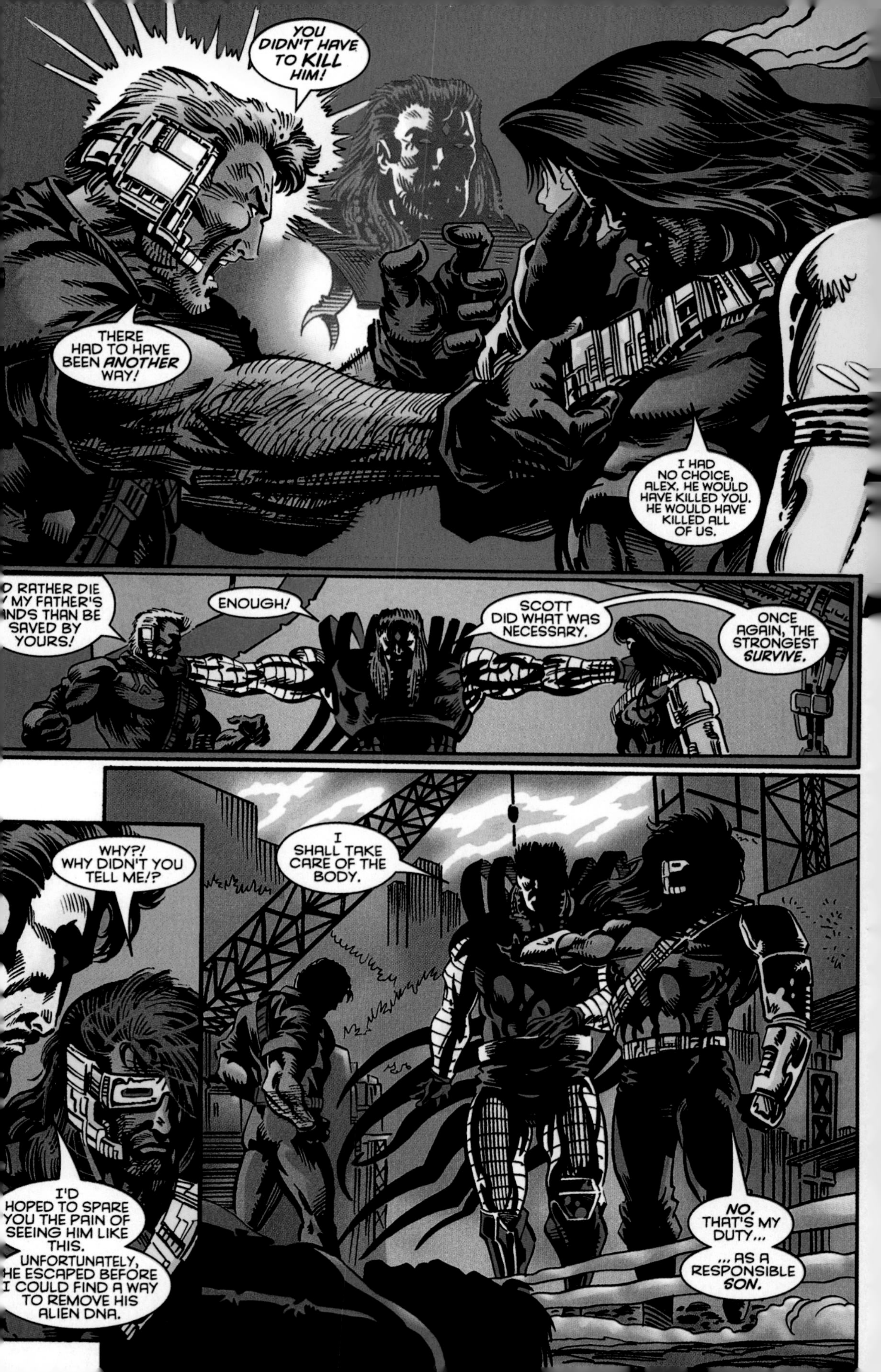
YOU DIDN'T HAVE TO KILL HIM!
THERE HAD TO HAVE BEEN ANOTHER WAY!
I HAD NO CHOICE, ALEX. HE WOULD HAVE KILLED YOU. HE WOULD HAVE KILLED ALL OF US.
D RATHER DIE Y MY FATHER'S NDS THAN BE SAVED BY YOURS!
ENOUGH!
SCOTT DID WHAT WAS NECESSARY.
ONCE AGAIN, THE STRONGEST SURVIVE.
WHY?! WHY DIDN'T YOU TELL ME!?
I'D HOPED TO SPARE YOU THE PAIN OF SEEING HIM LIKE THIS. UNFORTUNATELY, HE ESCAPED BEFORE I COULD FIND A WAY TO REMOVE HIS ALIEN DNA.
I SHALL TAKE CARE OF THE BODY.
NO. THAT'S MY DUTY...
... AS A RESPONSIBLE SON.

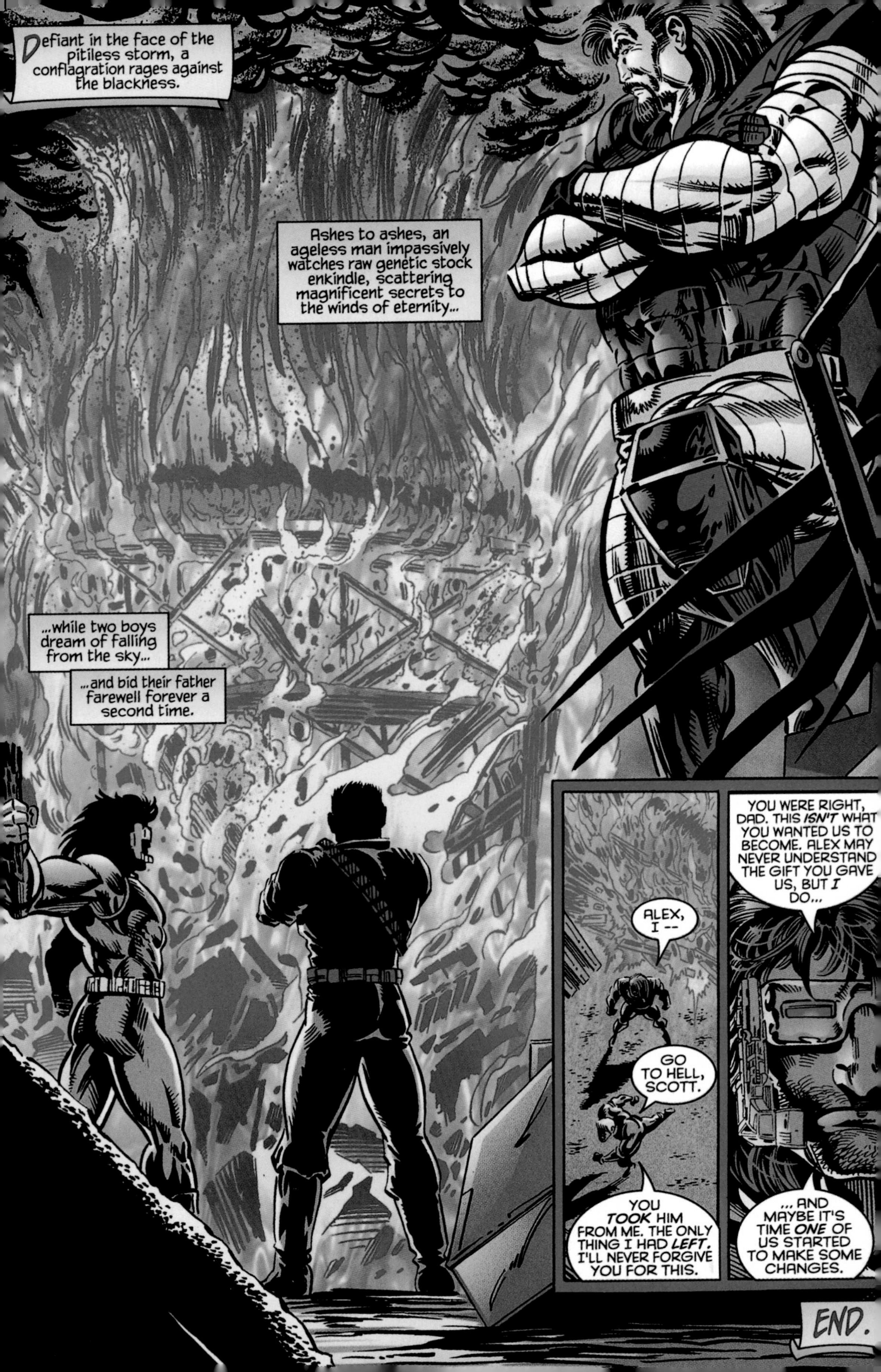
Defiant in the face of the pitiless storm, a conflagration rages against the blackness.
Ashes to ashes, an ageless man impassively watches raw genetic stock enkindle, scattering magnificent secrets to the winds of eternity...
...while two boys dream of falling from the sky...
...and bid their father farewell forever a second time.
ALEX, I --
GO TO HELL, SCOTT.
YOU TOOK HIM FROM ME. THE ONLY THING I HAD LEFT. I'LL NEVER FORGIVE YOU FOR THIS.
YOU WERE RIGHT, DAD. THIS ISN'T WHAT YOU WANTED US TO BECOME. ALEX MAY NEVER UNDERSTAND THE GIFT YOU GAVE US, BUT I DO...
... AND MAYBE IT'S TIME ONE OF US STARTED TO MAKE SOME CHANGES.
END.

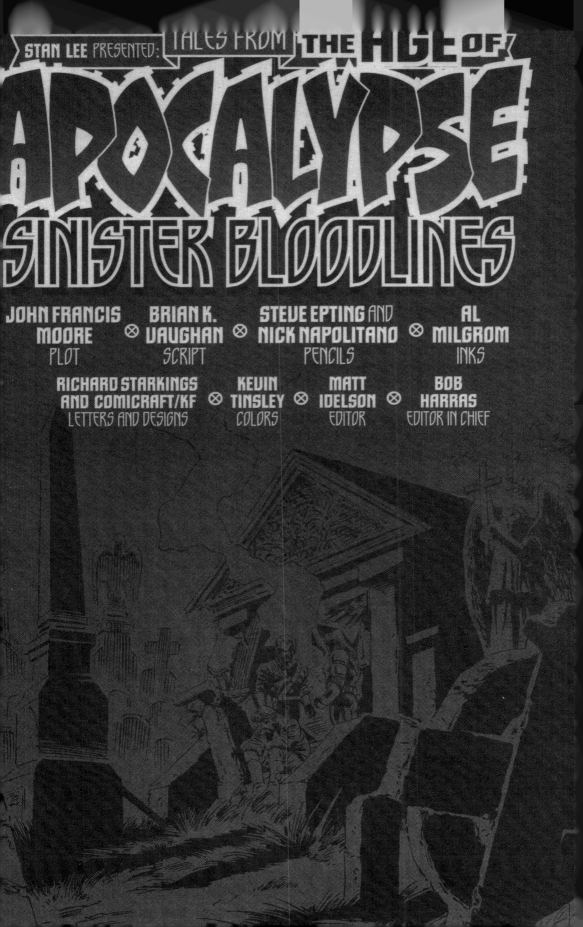

STAN LEE PRESENTED: TALES FROM THE AGE OF

APOCALYPSE

SINISTER BLOODLINES

JOHN FRANCIS MOORE PLOT ⊗ **BRIAN K. VAUGHAN** SCRIPT ⊗ **STEVE EPTING** AND **NICK NAPOLITANO** PENCILS ⊗ **AL MILGROM** INKS

RICHARD STARKINGS AND COMICRAFT/KF LETTERS AND DESIGNS ⊗ **KEVIN TINSLEY** COLORS ⊗ **MATT IDELSON** EDITOR ⊗ **BOB HARRAS** EDITOR IN CHIEF

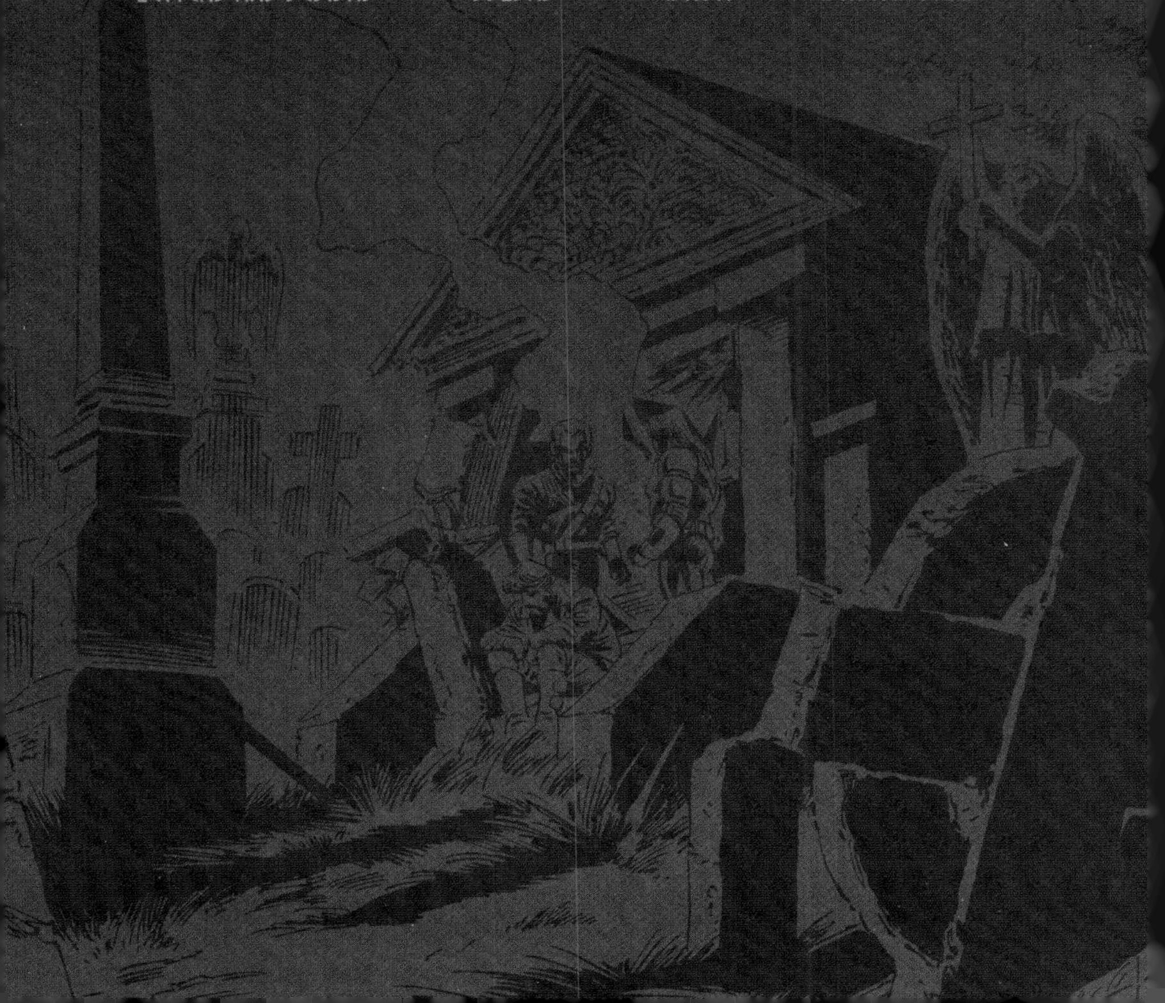

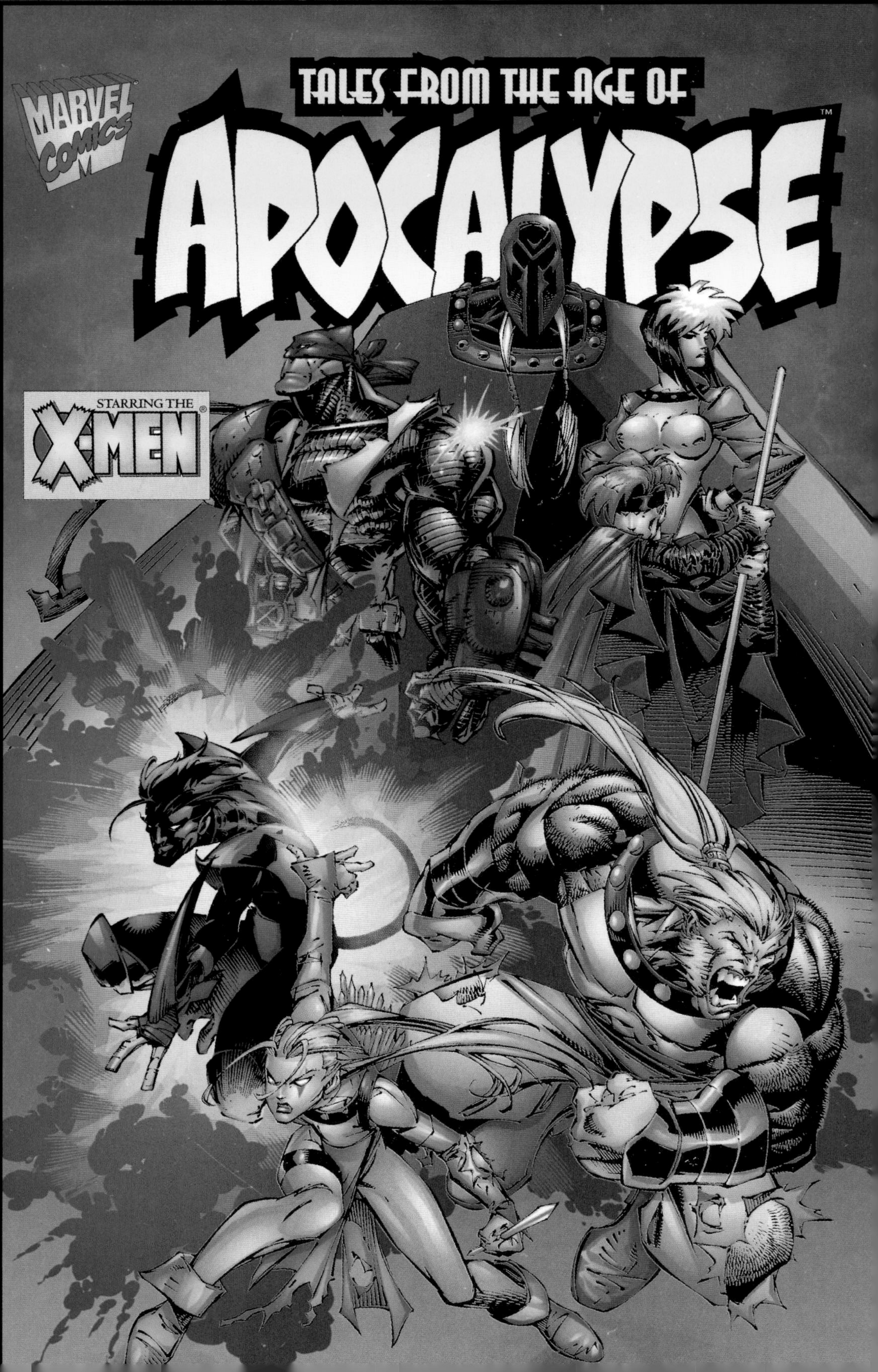

MARVEL COMICS
TALES FROM THE AGE OF
APOCALYPSE™
STARRING THE X-MEN®

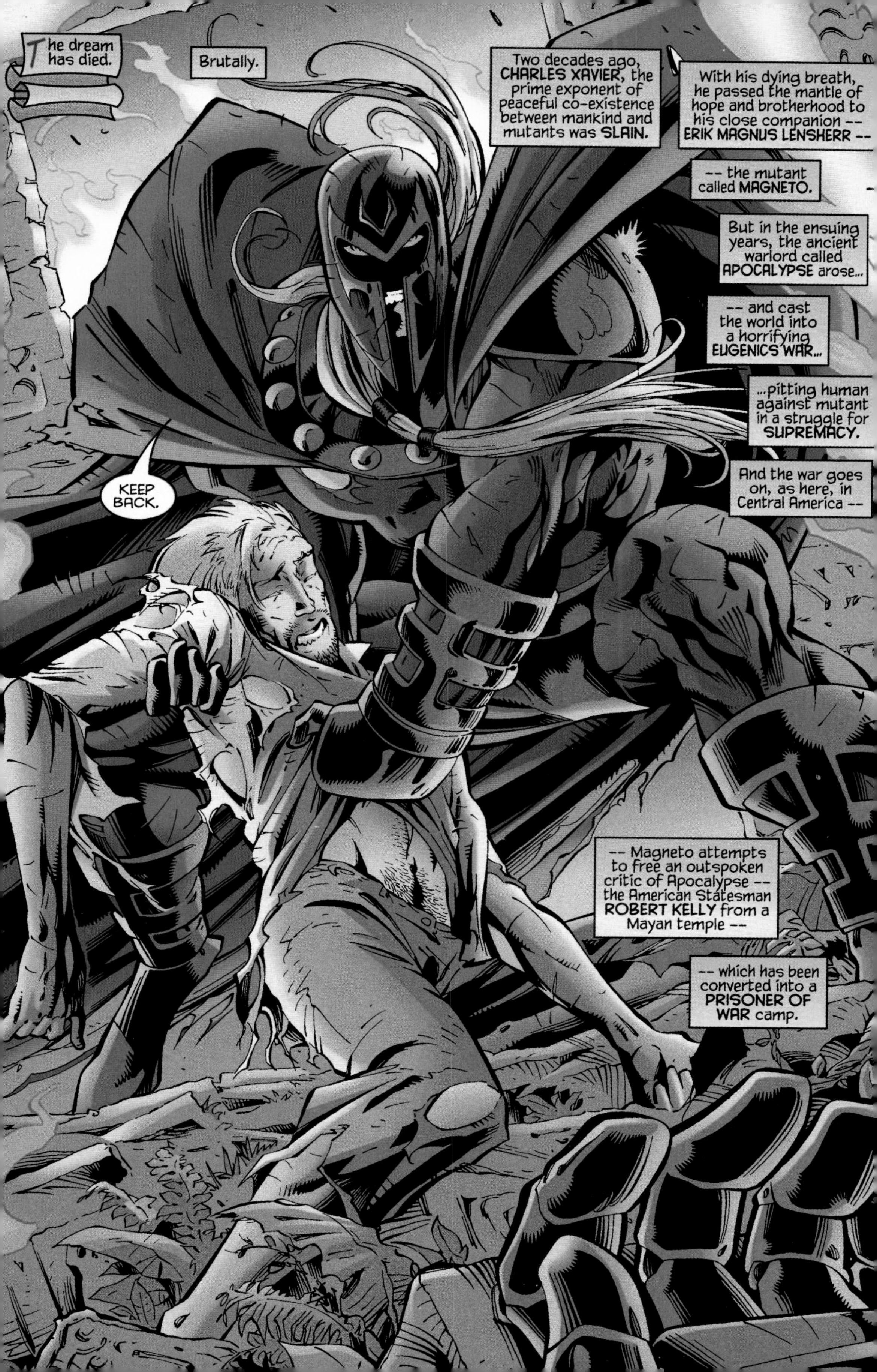
The dream has died.
Brutally.
Two decades ago, CHARLES XAVIER, the prime exponent of peaceful co-existence between mankind and mutants was SLAIN.
With his dying breath, he passed the mantle of hope and brotherhood to his close companion -- ERIK MAGNUS LENSHERR --
-- the mutant called MAGNETO.
But in the ensuing years, the ancient warlord called APOCALYPSE arose...
-- and cast the world into a horrifying EUGENICS WAR...
...pitting human against mutant in a struggle for SUPREMACY.
And the war goes on, as here, in Central America --
KEEP BACK.
-- Magneto attempts to free an outspoken critic of Apocalypse -- the American Statesman ROBERT KELLY from a Mayan temple --
-- which has been converted into a PRISONER OF WAR camp.

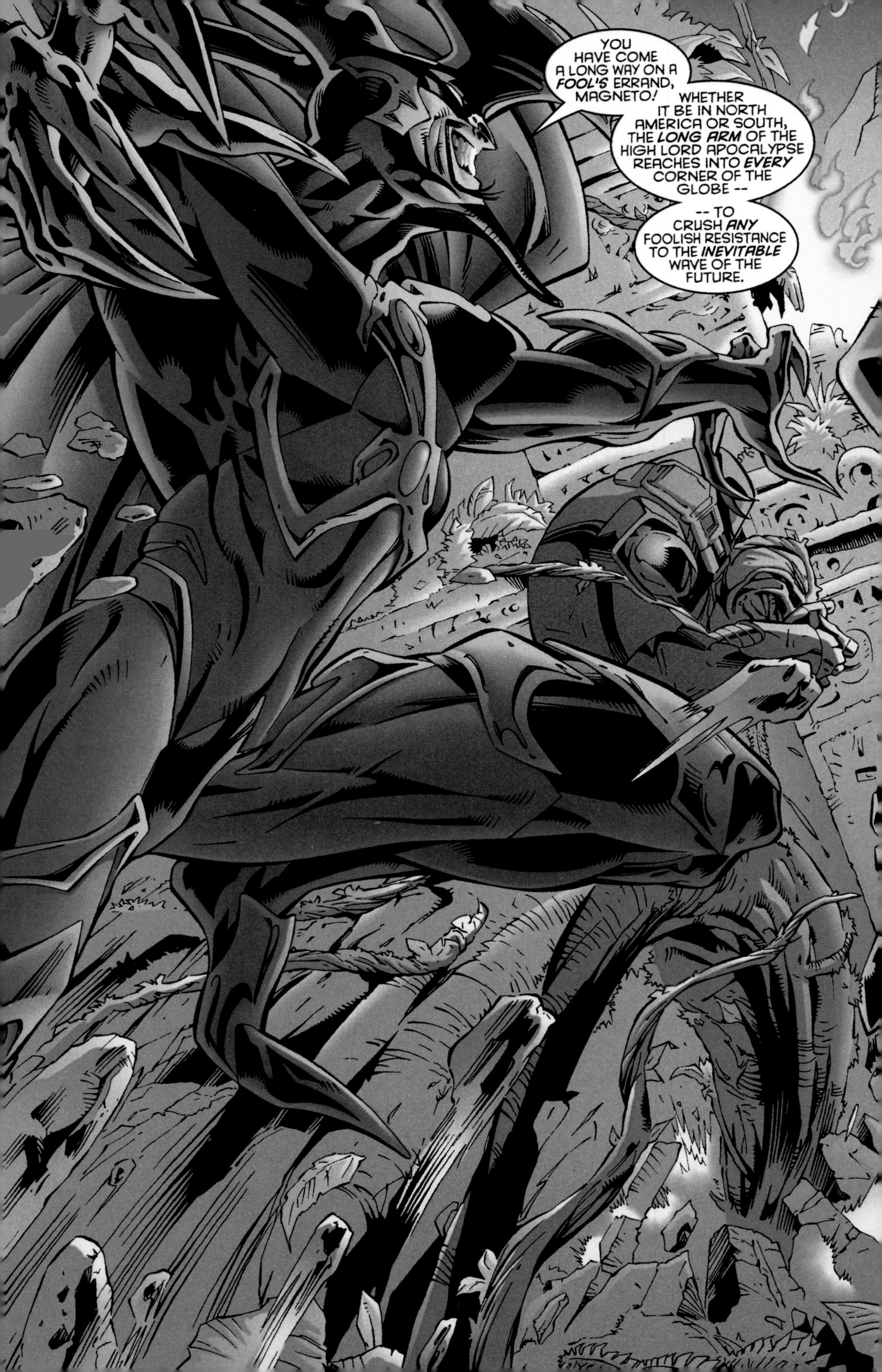
YOU HAVE COME A LONG WAY ON A *FOOL'S* ERRAND, MAGNETO!
WHETHER IT BE IN NORTH AMERICA OR SOUTH, THE *LONG ARM* OF THE HIGH LORD APOCALYPSE REACHES INTO *EVERY* CORNER OF THE GLOBE --
-- TO CRUSH *ANY* FOOLISH RESISTANCE TO THE *INEVITABLE* WAVE OF THE FUTURE.

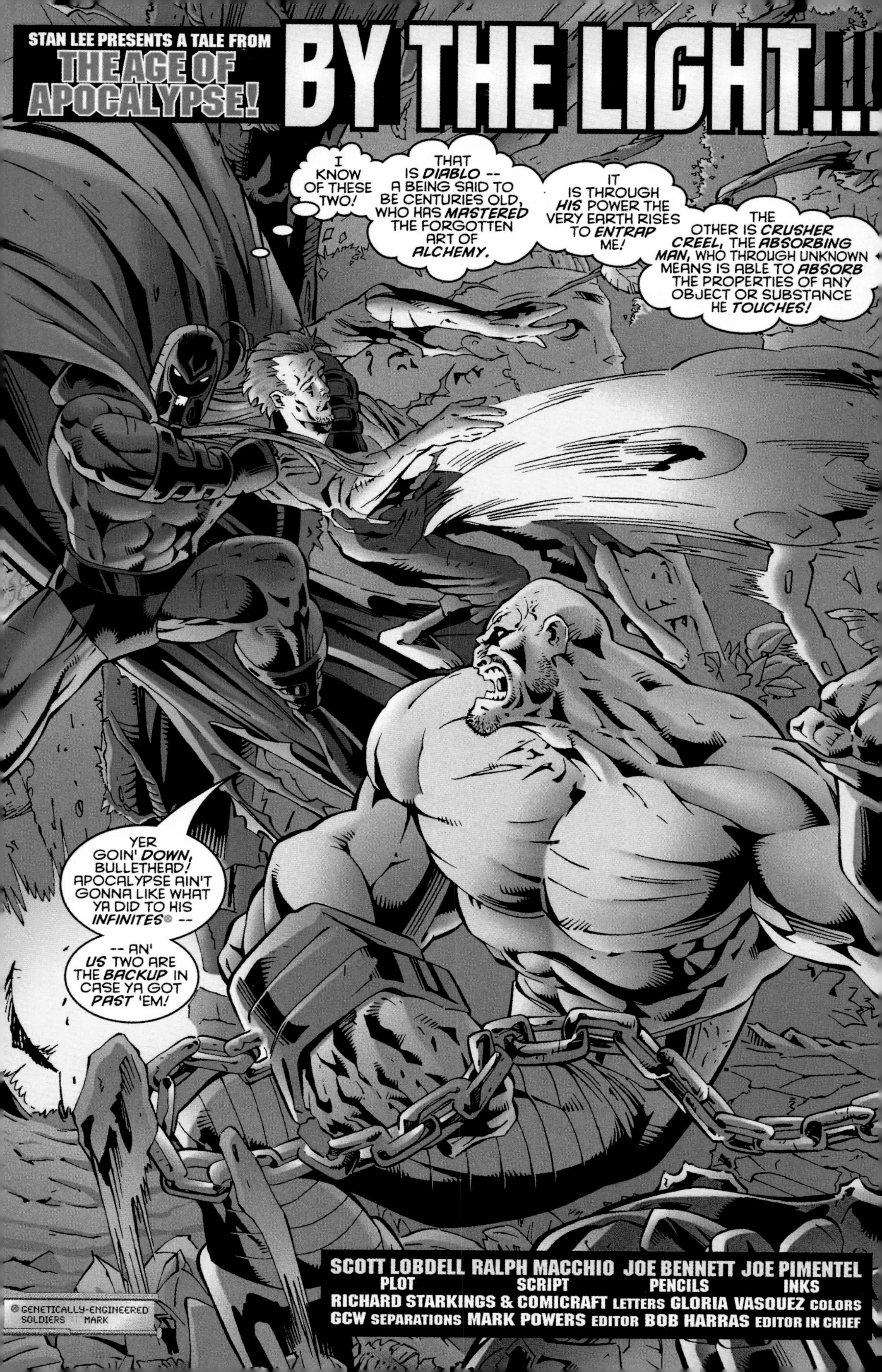
STAN LEE PRESENTS A TALE FROM
THE AGE OF APOCALYPSE!
BY THE LIGHT...!
I KNOW OF THESE TWO!
THAT IS DIABLO -- A BEING SAID TO BE CENTURIES OLD, WHO HAS MASTERED THE FORGOTTEN ART OF ALCHEMY.
IT IS THROUGH HIS POWER THE VERY EARTH RISES TO ENTRAP ME!
THE OTHER IS CRUSHER CREEL, THE ABSORBING MAN, WHO THROUGH UNKNOWN MEANS IS ABLE TO ABSORB THE PROPERTIES OF ANY OBJECT OR SUBSTANCE HE TOUCHES!
YER GOIN' DOWN, BULLETHEAD! APOCALYPSE AIN'T GONNA LIKE WHAT YA DID TO HIS INFINITES --
-- AN' US TWO ARE THE BACKUP IN CASE YA GOT PAST 'EM!
GENETICALLY-ENGINEERED SOLDIERS MARK
SCOTT LOBDELL PLOT RALPH MACCHIO SCRIPT JOE BENNETT PENCILS JOE PIMENTEL INKS
RICHARD STARKINGS & COMICRAFT LETTERS GLORIA VASQUEZ COLORS
GCW SEPARATIONS MARK POWERS EDITOR BOB HARRAS EDITOR IN CHIEF

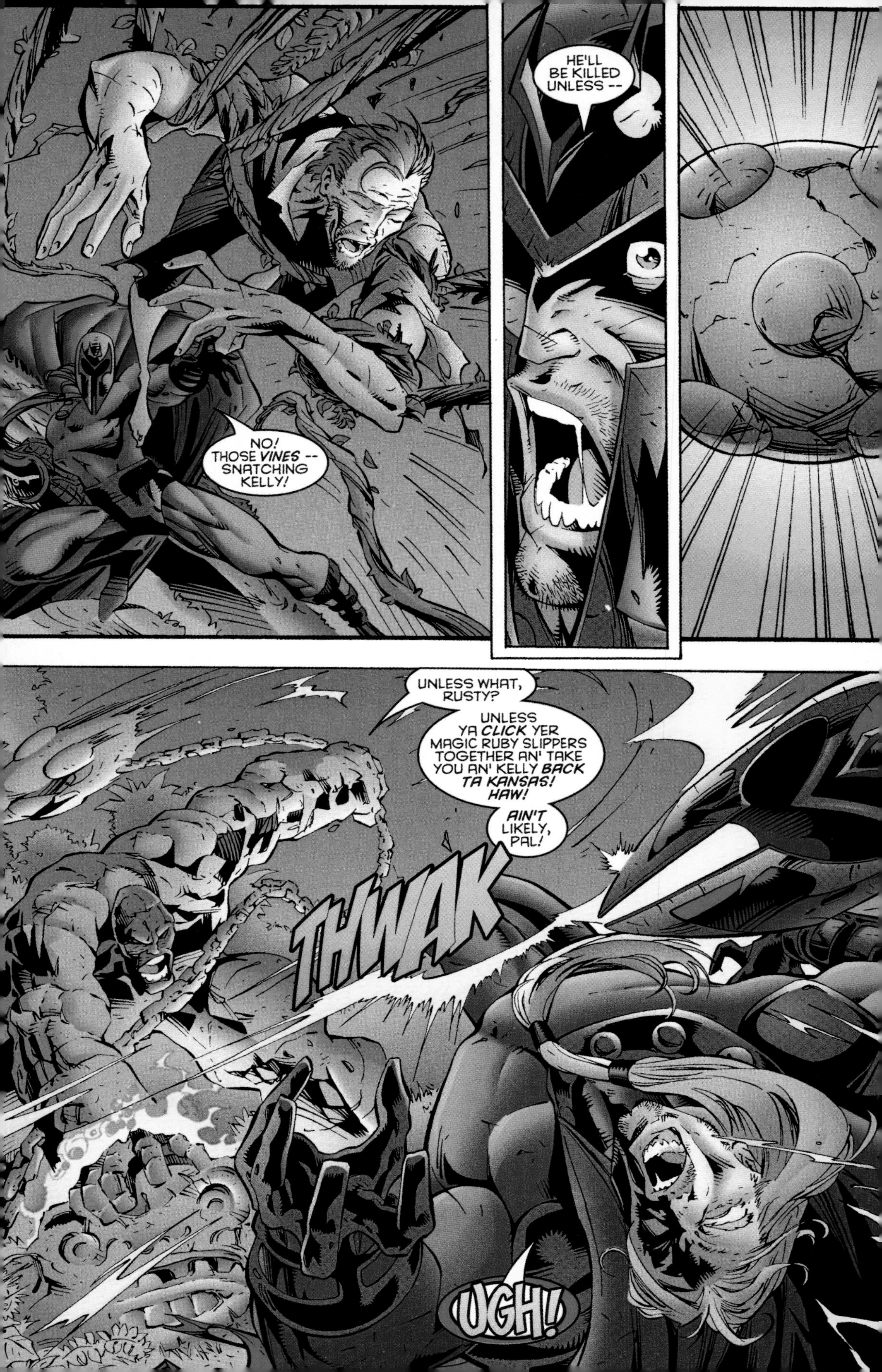
NO! THOSE *VINES* -- SNATCHING KELLY!
HE'LL BE KILLED UNLESS --
UNLESS WHAT, RUSTY?
UNLESS YA *CLICK* YER MAGIC RUBY SLIPPERS TOGETHER AN' TAKE YOU AN' KELLY *BACK TA KANSAS! HAW!*
AIN'T LIKELY, PAL!
THWAK
UGH!

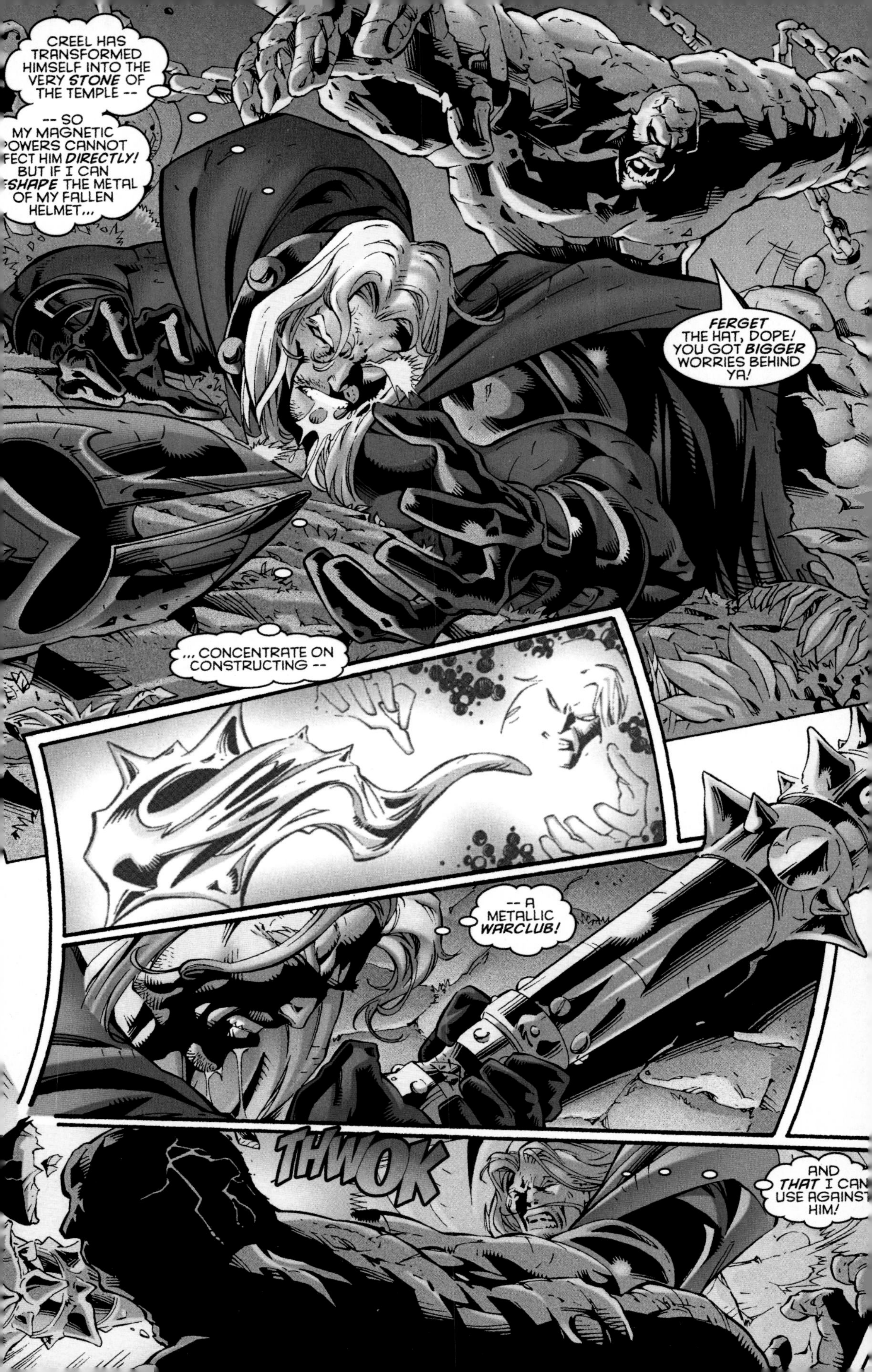
CREEL HAS TRANSFORMED HIMSELF INTO THE VERY STONE OF THE TEMPLE --
-- SO MY MAGNETIC POWERS CANNOT FECT HIM DIRECTLY! BUT IF I CAN SHAPE THE METAL OF MY FALLEN HELMET...
FERGET THE HAT, DOPE! YOU GOT BIGGER WORRIES BEHIND YA!
... CONCENTRATE ON CONSTRUCTING --
-- A METALLIC WARCLUB!
THWOK
AND THAT I CAN USE AGAINST HIM!

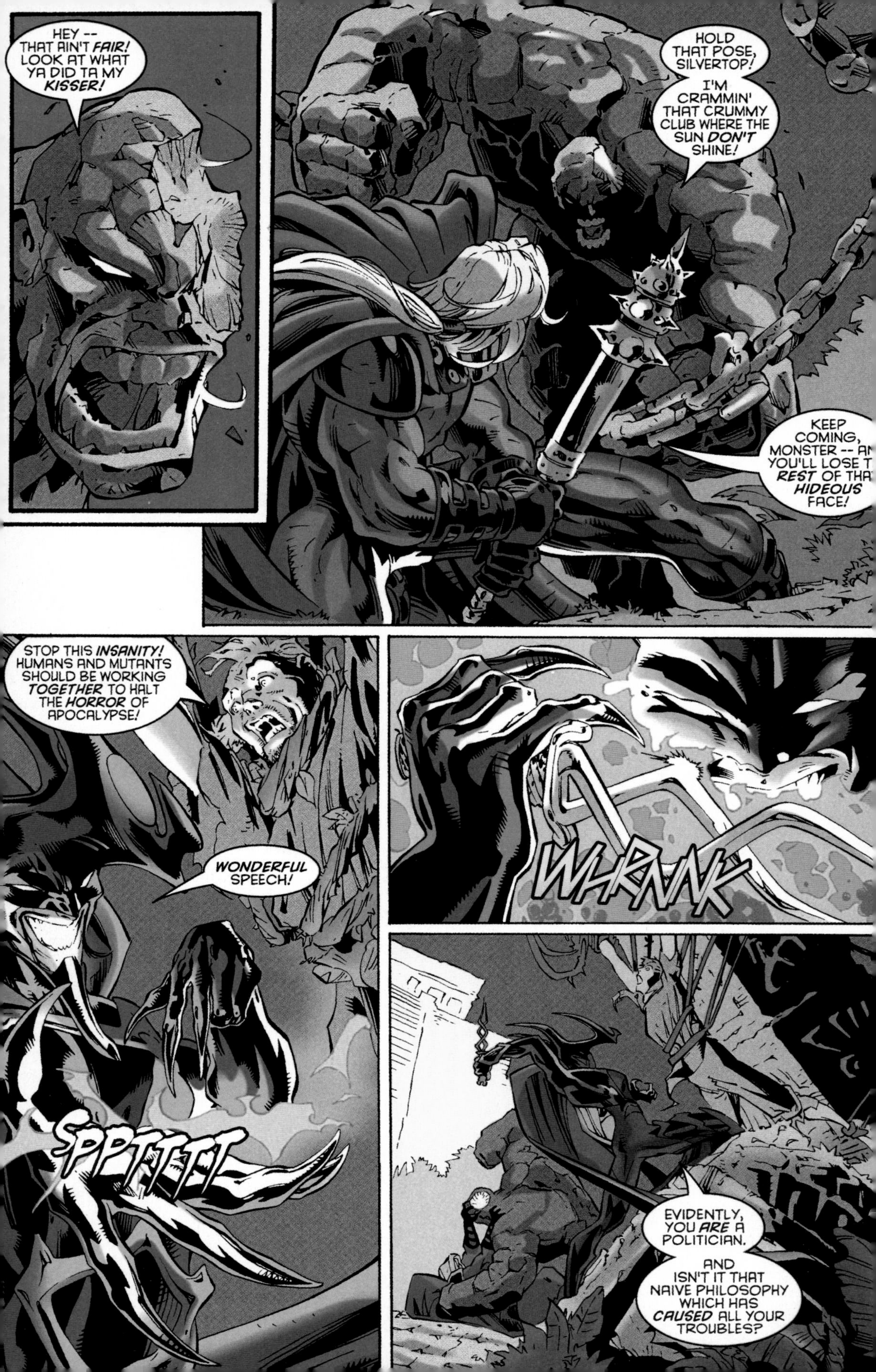

HEY -- THAT AIN'T FAIR! LOOK AT WHAT YA DID TA MY KISSER!
HOLD THAT POSE, SILVERTOP!
I'M CRAMMIN' THAT CRUMMY CLUB WHERE THE SUN DON'T SHINE!
KEEP COMING, MONSTER -- AN YOU'LL LOSE T REST OF THA HIDEOUS FACE!
STOP THIS INSANITY! HUMANS AND MUTANTS SHOULD BE WORKING TOGETHER TO HALT THE HORROR OF APOCALYPSE!
WONDERFUL SPEECH!
SPPTTTT
WHRNNK
EVIDENTLY, YOU ARE A POLITICIAN.
AND ISN'T IT THAT NAIVE PHILOSOPHY WHICH HAS CAUSED ALL YOUR TROUBLES?

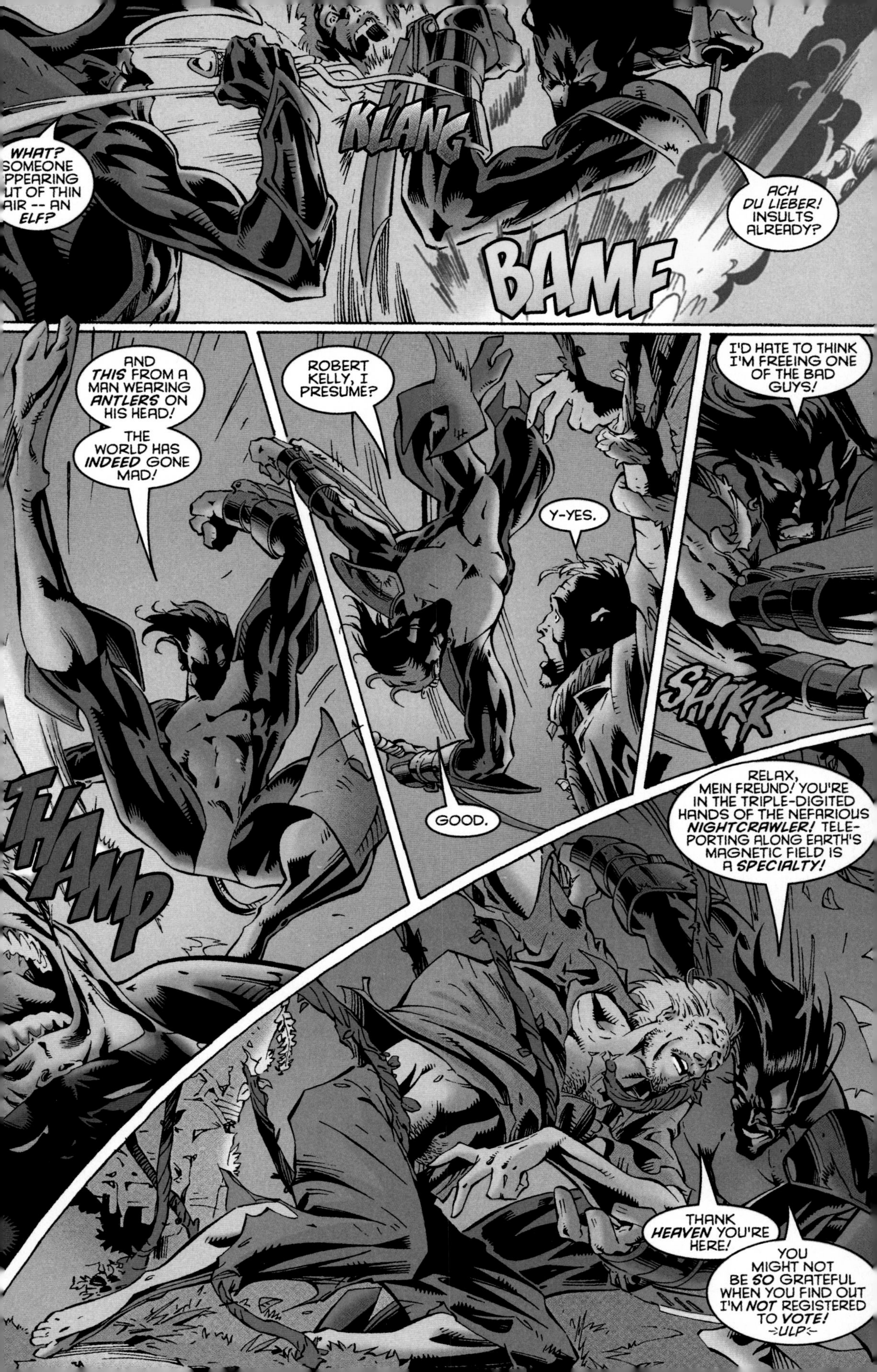
KLANG
WHAT? SOMEONE APPEARING OUT OF THIN AIR -- AN ELF?
ACH DU LIEBER! INSULTS ALREADY?
BAMF
AND THIS FROM A MAN WEARING ANTLERS ON HIS HEAD!
THE WORLD HAS INDEED GONE MAD!
THAMP
ROBERT KELLY, I PRESUME?
Y-YES.
GOOD.
I'D HATE TO THINK I'M FREEING ONE OF THE BAD GUYS!
SHIKK
RELAX, MEIN FREUND! YOU'RE IN THE TRIPLE-DIGITED HANDS OF THE NEFARIOUS NIGHTCRAWLER! TELE-PORTING ALONG EARTH'S MAGNETIC FIELD IS A SPECIALTY!
THANK HEAVEN YOU'RE HERE!
YOU MIGHT NOT BE SO GRATEFUL WHEN YOU FIND OUT I'M NOT REGISTERED TO VOTE!
ULP

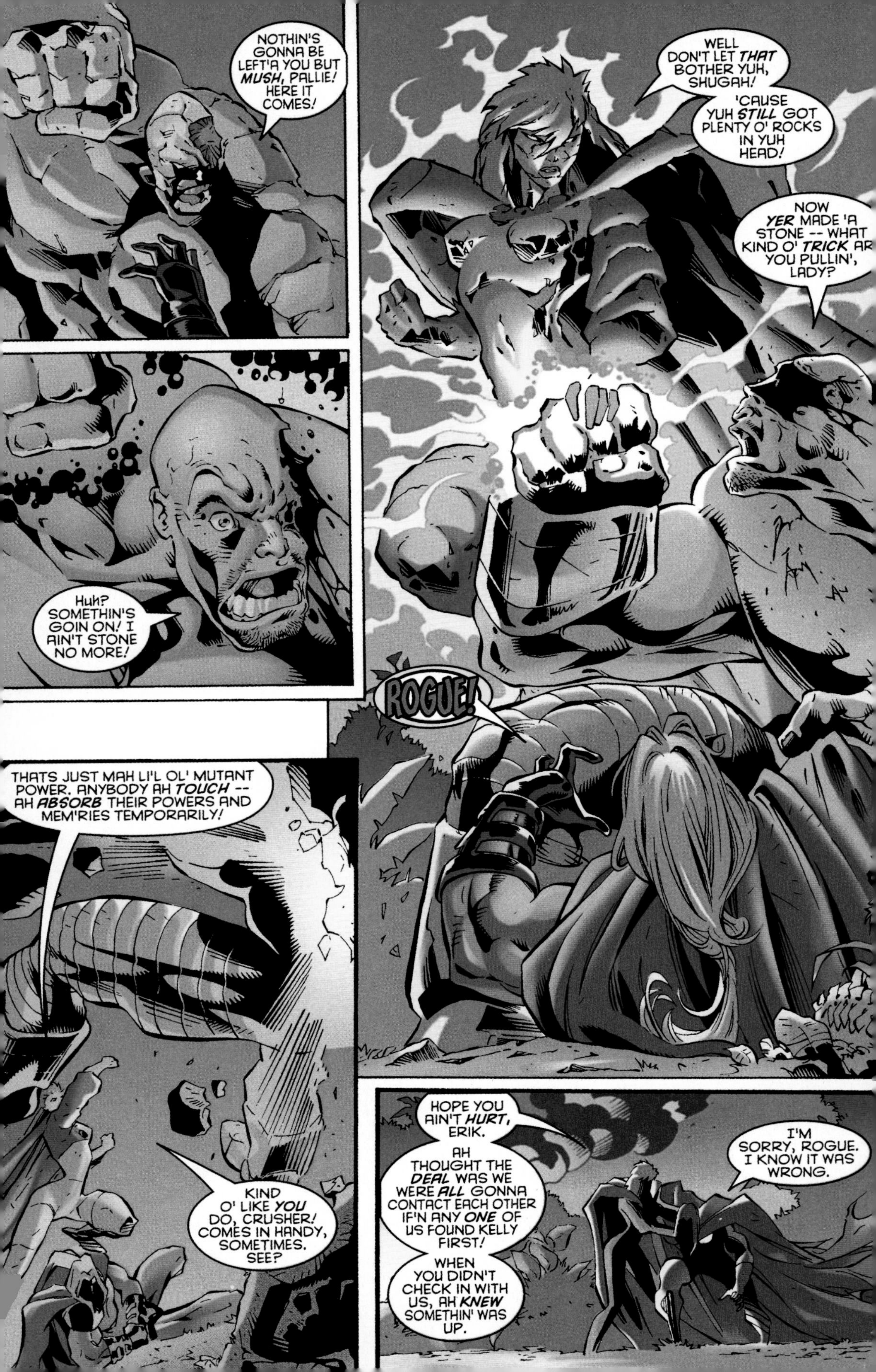
NOTHIN'S GONNA BE LEFT'A YOU BUT *MUSH*, PALLIE! HERE IT COMES!
Huh? SOMETHIN'S GOIN ON! I AIN'T STONE NO MORE!
WELL DON'T LET *THAT* BOTHER YUH, SHUGAH!
'CAUSE YUH *STILL* GOT PLENTY O' ROCKS IN YUH HEAD!
NOW *YER* MADE 'A STONE -- WHAT KIND O' *TRICK* AR YOU PULLIN', LADY?
ROGUE!
THATS JUST MAH LI'L OL' MUTANT POWER. ANYBODY AH *TOUCH* -- AH *ABSORB* THEIR POWERS AND MEM'RIES TEMPORARILY!
KIND O' LIKE *YOU* DO, CRUSHER! COMES IN HANDY, SOMETIMES. SEE?
HOPE YOU AIN'T *HURT*, ERIK.
AH THOUGHT THE *DEAL* WAS WE WERE *ALL* GONNA CONTACT EACH OTHER IF'N ANY *ONE* OF US FOUND KELLY FIRST!
WHEN YOU DIDN'T CHECK IN WITH US, AH *KNEW* SOMETHIN' WAS UP.
I'M SORRY, ROGUE. I KNOW IT WAS WRONG.

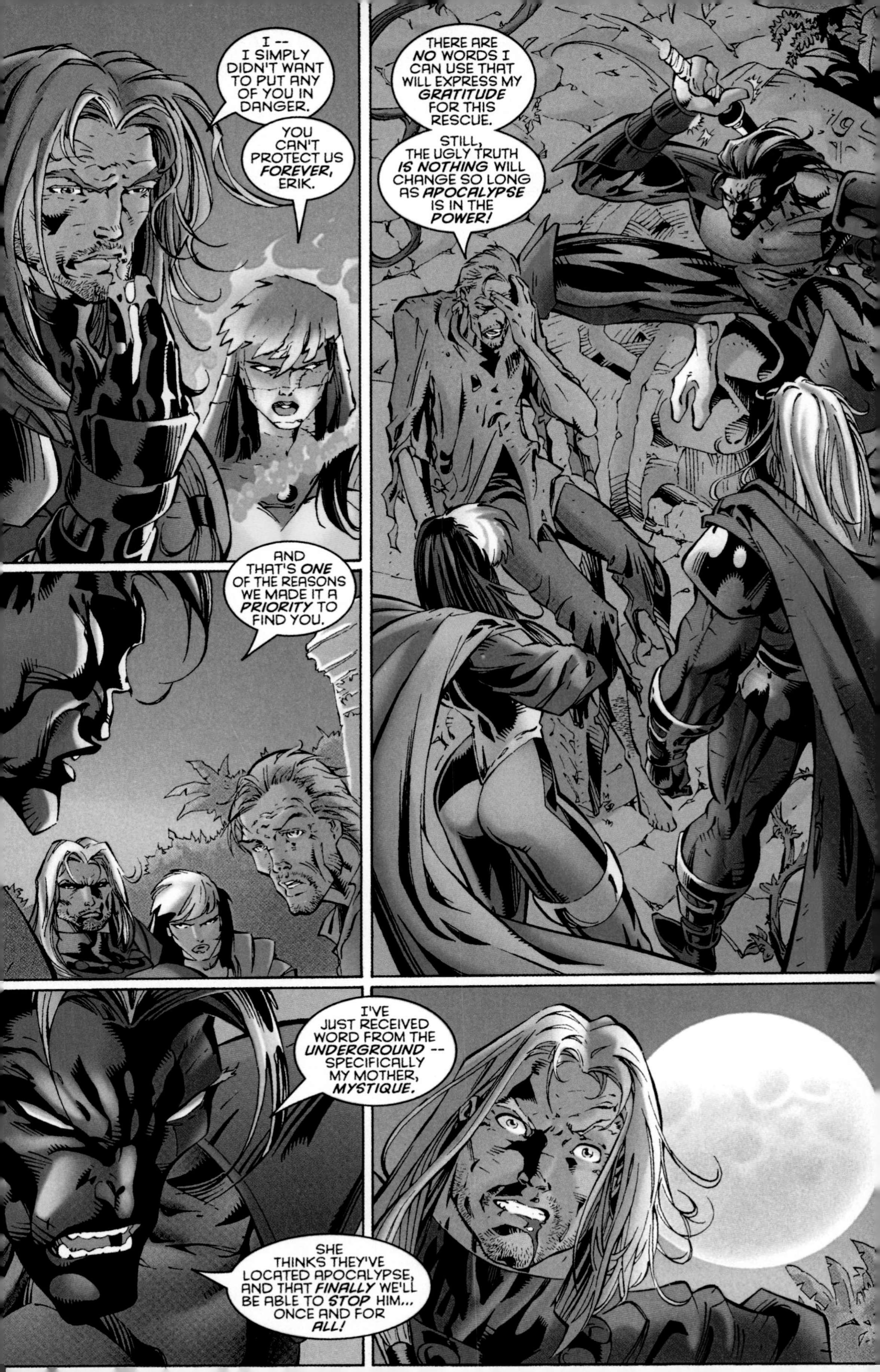
I -- I SIMPLY DIDN'T WANT TO PUT ANY OF YOU IN DANGER.
YOU CAN'T PROTECT US FOREVER, ERIK.
THERE ARE NO WORDS I CAN USE THAT WILL EXPRESS MY GRATITUDE FOR THIS RESCUE.
STILL, THE UGLY TRUTH IS NOTHING WILL CHANGE SO LONG AS APOCALYPSE IS IN THE POWER!
AND THAT'S ONE OF THE REASONS WE MADE IT A PRIORITY TO FIND YOU.
I'VE JUST RECEIVED WORD FROM THE UNDERGROUND -- SPECIFICALLY MY MOTHER, MYSTIQUE.
SHE THINKS THEY'VE LOCATED APOCALYPSE, AND THAT FINALLY WE'LL BE ABLE TO STOP HIM... ONCE AND FOR ALL!

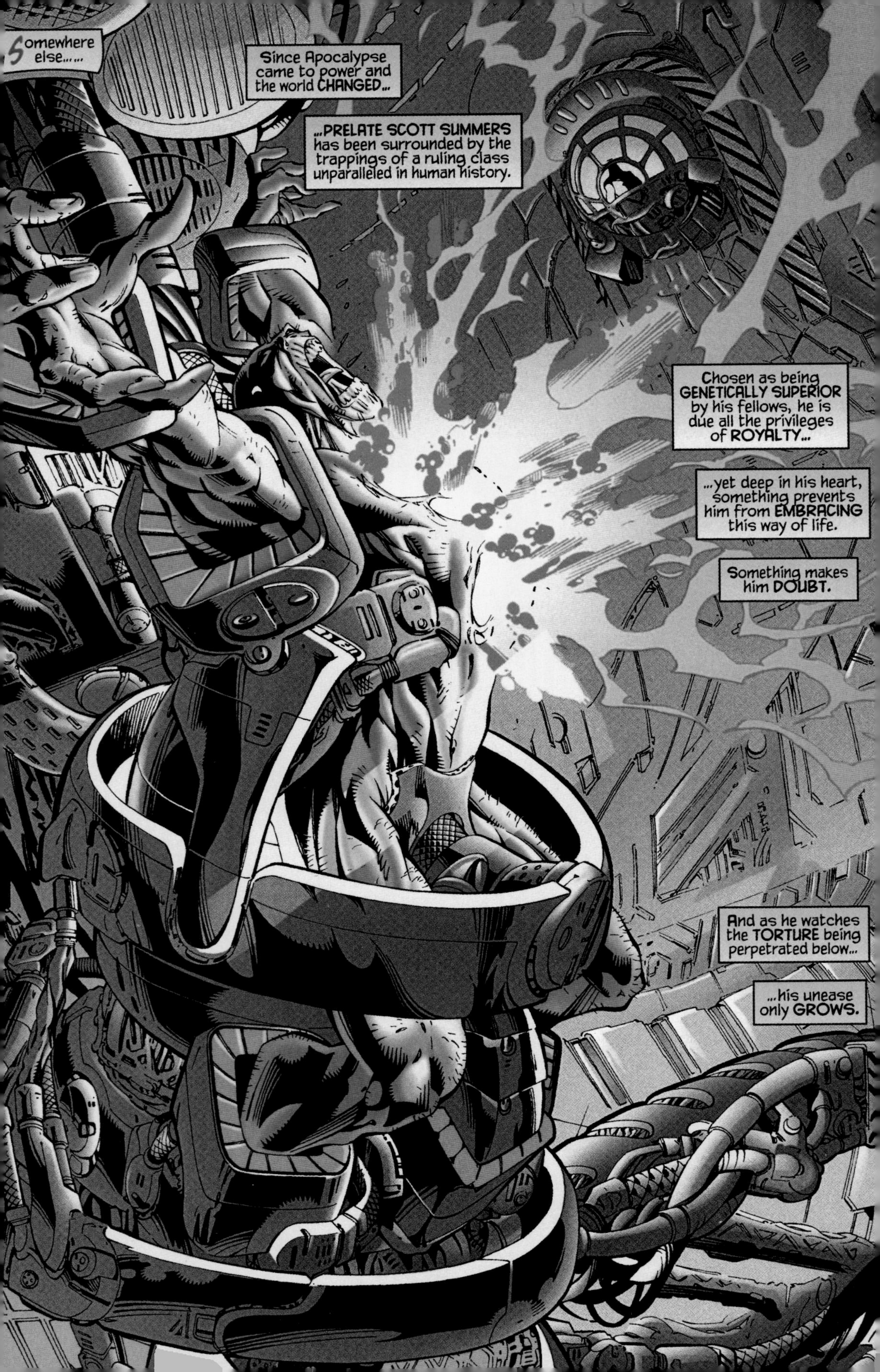
Somewhere else......
Since Apocalypse came to power and the world CHANGED...
...PRELATE SCOTT SUMMERS has been surrounded by the trappings of a ruling class unparalleled in human history.
Chosen as being GENETICALLY SUPERIOR by his fellows, he is due all the privileges of ROYALTY...
...yet deep in his heart, something prevents him from EMBRACING this way of life.
Something makes him DOUBT.
And as he watches the TORTURE being perpetrated below...
...his unease only GROWS.

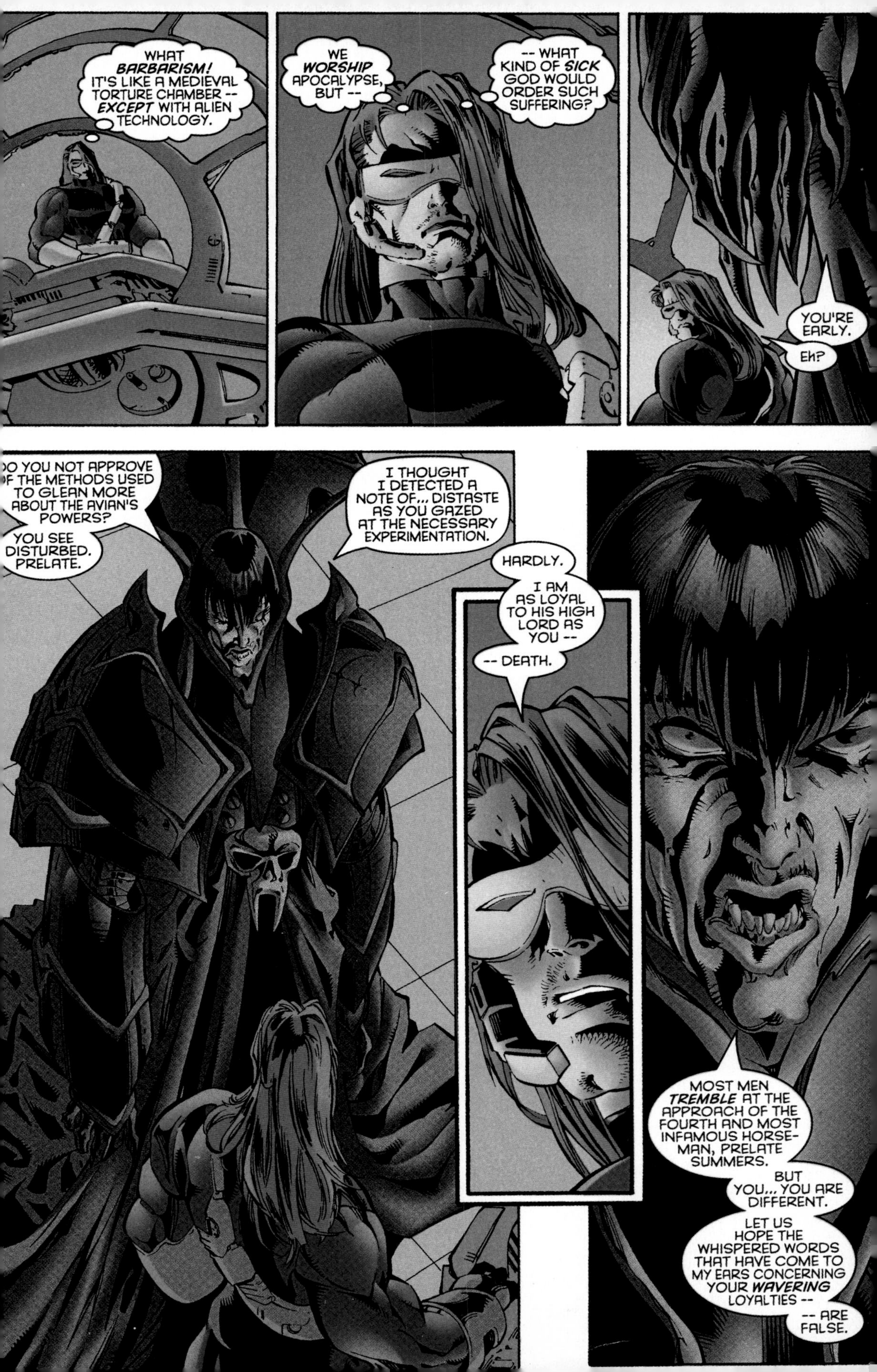
WHAT BARBARISM! IT'S LIKE A MEDIEVAL TORTURE CHAMBER -- EXCEPT WITH ALIEN TECHNOLOGY.
WE WORSHIP APOCALYPSE, BUT --
-- WHAT KIND OF SICK GOD WOULD ORDER SUCH SUFFERING?
YOU'RE EARLY.
Eh?
DO YOU NOT APPROVE OF THE METHODS USED TO GLEAN MORE ABOUT THE AVIAN'S POWERS?
YOU SEE DISTURBED. PRELATE.
I THOUGHT I DETECTED A NOTE OF... DISTASTE AS YOU GAZED AT THE NECESSARY EXPERIMENTATION.
HARDLY.
I AM AS LOYAL TO HIS HIGH LORD AS YOU --
-- DEATH.
MOST MEN TREMBLE AT THE APPROACH OF THE FOURTH AND MOST INFAMOUS HORSE-MAN, PRELATE SUMMERS.
BUT YOU... YOU ARE DIFFERENT.
LET US HOPE THE WHISPERED WORDS THAT HAVE COME TO MY EARS CONCERNING YOUR WAVERING LOYALTIES --
-- ARE FALSE.

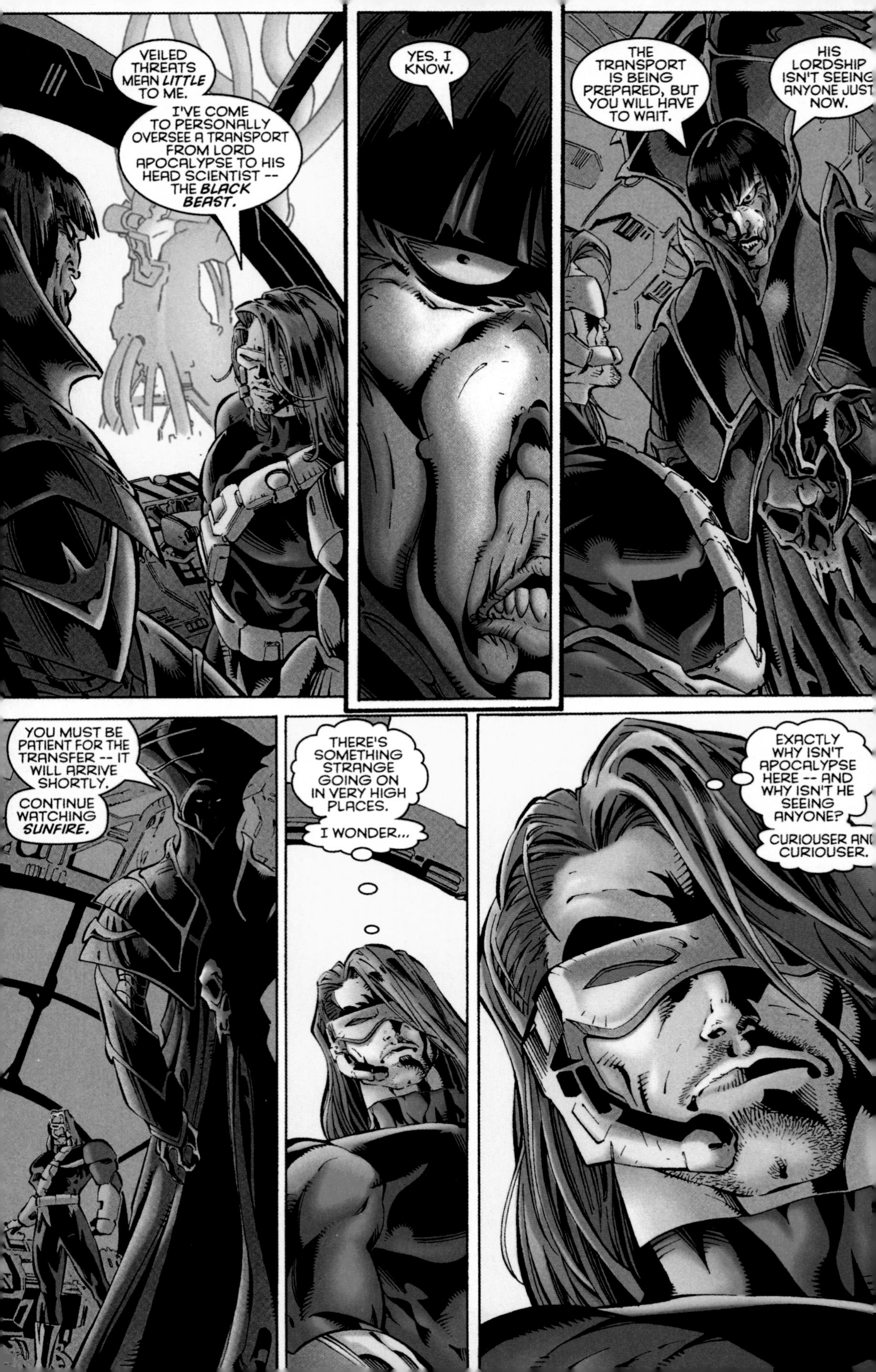
VEILED THREATS MEAN *LITTLE* TO ME.
I'VE COME TO PERSONALLY OVERSEE A TRANSPORT FROM LORD APOCALYPSE TO HIS HEAD SCIENTIST -- THE *BLACK BEAST.*
YES, I KNOW.
THE TRANSPORT IS BEING PREPARED, BUT YOU WILL HAVE TO WAIT.
HIS LORDSHIP ISN'T SEEING ANYONE JUST NOW.
YOU MUST BE PATIENT FOR THE TRANSFER -- IT WILL ARRIVE SHORTLY.
CONTINUE WATCHING *SUNFIRE.*
THERE'S SOMETHING STRANGE GOING ON IN VERY HIGH PLACES.
I WONDER...
EXACTLY WHY ISN'T APOCALYPSE HERE -- AND WHY ISN'T HE SEEING ANYONE?
CURIOUSER AND CURIOUSER.

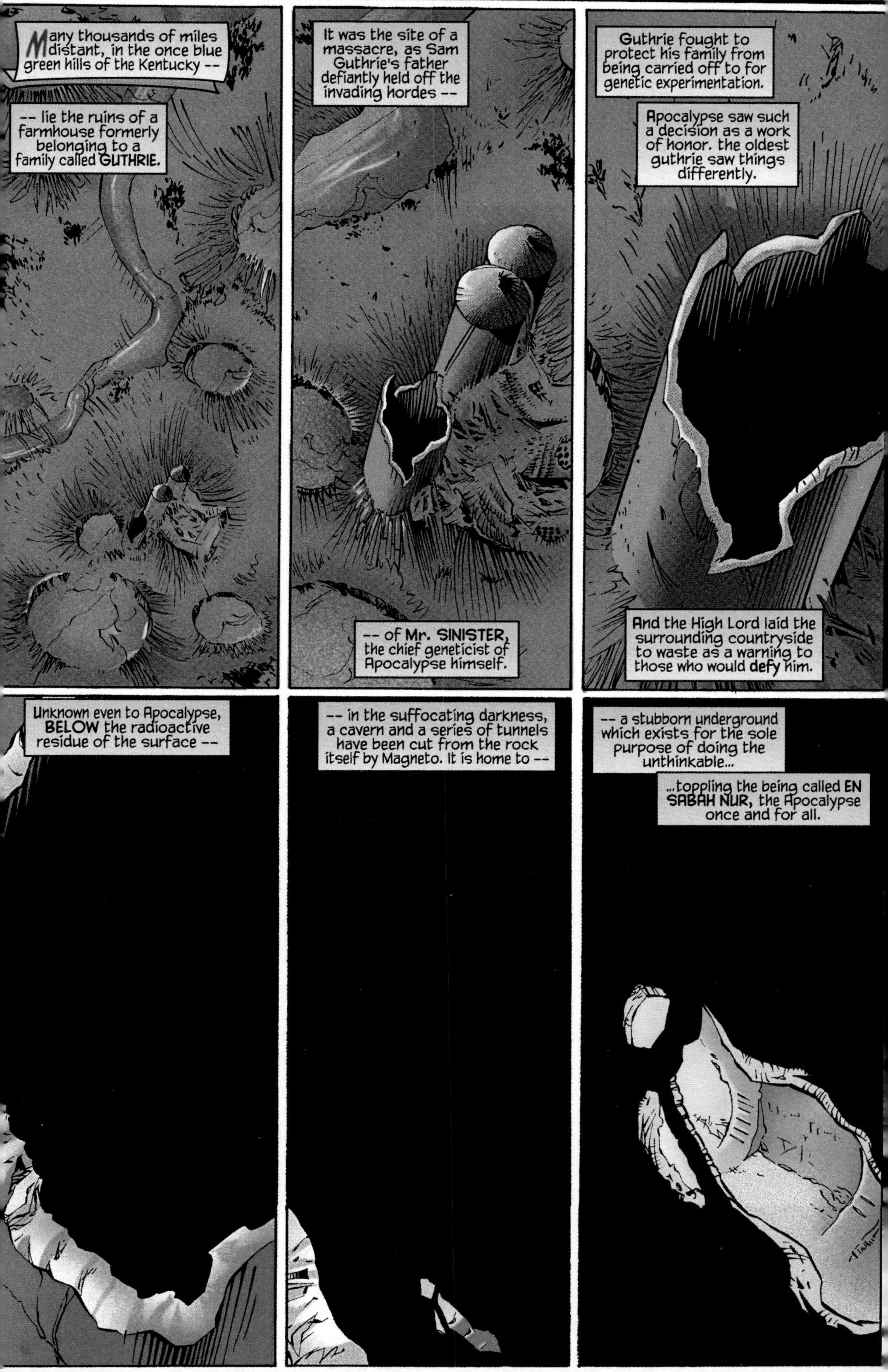
Many thousands of miles distant, in the once blue green hills of the Kentucky --
-- lie the ruins of a farmhouse formerly belonging to a family called GUTHRIE.
It was the site of a massacre, as Sam Guthrie's father defiantly held off the invading hordes --
-- of Mr. SINISTER, the chief geneticist of Apocalypse himself.
Guthrie fought to protect his family from being carried off to for genetic experimentation.
Apocalypse saw such a decision as a work of honor. the oldest guthrie saw things differently.
And the High Lord laid the surrounding countryside to waste as a warning to those who would defy him.
Unknown even to Apocalypse, BELOW the radioactive residue of the surface --
-- in the suffocating darkness, a cavern and a series of tunnels have been cut from the rock itself by Magneto. It is home to --
-- a stubborn underground which exists for the sole purpose of doing the unthinkable...
...toppling the being called EN SABAH NUR, the Apocalypse once and for all.

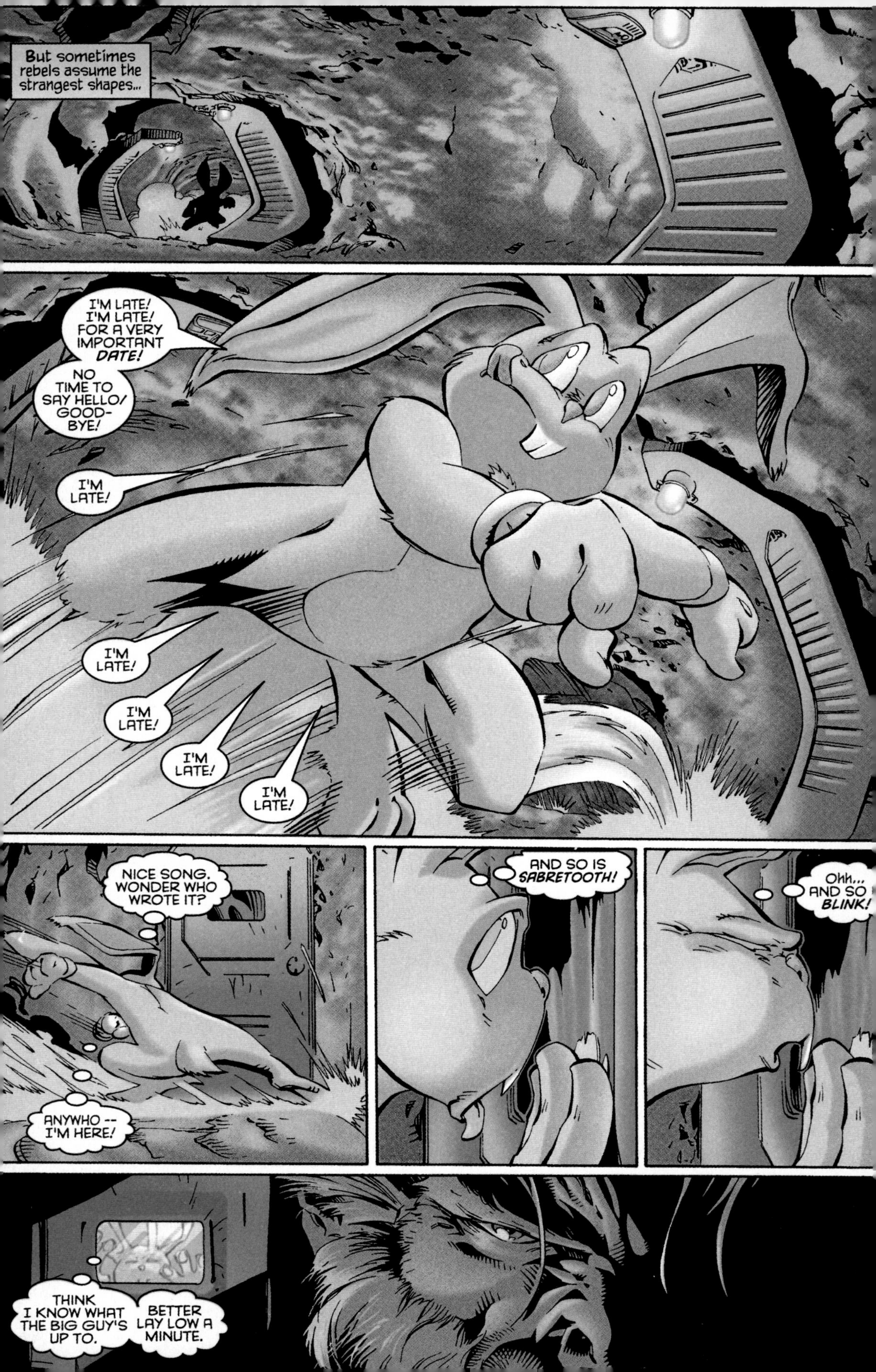

But sometimes rebels assume the strangest shapes...
I'M LATE! I'M LATE! FOR A VERY IMPORTANT DATE!
NO TIME TO SAY HELLO/ GOOD-BYE!
I'M LATE!
I'M LATE!
I'M LATE!
I'M LATE!
I'M LATE!
NICE SONG. WONDER WHO WROTE IT?
ANYWHO -- I'M HERE!
AND SO IS SABRETOOTH!
Ohh... AND SO BLINK!
THINK I KNOW WHAT THE BIG GUY'S UP TO.
BETTER LAY LOW A MINUTE.

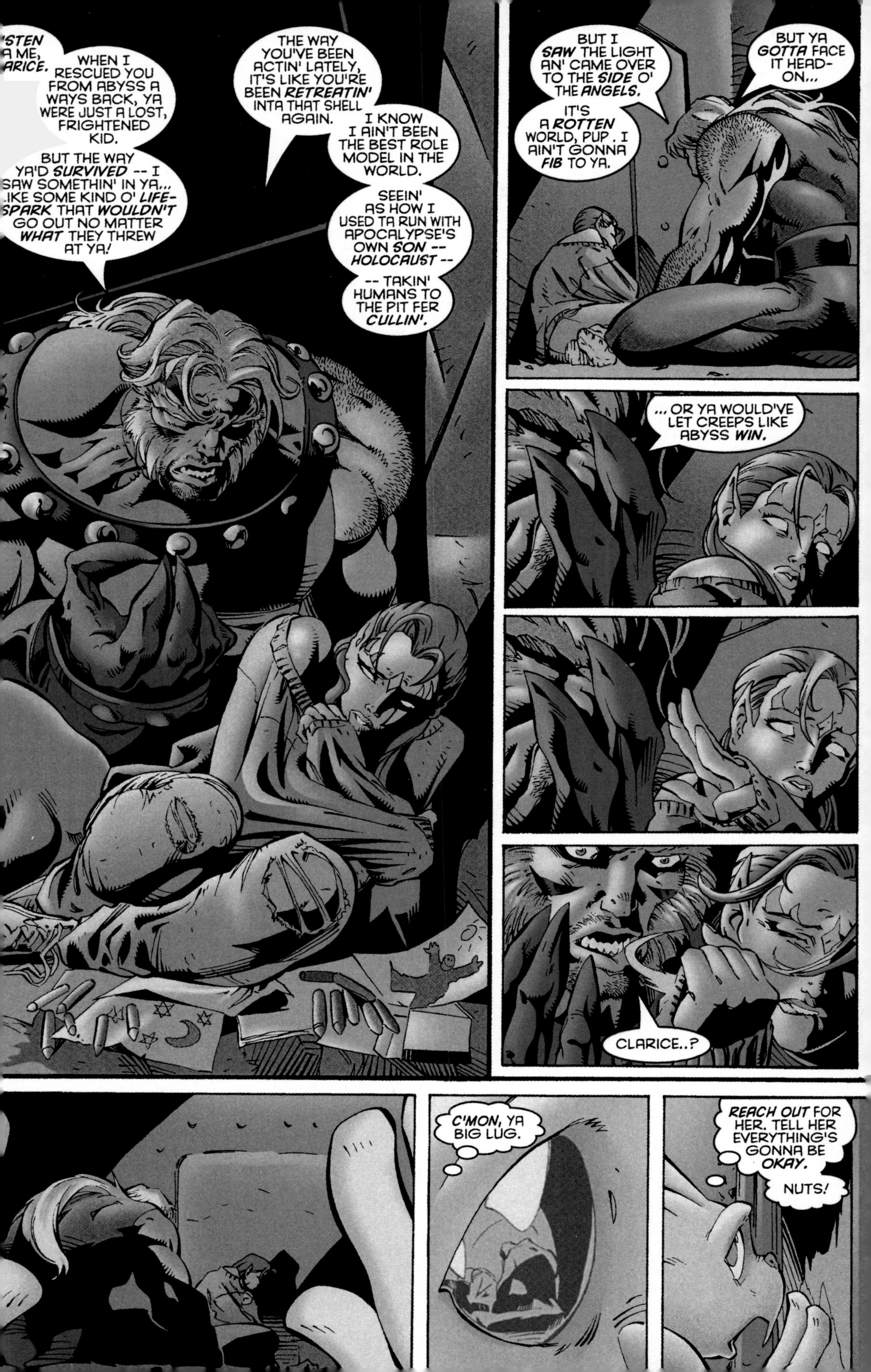
'STEN A ME, ARICE.
WHEN I RESCUED YOU FROM ABYSS A WAYS BACK, YA WERE JUST A LOST, FRIGHTENED KID.
BUT THE WAY YA'D SURVIVED -- I SAW SOMETHIN' IN YA... IKE SOME KIND O' LIFE-SPARK THAT WOULDN'T GO OUT NO MATTER WHAT THEY THREW AT YA!
THE WAY YOU'VE BEEN ACTIN' LATELY, IT'S LIKE YOU'RE BEEN RETREATIN' INTA THAT SHELL AGAIN.
I KNOW I AIN'T BEEN THE BEST ROLE MODEL IN THE WORLD.
SEEIN' AS HOW I USED TA RUN WITH APOCALYPSE'S OWN SON -- HOLOCAUST --
-- TAKIN' HUMANS TO THE PIT FER CULLIN'.
BUT I SAW THE LIGHT AN' CAME OVER TO THE SIDE O' THE ANGELS.
IT'S A ROTTEN WORLD, PUP. I AIN'T GONNA FIB TO YA.
BUT YA GOTTA FACE IT HEAD-ON...
... OR YA WOULD'VE LET CREEPS LIKE ABYSS WIN.
CLARICE..?
C'MON, YA BIG LUG.
REACH OUT FOR HER. TELL HER EVERYTHING'S GONNA BE OKAY.
NUTS!

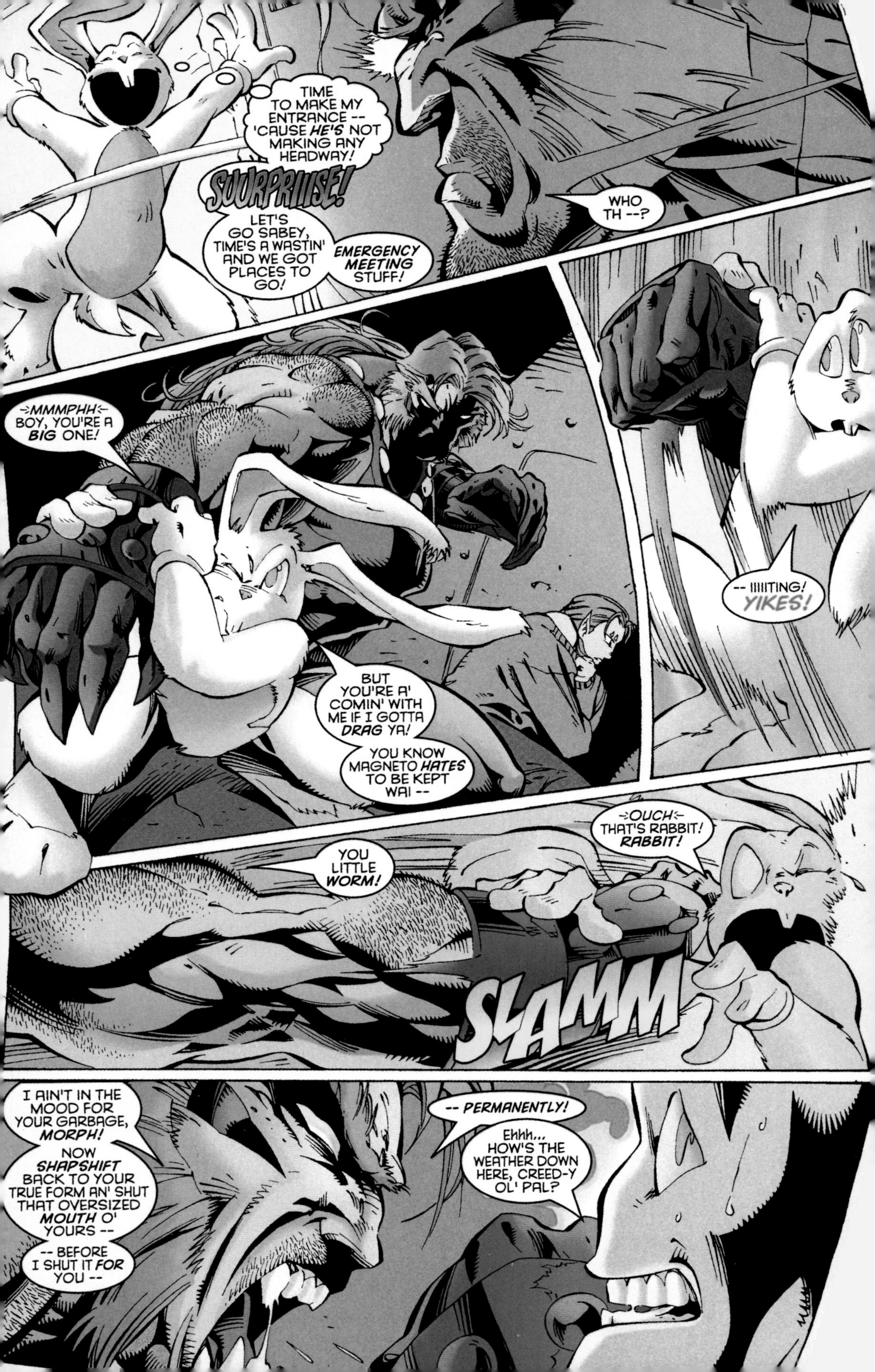
TIME TO MAKE MY ENTRANCE -- 'CAUSE HE'S NOT MAKING ANY HEADWAY!
SUURPRIIISE!
LET'S GO SABEY, TIME'S A WASTIN' AND WE GOT PLACES TO GO!
EMERGENCY MEETING STUFF!
WHO TH --?
-MMMPHH- BOY, YOU'RE A BIG ONE!
BUT YOU'RE A' COMIN' WITH ME IF I GOTTA DRAG YA!
YOU KNOW MAGNETO HATES TO BE KEPT WAI --
-- IIIIITING! YIKES!
YOU LITTLE WORM!
-OUCH- THAT'S RABBIT! RABBIT!
SLAMM
I AIN'T IN THE MOOD FOR YOUR GARBAGE, MORPH!
NOW SHAPSHIFT BACK TO YOUR TRUE FORM AN' SHUT THAT OVERSIZED MOUTH O' YOURS --
-- BEFORE I SHUT IT FOR YOU --
-- PERMANENTLY!
Ehhh... HOW'S THE WEATHER DOWN HERE, CREED-Y OL' PAL?

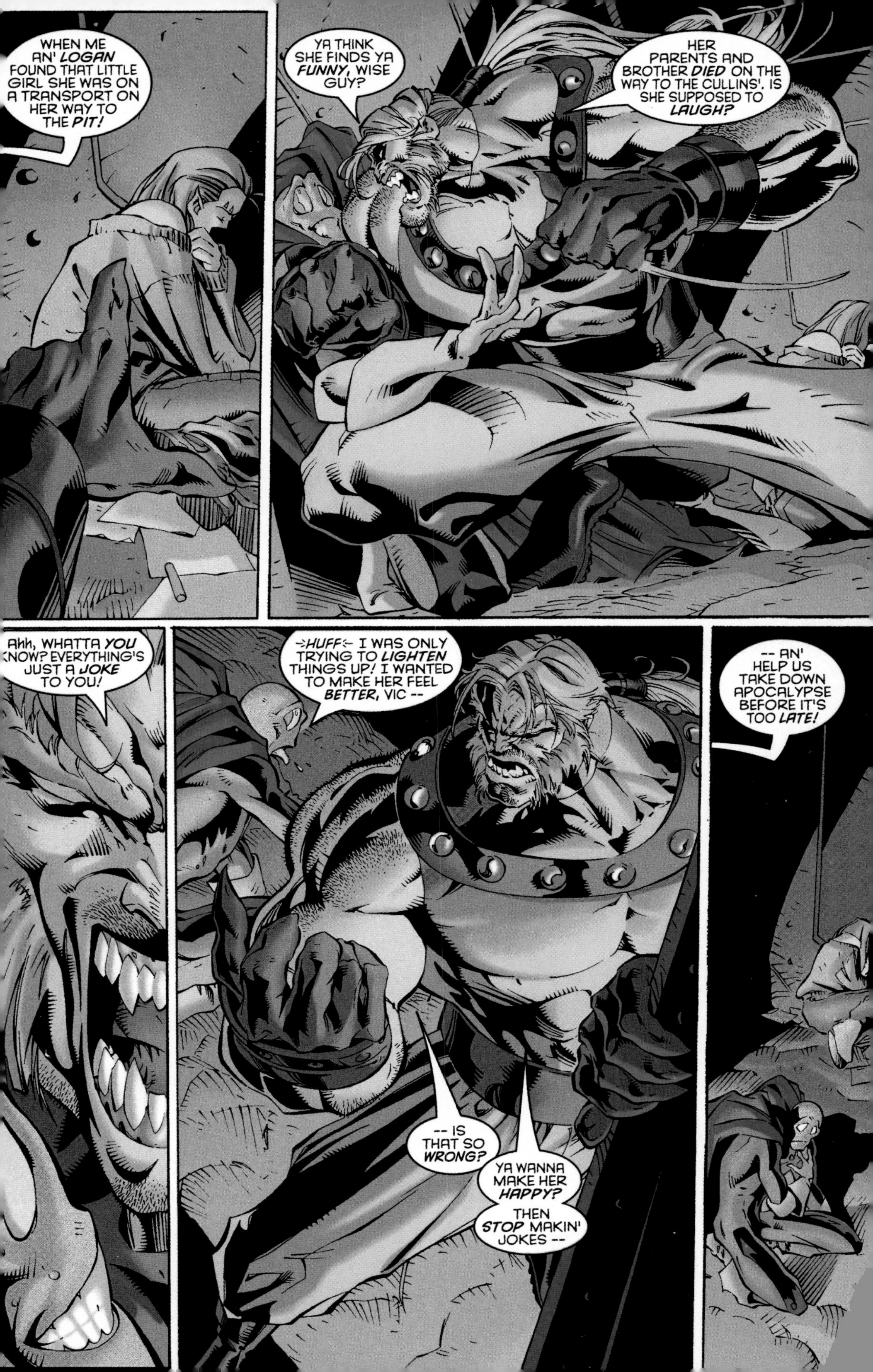
WHEN ME AN' LOGAN FOUND THAT LITTLE GIRL SHE WAS ON A TRANSPORT ON HER WAY TO THE PIT!
YA THINK SHE FINDS YA FUNNY, WISE GUY?
HER PARENTS AND BROTHER DIED ON THE WAY TO THE CULLINS'. IS SHE SUPPOSED TO LAUGH?
AHH, WHATTA YOU KNOW? EVERYTHING'S JUST A JOKE TO YOU!
-HUFF- I WAS ONLY TRYING TO LIGHTEN THINGS UP! I WANTED TO MAKE HER FEEL BETTER, VIC --
-- IS THAT SO WRONG?
YA WANNA MAKE HER HAPPY?
THEN STOP MAKIN' JOKES --
-- AN' HELP US TAKE DOWN APOCALYPSE BEFORE IT'S TOO LATE!

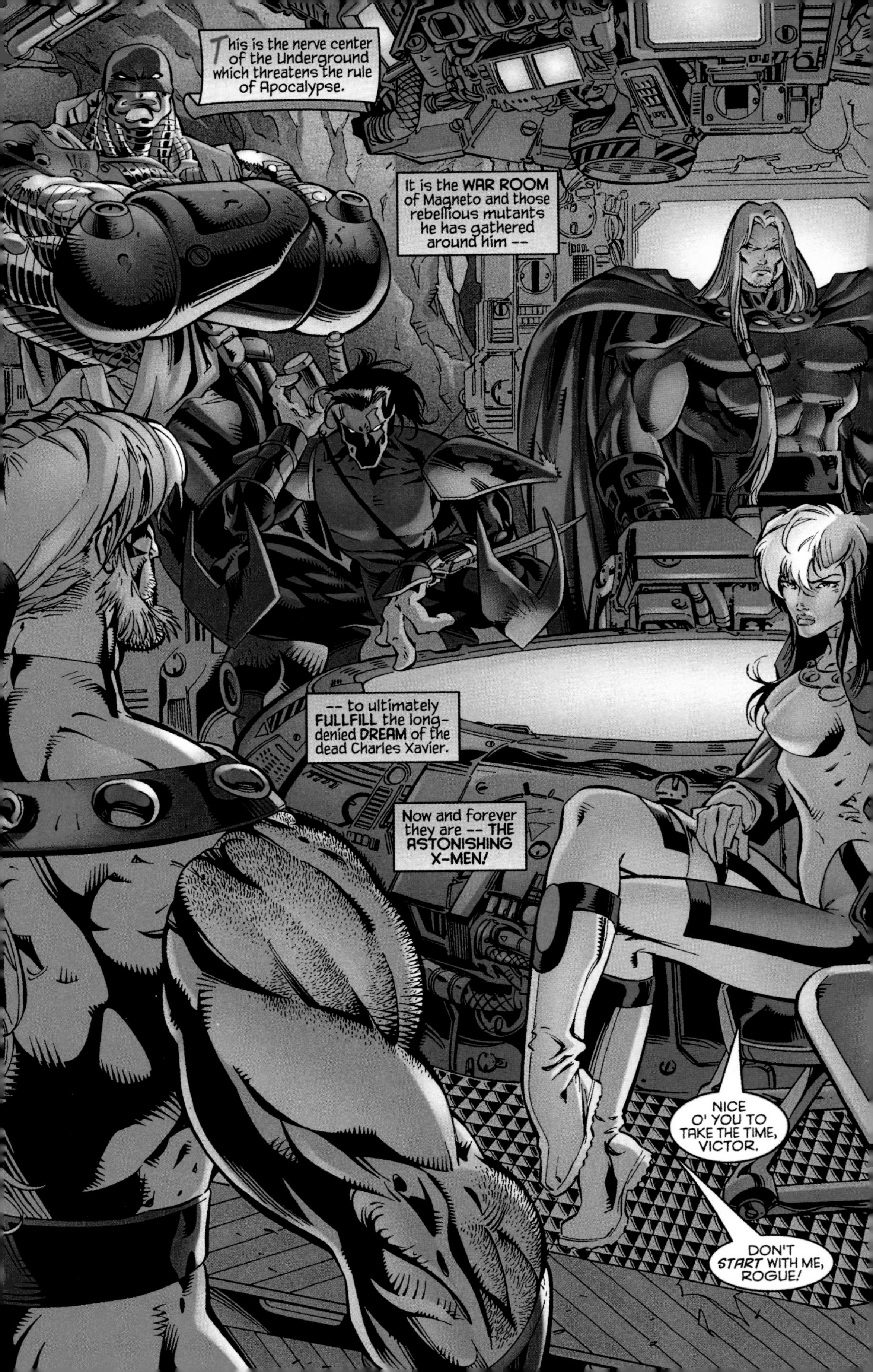
This is the nerve center of the Underground which threatens the rule of Apocalypse.
It is the WAR ROOM of Magneto and those rebellious mutants he has gathered around him --
-- to ultimately FULLFILL the long-denied DREAM of the dead Charles Xavier.
Now and forever they are -- THE ASTONISHING X-MEN!
NICE O' YOU TO TAKE THE TIME, VICTOR.
DON'T START WITH ME, ROGUE!

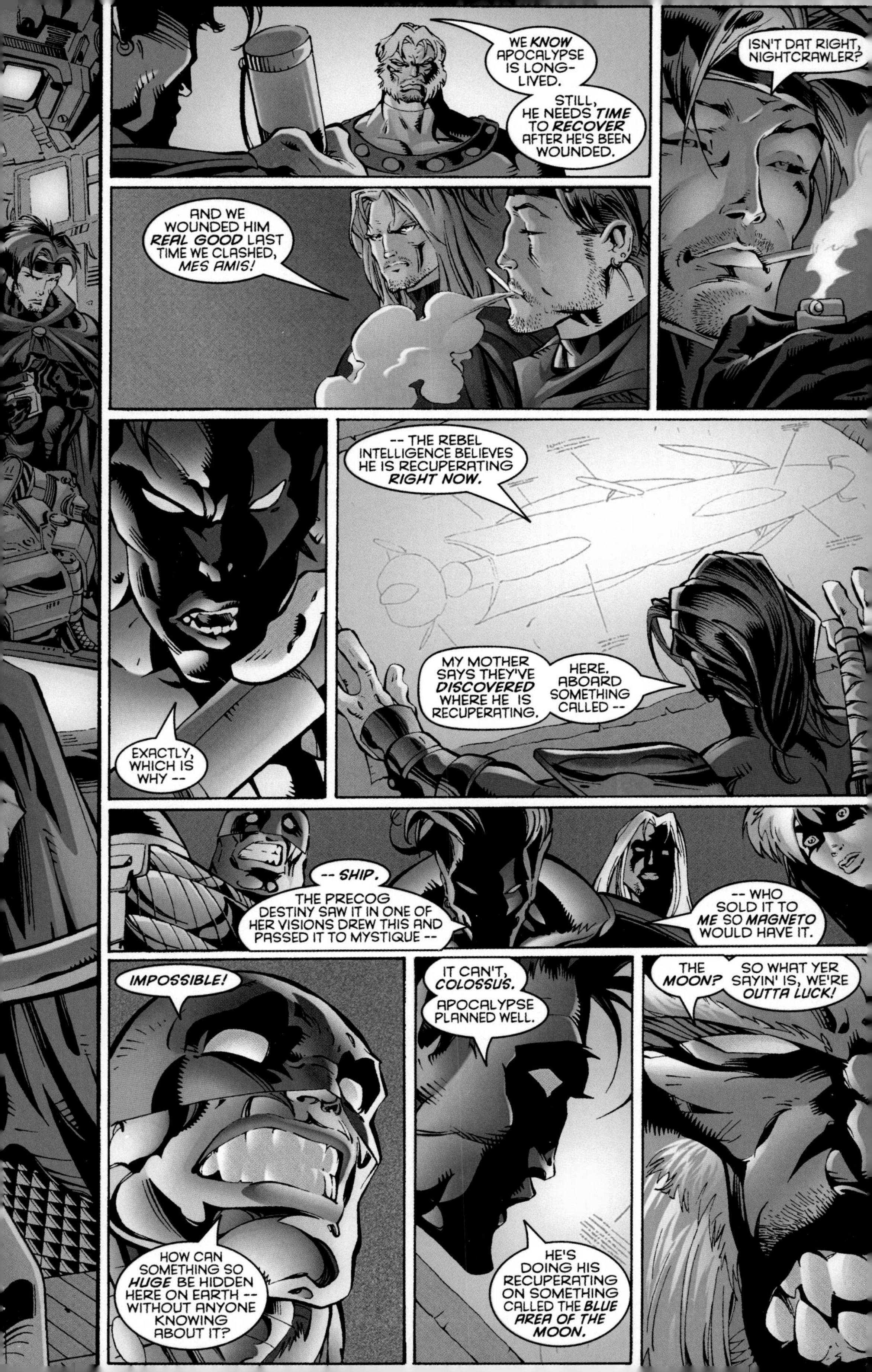
WE KNOW APOCALYPSE IS LONG-LIVED.
STILL, HE NEEDS TIME TO RECOVER AFTER HE'S BEEN WOUNDED.
ISN'T DAT RIGHT, NIGHTCRAWLER?
AND WE WOUNDED HIM REAL GOOD LAST TIME WE CLASHED, MES AMIS!
EXACTLY, WHICH IS WHY --
-- THE REBEL INTELLIGENCE BELIEVES HE IS RECUPERATING RIGHT NOW.
MY MOTHER SAYS THEY'VE DISCOVERED WHERE HE IS RECUPERATING.
HERE. ABOARD SOMETHING CALLED --
-- SHIP.
THE PRECOG DESTINY SAW IT IN ONE OF HER VISIONS DREW THIS AND PASSED IT TO MYSTIQUE --
-- WHO SOLD IT TO ME SO MAGNETO WOULD HAVE IT.
IMPOSSIBLE!
HOW CAN SOMETHING SO HUGE BE HIDDEN HERE ON EARTH -- WITHOUT ANYONE KNOWING ABOUT IT?
IT CAN'T, COLOSSUS.
APOCALYPSE PLANNED WELL.
HE'S DOING HIS RECUPERATING ON SOMETHING CALLED THE BLUE AREA OF THE MOON.
THE MOON?
SO WHAT YER SAYIN' IS, WE'RE OUTTA LUCK!

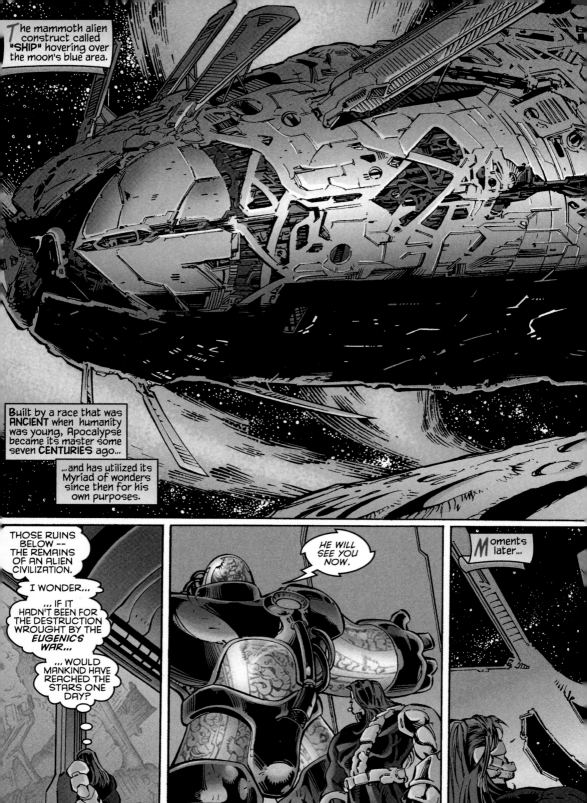

The mammoth alien construct called **"SHIP"** hovering over the moon's blue area.

Built by a race that was **ANCIENT** when humanity was young, Apocalypse became its master some seven **CENTURIES** ago...

...and has utilized its Myriad of wonders since then for his own purposes.

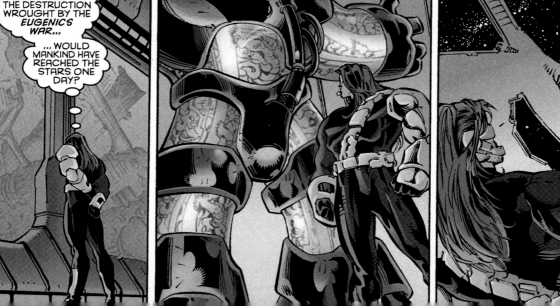

THOSE RUINS BELOW -- THE REMAINS OF AN ALIEN CIVILIZATION.

I WONDER...

... IF IT HADN'T BEEN FOR THE DESTRUCTION WROUGHT BY THE **EUGENICS WAR**...

... WOULD MANKIND HAVE REACHED THE STARS ONE DAY?

HE WILL SEE YOU NOW.

Moments later...

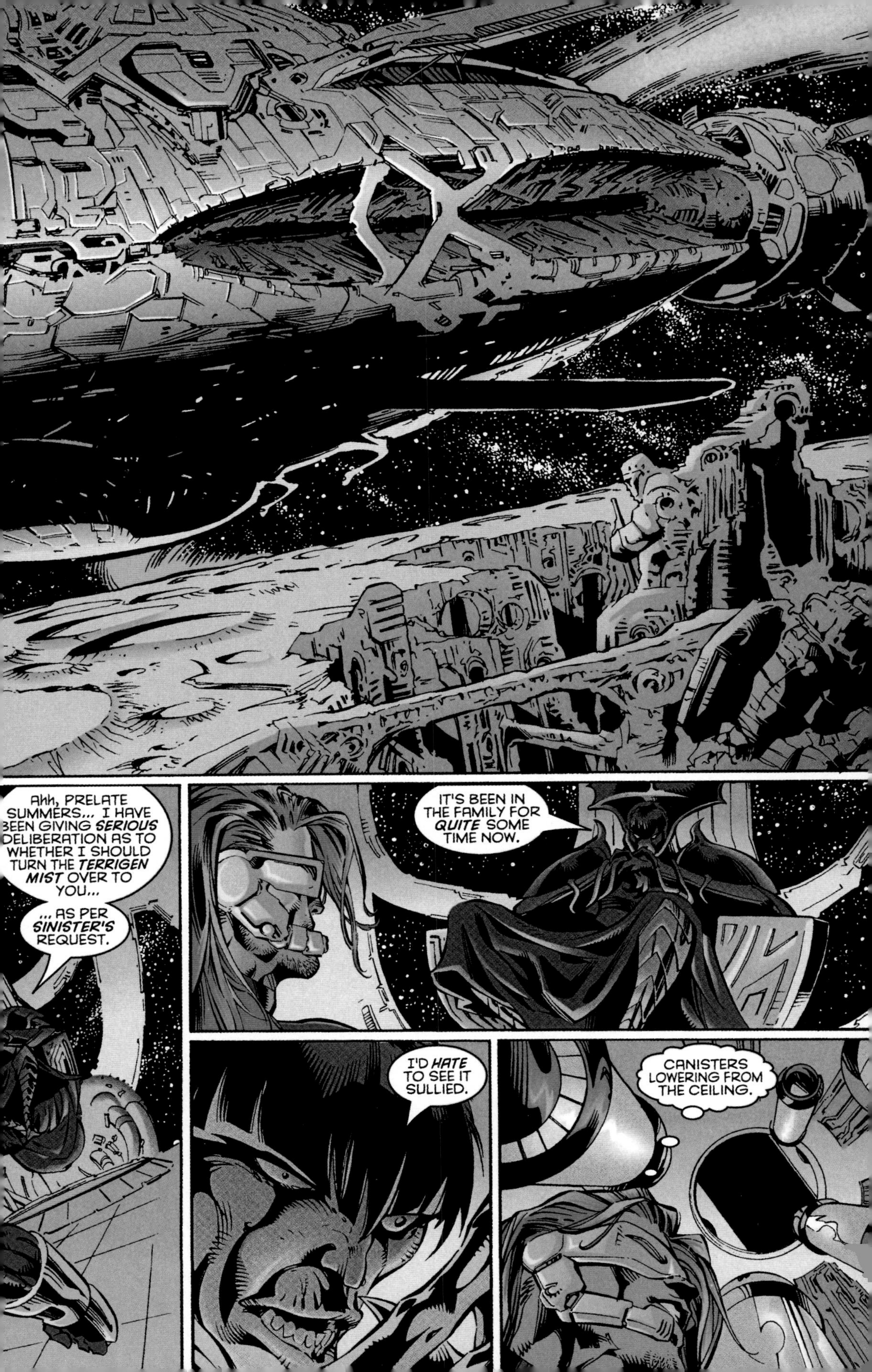
AHH, PRELATE SUMMERS... I HAVE BEEN GIVING SERIOUS DELIBERATION AS TO WHETHER I SHOULD TURN THE TERRIGEN MIST OVER TO YOU...
...AS PER SINISTER'S REQUEST.
IT'S BEEN IN THE FAMILY FOR QUITE SOME TIME NOW.
I'D HATE TO SEE IT SULLIED.
CANISTERS LOWERING FROM THE CEILING.

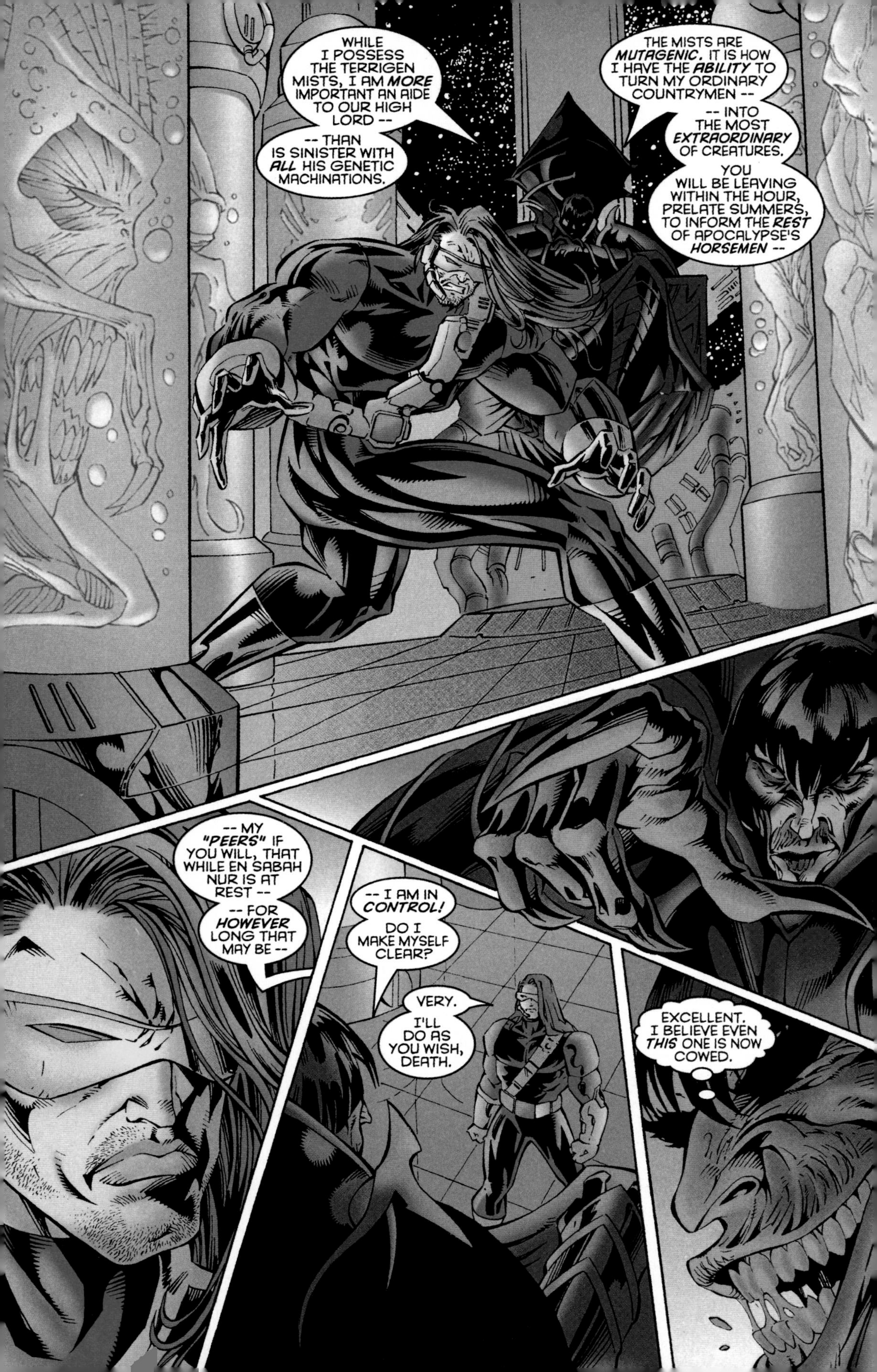
WHILE I POSSESS THE TERRIGEN MISTS, I AM *MORE* IMPORTANT AN AIDE TO OUR HIGH LORD --
-- THAN IS SINISTER WITH *ALL* HIS GENETIC MACHINATIONS.
THE MISTS ARE *MUTAGENIC.* IT IS HOW I HAVE THE *ABILITY* TO TURN MY ORDINARY COUNTRYMEN --
-- INTO THE MOST *EXTRAORDINARY* OF CREATURES.
YOU WILL BE LEAVING WITHIN THE HOUR, PRELATE SUMMERS, TO INFORM THE *REST* OF APOCALYPSE'S *HORSEMEN* --
-- MY *"PEERS"* IF YOU WILL, THAT WHILE EN SABAH NUR IS AT REST --
-- FOR *HOWEVER* LONG THAT MAY BE --
-- I AM IN *CONTROL!*
DO I MAKE MYSELF CLEAR?
VERY.
I'LL DO AS YOU WISH, DEATH.
EXCELLENT. I BELIEVE EVEN *THIS* ONE IS NOW COWED.

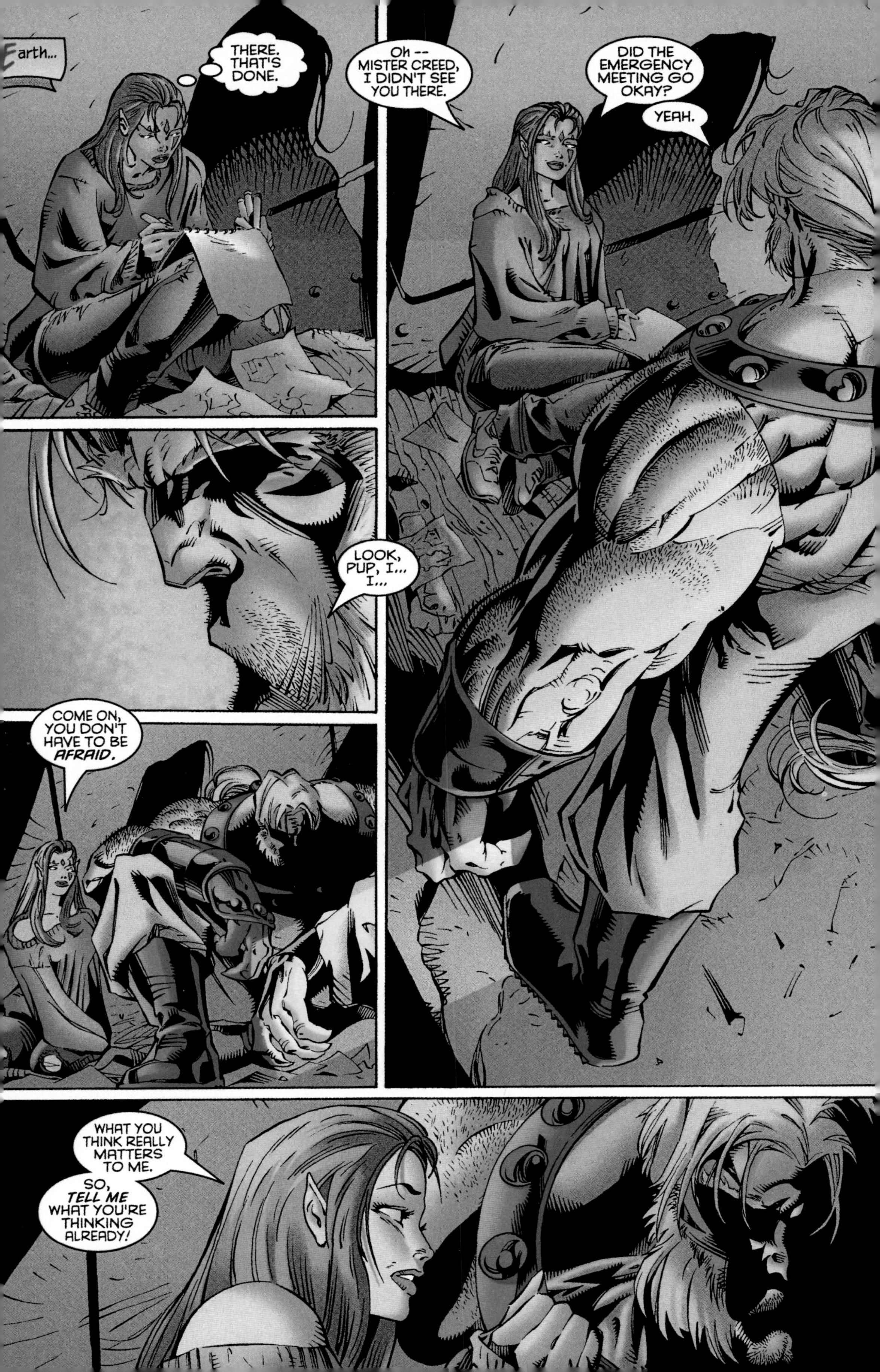
Earth...
THERE. THAT'S DONE.
Oh -- MISTER CREED, I DIDN'T SEE YOU THERE.
DID THE EMERGENCY MEETING GO OKAY?
YEAH.
LOOK, PUP, I... I...
COME ON, YOU DON'T HAVE TO BE AFRAID.
WHAT YOU THINK REALLY MATTERS TO ME.
SO, TELL ME WHAT YOU'RE THINKING ALREADY!

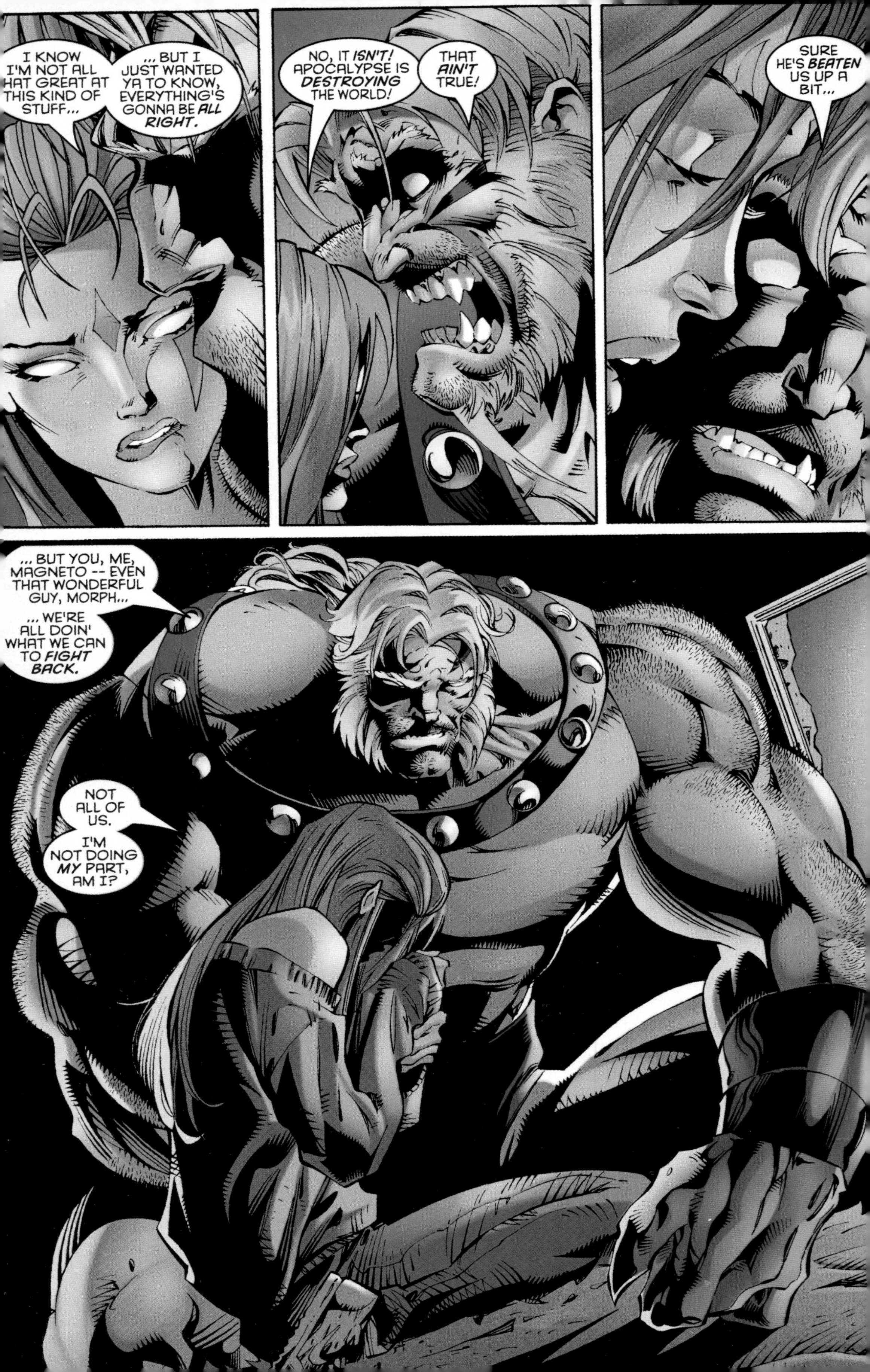
I KNOW I'M NOT ALL HAT GREAT AT THIS KIND OF STUFF...
... BUT I JUST WANTED YA TO KNOW, EVERYTHING'S GONNA BE ALL RIGHT.
NO, IT ISN'T! APOCALYPSE IS DESTROYING THE WORLD!
THAT AIN'T TRUE!
SURE HE'S BEATEN US UP A BIT...
... BUT YOU, ME, MAGNETO -- EVEN THAT WONDERFUL GUY, MORPH...
... WE'RE ALL DOIN' WHAT WE CAN TO FIGHT BACK.
NOT ALL OF US.
I'M NOT DOING MY PART, AM I?

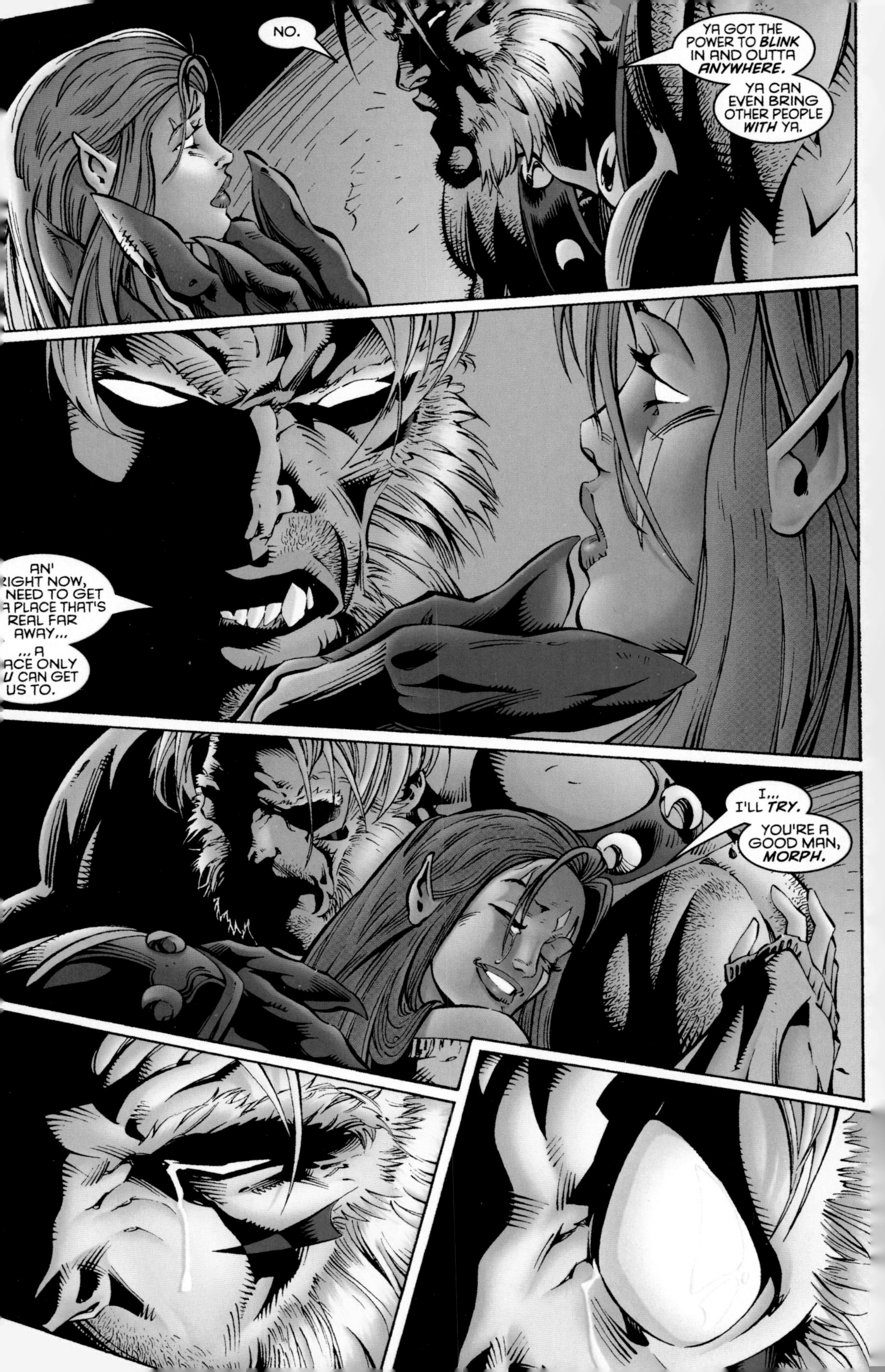
NO.
YA GOT THE POWER TO *BLINK* IN AND OUTTA *ANYWHERE.*
YA CAN EVEN BRING OTHER PEOPLE *WITH* YA.
AN' RIGHT NOW, NEED TO GET A PLACE THAT'S REAL FAR AWAY...
...A ACE ONLY U CAN GET US TO.
I... I'LL *TRY.*
YOU'RE A GOOD MAN, *MORPH.*

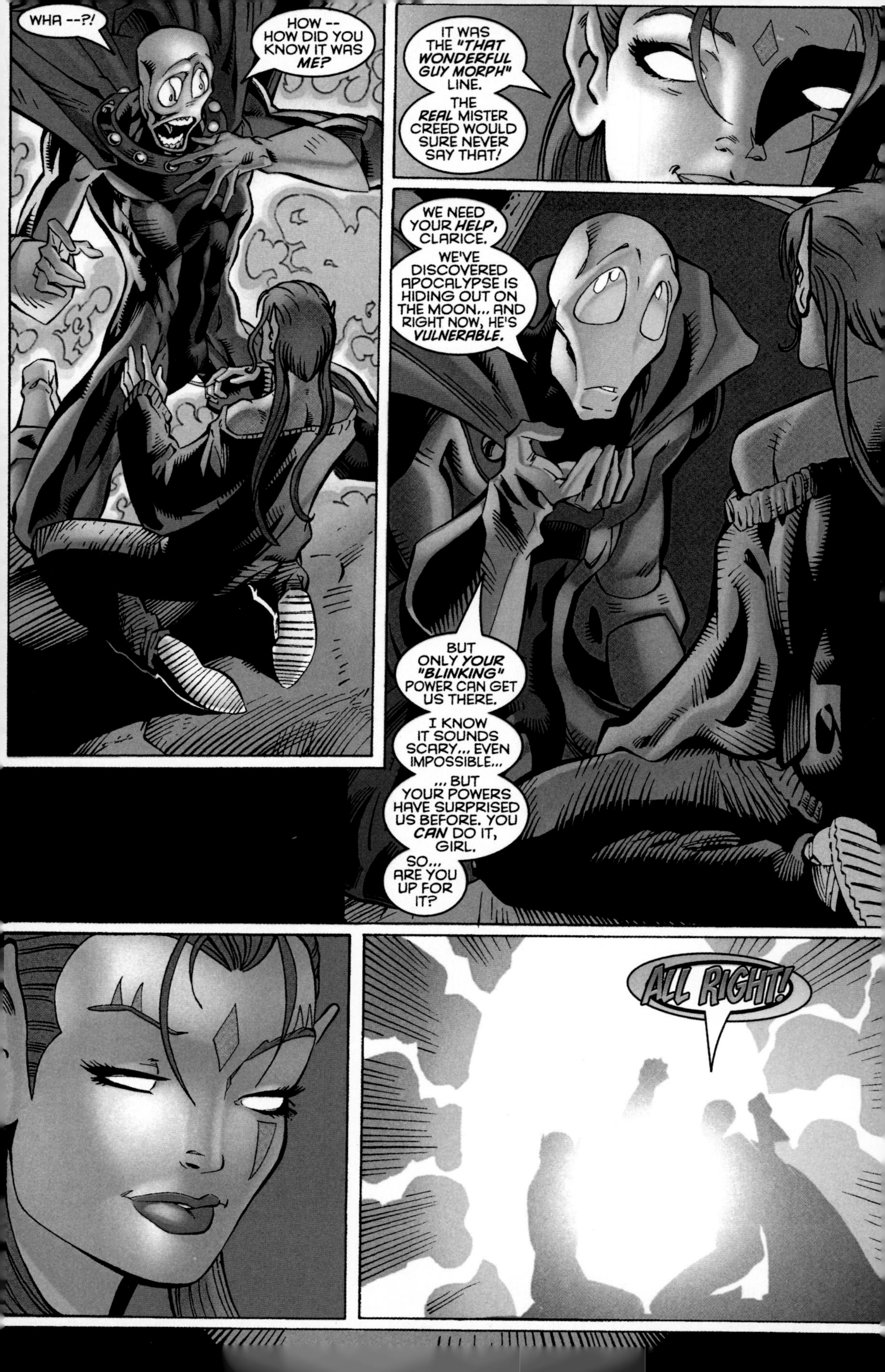
WHA --?!
HOW -- HOW DID YOU KNOW IT WAS ME?
IT WAS THE "THAT WONDERFUL GUY MORPH" LINE.
THE REAL MISTER CREED WOULD SURE NEVER SAY THAT!
WE NEED YOUR HELP, CLARICE.
WE'VE DISCOVERED APOCALYPSE IS HIDING OUT ON THE MOON... AND RIGHT NOW, HE'S VULNERABLE.
BUT ONLY YOUR "BLINKING" POWER CAN GET US THERE.
I KNOW IT SOUNDS SCARY... EVEN IMPOSSIBLE...
... BUT YOUR POWERS HAVE SURPRISED US BEFORE. YOU CAN DO IT, GIRL.
SO... ARE YOU UP FOR IT?
ALL RIGHT!

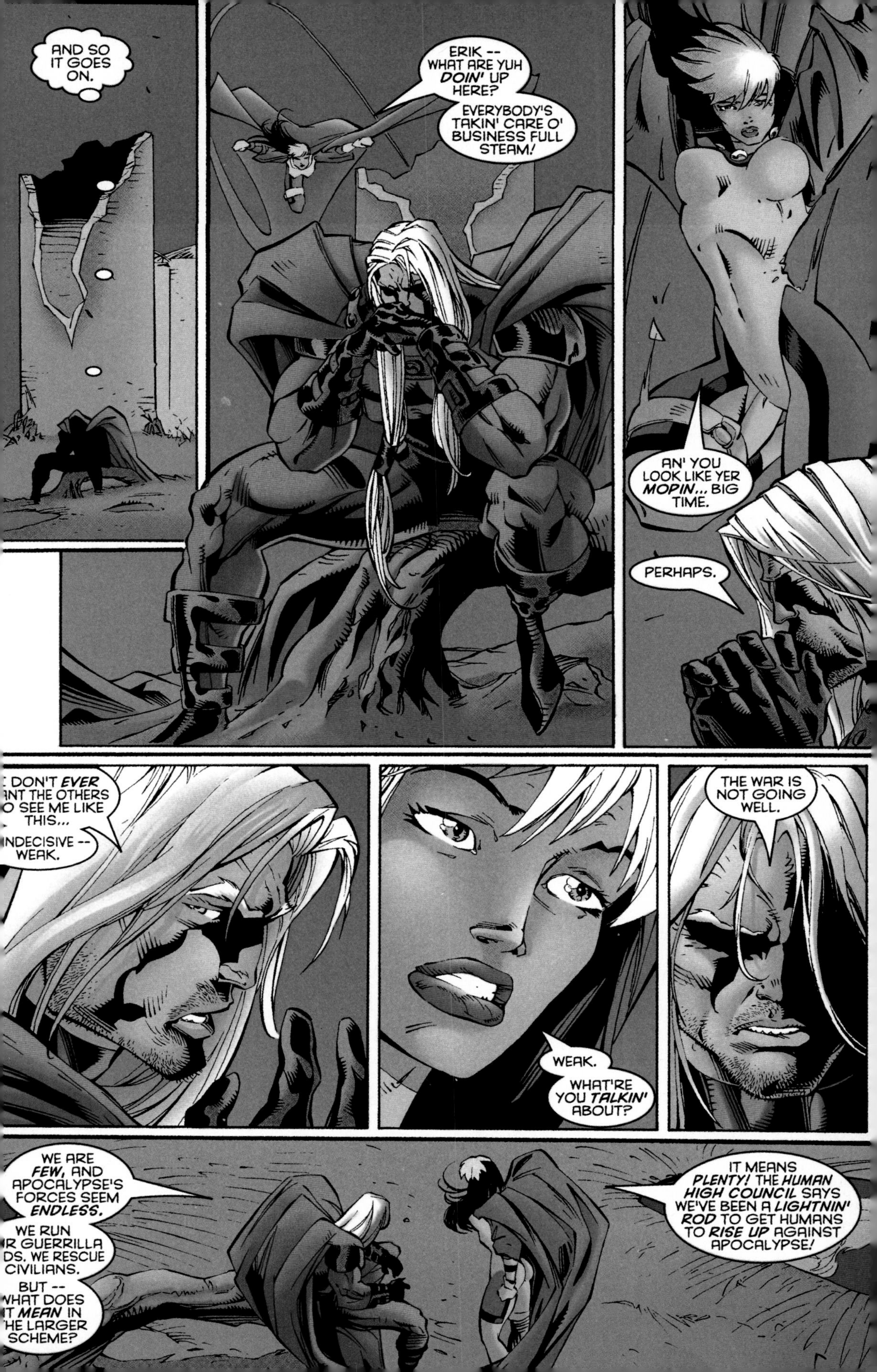

AND SO IT GOES ON.
ERIK -- WHAT ARE YUH DOIN' UP HERE?
EVERYBODY'S TAKIN' CARE O' BUSINESS FULL STEAM!
AN' YOU LOOK LIKE YER MOPIN... BIG TIME.
PERHAPS.
I DON'T EVER ANT THE OTHERS O SEE ME LIKE THIS...
NDECISIVE -- WEAK.
WEAK.
WHAT'RE YOU TALKIN' ABOUT?
THE WAR IS NOT GOING WELL.
WE ARE FEW, AND APOCALYPSE'S FORCES SEEM ENDLESS.
WE RUN R GUERRILLA DS. WE RESCUE CIVILIANS.
BUT -- WHAT DOES T MEAN IN HE LARGER SCHEME?
IT MEANS PLENTY! THE HUMAN HIGH COUNCIL SAYS WE'VE BEEN A LIGHTNIN' ROD TO GET HUMANS TO RISE UP AGAINST APOCALYPSE!

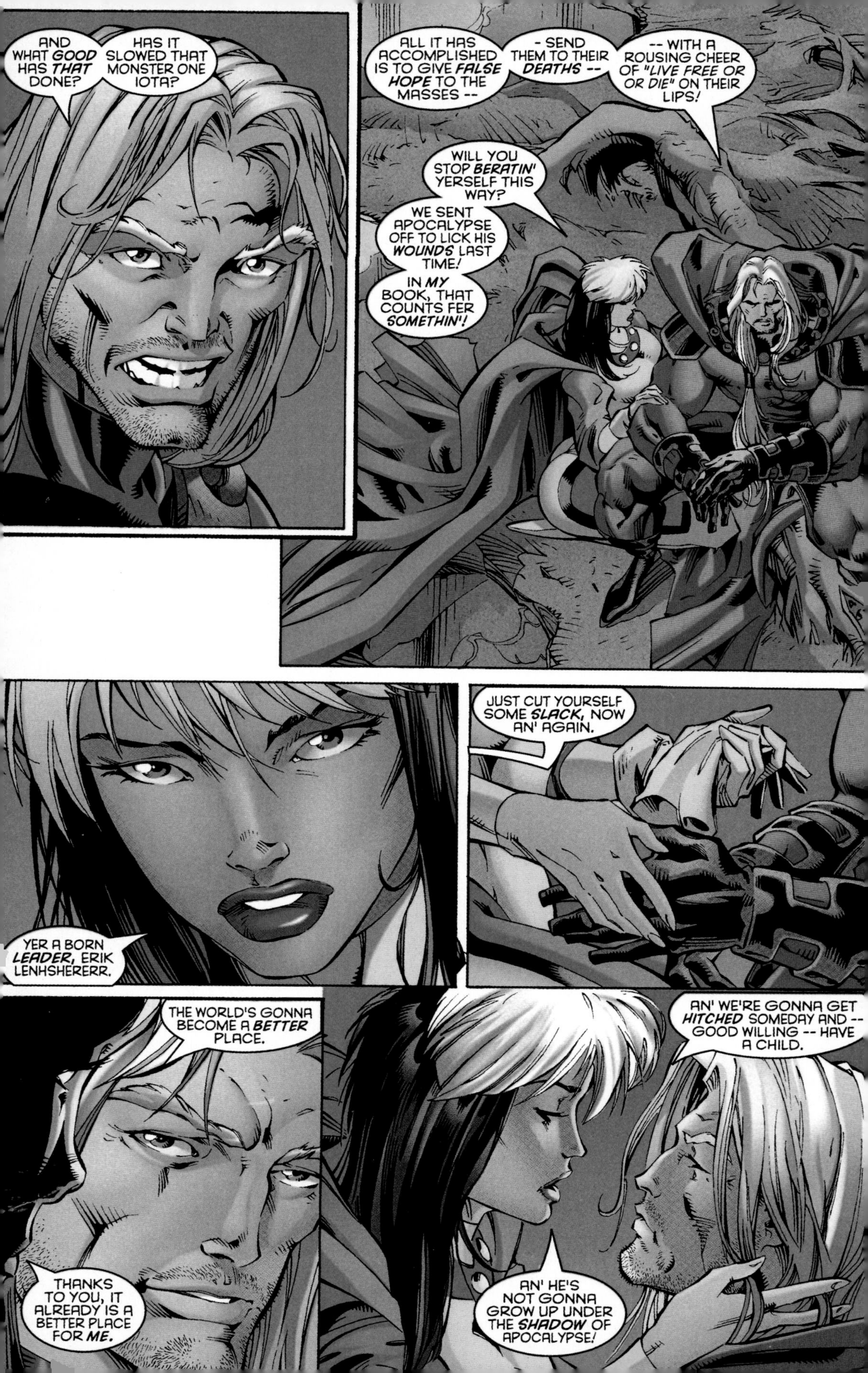

AND WHAT GOOD HAS THAT DONE?
HAS IT SLOWED THAT MONSTER ONE IOTA?
ALL IT HAS ACCOMPLISHED IS TO GIVE FALSE HOPE TO THE MASSES --
- SEND THEM TO THEIR DEATHS --
-- WITH A ROUSING CHEER OF "LIVE FREE OR OR DIE" ON THEIR LIPS!
WILL YOU STOP BERATIN' YERSELF THIS WAY?
WE SENT APOCALYPSE OFF TO LICK HIS WOUNDS LAST TIME!
IN MY BOOK, THAT COUNTS FER SOMETHIN'!
YER A BORN LEADER, ERIK LENHSHERERR.
JUST CUT YOURSELF SOME SLACK, NOW AN' AGAIN.
THE WORLD'S GONNA BECOME A BETTER PLACE.
THANKS TO YOU, IT ALREADY IS A BETTER PLACE FOR ME.
AN' WE'RE GONNA GET HITCHED SOMEDAY AND -- GOOD WILLING -- HAVE A CHILD.
AN' HE'S NOT GONNA GROW UP UNDER THE SHADOW OF APOCALYPSE!

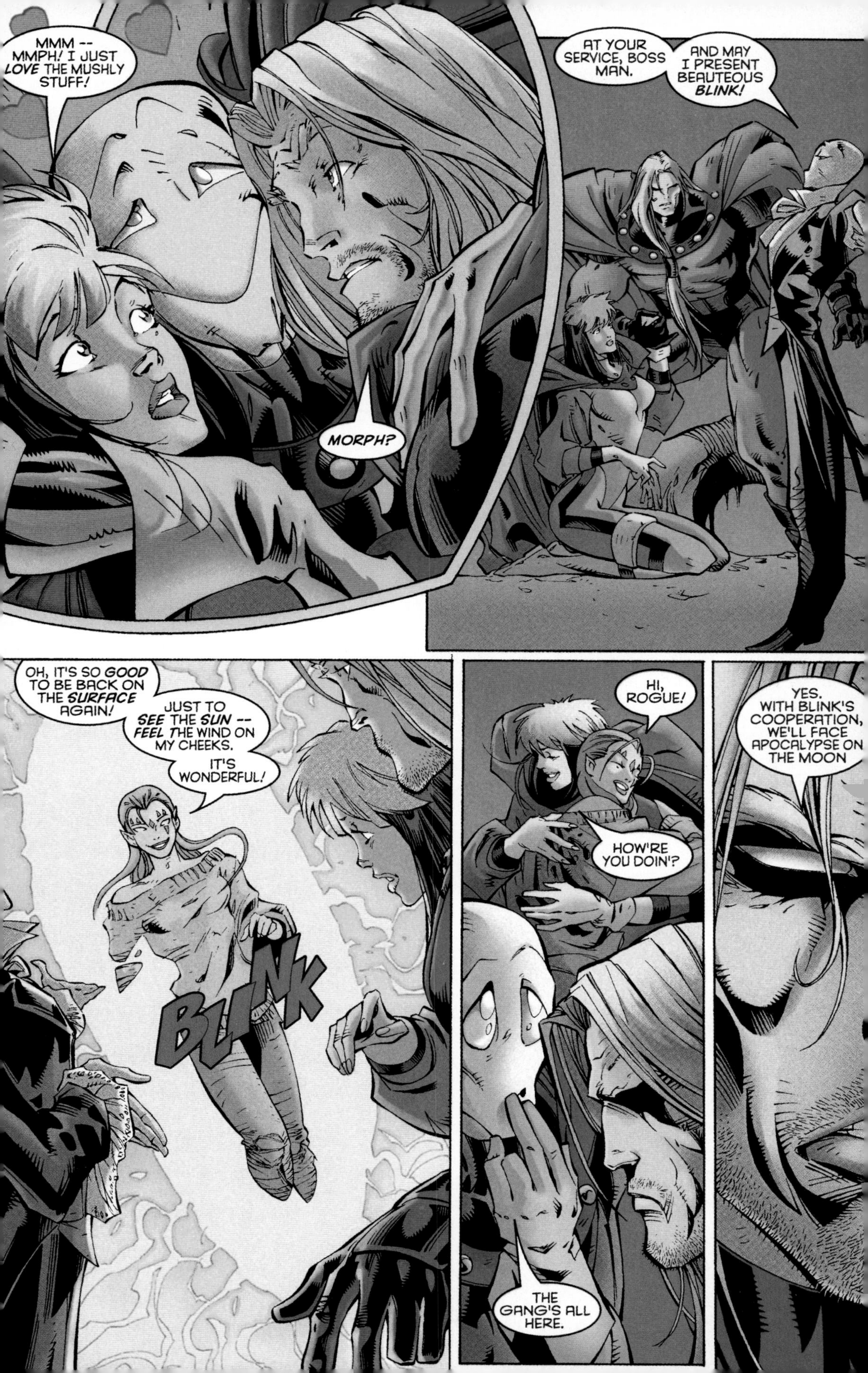

MMM -- MMPH! I JUST LOVE THE MUSHLY STUFF!
MORPH?
AT YOUR SERVICE, BOSS MAN.
AND MAY I PRESENT BEAUTEOUS BLINK!
OH, IT'S SO GOOD TO BE BACK ON THE SURFACE AGAIN!
JUST TO SEE THE SUN -- FEEL THE WIND ON MY CHEEKS.
IT'S WONDERFUL!
BLINK
HI, ROGUE!
HOW'RE YOU DOIN'?
THE GANG'S ALL HERE.
YES. WITH BLINK'S COOPERATION, WE'LL FACE APOCALYPSE ON THE MOON

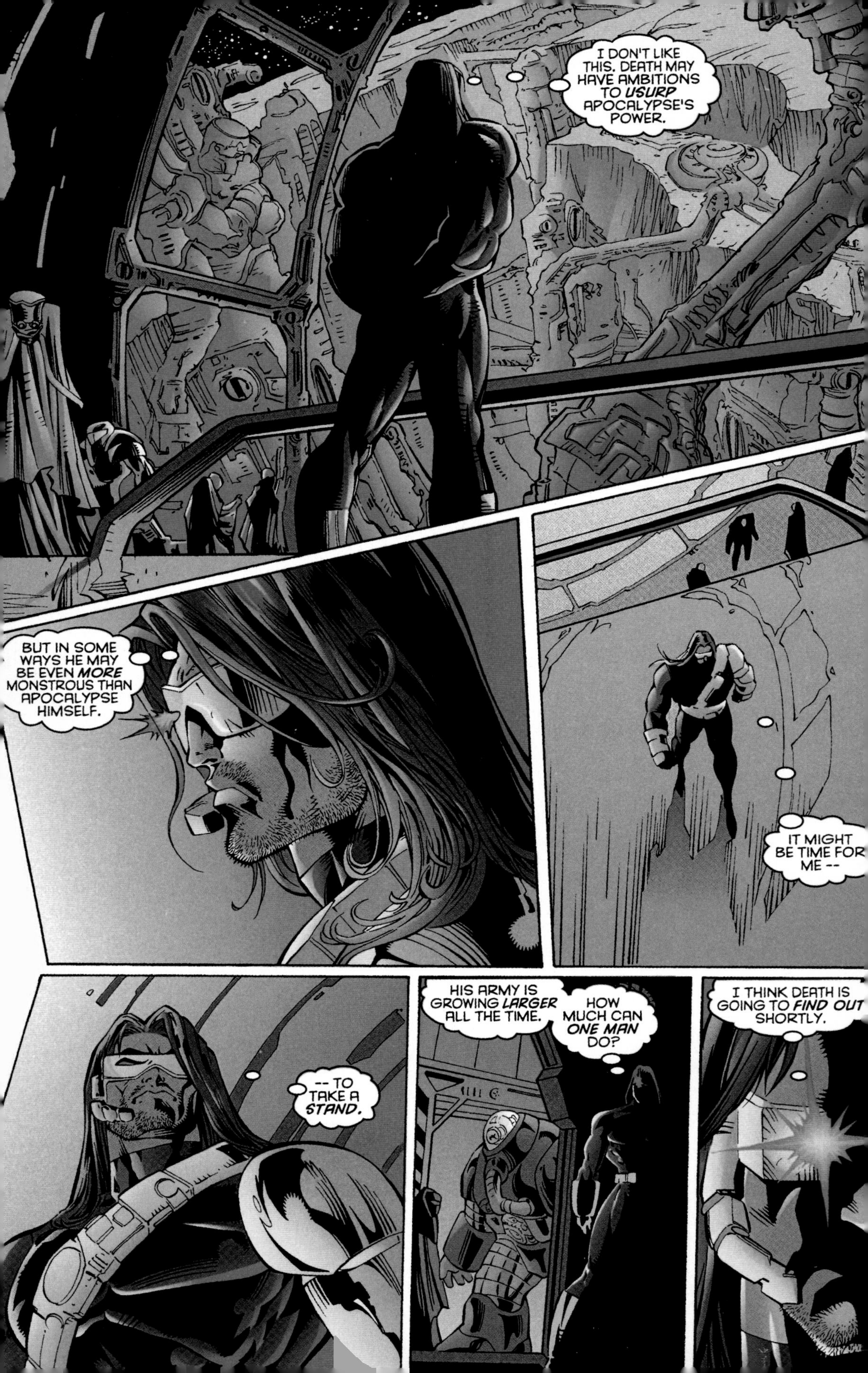
I DON'T LIKE THIS. DEATH MAY HAVE AMBITIONS TO *USURP* APOCALYPSE'S POWER.
BUT IN SOME WAYS HE MAY BE EVEN *MORE* MONSTROUS THAN APOCALYPSE HIMSELF.
IT MIGHT BE TIME FOR ME --
-- TO TAKE A *STAND.*
HIS ARMY IS GROWING *LARGER* ALL THE TIME.
HOW MUCH CAN *ONE MAN* DO?
I THINK DEATH IS GOING TO *FIND OUT* SHORTLY.

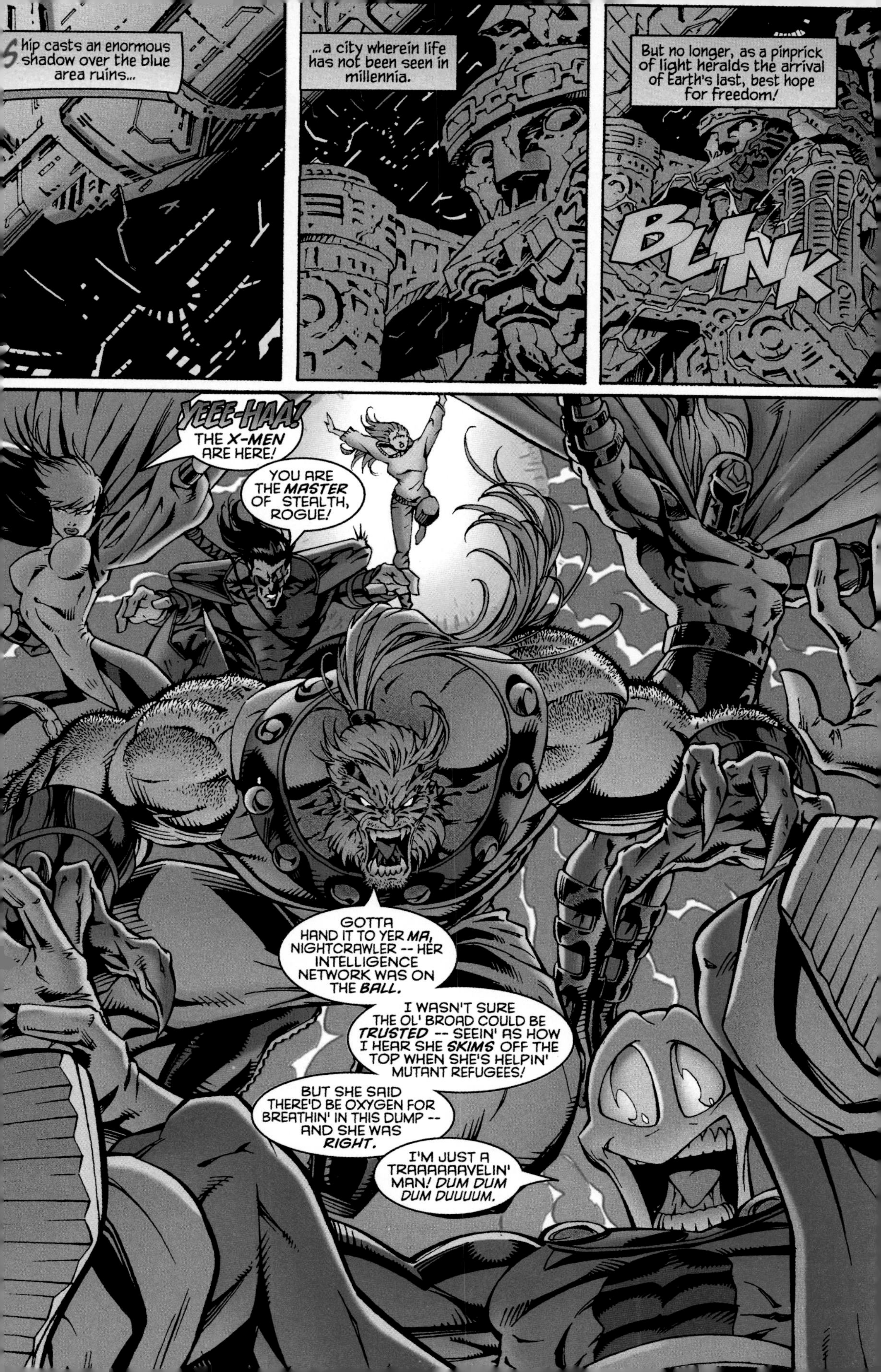
Ship casts an enormous shadow over the blue area ruins...
...a city wherein life has not been seen in millennia.
But no longer, as a pinprick of light heralds the arrival of Earth's last, best hope for freedom!
BLINK
YEEE-HAA! THE X-MEN ARE HERE!
YOU ARE THE MASTER OF STEALTH, ROGUE!
GOTTA HAND IT TO YER MA, NIGHTCRAWLER -- HER INTELLIGENCE NETWORK WAS ON THE BALL.
I WASN'T SURE THE OL' BROAD COULD BE TRUSTED -- SEEIN' AS HOW I HEAR SHE SKIMS OFF THE TOP WHEN SHE'S HELPIN' MUTANT REFUGEES!
BUT SHE SAID THERE'D BE OXYGEN FOR BREATHIN' IN THIS DUMP -- AND SHE WAS RIGHT.
I'M JUST A TRAAAAAAVELIN' MAN! DUM DUM DUM DUUUUM.

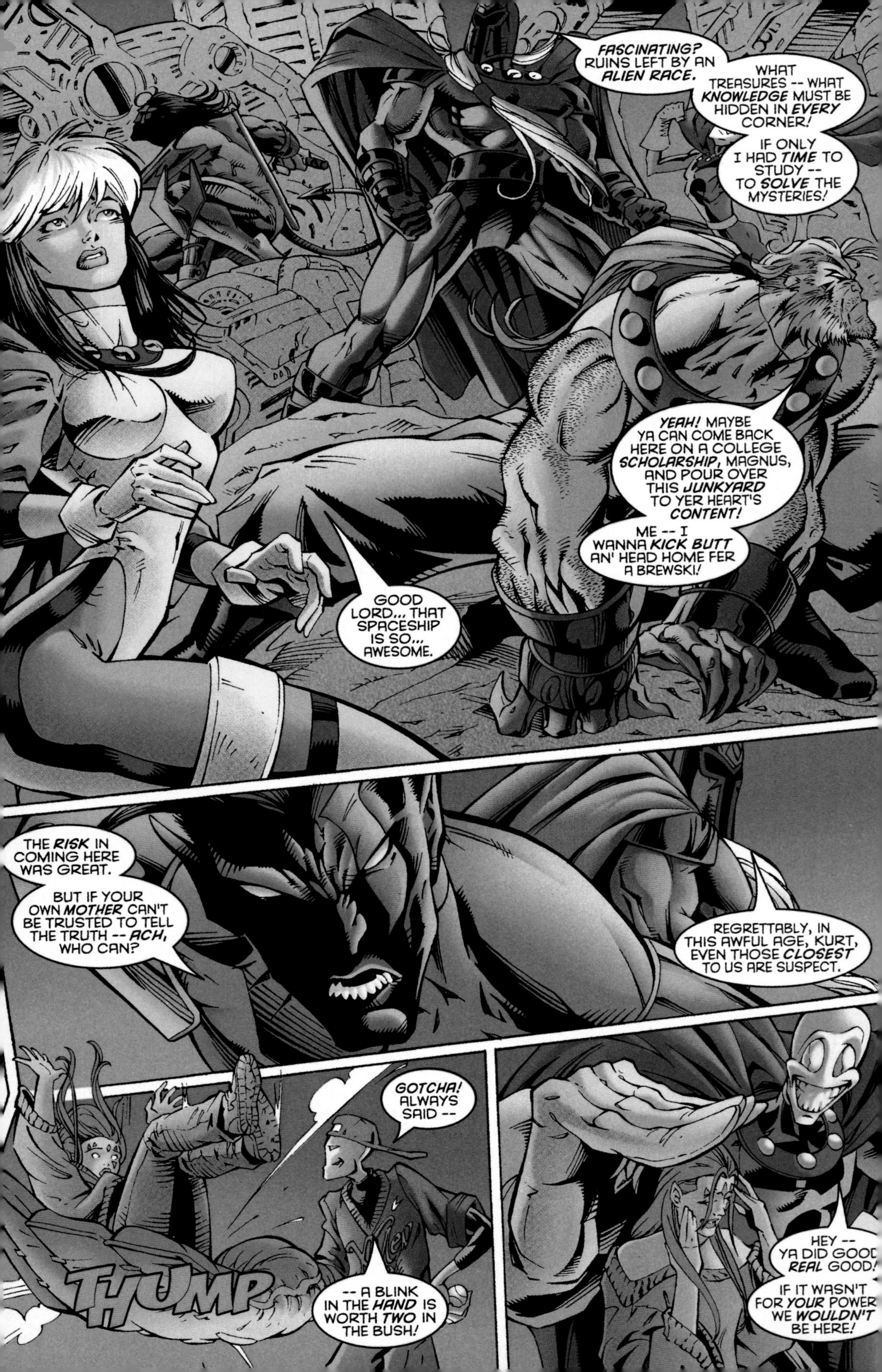
FASCINATING? RUINS LEFT BY AN ALIEN RACE.
WHAT TREASURES -- WHAT KNOWLEDGE MUST BE HIDDEN IN EVERY CORNER!
IF ONLY I HAD TIME TO STUDY -- TO SOLVE THE MYSTERIES!
YEAH! MAYBE YA CAN COME BACK HERE ON A COLLEGE SCHOLARSHIP, MAGNUS, AND POUR OVER THIS JUNKYARD TO YER HEART'S CONTENT!
ME -- I WANNA KICK BUTT AN' HEAD HOME FER A BREWSKI!
GOOD LORD... THAT SPACESHIP IS SO... AWESOME.
THE RISK IN COMING HERE WAS GREAT.
BUT IF YOUR OWN MOTHER CAN'T BE TRUSTED TO TELL THE TRUTH -- ACH, WHO CAN?
REGRETTABLY, IN THIS AWFUL AGE, KURT, EVEN THOSE CLOSEST TO US ARE SUSPECT.
THUMP
GOTCHA! ALWAYS SAID --
-- A BLINK IN THE HAND IS WORTH TWO IN THE BUSH!
HEY -- YA DID GOOD REAL GOOD!
IF IT WASN'T FOR YOUR POWER WE WOULDN'T BE HERE!

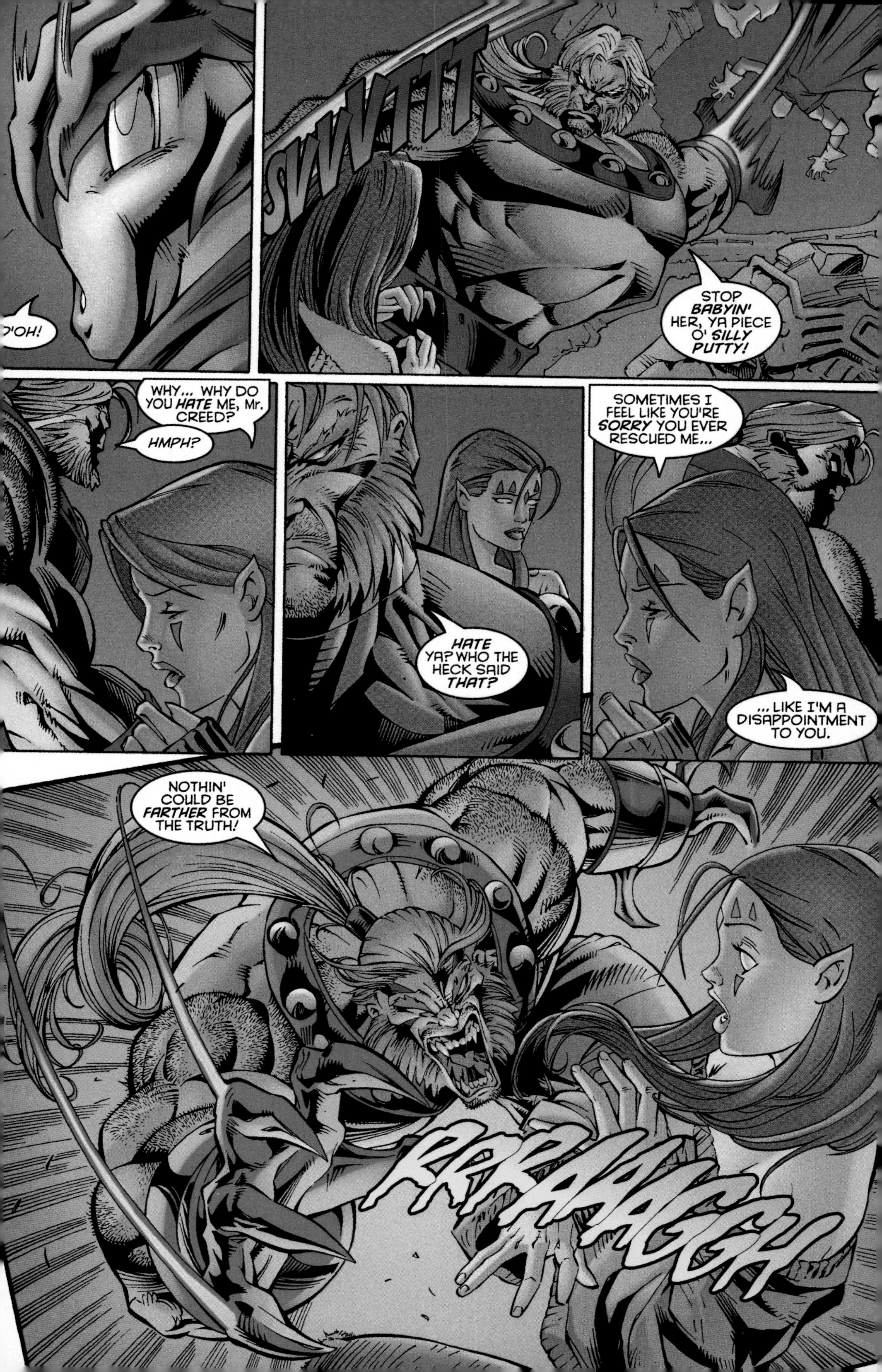
D'OH!
SVVVTTT
STOP BABYIN' HER, YA PIECE O' SILLY PUTTY!
WHY... WHY DO YOU HATE ME, Mr. CREED?
HMPH?
HATE YA? WHO THE HECK SAID THAT?
SOMETIMES I FEEL LIKE YOU'RE SORRY YOU EVER RESCUED ME...
... LIKE I'M A DISAPPOINTMENT TO YOU.
NOTHIN' COULD BE FARTHER FROM THE TRUTH!
RRRAAAGGH

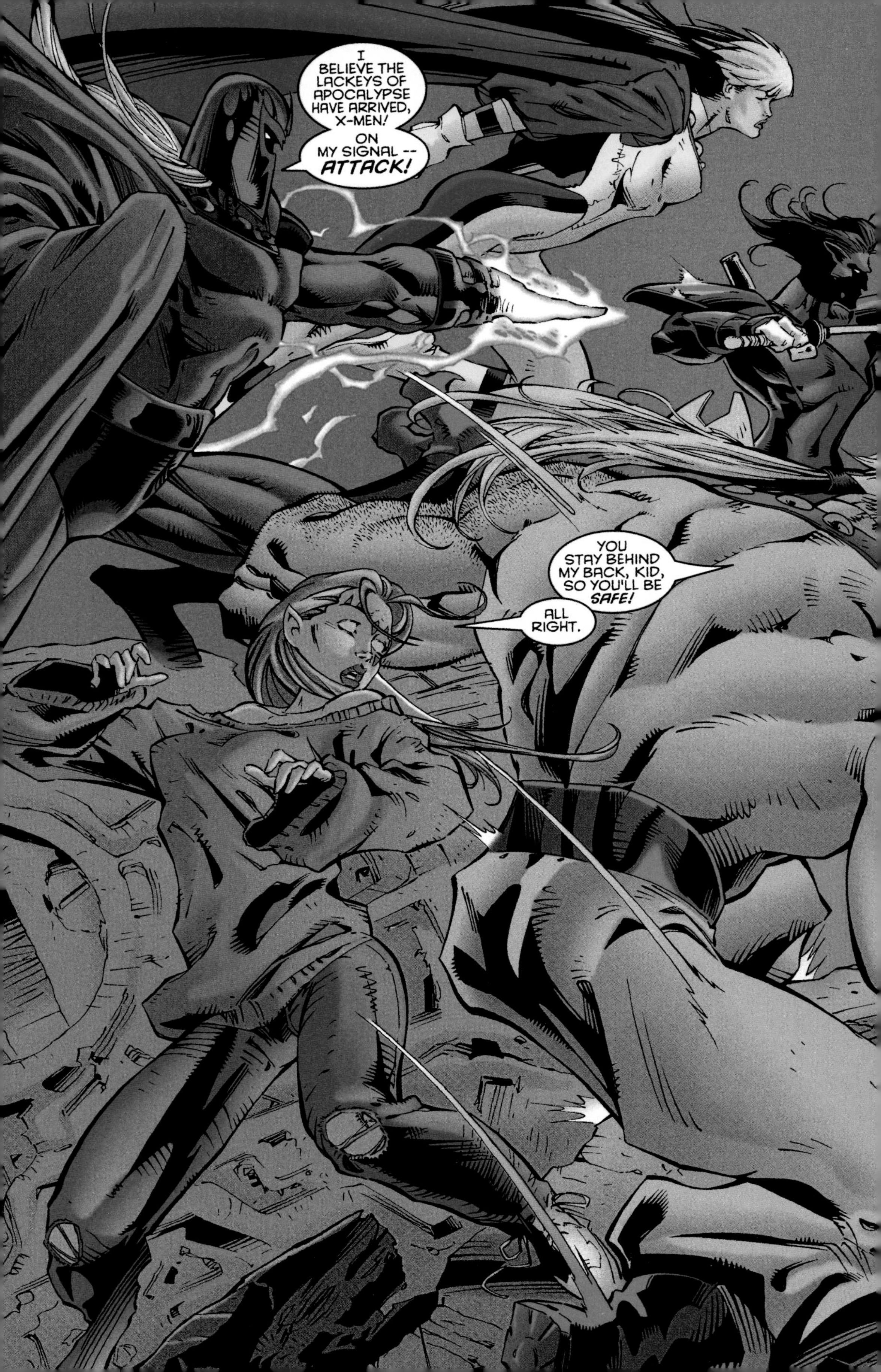
I BELIEVE THE LACKEYS OF APOCALYPSE HAVE ARRIVED, X-MEN!
ON MY SIGNAL -- ATTACK!
YOU STAY BEHIND MY BACK, KID, SO YOU'LL BE SAFE!
ALL RIGHT.

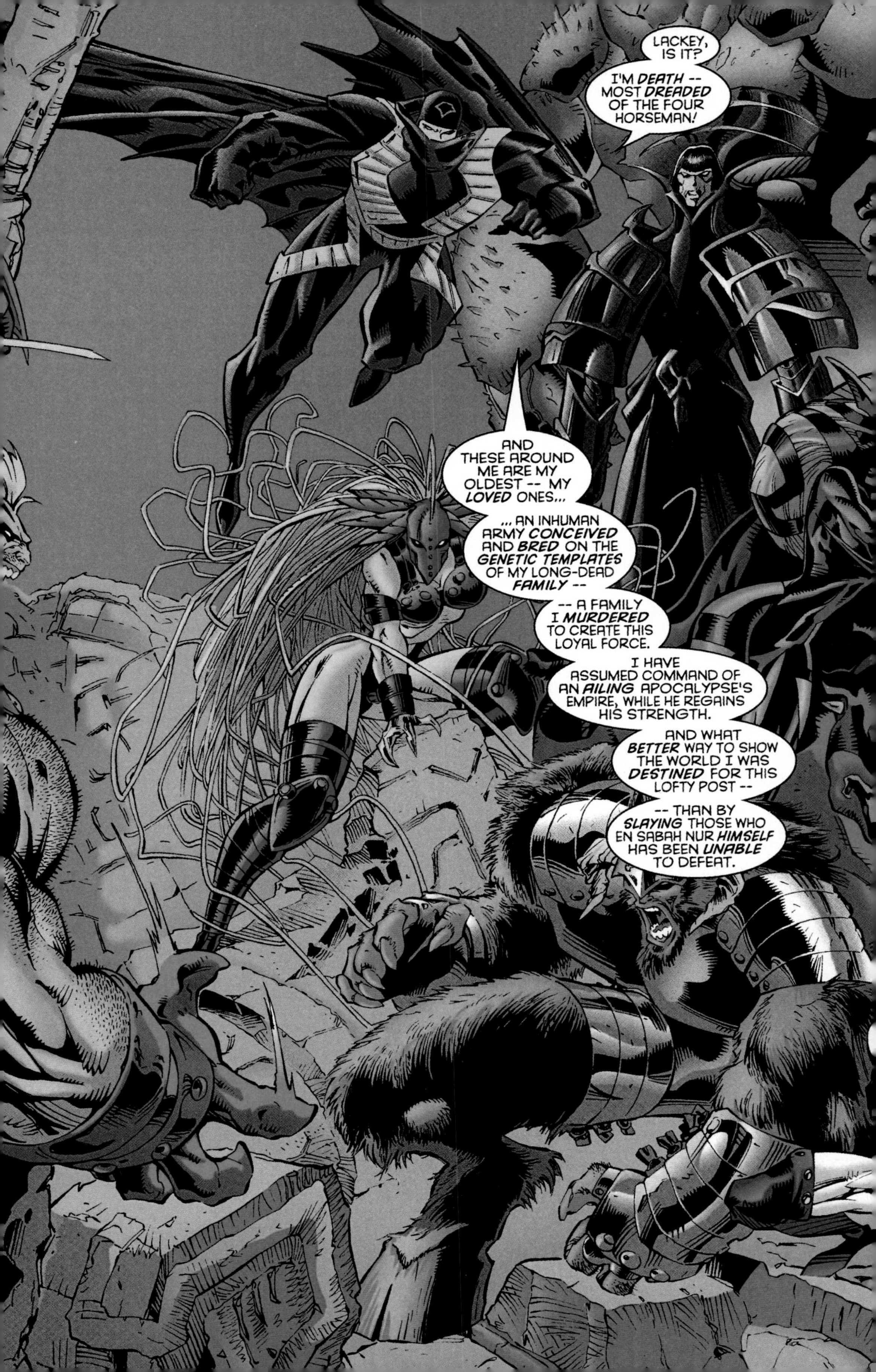
LACKEY, IS IT?
I'M DEATH -- MOST DREADED OF THE FOUR HORSEMAN!
AND THESE AROUND ME ARE MY OLDEST -- MY LOVED ONES...
... AN INHUMAN ARMY CONCEIVED AND BRED ON THE GENETIC TEMPLATES OF MY LONG-DEAD FAMILY --
-- A FAMILY I MURDERED TO CREATE THIS LOYAL FORCE.
I HAVE ASSUMED COMMAND OF AN AILING APOCALYPSE'S EMPIRE, WHILE HE REGAINS HIS STRENGTH.
AND WHAT BETTER WAY TO SHOW THE WORLD I WAS DESTINED FOR THIS LOFTY POST --
-- THAN BY SLAYING THOSE WHO EN SABAH NUR HIMSELF HAS BEEN UNABLE TO DEFEAT.

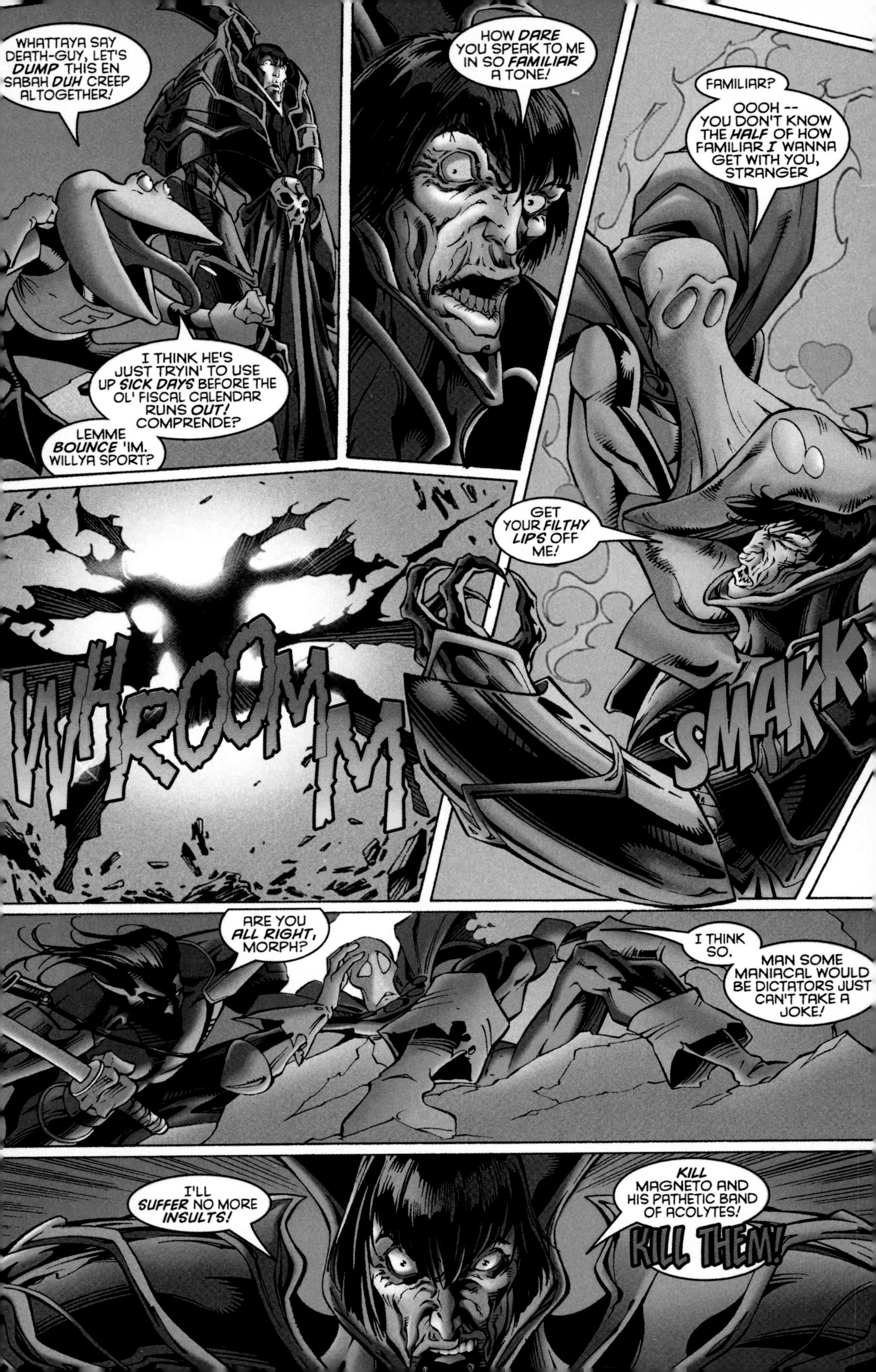
WHATTAYA SAY DEATH-GUY, LET'S DUMP THIS EN SABAH DUH CREEP ALTOGETHER!
I THINK HE'S JUST TRYIN' TO USE UP SICK DAYS BEFORE THE OL' FISCAL CALENDAR RUNS OUT! COMPRENDE?
LEMME BOUNCE 'IM. WILLYA SPORT?
HOW DARE YOU SPEAK TO ME IN SO FAMILIAR A TONE!
FAMILIAR?
OOOH -- YOU DON'T KNOW THE HALF OF HOW FAMILIAR I WANNA GET WITH YOU, STRANGER
GET YOUR FILTHY LIPS OFF ME!
WHROOMM
SMAKK
ARE YOU ALL RIGHT, MORPH?
I THINK SO.
MAN SOME MANIACAL WOULD BE DICTATORS JUST CAN'T TAKE A JOKE!
I'LL SUFFER NO MORE INSULTS!
KILL MAGNETO AND HIS PATHETIC BAND OF ACOLYTES!
KILL THEM!

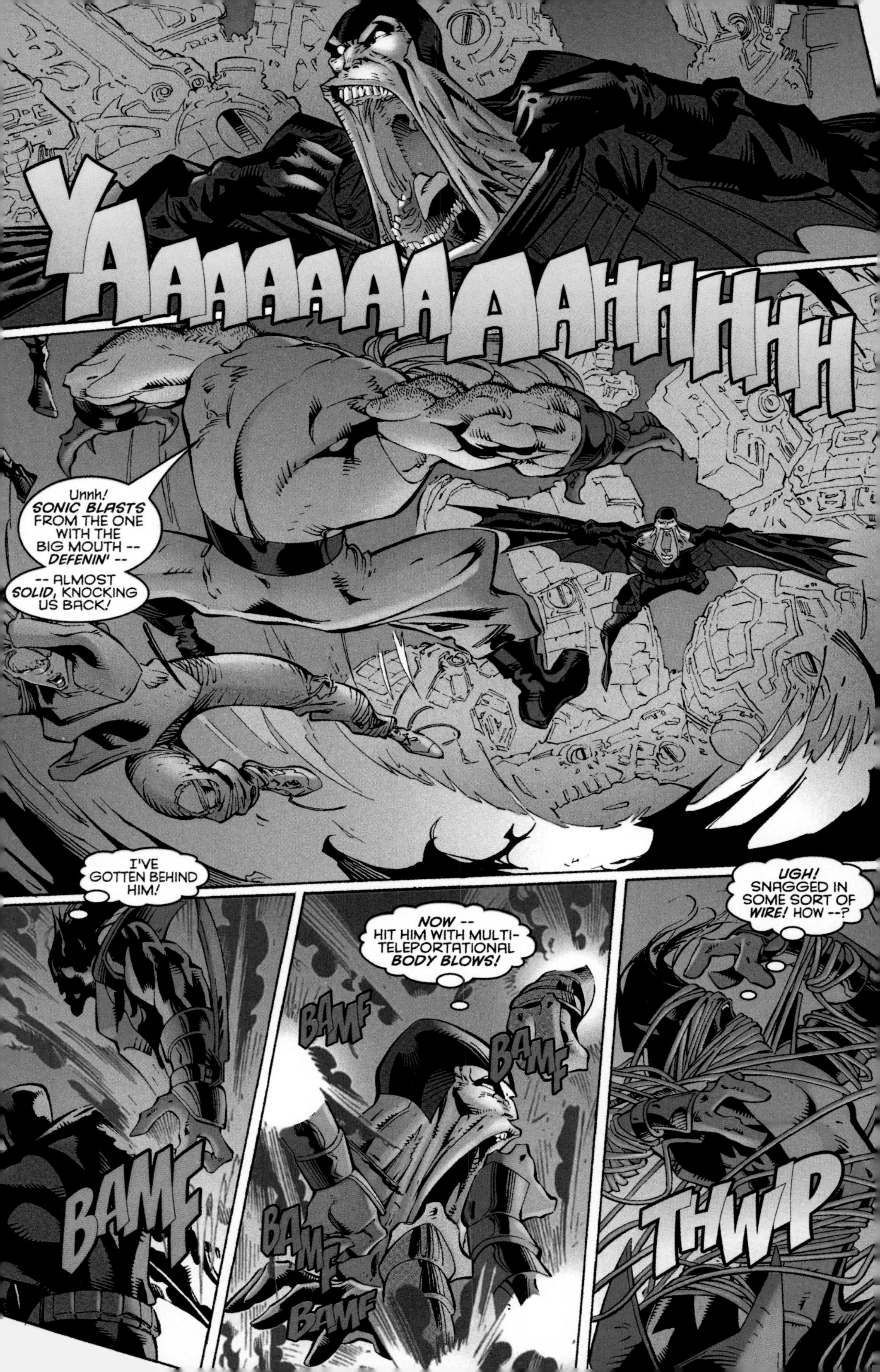
YAAAAAAAAAAHHHHHH
Unnh! SONIC BLASTS FROM THE ONE WITH THE BIG MOUTH -- DEFENIN' --
-- ALMOST SOLID, KNOCKING US BACK!
I'VE GOTTEN BEHIND HIM!
BAMF
NOW -- HIT HIM WITH MULTI-TELEPORTATIONAL BODY BLOWS!
BAMF
BAMF
BAMF
BAMF
UGH! SNAGGED IN SOME SORT OF WIRE! HOW --?
THWIP

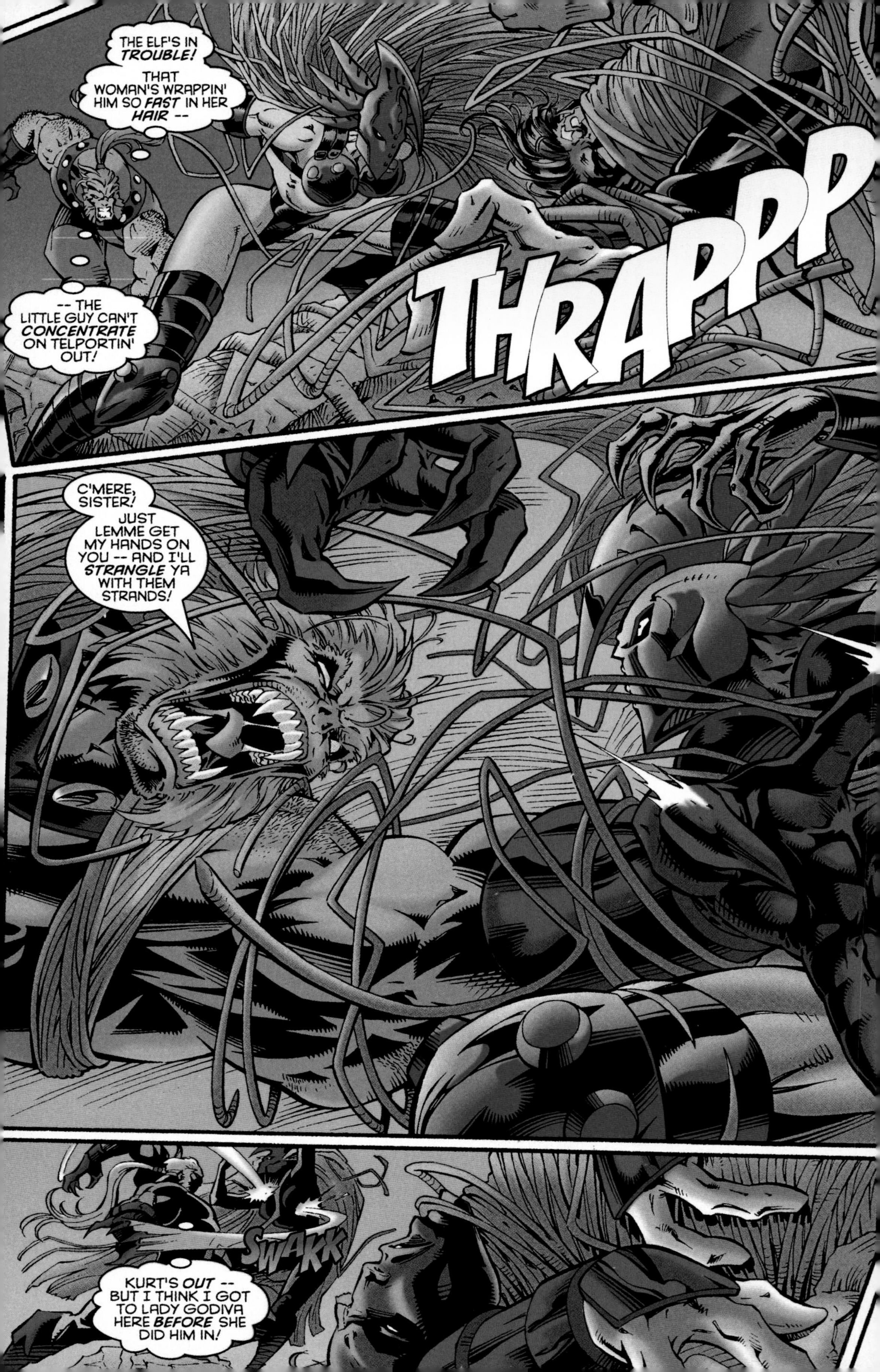
THE ELF'S IN *TROUBLE!* THAT WOMAN'S WRAPPIN' HIM SO *FAST* IN HER *HAIR* --
-- THE LITTLE GUY CAN'T *CONCENTRATE* ON TELPORTIN' OUT!
THRAPPP
C'MERE, SISTER! JUST LEMME GET MY HANDS ON YOU -- AND I'LL *STRANGLE* YA WITH THEM STRANDS!
SWAKK
KURT'S *OUT* -- BUT I THINK I GOT TO LADY GODIVA HERE *BEFORE* SHE DID HIM IN!

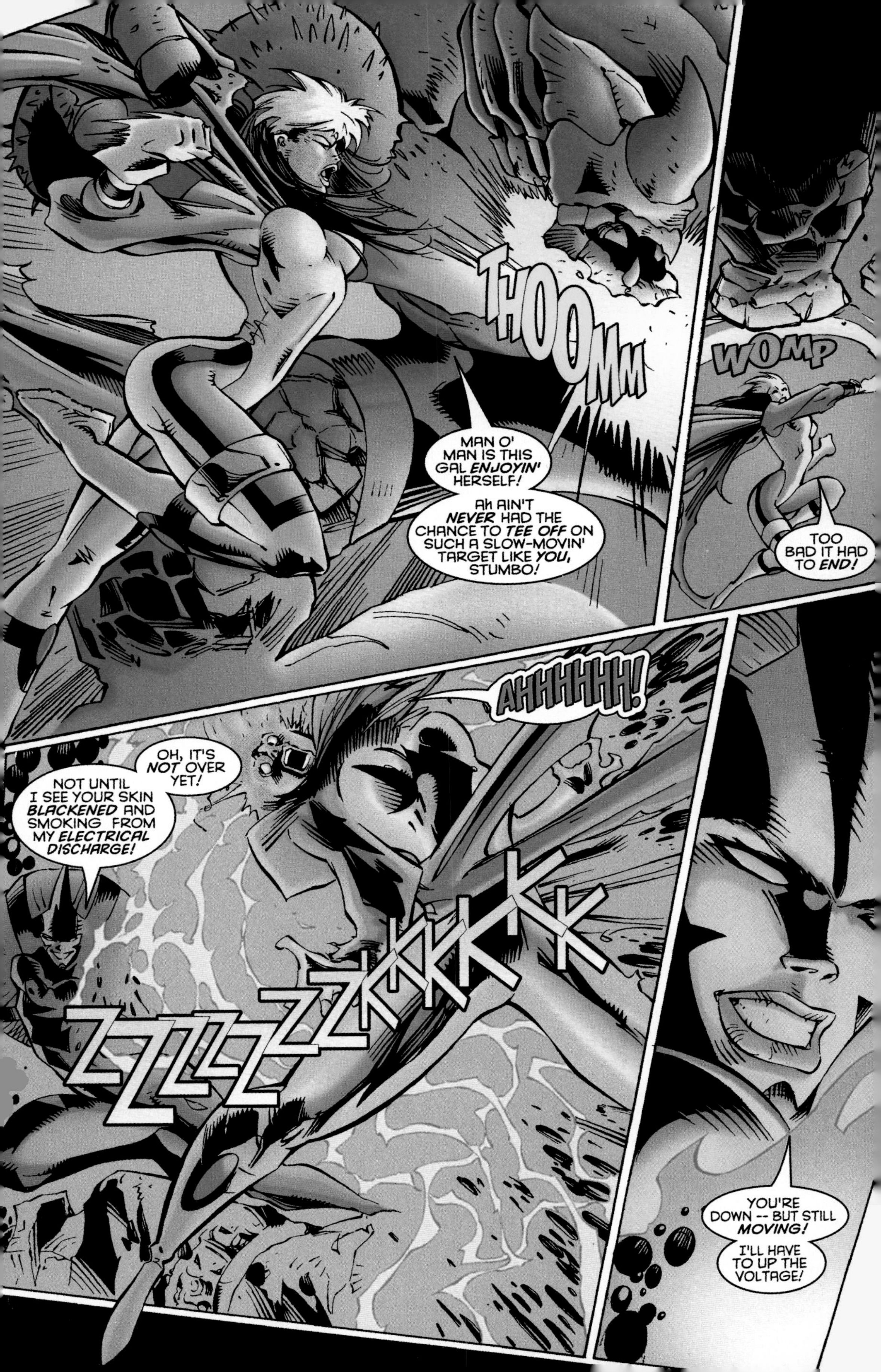
THOOMMM
MAN O' MAN IS THIS GAL ENJOYIN' HERSELF!
AH AIN'T NEVER HAD THE CHANCE TO TEE OFF ON SUCH A SLOW-MOVIN' TARGET LIKE YOU, STUMBO!
WOMP
TOO BAD IT HAD TO END!
AHHHHHH!
OH, IT'S NOT OVER YET!
NOT UNTIL I SEE YOUR SKIN BLACKENED AND SMOKING FROM MY ELECTRICAL DISCHARGE!
ZZZZZZZKKKKKKK
YOU'RE DOWN -- BUT STILL MOVING!
I'LL HAVE TO UP THE VOLTAGE!

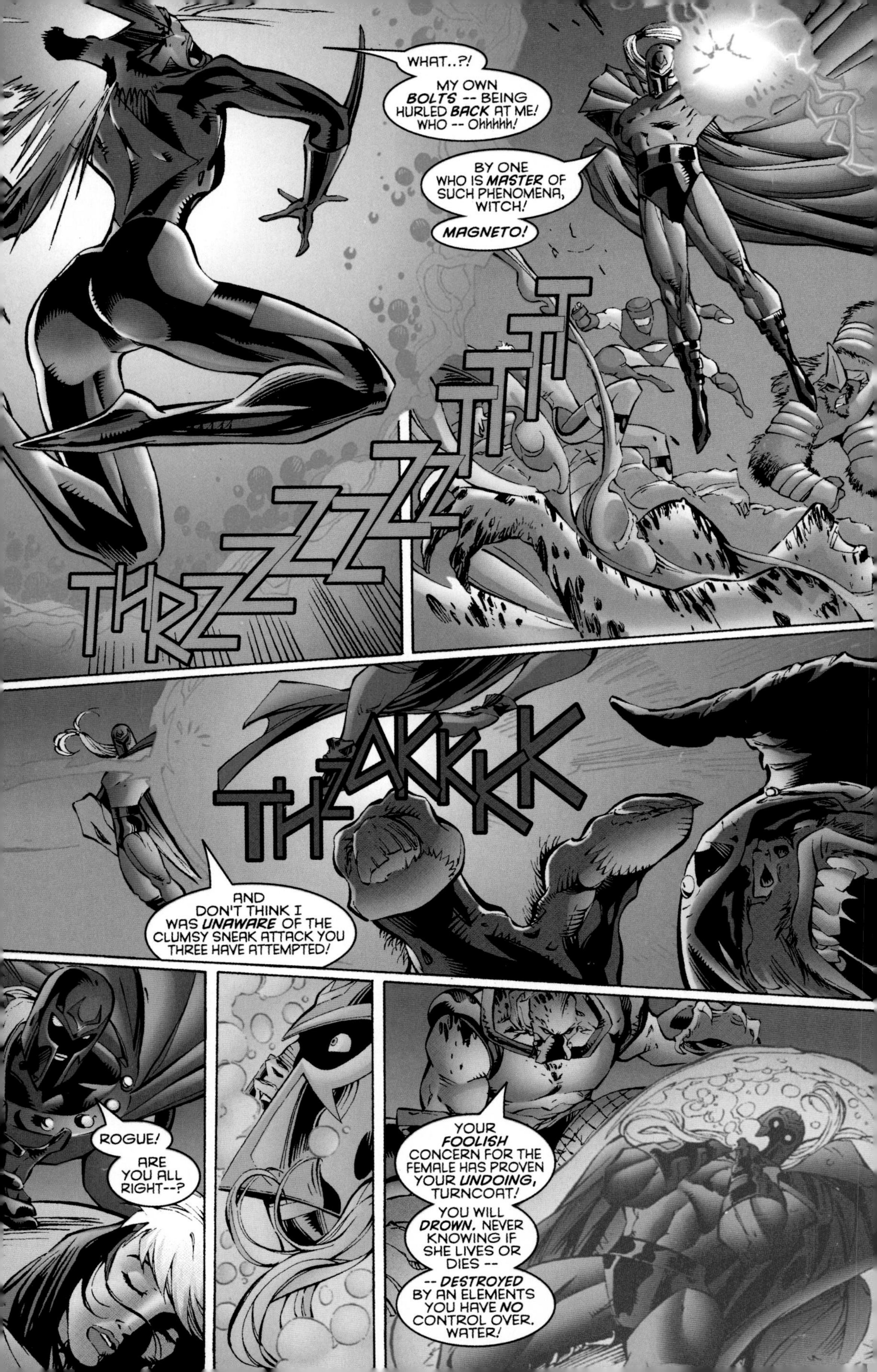
WHAT..?! MY OWN BOLTS -- BEING HURLED BACK AT ME! WHO -- Ohhhhh!
BY ONE WHO IS MASTER OF SUCH PHENOMENA, WITCH!
MAGNETO!
THRZZZZTTTTT
THZAKKKK
AND DON'T THINK I WAS UNAWARE OF THE CLUMSY SNEAK ATTACK YOU THREE HAVE ATTEMPTED!
ROGUE!
ARE YOU ALL RIGHT--?
YOUR FOOLISH CONCERN FOR THE FEMALE HAS PROVEN YOUR UNDOING, TURNCOAT!
YOU WILL DROWN, NEVER KNOWING IF SHE LIVES OR DIES --
-- DESTROYED BY AN ELEMENTS YOU HAVE NO CONTROL OVER. WATER!

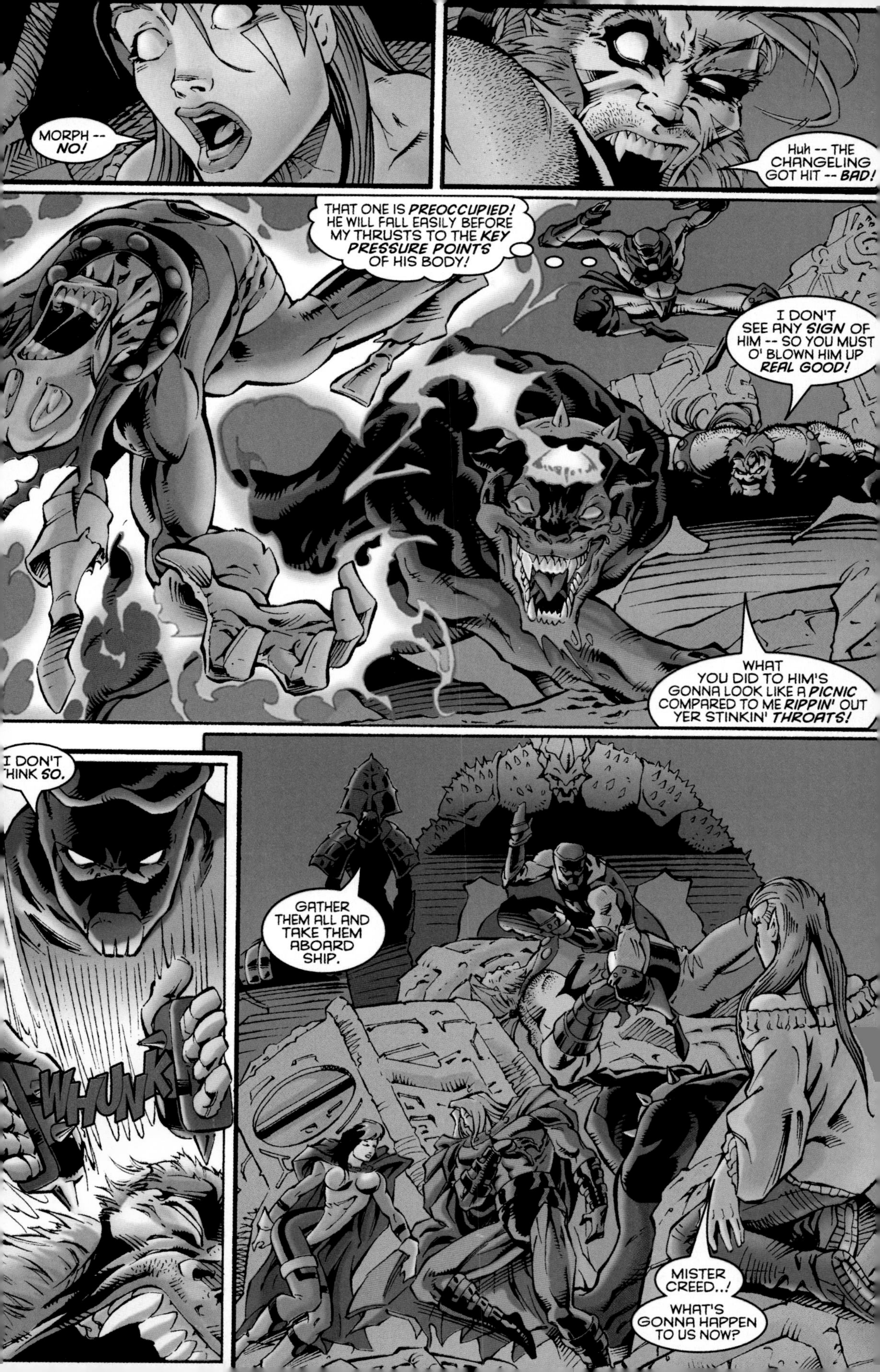
MORPH -- NO!
Huh -- THE CHANGELING GOT HIT -- BAD!
THAT ONE IS PREOCCUPIED! HE WILL FALL EASILY BEFORE MY THRUSTS TO THE KEY PRESSURE POINTS OF HIS BODY!
I DON'T SEE ANY SIGN OF HIM -- SO YOU MUST O' BLOWN HIM UP REAL GOOD!
WHAT YOU DID TO HIM'S GONNA LOOK LIKE A PICNIC COMPARED TO ME RIPPIN' OUT YER STINKIN' THROATS!
I DON'T THINK SO.
WHUNK
GATHER THEM ALL AND TAKE THEM ABOARD SHIP.
MISTER CREED..! WHAT'S GONNA HAPPEN TO US NOW?

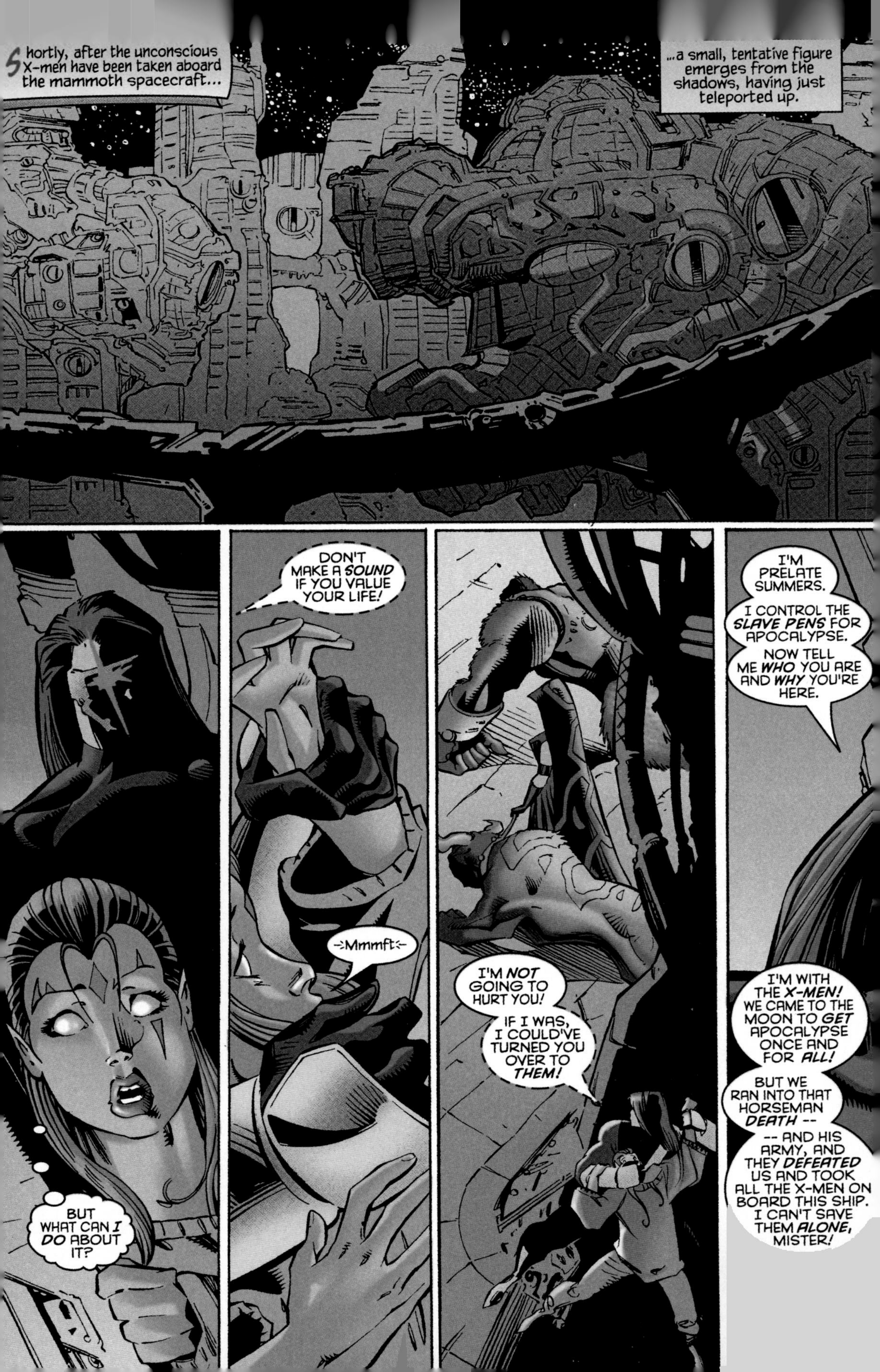
Shortly, after the unconscious X-men have been taken aboard the mammoth spacecraft...
...a small, tentative figure emerges from the shadows, having just teleported up.
BUT WHAT CAN I DO ABOUT IT?
DON'T MAKE A SOUND IF YOU VALUE YOUR LIFE!
Mmmft
I'M NOT GOING TO HURT YOU!
IF I WAS, I COULD'VE TURNED YOU OVER TO THEM!
I'M PRELATE SUMMERS.
I CONTROL THE SLAVE PENS FOR APOCALYPSE.
NOW TELL ME WHO YOU ARE AND WHY YOU'RE HERE.
I'M WITH THE X-MEN! WE CAME TO THE MOON TO GET APOCALYPSE ONCE AND FOR ALL!
BUT WE RAN INTO THAT HORSEMAN DEATH --
-- AND HIS ARMY, AND THEY DEFEATED US AND TOOK ALL THE X-MEN ON BOARD THIS SHIP. I CAN'T SAVE THEM ALONE, MISTER!

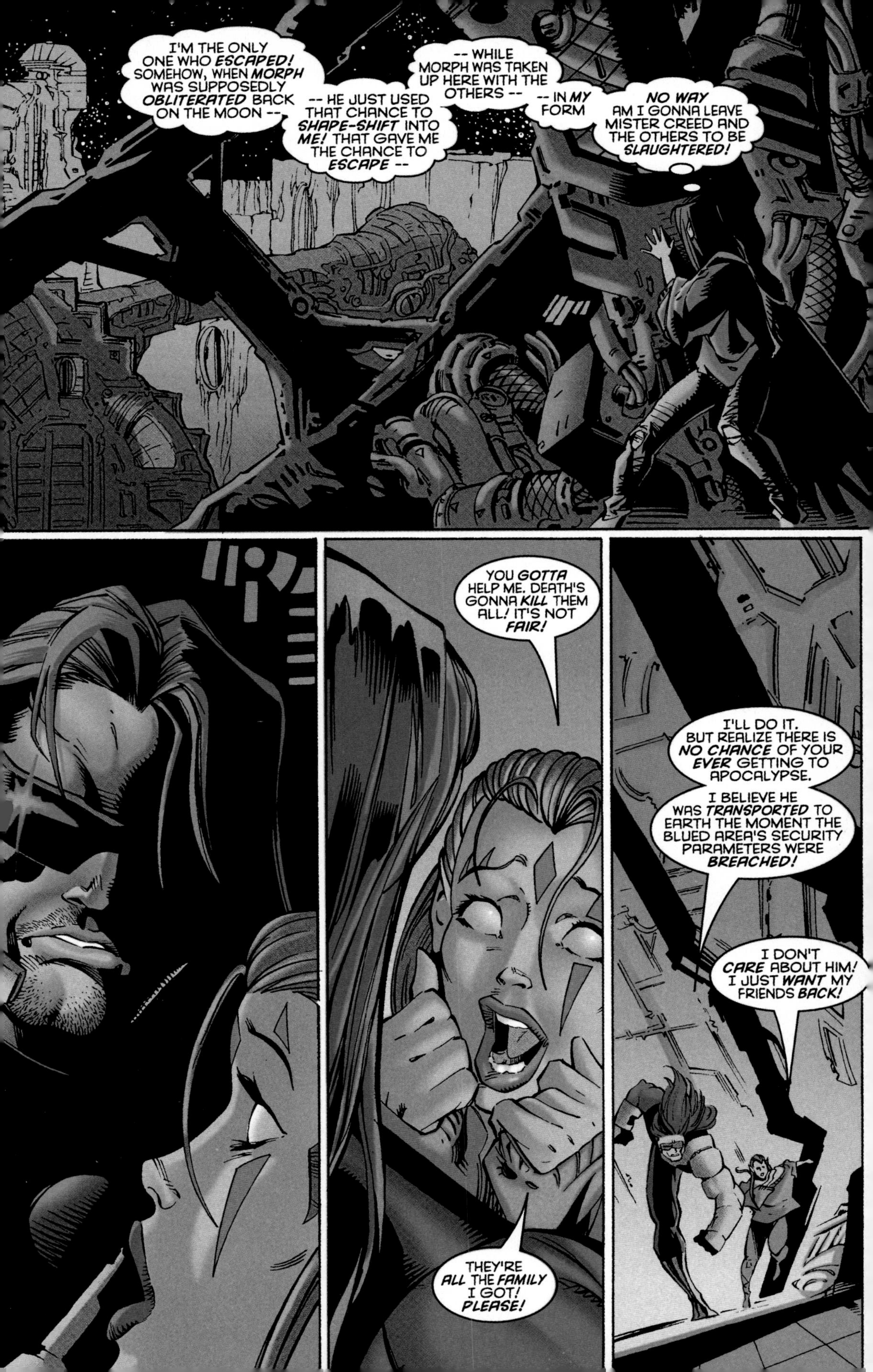
I'M THE ONLY ONE WHO ESCAPED! SOMEHOW, WHEN MORPH WAS SUPPOSEDLY OBLITERATED BACK ON THE MOON --
-- HE JUST USED THAT CHANCE TO SHAPE-SHIFT INTO ME! THAT GAVE ME THE CHANCE TO ESCAPE --
-- WHILE MORPH WAS TAKEN UP HERE WITH THE OTHERS --
-- IN MY FORM
NO WAY AM I GONNA LEAVE MISTER CREED AND THE OTHERS TO BE SLAUGHTERED!
YOU GOTTA HELP ME. DEATH'S GONNA KILL THEM ALL! IT'S NOT FAIR!
THEY'RE ALL THE FAMILY I GOT! PLEASE!
I'LL DO IT. BUT REALIZE THERE IS NO CHANCE OF YOUR EVER GETTING TO APOCALYPSE.
I BELIEVE HE WAS TRANSPORTED TO EARTH THE MOMENT THE BLUED AREA'S SECURITY PARAMETERS WERE BREACHED!
I DON'T CARE ABOUT HIM! I JUST WANT MY FRIENDS BACK!

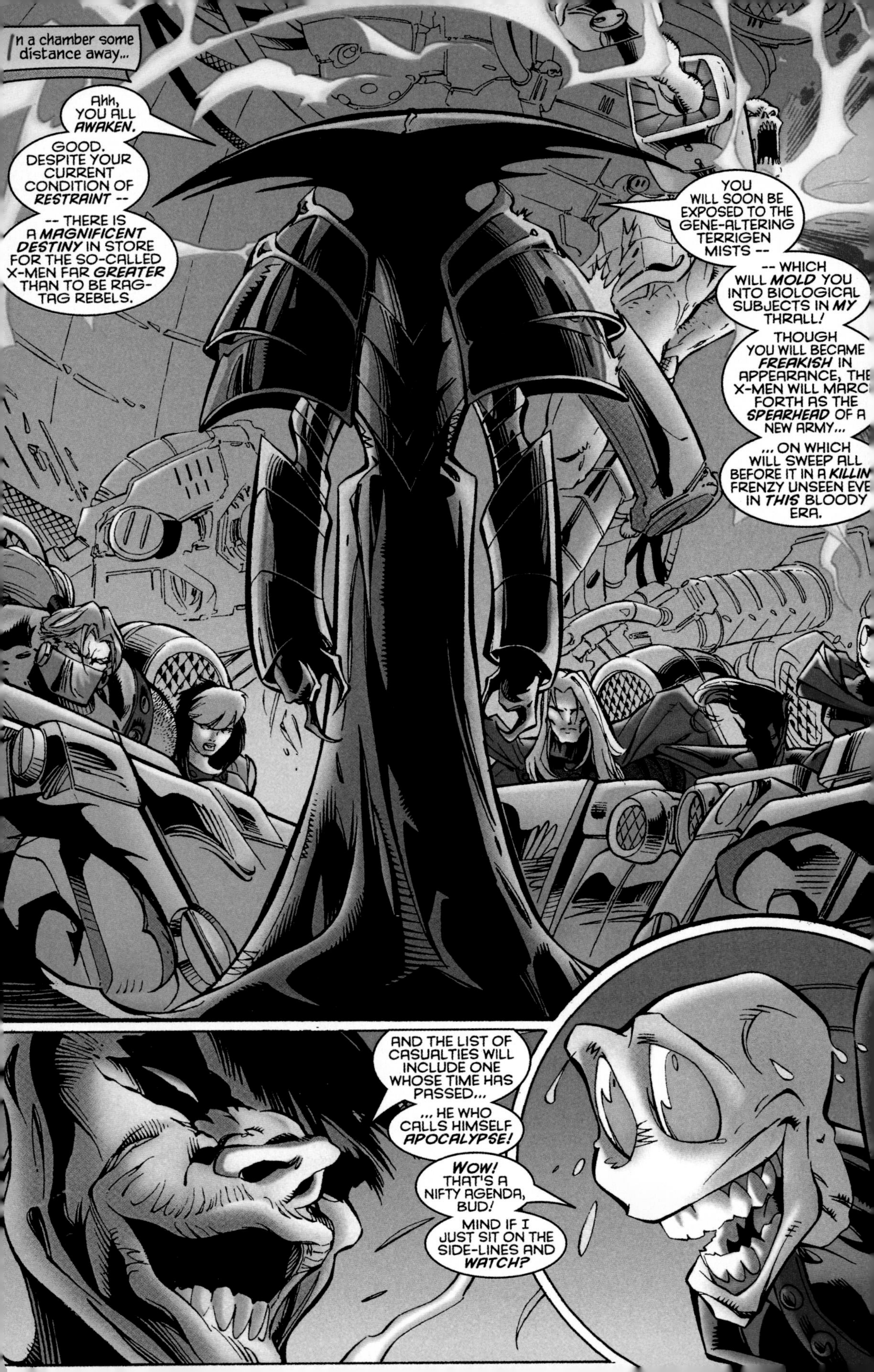
In a chamber some distance away...
Ahh, YOU ALL AWAKEN.
GOOD. DESPITE YOUR CURRENT CONDITION OF RESTRAINT --
-- THERE IS A MAGNIFICENT DESTINY IN STORE FOR THE SO-CALLED X-MEN FAR GREATER THAN TO BE RAG-TAG REBELS.
YOU WILL SOON BE EXPOSED TO THE GENE-ALTERING TERRIGEN MISTS --
-- WHICH WILL MOLD YOU INTO BIOLOGICAL SUBJECTS IN MY THRALL!
THOUGH YOU WILL BECAME FREAKISH IN APPEARANCE, THE X-MEN WILL MARCH FORTH AS THE SPEARHEAD OF A NEW ARMY...
... ON WHICH WILL SWEEP ALL BEFORE IT IN A KILLING FRENZY UNSEEN EVEN IN THIS BLOODY ERA.
AND THE LIST OF CASUALTIES WILL INCLUDE ONE WHOSE TIME HAS PASSED...
... HE WHO CALLS HIMSELF APOCALYPSE!
WOW! THAT'S A NIFTY AGENDA, BUD!
MIND IF I JUST SIT ON THE SIDE-LINES AND WATCH?

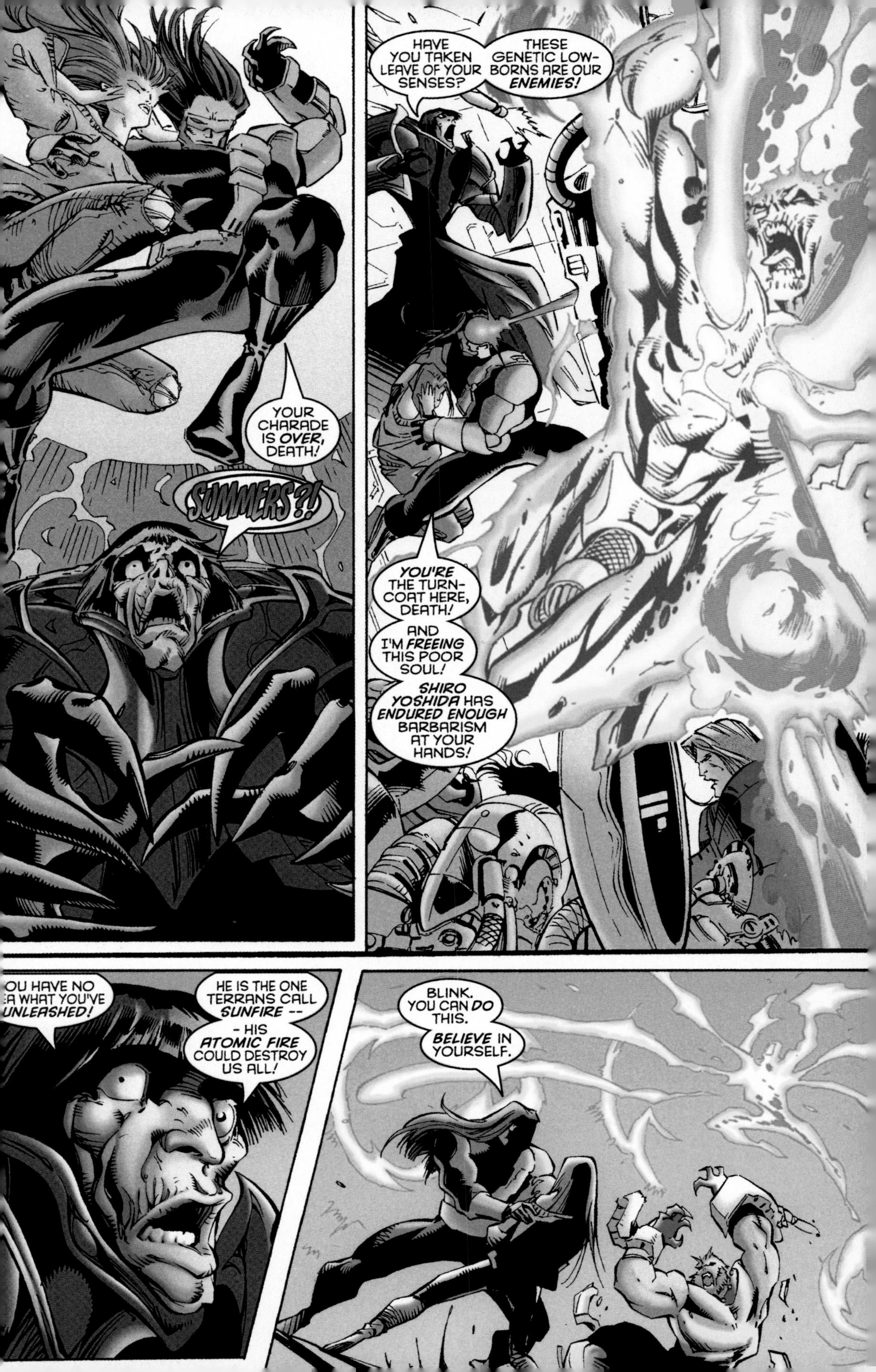
YOUR CHARADE IS *OVER*, DEATH!
SUMMERS?!
HAVE YOU TAKEN LEAVE OF YOUR SENSES?
THESE GENETIC LOW-BORNS ARE OUR *ENEMIES!*
YOU'RE THE TURN-COAT HERE, DEATH!
AND I'M *FREEING* THIS POOR SOUL!
SHIRO YOSHIDA HAS *ENDURED ENOUGH* BARBARISM AT YOUR HANDS!
OU HAVE NO EA WHAT YOU'VE *UNLEASHED!*
HE IS THE ONE TERRANS CALL *SUNFIRE* --
- HIS *ATOMIC FIRE* COULD DESTROY US ALL!
BLINK. YOU CAN *DO* THIS.
BELIEVE IN YOURSELF.

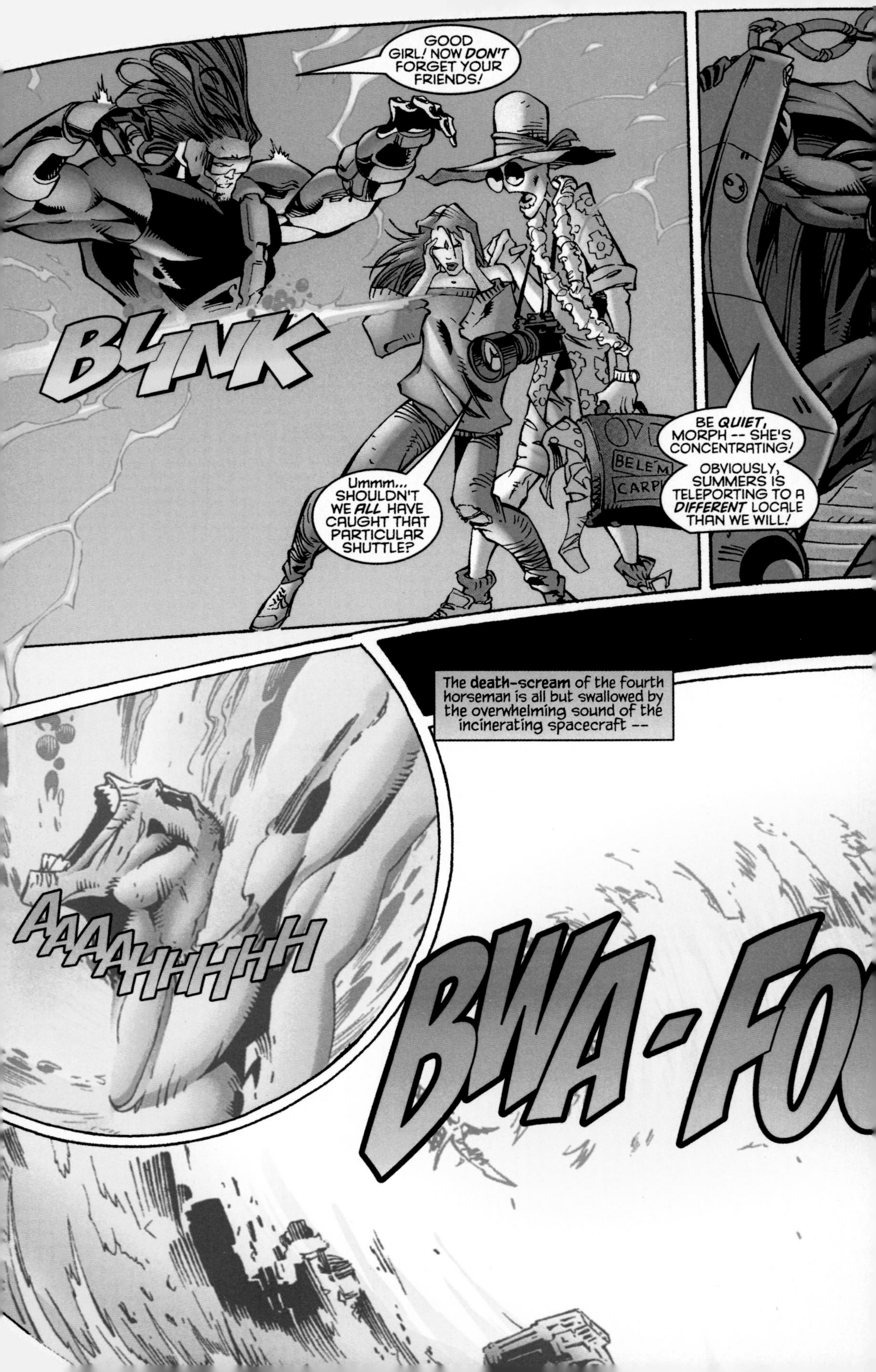
GOOD GIRL! NOW DON'T FORGET YOUR FRIENDS!
BLINK
Ummm... SHOULDN'T WE ALL HAVE CAUGHT THAT PARTICULAR SHUTTLE?
BE QUIET, MORPH -- SHE'S CONCENTRATING!
OBVIOUSLY, SUMMERS IS TELEPORTING TO A DIFFERENT LOCALE THAN WE WILL!
BELE'M
CARP
The death-scream of the fourth horseman is all but swallowed by the overwhelming sound of the incinerating spacecraft --
AAAAHHHHHH
BWA-FOO

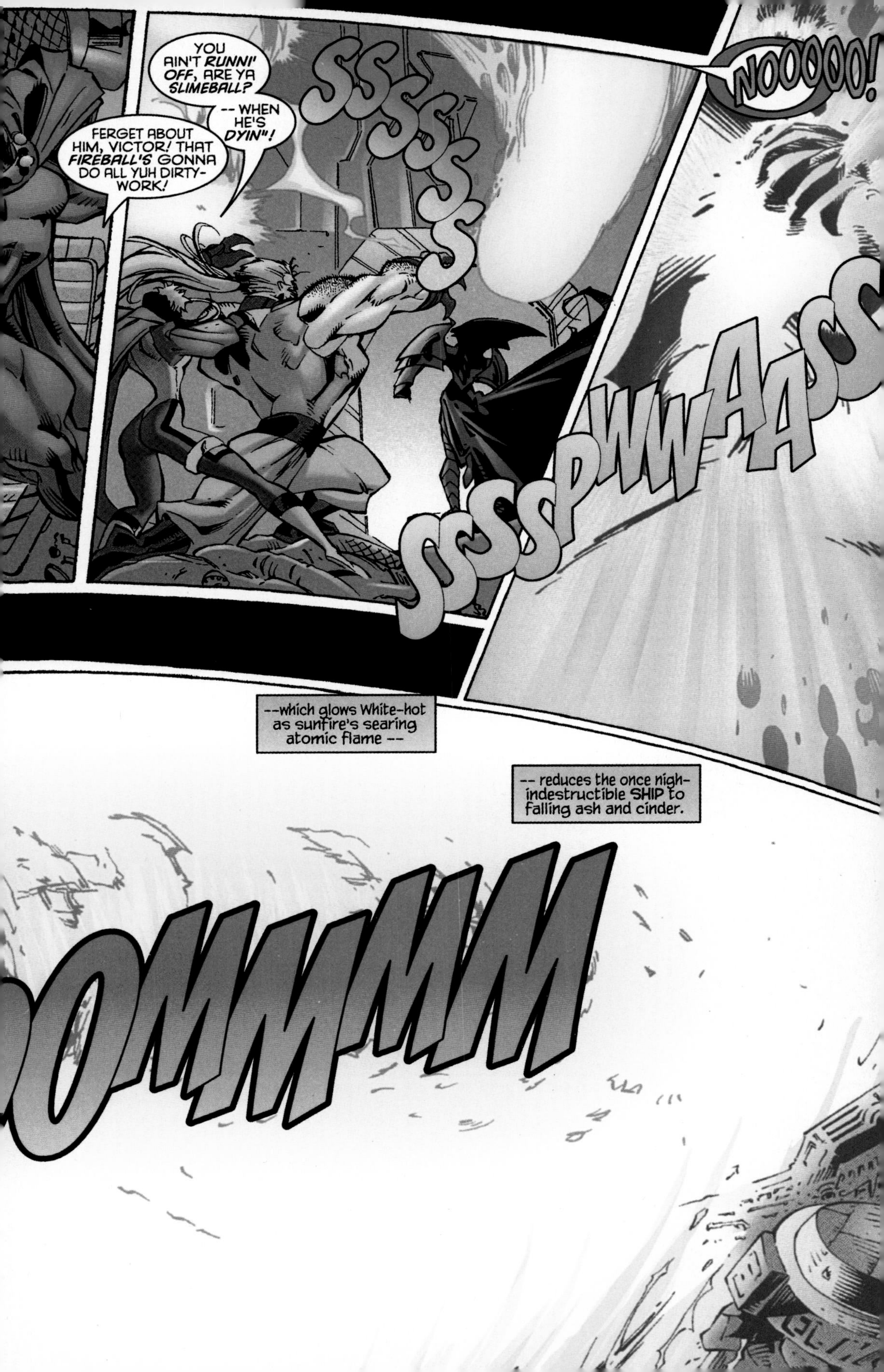
YOU AIN'T RUNNI' OFF, ARE YA SLIMEBALL?
-- WHEN HE'S DYIN'!
FERGET ABOUT HIM, VICTOR! THAT FIREBALL'S GONNA DO ALL YUH DIRTY-WORK!
SSSSSSS
NOOOOO!
SSSSPWWAASS
--which glows white-hot as sunfire's searing atomic flame --
-- reduces the once nigh-indestructible SHIP to falling ash and cinder.
OMMMMM

The Earth...

BLINK

SUNFIRE IS SPENT-- -- BUT STILL LIVES.

GOOD. I GOT A HUNCH HE'S GONNA COME IN HANDY FER OUR SIDE IN THE FUTURE.

DID I HELP ENOUGH, MISTER CREED?

KID, YOU'RE THE BEST.

THANKS.

OHH-- YOU ARE ONE HOT TAMALE!

YOU ASKED ME IF I STILL HAVE FAITH, ROGUE.

I DO.

THE WAR STILL RAGES, THOUGH.

ERIK, ONE THING STILL BOTHERS ME. WHY DID SUMMERS HELP US?

WAS IT OUT OF LOYALTY TO APOCALYPSE... ...OR SOMETHING MORE?

ONLY TIME WILL TELL.

BUT I SENSE A INNER STRENGT A NOBILITY IN T MAN CALLED CYCLOPS.

PERHAPS, WHEN THE DAY OF OUR FINAL BATTLE WITH APOCALYPSE ARRIVES...

...WE WILL BE AB TO CALL H ALLY.

AND WOULD THAT NOT BE THE GREATEST TRIBUTE TO CHARLES XAVIER?

THAT DESPITE OUR DIFFERENCES--

-- AND VARYING BACK- GROUNDS--

-- IN TIMES OF NEED, SOMETHING COMMON TO ALL HUMAN SOULS WILL BIND US TOGETHER.

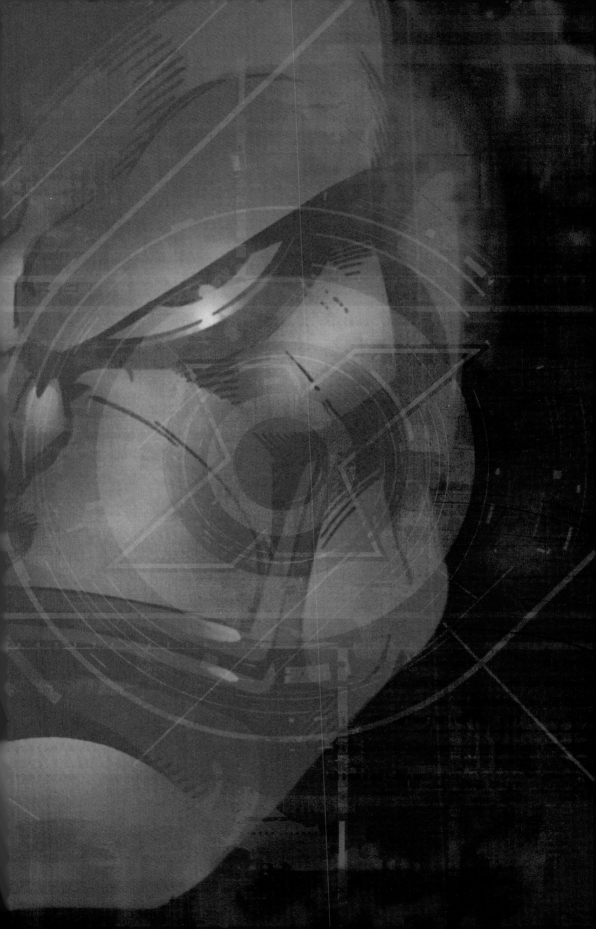

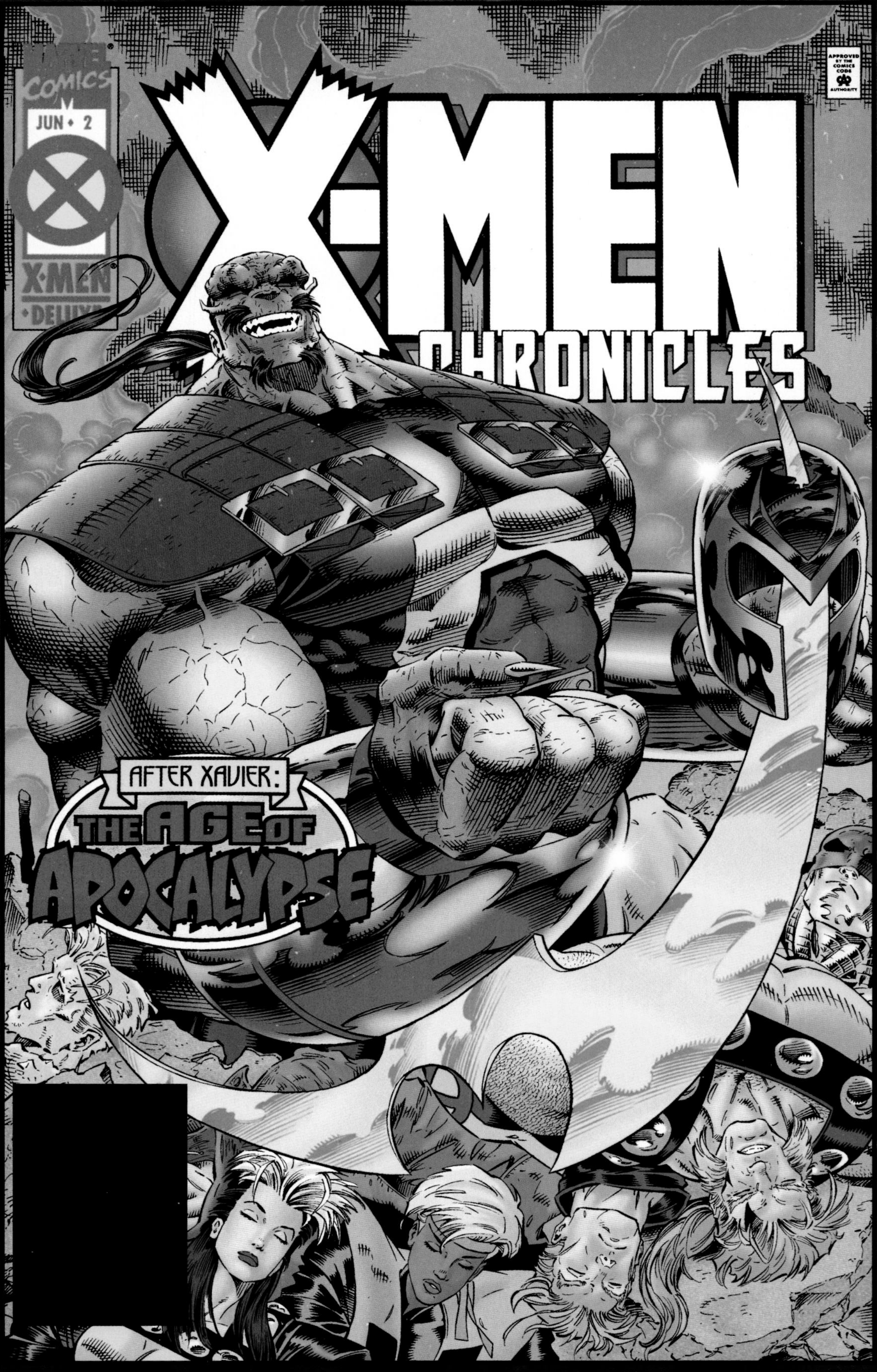
MARVEL COMICS
JUN • 2
X-MEN
DELUXE
APPROVED BY THE COMICS CODE AUTHORITY
X-MEN
CHRONICLES
AFTER XAVIER:
THE AGE OF APOCALYPSE

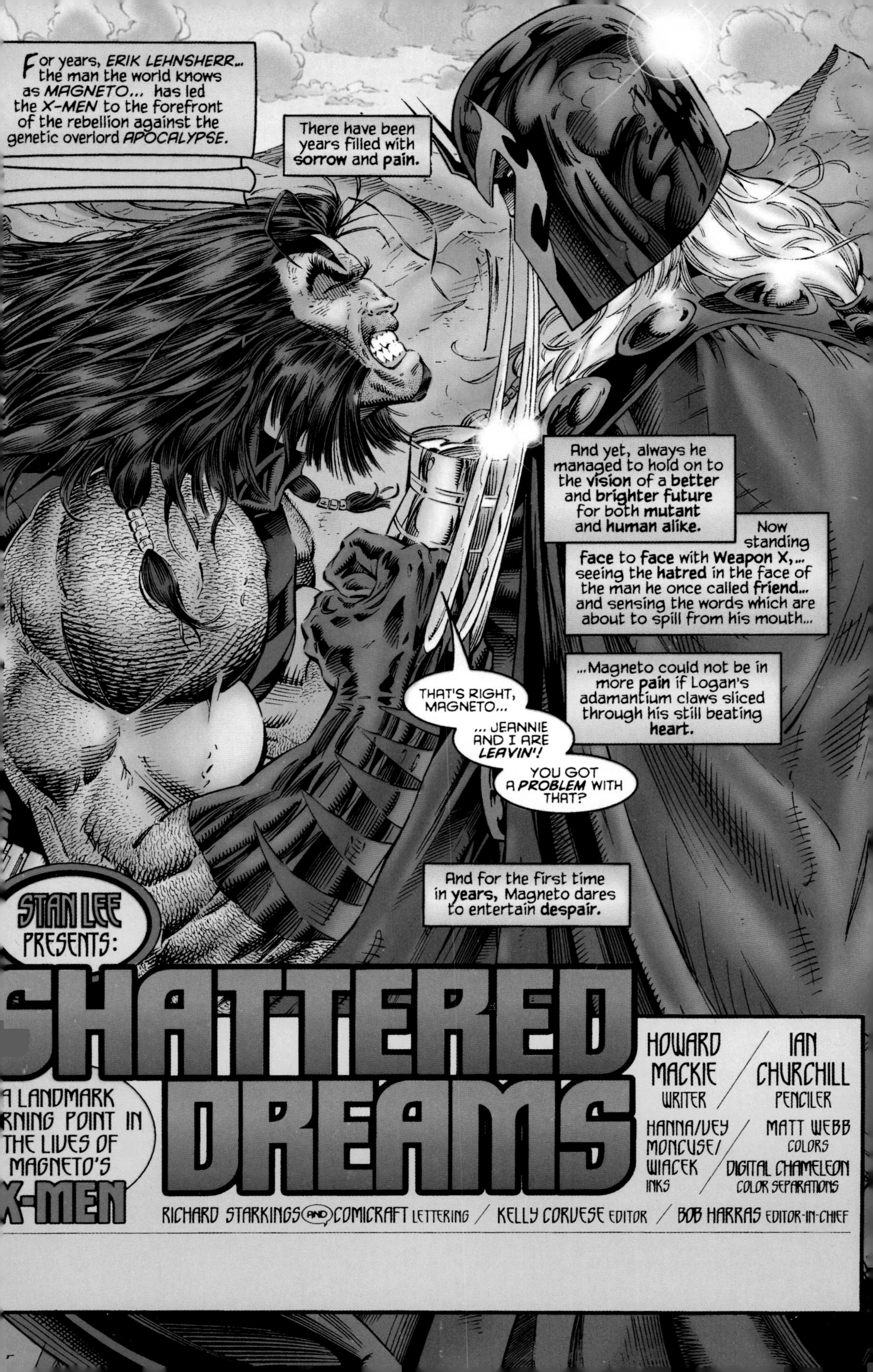
For years, ERIK LEHNSHERR... the man the world knows as MAGNETO... has led the X-MEN to the forefront of the rebellion against the genetic overlord APOCALYPSE.
There have been years filled with sorrow and pain.
And yet, always he managed to hold on to the vision of a better and brighter future for both mutant and human alike.
Now standing face to face with Weapon X,... seeing the hatred in the face of the man he once called friend... and sensing the words which are about to spill from his mouth...
...Magneto could not be in more pain if Logan's adamantium claws sliced through his still beating heart.
THAT'S RIGHT, MAGNETO...
... JEANNIE AND I ARE LEAVIN'!
YOU GOT A PROBLEM WITH THAT?
And for the first time in years, Magneto dares to entertain despair.
STAN LEE PRESENTS:
SHATTERED DREAMS
A LANDMARK RNING POINT IN THE LIVES OF MAGNETO'S X-MEN
HOWARD MACKIE WRITER / IAN CHURCHILL PENCILER
HANNA/VEY MONCUSE/ WIACEK INKS / MATT WEBB COLORS
DIGITAL CHAMELEON COLOR SEPARATIONS
RICHARD STARKINGS AND COMICRAFT LETTERING / KELLY CORVESE EDITOR / BOB HARRAS EDITOR-IN-CHIEF

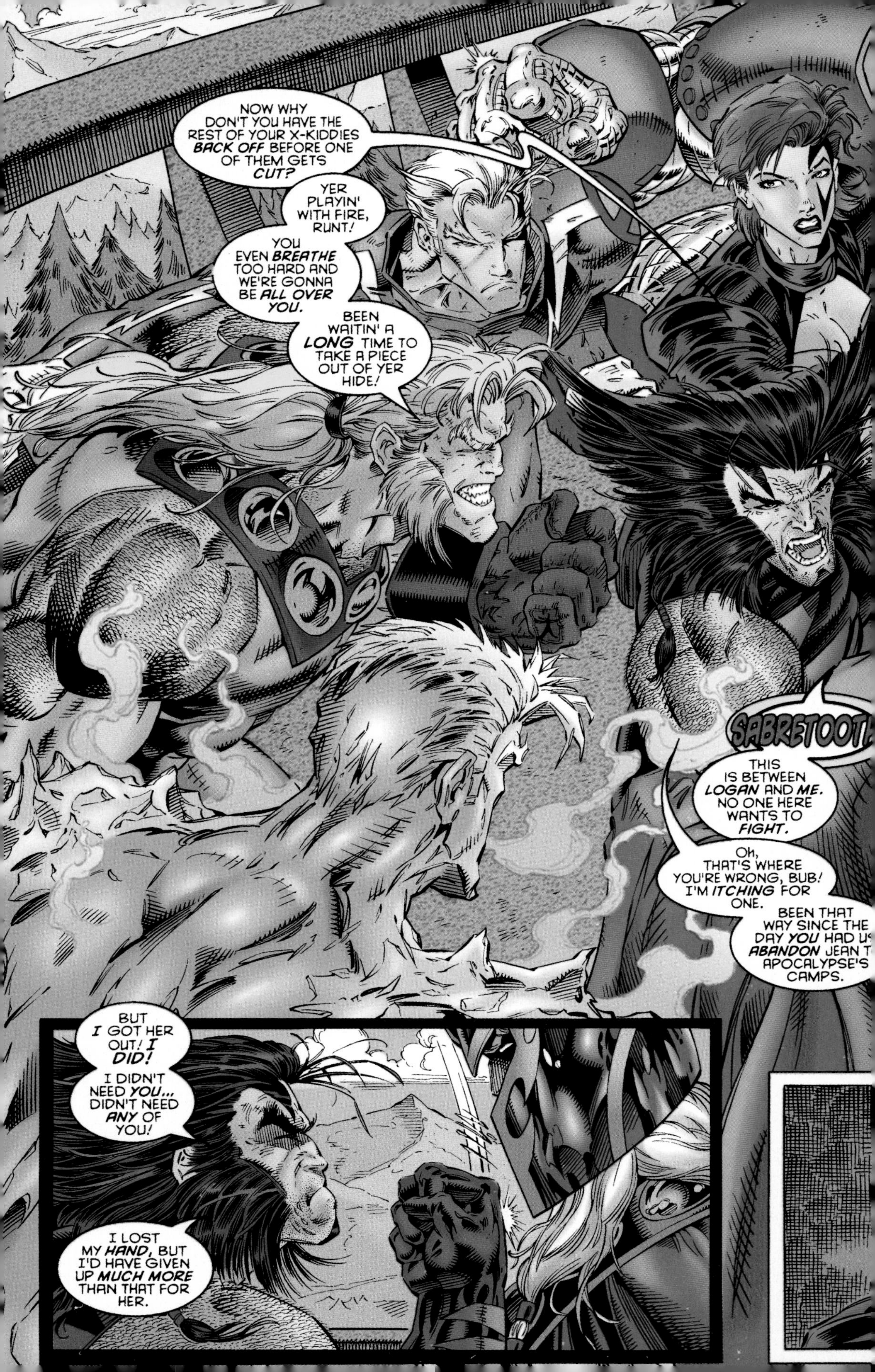
NOW WHY DON'T YOU HAVE THE REST OF YOUR X-KIDDIES BACK OFF BEFORE ONE OF THEM GETS CUT?
YER PLAYIN' WITH FIRE, RUNT!
YOU EVEN BREATHE TOO HARD AND WE'RE GONNA BE ALL OVER YOU.
BEEN WAITIN' A LONG TIME TO TAKE A PIECE OUT OF YER HIDE!
SABRETOOTH
THIS IS BETWEEN LOGAN AND ME. NO ONE HERE WANTS TO FIGHT.
Oh, THAT'S WHERE YOU'RE WRONG, BUB! I'M ITCHING FOR ONE.
BEEN THAT WAY SINCE THE DAY YOU HAD US ABANDON JEAN T APOCALYPSE'S CAMPS.
BUT I GOT HER OUT! I DID!
I DIDN'T NEED YOU... DIDN'T NEED ANY OF YOU!
I LOST MY HAND, BUT I'D HAVE GIVEN UP MUCH MORE THAN THAT FOR HER.

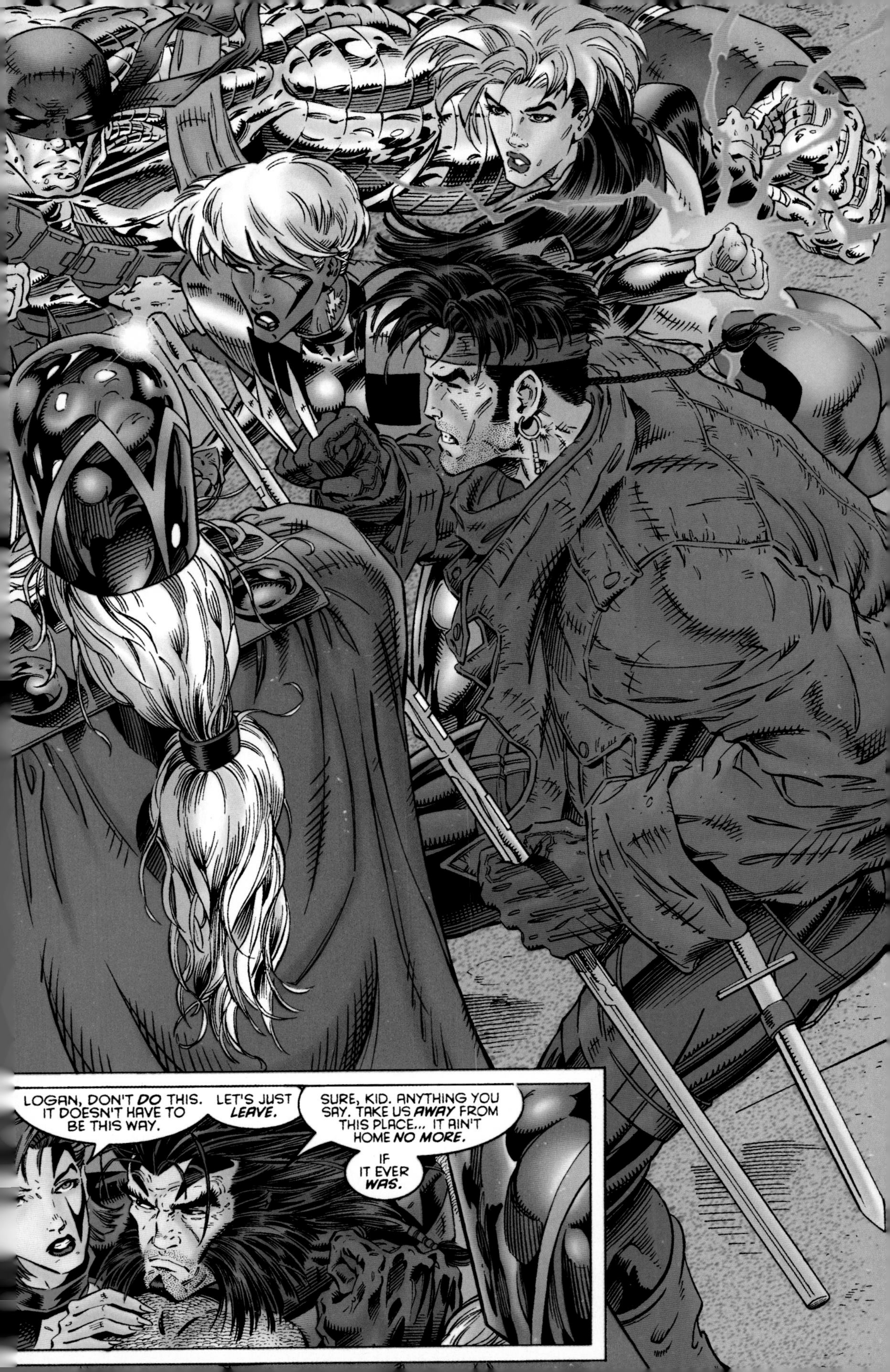
LOGAN, DON'T DO THIS. IT DOESN'T HAVE TO BE THIS WAY.
LET'S JUST LEAVE.
SURE, KID. ANYTHING YOU SAY. TAKE US AWAY FROM THIS PLACE... IT AIN'T HOME NO MORE.
IF IT EVER WAS.

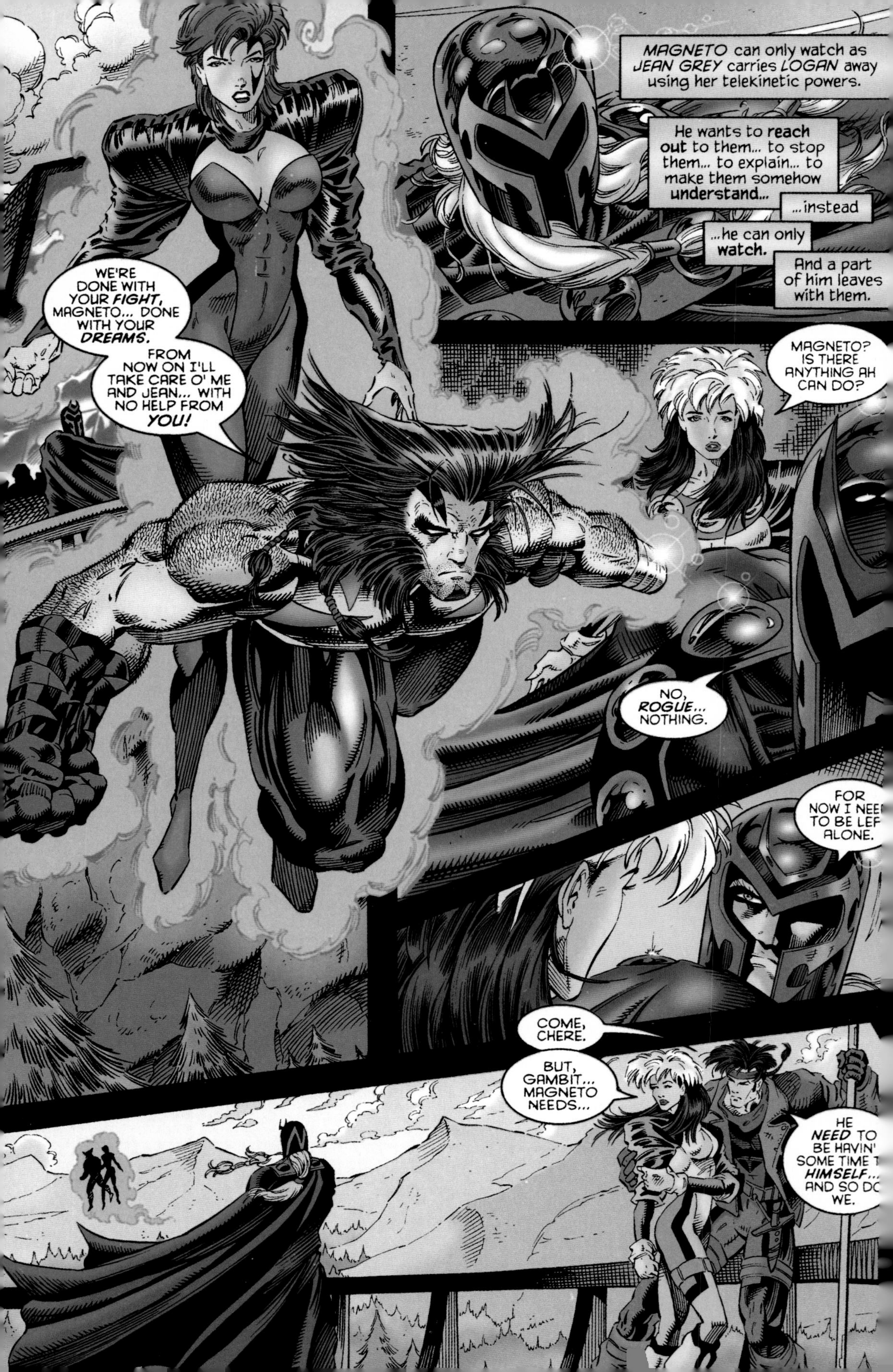
MAGNETO can only watch as JEAN GREY carries LOGAN away using her telekinetic powers.
He wants to reach out to them... to stop them... to explain... to make them somehow understand...
...instead
...he can only watch.
And a part of him leaves with them.
WE'RE DONE WITH YOUR FIGHT, MAGNETO... DONE WITH YOUR DREAMS.
FROM NOW ON I'LL TAKE CARE O' ME AND JEAN... WITH NO HELP FROM YOU!
MAGNETO? IS THERE ANYTHING AH CAN DO?
NO, ROGUE... NOTHING.
FOR NOW I NEE TO BE LEF ALONE.
COME, CHERE.
BUT, GAMBIT... MAGNETO NEEDS...
HE NEED TO BE HAVIN' SOME TIME T HIMSELF... AND SO DO WE.

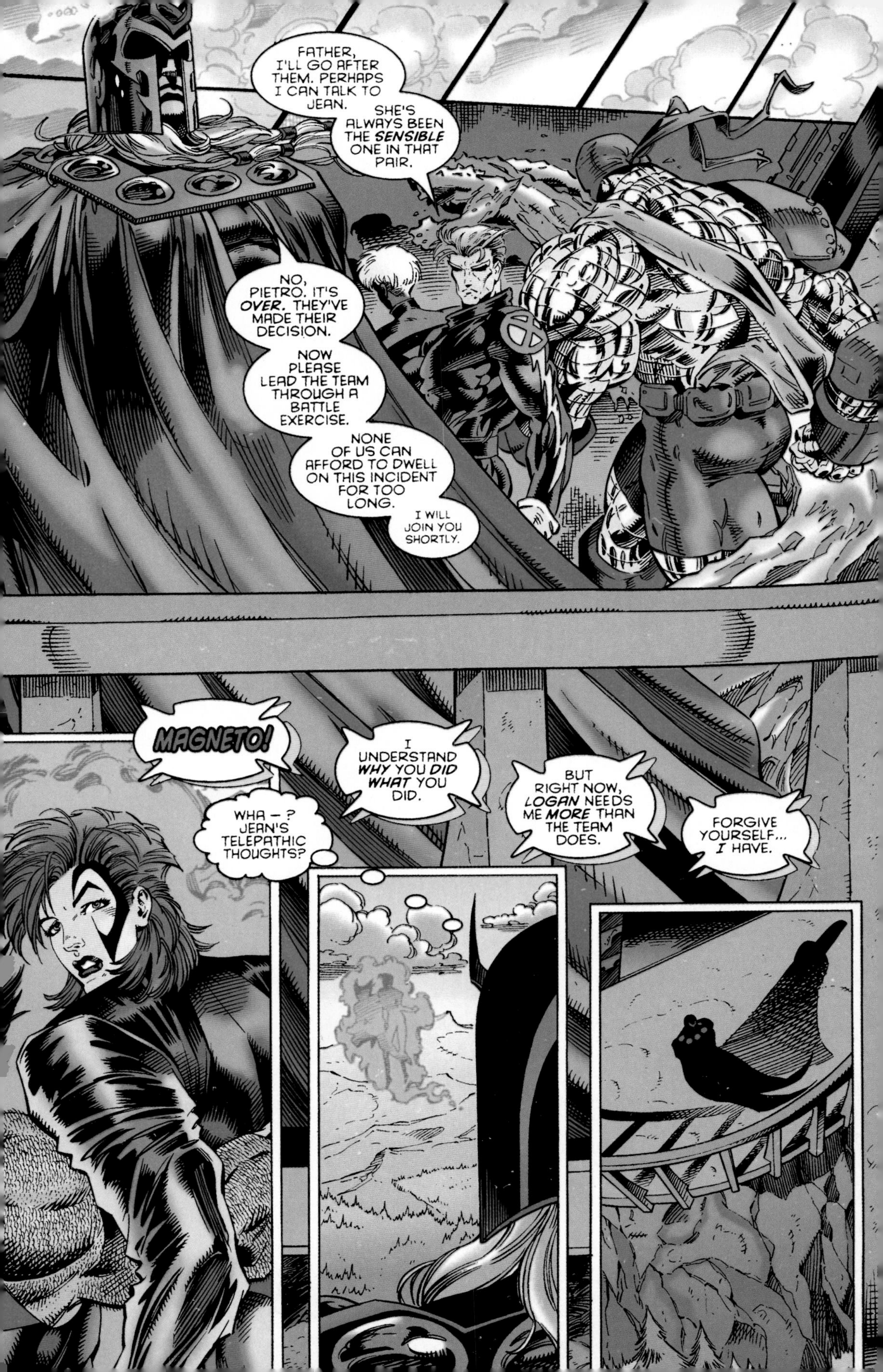
FATHER, I'LL GO AFTER THEM. PERHAPS I CAN TALK TO JEAN.
SHE'S ALWAYS BEEN THE *SENSIBLE* ONE IN THAT PAIR.
NO, PIETRO. IT'S *OVER.* THEY'VE MADE THEIR DECISION.
NOW PLEASE LEAD THE TEAM THROUGH A BATTLE EXERCISE.
NONE OF US CAN AFFORD TO DWELL ON THIS INCIDENT FOR TOO LONG.
I WILL JOIN YOU SHORTLY.
MAGNETO!
WHA -- ? JEAN'S TELEPATHIC THOUGHTS?
I UNDERSTAND *WHY* YOU *DID WHAT* YOU DID.
BUT RIGHT NOW, *LOGAN* NEEDS ME *MORE* THAN THE TEAM DOES.
FORGIVE YOURSELF... *I* HAVE.

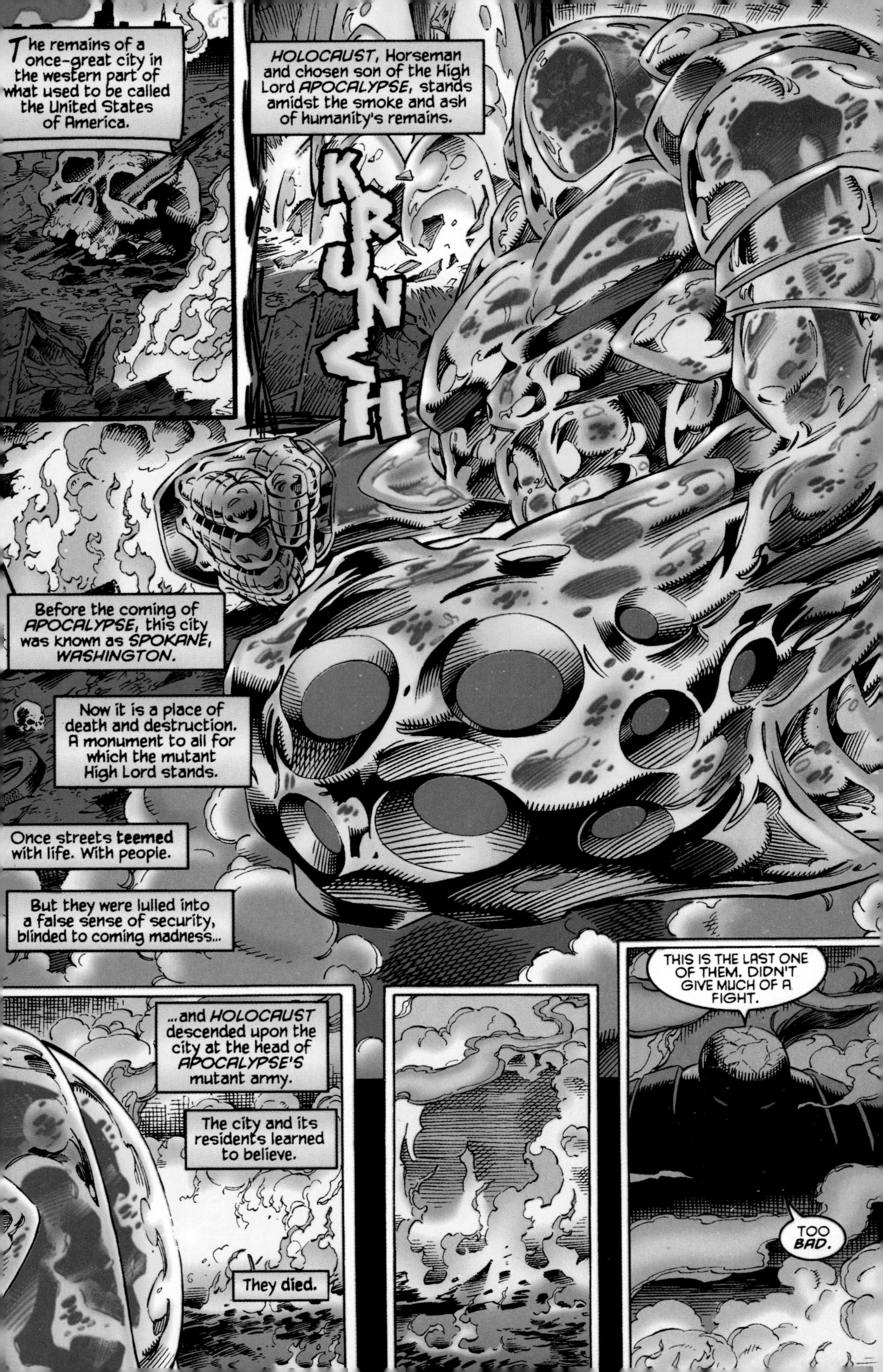

The remains of a once-great city in the western part of what used to be called the United States of America.
HOLOCAUST, Horseman and chosen son of the High Lord APOCALYPSE, stands amidst the smoke and ash of humanity's remains.
KRUNCH
Before the coming of APOCALYPSE, this city was known as SPOKANE, WASHINGTON.
Now it is a place of death and destruction. A monument to all for which the mutant High Lord stands.
Once streets teemed with life. With people.
But they were lulled into a false sense of security, blinded to coming madness...
...and HOLOCAUST descended upon the city at the head of APOCALYPSE'S mutant army.
The city and its residents learned to believe.
They died.
THIS IS THE LAST ONE OF THEM. DIDN'T GIVE MUCH OF A FIGHT.
TOO BAD.

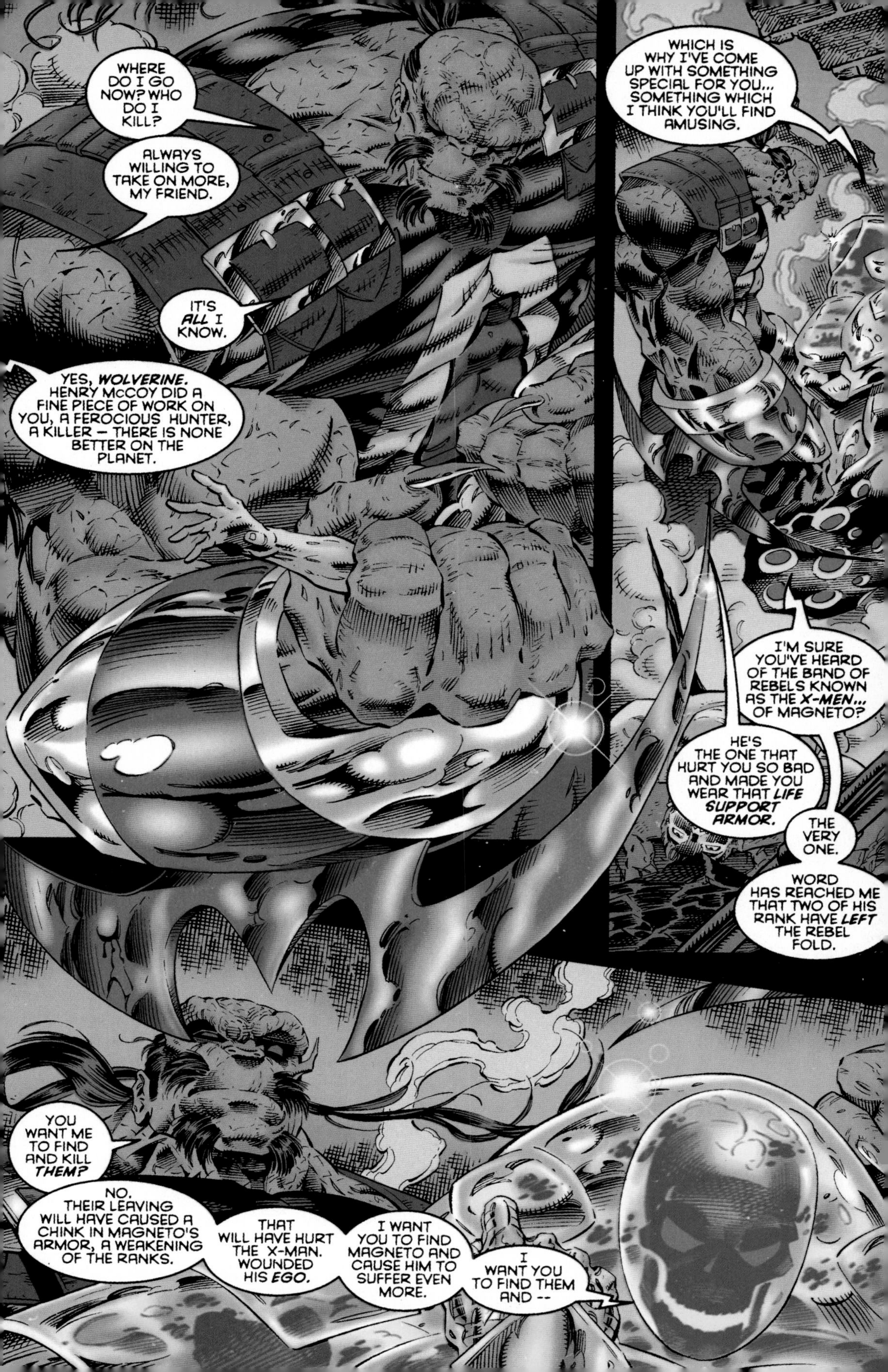
WHERE DO I GO NOW? WHO DO I KILL?
ALWAYS WILLING TO TAKE ON MORE, MY FRIEND.
IT'S ALL I KNOW.
YES, WOLVERINE. HENRY McCOY DID A FINE PIECE OF WORK ON YOU, A FEROCIOUS HUNTER, A KILLER — THERE IS NONE BETTER ON THE PLANET.
WHICH IS WHY I'VE COME UP WITH SOMETHING SPECIAL FOR YOU... SOMETHING WHICH I THINK YOU'LL FIND AMUSING.
I'M SURE YOU'VE HEARD OF THE BAND OF REBELS KNOWN AS THE X-MEN... OF MAGNETO?
HE'S THE ONE THAT HURT YOU SO BAD AND MADE YOU WEAR THAT LIFE SUPPORT ARMOR.
THE VERY ONE.
WORD HAS REACHED ME THAT TWO OF HIS RANK HAVE LEFT THE REBEL FOLD.
YOU WANT ME TO FIND AND KILL THEM?
NO. THEIR LEAVING WILL HAVE CAUSED A CHINK IN MAGNETO'S ARMOR, A WEAKENING OF THE RANKS.
THAT WILL HAVE HURT THE X-MAN. WOUNDED HIS EGO.
I WANT YOU TO FIND MAGNETO AND CAUSE HIM TO SUFFER EVEN MORE.
I WANT YOU TO FIND THEM AND --

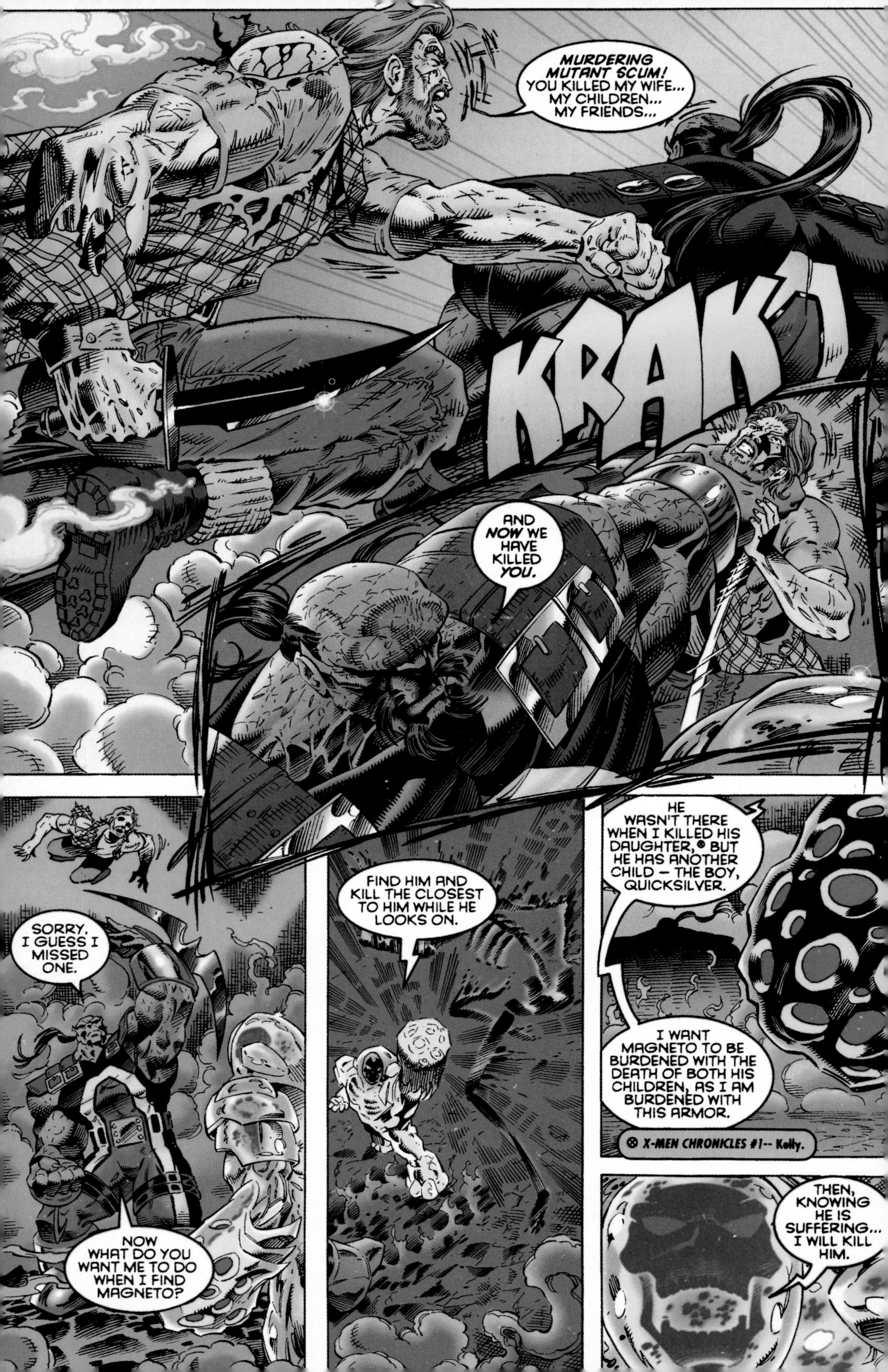
MURDERING MUTANT SCUM! YOU KILLED MY WIFE... MY CHILDREN... MY FRIENDS...
KRAK'T
AND NOW WE HAVE KILLED YOU.
SORRY. I GUESS I MISSED ONE.
NOW WHAT DO YOU WANT ME TO DO WHEN I FIND MAGNETO?
FIND HIM AND KILL THE CLOSEST TO HIM WHILE HE LOOKS ON.
HE WASN'T THERE WHEN I KILLED HIS DAUGHTER,⊗ BUT HE HAS ANOTHER CHILD — THE BOY, QUICKSILVER.
I WANT MAGNETO TO BE BURDENED WITH THE DEATH OF BOTH HIS CHILDREN, AS I AM BURDENED WITH THIS ARMOR.
⊗ X-MEN CHRONICLES #1-- Kelly.
THEN, KNOWING HE IS SUFFERING... I WILL KILL HIM.

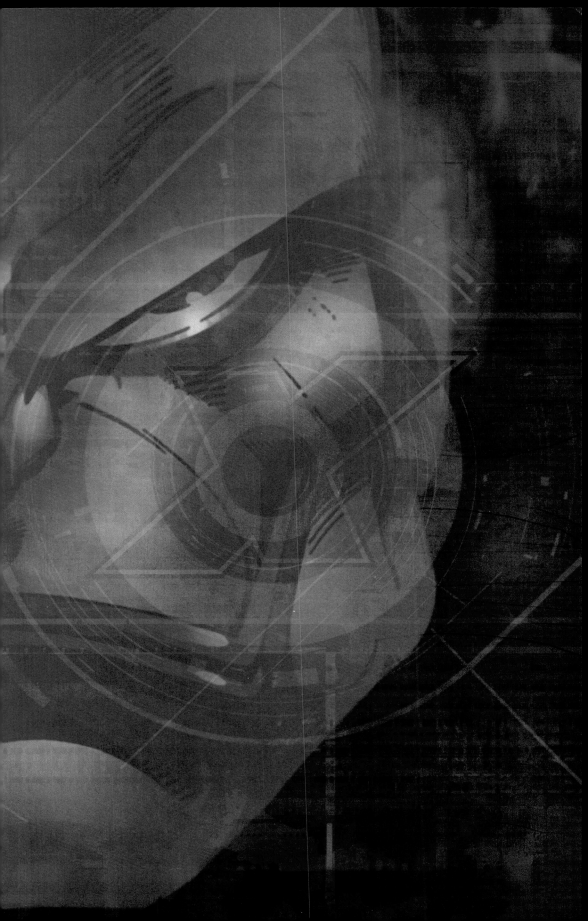

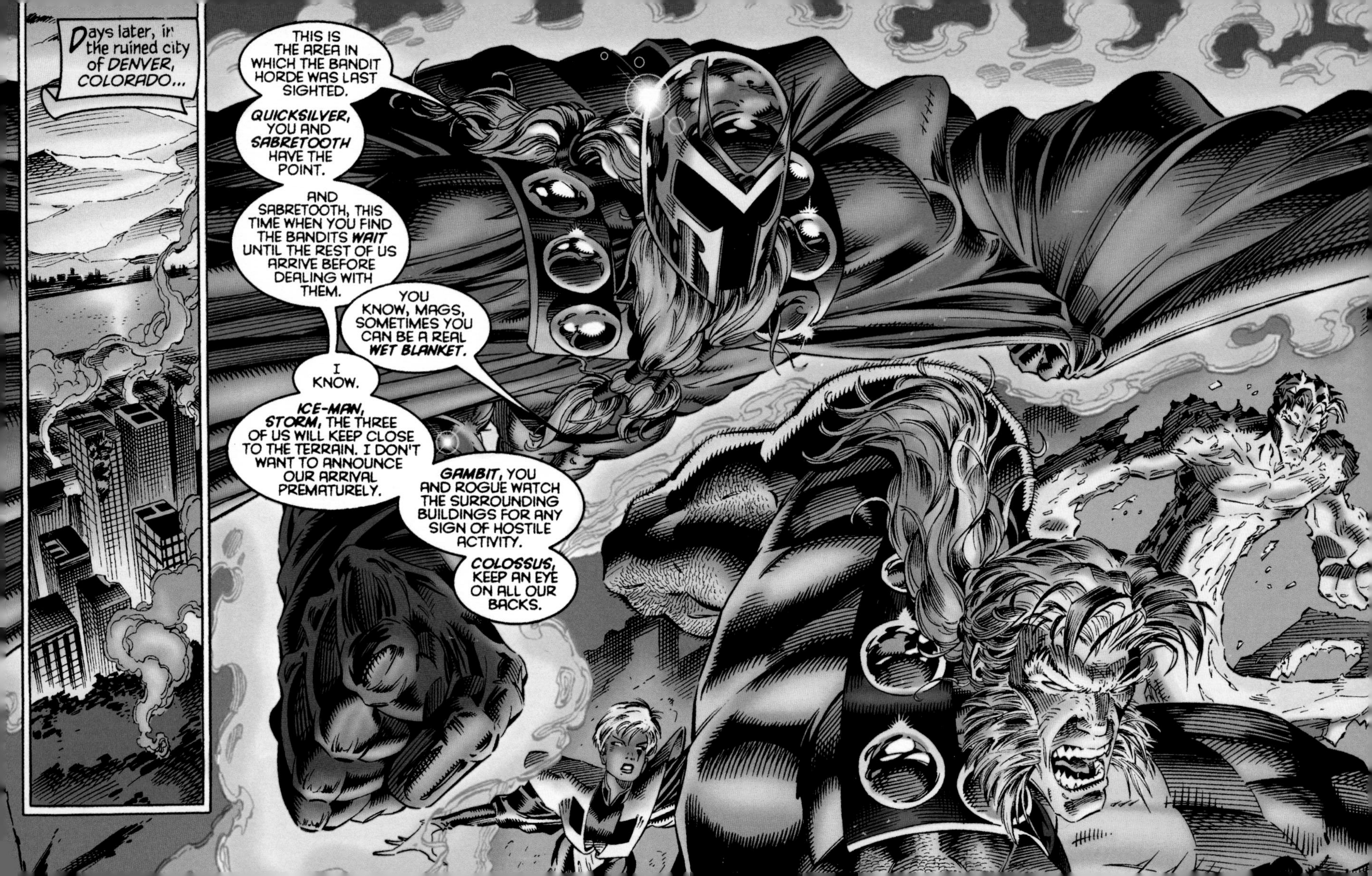
Days later, in the ruined city of DENVER, COLORADO...
THIS IS THE AREA IN WHICH THE BANDIT HORDE WAS LAST SIGHTED.
QUICKSILVER, YOU AND SABRETOOTH HAVE THE POINT.
AND SABRETOOTH, THIS TIME WHEN YOU FIND THE BANDITS WAIT UNTIL THE REST OF US ARRIVE BEFORE DEALING WITH THEM.
YOU KNOW, MAGS, SOMETIMES YOU CAN BE A REAL WET BLANKET.
I KNOW.
ICE-MAN, STORM, THE THREE OF US WILL KEEP CLOSE TO THE TERRAIN. I DON'T WANT TO ANNOUNCE OUR ARRIVAL PREMATURELY.
GAMBIT, YOU AND ROGUE WATCH THE SURROUNDING BUILDINGS FOR ANY SIGN OF HOSTILE ACTIVITY.
COLOSSUS, KEEP AN EYE ON ALL OUR BACKS.

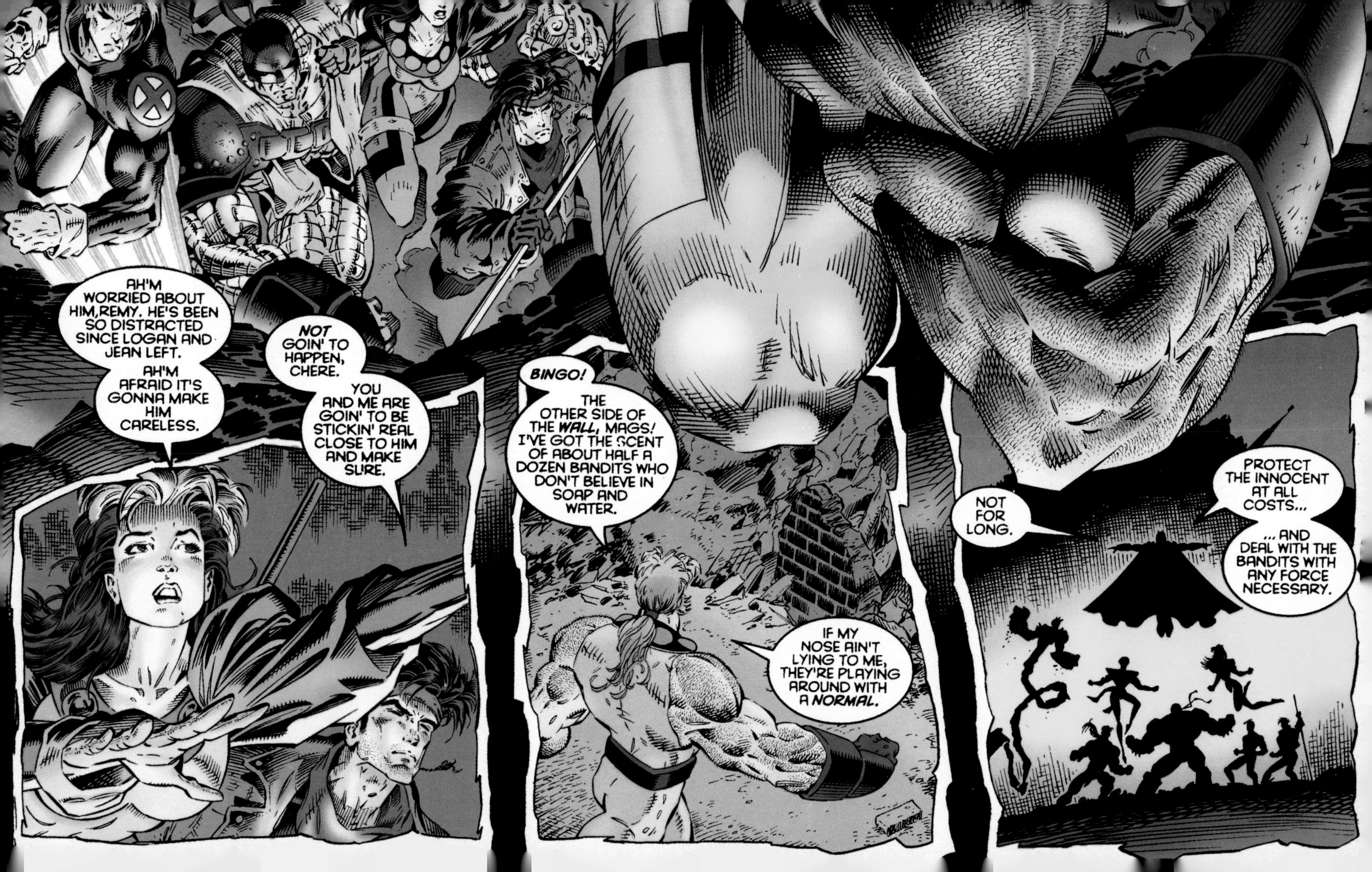
AH'M WORRIED ABOUT HIM, REMY. HE'S BEEN SO DISTRACTED SINCE LOGAN AND JEAN LEFT.
AH'M AFRAID IT'S GONNA MAKE HIM CARELESS.
NOT GOIN' TO HAPPEN, CHERE.
YOU AND ME ARE GOIN' TO BE STICKIN' REAL CLOSE TO HIM AND MAKE SURE.
BINGO!
THE OTHER SIDE OF THE WALL, MAGS! I'VE GOT THE SCENT OF ABOUT HALF A DOZEN BANDITS WHO DON'T BELIEVE IN SOAP AND WATER.
IF MY NOSE AIN'T LYING TO ME, THEY'RE PLAYING AROUND WITH A NORMAL.
NOT FOR LONG.
PROTECT THE INNOCENT AT ALL COSTS...
...AND DEAL WITH THE BANDITS WITH ANY FORCE NECESSARY.

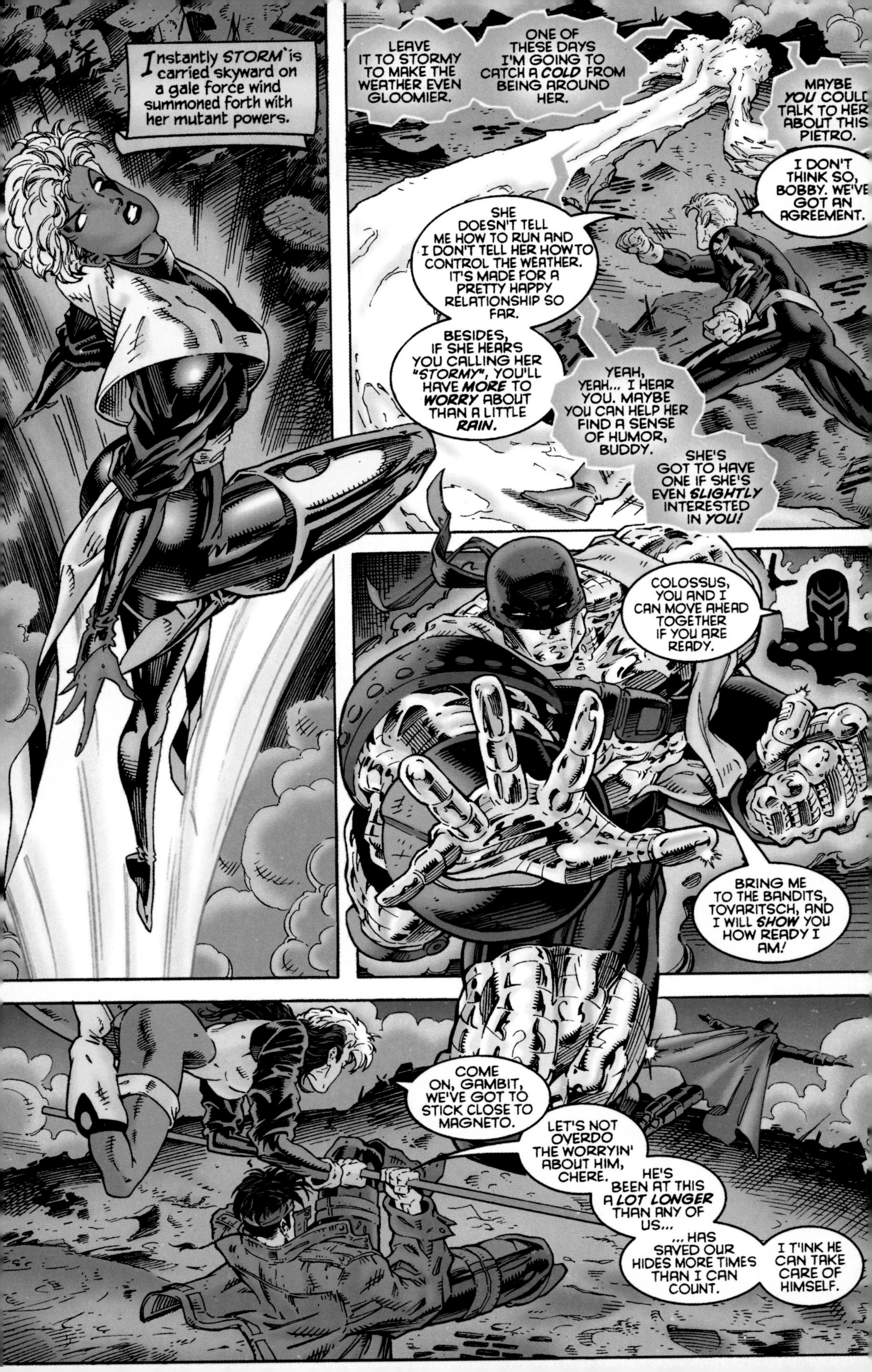
Instantly STORM is carried skyward on a gale force wind summoned forth with her mutant powers.
LEAVE IT TO STORMY TO MAKE THE WEATHER EVEN GLOOMIER.
ONE OF THESE DAYS I'M GOING TO CATCH A COLD FROM BEING AROUND HER.
MAYBE YOU COULD TALK TO HER ABOUT THIS PIETRO.
I DON'T THINK SO, BOBBY. WE'VE GOT AN AGREEMENT.
SHE DOESN'T TELL ME HOW TO RUN AND I DON'T TELL HER HOW TO CONTROL THE WEATHER. IT'S MADE FOR A PRETTY HAPPY RELATIONSHIP SO FAR.
BESIDES, IF SHE HEARS YOU CALLING HER "STORMY", YOU'LL HAVE MORE TO WORRY ABOUT THAN A LITTLE RAIN.
YEAH, YEAH... I HEAR YOU. MAYBE YOU CAN HELP HER FIND A SENSE OF HUMOR, BUDDY.
SHE'S GOT TO HAVE ONE IF SHE'S EVEN SLIGHTLY INTERESTED IN YOU!
COLOSSUS, YOU AND I CAN MOVE AHEAD TOGETHER IF YOU ARE READY.
BRING ME TO THE BANDITS, TOVARITSCH, AND I WILL SHOW YOU HOW READY I AM!
COME ON, GAMBIT, WE'VE GOT TO STICK CLOSE TO MAGNETO.
LET'S NOT OVERDO THE WORRYIN' ABOUT HIM, CHERE.
HE'S BEEN AT THIS A LOT LONGER THAN ANY OF US...
... HAS SAVED OUR HIDES MORE TIMES THAN I CAN COUNT.
I T'INK HE CAN TAKE CARE OF HIMSELF.

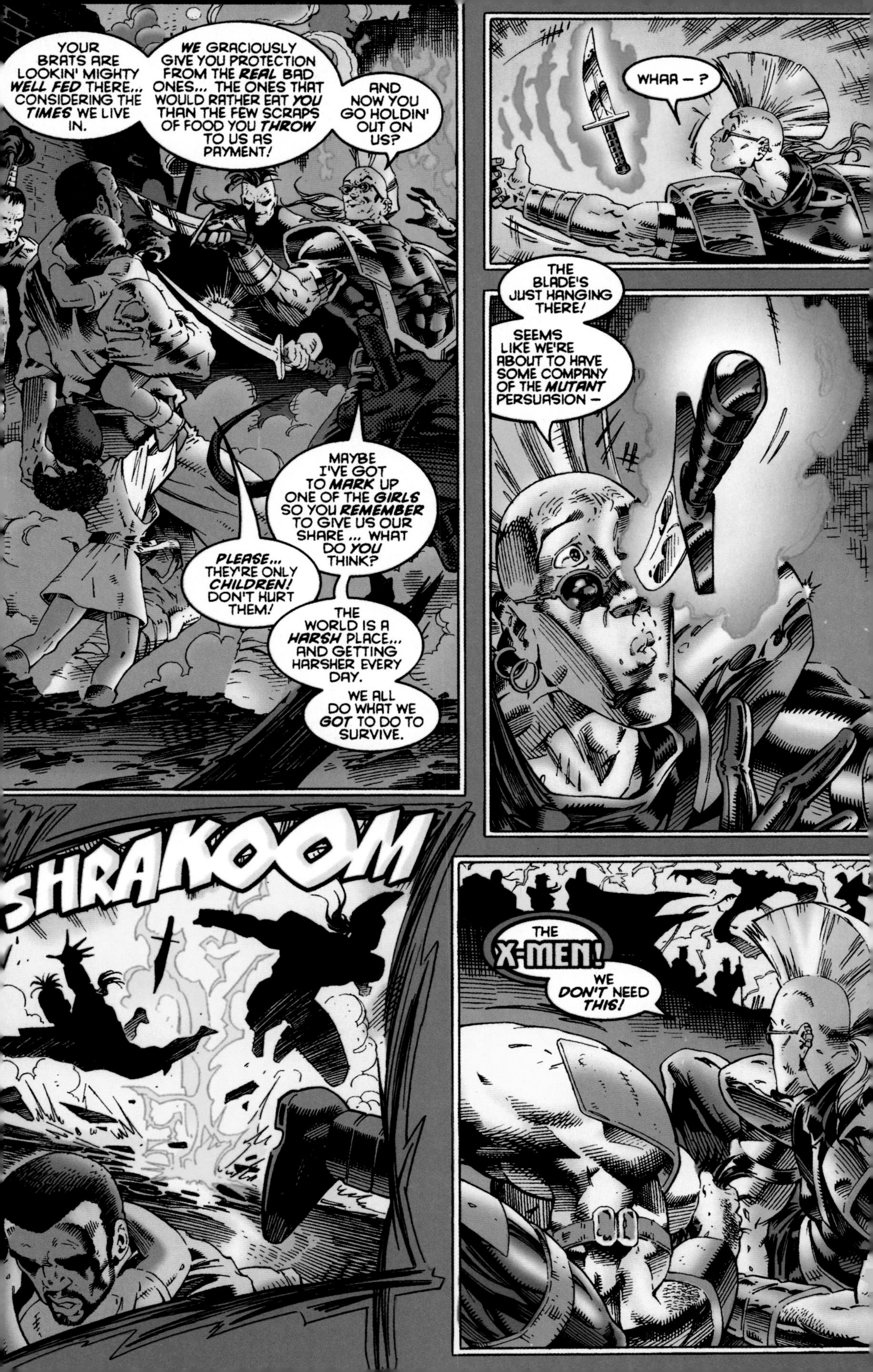

YOUR BRATS ARE LOOKIN' MIGHTY WELL FED THERE... CONSIDERING THE TIMES WE LIVE IN.
WE GRACIOUSLY GIVE YOU PROTECTION FROM THE REAL BAD ONES... THE ONES THAT WOULD RATHER EAT YOU THAN THE FEW SCRAPS OF FOOD YOU THROW TO US AS PAYMENT!
AND NOW YOU GO HOLDIN' OUT ON US?
MAYBE I'VE GOT TO MARK UP ONE OF THE GIRLS SO YOU REMEMBER TO GIVE US OUR SHARE ... WHAT DO YOU THINK?
PLEASE... THEY'RE ONLY CHILDREN! DON'T HURT THEM!
THE WORLD IS A HARSH PLACE... AND GETTING HARSHER EVERY DAY.
WE ALL DO WHAT WE GOT TO DO TO SURVIVE.
WHAA — ?
THE BLADE'S JUST HANGING THERE!
SEEMS LIKE WE'RE ABOUT TO HAVE SOME COMPANY OF THE MUTANT PERSUASION —
SHRAKOOM
THE X-MEN! WE DON'T NEED THIS!

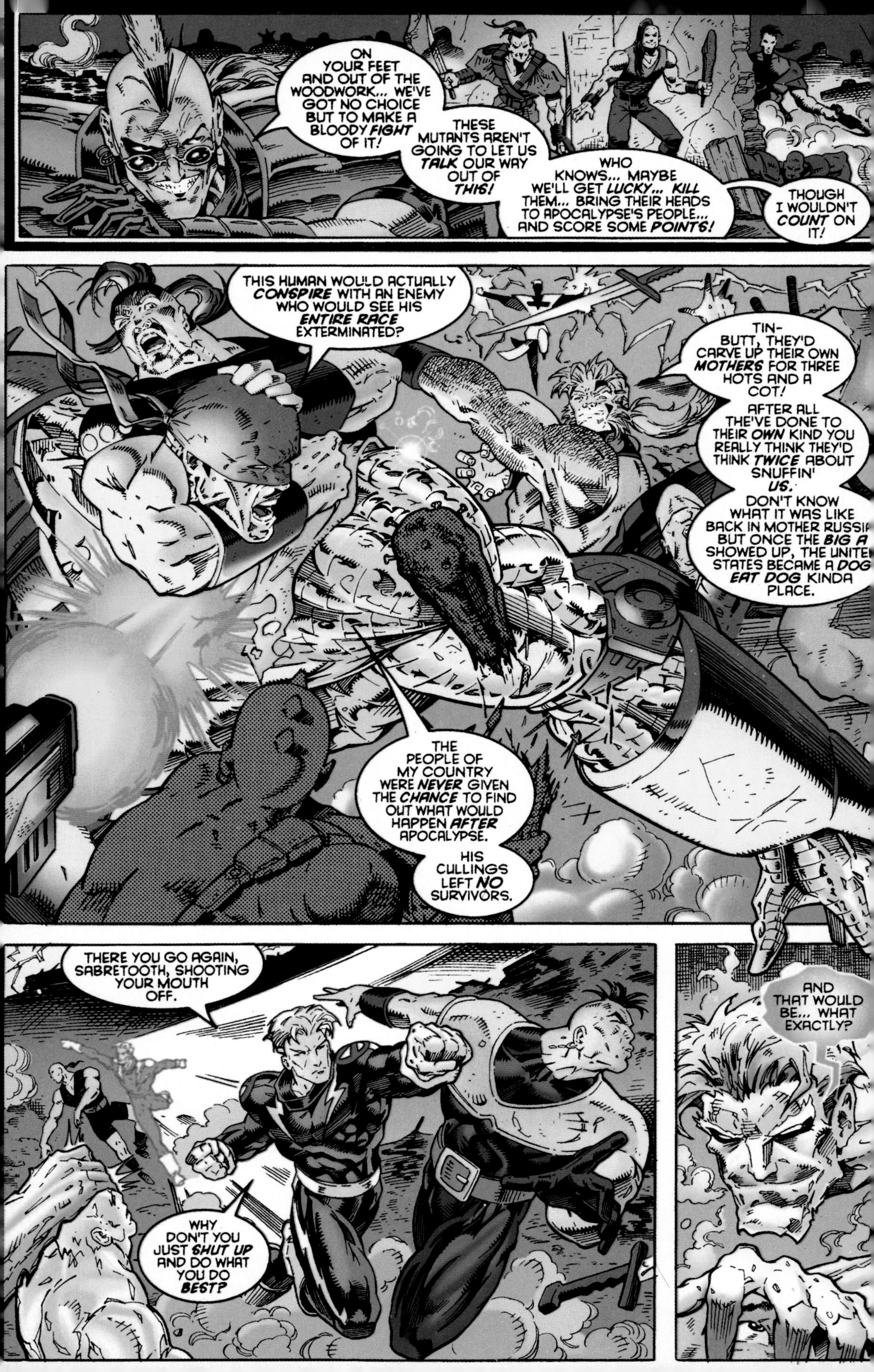
ON YOUR FEET AND OUT OF THE WOODWORK... WE'VE GOT NO CHOICE BUT TO MAKE A BLOODY FIGHT OF IT!
THESE MUTANTS AREN'T GOING TO LET US TALK OUR WAY OUT OF THIS!
WHO KNOWS... MAYBE WE'LL GET LUCKY... KILL THEM... BRING THEIR HEADS TO APOCALYPSE'S PEOPLE... AND SCORE SOME POINTS!
THOUGH I WOULDN'T COUNT ON IT!
THIS HUMAN WOULD ACTUALLY CONSPIRE WITH AN ENEMY WHO WOULD SEE HIS ENTIRE RACE EXTERMINATED?
TIN-BUTT, THEY'D CARVE UP THEIR OWN MOTHERS FOR THREE HOTS AND A COT!
AFTER ALL THE'VE DONE TO THEIR OWN KIND YOU REALLY THINK THEY'D THINK TWICE ABOUT SNUFFIN' US.
DON'T KNOW WHAT IT WAS LIKE BACK IN MOTHER RUSSIA BUT ONCE THE BIG A SHOWED UP, THE UNITED STATES BECAME A DOG EAT DOG KINDA PLACE.
THE PEOPLE OF MY COUNTRY WERE NEVER GIVEN THE CHANCE TO FIND OUT WHAT WOULD HAPPEN AFTER APOCALYPSE.
HIS CULLINGS LEFT NO SURVIVORS.
THERE YOU GO AGAIN, SABRETOOTH, SHOOTING YOUR MOUTH OFF.
WHY DON'T YOU JUST SHUT UP AND DO WHAT YOU DO BEST?
AND THAT WOULD BE... WHAT EXACTLY?

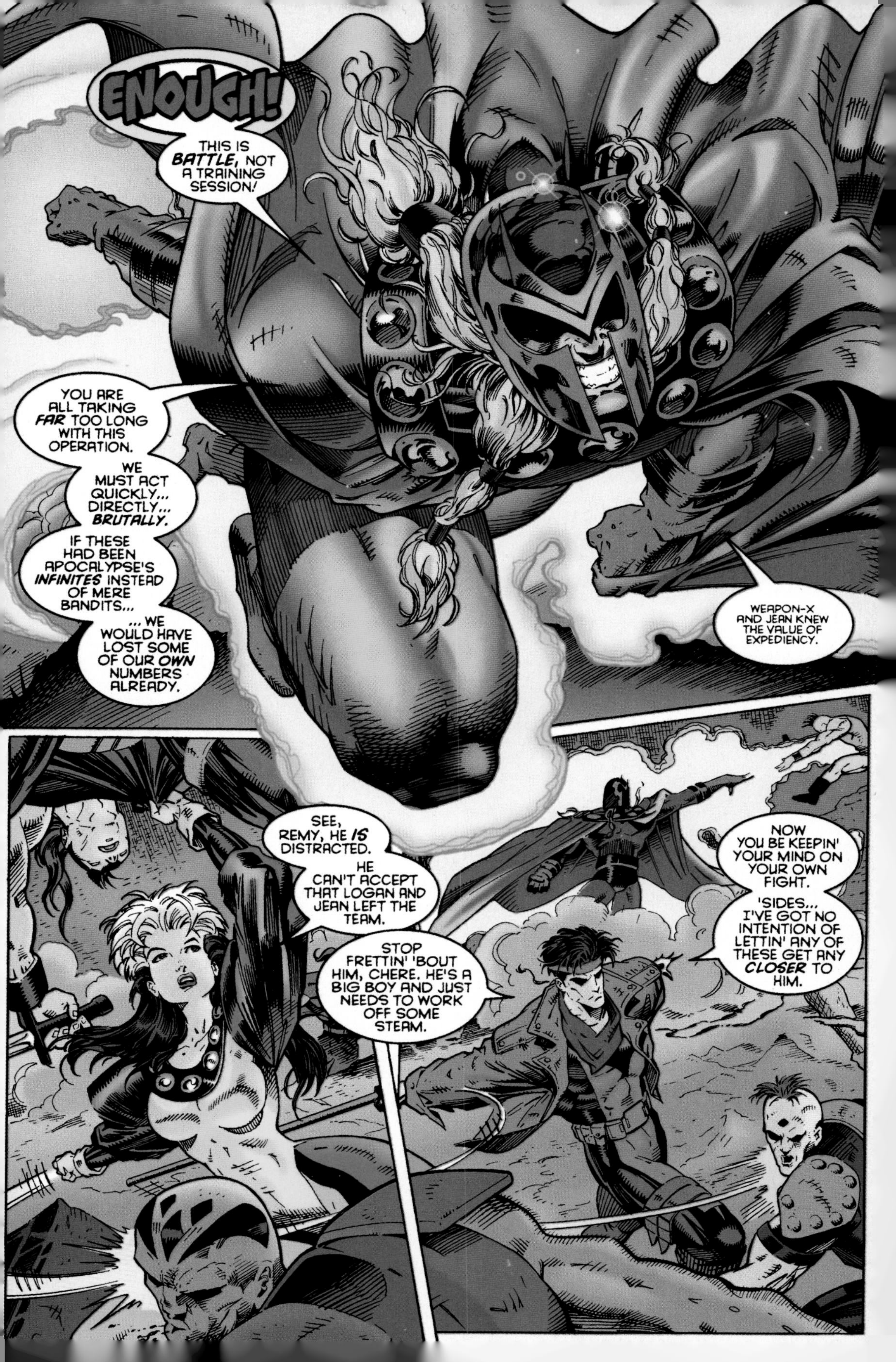
ENOUGH!
THIS IS BATTLE, NOT A TRAINING SESSION!
YOU ARE ALL TAKING FAR TOO LONG WITH THIS OPERATION.
WE MUST ACT QUICKLY... DIRECTLY... BRUTALLY.
IF THESE HAD BEEN APOCALYPSE'S INFINITES INSTEAD OF MERE BANDITS...
...WE WOULD HAVE LOST SOME OF OUR OWN NUMBERS ALREADY.
WEAPON-X AND JEAN KNEW THE VALUE OF EXPEDIENCY.
SEE, REMY, HE IS DISTRACTED.
HE CAN'T ACCEPT THAT LOGAN AND JEAN LEFT THE TEAM.
STOP FRETTIN' 'BOUT HIM, CHERE. HE'S A BIG BOY AND JUST NEEDS TO WORK OFF SOME STEAM.
NOW YOU BE KEEPIN' YOUR MIND ON YOUR OWN FIGHT.
'SIDES... I'VE GOT NO INTENTION OF LETTIN' ANY OF THESE GET ANY CLOSER TO HIM.

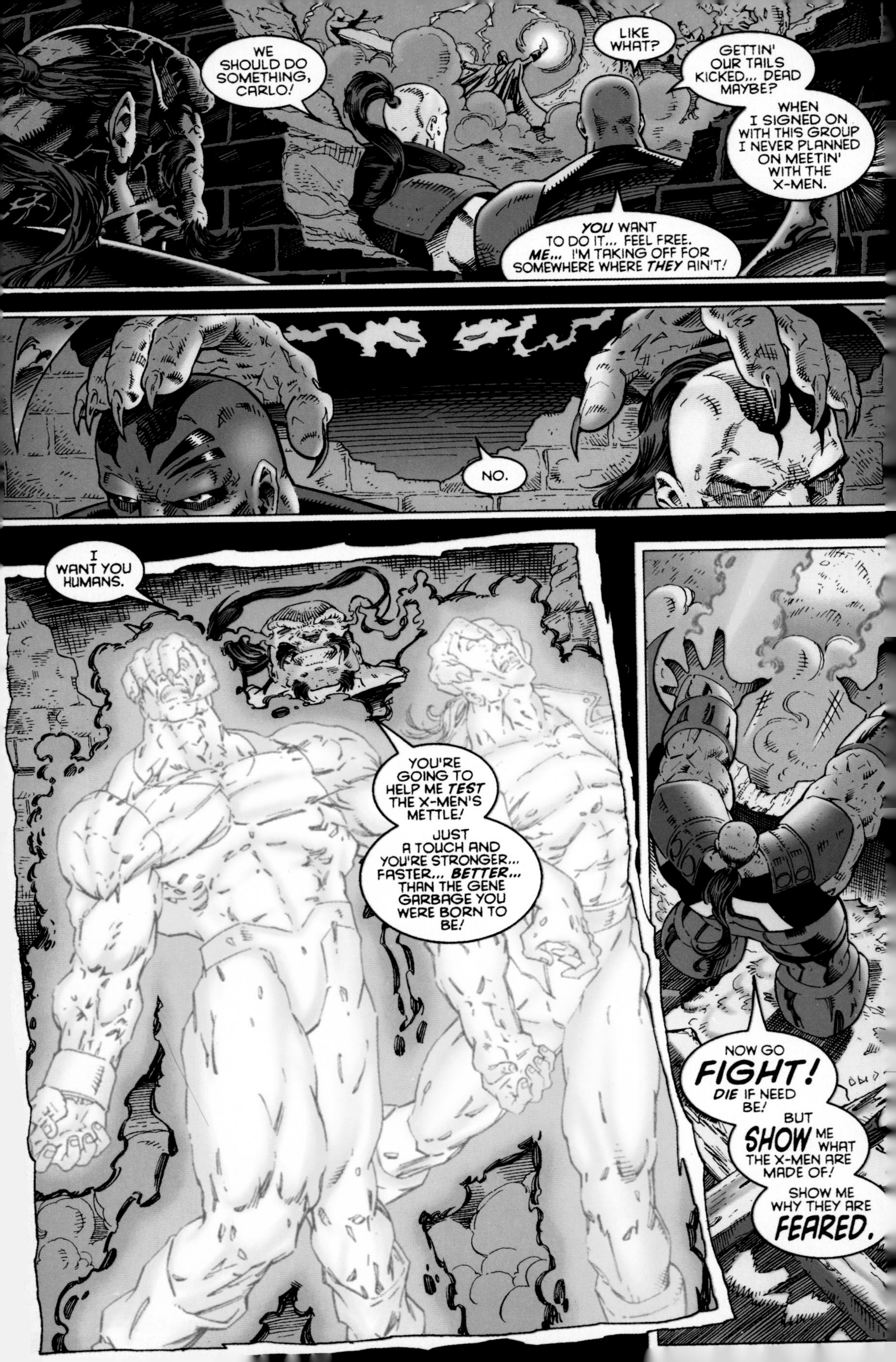
WE SHOULD DO SOMETHING, CARLO!
LIKE WHAT?
GETTIN' OUR TAILS KICKED... DEAD MAYBE?
WHEN I SIGNED ON WITH THIS GROUP I NEVER PLANNED ON MEETIN' WITH THE X-MEN.
YOU WANT TO DO IT... FEEL FREE. ME... I'M TAKING OFF FOR SOMEWHERE WHERE THEY AIN'T!
NO.
I WANT YOU HUMANS.
YOU'RE GOING TO HELP ME TEST THE X-MEN'S METTLE!
JUST A TOUCH AND YOU'RE STRONGER... FASTER... BETTER... THAN THE GENE GARBAGE YOU WERE BORN TO BE!
NOW GO FIGHT! DIE IF NEED BE!
BUT SHOW ME WHAT THE X-MEN ARE MADE OF!
SHOW ME WHY THEY ARE FEARED.

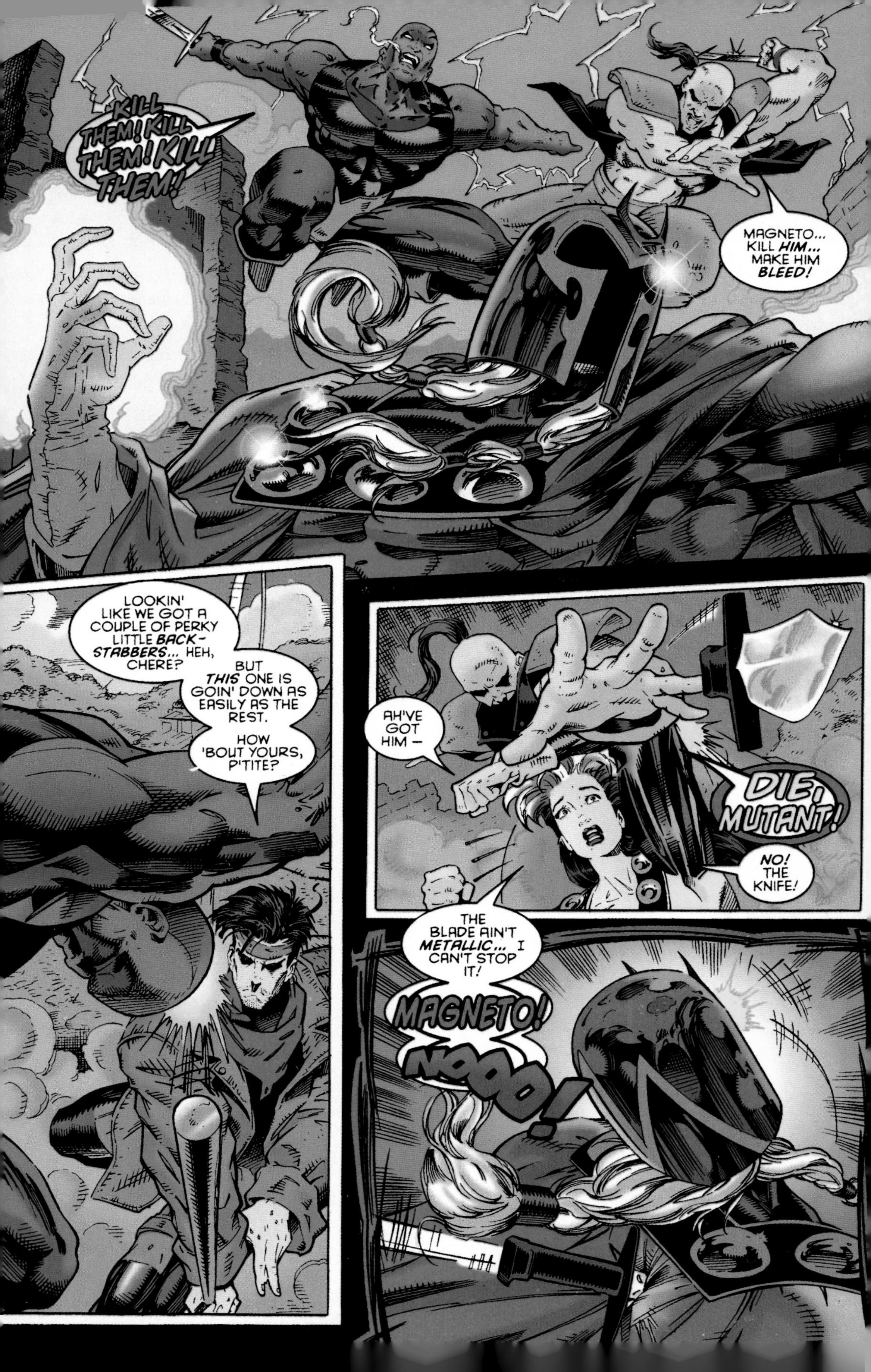
KILL THEM! KILL THEM! KILL THEM!
MAGNETO... KILL HIM... MAKE HIM BLEED!
LOOKIN' LIKE WE GOT A COUPLE OF PERKY LITTLE BACK-STABBERS... HEH, CHERE?
BUT THIS ONE IS GOIN' DOWN AS EASILY AS THE REST.
HOW 'BOUT YOURS, P'TITE?
AH'VE GOT HIM —
DIE, MUTANT!
NO! THE KNIFE!
THE BLADE AIN'T METALLIC... I CAN'T STOP IT!
MAGNETO!
NOOO!

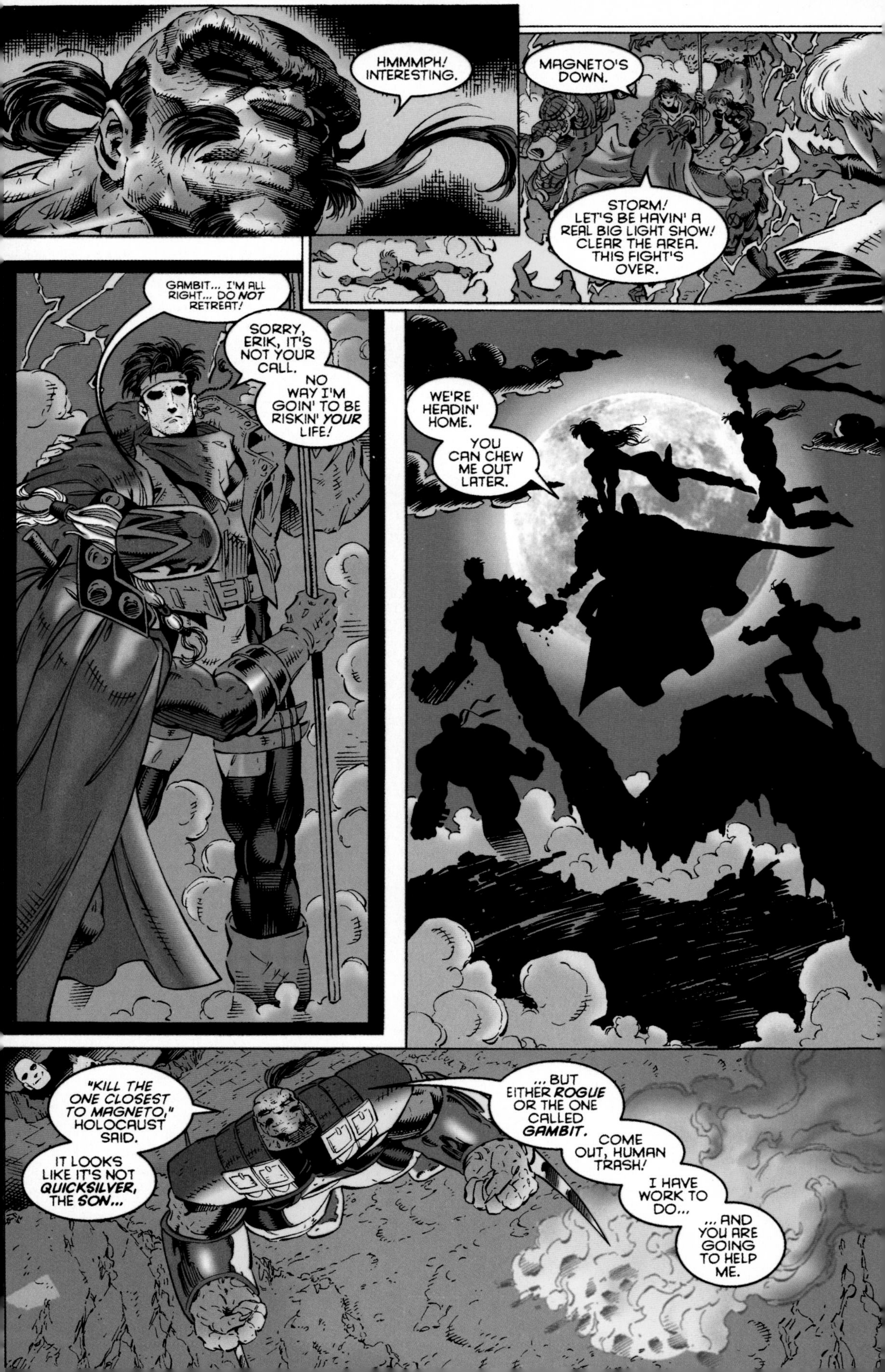
HMMMPH! INTERESTING.
MAGNETO'S DOWN.
STORM! LET'S BE HAVIN' A REAL BIG LIGHT SHOW! CLEAR THE AREA. THIS FIGHT'S OVER.
GAMBIT... I'M ALL RIGHT... DO *NOT* RETREAT!
SORRY, ERIK, IT'S NOT YOUR CALL.
NO WAY I'M GOIN' TO BE RISKIN' *YOUR* LIFE!
WE'RE HEADIN' HOME.
YOU CAN CHEW ME OUT LATER.
"KILL THE ONE CLOSEST TO MAGNETO," HOLOCAUST SAID.
IT LOOKS LIKE IT'S NOT *QUICKSILVER*, THE *SON*...
... BUT EITHER *ROGUE* OR THE ONE CALLED *GAMBIT*.
COME OUT, HUMAN TRASH!
I HAVE WORK TO DO...
... AND YOU ARE GOING TO HELP ME.

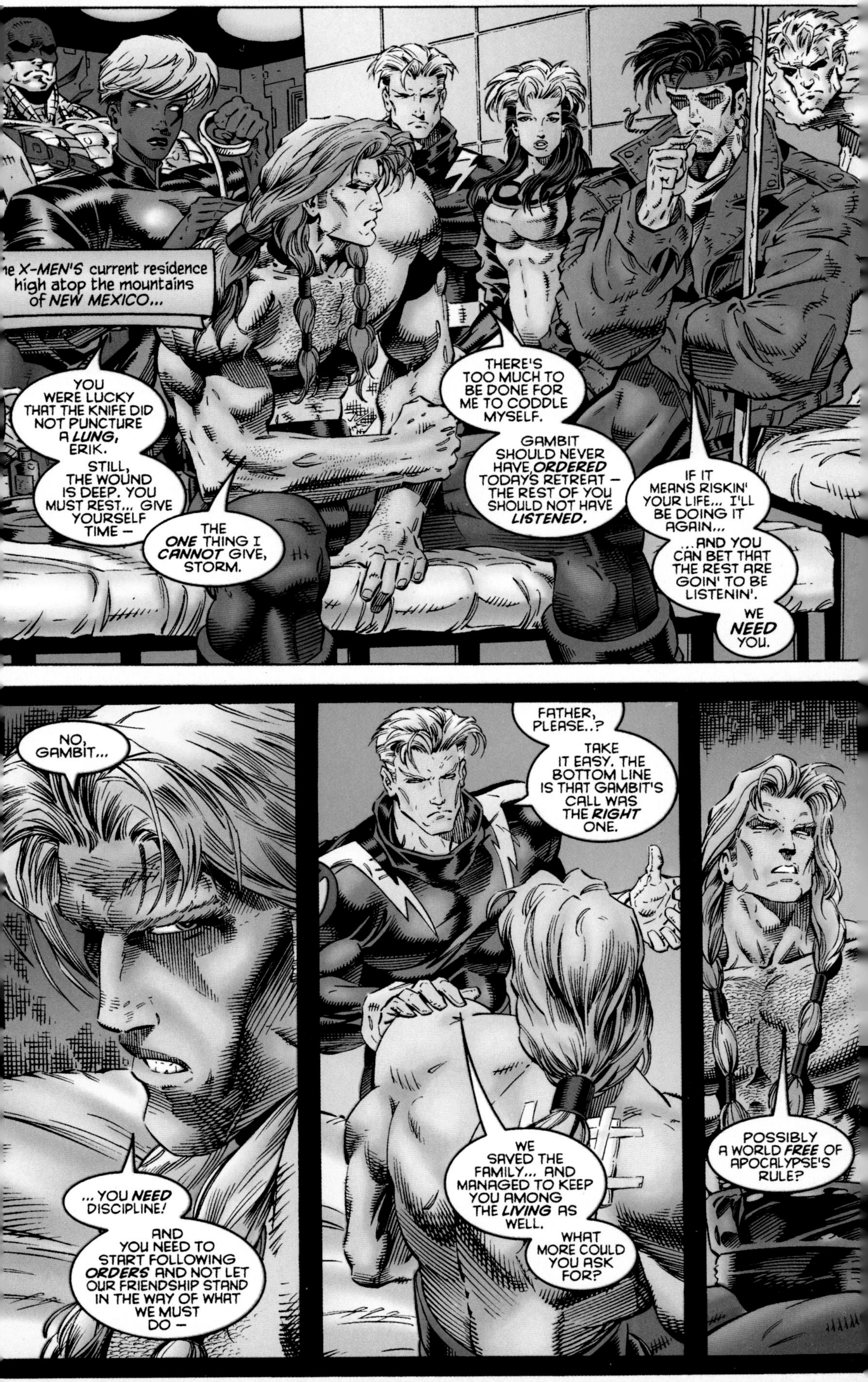

...the X-MEN'S current residence high atop the mountains of NEW MEXICO...
YOU WERE LUCKY THAT THE KNIFE DID NOT PUNCTURE A LUNG, ERIK.
STILL, THE WOUND IS DEEP. YOU MUST REST... GIVE YOURSELF TIME —
THE ONE THING I CANNOT GIVE, STORM.
THERE'S TOO MUCH TO BE DONE FOR ME TO CODDLE MYSELF.
GAMBIT SHOULD NEVER HAVE ORDERED TODAY'S RETREAT — THE REST OF YOU SHOULD NOT HAVE LISTENED.
IF IT MEANS RISKIN' YOUR LIFE... I'LL BE DOING IT AGAIN...
...AND YOU CAN BET THAT THE REST ARE GOIN' TO BE LISTENIN'.
WE NEED YOU.
NO, GAMBIT...
...YOU NEED DISCIPLINE!
AND YOU NEED TO START FOLLOWING ORDERS AND NOT LET OUR FRIENDSHIP STAND IN THE WAY OF WHAT WE MUST DO —
FATHER, PLEASE..?
TAKE IT EASY. THE BOTTOM LINE IS THAT GAMBIT'S CALL WAS THE RIGHT ONE.
WE SAVED THE FAMILY... AND MANAGED TO KEEP YOU AMONG THE LIVING AS WELL.
WHAT MORE COULD YOU ASK FOR?
POSSIBLY A WORLD FREE OF APOCALYPSE'S RULE?

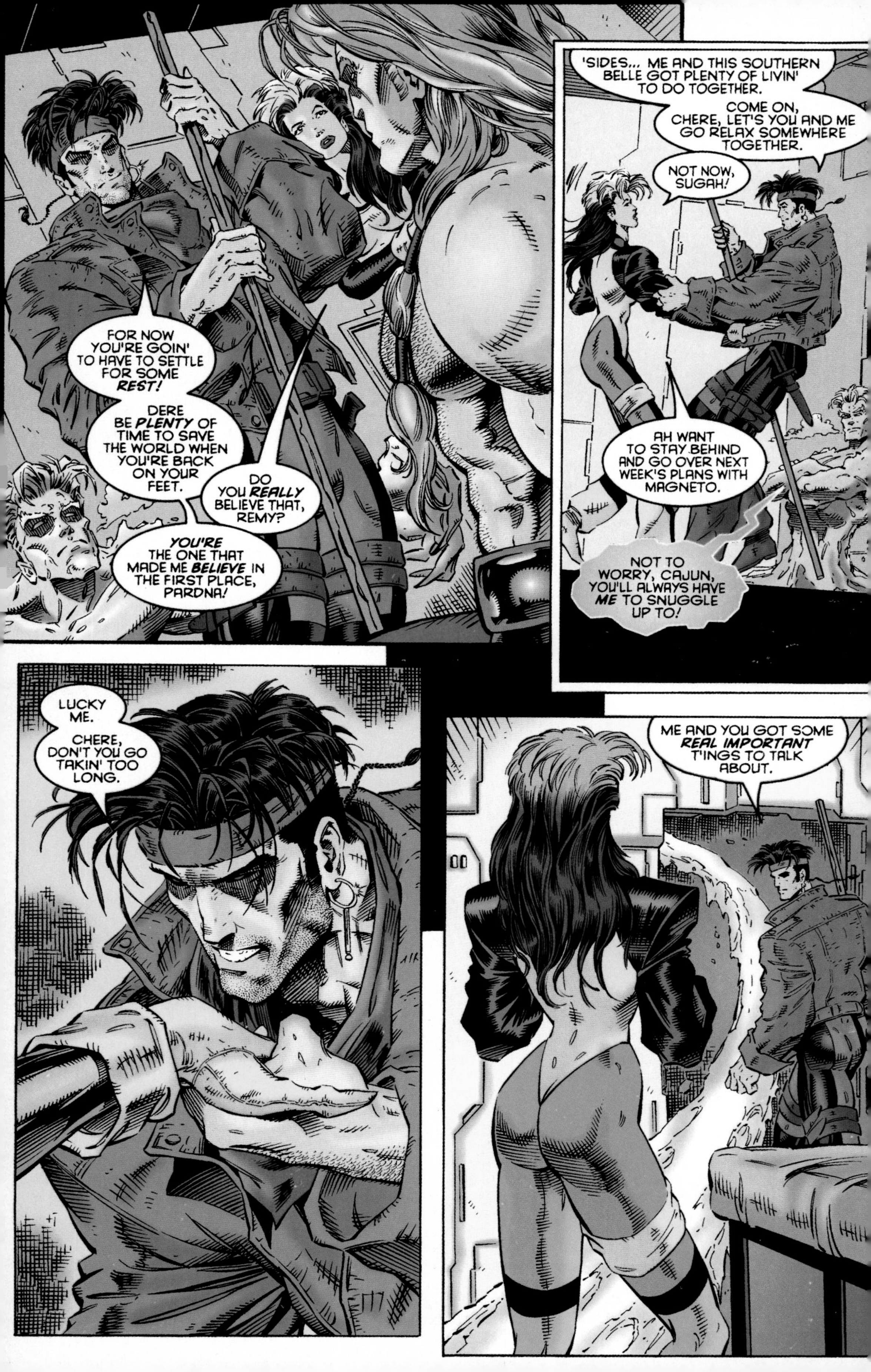
FOR NOW YOU'RE GOIN' TO HAVE TO SETTLE FOR SOME REST!
DERE BE PLENTY OF TIME TO SAVE THE WORLD WHEN YOU'RE BACK ON YOUR FEET.
DO YOU REALLY BELIEVE THAT, REMY?
YOU'RE THE ONE THAT MADE ME BELIEVE IN THE FIRST PLACE, PARDNA!
'SIDES... ME AND THIS SOUTHERN BELLE GOT PLENTY OF LIVIN' TO DO TOGETHER.
COME ON, CHERE, LET'S YOU AND ME GO RELAX SOMEWHERE TOGETHER.
NOT NOW, SUGAH!
AH WANT TO STAY BEHIND AND GO OVER NEXT WEEK'S PLANS WITH MAGNETO.
NOT TO WORRY, CAJUN, YOU'LL ALWAYS HAVE ME TO SNUGGLE UP TO!
LUCKY ME.
CHERE, DON'T YOU GO TAKIN' TOO LONG.
ME AND YOU GOT SOME REAL IMPORTANT T'INGS TO TALK ABOUT.

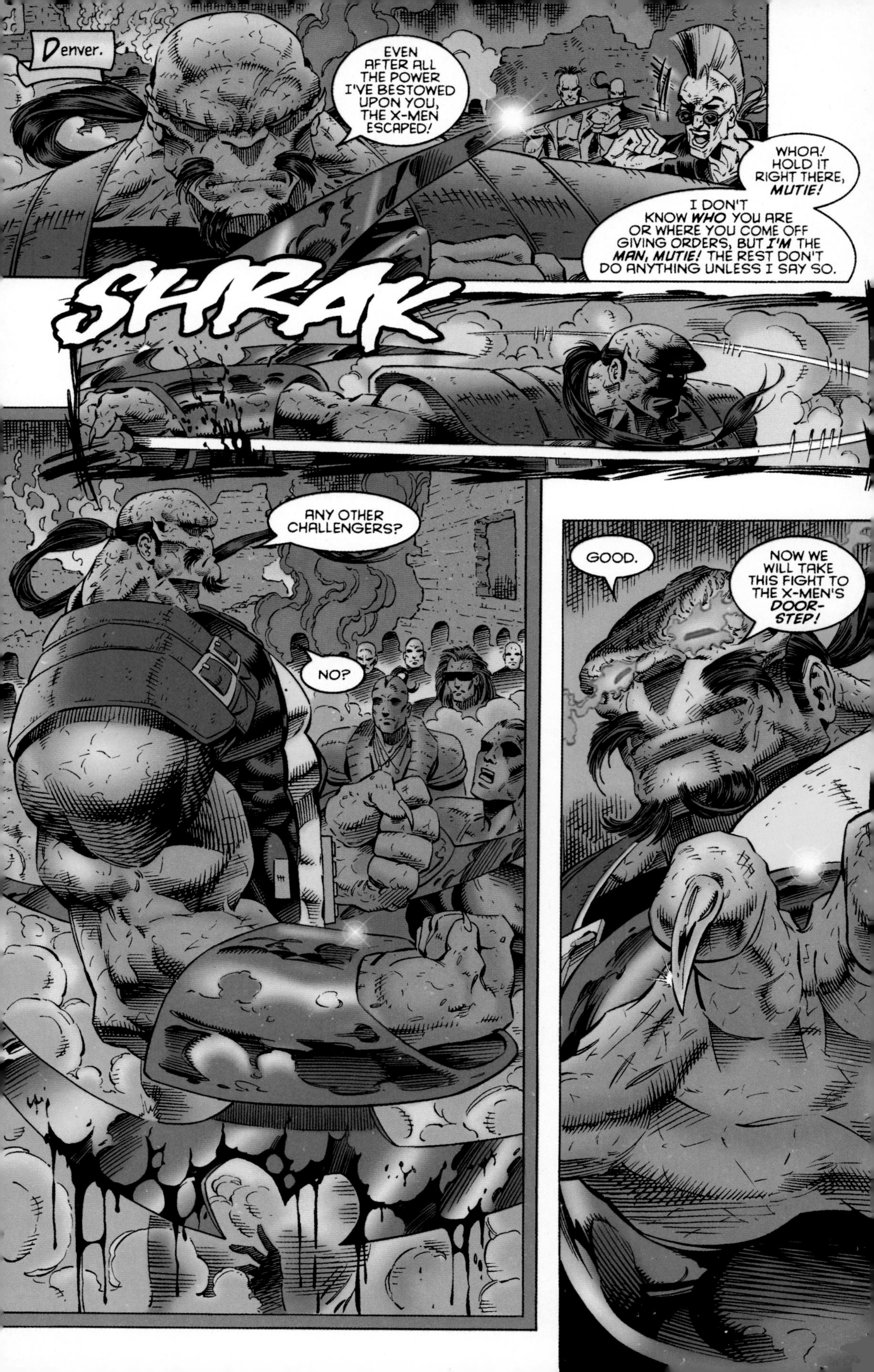
Denver.
EVEN AFTER ALL THE POWER I'VE BESTOWED UPON YOU, THE X-MEN ESCAPED!
WHOA! HOLD IT RIGHT THERE, MUTIE!
I DON'T KNOW WHO YOU ARE OR WHERE YOU COME OFF GIVING ORDERS, BUT I'M THE MAN, MUTIE! THE REST DON'T DO ANYTHING UNLESS I SAY SO.
SHRAK
ANY OTHER CHALLENGERS?
NO?
GOOD.
NOW WE WILL TAKE THIS FIGHT TO THE X-MEN'S DOOR-STEP!

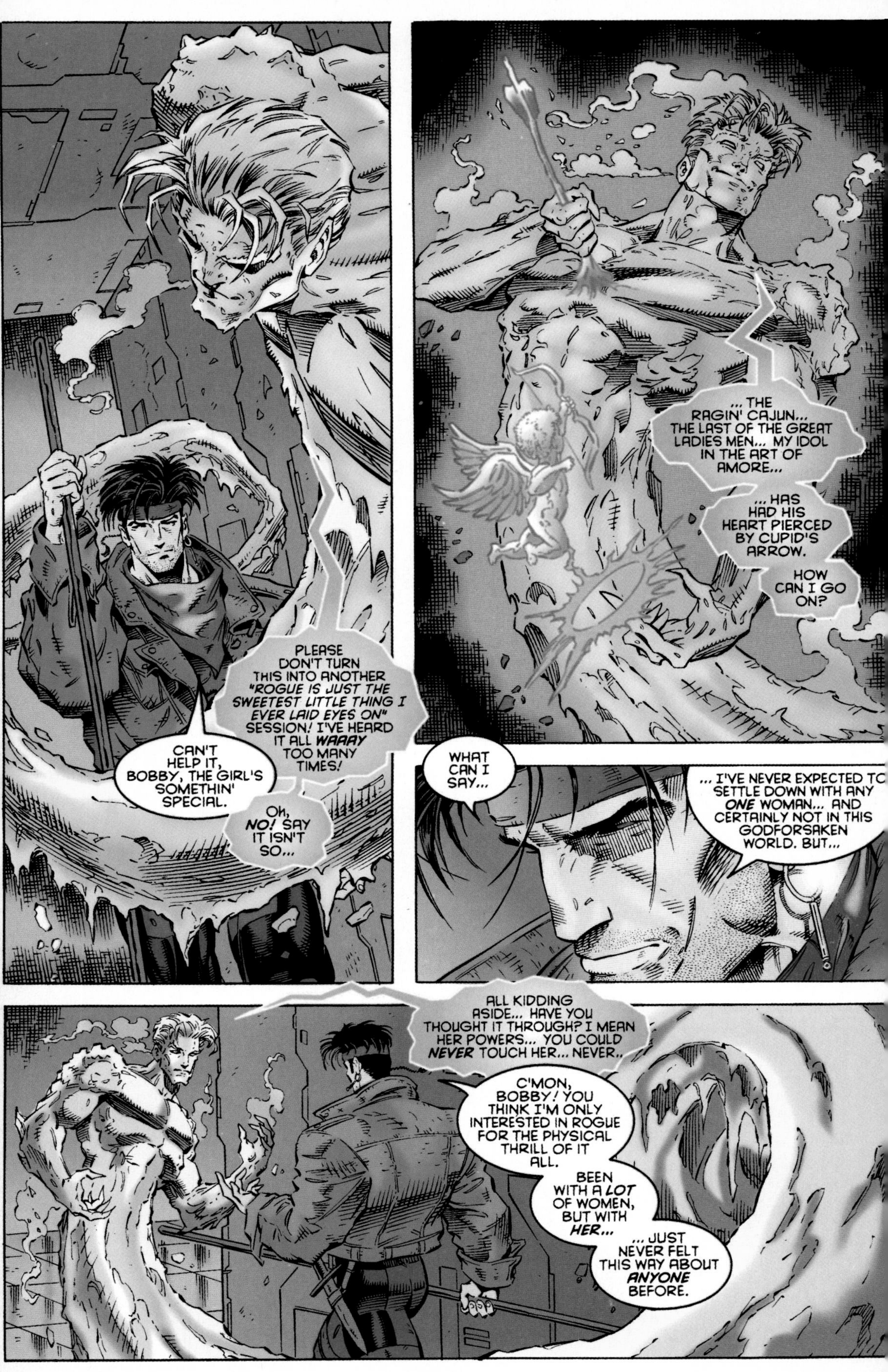
PLEASE DON'T TURN THIS INTO ANOTHER "ROGUE IS JUST THE SWEETEST LITTLE THING I EVER LAID EYES ON" SESSION! I'VE HEARD IT ALL WAAAY TOO MANY TIMES!
CAN'T HELP IT, BOBBY, THE GIRL'S SOMETHIN' SPECIAL.
Oh, NO! SAY IT ISN'T SO...
... THE RAGIN' CAJUN... THE LAST OF THE GREAT LADIES MEN... MY IDOL IN THE ART OF AMORE...
... HAS HAD HIS HEART PIERCED BY CUPID'S ARROW.
HOW CAN I GO ON?
WHAT CAN I SAY...
... I'VE NEVER EXPECTED TO SETTLE DOWN WITH ANY ONE WOMAN... AND CERTAINLY NOT IN THIS GODFORSAKEN WORLD. BUT...
ALL KIDDING ASIDE... HAVE YOU THOUGHT IT THROUGH? I MEAN HER POWERS... YOU COULD NEVER TOUCH HER... NEVER..
C'MON, BOBBY! YOU THINK I'M ONLY INTERESTED IN ROGUE FOR THE PHYSICAL THRILL OF IT ALL.
BEEN WITH A LOT OF WOMEN, BUT WITH HER...
... JUST NEVER FELT THIS WAY ABOUT ANYONE BEFORE.

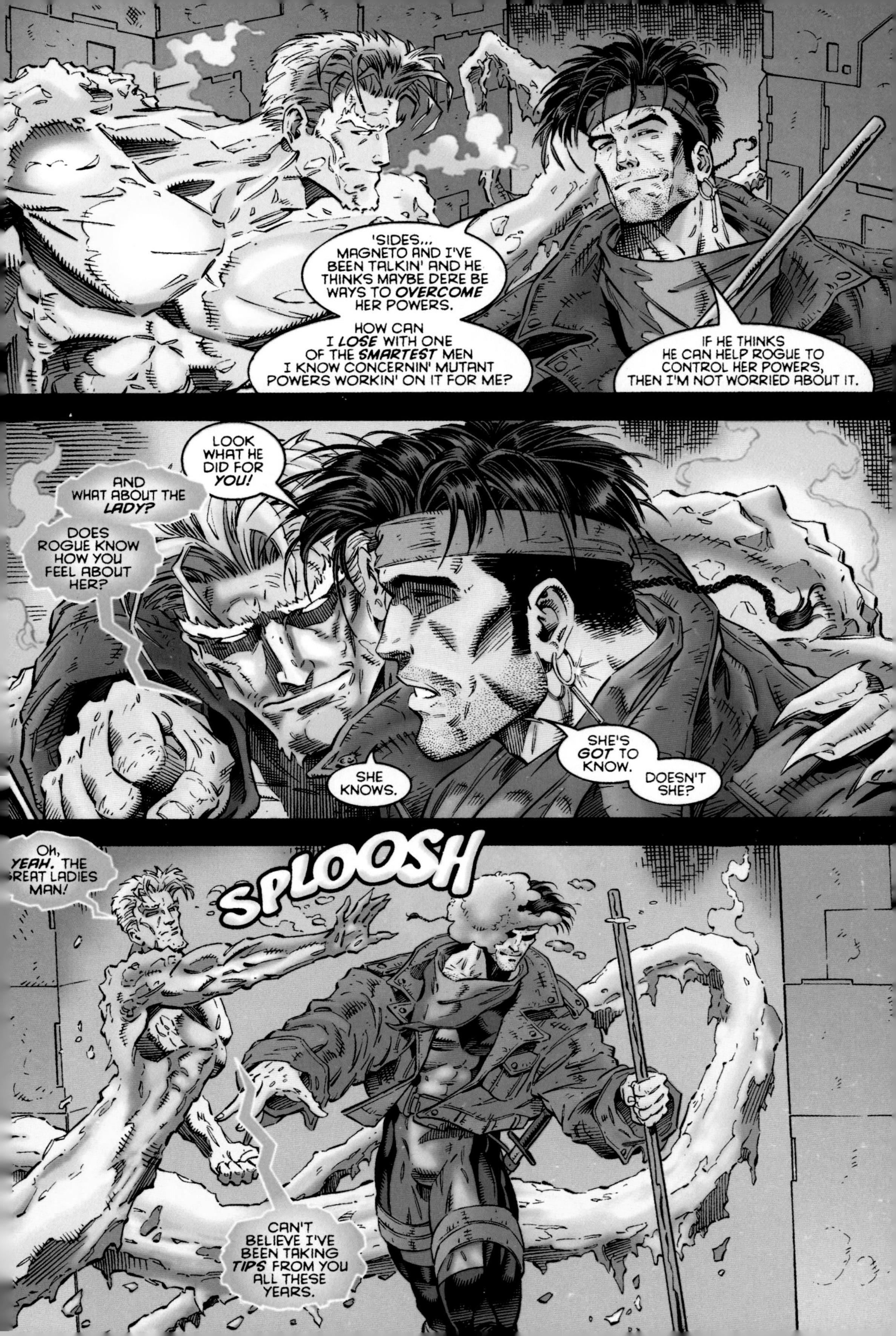
'SIDES... MAGNETO AND I'VE BEEN TALKIN' AND HE THINKS MAYBE DERE BE WAYS TO OVERCOME HER POWERS.
HOW CAN I LOSE WITH ONE OF THE SMARTEST MEN I KNOW CONCERNIN' MUTANT POWERS WORKIN' ON IT FOR ME?
IF HE THINKS HE CAN HELP ROGUE TO CONTROL HER POWERS, THEN I'M NOT WORRIED ABOUT IT.
LOOK WHAT HE DID FOR YOU!
AND WHAT ABOUT THE LADY?
DOES ROGUE KNOW HOW YOU FEEL ABOUT HER?
SHE KNOWS.
SHE'S GOT TO KNOW.
DOESN'T SHE?
OH, YEAH. THE GREAT LADIES MAN!
SPLOOSH
CAN'T BELIEVE I'VE BEEN TAKING TIPS FROM YOU ALL THESE YEARS.

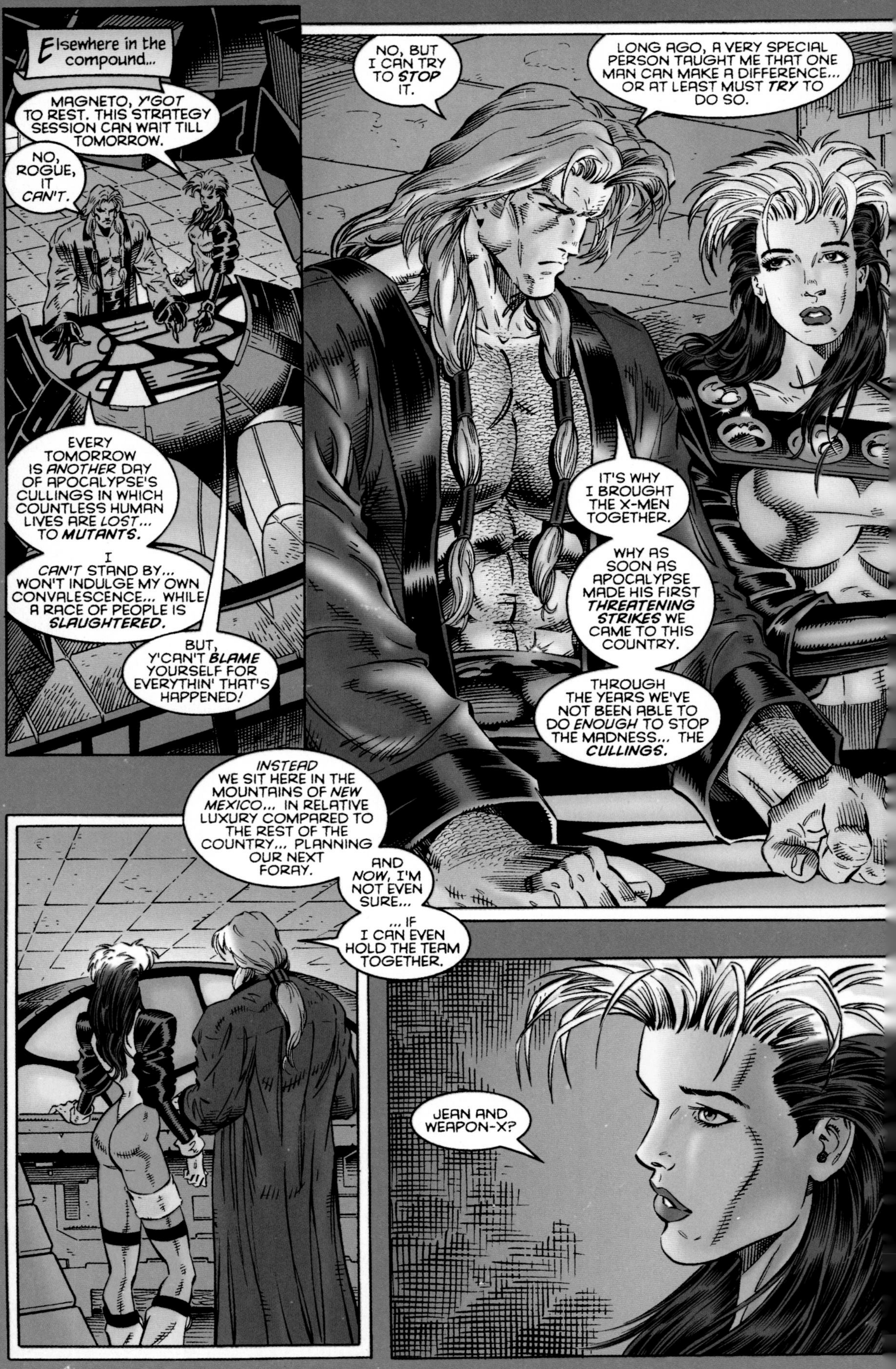
Elsewhere in the compound...
MAGNETO, Y'GOT TO REST. THIS STRATEGY SESSION CAN WAIT TILL TOMORROW.
NO, ROGUE, IT CAN'T.
EVERY TOMORROW IS ANOTHER DAY OF APOCALYPSE'S CULLINGS IN WHICH COUNTLESS HUMAN LIVES ARE LOST... TO MUTANTS.
I CAN'T STAND BY... WON'T INDULGE MY OWN CONVALESCENCE... WHILE A RACE OF PEOPLE IS SLAUGHTERED.
BUT, Y'CAN'T BLAME YOURSELF FOR EVERYTHIN' THAT'S HAPPENED!
NO, BUT I CAN TRY TO STOP IT.
LONG AGO, A VERY SPECIAL PERSON TAUGHT ME THAT ONE MAN CAN MAKE A DIFFERENCE... OR AT LEAST MUST TRY TO DO SO.
IT'S WHY I BROUGHT THE X-MEN TOGETHER.
WHY AS SOON AS APOCALYPSE MADE HIS FIRST THREATENING STRIKES WE CAME TO THIS COUNTRY.
THROUGH THE YEARS WE'VE NOT BEEN ABLE TO DO ENOUGH TO STOP THE MADNESS... THE CULLINGS.
INSTEAD WE SIT HERE IN THE MOUNTAINS OF NEW MEXICO... IN RELATIVE LUXURY COMPARED TO THE REST OF THE COUNTRY... PLANNING OUR NEXT FORAY.
AND NOW, I'M NOT EVEN SURE...
...IF I CAN EVEN HOLD THE TEAM TOGETHER.
JEAN AND WEAPON-X?

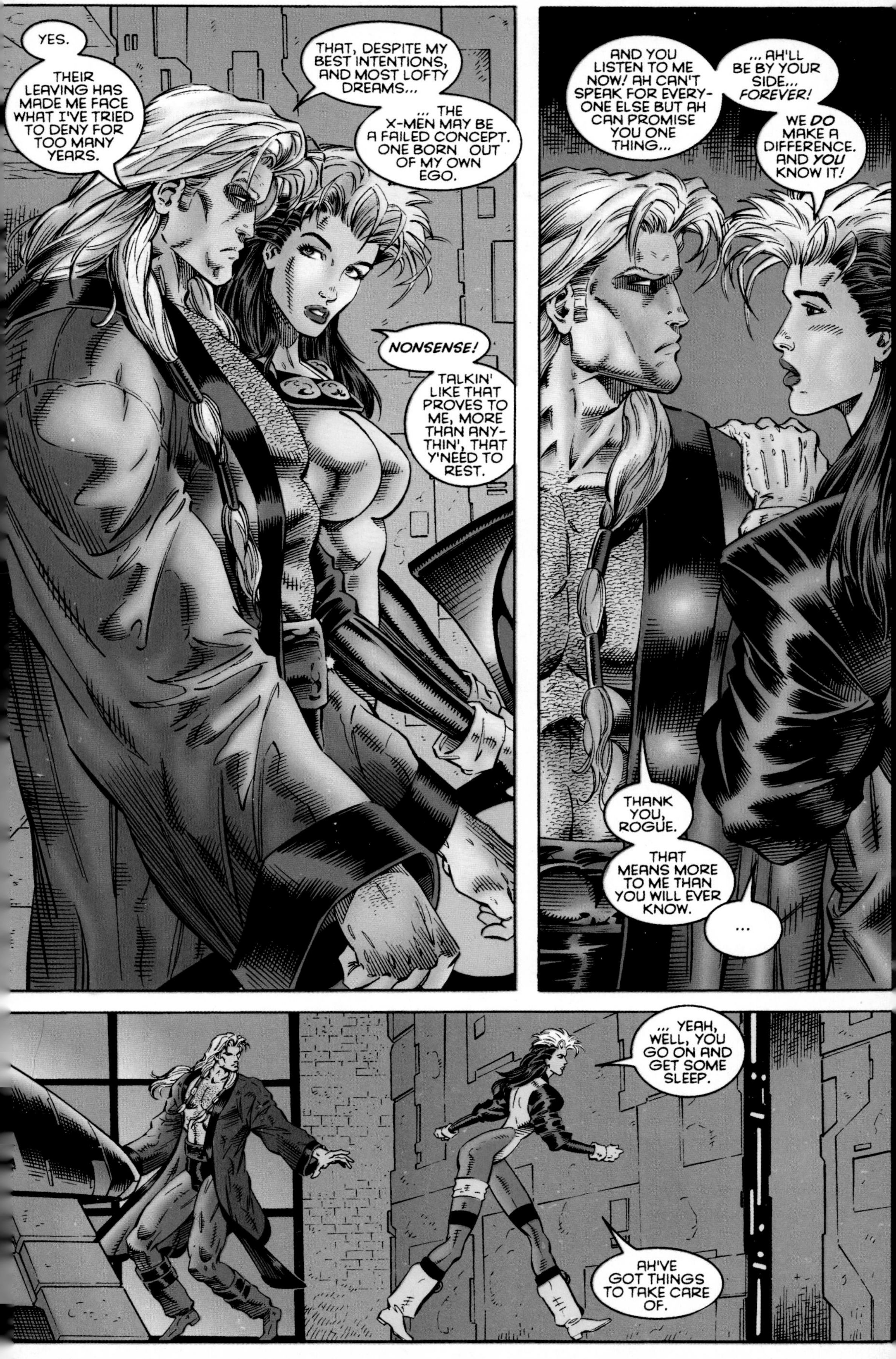
YES.
THEIR LEAVING HAS MADE ME FACE WHAT I'VE TRIED TO DENY FOR TOO MANY YEARS.
THAT, DESPITE MY BEST INTENTIONS, AND MOST LOFTY DREAMS...
... THE X-MEN MAY BE A FAILED CONCEPT. ONE BORN OUT OF MY OWN EGO.
NONSENSE!
TALKIN' LIKE THAT PROVES TO ME, MORE THAN ANY-THIN', THAT Y'NEED TO REST.
AND YOU LISTEN TO ME NOW! AH CAN'T SPEAK FOR EVERY-ONE ELSE BUT AH CAN PROMISE YOU ONE THING...
... AH'LL BE BY YOUR SIDE... FOREVER!
WE DO MAKE A DIFFERENCE. AND YOU KNOW IT!
THANK YOU, ROGUE.
THAT MEANS MORE TO ME THAN YOU WILL EVER KNOW.
...
... YEAH, WELL, YOU GO ON AND GET SOME SLEEP.
AH'VE GOT THINGS TO TAKE CARE OF.

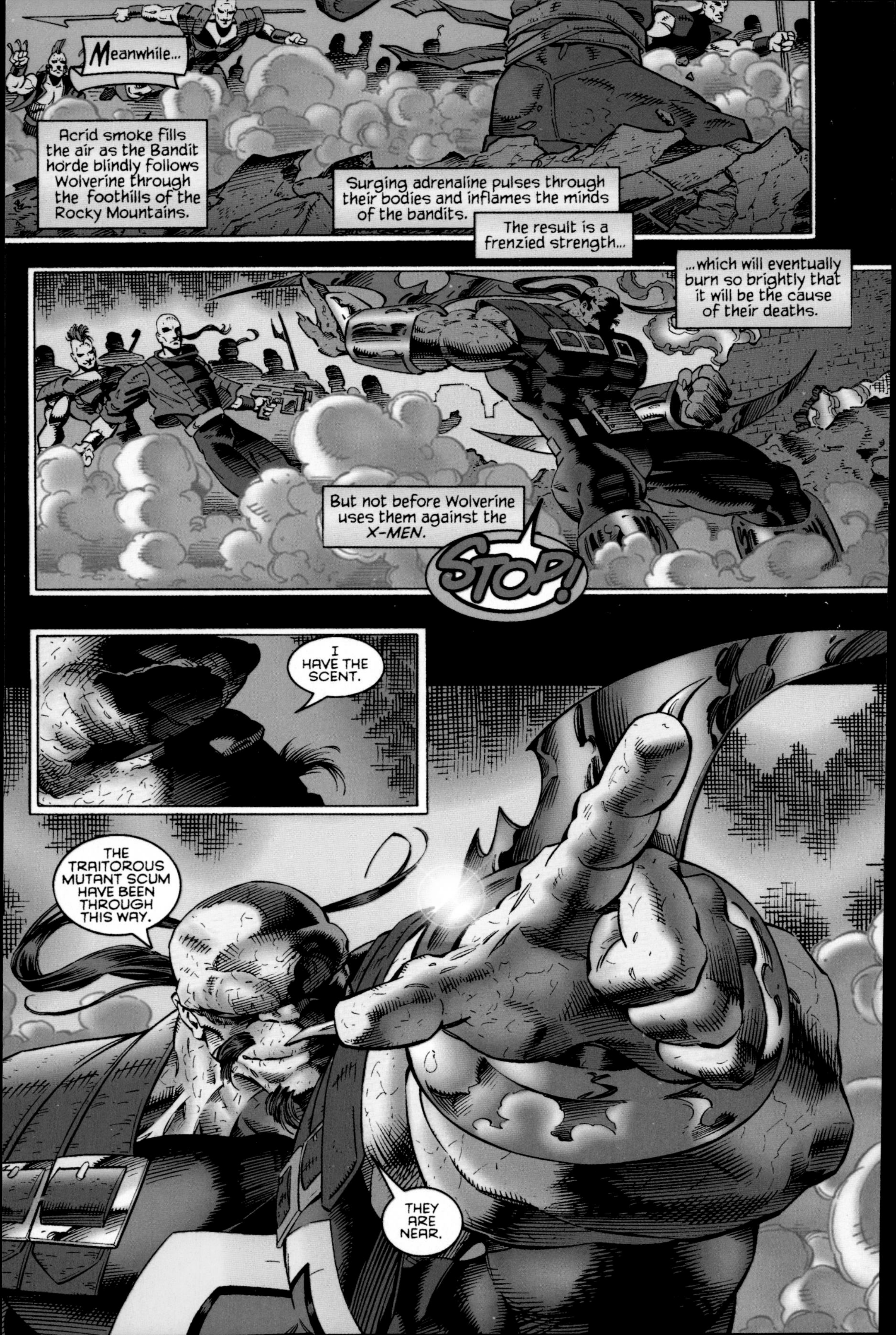
Meanwhile...
Acrid smoke fills the air as the Bandit horde blindly follows Wolverine through the foothills of the Rocky Mountains.
Surging adrenaline pulses through their bodies and inflames the minds of the bandits.
The result is a frenzied strength...
...which will eventually burn so brightly that it will be the cause of their deaths.
But not before Wolverine uses them against the X-MEN.
STOP!
I HAVE THE SCENT.
THE TRAITOROUS MUTANT SCUM HAVE BEEN THROUGH THIS WAY.
THEY ARE NEAR.

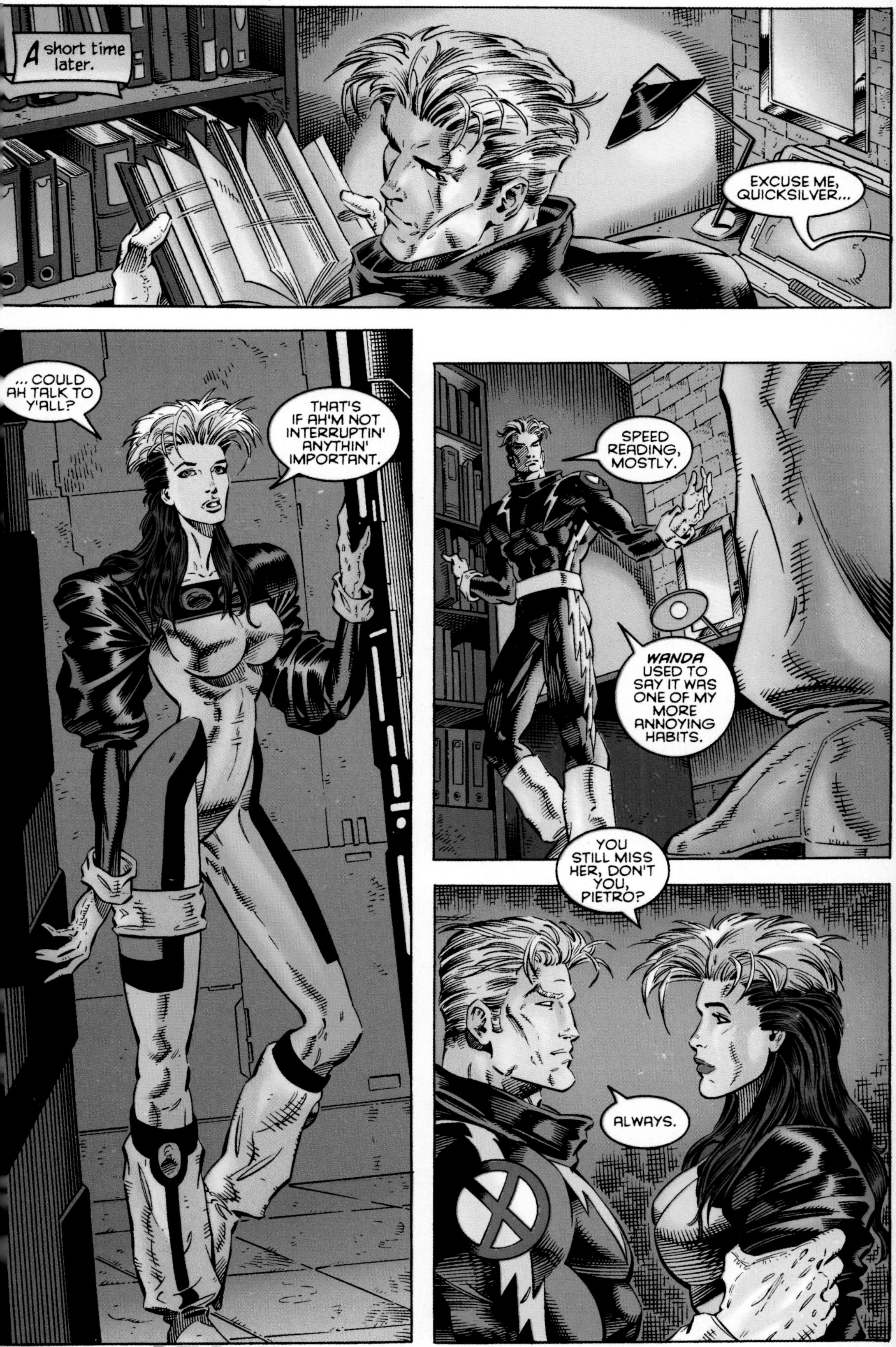
A short time later.
EXCUSE ME, QUICKSILVER...
... COULD AH TALK TO Y'ALL?
THAT'S IF AH'M NOT INTERRUPTIN' ANYTHIN' IMPORTANT.
SPEED READING, MOSTLY.
WANDA USED TO SAY IT WAS ONE OF MY MORE ANNOYING HABITS.
YOU STILL MISS HER, DON'T YOU, PIETRO?
ALWAYS.

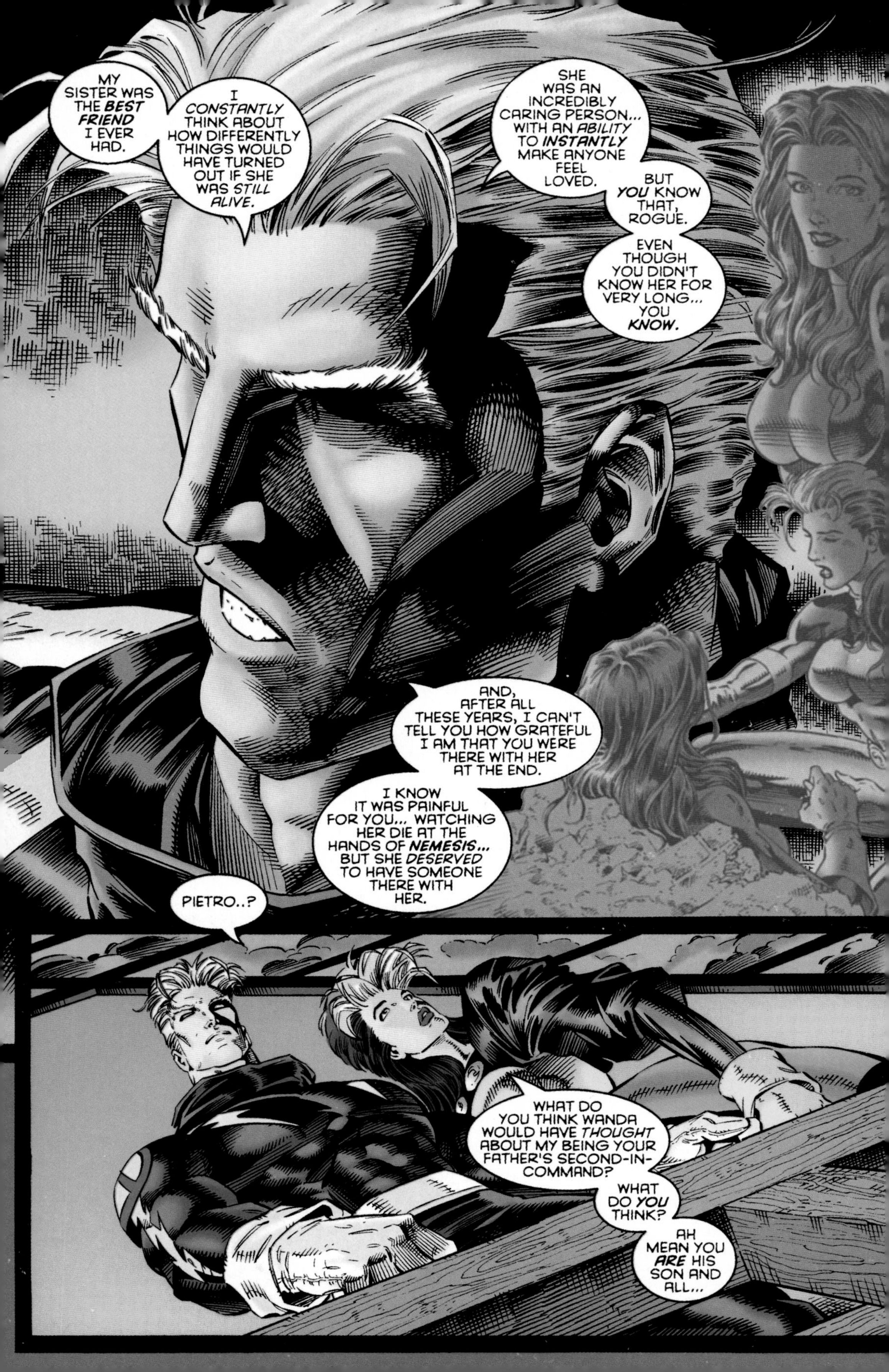
MY SISTER WAS THE BEST FRIEND I EVER HAD.
I CONSTANTLY THINK ABOUT HOW DIFFERENTLY THINGS WOULD HAVE TURNED OUT IF SHE WAS STILL ALIVE.
SHE WAS AN INCREDIBLY CARING PERSON... WITH AN ABILITY TO INSTANTLY MAKE ANYONE FEEL LOVED.
BUT YOU KNOW THAT, ROGUE.
EVEN THOUGH YOU DIDN'T KNOW HER FOR VERY LONG... YOU KNOW.
AND, AFTER ALL THESE YEARS, I CAN'T TELL YOU HOW GRATEFUL I AM THAT YOU WERE THERE WITH HER AT THE END.
I KNOW IT WAS PAINFUL FOR YOU... WATCHING HER DIE AT THE HANDS OF NEMESIS... BUT SHE DESERVED TO HAVE SOMEONE THERE WITH HER.
PIETRO..?
WHAT DO YOU THINK WANDA WOULD HAVE THOUGHT ABOUT MY BEING YOUR FATHER'S SECOND-IN-COMMAND?
WHAT DO YOU THINK?
AH MEAN YOU ARE HIS SON AND ALL...

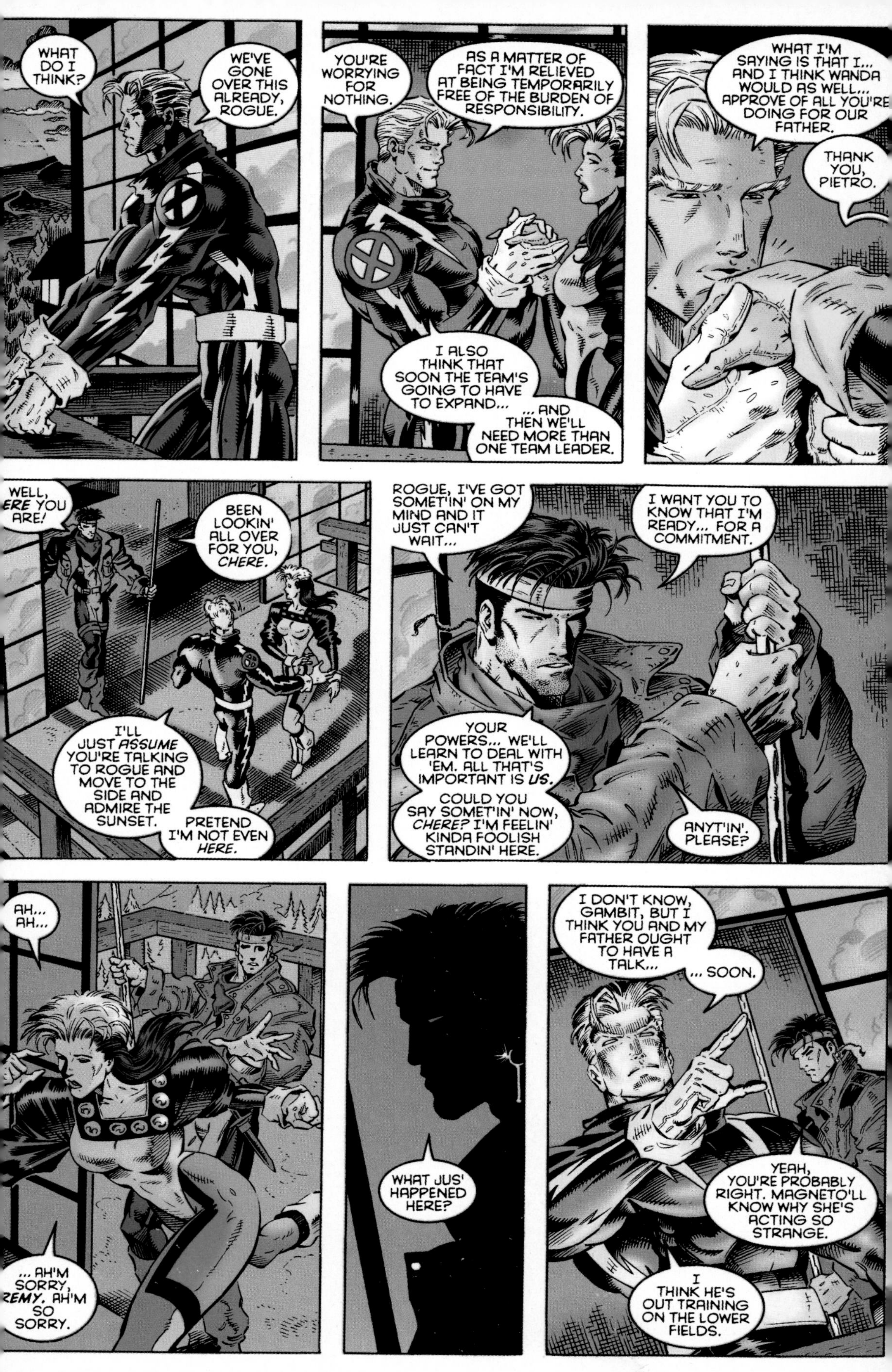
WHAT DO I THINK?
WE'VE GONE OVER THIS ALREADY, ROGUE.
YOU'RE WORRYING FOR NOTHING.
AS A MATTER OF FACT I'M RELIEVED AT BEING TEMPORARILY FREE OF THE BURDEN OF RESPONSIBILITY.
I ALSO THINK THAT SOON THE TEAM'S GOING TO HAVE TO EXPAND...
... AND THEN WE'LL NEED MORE THAN ONE TEAM LEADER.
WHAT I'M SAYING IS THAT I... AND I THINK WANDA WOULD AS WELL... APPROVE OF ALL YOU'RE DOING FOR OUR FATHER.
THANK YOU, PIETRO.
WELL, ERE YOU ARE!
BEEN LOOKIN' ALL OVER FOR YOU, CHERE.
I'LL JUST ASSUME YOU'RE TALKING TO ROGUE AND MOVE TO THE SIDE AND ADMIRE THE SUNSET.
PRETEND I'M NOT EVEN HERE.
ROGUE, I'VE GOT SOMET'IN' ON MY MIND AND IT JUST CAN'T WAIT...
I WANT YOU TO KNOW THAT I'M READY... FOR A COMMITMENT.
YOUR POWERS... WE'LL LEARN TO DEAL WITH 'EM. ALL THAT'S IMPORTANT IS US.
COULD YOU SAY SOMET'IN' NOW, CHERE? I'M FEELIN' KINDA FOOLISH STANDIN' HERE.
ANYT'IN'. PLEASE?
AH... AH...
... AH'M SORRY, REMY. AH'M SO SORRY.
WHAT JUS' HAPPENED HERE?
I DON'T KNOW, GAMBIT, BUT I THINK YOU AND MY FATHER OUGHT TO HAVE A TALK...
... SOON.
YEAH, YOU'RE PROBABLY RIGHT. MAGNETO'LL KNOW WHY SHE'S ACTING SO STRANGE.
I THINK HE'S OUT TRAINING ON THE LOWER FIELDS.

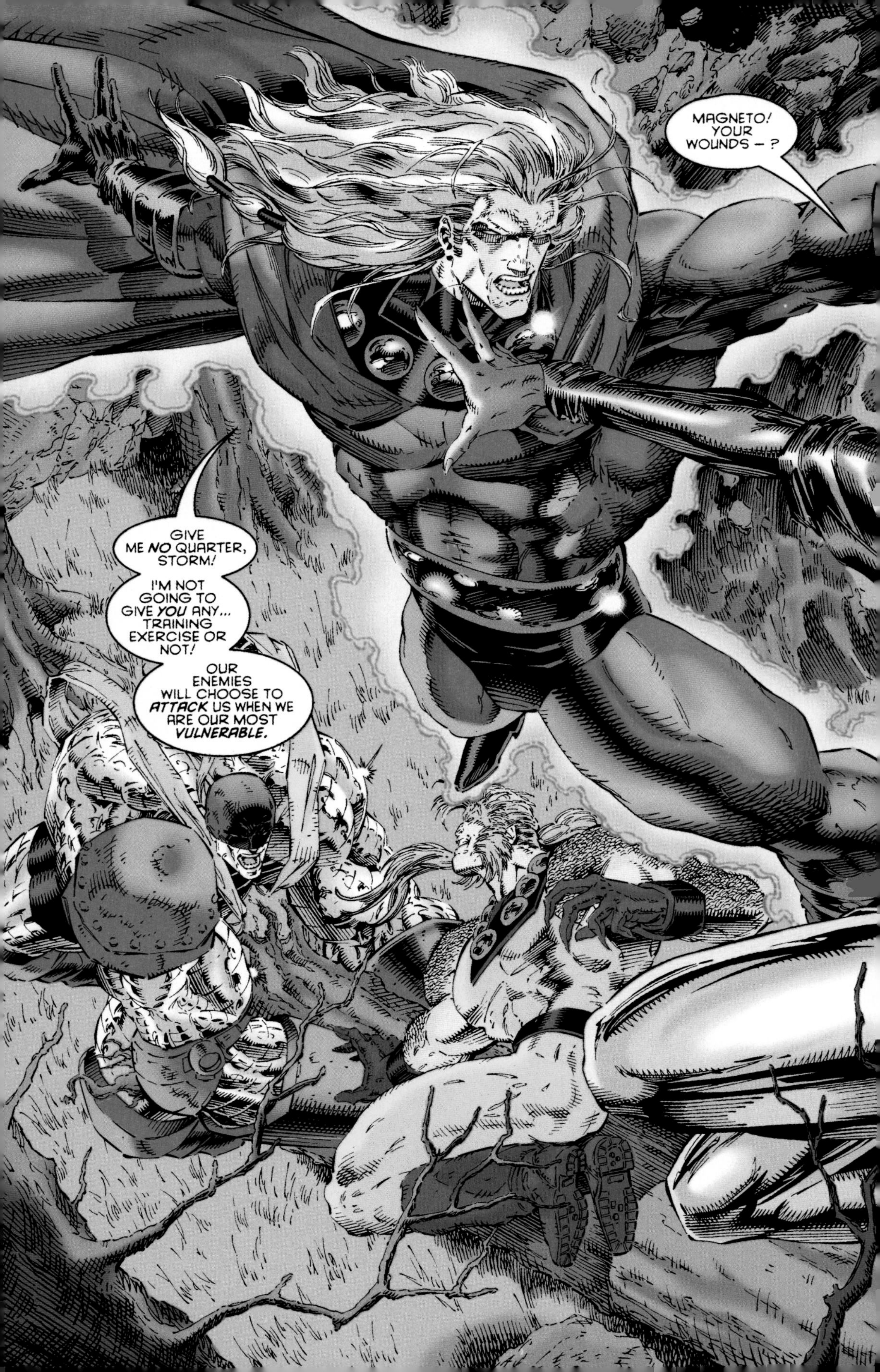
MAGNETO! YOUR WOUNDS -- ?
GIVE ME NO QUARTER, STORM!
I'M NOT GOING TO GIVE YOU ANY... TRAINING EXERCISE OR NOT!
OUR ENEMIES WILL CHOOSE TO ATTACK US WHEN WE ARE OUR MOST VULNERABLE.

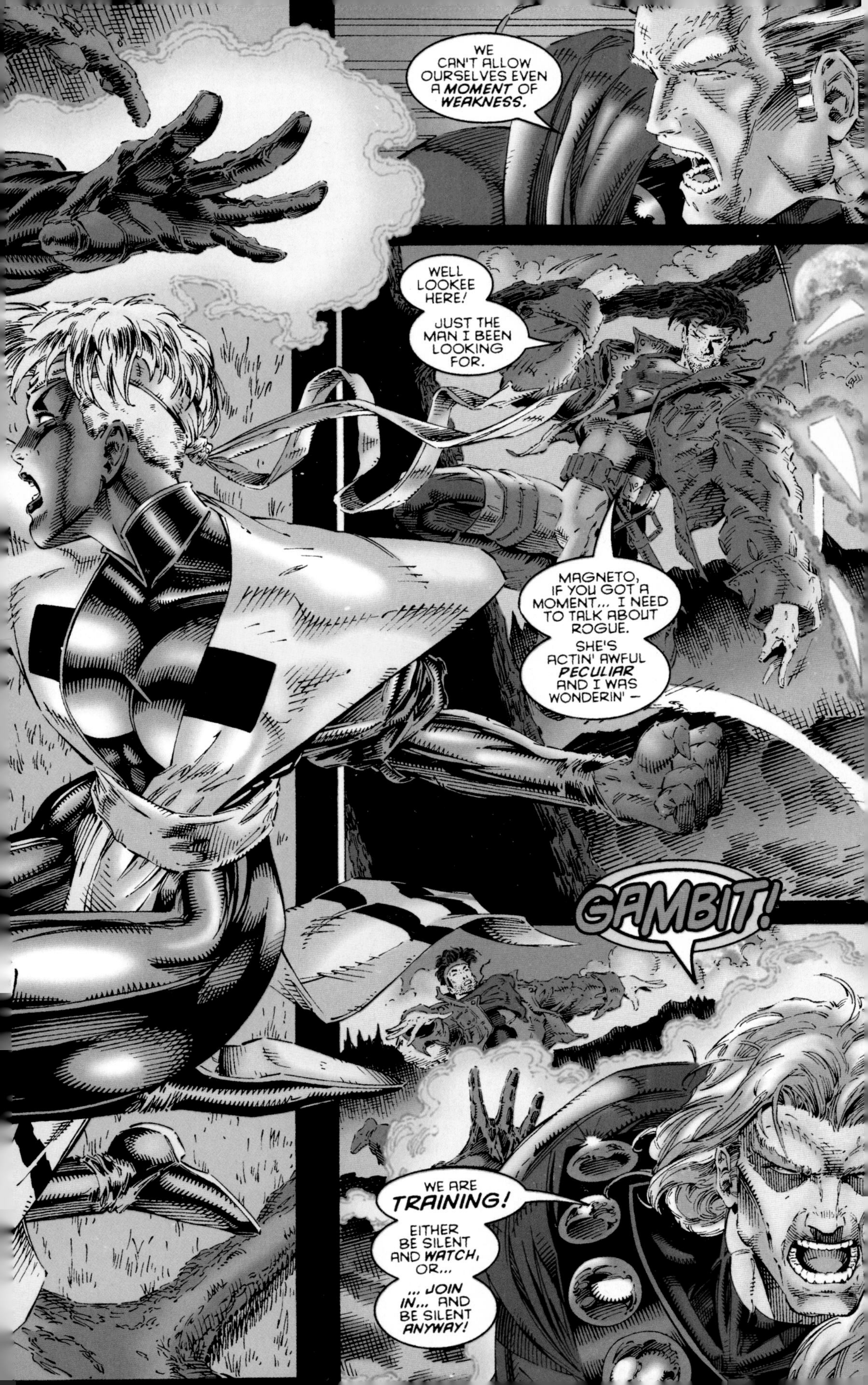
WE CAN'T ALLOW OURSELVES EVEN A MOMENT OF WEAKNESS.
WELL LOOKEE HERE!
JUST THE MAN I BEEN LOOKING FOR.
MAGNETO, IF YOU GOT A MOMENT... I NEED TO TALK ABOUT ROGUE.
SHE'S ACTIN' AWFUL PECULIAR AND I WAS WONDERIN' --
GAMBIT!
WE ARE TRAINING!
EITHER BE SILENT AND WATCH, OR...
...JOIN IN... AND BE SILENT ANYWAY!

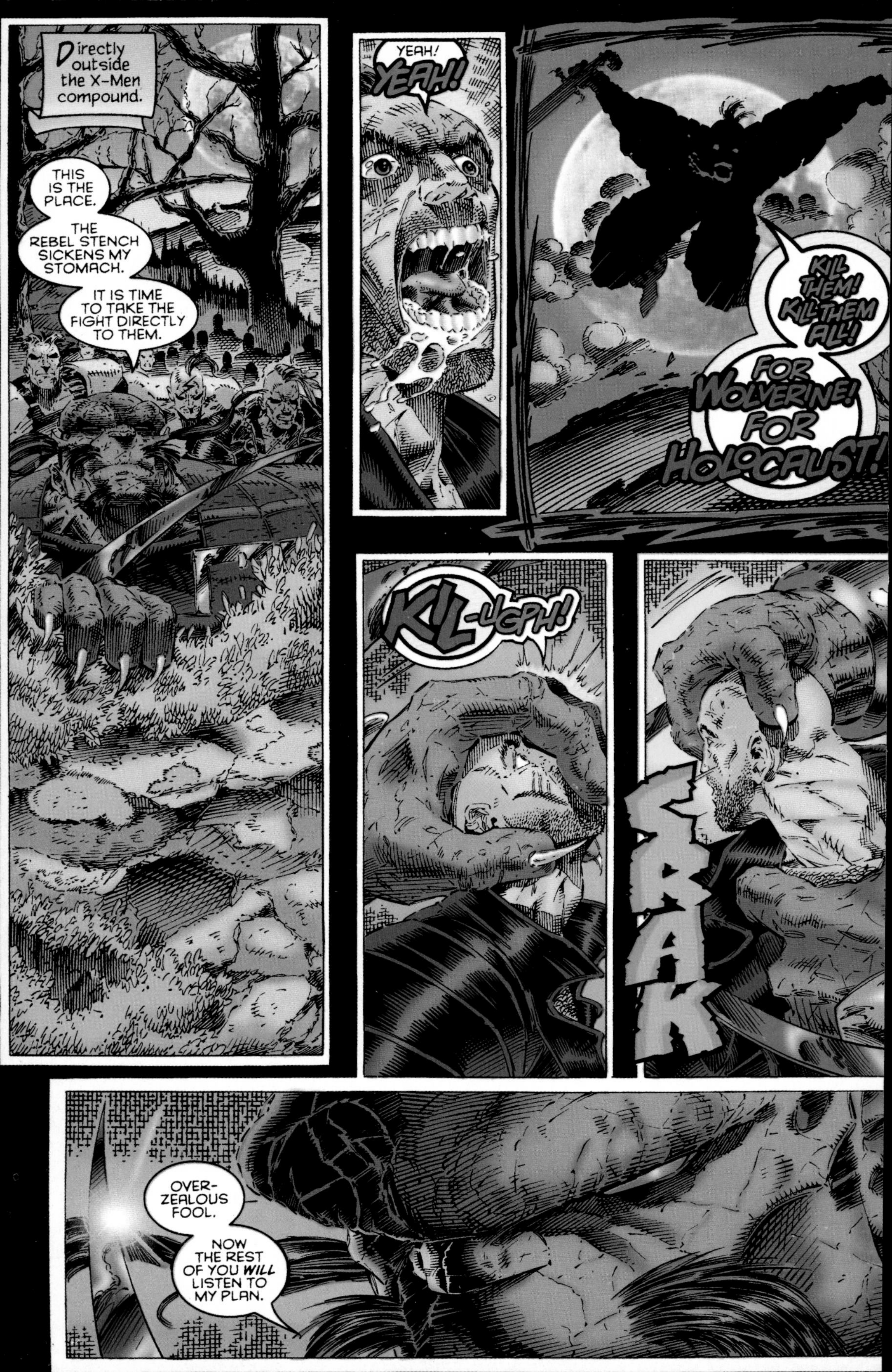
Directly outside the X-Men compound.
THIS IS THE PLACE.
THE REBEL STENCH SICKENS MY STOMACH.
IT IS TIME TO TAKE THE FIGHT DIRECTLY TO THEM.
YEAH! YEAH!
KILL THEM! KILL THEM ALL!
FOR WOLVERINE! FOR HOLOCAUST!
KIL-UGPH!
RAK
OVER-ZEALOUS FOOL.
NOW THE REST OF YOU WILL LISTEN TO MY PLAN.

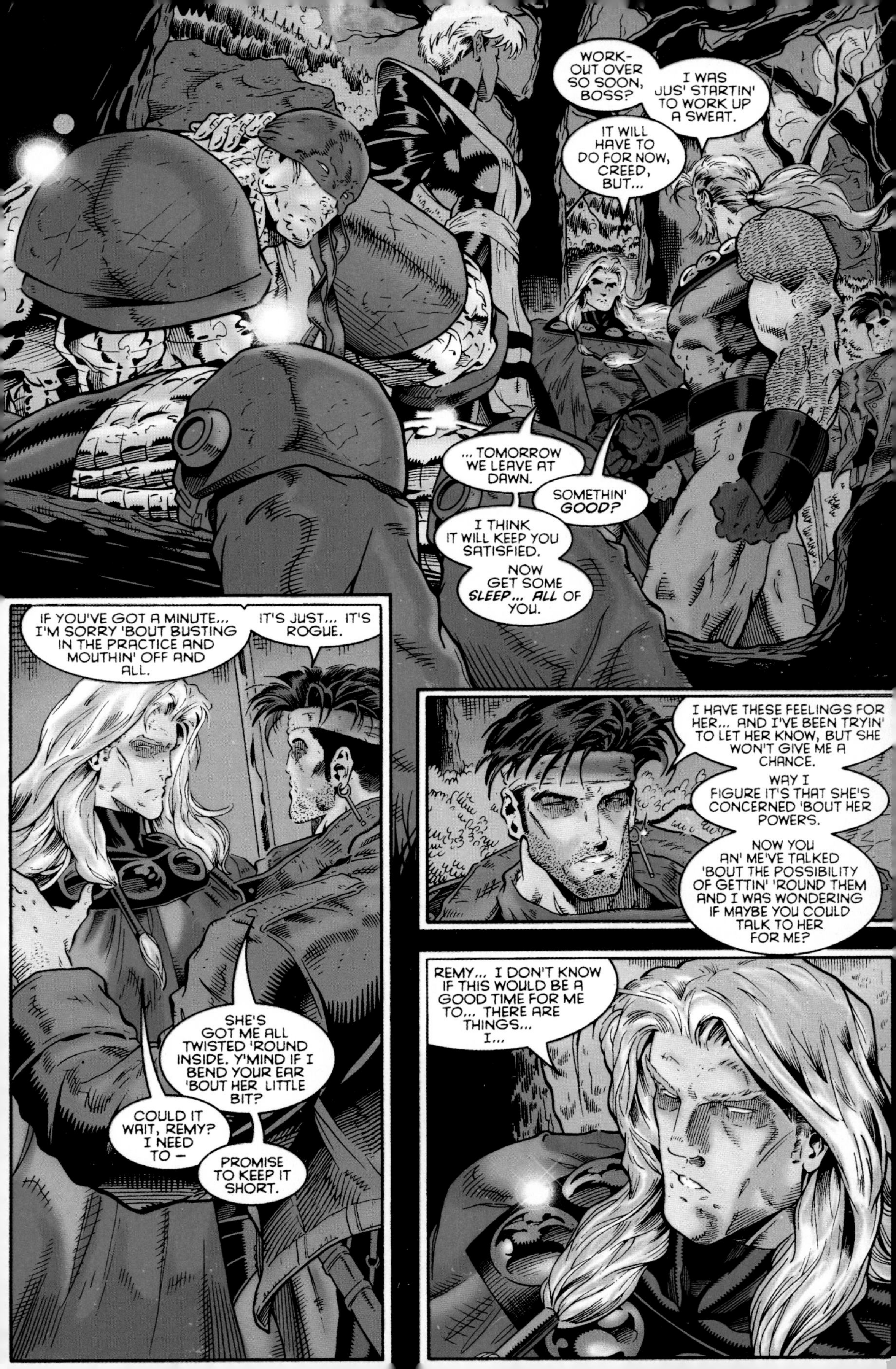
WORK-OUT OVER SO SOON, BOSS?
I WAS JUS' STARTIN' TO WORK UP A SWEAT.
IT WILL HAVE TO DO FOR NOW, CREED, BUT...
...TOMORROW WE LEAVE AT DAWN.
SOMETHIN' GOOD?
I THINK IT WILL KEEP YOU SATISFIED.
NOW GET SOME SLEEP... ALL OF YOU.
IF YOU'VE GOT A MINUTE... I'M SORRY 'BOUT BUSTING IN THE PRACTICE AND MOUTHIN' OFF AND ALL.
IT'S JUST... IT'S ROGUE.
SHE'S GOT ME ALL TWISTED 'ROUND INSIDE. Y'MIND IF I BEND YOUR EAR 'BOUT HER LITTLE BIT?
COULD IT WAIT, REMY? I NEED TO —
PROMISE TO KEEP IT SHORT.
I HAVE THESE FEELINGS FOR HER... AND I'VE BEEN TRYIN' TO LET HER KNOW, BUT SHE WON'T GIVE ME A CHANCE.
WAY I FIGURE IT'S THAT SHE'S CONCERNED 'BOUT HER POWERS.
NOW YOU AN' ME'VE TALKED 'BOUT THE POSSIBILITY OF GETTIN' 'ROUND THEM AND I WAS WONDERING IF MAYBE YOU COULD TALK TO HER FOR ME?
REMY... I DON'T KNOW IF THIS WOULD BE A GOOD TIME FOR ME TO... THERE ARE THINGS... I...

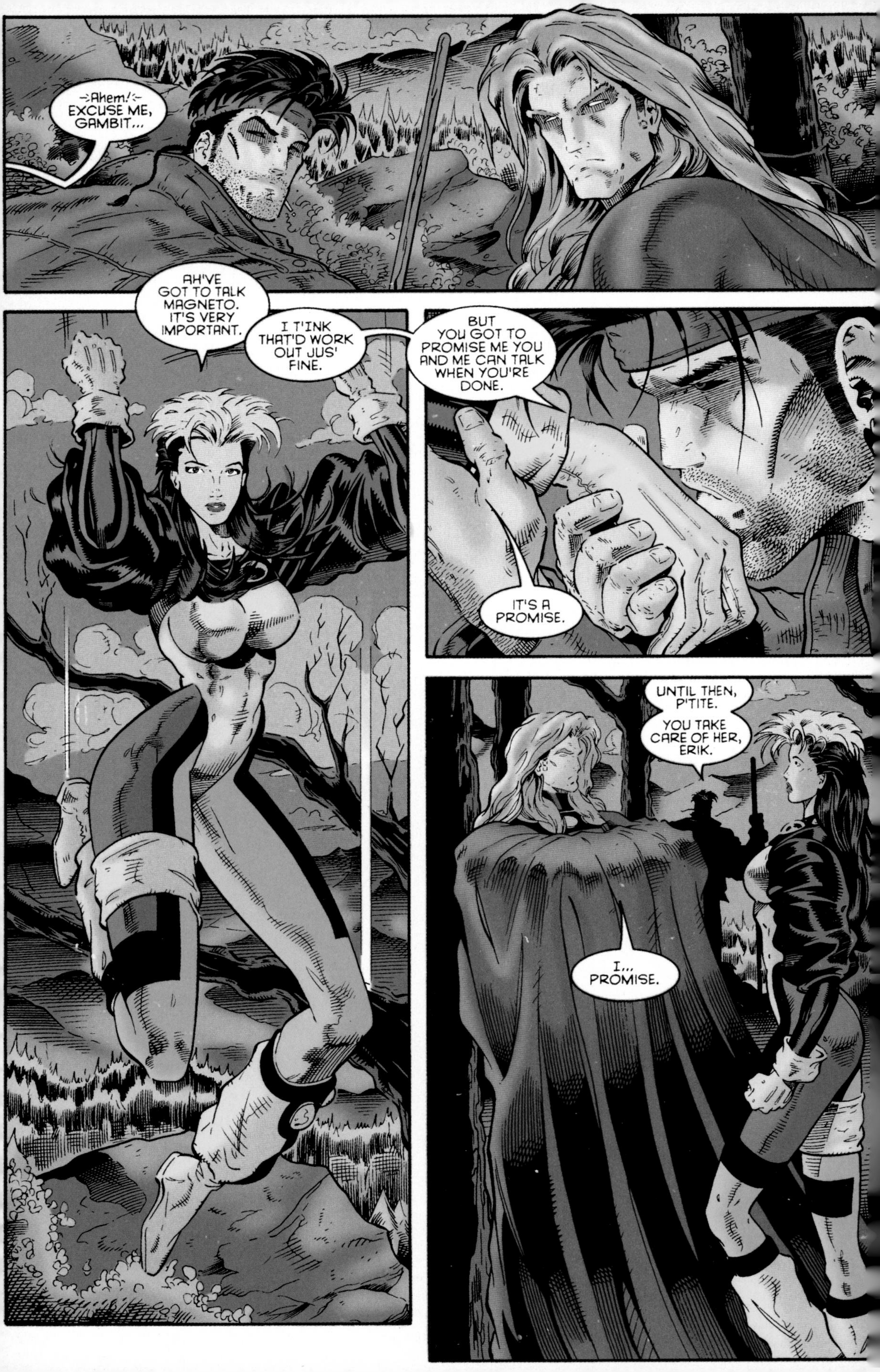

-Ahem!- EXCUSE ME, GAMBIT...
AH'VE GOT TO TALK MAGNETO. IT'S VERY IMPORTANT.
I T'INK THAT'D WORK OUT JUS' FINE.
BUT YOU GOT TO PROMISE ME YOU AND ME CAN TALK WHEN YOU'RE DONE.
IT'S A PROMISE.
UNTIL THEN, P'TITE.
YOU TAKE CARE OF HER, ERIK.
I... PROMISE.

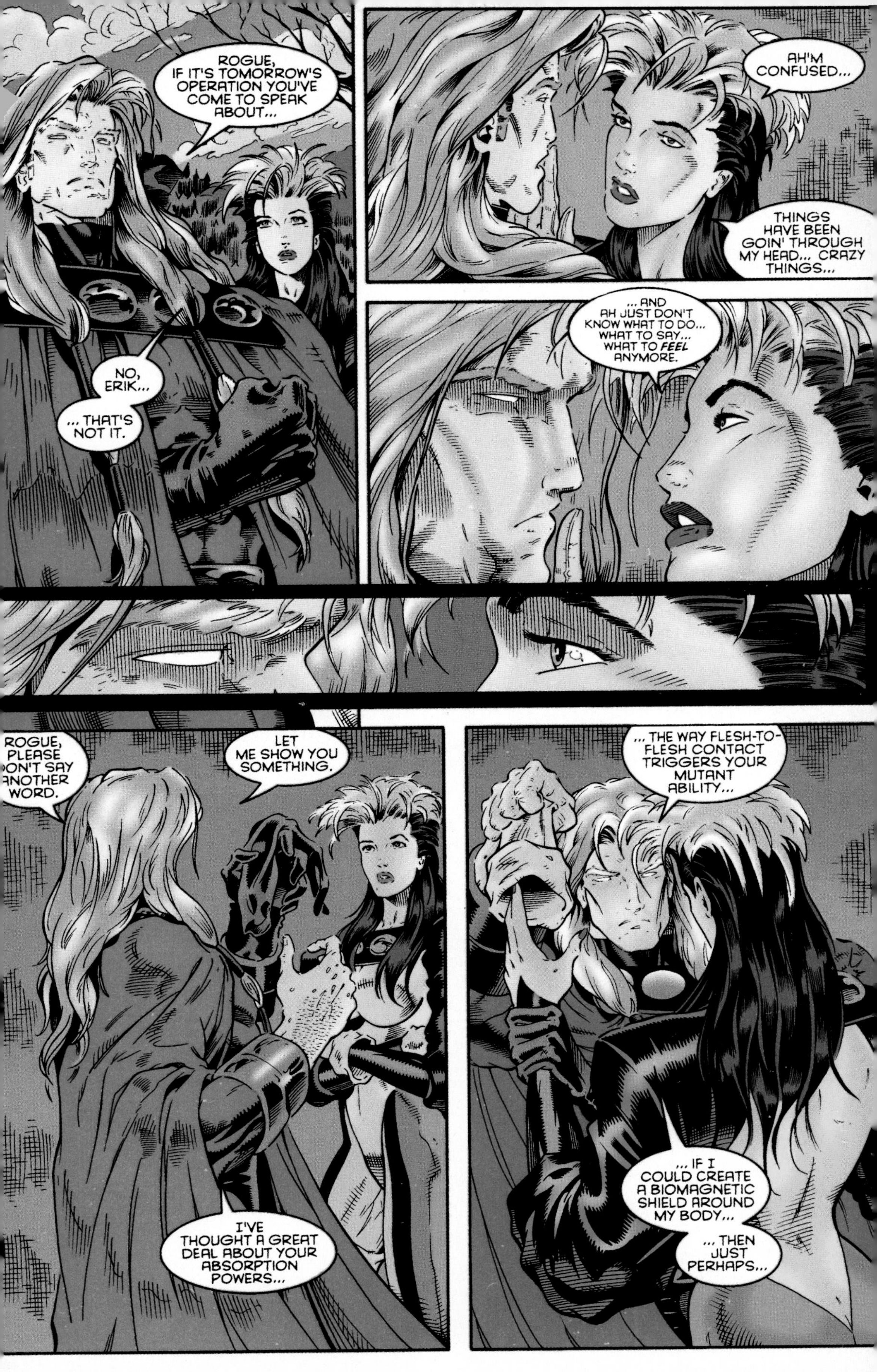

ROGUE, IF IT'S TOMORROW'S OPERATION YOU'VE COME TO SPEAK ABOUT...
NO, ERIK...
... THAT'S NOT IT.
AH'M CONFUSED...
THINGS HAVE BEEN GOIN' THROUGH MY HEAD... CRAZY THINGS...
... AND AH JUST DON'T KNOW WHAT TO DO... WHAT TO SAY... WHAT TO FEEL ANYMORE.
ROGUE, PLEASE DON'T SAY ANOTHER WORD.
LET ME SHOW YOU SOMETHING.
I'VE THOUGHT A GREAT DEAL ABOUT YOUR ABSORPTION POWERS...
... THE WAY FLESH-TO-FLESH CONTACT TRIGGERS YOUR MUTANT ABILITY...
... IF I COULD CREATE A BIOMAGNETIC SHIELD AROUND MY BODY...
... THEN JUST PERHAPS...

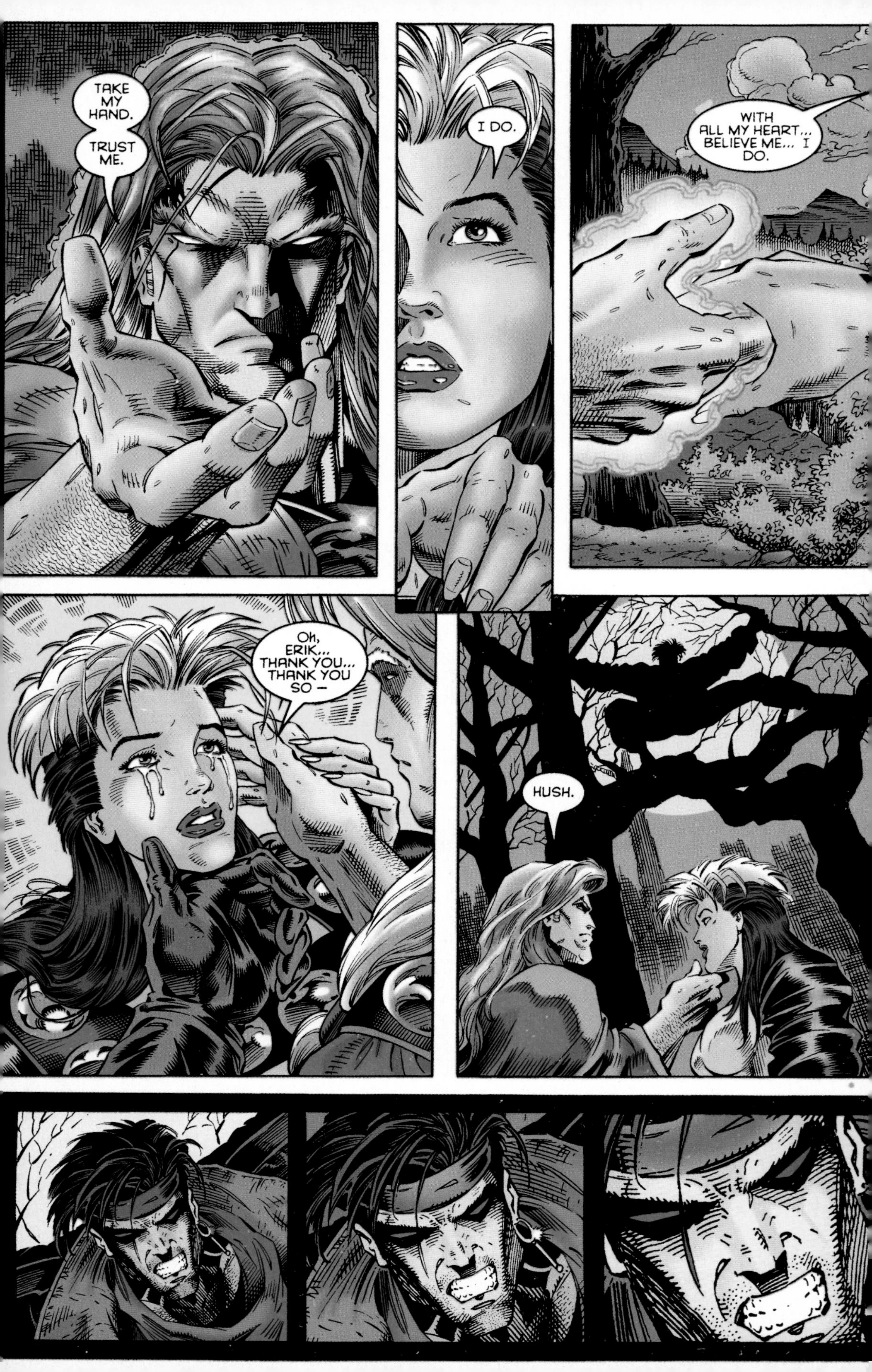
TAKE MY HAND.
TRUST ME.
I DO.
WITH ALL MY HEART... BELIEVE ME... I DO.
Oh, ERIK... THANK YOU... THANK YOU SO –
HUSH.

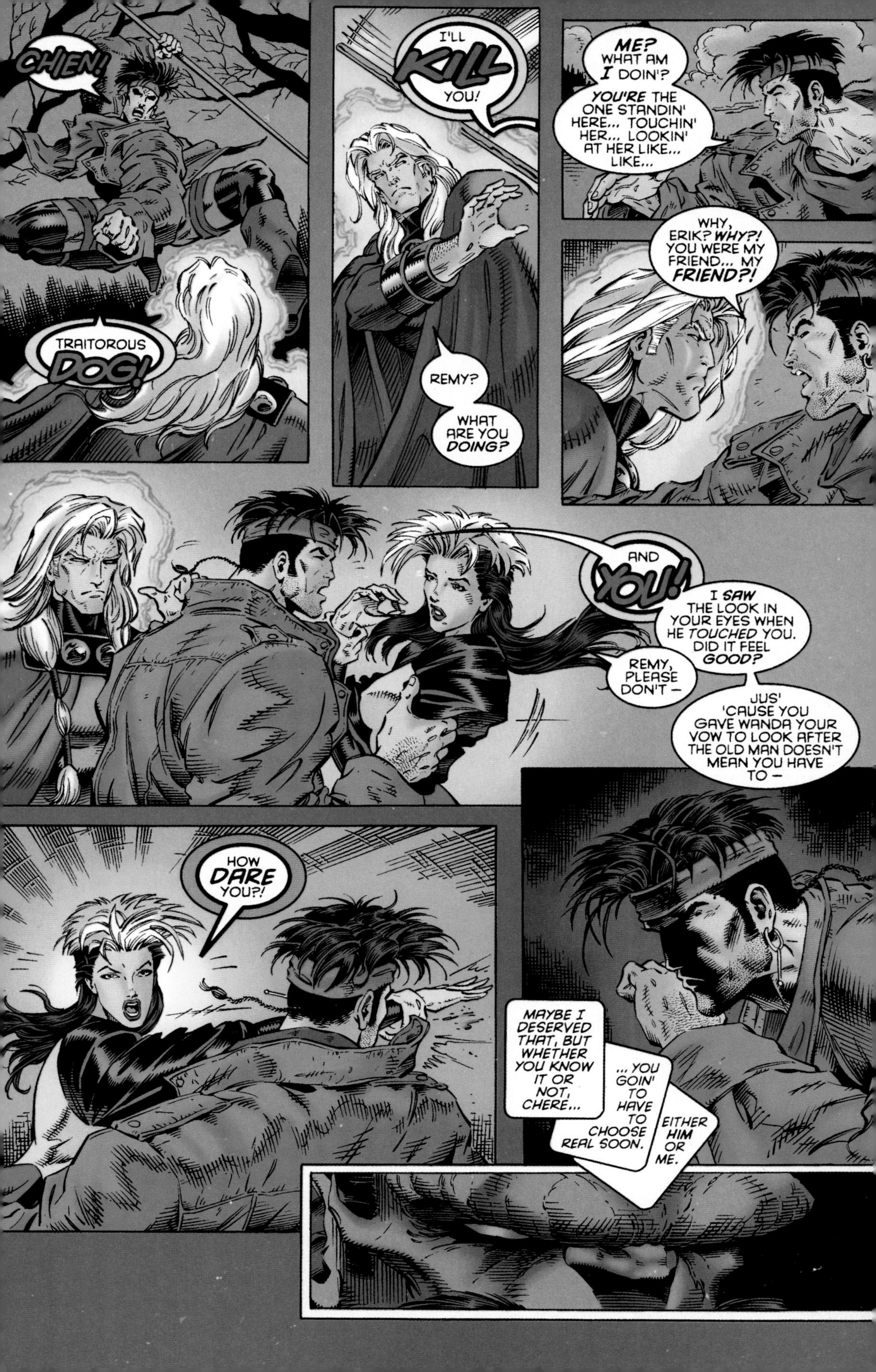
CHIEN!
TRAITOROUS DOG!
I'LL KILL YOU!
REMY?
WHAT ARE YOU DOING?
ME? WHAT AM I DOIN'?
YOU'RE THE ONE STANDIN' HERE... TOUCHIN' HER... LOOKIN' AT HER LIKE... LIKE...
WHY, ERIK? WHY?! YOU WERE MY FRIEND... MY FRIEND?!
AND YOU!
I SAW THE LOOK IN YOUR EYES WHEN HE TOUCHED YOU. DID IT FEEL GOOD?
REMY, PLEASE DON'T —
JUS' 'CAUSE YOU GAVE WANDA YOUR VOW TO LOOK AFTER THE OLD MAN DOESN'T MEAN YOU HAVE TO —
HOW DARE YOU?!
MAYBE I DESERVED THAT, BUT WHETHER YOU KNOW IT OR NOT, CHERE...
... YOU GOIN' TO HAVE TO CHOOSE REAL SOON.
EITHER HIM OR ME.

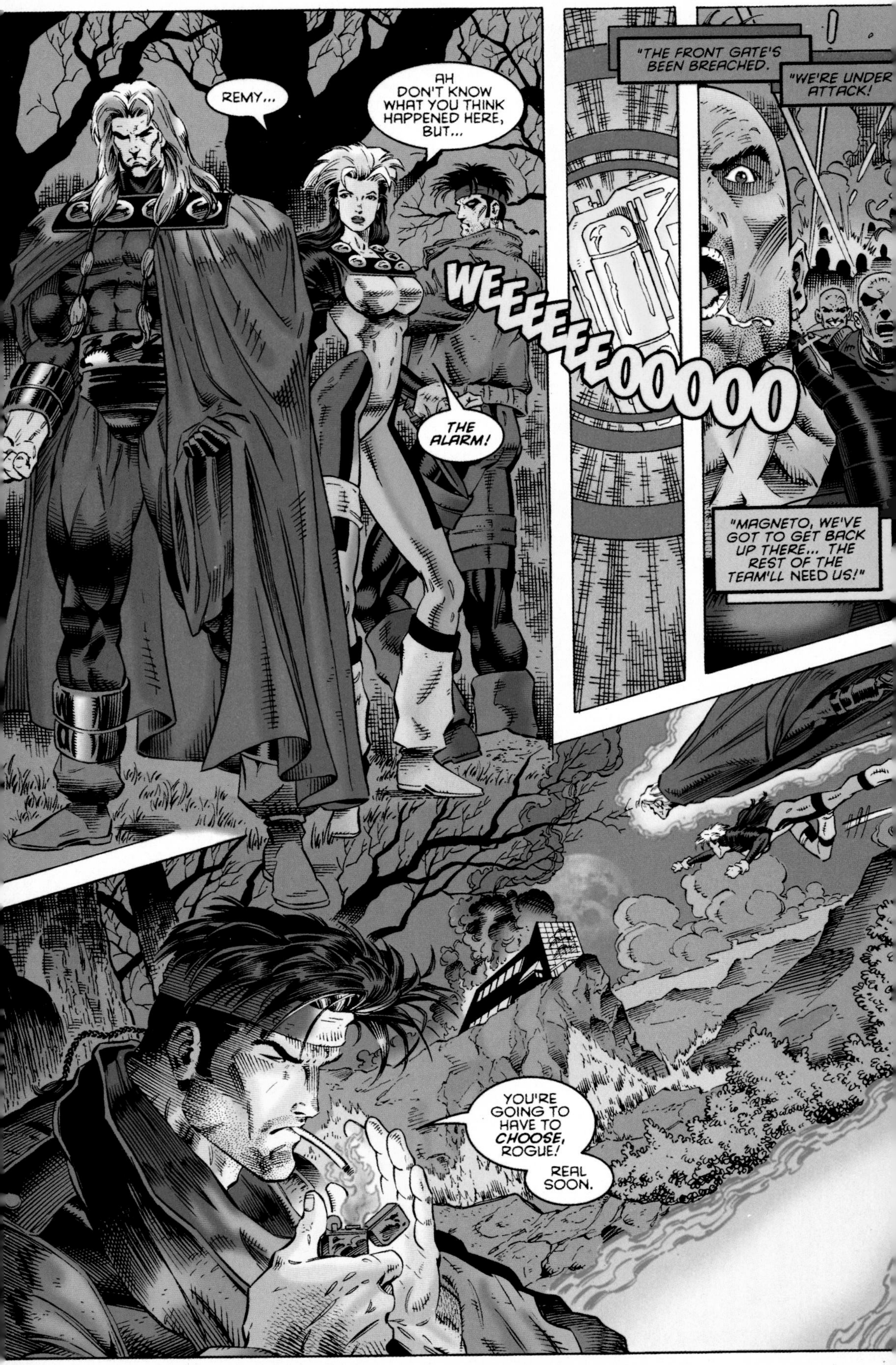
REMY...
AH DON'T KNOW WHAT YOU THINK HAPPENED HERE, BUT...
"THE FRONT GATE'S BEEN BREACHED.
"WE'RE UNDER ATTACK!
WEEEEEEOOOOO
THE ALARM!
"MAGNETO, WE'VE GOT TO GET BACK UP THERE... THE REST OF THE TEAM'LL NEED US!"
YOU'RE GOING TO HAVE TO CHOOSE, ROGUE!
REAL SOON.

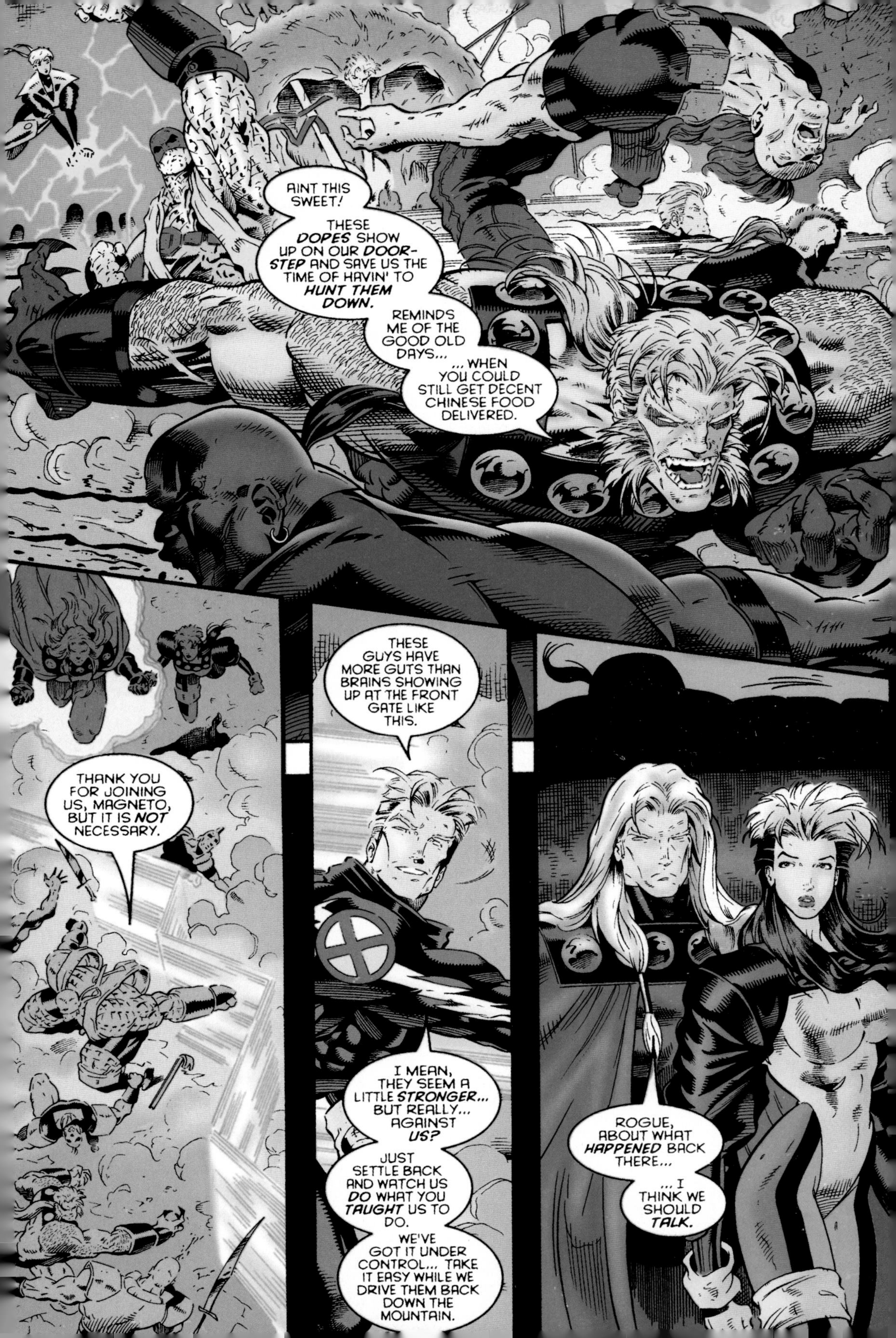
AINT THIS SWEET!
THESE DOPES SHOW UP ON OUR DOOR-STEP AND SAVE US THE TIME OF HAVIN' TO HUNT THEM DOWN.
REMINDS ME OF THE GOOD OLD DAYS...
...WHEN YOU COULD STILL GET DECENT CHINESE FOOD DELIVERED.
THANK YOU FOR JOINING US, MAGNETO, BUT IT IS NOT NECESSARY.
THESE GUYS HAVE MORE GUTS THAN BRAINS SHOWING UP AT THE FRONT GATE LIKE THIS.
I MEAN, THEY SEEM A LITTLE STRONGER... BUT REALLY... AGAINST US?
JUST SETTLE BACK AND WATCH US DO WHAT YOU TAUGHT US TO DO.
WE'VE GOT IT UNDER CONTROL... TAKE IT EASY WHILE WE DRIVE THEM BACK DOWN THE MOUNTAIN.
ROGUE, ABOUT WHAT HAPPENED BACK THERE...
...I THINK WE SHOULD TALK.

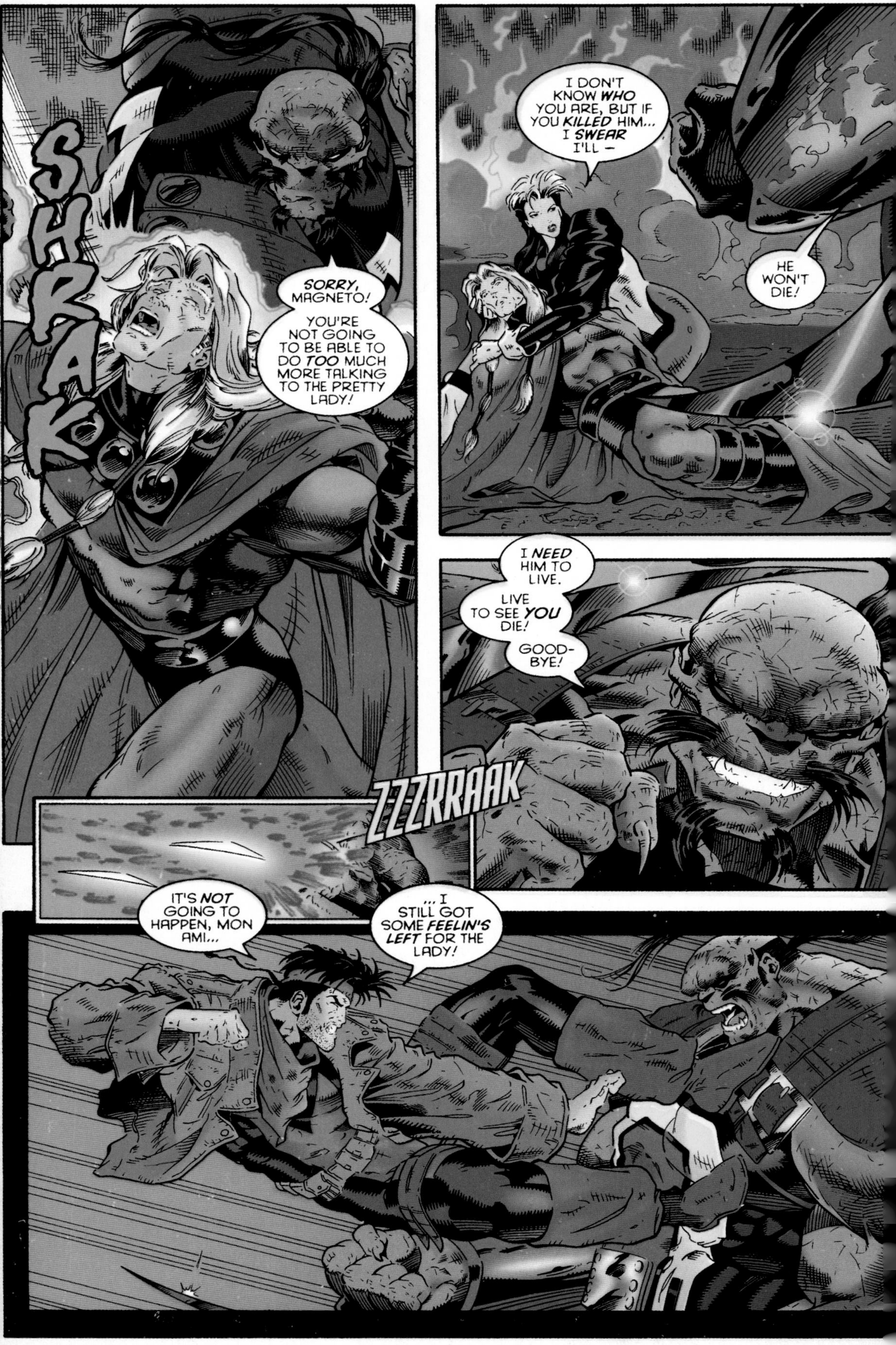
SHRAK
SORRY, MAGNETO!
YOU'RE NOT GOING TO BE ABLE TO DO TOO MUCH MORE TALKING TO THE PRETTY LADY!
I DON'T KNOW WHO YOU ARE, BUT IF YOU KILLED HIM... I SWEAR I'LL —
HE WON'T DIE!
I NEED HIM TO LIVE.
LIVE TO SEE YOU DIE!
GOOD-BYE!
ZZZRRAAK
IT'S NOT GOING TO HAPPEN, MON AMI...
... I STILL GOT SOME FEELIN'S LEFT FOR THE LADY!

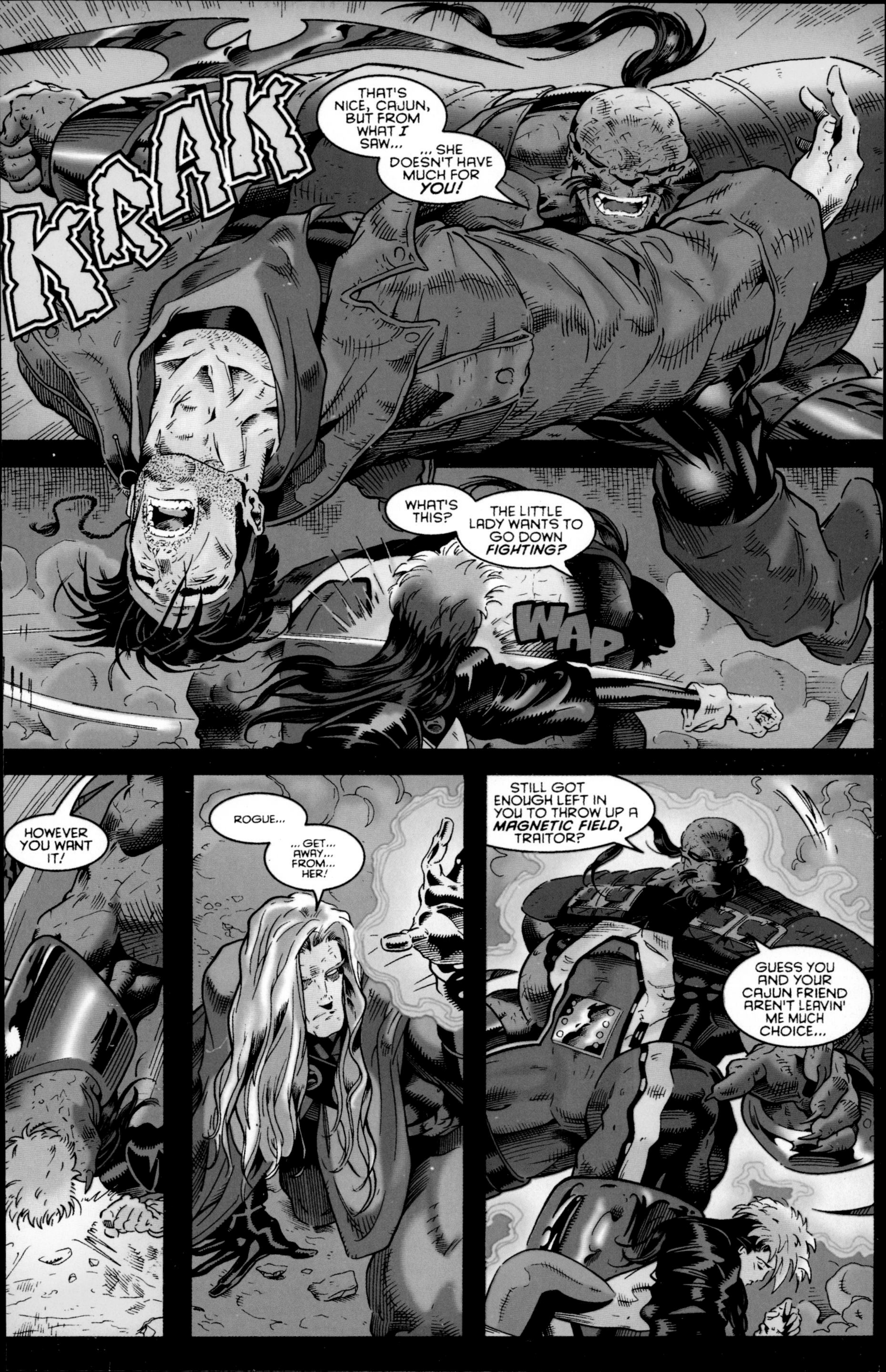
KRAK
THAT'S NICE, CAJUN, BUT FROM WHAT I SAW...
..., SHE DOESN'T HAVE MUCH FOR YOU!
WHAT'S THIS?
THE LITTLE LADY WANTS TO GO DOWN FIGHTING?
WAP
HOWEVER YOU WANT IT!
ROGUE...
..., GET... AWAY... FROM... HER!
STILL GOT ENOUGH LEFT IN YOU TO THROW UP A MAGNETIC FIELD, TRAITOR?
GUESS YOU AND YOUR CAJUN FRIEND AREN'T LEAVIN' ME MUCH CHOICE...

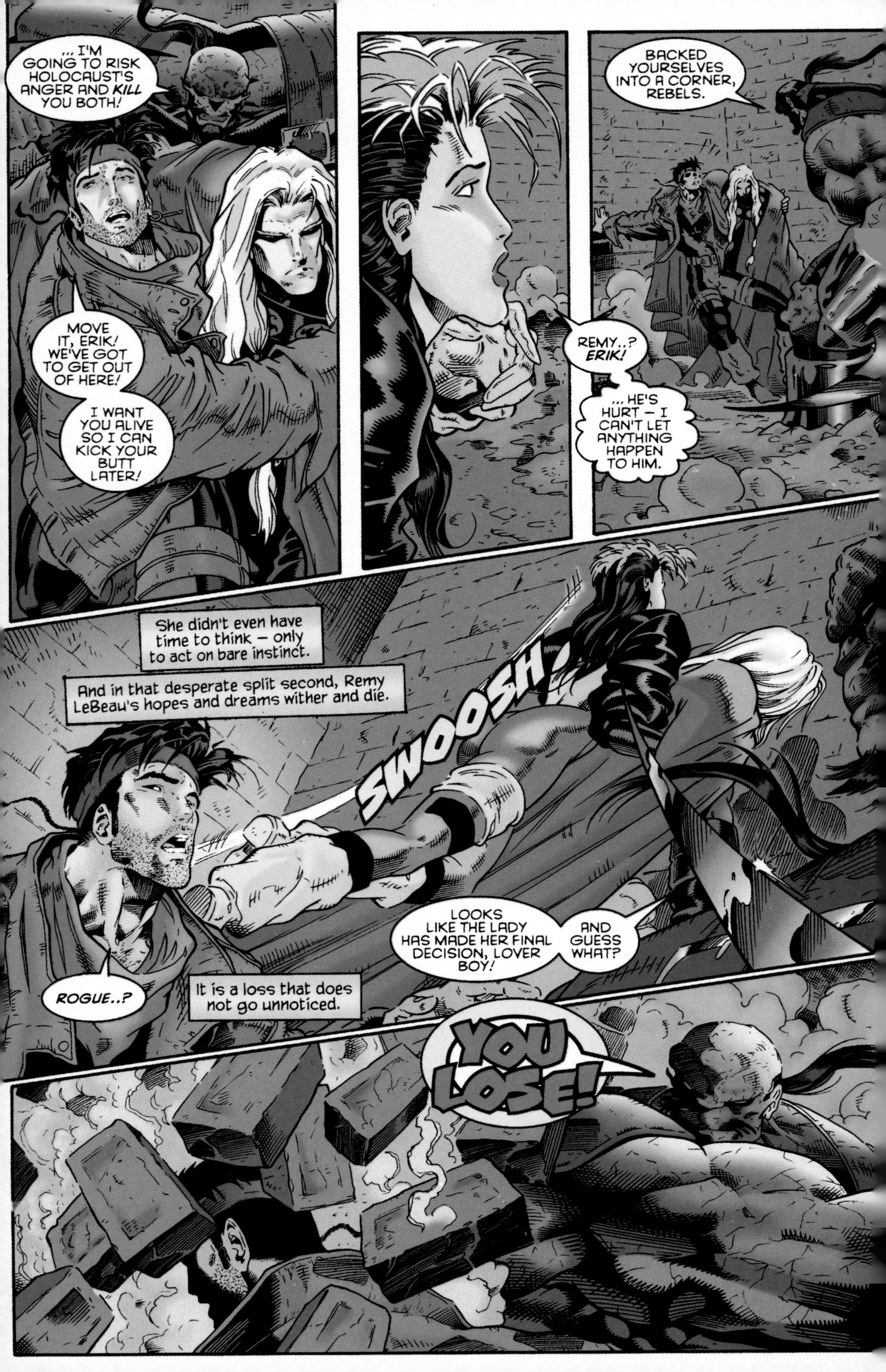
...I'M GOING TO RISK HOLOCAUST'S ANGER AND KILL YOU BOTH!
MOVE IT, ERIK! WE'VE GOT TO GET OUT OF HERE!
I WANT YOU ALIVE SO I CAN KICK YOUR BUTT LATER!
REMY..? ERIK!
...HE'S HURT — I CAN'T LET ANYTHING HAPPEN TO HIM.
BACKED YOURSELVES INTO A CORNER, REBELS.
She didn't even have time to think — only to act on bare instinct.
And in that desperate split second, Remy LeBeau's hopes and dreams wither and die.
SWOOSH
ROGUE..?
It is a loss that does not go unnoticed.
LOOKS LIKE THE LADY HAS MADE HER FINAL DECISION, LOVER BOY!
AND GUESS WHAT?
YOU LOSE!

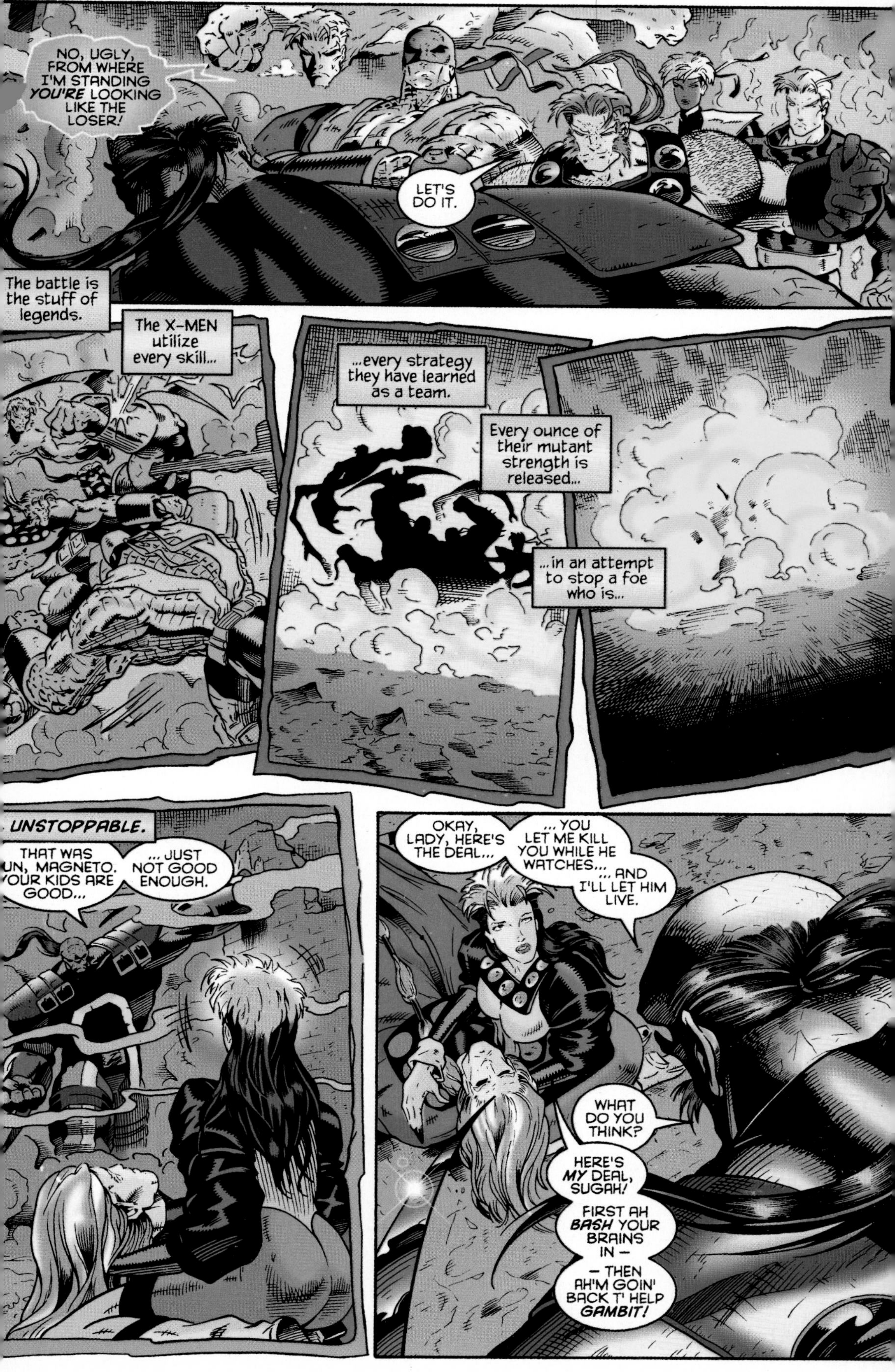
NO, UGLY, FROM WHERE I'M STANDING *YOU'RE* LOOKING LIKE THE LOSER!
LET'S DO IT.
The battle is the stuff of legends.
The X-MEN utilize every skill...
...every strategy they have learned as a team.
Every ounce of their mutant strength is released...
...in an attempt to stop a foe who is...
UNSTOPPABLE.
THAT WAS UN, MAGNETO. YOUR KIDS ARE GOOD...
... JUST NOT GOOD ENOUGH.
OKAY, LADY, HERE'S THE DEAL...
... YOU LET ME KILL YOU WHILE HE WATCHES...
... AND I'LL LET HIM LIVE.
WHAT DO YOU THINK?
HERE'S *MY* DEAL, SUGAH!
FIRST AH *BASH* YOUR BRAINS IN —
— THEN AH'M GOIN' BACK T' HELP *GAMBIT!*

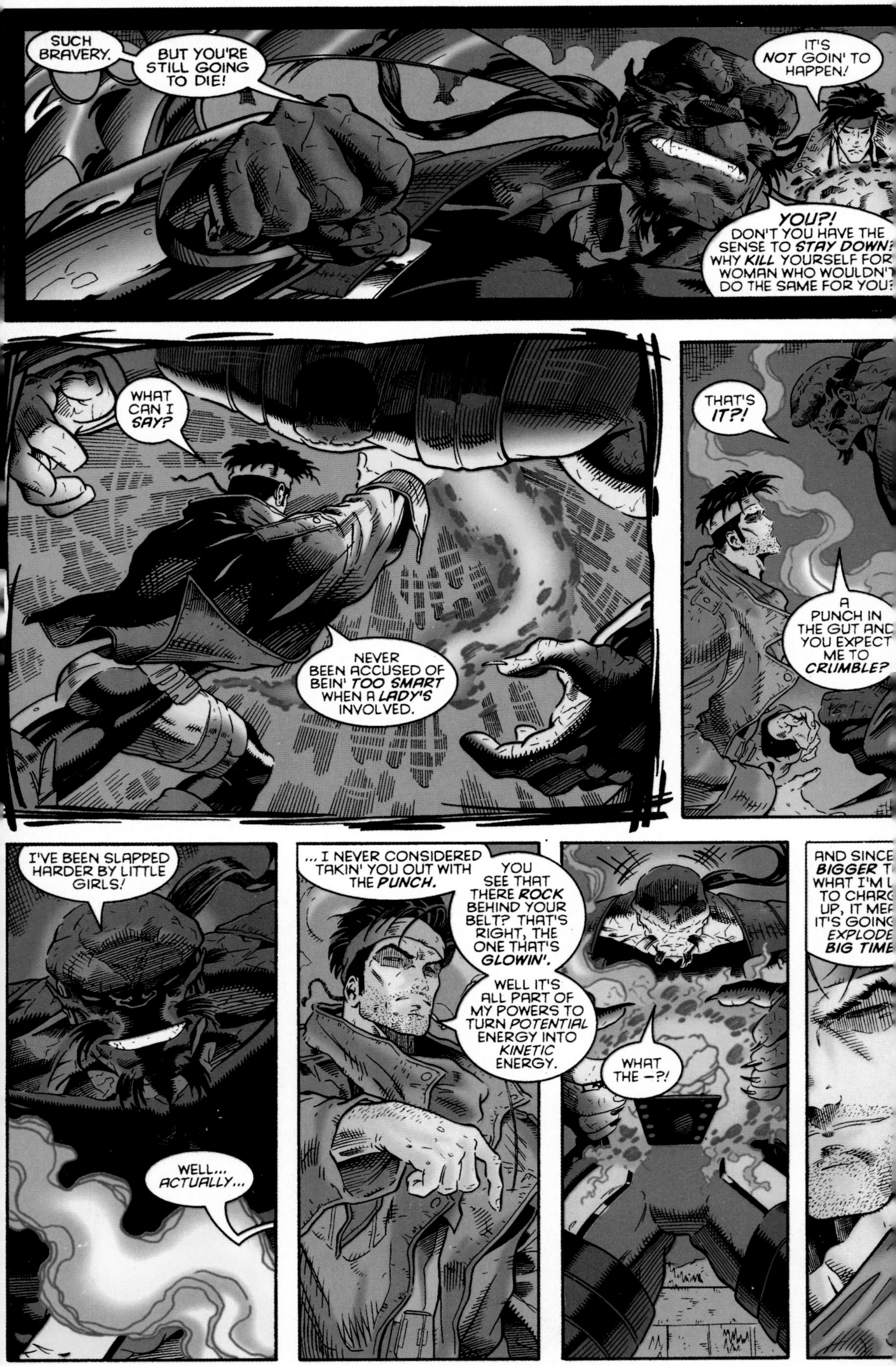
SUCH BRAVERY.
BUT YOU'RE STILL GOING TO DIE!
IT'S *NOT* GOIN' TO HAPPEN!
YOU?! DON'T YOU HAVE THE SENSE TO *STAY DOWN?* WHY *KILL* YOURSELF FOR WOMAN WHO WOULDN'T DO THE SAME FOR YOU?
WHAT CAN I *SAY?*
NEVER BEEN ACCUSED OF BEIN' *TOO SMART* WHEN A *LADY'S* INVOLVED.
THAT'S *IT?!*
A PUNCH IN THE GUT AND YOU EXPECT ME TO *CRUMBLE?*
I'VE BEEN SLAPPED HARDER BY LITTLE GIRLS!
WELL... *ACTUALLY*...
... I NEVER CONSIDERED TAKIN' YOU OUT WITH THE *PUNCH.*
YOU SEE THAT THERE *ROCK* BEHIND YOUR BELT? THAT'S RIGHT, THE ONE THAT'S *GLOWIN'.*
WELL IT'S ALL PART OF MY POWERS TO TURN *POTENTIAL* ENERGY INTO *KINETIC* ENERGY.
WHAT THE --?!
AND SINCE *BIGGER* WHAT I'M TO CHARG UP, IT MEA IT'S GOING *EXPLODE BIG TIME*

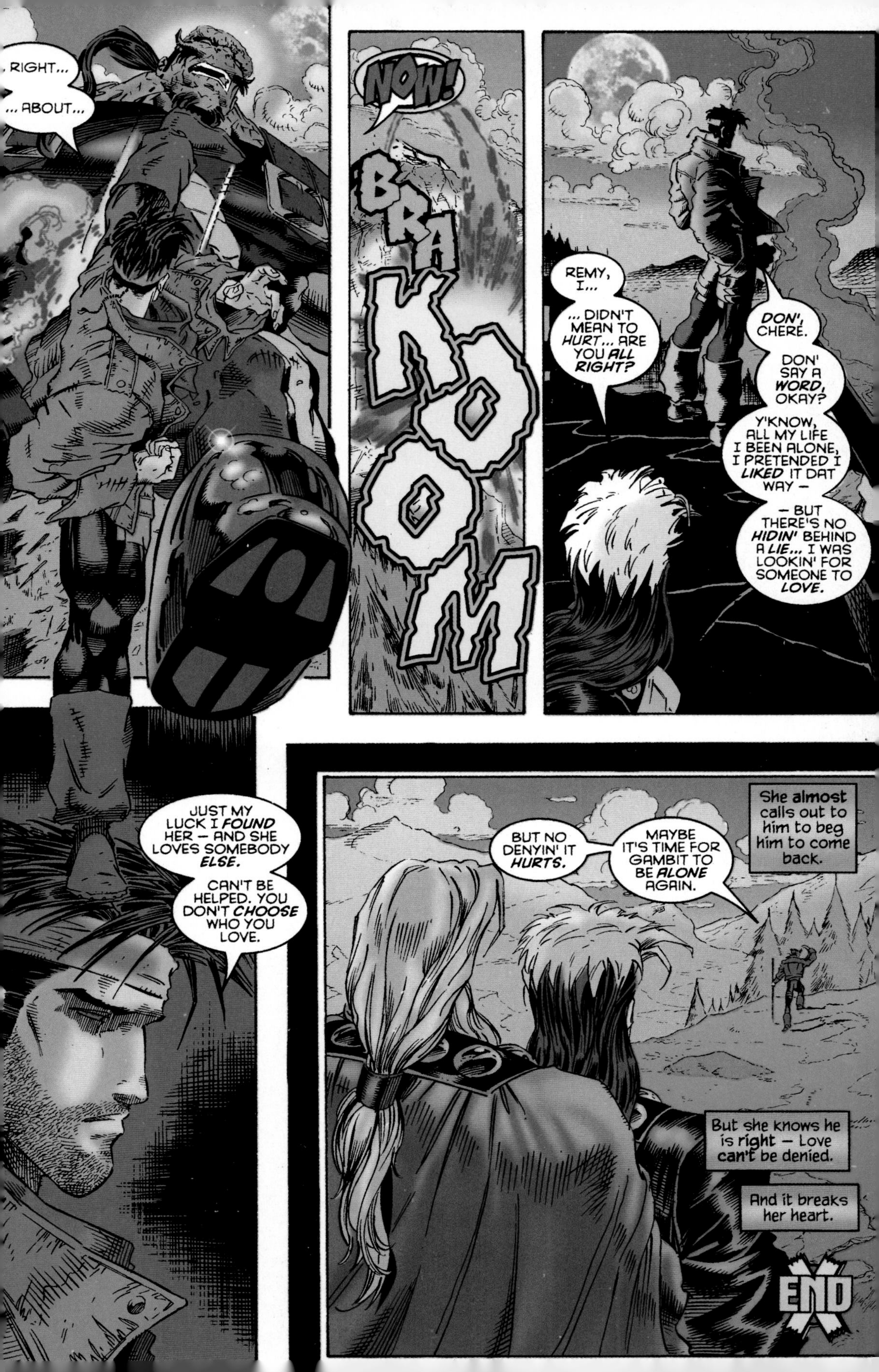

... RIGHT...
... ABOUT...
NOW!
BRA KOOM
REMY, I...
... DIDN'T MEAN TO HURT... ARE YOU ALL RIGHT?
DON', CHERE.
DON' SAY A WORD, OKAY?
Y'KNOW, ALL MY LIFE I BEEN ALONE, I PRETENDED I LIKED IT DAT WAY —
— BUT THERE'S NO HIDIN' BEHIND A LIE... I WAS LOOKIN' FOR SOMEONE TO LOVE.
JUST MY LUCK I FOUND HER — AND SHE LOVES SOMEBODY ELSE.
CAN'T BE HELPED. YOU DON'T CHOOSE WHO YOU LOVE.
BUT NO DENYIN' IT HURTS.
MAYBE IT'S TIME FOR GAMBIT TO BE ALONE AGAIN.
She almost calls out to him to beg him to come back.
But she knows he is right — Love can't be denied.
And it breaks her heart.
END

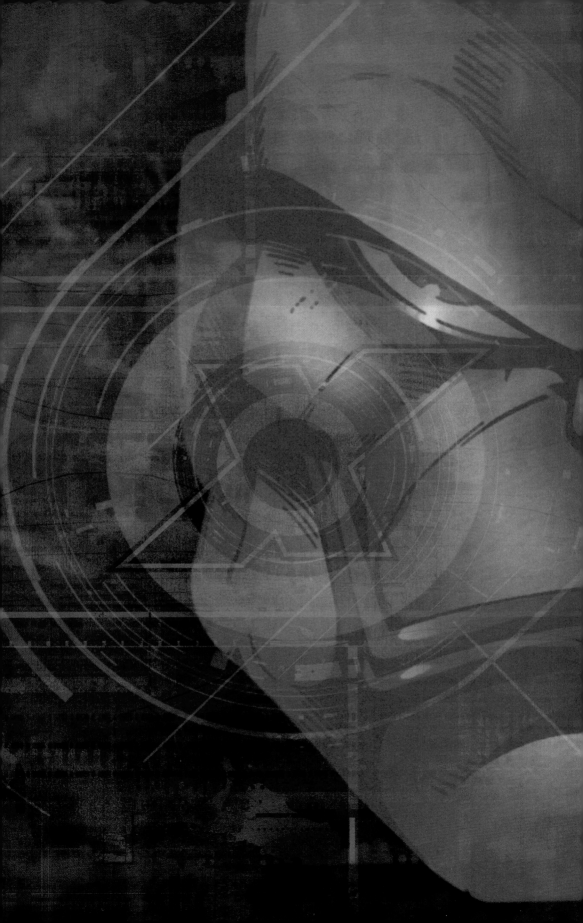

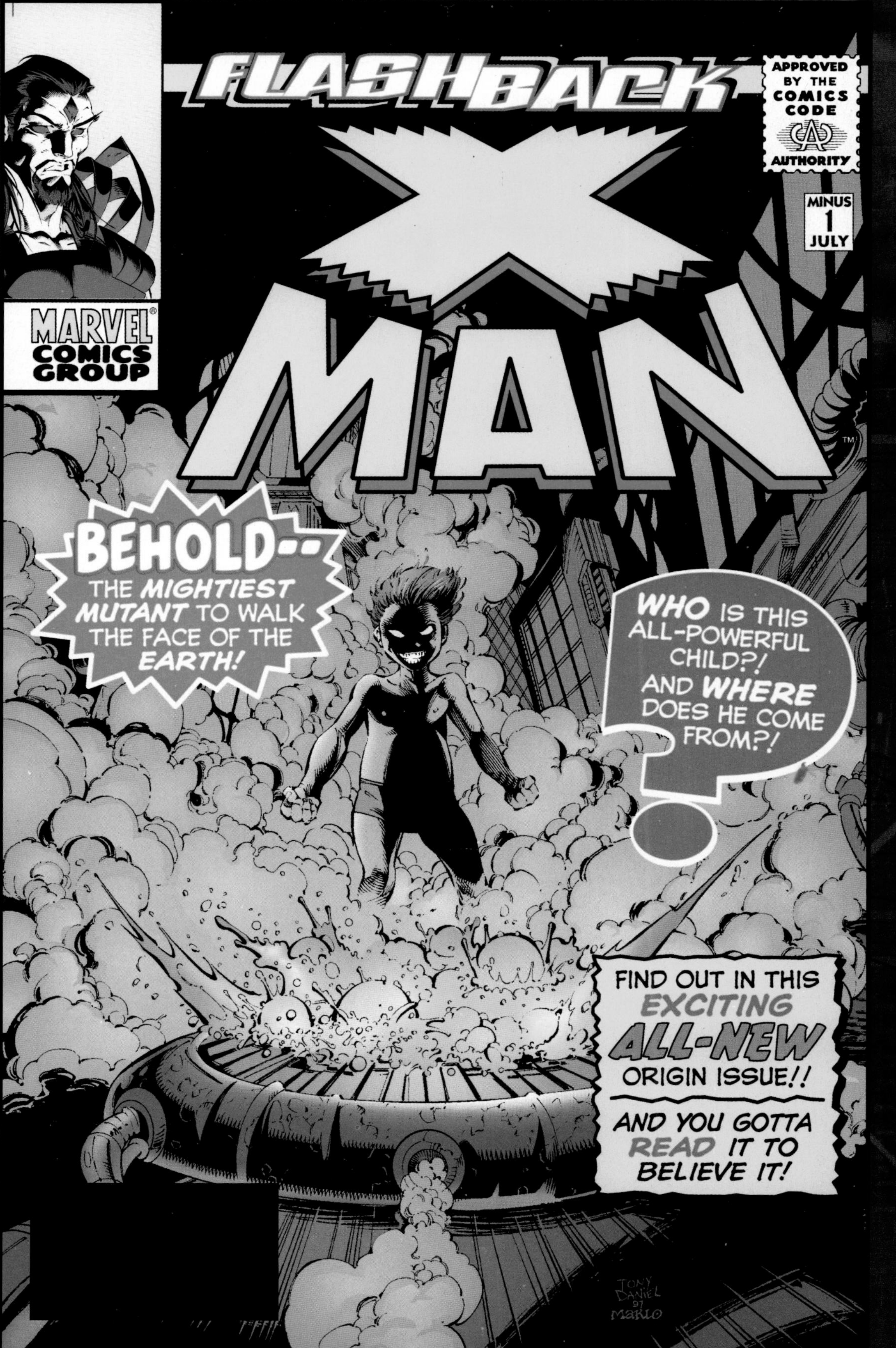

FLASHBACK
APPROVED BY THE COMICS CODE AUTHORITY
MINUS 1 JULY
X-MAN
MARVEL COMICS GROUP
BEHOLD-- THE MIGHTIEST MUTANT TO WALK THE FACE OF THE EARTH!
WHO IS THIS ALL-POWERFUL CHILD?! AND WHERE DOES HE COME FROM?!
FIND OUT IN THIS EXCITING ALL-NEW ORIGIN ISSUE!!
AND YOU GOTTA READ IT TO BELIEVE IT!
TONY DANIEL 97 MARLO

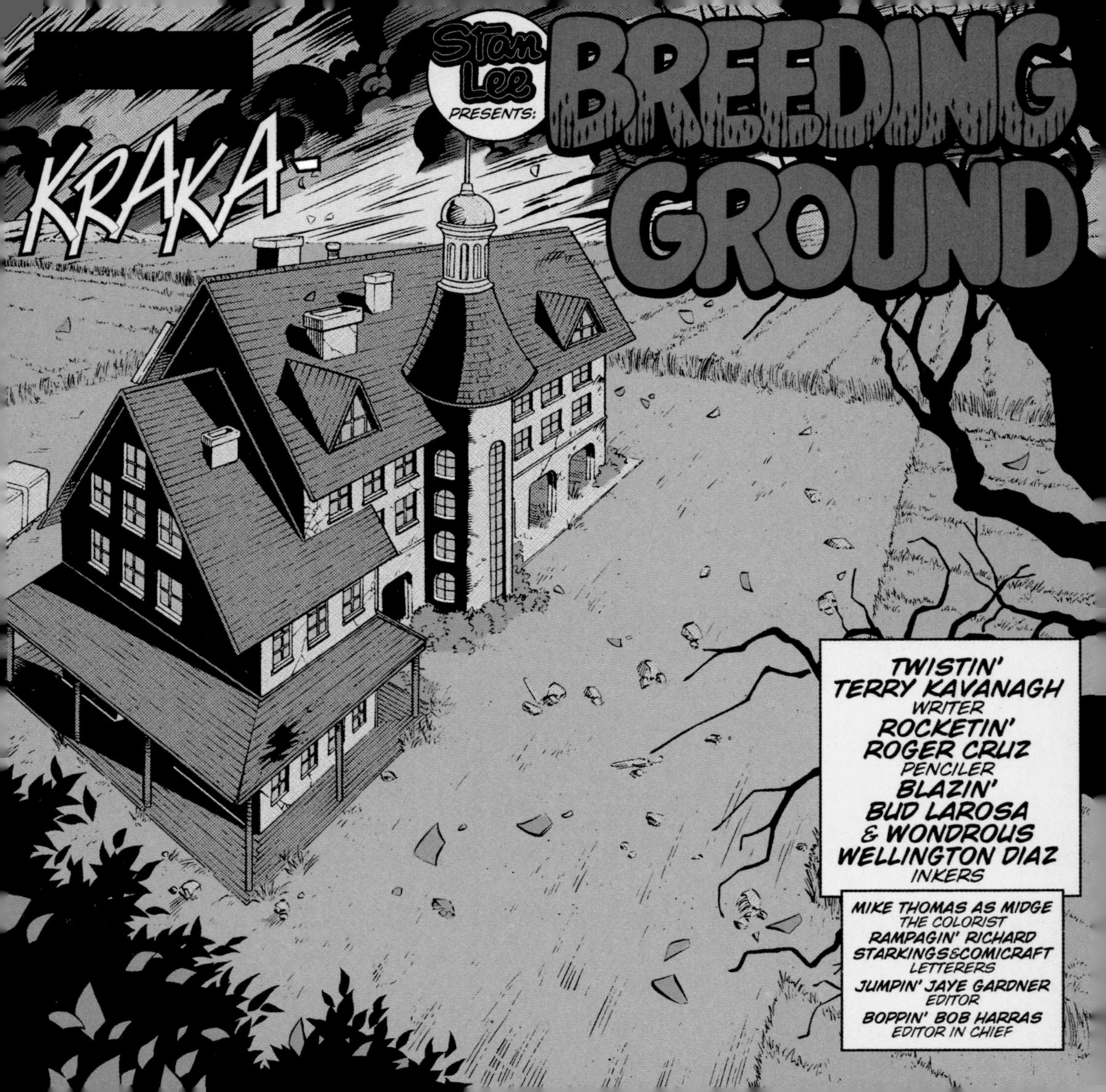
[redacted]
Stan Lee PRESENTS:
BREEDING GROUND
KRAKA-
TWISTIN' TERRY KAVANAGH WRITER
ROCKETIN' ROGER CRUZ PENCILER
BLAZIN' BUD LAROSA & WONDROUS WELLINGTON DIAZ INKERS
MIKE THOMAS AS MIDGE THE COLORIST
RAMPAGIN' RICHARD STARKINGS&COMICRAFT LETTERERS
JUMPIN' JAYE GARDNER EDITOR
BOPPIN' BOB HARRAS EDITOR IN CHIEF

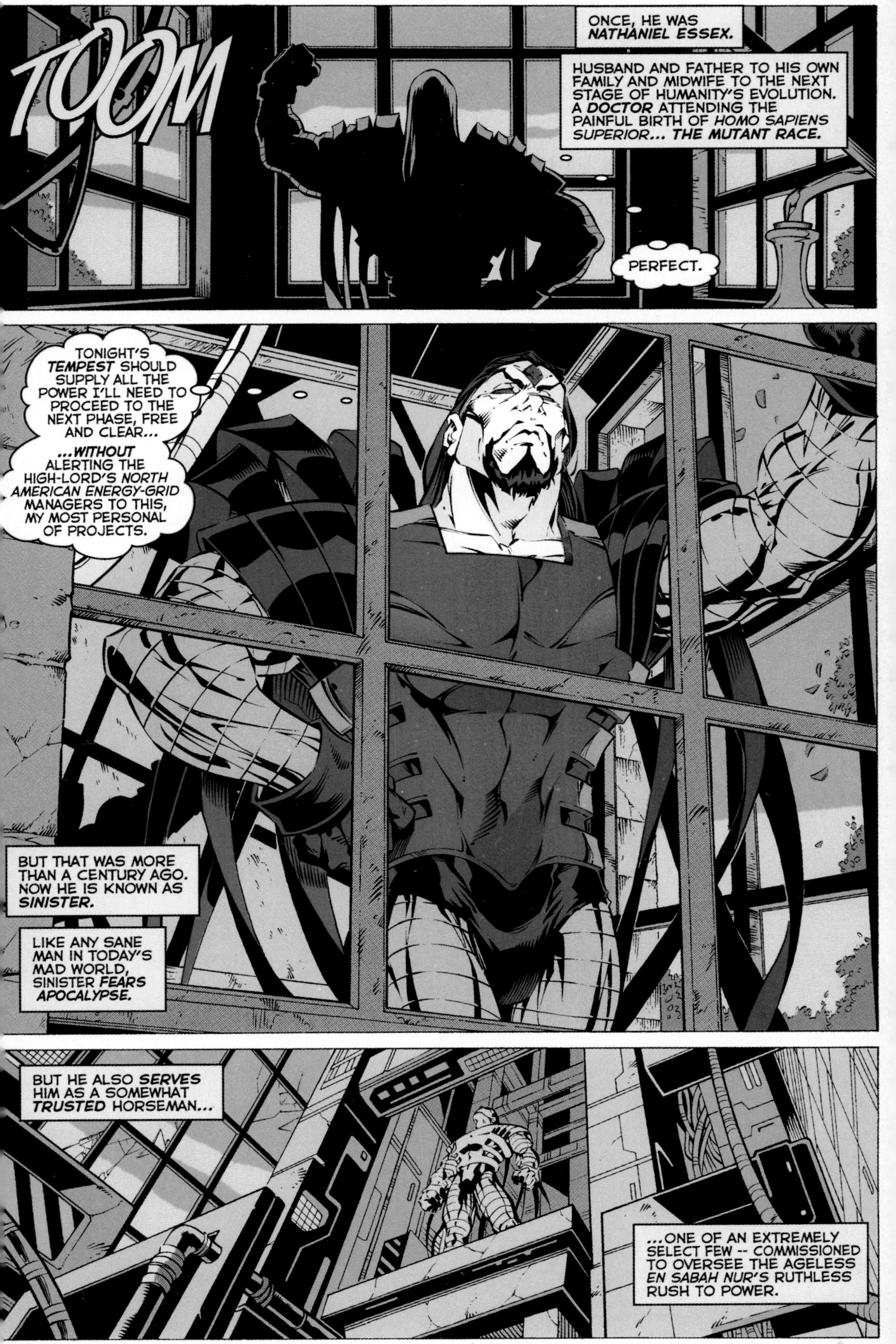
TOOM
ONCE, HE WAS *NATHANIEL ESSEX.*
HUSBAND AND FATHER TO HIS OWN FAMILY AND MIDWIFE TO THE NEXT STAGE OF HUMANITY'S EVOLUTION. A *DOCTOR* ATTENDING THE PAINFUL BIRTH OF *HOMO SAPIENS SUPERIOR... THE MUTANT RACE.*
PERFECT.
TONIGHT'S *TEMPEST* SHOULD SUPPLY ALL THE POWER I'LL NEED TO PROCEED TO THE NEXT PHASE, FREE AND CLEAR...
...WITHOUT ALERTING THE HIGH-LORD'S *NORTH AMERICAN ENERGY-GRID* MANAGERS TO THIS, MY MOST PERSONAL OF PROJECTS.
BUT THAT WAS MORE THAN A CENTURY AGO. NOW HE IS KNOWN AS *SINISTER.*
LIKE ANY SANE MAN IN TODAY'S MAD WORLD, SINISTER *FEARS APOCALYPSE.*
BUT HE ALSO *SERVES* HIM AS A SOMEWHAT *TRUSTED* HORSEMAN...
...ONE OF AN EXTREMELY SELECT FEW -- COMMISSIONED TO OVERSEE THE AGELESS *EN SABAH NUR'S* RUTHLESS RUSH TO POWER.

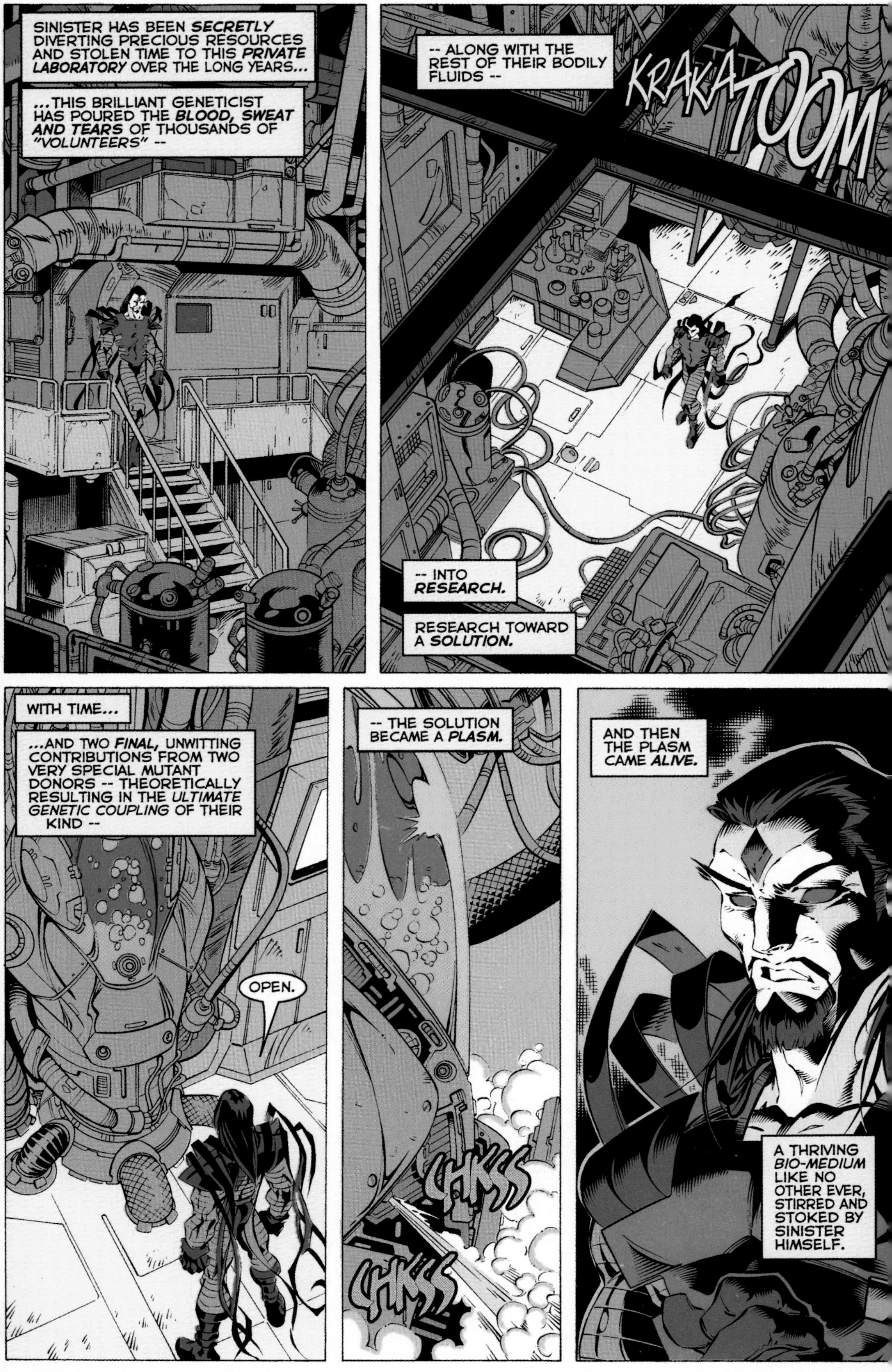
SINISTER HAS BEEN SECRETLY DIVERTING PRECIOUS RESOURCES AND STOLEN TIME TO THIS PRIVATE LABORATORY OVER THE LONG YEARS...
...THIS BRILLIANT GENETICIST HAS POURED THE BLOOD, SWEAT AND TEARS OF THOUSANDS OF "VOLUNTEERS" --
-- ALONG WITH THE REST OF THEIR BODILY FLUIDS --
KRAKATOOM
-- INTO RESEARCH.
RESEARCH TOWARD A SOLUTION.
WITH TIME...
...AND TWO FINAL, UNWITTING CONTRIBUTIONS FROM TWO VERY SPECIAL MUTANT DONORS -- THEORETICALLY RESULTING IN THE ULTIMATE GENETIC COUPLING OF THEIR KIND --
OPEN.
-- THE SOLUTION BECAME A PLASM.
CHKSS
CHKSS
AND THEN THE PLASM CAME ALIVE.
A THRIVING BIO-MEDIUM LIKE NO OTHER EVER, STIRRED AND STOKED BY SINISTER HIMSELF.

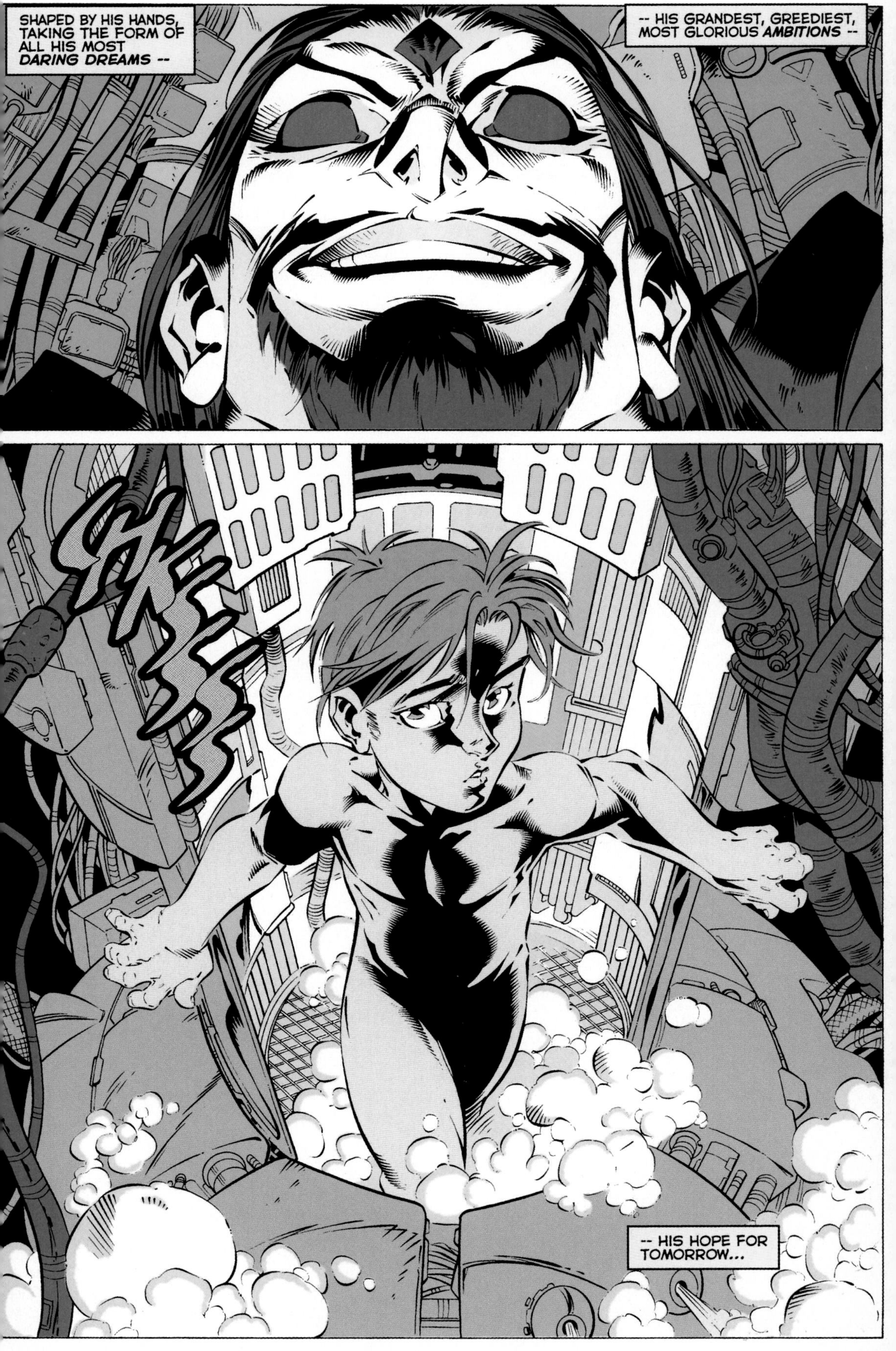
SHAPED BY HIS HANDS, TAKING THE FORM OF ALL HIS MOST DARING DREAMS --
-- HIS GRANDEST, GREEDIEST, MOST GLORIOUS AMBITIONS --
-- HIS HOPE FOR TOMORROW...

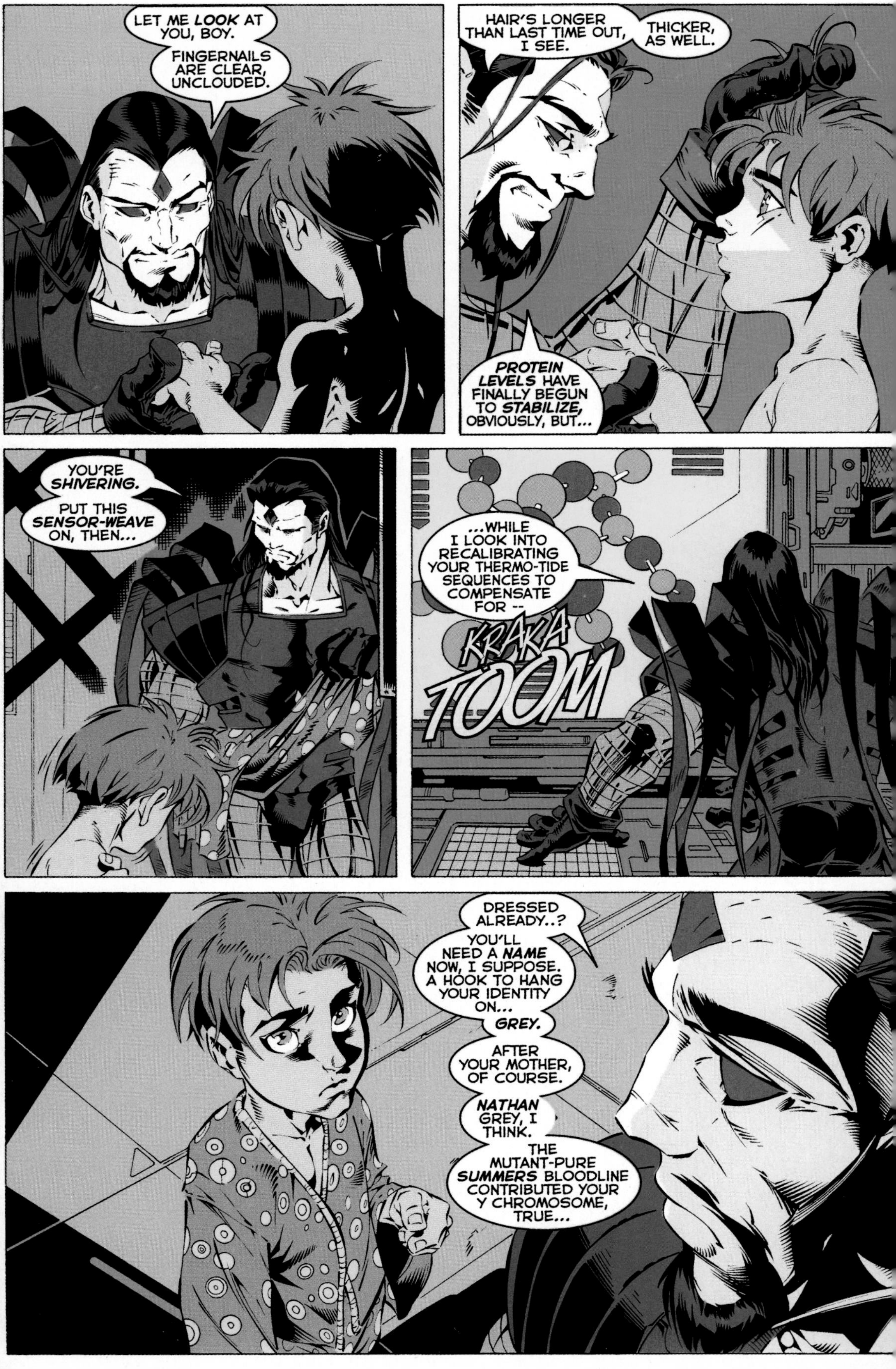
LET ME LOOK AT YOU, BOY.
FINGERNAILS ARE CLEAR, UNCLOUDED.
HAIR'S LONGER THAN LAST TIME OUT, I SEE.
THICKER, AS WELL.
PROTEIN LEVELS HAVE FINALLY BEGUN TO STABILIZE, OBVIOUSLY, BUT...
YOU'RE SHIVERING.
PUT THIS SENSOR-WEAVE ON, THEN...
...WHILE I LOOK INTO RECALIBRATING YOUR THERMO-TIDE SEQUENCES TO COMPENSATE FOR --
KRAKA TOOM
DRESSED ALREADY..?
YOU'LL NEED A NAME NOW, I SUPPOSE. A HOOK TO HANG YOUR IDENTITY ON...
GREY.
AFTER YOUR MOTHER, OF COURSE.
NATHAN GREY, I THINK.
THE MUTANT-PURE SUMMERS BLOODLINE CONTRIBUTED YOUR Y CHROMOSOME, TRUE...

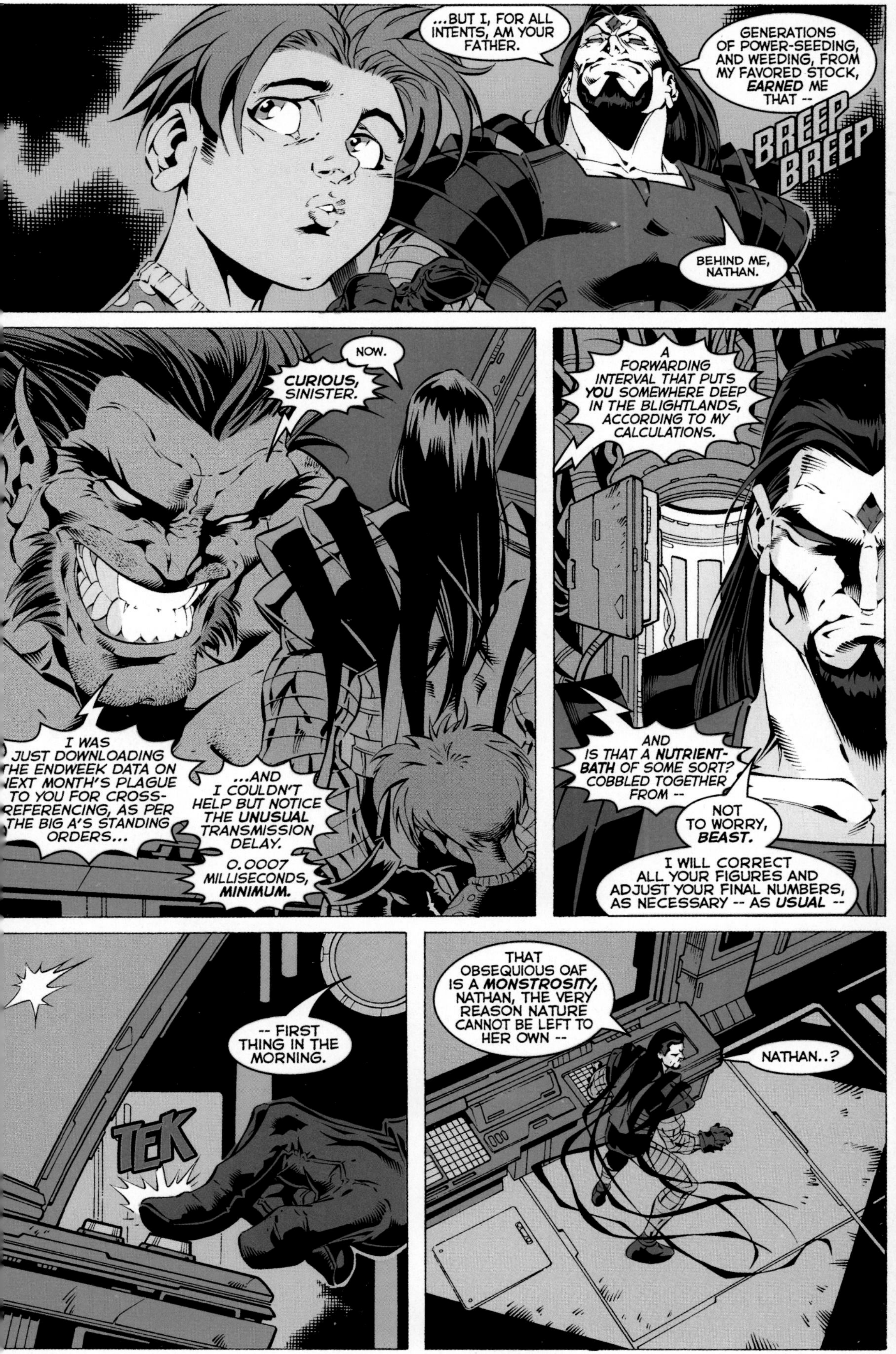
...BUT I, FOR ALL INTENTS, AM YOUR FATHER.
GENERATIONS OF POWER-SEEDING, AND WEEDING, FROM MY FAVORED STOCK, EARNED ME THAT --
BREEP BREEP
BEHIND ME, NATHAN.
NOW.
CURIOUS, SINISTER.
I WAS JUST DOWNLOADING THE ENDWEEK DATA ON NEXT MONTH'S PLAGUE TO YOU FOR CROSS-REFERENCING, AS PER THE BIG A'S STANDING ORDERS...
...AND I COULDN'T HELP BUT NOTICE THE UNUSUAL TRANSMISSION DELAY.
0.0007 MILLISECONDS, MINIMUM.
A FORWARDING INTERVAL THAT PUTS YOU SOMEWHERE DEEP IN THE BLIGHTLANDS, ACCORDING TO MY CALCULATIONS.
AND IS THAT A NUTRIENT-BATH OF SOME SORT? COBBLED TOGETHER FROM --
NOT TO WORRY, BEAST.
I WILL CORRECT ALL YOUR FIGURES AND ADJUST YOUR FINAL NUMBERS, AS NECESSARY -- AS USUAL --
-- FIRST THING IN THE MORNING.
TEK
THAT OBSEQUIOUS OAF IS A MONSTROSITY, NATHAN, THE VERY REASON NATURE CANNOT BE LEFT TO HER OWN --
NATHAN..?

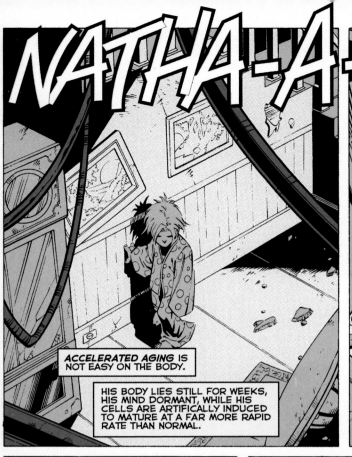

ACCELERATED AGING IS NOT EASY ON THE BODY.

HIS BODY LIES STILL FOR WEEKS, HIS MIND DORMANT, WHILE HIS CELLS ARE ARTIFICIALLY INDUCED TO MATURE AT A FAR MORE RAPID RATE THAN NORMAL.

SO EACH AWAKENING IS A *REBIRTH* TO THE JUST-CHRISTENED *NATHAN GREY.*

AN OPPORTUNITY TO REDISCOVER, TO EXPLORE THE BOUNDARIES OF HIS EXPANDING WORLD...

...TO *TEST* THE LIMITS OF HIS GROWING BODY.

HE HAS A LOT OF CATCHING UP TO DO.

EVERYTHING OLD IS *NEW* AGAIN.

KING OF THE HILL!

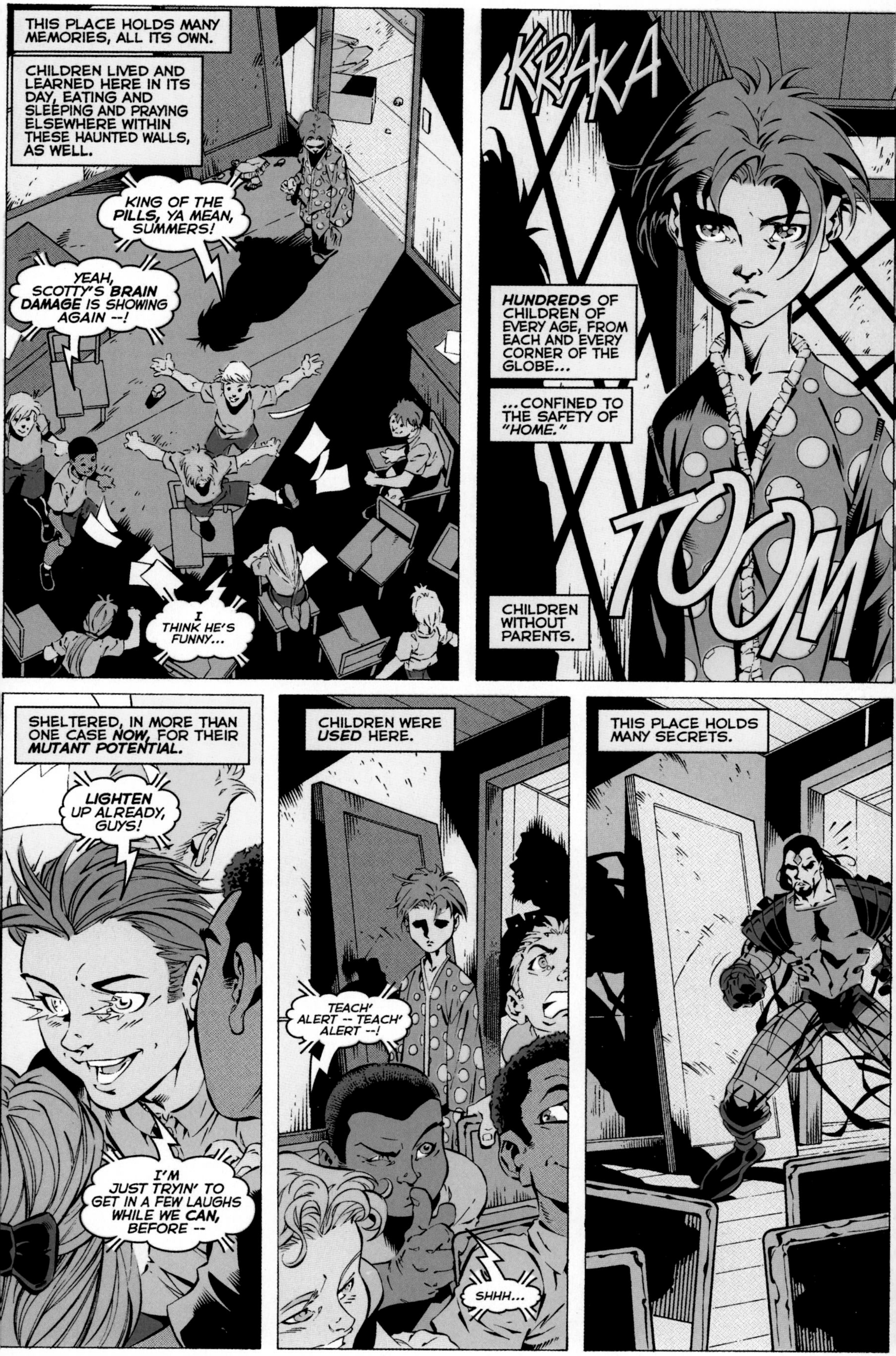

THIS PLACE HOLDS MANY MEMORIES, ALL ITS OWN.
CHILDREN LIVED AND LEARNED HERE IN ITS DAY, EATING AND SLEEPING AND PRAYING ELSEWHERE WITHIN THESE HAUNTED WALLS, AS WELL.
KING OF THE PILLS, YA MEAN, SUMMERS!
YEAH, SCOTTY'S BRAIN DAMAGE IS SHOWING AGAIN --!
I THINK HE'S FUNNY...
KRAKA
HUNDREDS OF CHILDREN OF EVERY AGE, FROM EACH AND EVERY CORNER OF THE GLOBE...
...CONFINED TO THE SAFETY OF "HOME."
TOOM
CHILDREN WITHOUT PARENTS.
SHELTERED, IN MORE THAN ONE CASE NOW, FOR THEIR MUTANT POTENTIAL.
LIGHTEN UP ALREADY, GUYS!
I'M JUST TRYIN' TO GET IN A FEW LAUGHS WHILE WE CAN, BEFORE --
CHILDREN WERE USED HERE.
TEACH' ALERT -- TEACH' ALERT --!
SHHH...
THIS PLACE HOLDS MANY SECRETS.

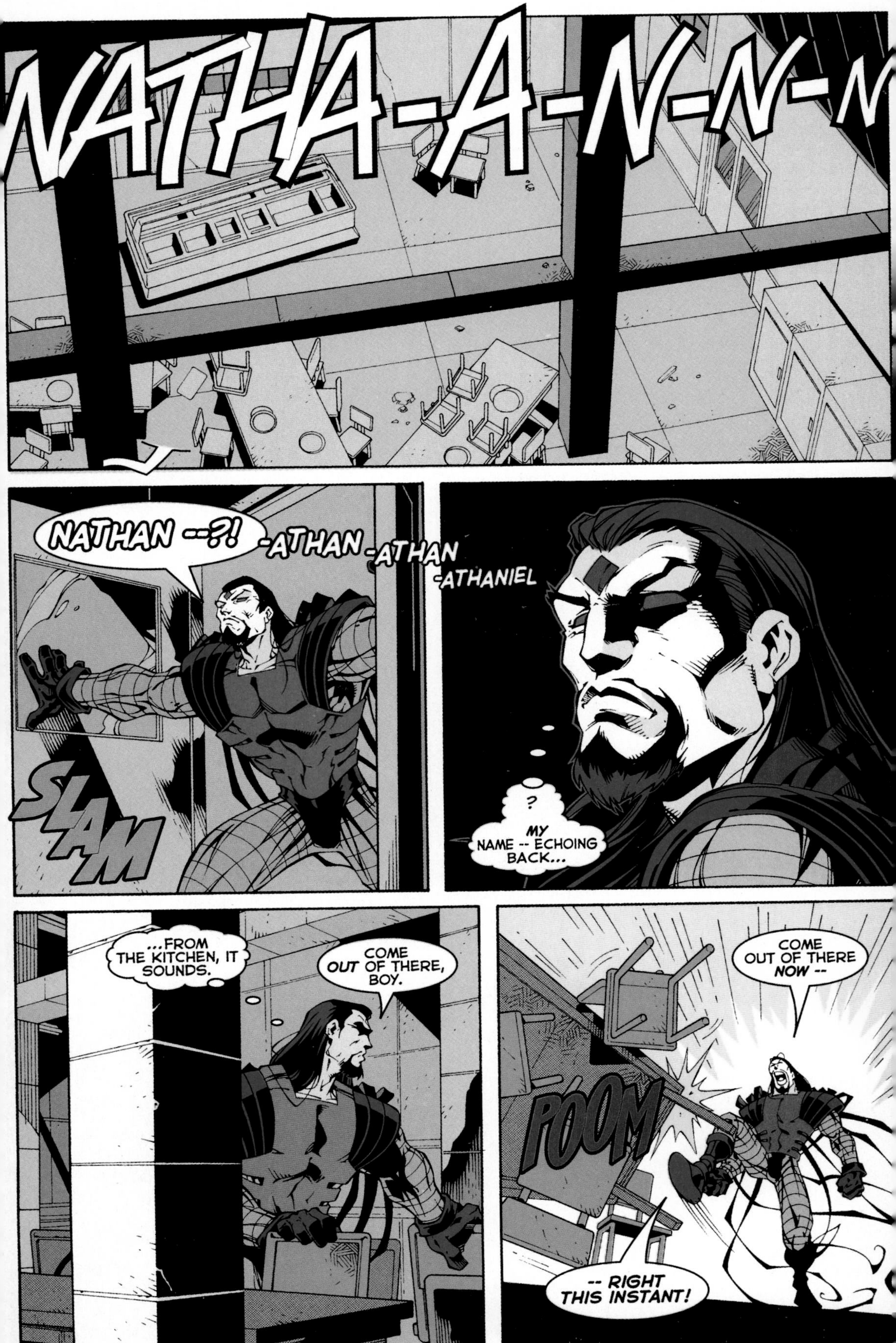
NATHA-A-N-N-N
NATHAN --?!
-ATHAN -ATHAN -ATHANIEL
SLAM
? MY NAME -- ECHOING BACK...
...FROM THE KITCHEN, IT SOUNDS.
COME OUT OF THERE, BOY.
COME OUT OF THERE NOW --
POOM
-- RIGHT THIS INSTANT!

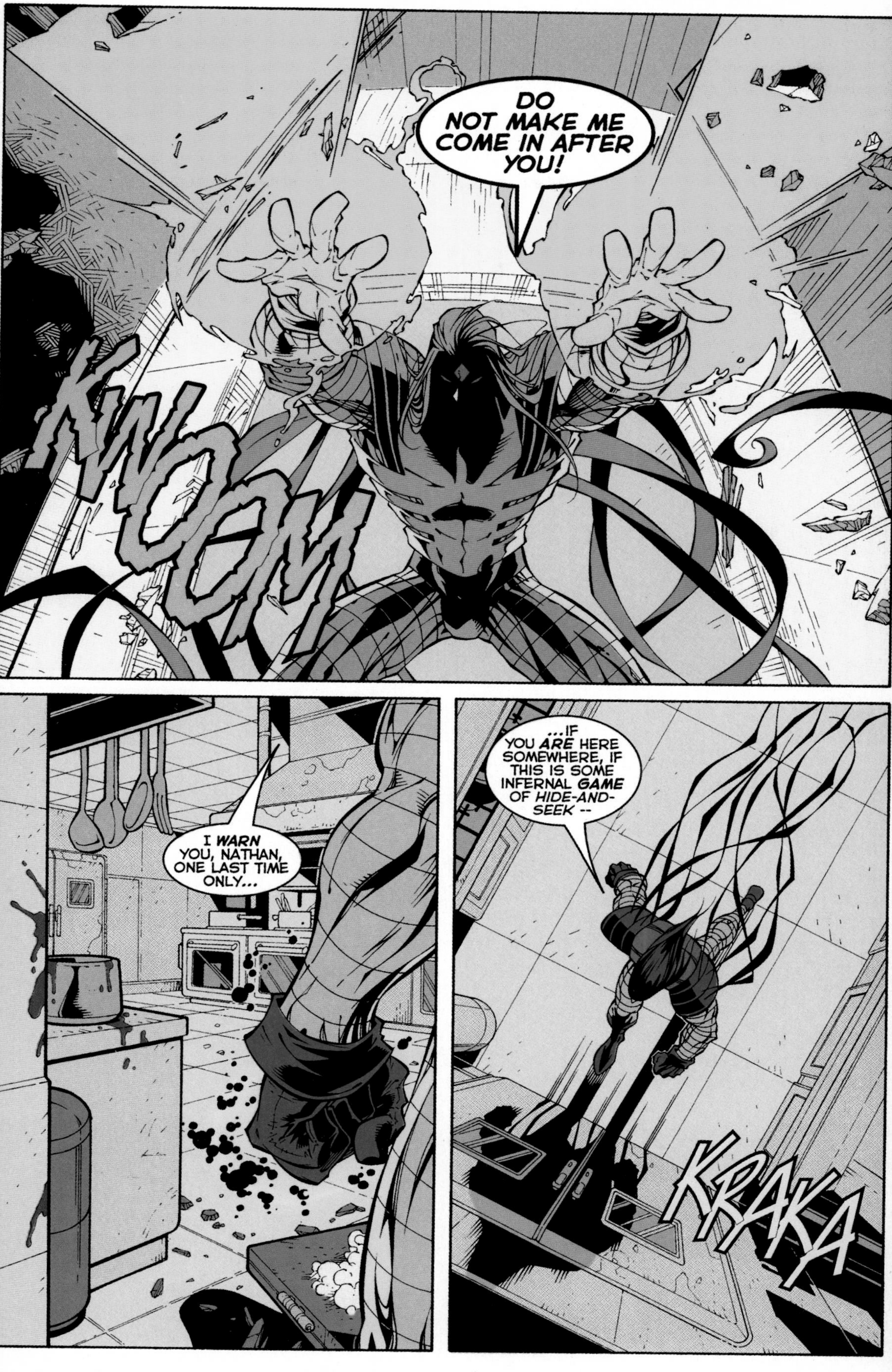
DO NOT MAKE ME COME IN AFTER YOU!
KWOOM
I WARN YOU, NATHAN, ONE LAST TIME ONLY...
...IF YOU ARE HERE SOMEWHERE, IF THIS IS SOME INFERNAL GAME OF HIDE-AND-SEEK --
KRAKA

TOOM

SORRY.

I GOT LOST.

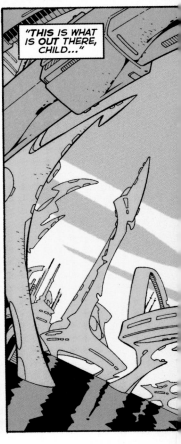

"THIS IS WHAT IS OUT THERE, CHILD..."

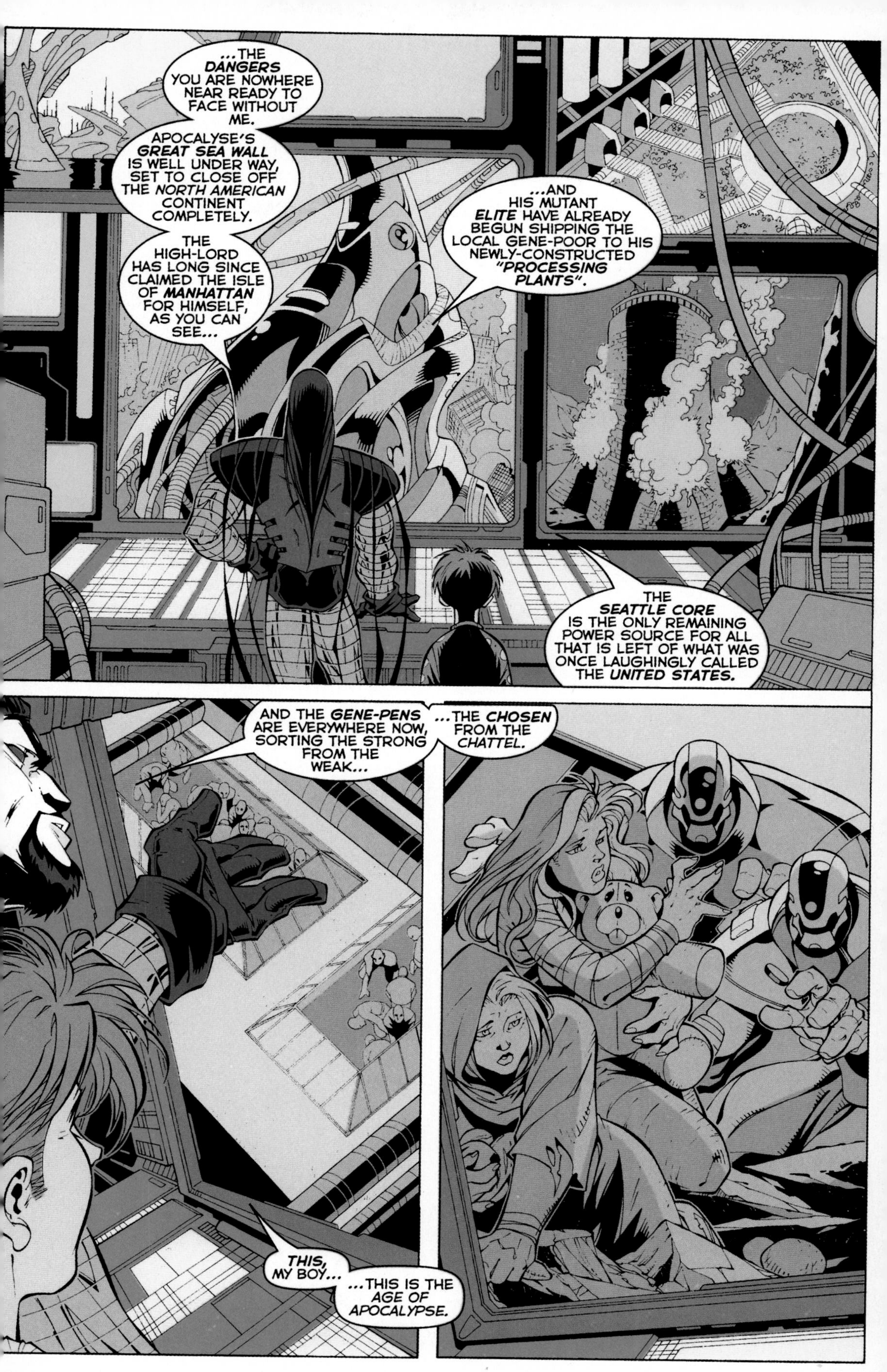
...THE *DANGERS* YOU ARE NOWHERE NEAR READY TO FACE WITHOUT ME.
APOCALYSE'S *GREAT SEA WALL* IS WELL UNDER WAY, SET TO CLOSE OFF THE *NORTH AMERICAN* CONTINENT COMPLETELY.
THE HIGH-LORD HAS LONG SINCE CLAIMED THE ISLE OF *MANHATTAN* FOR HIMSELF, AS YOU CAN SEE...
...AND HIS MUTANT *ELITE* HAVE ALREADY BEGUN SHIPPING THE LOCAL GENE-POOR TO HIS NEWLY-CONSTRUCTED *"PROCESSING PLANTS"*.
THE *SEATTLE CORE* IS THE ONLY REMAINING POWER SOURCE FOR ALL THAT IS LEFT OF WHAT WAS ONCE LAUGHINGLY CALLED THE *UNITED STATES.*
AND THE *GENE-PENS* ARE EVERYWHERE NOW, SORTING THE STRONG FROM THE WEAK...
...THE *CHOSEN* FROM THE *CHATTEL.*
THIS, MY BOY...
...THIS IS THE *AGE OF APOCALYPSE.*

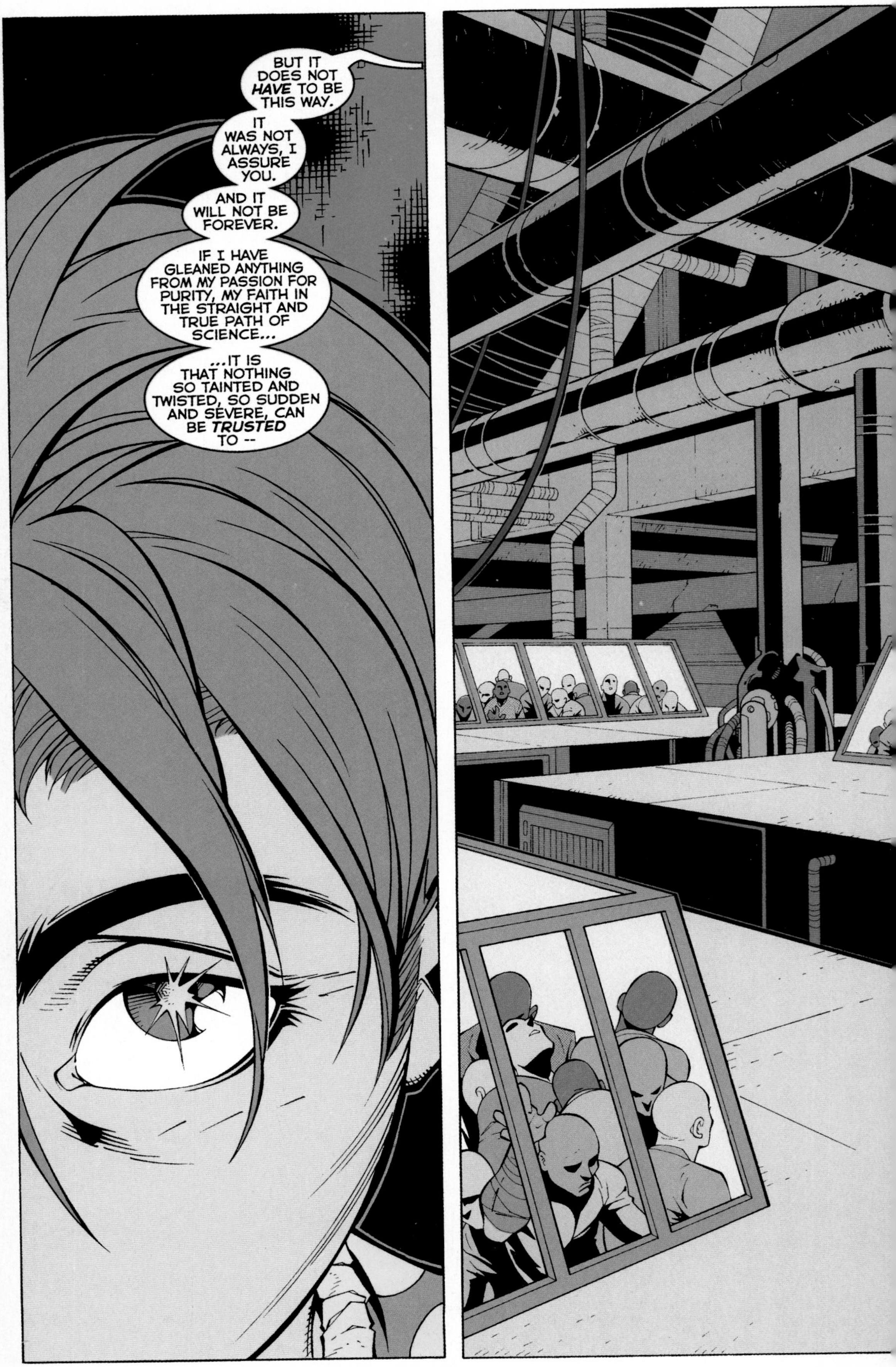
BUT IT DOES NOT *HAVE* TO BE THIS WAY.
IT WAS NOT ALWAYS, I ASSURE YOU.
AND IT WILL NOT BE FOREVER.
IF I HAVE GLEANED ANYTHING FROM MY PASSION FOR PURITY, MY FAITH IN THE STRAIGHT AND TRUE PATH OF SCIENCE...
...IT IS THAT NOTHING SO TAINTED AND TWISTED, SO SUDDEN AND SEVERE, CAN BE *TRUSTED* TO --

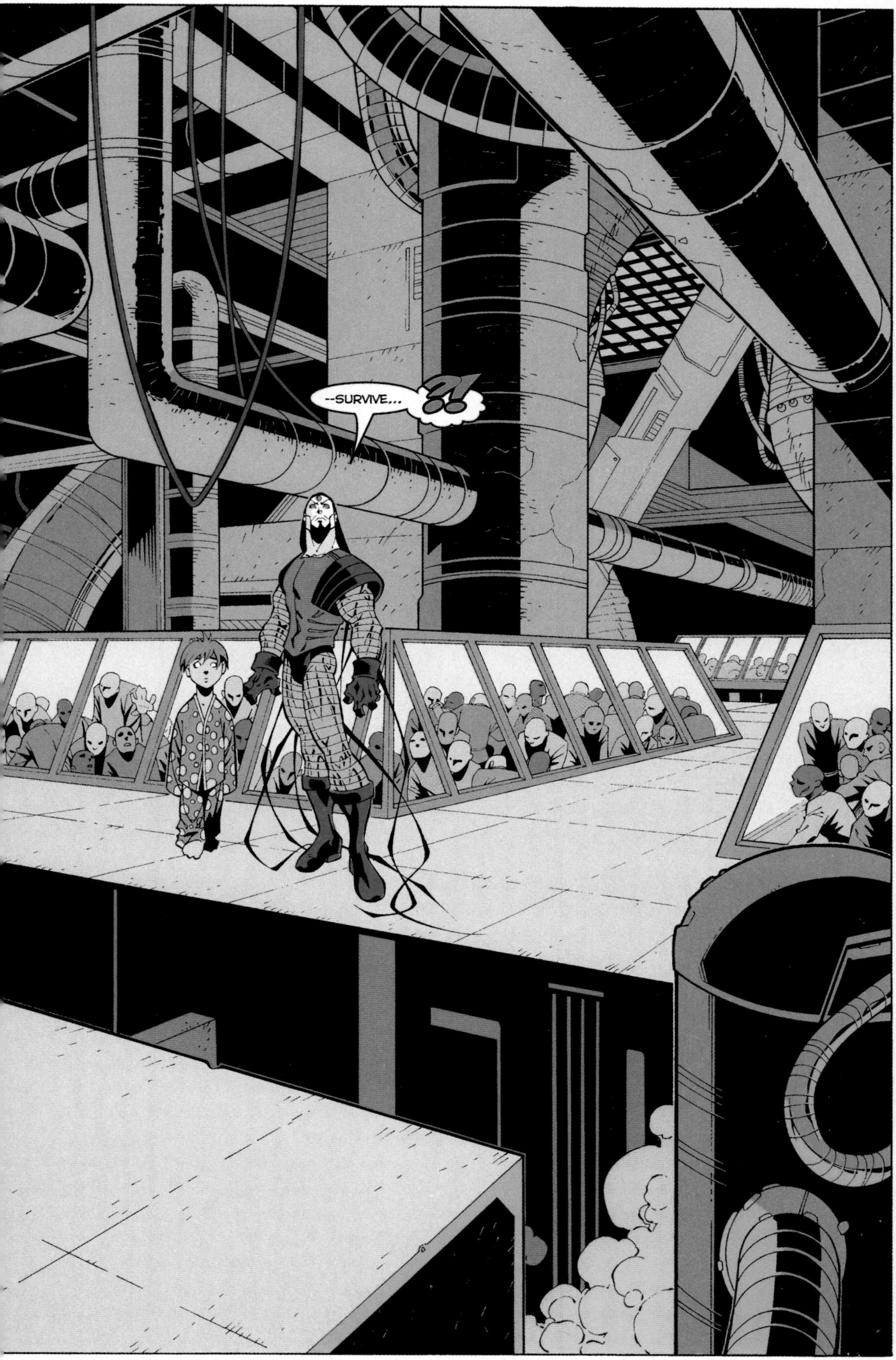
--SURVIVE...
?!

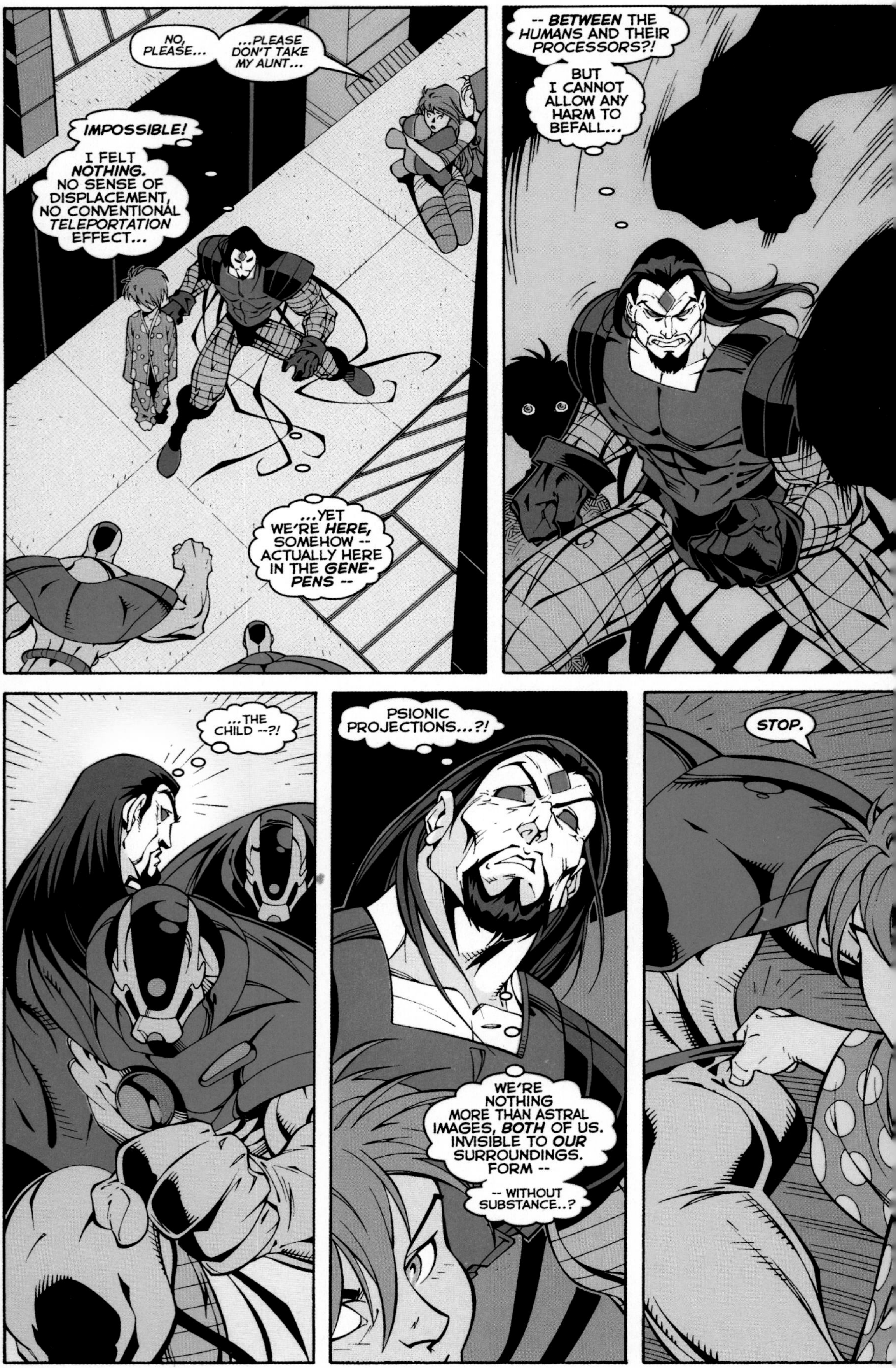
NO, PLEASE...
...PLEASE DON'T TAKE MY AUNT...
IMPOSSIBLE!
I FELT NOTHING. NO SENSE OF DISPLACEMENT, NO CONVENTIONAL TELEPORTATION EFFECT...
...YET WE'RE HERE, SOMEHOW -- ACTUALLY HERE IN THE GENE-PENS --
-- BETWEEN THE HUMANS AND THEIR PROCESSORS?!
BUT I CANNOT ALLOW ANY HARM TO BEFALL...
...THE CHILD --?!
PSIONIC PROJECTIONS...?!
WE'RE NOTHING MORE THAN ASTRAL IMAGES, BOTH OF US. INVISIBLE TO OUR SURROUNDINGS. FORM --
-- WITHOUT SUBSTANCE..?
STOP.

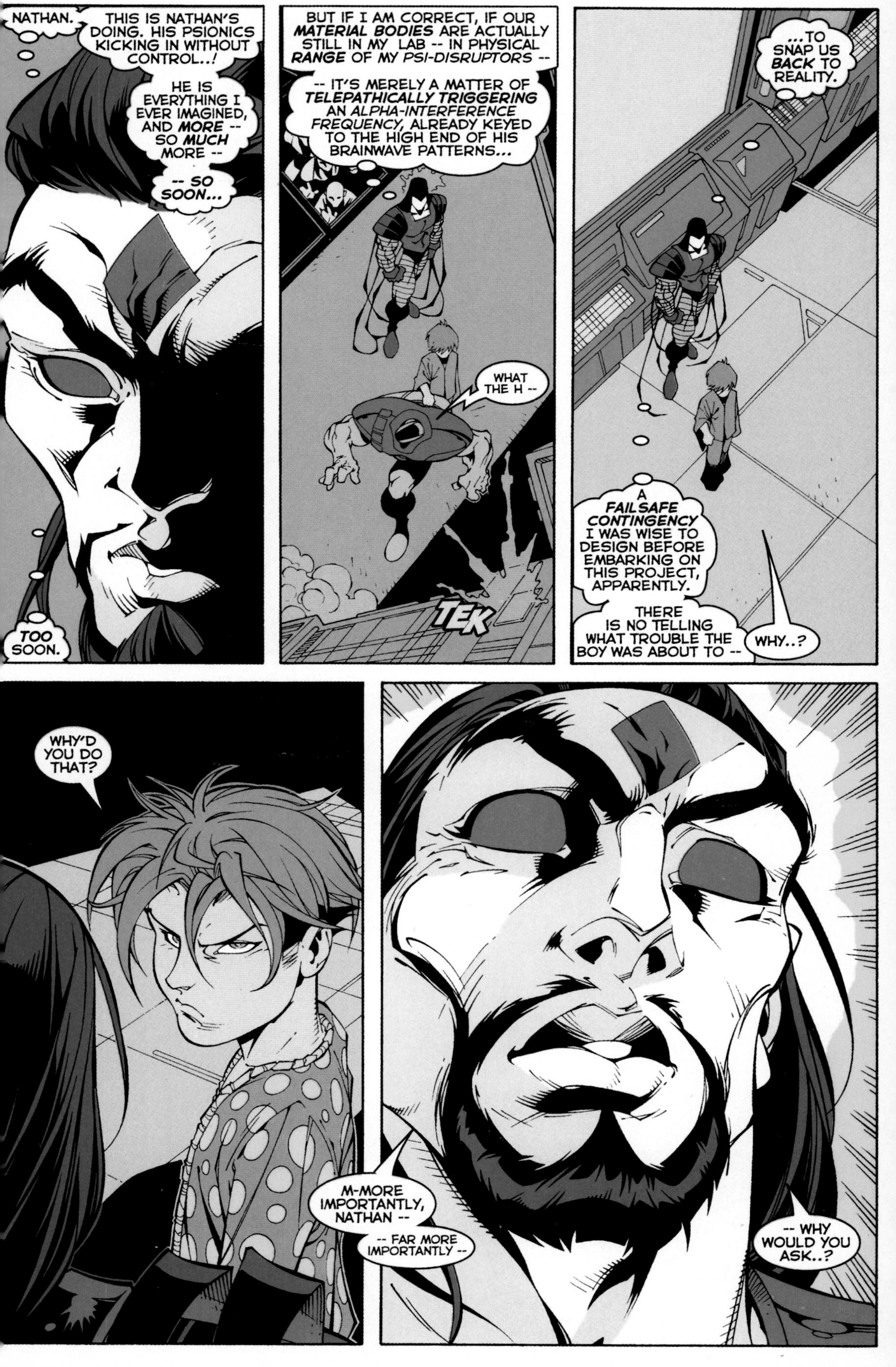
NATHAN.
THIS IS NATHAN'S DOING. HIS PSIONICS KICKING IN WITHOUT CONTROL..!
HE IS EVERYTHING I EVER IMAGINED, AND MORE -- SO MUCH MORE --
-- SO SOON...
TOO SOON.
BUT IF I AM CORRECT, IF OUR MATERIAL BODIES ARE ACTUALLY STILL IN MY LAB -- IN PHYSICAL RANGE OF MY PSI-DISRUPTORS --
-- IT'S MERELY A MATTER OF TELEPATHICALLY TRIGGERING AN ALPHA-INTERFERENCE FREQUENCY, ALREADY KEYED TO THE HIGH END OF HIS BRAINWAVE PATTERNS...
WHAT THE H --
TEK
...TO SNAP US BACK TO REALITY.
A FAILSAFE CONTINGENCY I WAS WISE TO DESIGN BEFORE EMBARKING ON THIS PROJECT, APPARENTLY.
THERE IS NO TELLING WHAT TROUBLE THE BOY WAS ABOUT TO --
WHY..?
WHY'D YOU DO THAT?
M-MORE IMPORTANTLY, NATHAN --
-- FAR MORE IMPORTANTLY --
-- WHY WOULD YOU ASK..?

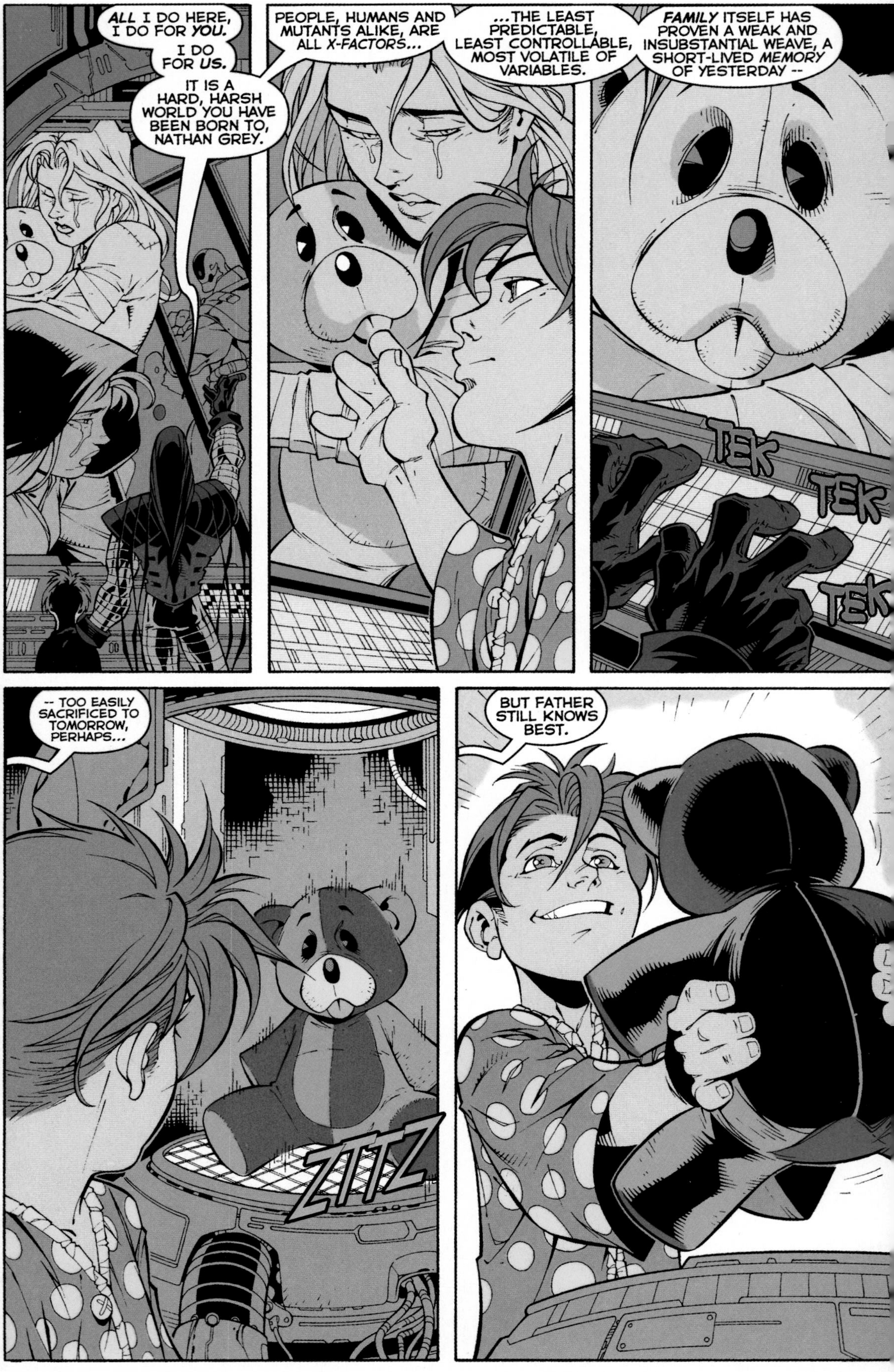
ALL I DO HERE, I DO FOR YOU.
I DO FOR US.
IT IS A HARD, HARSH WORLD YOU HAVE BEEN BORN TO, NATHAN GREY.
PEOPLE, HUMANS AND MUTANTS ALIKE, ARE ALL X-FACTORS...
...THE LEAST PREDICTABLE, LEAST CONTROLLABLE, MOST VOLATILE OF VARIABLES.
FAMILY ITSELF HAS PROVEN A WEAK AND INSUBSTANTIAL WEAVE, A SHORT-LIVED MEMORY OF YESTERDAY --
TEK
TEK
TEK
-- TOO EASILY SACRIFICED TO TOMORROW, PERHAPS...
ZTTZ
BUT FATHER STILL KNOWS BEST.

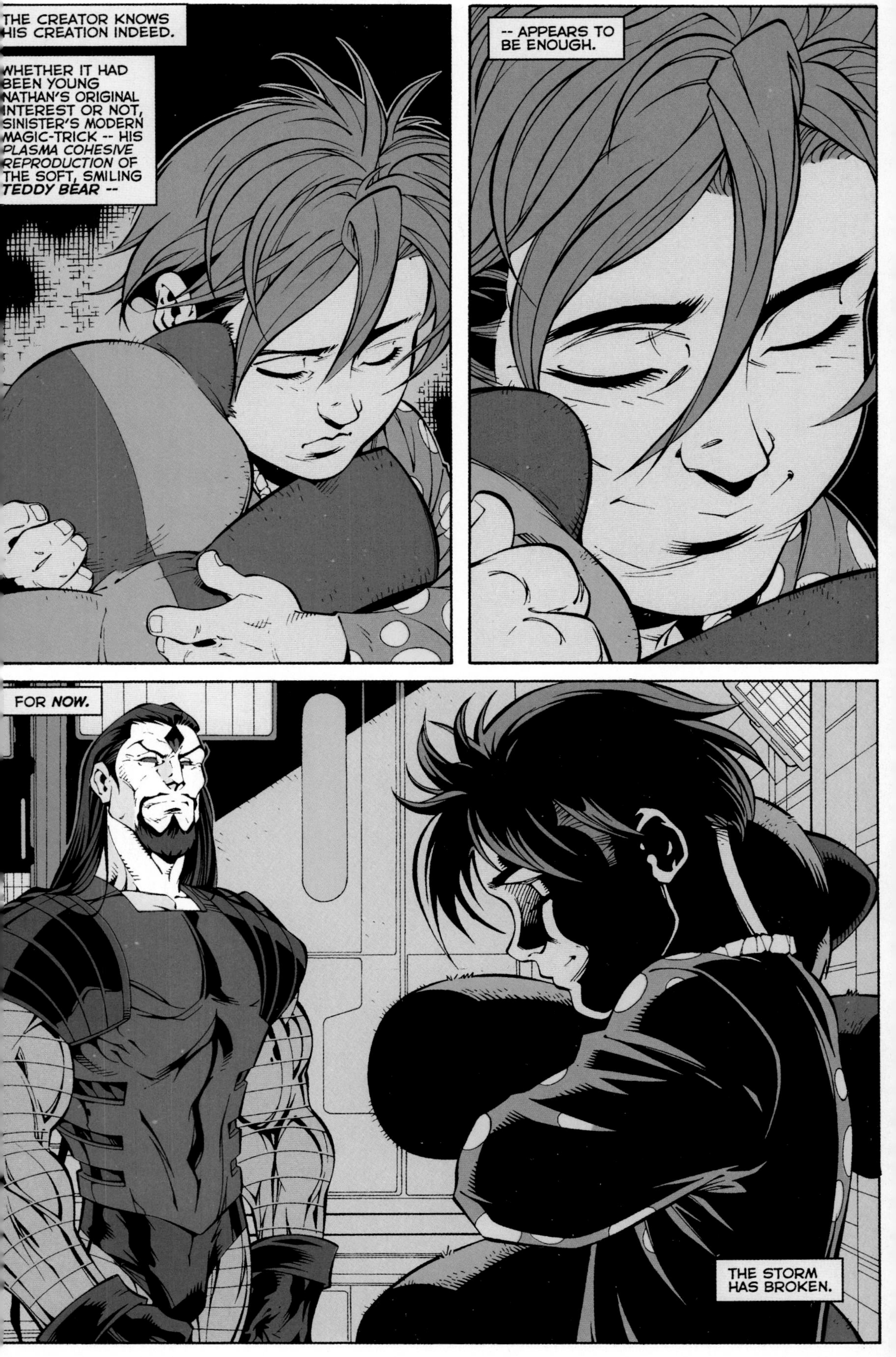
THE CREATOR KNOWS HIS CREATION INDEED.
WHETHER IT HAD BEEN YOUNG NATHAN'S ORIGINAL INTEREST OR NOT, SINISTER'S MODERN MAGIC-TRICK -- HIS *PLASMA COHESIVE REPRODUCTION* OF THE SOFT, SMILING ***TEDDY BEAR*** --
-- APPEARS TO BE ENOUGH.
FOR ***NOW.***
THE STORM HAS BROKEN.

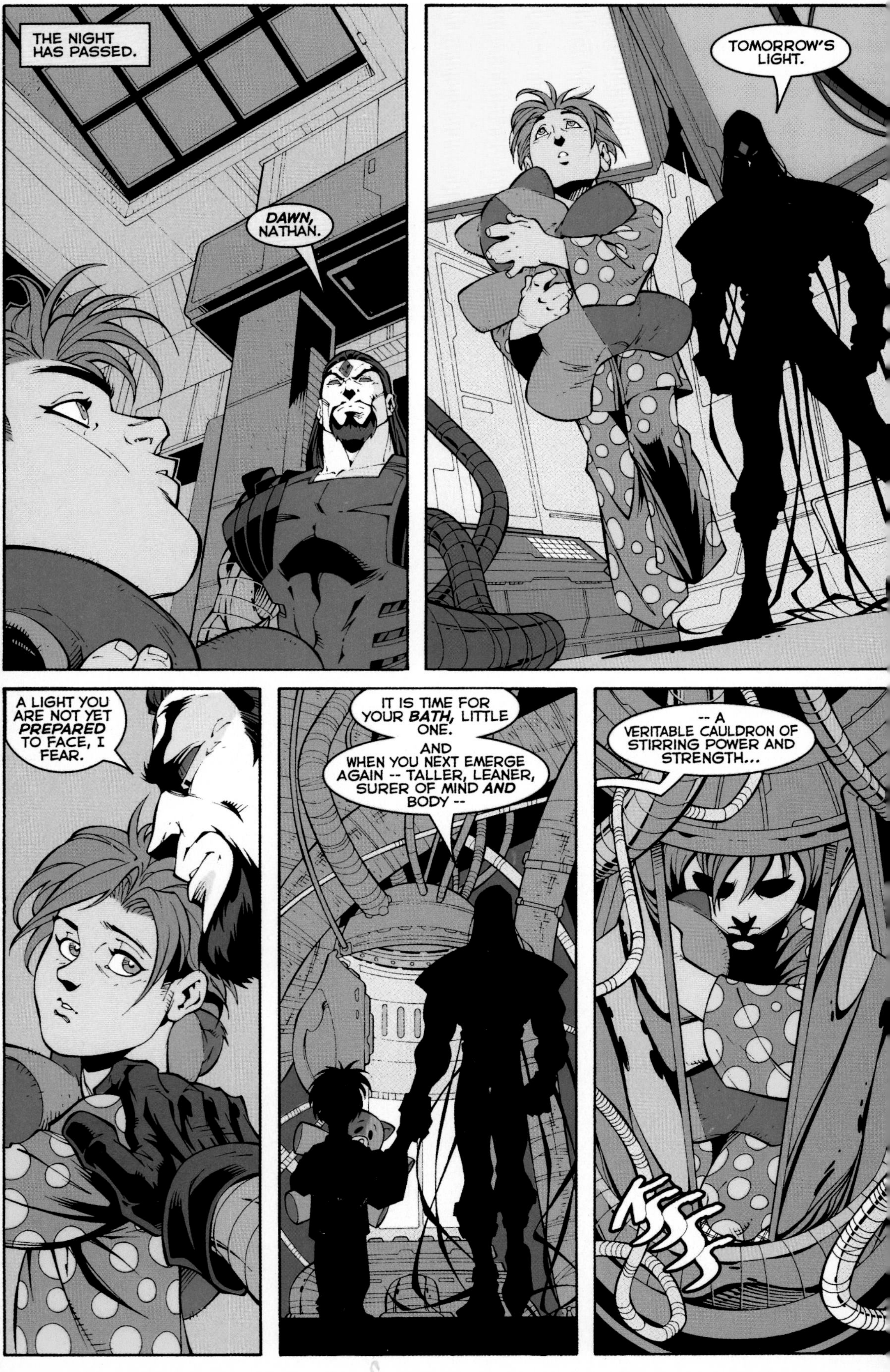
THE NIGHT HAS PASSED.
DAWN, NATHAN.
TOMORROW'S LIGHT.
A LIGHT YOU ARE NOT YET PREPARED TO FACE, I FEAR.
IT IS TIME FOR YOUR BATH, LITTLE ONE.
AND WHEN YOU NEXT EMERGE AGAIN -- TALLER, LEANER, SURER OF MIND AND BODY --
-- A VERITABLE CAULDRON OF STIRRING POWER AND STRENGTH...
KSSSS

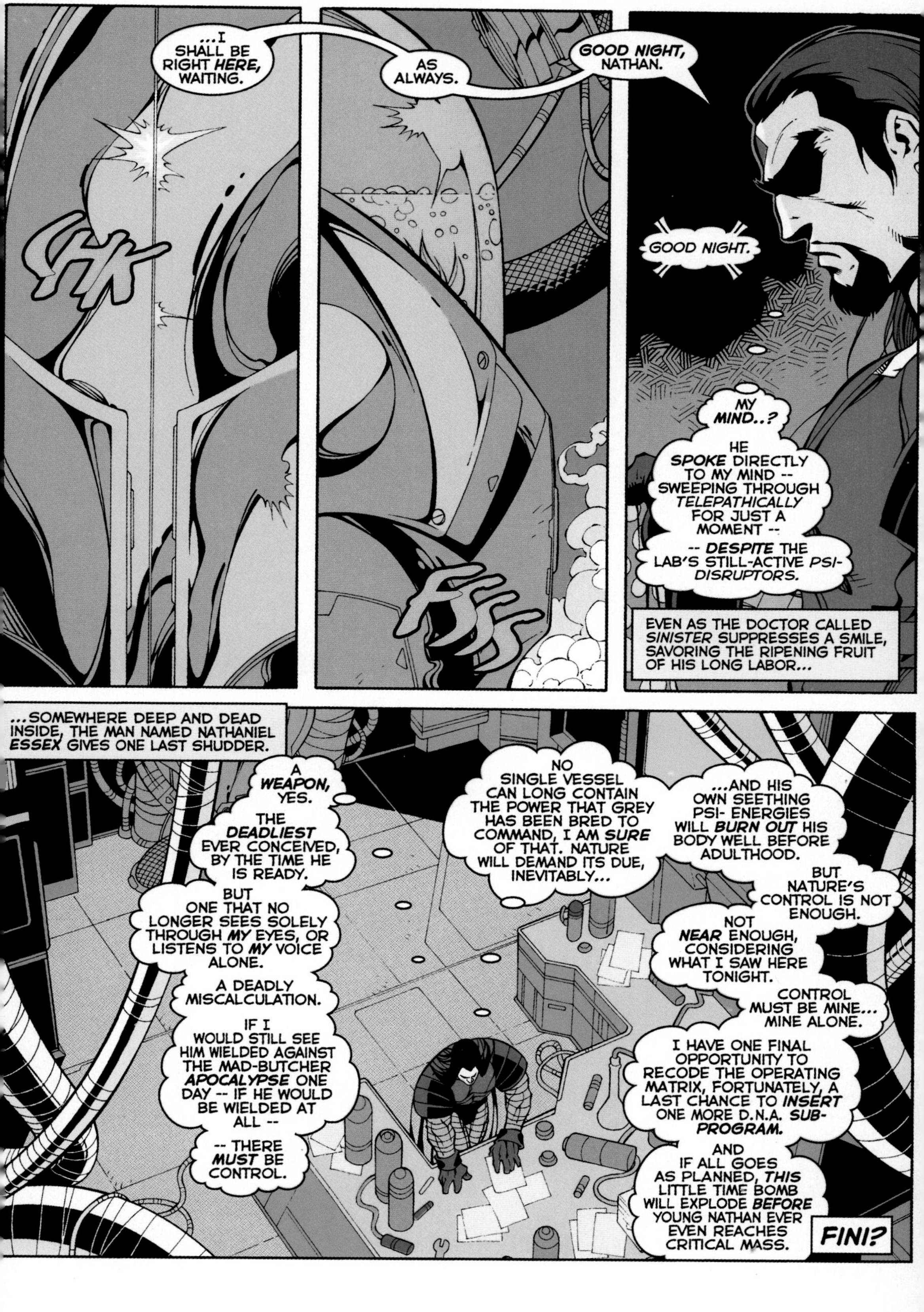
...I SHALL BE RIGHT HERE, WAITING.
SHK
AS ALWAYS.
GOOD NIGHT, NATHAN.
FSSS
GOOD NIGHT.
MY MIND..?
HE SPOKE DIRECTLY TO MY MIND -- SWEEPING THROUGH TELEPATHICALLY FOR JUST A MOMENT --
-- DESPITE THE LAB'S STILL-ACTIVE PSI-DISRUPTORS.
EVEN AS THE DOCTOR CALLED SINISTER SUPPRESSES A SMILE, SAVORING THE RIPENING FRUIT OF HIS LONG LABOR...
...SOMEWHERE DEEP AND DEAD INSIDE, THE MAN NAMED NATHANIEL ESSEX GIVES ONE LAST SHUDDER.
A WEAPON, YES.
THE DEADLIEST EVER CONCEIVED, BY THE TIME HE IS READY.
BUT ONE THAT NO LONGER SEES SOLELY THROUGH MY EYES, OR LISTENS TO MY VOICE ALONE.
A DEADLY MISCALCULATION.
IF I WOULD STILL SEE HIM WIELDED AGAINST THE MAD-BUTCHER APOCALYPSE ONE DAY -- IF HE WOULD BE WIELDED AT ALL --
-- THERE MUST BE CONTROL.
NO SINGLE VESSEL CAN LONG CONTAIN THE POWER THAT GREY HAS BEEN BRED TO COMMAND, I AM SURE OF THAT. NATURE WILL DEMAND ITS DUE, INEVITABLY...
...AND HIS OWN SEETHING PSI- ENERGIES WILL BURN OUT HIS BODY WELL BEFORE ADULTHOOD.
BUT NATURE'S CONTROL IS NOT ENOUGH.
NOT NEAR ENOUGH, CONSIDERING WHAT I SAW HERE TONIGHT.
CONTROL MUST BE MINE... MINE ALONE.
I HAVE ONE FINAL OPPORTUNITY TO RECODE THE OPERATING MATRIX, FORTUNATELY, A LAST CHANCE TO INSERT ONE MORE D.N.A. SUB-PROGRAM.
AND IF ALL GOES AS PLANNED, THIS LITTLE TIME BOMB WILL EXPLODE BEFORE YOUNG NATHAN EVER EVEN REACHES CRITICAL MASS.
FINI?

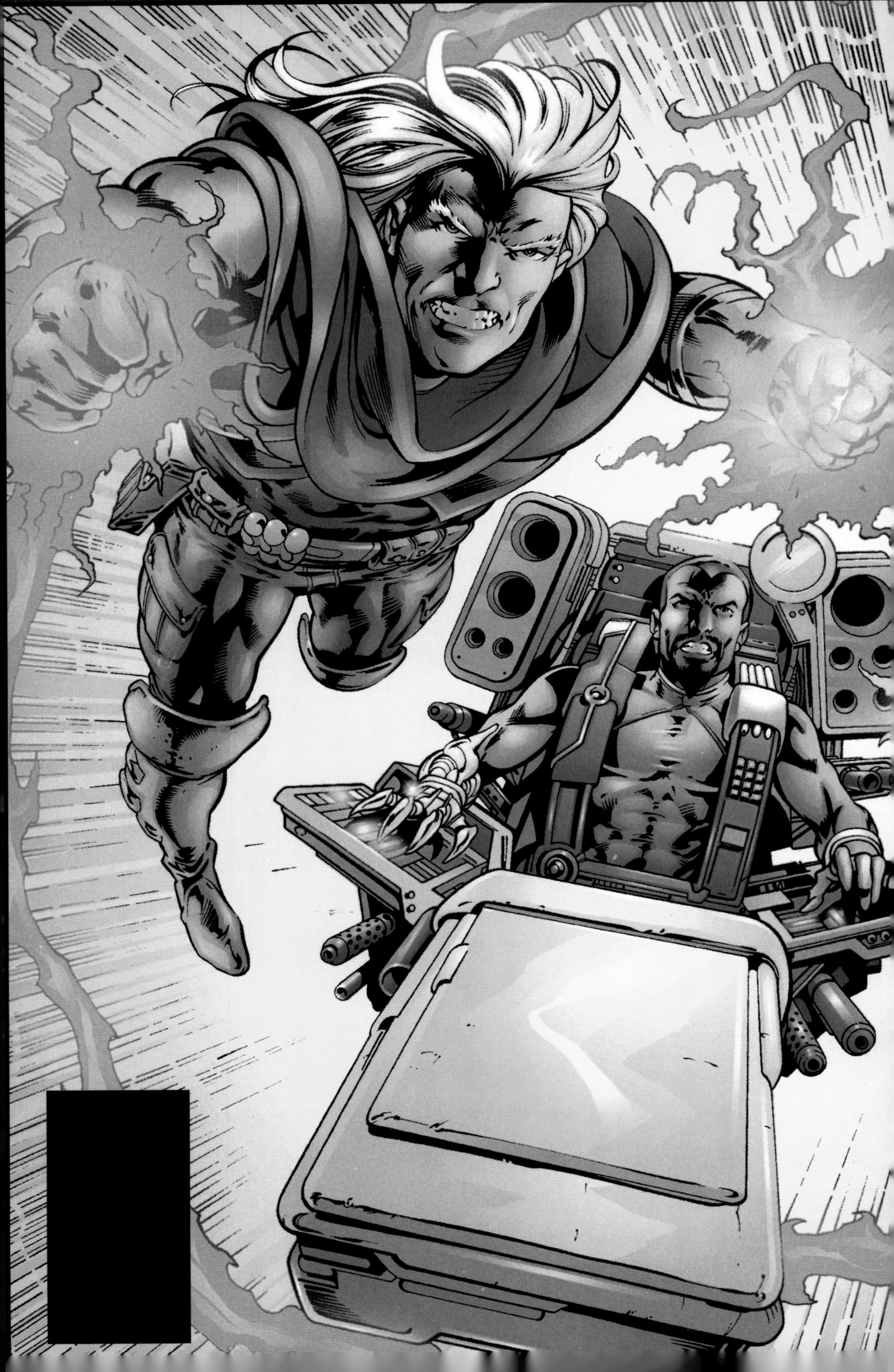

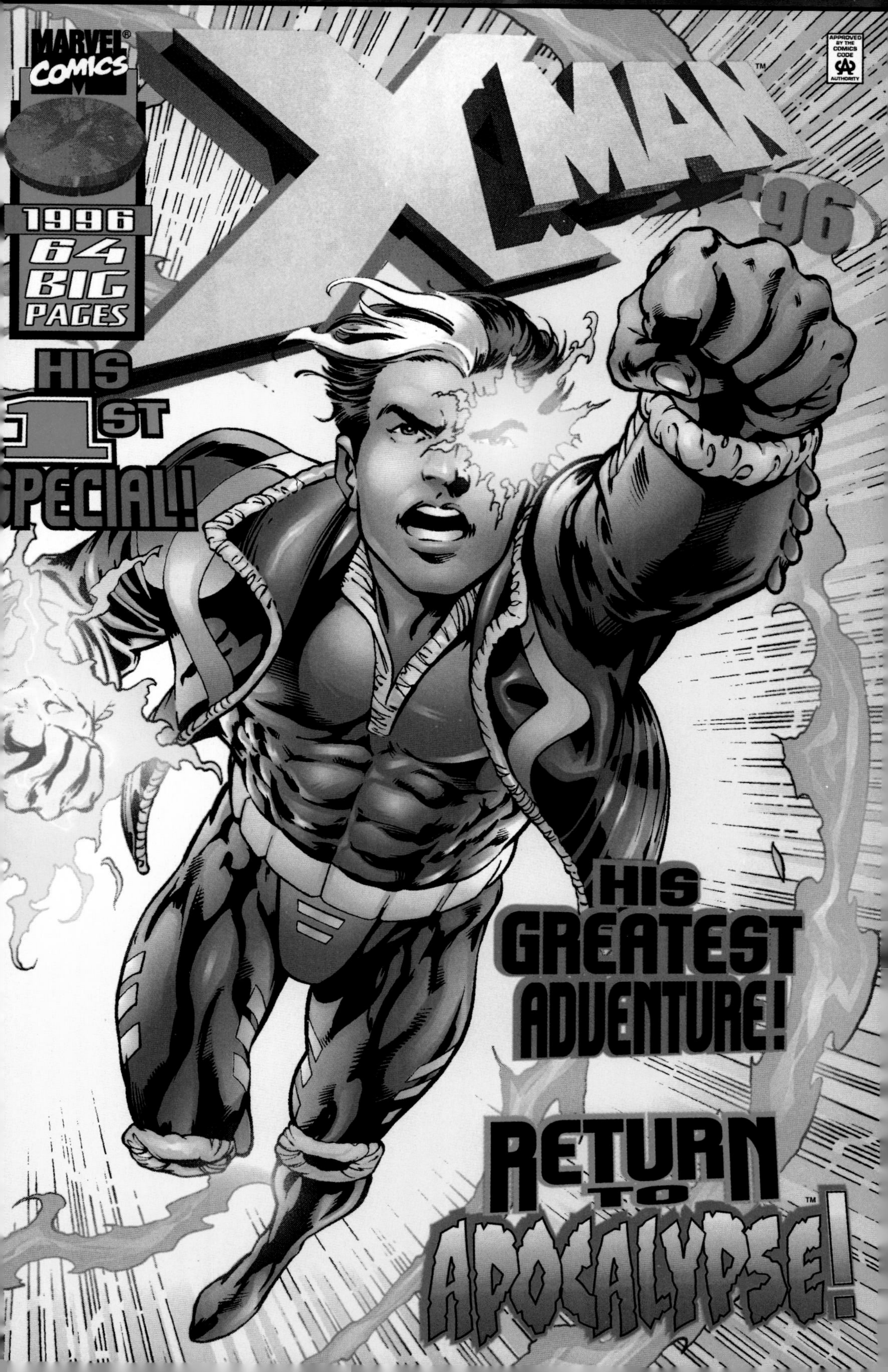
MARVEL COMICS
X-MAN '96
APPROVED BY THE COMICS CODE AUTHORITY
1996
64 BIG PAGES
HIS 1ST SPECIAL!
HIS GREATEST ADVENTURE!
RETURN TO APOCALYPSE!

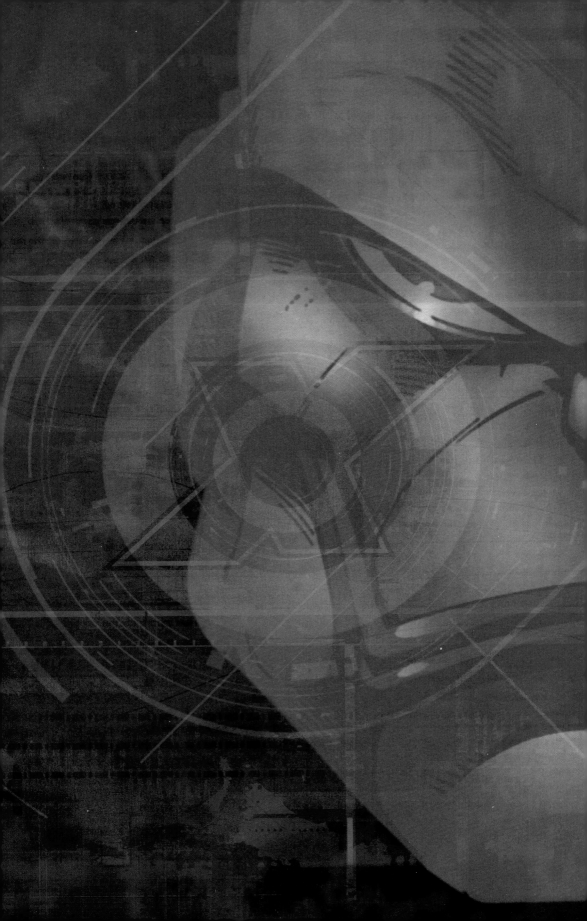

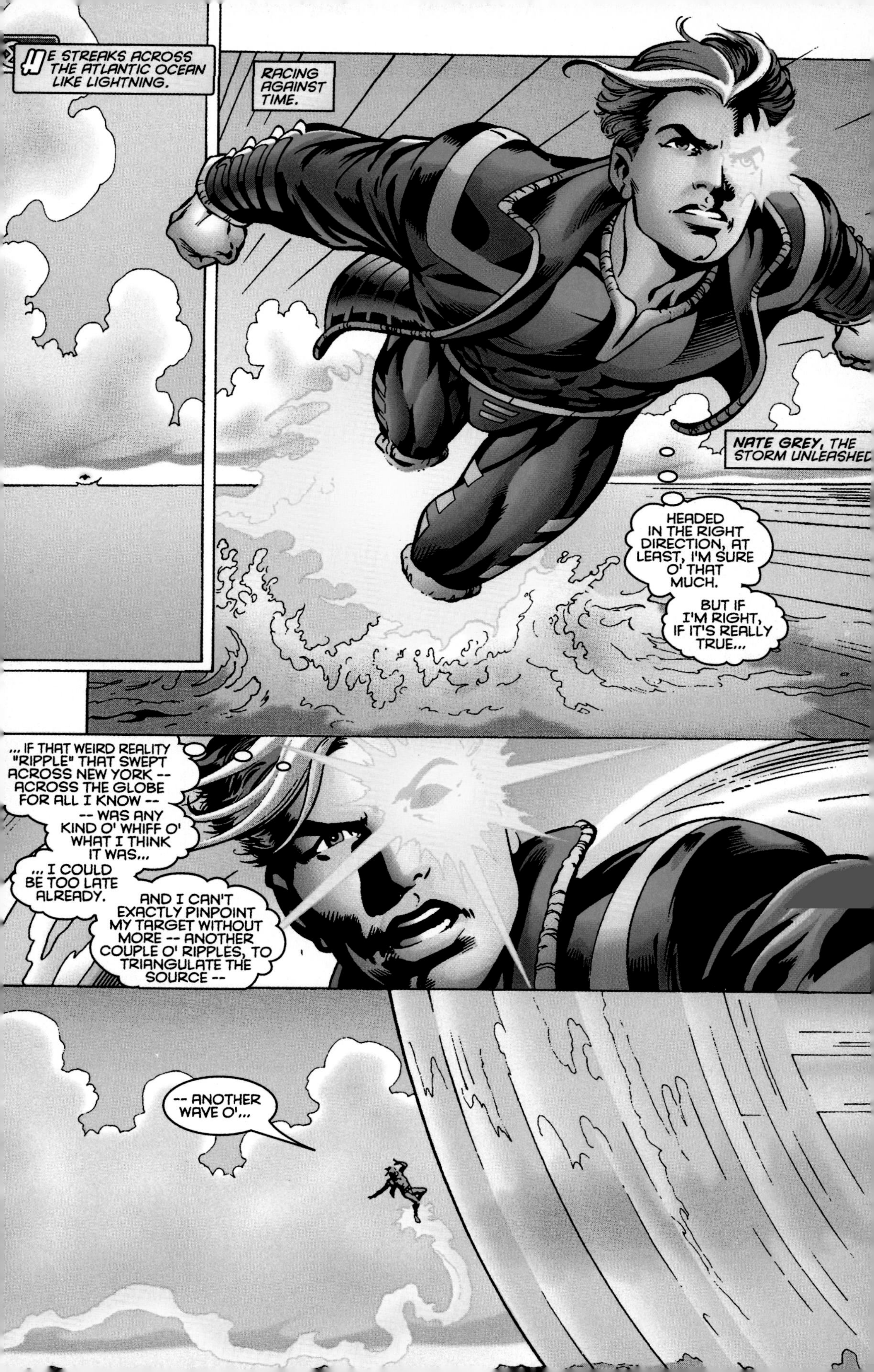
HE STREAKS ACROSS THE ATLANTIC OCEAN LIKE LIGHTNING.
RACING AGAINST TIME.
NATE GREY, THE STORM UNLEASHED
HEADED IN THE RIGHT DIRECTION, AT LEAST, I'M SURE O' THAT MUCH.
BUT IF I'M RIGHT, IF IT'S REALLY TRUE...
... IF THAT WEIRD REALITY "RIPPLE" THAT SWEPT ACROSS NEW YORK -- ACROSS THE GLOBE FOR ALL I KNOW --
-- WAS ANY KIND O' WHIFF O' WHAT I THINK IT WAS...
... I COULD BE TOO LATE ALREADY.
AND I CAN'T EXACTLY PINPOINT MY TARGET WITHOUT MORE -- ANOTHER COUPLE O' RIPPLES, TO TRIANGULATE THE SOURCE --
-- ANOTHER WAVE O'...

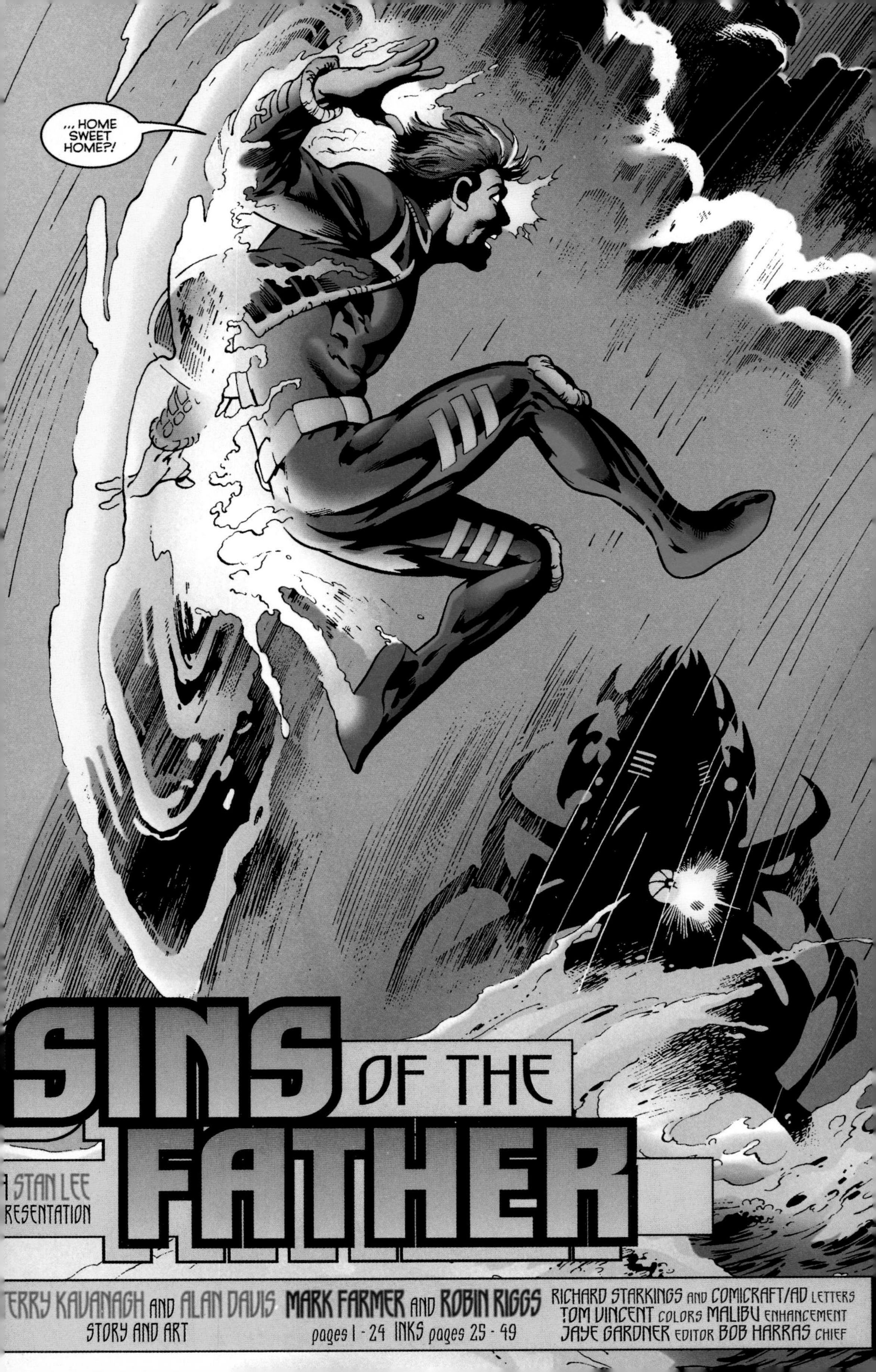
...HOME SWEET HOME?!
SINS OF THE FATHER
A STAN LEE PRESENTATION
TERRY KAVANAGH AND ALAN DAVIS STORY AND ART
MARK FARMER AND ROBIN RIGGS pages 1 - 24 INKS pages 25 - 49
RICHARD STARKINGS AND COMICRAFT/AD LETTERS
TOM VINCENT COLORS MALIBU ENHANCEMENT
JAYE GARDNER EDITOR BOB HARRAS CHIEF

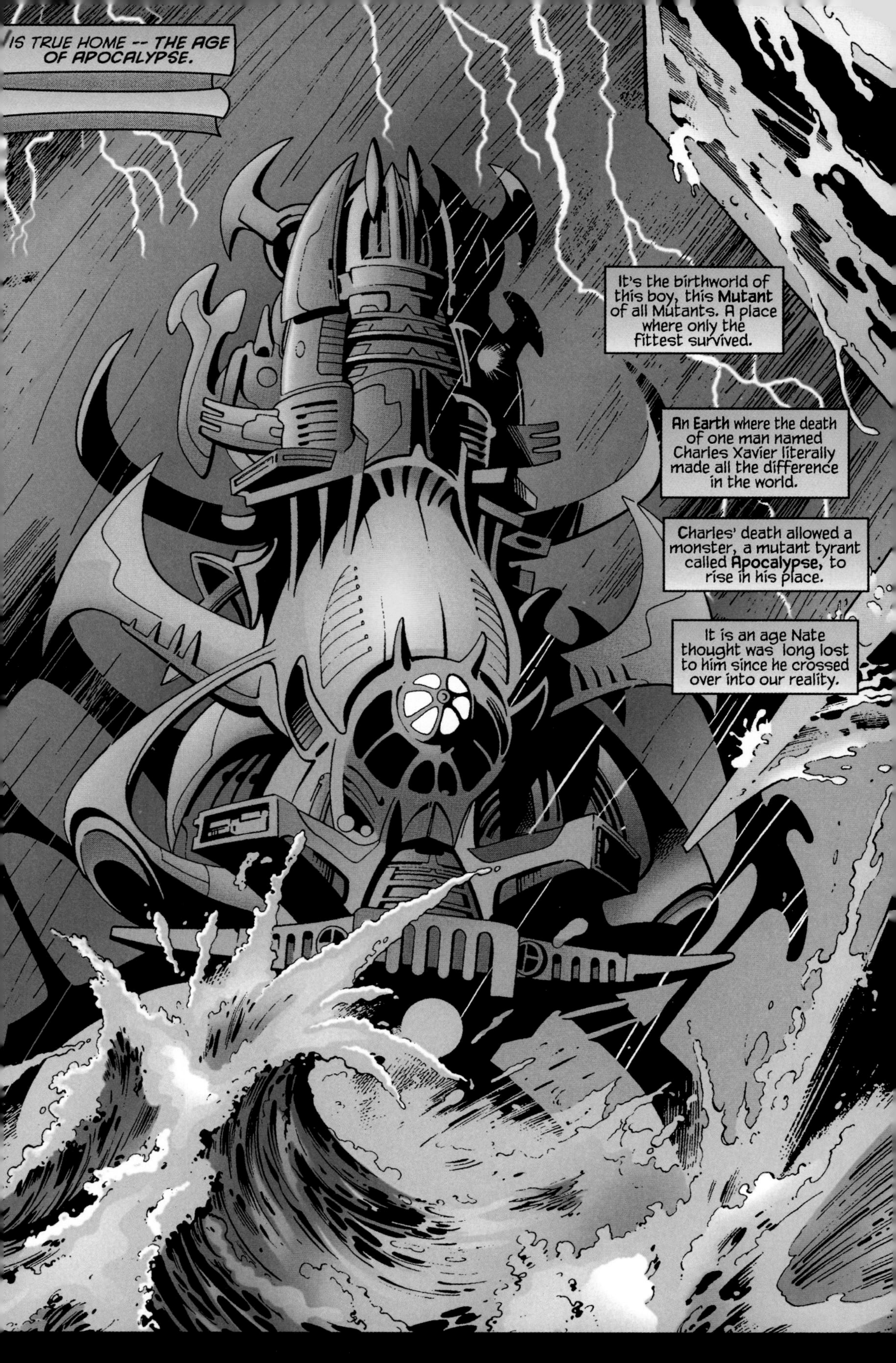
IS TRUE HOME -- THE AGE OF APOCALYPSE.
It's the birthworld of this boy, this Mutant of all Mutants. A place where only the fittest survived.
An Earth where the death of one man named Charles Xavier literally made all the difference in the world.
Charles' death allowed a monster, a mutant tyrant called Apocalypse, to rise in his place.
It is an age Nate thought was long lost to him since he crossed over into our reality.

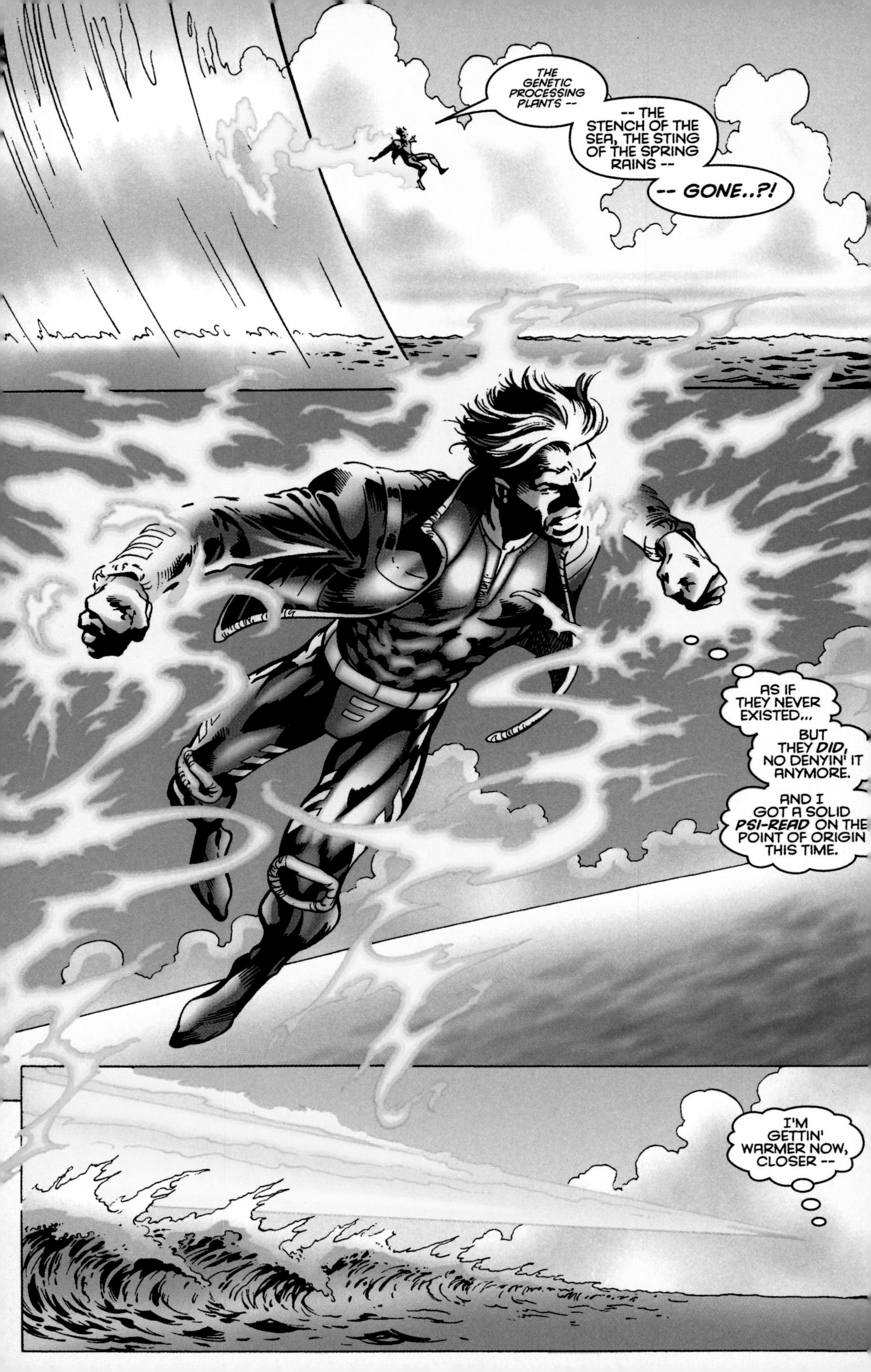
THE GENETIC PROCESSING PLANTS --
-- THE STENCH OF THE SEA, THE STING OF THE SPRING RAINS --
-- GONE..?!
AS IF THEY NEVER EXISTED...
BUT THEY DID, NO DENYIN' IT ANYMORE.
AND I GOT A SOLID PSI-READ ON THE POINT OF ORIGIN THIS TIME.
I'M GETTIN' WARMER NOW, CLOSER --

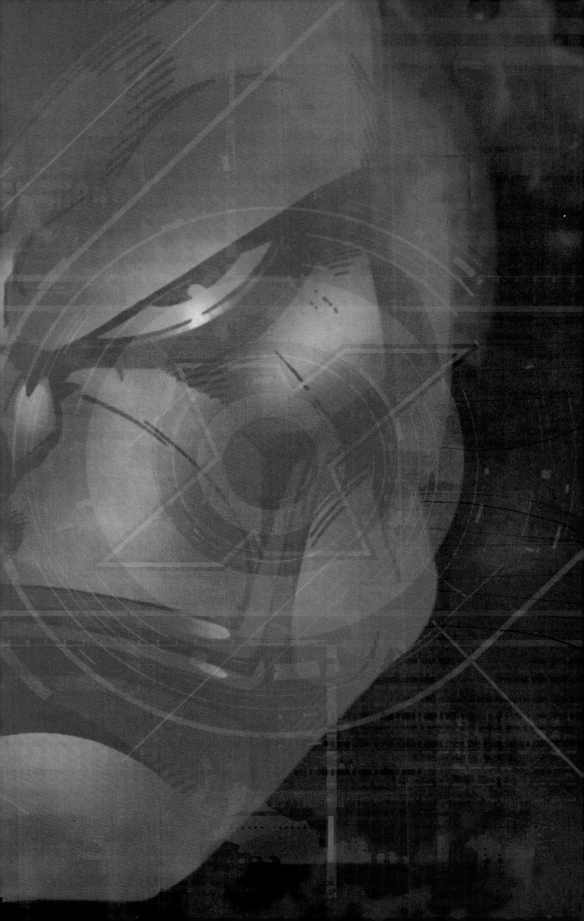

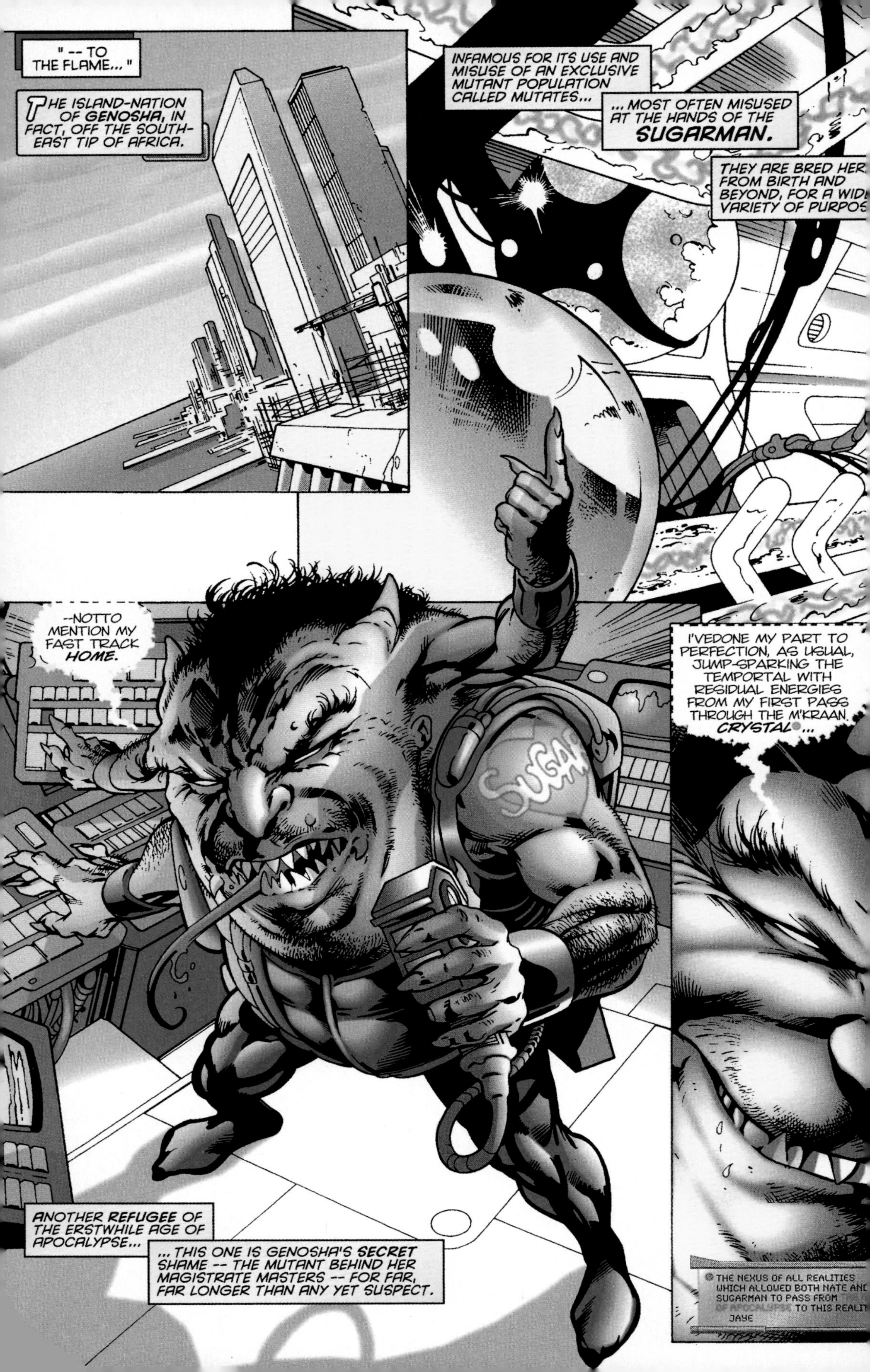

" -- TO THE FLAME... "
THE ISLAND-NATION OF GENOSHA, IN FACT, OFF THE SOUTH-EAST TIP OF AFRICA.
INFAMOUS FOR ITS USE AND MISUSE OF AN EXCLUSIVE MUTANT POPULATION CALLED MUTATES...
... MOST OFTEN MISUSED AT THE HANDS OF THE SUGARMAN.
THEY ARE BRED HER FROM BIRTH AND BEYOND, FOR A WID VARIETY OF PURPOS
--NOTTO MENTION MY FAST TRACK HOME.
I'VEDONE MY PART TO PERFECTION, AS USUAL, JUMP-SPARKING THE TEMPORTAL WITH RESIDUAL ENERGIES FROM MY FIRST PASS THROUGH THE M'KRAAN CRYSTAL...
SUGAR
ANOTHER REFUGEE OF THE ERSTWHILE AGE OF APOCALYPSE...
... THIS ONE IS GENOSHA'S SECRET SHAME -- THE MUTANT BEHIND HER MAGISTRATE MASTERS -- FOR FAR, FAR LONGER THAN ANY YET SUSPECT.
THE NEXUS OF ALL REALITIES WHICH ALLOWED BOTH NATE AND SUGARMAN TO PASS FROM TO THIS REALIT
JAYE

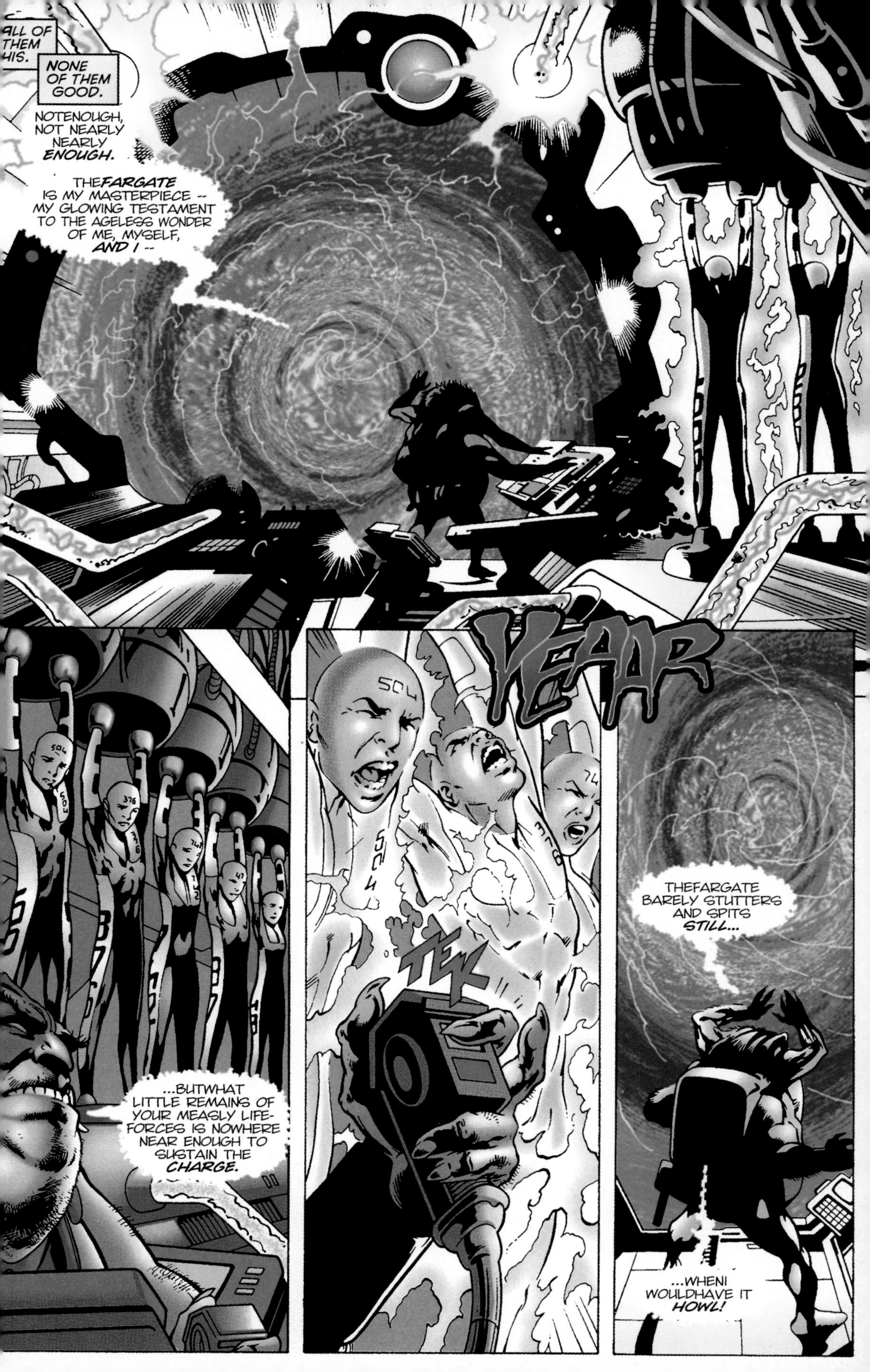
ALL OF THEM HIS.
NONE OF THEM GOOD.
NOTENOUGH, NOT NEARLY NEARLY ENOUGH.
THEFARGATE IS MY MASTERPIECE -- MY GLOWING TESTAMENT TO THE AGELESS WONDER OF ME, MYSELF, AND I --
...BUTWHAT LITTLE REMAINS OF YOUR MEASLY LIFE-FORCES IS NOWHERE NEAR ENOUGH TO SUSTAIN THE CHARGE.
YEAAR
TEK
THEFARGATE BARELY STUTTERS AND SPITS STILL...
...WHENI WOULDHAVE IT HOWL!

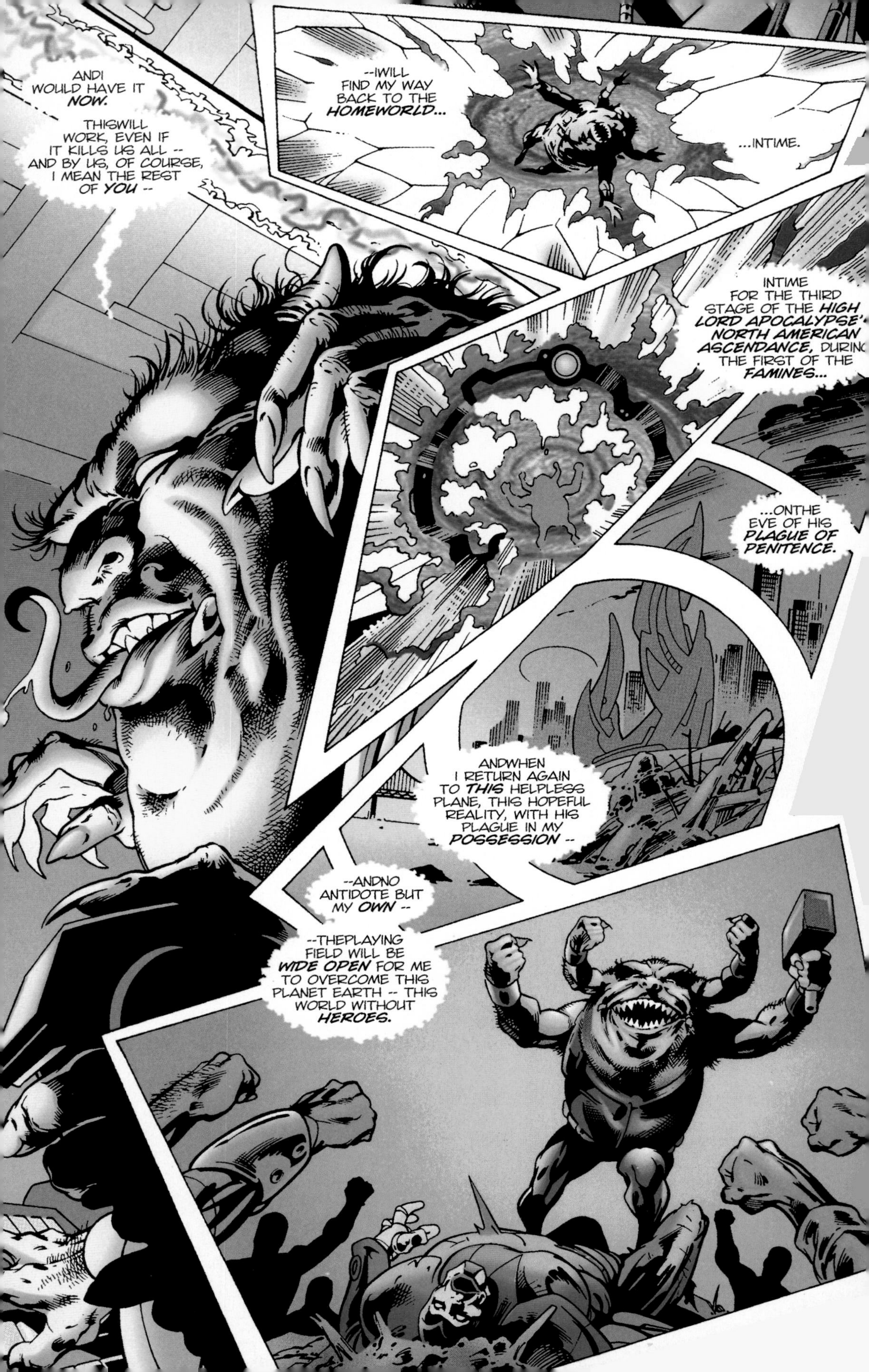

ANDI WOULD HAVE IT NOW.
THISWILL WORK, EVEN IF IT KILLS US ALL -- AND BY US, OF COURSE, I MEAN THE REST OF YOU --
--IWILL FIND MY WAY BACK TO THE HOMEWORLD...
...INTIME.
INTIME FOR THE THIRD STAGE OF THE HIGH LORD APOCALYPSE'S NORTH AMERICAN ASCENDANCE, DURING THE FIRST OF THE FAMINES...
...ONTHE EVE OF HIS PLAGUE OF PENITENCE.
ANDWHEN I RETURN AGAIN TO THIS HELPLESS PLANE, THIS HOPEFUL REALITY, WITH HIS PLAGUE IN MY POSSESSION --
--ANDNO ANTIDOTE BUT MY OWN --
--THEPLAYING FIELD WILL BE WIDE OPEN FOR ME TO OVERCOME THIS PLANET EARTH -- THIS WORLD WITHOUT HEROES.

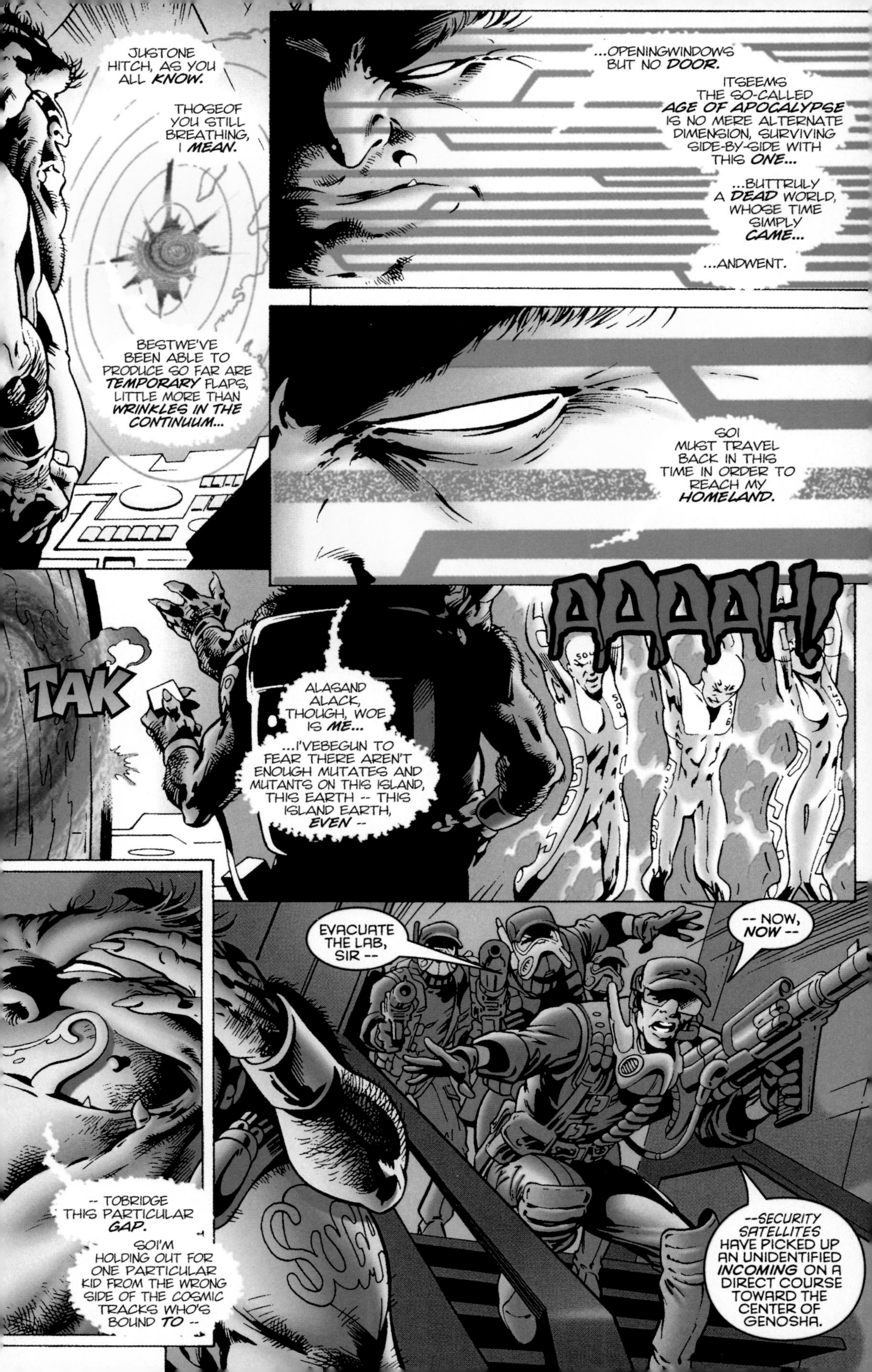
JUSTONE HITCH, AS YOU ALL KNOW.
THOSEOF YOU STILL BREATHING, I MEAN.
BESTWE'VE BEEN ABLE TO PRODUCE SO FAR ARE TEMPORARY FLAPS, LITTLE MORE THAN WRINKLES IN THE CONTINUUM...
...OPENINGWINDOWS BUT NO DOOR.
ITSEEMS THE SO-CALLED AGE OF APOCALYPSE IS NO MERE ALTERNATE DIMENSION, SURVIVING SIDE-BY-SIDE WITH THIS ONE...
...BUTTRULY A DEAD WORLD, WHOSE TIME SIMPLY CAME...
...ANDWENT.
SOI MUST TRAVEL BACK IN THIS TIME IN ORDER TO REACH MY HOMELAND.
TAK
ALASAND ALACK, THOUGH, WOE IS ME...
...I'VEBEGUN TO FEAR THERE AREN'T ENOUGH MUTATES AND MUTANTS ON THIS ISLAND, THIS EARTH -- THIS ISLAND EARTH, EVEN --
AAAAH!
-- TOBRIDGE THIS PARTICULAR GAP.
SOI'M HOLDING OUT FOR ONE PARTICULAR KID FROM THE WRONG SIDE OF THE COSMIC TRACKS WHO'S BOUND TO --
EVACUATE THE LAB, SIR --
-- NOW, NOW --
--SECURITY SATELLITES HAVE PICKED UP AN UNIDENTIFIED INCOMING ON A DIRECT COURSE TOWARD THE CENTER OF GENOSHA.

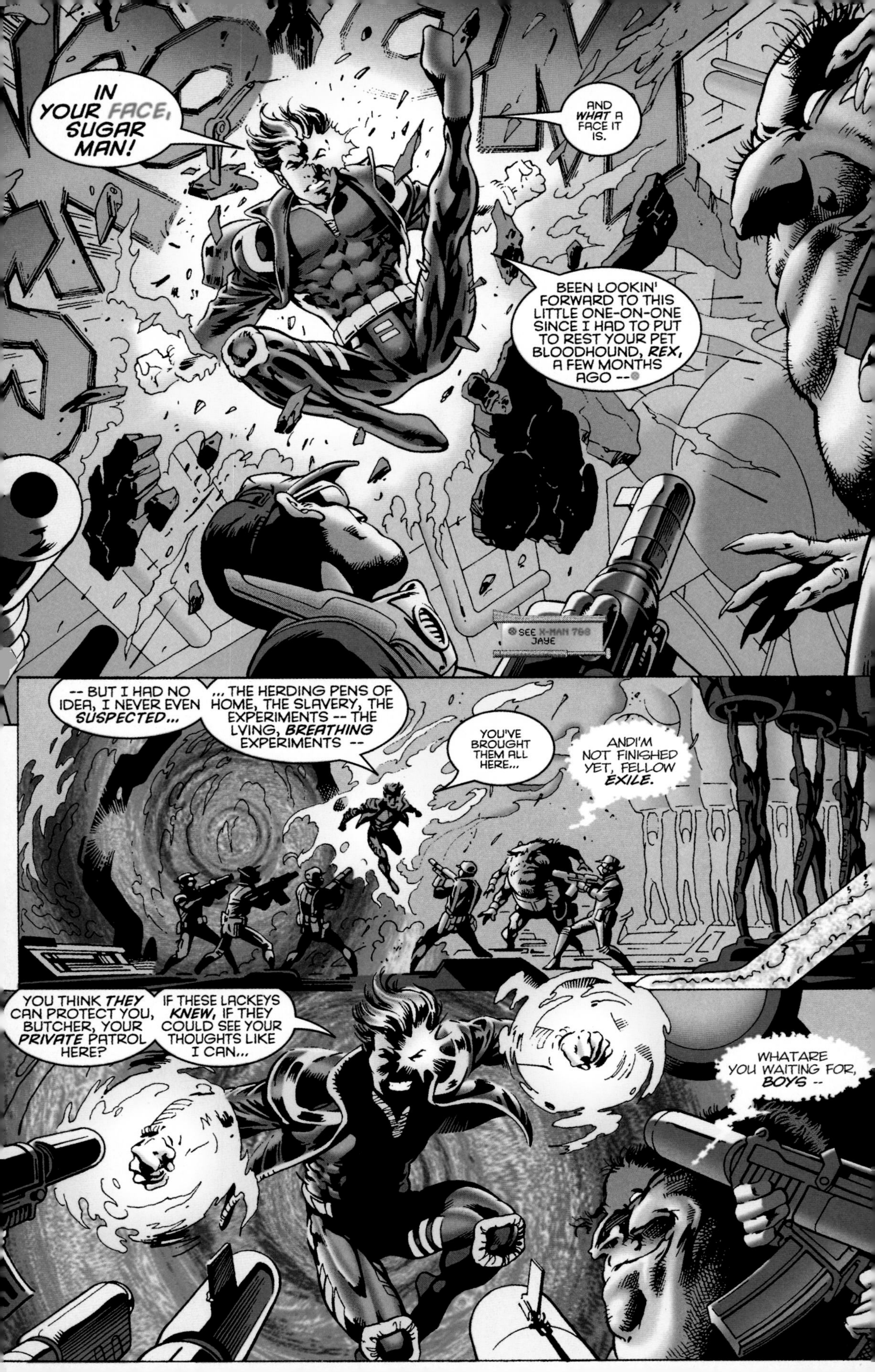
IN YOUR FACE, SUGAR MAN!
AND WHAT A FACE IT IS.
BEEN LOOKIN' FORWARD TO THIS LITTLE ONE-ON-ONE SINCE I HAD TO PUT TO REST YOUR PET BLOODHOUND, REX, A FEW MONTHS AGO --
SEE X-MAN 76 JAYE
-- BUT I HAD NO IDEA, I NEVER EVEN SUSPECTED...
... THE HERDING PENS OF HOME, THE SLAVERY, THE EXPERIMENTS -- THE LIVING, BREATHING EXPERIMENTS --
YOU'VE BROUGHT THEM ALL HERE...
AND I'M NOT FINISHED YET, FELLOW EXILE.
YOU THINK THEY CAN PROTECT YOU, BUTCHER, YOUR PRIVATE PATROL HERE?
IF THESE LACKEYS KNEW, IF THEY COULD SEE YOUR THOUGHTS LIKE I CAN...
WHAT ARE YOU WAITING FOR, BOYS --

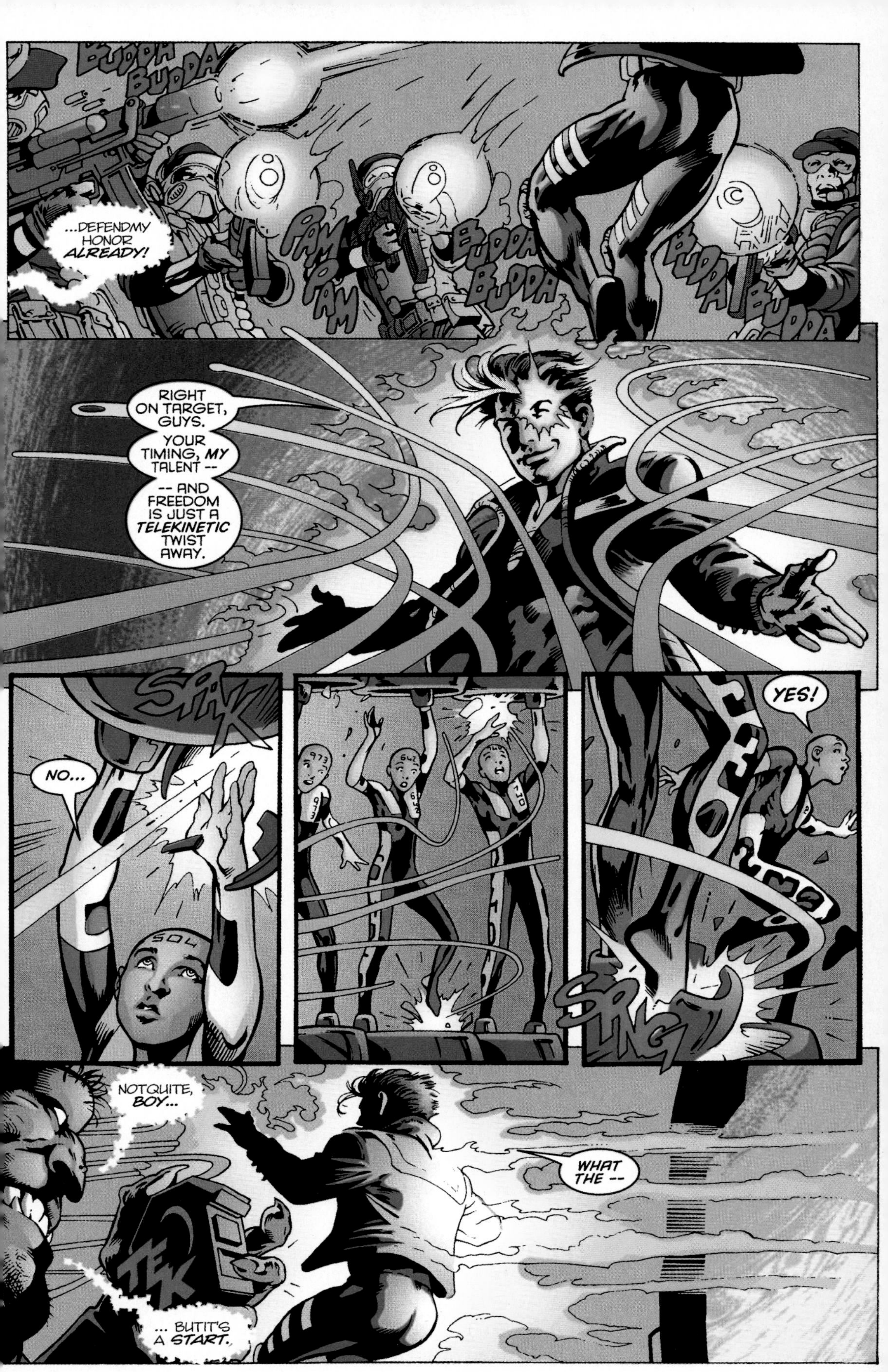
BUDDA BUDDA
...DEFENDMY HONOR ALREADY!
PAM PAM
BUDDA BUDDA
BUDDA BUDDA
RIGHT ON TARGET, GUYS.
YOUR TIMING, MY TALENT --
-- AND FREEDOM IS JUST A TELEKINETIC TWIST AWAY.
SPAK
NO...
YES!
SPLING
NOTQUITE, BOY...
WHAT THE --
TEK
... BUTIT'S A START.

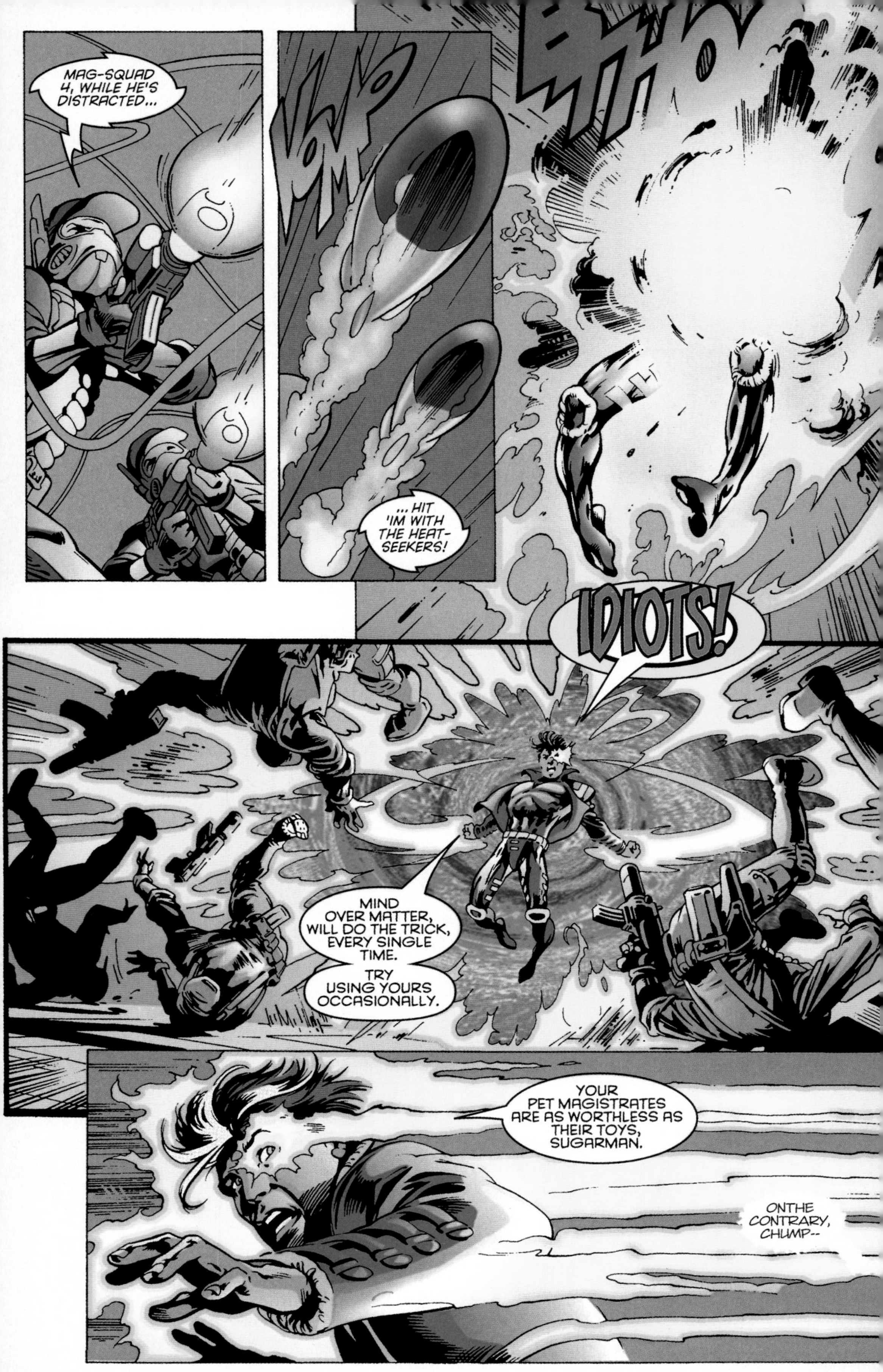
MAG-SQUAD 4, WHILE HE'S DISTRACTED...
VOMP
...HIT 'IM WITH THE HEAT-SEEKERS!
IDIOTS!
MIND OVER MATTER, WILL DO THE TRICK, EVERY SINGLE TIME.
TRY USING YOURS OCCASIONALLY.
YOUR PET MAGISTRATES ARE AS WORTHLESS AS THEIR TOYS, SUGARMAN.
ONTHE CONTRARY, CHUMP--

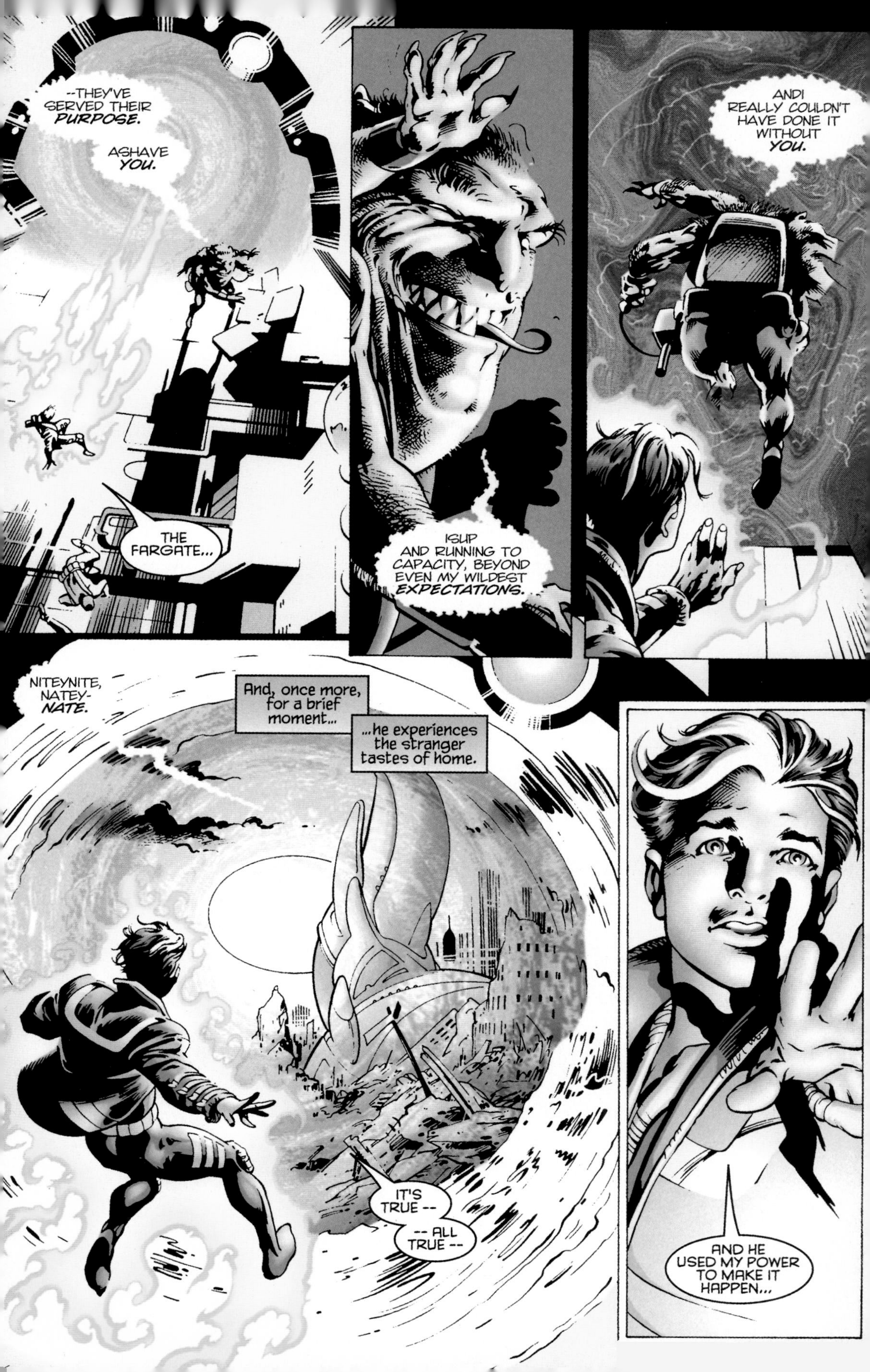
--THEY'VE SERVED THEIR PURPOSE.
ASHAVE YOU.
THE FARGATE...
ISUP AND RUNNING TO CAPACITY, BEYOND EVEN MY WILDEST EXPECTATIONS.
ANDI REALLY COULDN'T HAVE DONE IT WITHOUT YOU.
NITEYNITE, NATEY-NATE.
And, once more, for a brief moment...
...he experiences the stranger tastes of home.
IT'S TRUE --
-- ALL TRUE --
AND HE USED MY POWER TO MAKE IT HAPPEN...

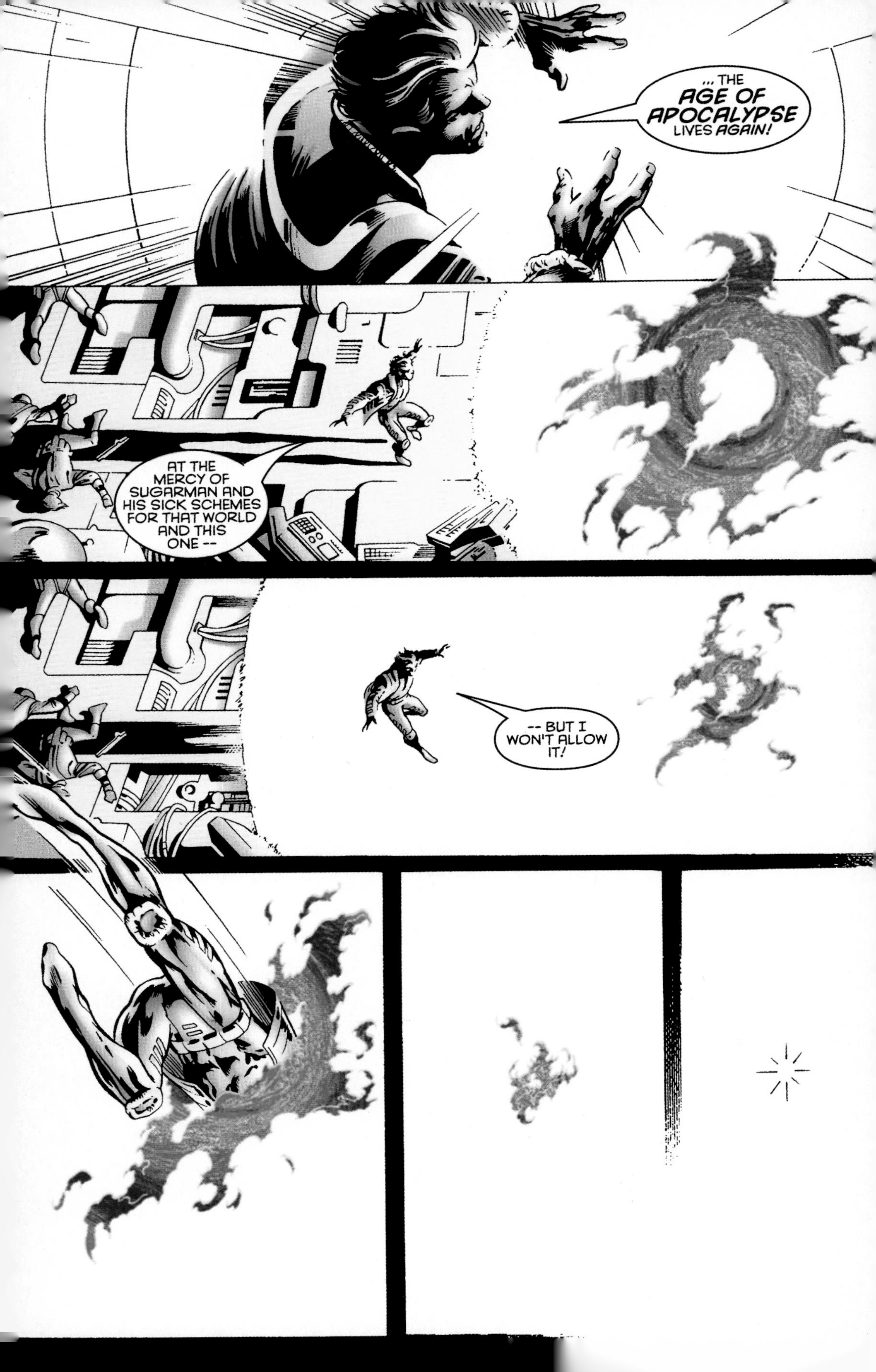
... THE
AGE OF
APOCALYPSE
LIVES AGAIN!
AT THE MERCY OF SUGARMAN AND HIS SICK SCHEMES FOR THAT WORLD AND THIS ONE --
-- BUT I WON'T ALLOW IT!

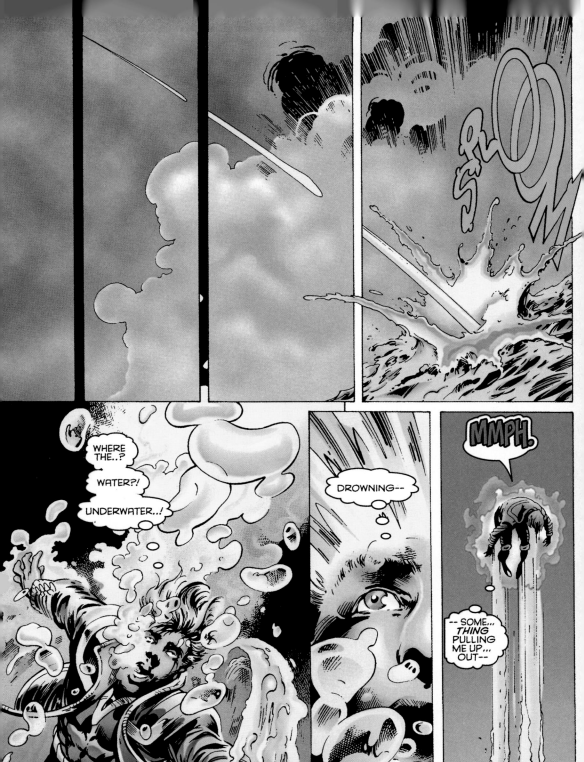

WHERE THE..?

WATER?!

UNDERWATER..!

DROWNING--

MMPH.

-- SOME... *THING* PULLING ME UP... OUT--

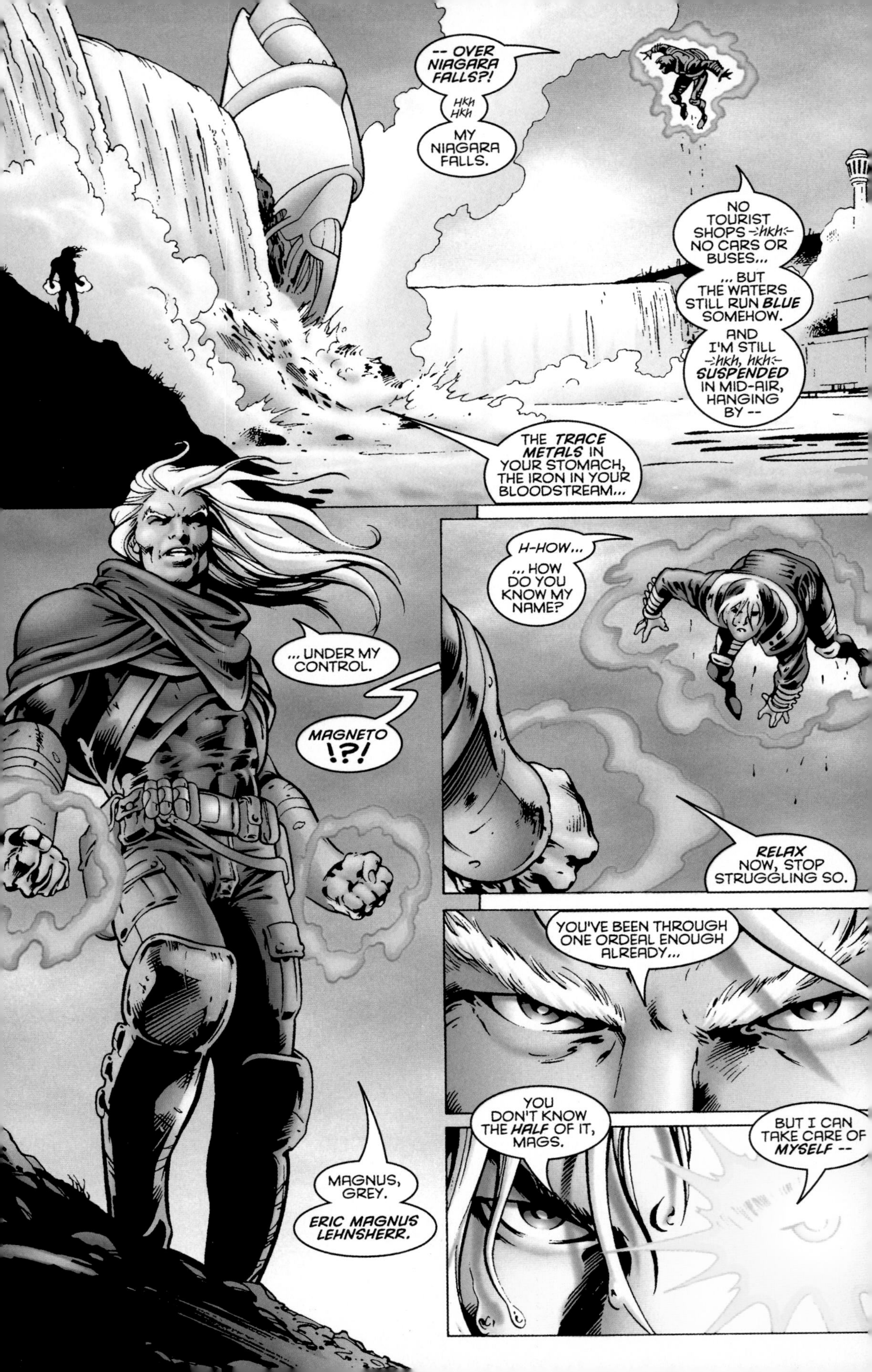

-- OVER NIAGARA FALLS?!
HKH HKH
MY NIAGARA FALLS.
NO TOURIST SHOPS -hkh- NO CARS OR BUSES...
... BUT THE WATERS STILL RUN BLUE SOMEHOW.
AND I'M STILL -hkh, hkh- SUSPENDED IN MID-AIR, HANGING BY --
THE TRACE METALS IN YOUR STOMACH, THE IRON IN YOUR BLOODSTREAM...
... UNDER MY CONTROL.
MAGNETO !?!
H-HOW...
... HOW DO YOU KNOW MY NAME?
RELAX NOW, STOP STRUGGLING SO.
MAGNUS, GREY.
ERIC MAGNUS LEHNSHERR.
YOU'VE BEEN THROUGH ONE ORDEAL ENOUGH ALREADY...
YOU DON'T KNOW THE HALF OF IT, MAGS.
BUT I CAN TAKE CARE OF MYSELF --

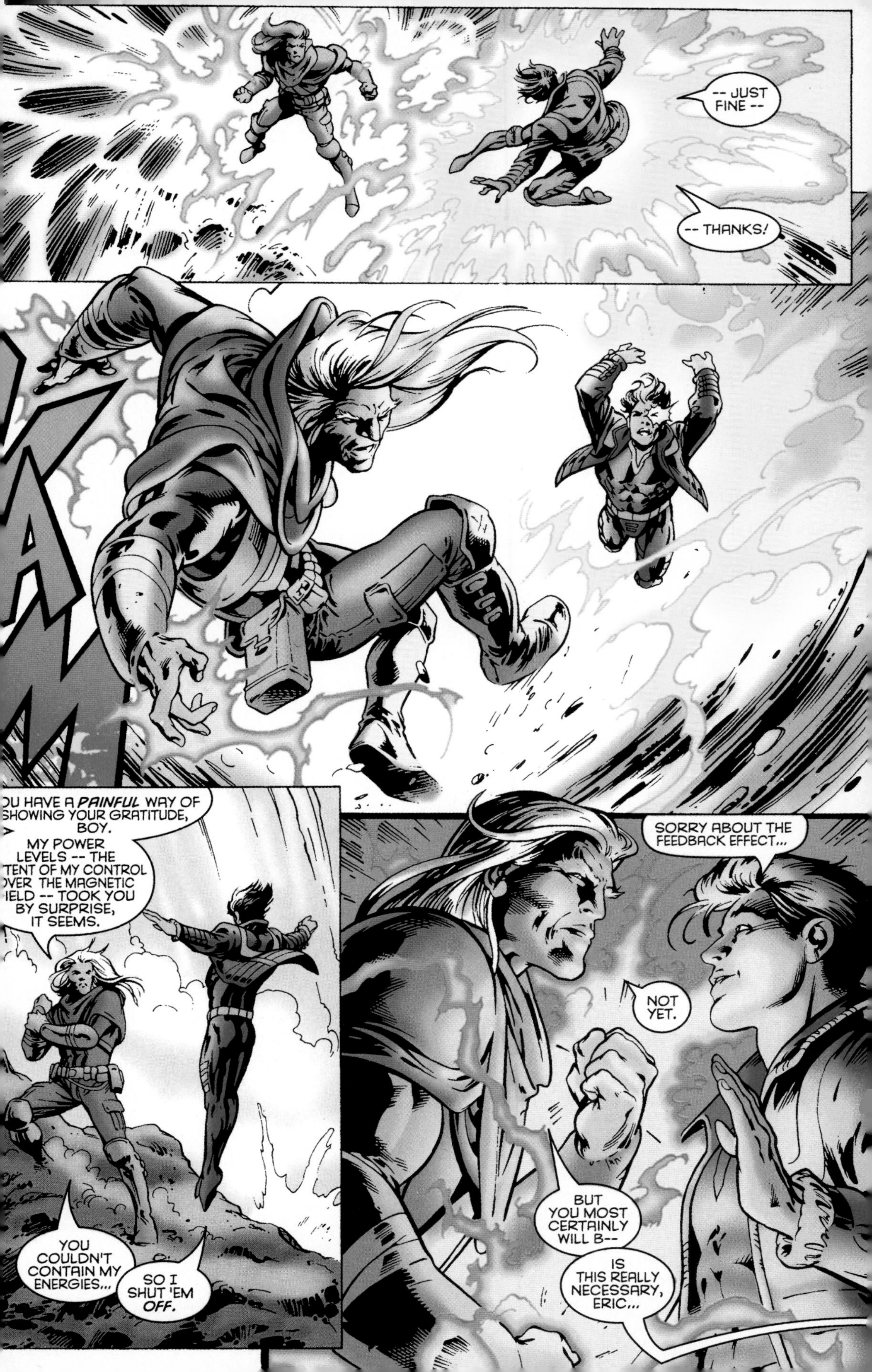
-- JUST FINE --
-- THANKS!
OU HAVE A PAINFUL WAY OF SHOWING YOUR GRATITUDE, BOY.
MY POWER LEVELS -- THE TENT OF MY CONTROL OVER THE MAGNETIC IELD -- TOOK YOU BY SURPRISE, IT SEEMS.
YOU COULDN'T CONTAIN MY ENERGIES...
SO I SHUT 'EM OFF.
SORRY ABOUT THE FEEDBACK EFFECT...
NOT YET.
BUT YOU MOST CERTAINLY WILL B--
IS THIS REALLY NECESSARY, ERIC...

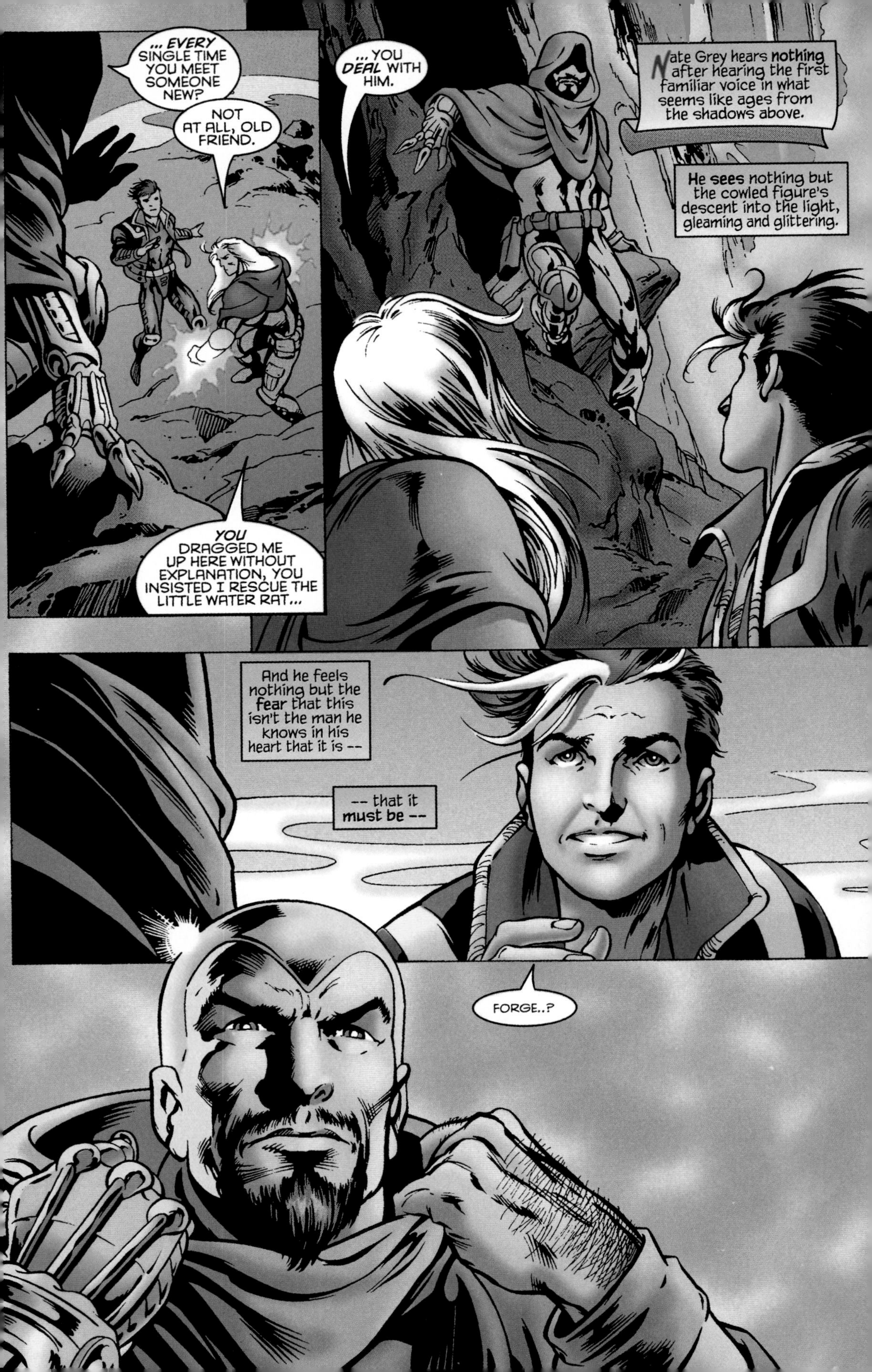
... EVERY SINGLE TIME YOU MEET SOMEONE NEW?
NOT AT ALL, OLD FRIEND.
YOU DRAGGED ME UP HERE WITHOUT EXPLANATION, YOU INSISTED I RESCUE THE LITTLE WATER RAT...
... YOU DEAL WITH HIM.
Nate Grey hears nothing after hearing the first familiar voice in what seems like ages from the shadows above.
He sees nothing but the cowled figure's descent into the light, gleaming and glittering.
And he feels nothing but the fear that this isn't the man he knows in his heart that it is --
-- that it must be --
FORGE..?

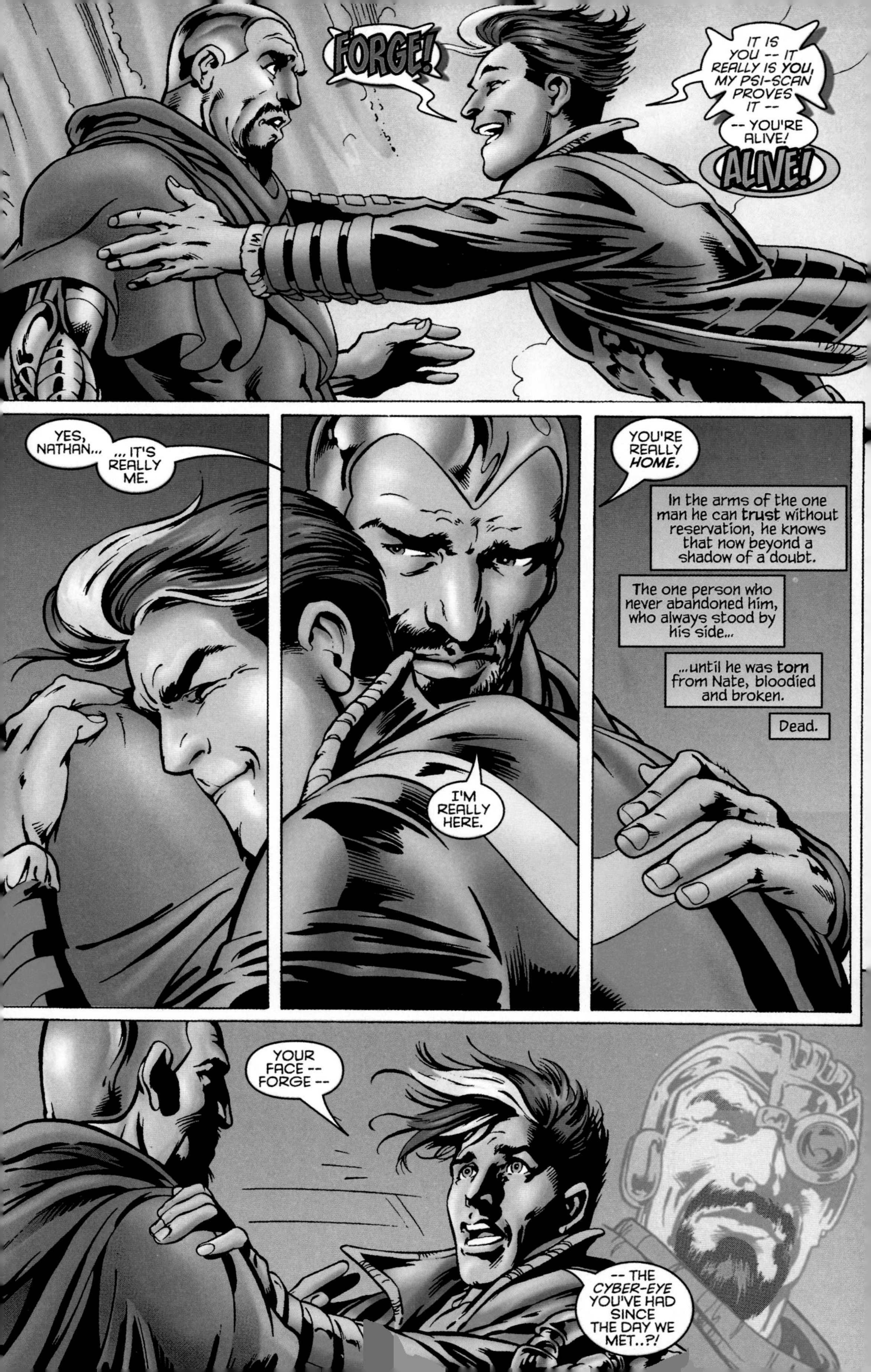
FORGE!
IT IS YOU -- IT REALLY IS YOU, MY PSI-SCAN PROVES IT --
-- YOU'RE ALIVE!
ALIVE!
YES, NATHAN...
...IT'S REALLY ME.
I'M REALLY HERE.
YOU'RE REALLY HOME.
In the arms of the one man he can trust without reservation, he knows that now beyond a shadow of a doubt.
The one person who never abandoned him, who always stood by his side...
...until he was torn from Nate, bloodied and broken.
Dead.
YOUR FACE -- FORGE --
-- THE CYBER-EYE YOU'VE HAD SINCE THE DAY WE MET..?!

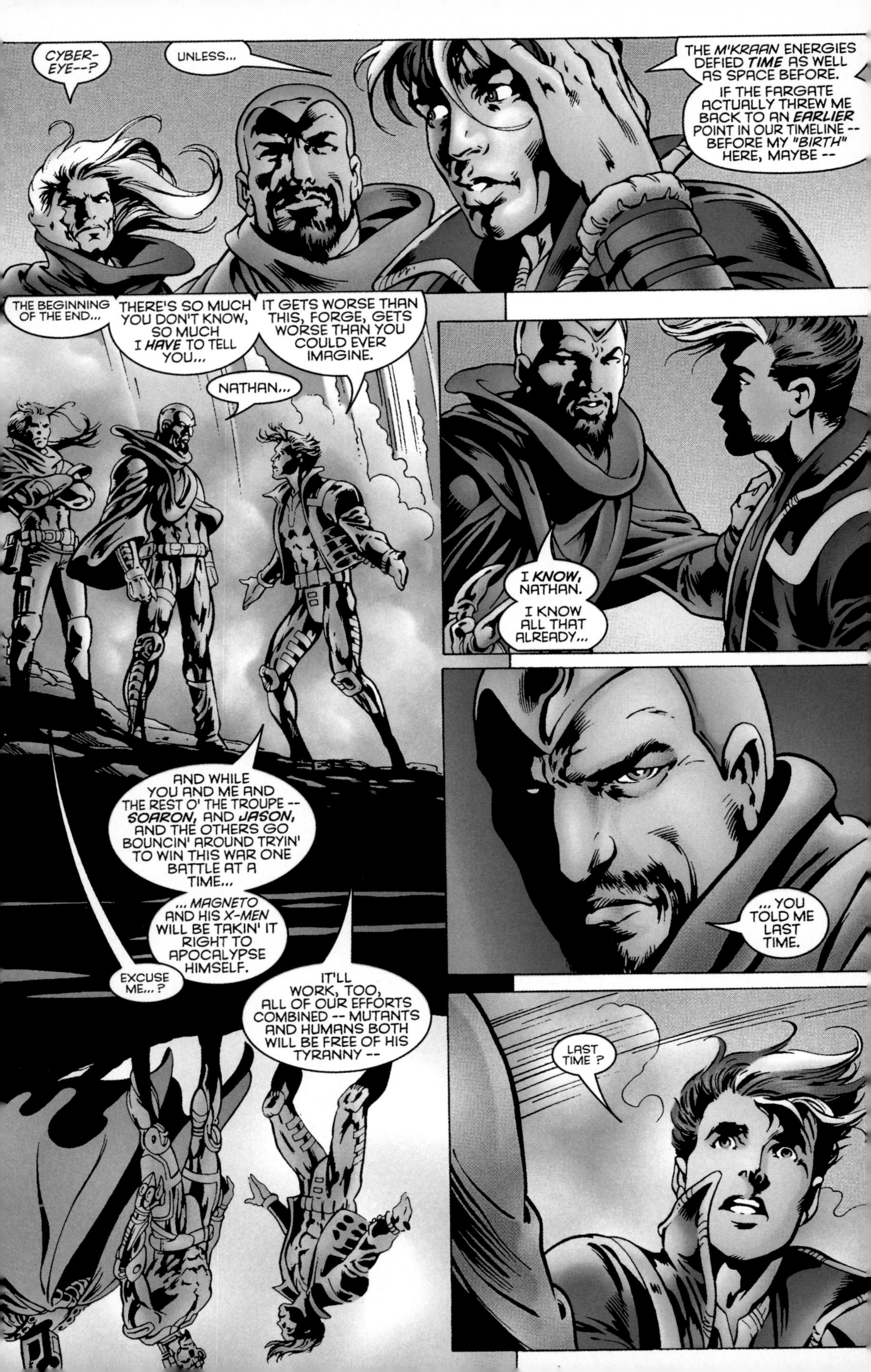
CYBER-EYE--?
UNLESS...
THE M'KRAAN ENERGIES DEFIED TIME AS WELL AS SPACE BEFORE.
IF THE FARGATE ACTUALLY THREW ME BACK TO AN EARLIER POINT IN OUR TIMELINE -- BEFORE MY "BIRTH" HERE, MAYBE --
THE BEGINNING OF THE END...
THERE'S SO MUCH YOU DON'T KNOW, SO MUCH I HAVE TO TELL YOU...
IT GETS WORSE THAN THIS, FORGE, GETS WORSE THAN YOU COULD EVER IMAGINE.
NATHAN...
I KNOW, NATHAN.
I KNOW ALL THAT ALREADY...
AND WHILE YOU AND ME AND THE REST O' THE TROUPE -- SOARON, AND JASON, AND THE OTHERS GO BOUNCIN' AROUND TRYIN' TO WIN THIS WAR ONE BATTLE AT A TIME...
... MAGNETO AND HIS X-MEN WILL BE TAKIN' IT RIGHT TO APOCALYPSE HIMSELF.
EXCUSE ME... ?
IT'LL WORK, TOO, ALL OF OUR EFFORTS COMBINED -- MUTANTS AND HUMANS BOTH WILL BE FREE OF HIS TYRANNY --
... YOU TOLD ME LAST TIME.
LAST TIME ?

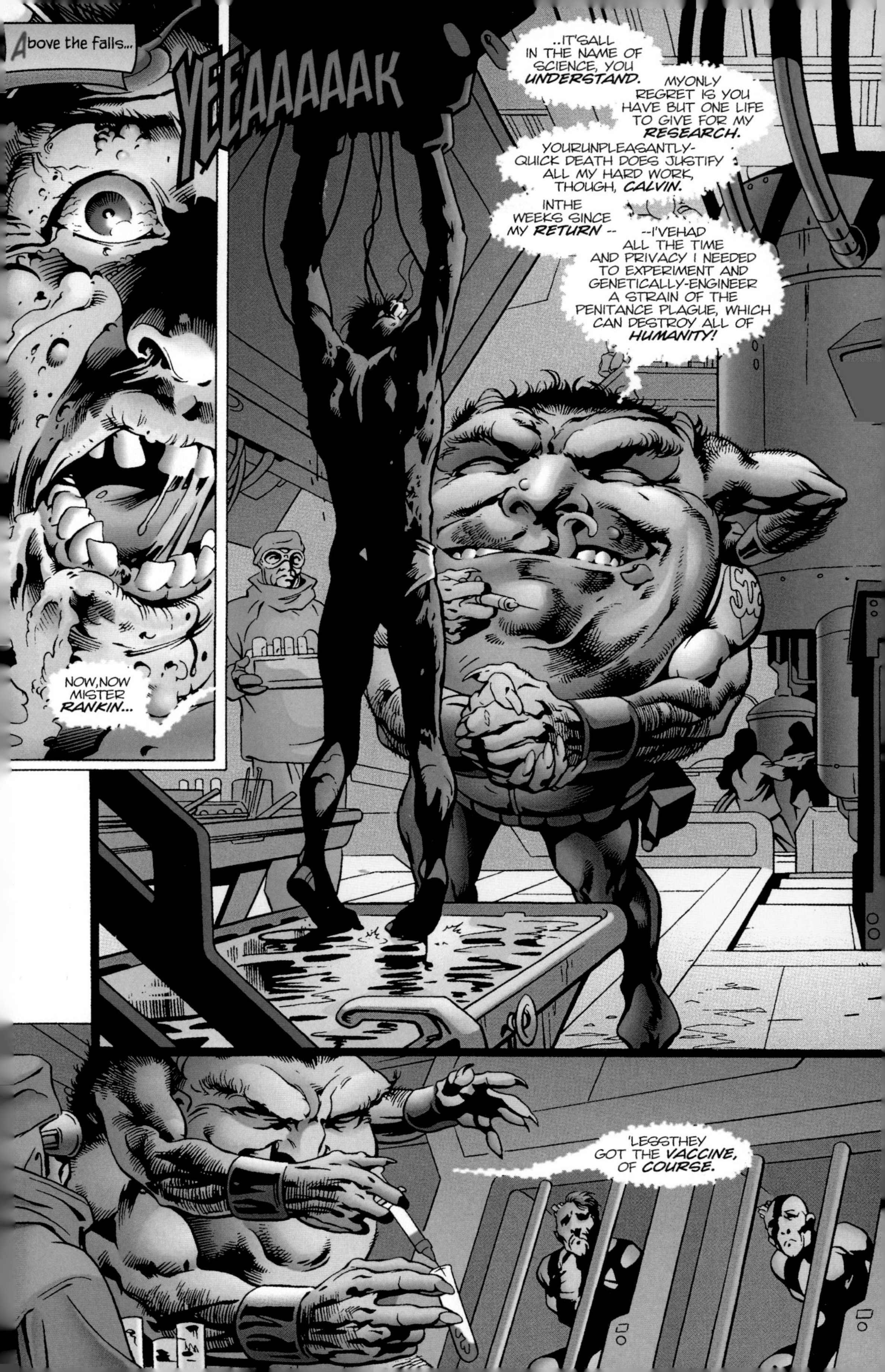
Above the falls...
YEEAAAAAK
NOW, NOW MISTER RANKIN...
..IT'S ALL IN THE NAME OF SCIENCE, YOU UNDERSTAND.
MY ONLY REGRET IS YOU HAVE BUT ONE LIFE TO GIVE FOR MY RESEARCH.
YOUR UNPLEASANTLY-QUICK DEATH DOES JUSTIFY ALL MY HARD WORK, THOUGH, CALVIN.
IN THE WEEKS SINCE MY RETURN --
--I'VE HAD ALL THE TIME AND PRIVACY I NEEDED TO EXPERIMENT AND GENETICALLY-ENGINEER A STRAIN OF THE PENITANCE PLAGUE, WHICH CAN DESTROY ALL OF HUMANITY!
'LESS THEY GOT THE VACCINE, OF COURSE.

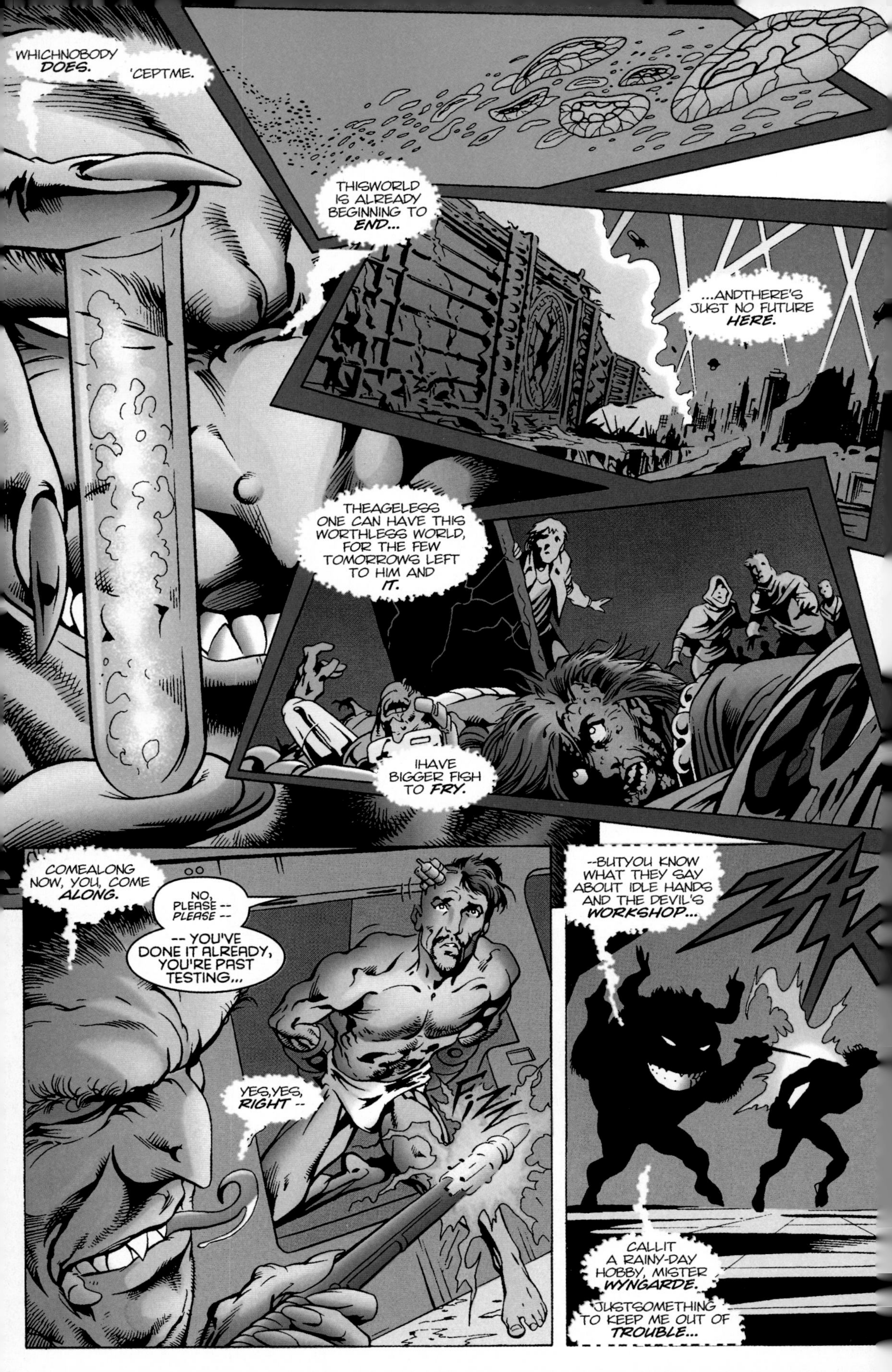

WHICH NOBODY DOES.
'CEPT ME.
THIS WORLD IS ALREADY BEGINNING TO END...
...AND THERE'S JUST NO FUTURE HERE.
THE AGELESS ONE CAN HAVE THIS WORTHLESS WORLD, FOR THE FEW TOMORROWS LEFT TO HIM AND IT.
I HAVE BIGGER FISH TO FRY.
COME ALONG NOW, YOU, COME ALONG.
NO, PLEASE -- PLEASE --
-- YOU'VE DONE IT ALREADY, YOU'RE PAST TESTING...
YES, YES, RIGHT --
--BUT YOU KNOW WHAT THEY SAY ABOUT IDLE HANDS AND THE DEVIL'S WORKSHOP...
CALL IT A RAINY-DAY HOBBY, MISTER WYNGARDE.
JUST SOMETHING TO KEEP ME OUT OF TROUBLE...

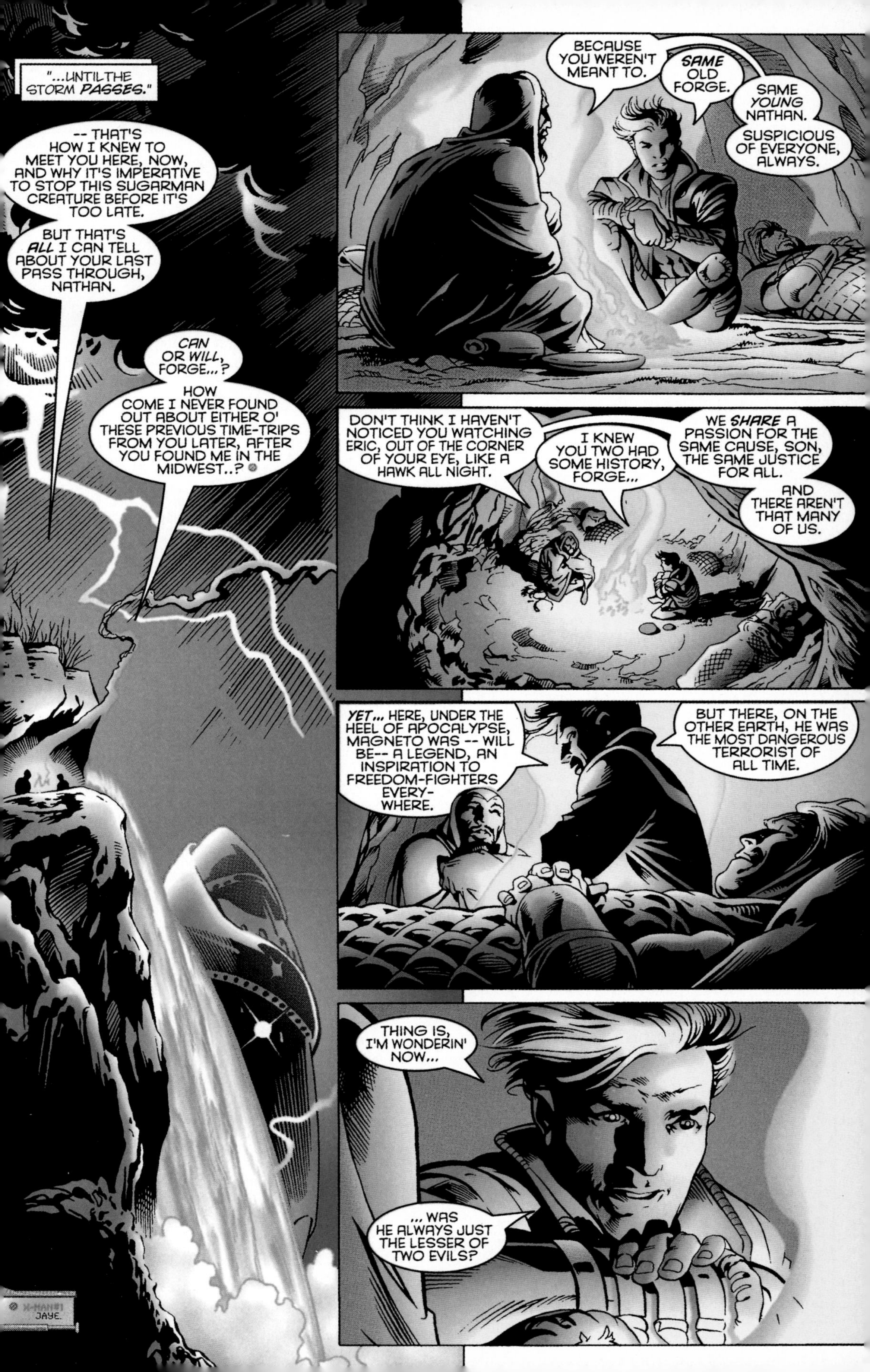
"...UNTIL THE STORM PASSES."
-- THAT'S HOW I KNEW TO MEET YOU HERE, NOW, AND WHY IT'S IMPERATIVE TO STOP THIS SUGARMAN CREATURE BEFORE IT'S TOO LATE.
BUT THAT'S ALL I CAN TELL ABOUT YOUR LAST PASS THROUGH, NATHAN.
CAN OR WILL, FORGE...?
HOW COME I NEVER FOUND OUT ABOUT EITHER O' THESE PREVIOUS TIME-TRIPS FROM YOU LATER, AFTER YOU FOUND ME IN THE MIDWEST..?
X-MAN#1 JAYE.
BECAUSE YOU WEREN'T MEANT TO.
SAME OLD FORGE.
SAME YOUNG NATHAN.
SUSPICIOUS OF EVERYONE, ALWAYS.
DON'T THINK I HAVEN'T NOTICED YOU WATCHING ERIC, OUT OF THE CORNER OF YOUR EYE, LIKE A HAWK ALL NIGHT.
I KNEW YOU TWO HAD SOME HISTORY, FORGE...
WE SHARE A PASSION FOR THE SAME CAUSE, SON, THE SAME JUSTICE FOR ALL.
AND THERE AREN'T THAT MANY OF US.
YET... HERE, UNDER THE HEEL OF APOCALYPSE, MAGNETO WAS -- WILL BE-- A LEGEND, AN INSPIRATION TO FREEDOM-FIGHTERS EVERYWHERE.
BUT THERE, ON THE OTHER EARTH, HE WAS THE MOST DANGEROUS TERRORIST OF ALL TIME.
THING IS, I'M WONDERIN' NOW...
...WAS HE ALWAYS JUST THE LESSER OF TWO EVILS?

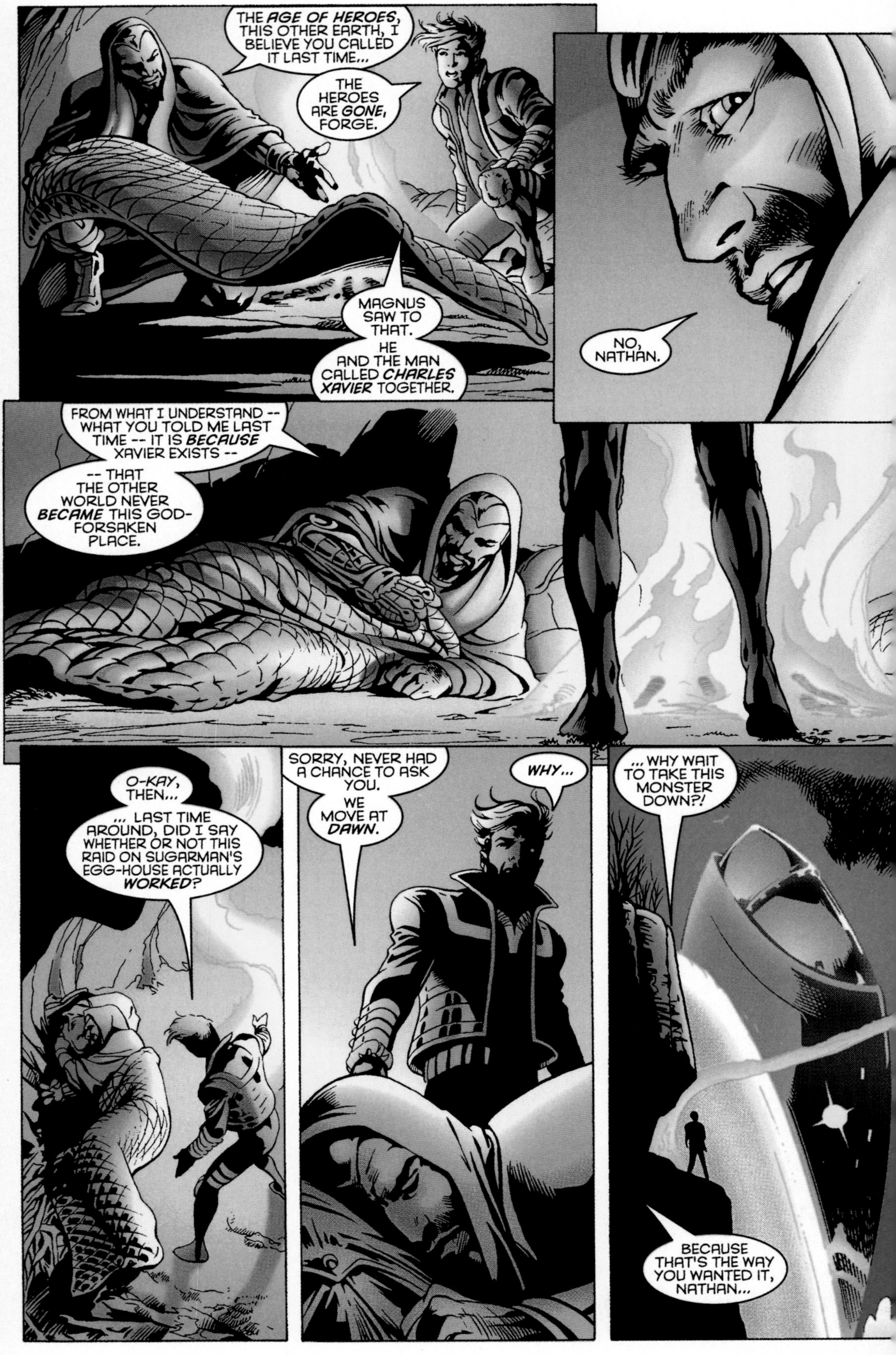
THE AGE OF HEROES, THIS OTHER EARTH, I BELIEVE YOU CALLED IT LAST TIME...
THE HEROES ARE GONE, FORGE.
MAGNUS SAW TO THAT.
HE AND THE MAN CALLED CHARLES XAVIER TOGETHER.
NO, NATHAN.
FROM WHAT I UNDERSTAND -- WHAT YOU TOLD ME LAST TIME -- IT IS BECAUSE XAVIER EXISTS --
-- THAT THE OTHER WORLD NEVER BECAME THIS GOD-FORSAKEN PLACE.
O-KAY, THEN...
... LAST TIME AROUND, DID I SAY WHETHER OR NOT THIS RAID ON SUGARMAN'S EGG-HOUSE ACTUALLY WORKED?
SORRY, NEVER HAD A CHANCE TO ASK YOU.
WE MOVE AT DAWN.
WHY...
... WHY WAIT TO TAKE THIS MONSTER DOWN?!
BECAUSE THAT'S THE WAY YOU WANTED IT, NATHAN...

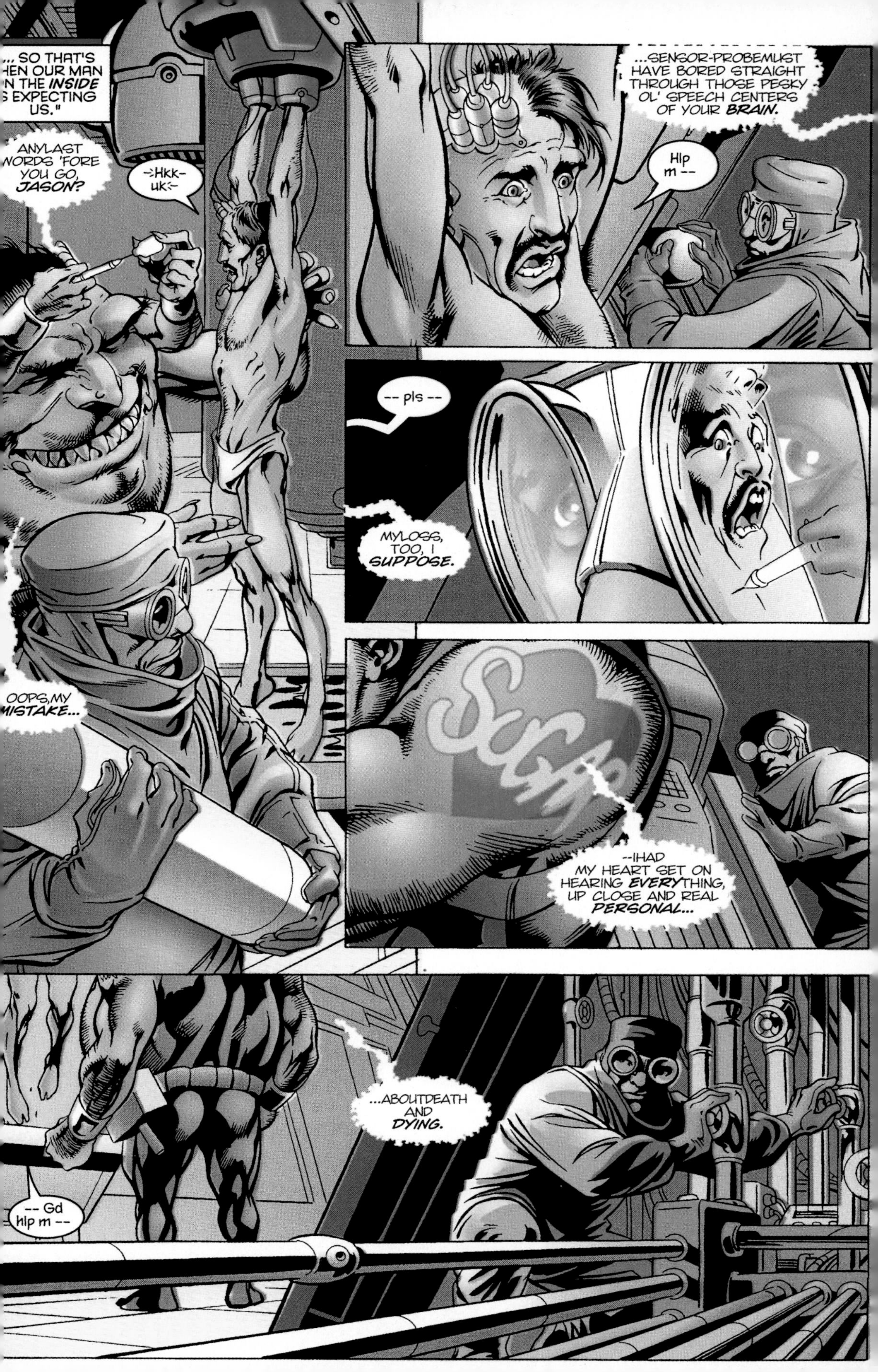
... SO THAT'S
HEN OUR MAN
N THE INSIDE
S EXPECTING
US."
...SENSOR-PROBE MUST HAVE BORED STRAIGHT THROUGH THOSE PESKY OL' SPEECH CENTERS OF YOUR BRAIN.
ANY LAST WORDS 'FORE YOU GO, JASON?
Hkk-uk
Hlp m --
-- pls --
MY LOSS, TOO, I SUPPOSE.
OOPS, MY MISTAKE...
--I HAD MY HEART SET ON HEARING EVERYTHING, UP CLOSE AND REAL PERSONAL...
...ABOUT DEATH AND DYING.
-- Gd hlp m --

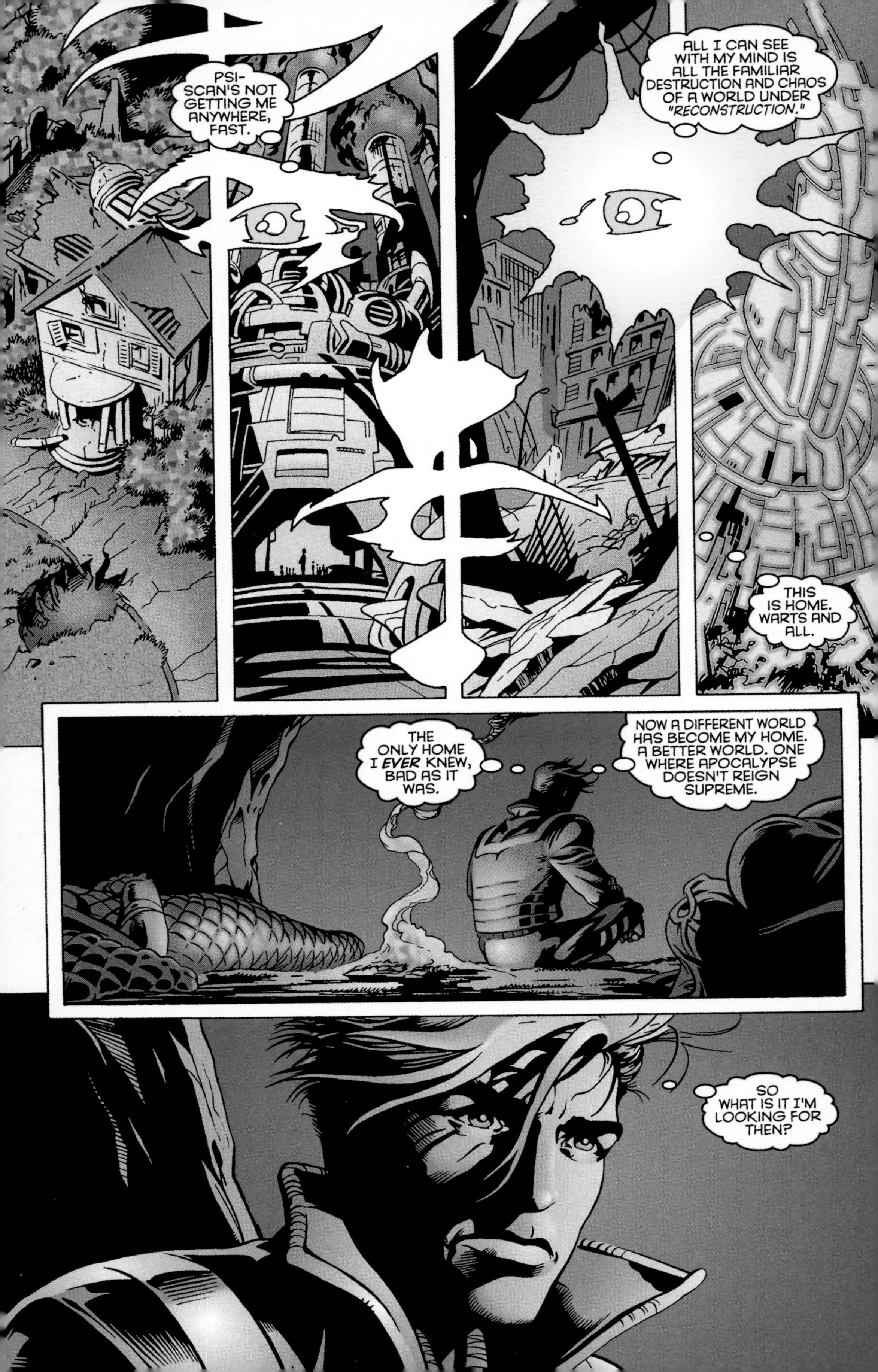
PSI-SCAN'S NOT GETTING ME ANYWHERE, FAST.
ALL I CAN SEE WITH MY MIND IS ALL THE FAMILIAR DESTRUCTION AND CHAOS OF A WORLD UNDER "RECONSTRUCTION."
THIS IS HOME. WARTS AND ALL.
THE ONLY HOME I EVER KNEW, BAD AS IT WAS.
NOW A DIFFERENT WORLD HAS BECOME MY HOME. A BETTER WORLD. ONE WHERE APOCALYPSE DOESN'T REIGN SUPREME.
SO WHAT IS IT I'M LOOKING FOR THEN?

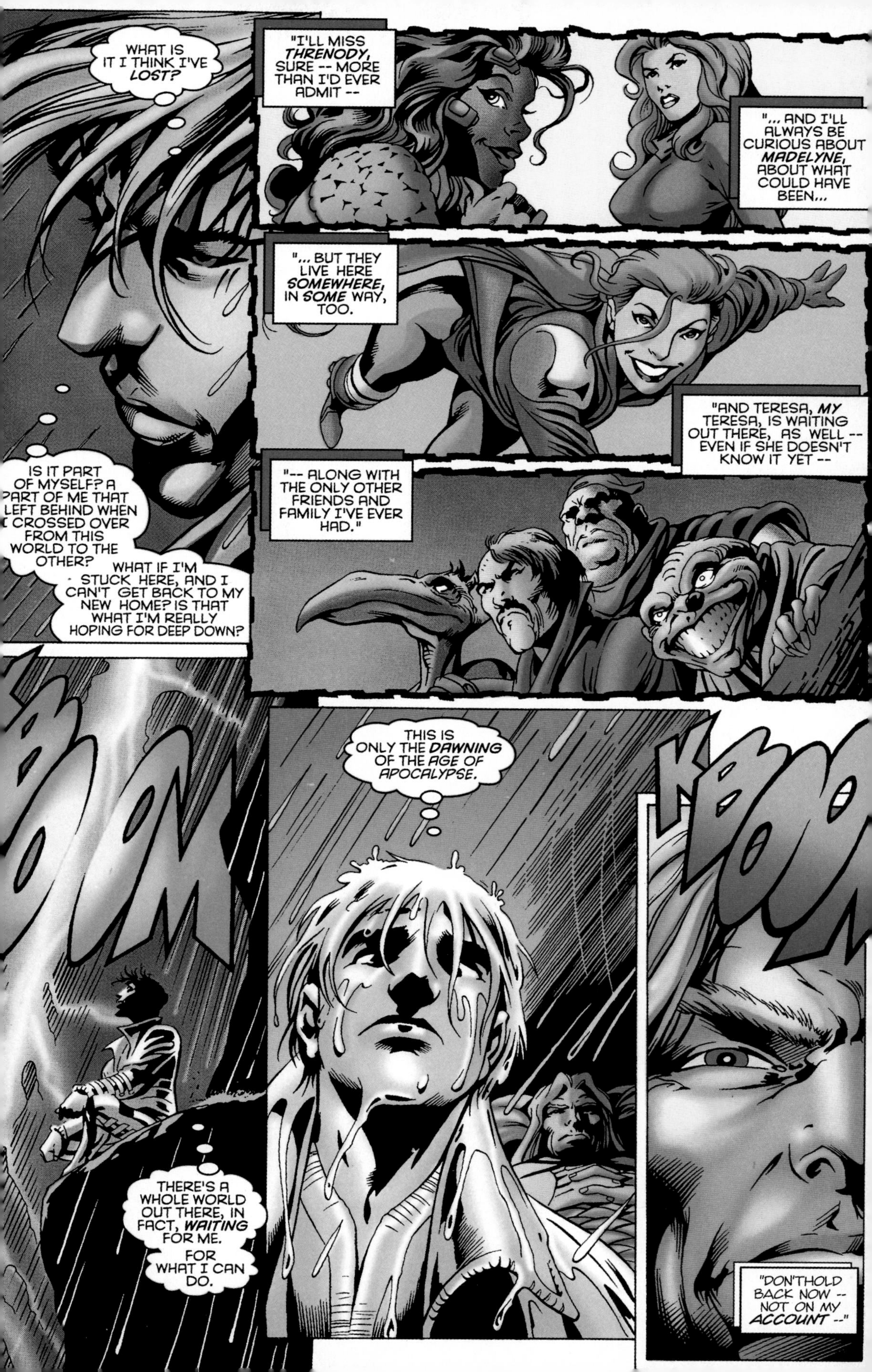
WHAT IS IT I THINK I'VE LOST?
"I'LL MISS THRENODY, SURE -- MORE THAN I'D EVER ADMIT --
"... AND I'LL ALWAYS BE CURIOUS ABOUT MADELYNE, ABOUT WHAT COULD HAVE BEEN...
"... BUT THEY LIVE HERE SOMEWHERE, IN SOME WAY, TOO.
"AND TERESA, MY TERESA, IS WAITING OUT THERE, AS WELL -- EVEN IF SHE DOESN'T KNOW IT YET --
IS IT PART OF MYSELF? A PART OF ME THAT I LEFT BEHIND WHEN I CROSSED OVER FROM THIS WORLD TO THE OTHER?
WHAT IF I'M STUCK HERE, AND I CAN'T GET BACK TO MY NEW HOME? IS THAT WHAT I'M REALLY HOPING FOR DEEP DOWN?
"-- ALONG WITH THE ONLY OTHER FRIENDS AND FAMILY I'VE EVER HAD."
BOOM
THIS IS ONLY THE DAWNING OF THE AGE OF APOCALYPSE.
KA-BOOM
THERE'S A WHOLE WORLD OUT THERE, IN FACT, WAITING FOR ME.
FOR WHAT I CAN DO.
"DON'T HOLD BACK NOW -- NOT ON MY ACCOUNT --"

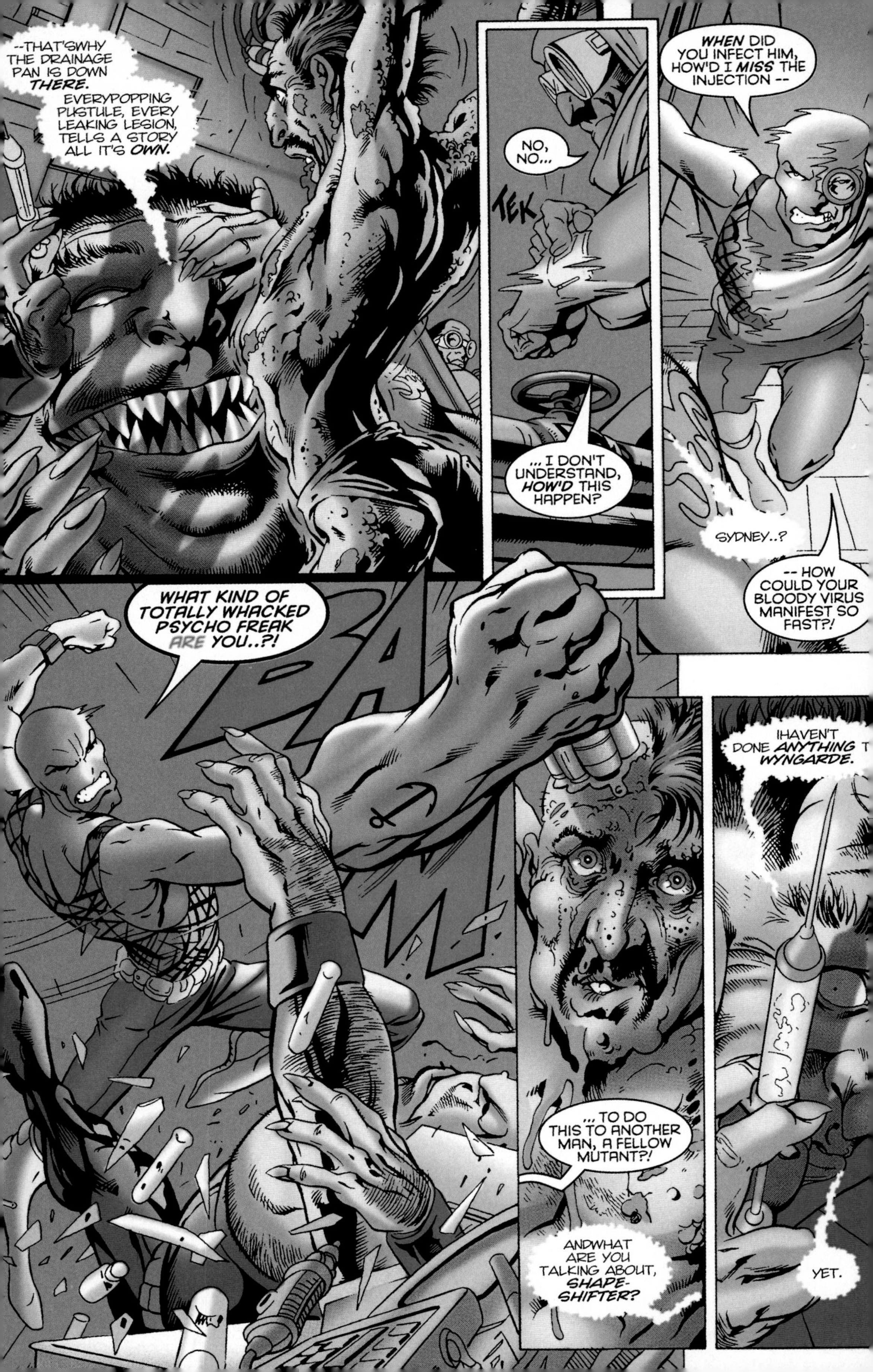
--THAT'SWHY THE DRAINAGE PAN IS DOWN THERE.
EVERYPOPPING PUSTULE, EVERY LEAKING LESION, TELLS A STORY ALL IT'S OWN.
NO, NO...
TEK
WHEN DID YOU INFECT HIM, HOW'D I MISS THE INJECTION --
...I DON'T UNDERSTAND, HOW'D THIS HAPPEN?
SYDNEY..?
-- HOW COULD YOUR BLOODY VIRUS MANIFEST SO FAST?!
WHAT KIND OF TOTALLY WHACKED PSYCHO FREAK ARE YOU..?!
IHAVEN'T DONE ANYTHING T WYNGARDE.
...TO DO THIS TO ANOTHER MAN, A FELLOW MUTANT?!
ANDWHAT ARE YOU TALKING ABOUT, SHAPE-SHIFTER?
YET.

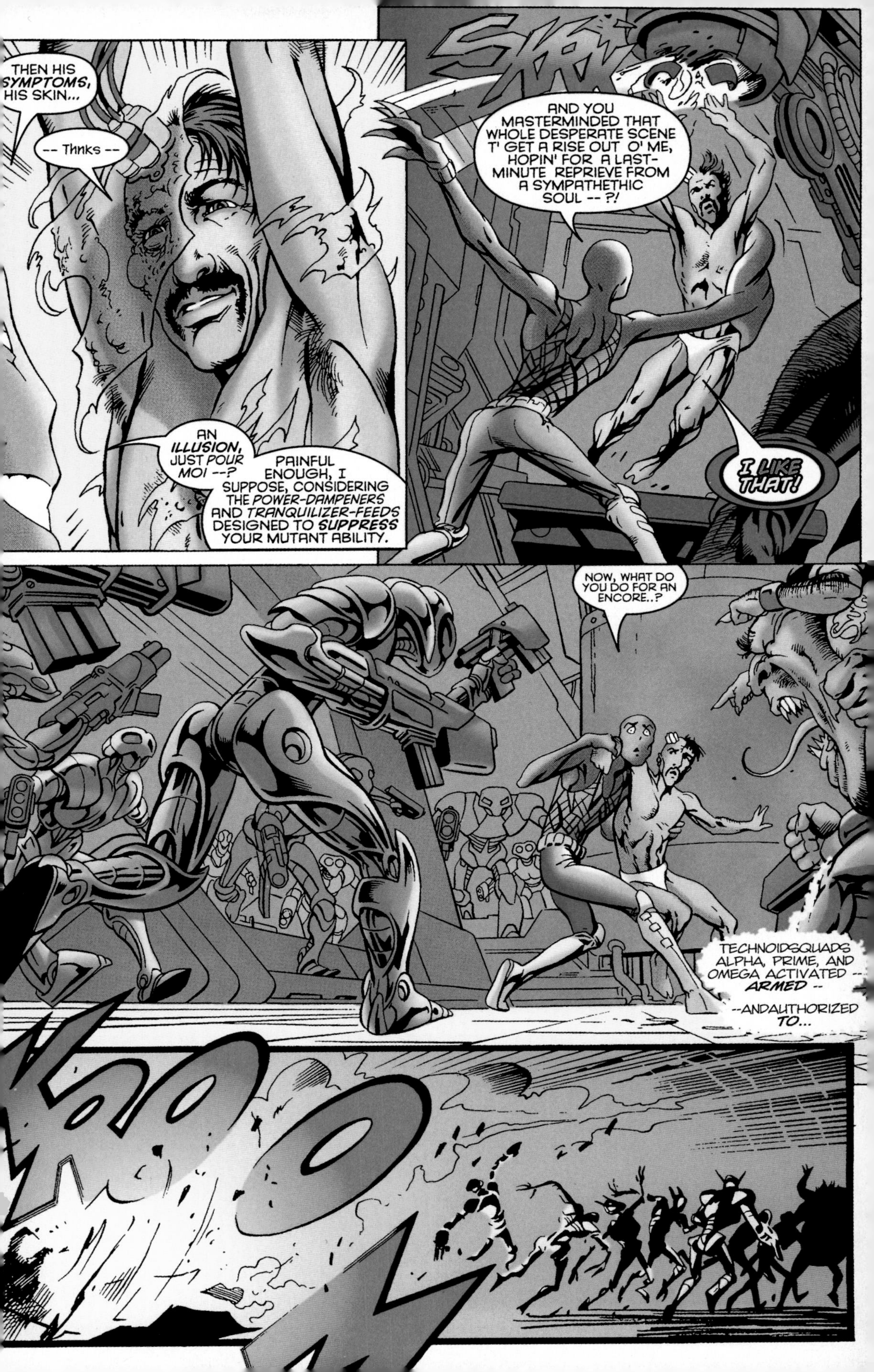
SKRK
THEN HIS SYMPTOMS, HIS SKIN...
-- Thnks --
AND YOU MASTERMINDED THAT WHOLE DESPERATE SCENE T' GET A RISE OUT O' ME, HOPIN' FOR A LAST-MINUTE REPRIEVE FROM A SYMPATHETHIC SOUL --?!
AN ILLUSION, JUST POUR MOI --?
PAINFUL ENOUGH, I SUPPOSE, CONSIDERING THE POWER-DAMPENERS AND TRANQUILIZER-FEEDS DESIGNED TO SUPPRESS YOUR MUTANT ABILITY.
I LIKE THAT!
NOW, WHAT DO YOU DO FOR AN ENCORE..?
TECHNOIDSQUADS ALPHA, PRIME, AND OMEGA ACTIVATED -- ARMED --
--ANDAUTHORIZED TO...
WHOOM

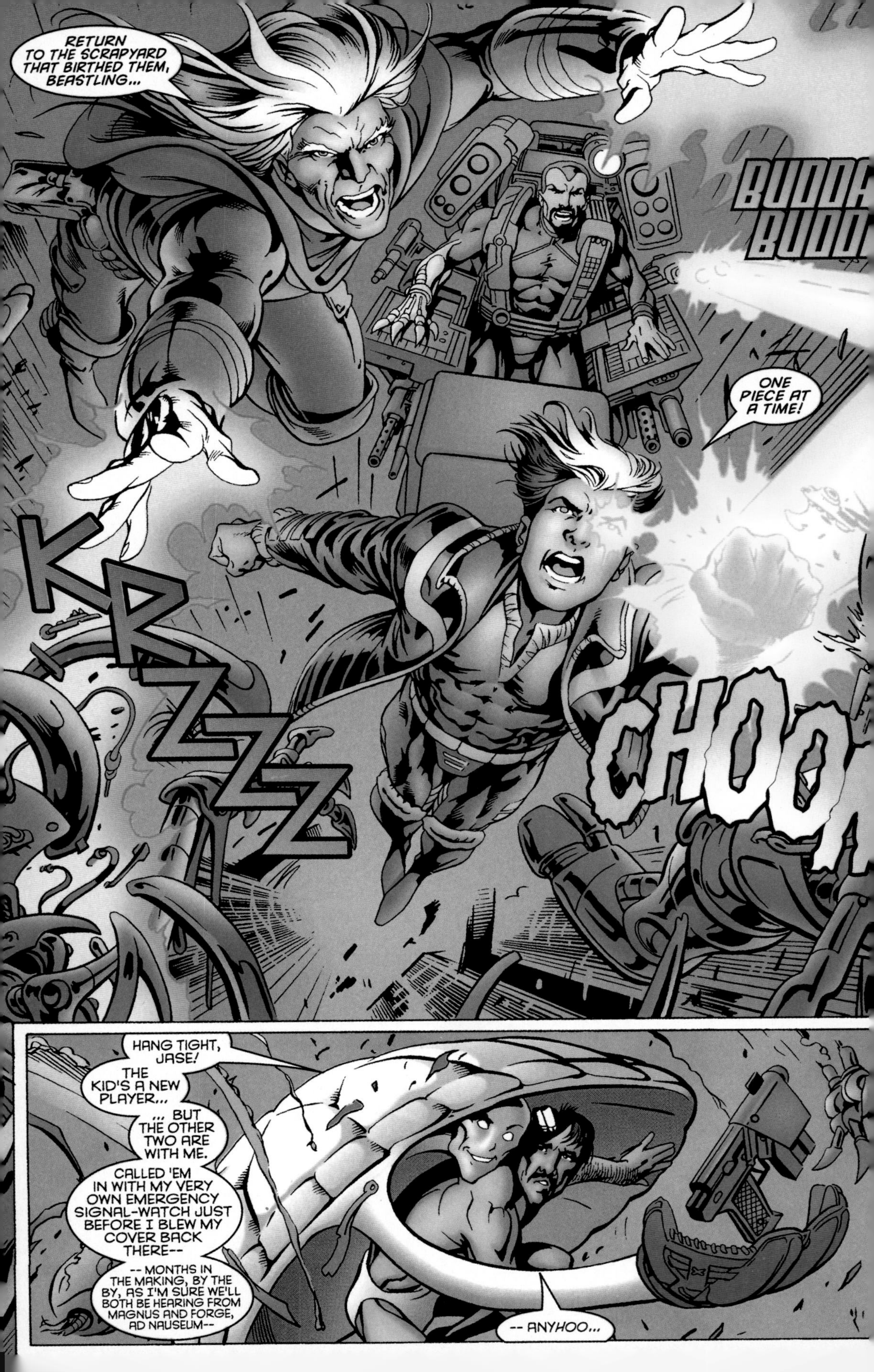
RETURN TO THE SCRAPYARD THAT BIRTHED THEM, BEASTLING...
BUDDA BUDD
ONE PIECE AT A TIME!
KRZZZZ
CHOO
HANG TIGHT, JASE!
THE KID'S A NEW PLAYER...
... BUT THE OTHER TWO ARE WITH ME.
CALLED 'EM IN WITH MY VERY OWN EMERGENCY SIGNAL-WATCH JUST BEFORE I BLEW MY COVER BACK THERE--
-- MONTHS IN THE MAKING, BY THE BY, AS I'M SURE WE'LL BOTH BE HEARING FROM MAGNUS AND FORGE, AD NAUSEUM--
-- ANYHOO...

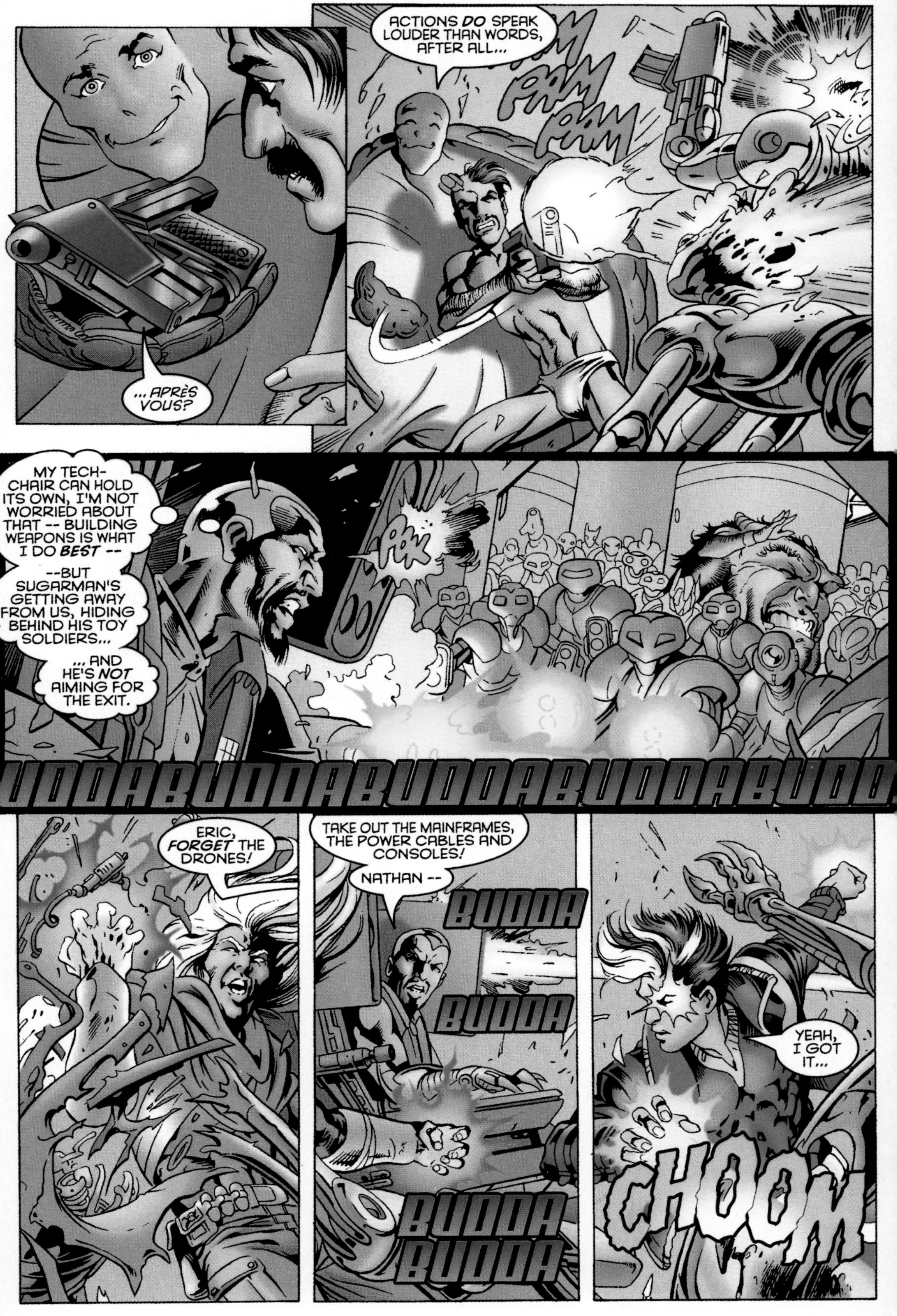
...APRÈS VOUS?
ACTIONS DO SPEAK LOUDER THAN WORDS, AFTER ALL...
PAM PAM PAM
MY TECH-CHAIR CAN HOLD ITS OWN, I'M NOT WORRIED ABOUT THAT -- BUILDING WEAPONS IS WHAT I DO BEST --
--BUT SUGARMAN'S GETTING AWAY FROM US, HIDING BEHIND HIS TOY SOLDIERS...
...AND HE'S NOT AIMING FOR THE EXIT.
POK
UDDABUDDABUDDABUDD
ERIC, FORGET THE DRONES!
TAKE OUT THE MAINFRAMES, THE POWER CABLES AND CONSOLES!
NATHAN --
BUDDA
BUDDA
BUDDA BUDDA
YEAH, I GOT IT...
CHOOM

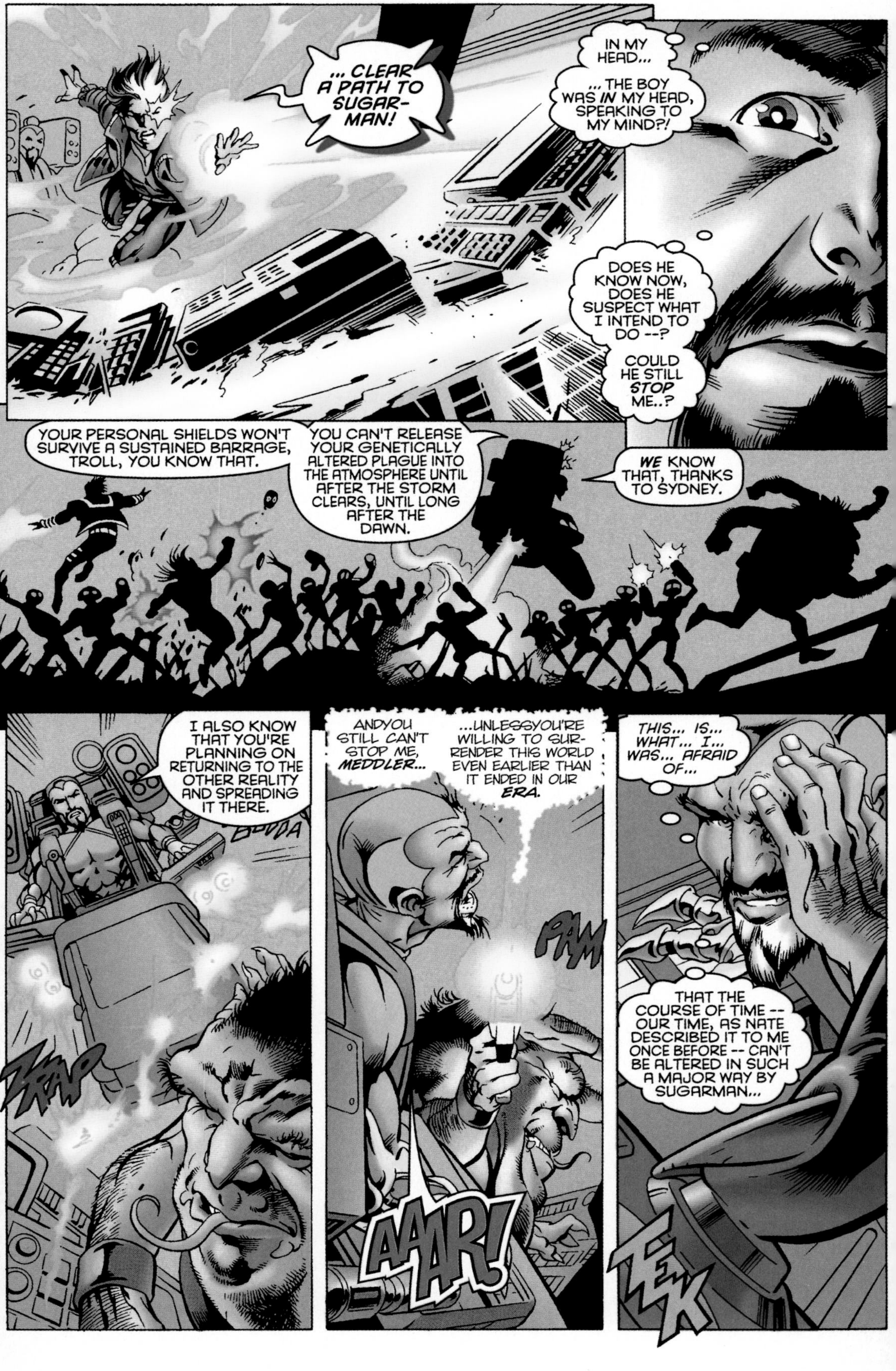

...CLEAR A PATH TO SUGAR-MAN!
IN MY HEAD...
...THE BOY WAS IN MY HEAD, SPEAKING TO MY MIND?!
DOES HE KNOW NOW, DOES HE SUSPECT WHAT I INTEND TO DO --?
COULD HE STILL STOP ME..?
YOUR PERSONAL SHIELDS WON'T SURVIVE A SUSTAINED BARRAGE, TROLL, YOU KNOW THAT.
YOU CAN'T RELEASE YOUR GENETICALLY ALTERED PLAGUE INTO THE ATMOSPHERE UNTIL AFTER THE STORM CLEARS, UNTIL LONG AFTER THE DAWN.
WE KNOW THAT, THANKS TO SYDNEY.
I ALSO KNOW THAT YOU'RE PLANNING ON RETURNING TO THE OTHER REALITY AND SPREADING IT THERE.
BUDDA
ZKRAK
ANDYOU STILL CAN'T STOP ME, MEDDLER...
...UNLESSYOU'RE WILLING TO SUR-RENDER THIS WORLD EVEN EARLIER THAN IT ENDED IN OUR ERA.
PAM
AAAR!
THIS... IS... WHAT... I... WAS... AFRAID OF...
THAT THE COURSE OF TIME -- OUR TIME, AS NATE DESCRIBED IT TO ME ONCE BEFORE -- CAN'T BE ALTERED IN SUCH A MAJOR WAY BY SUGARMAN...
TEK

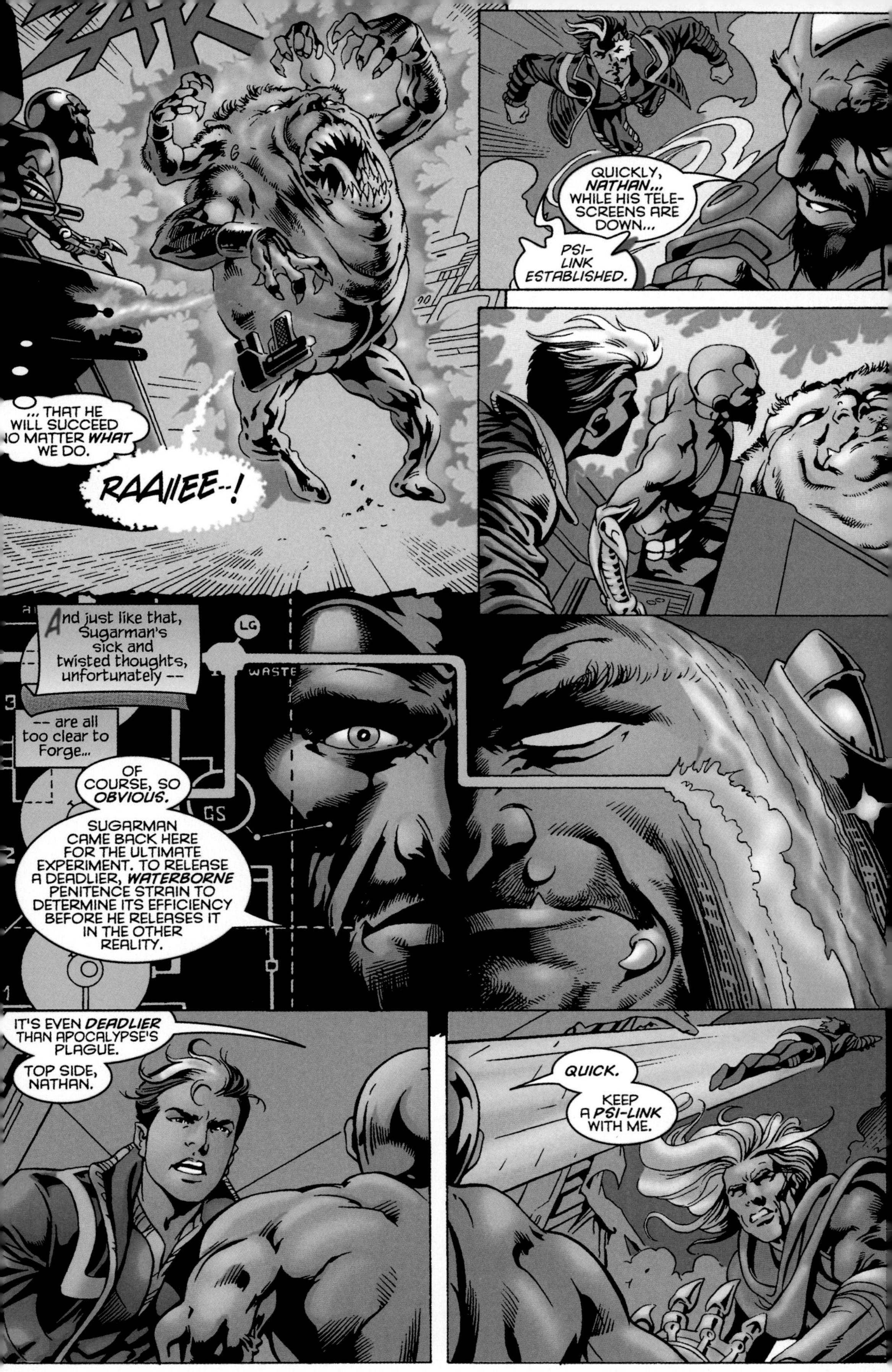

... THAT HE WILL SUCCEED NO MATTER WHAT WE DO.
RAAIIEE--!
QUICKLY, NATHAN... WHILE HIS TELE-SCREENS ARE DOWN...
PSI-LINK ESTABLISHED.
And just like that, Sugarman's sick and twisted thoughts, unfortunately --
-- are all too clear to Forge...
OF COURSE, SO OBVIOUS.
SUGARMAN CAME BACK HERE FOR THE ULTIMATE EXPERIMENT. TO RELEASE A DEADLIER, WATERBORNE PENITENCE STRAIN TO DETERMINE ITS EFFICIENCY BEFORE HE RELEASES IT IN THE OTHER REALITY.
IT'S EVEN DEADLIER THAN APOCALYPSE'S PLAGUE.
TOP SIDE, NATHAN.
QUICK.
KEEP A PSI-LINK WITH ME.

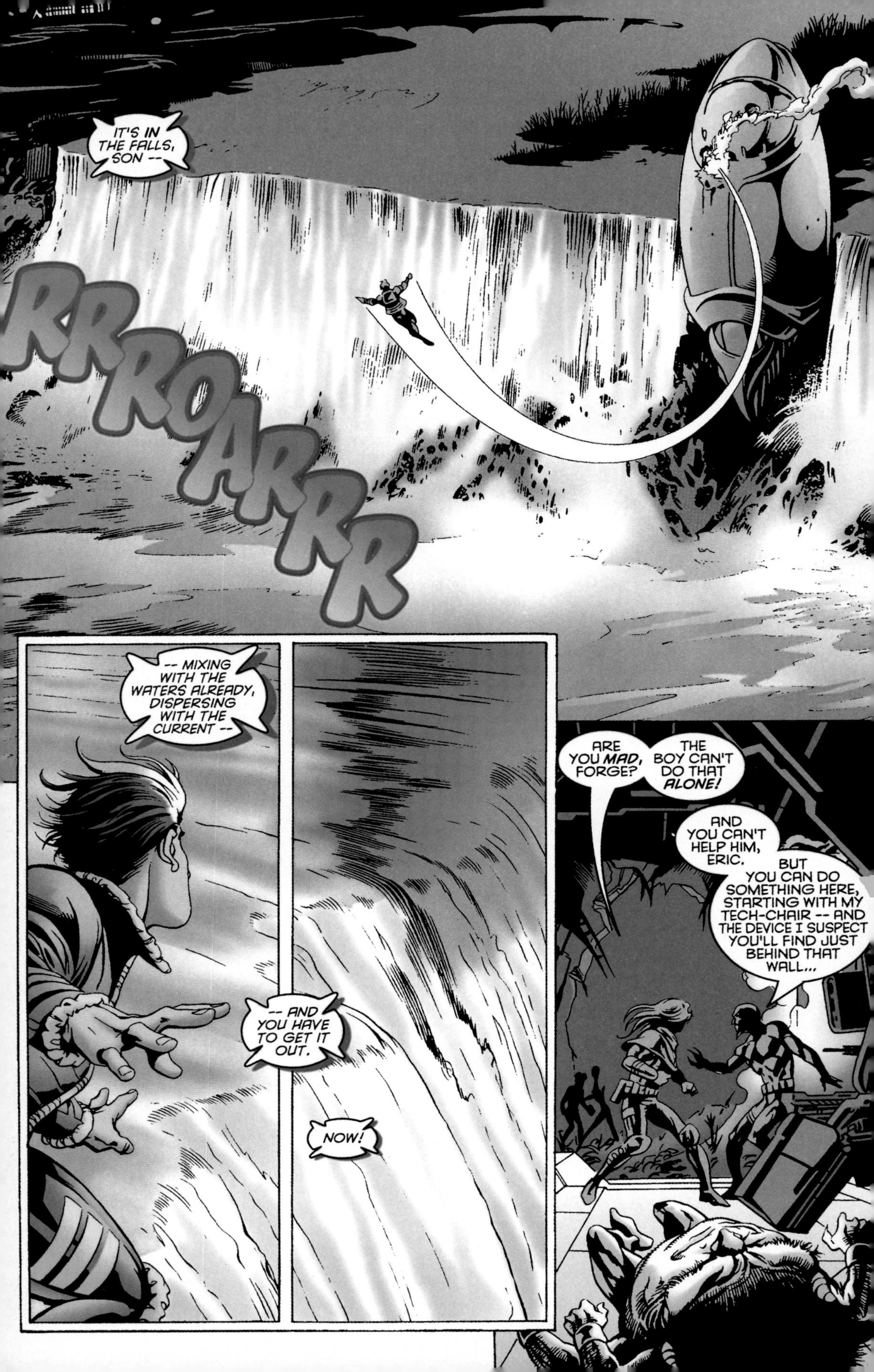
IT'S IN THE FALLS, SON --
RRROARRR
-- MIXING WITH THE WATERS ALREADY, DISPERSING WITH THE CURRENT --
-- AND YOU HAVE TO GET IT OUT.
NOW!
ARE YOU MAD, FORGE?
THE BOY CAN'T DO THAT ALONE!
AND YOU CAN'T HELP HIM, ERIC.
BUT YOU CAN DO SOMETHING HERE, STARTING WITH MY TECH-CHAIR -- AND THE DEVICE I SUSPECT YOU'LL FIND JUST BEHIND THAT WALL...

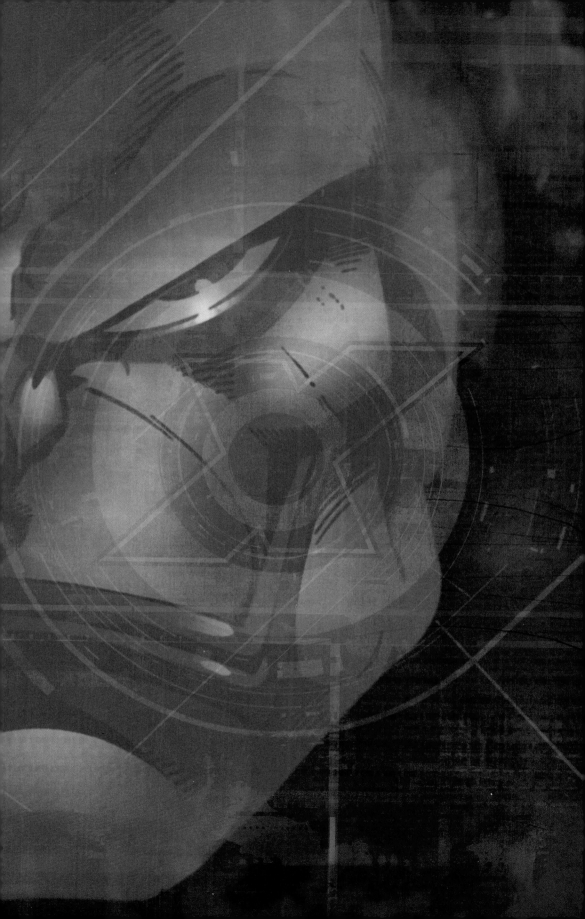

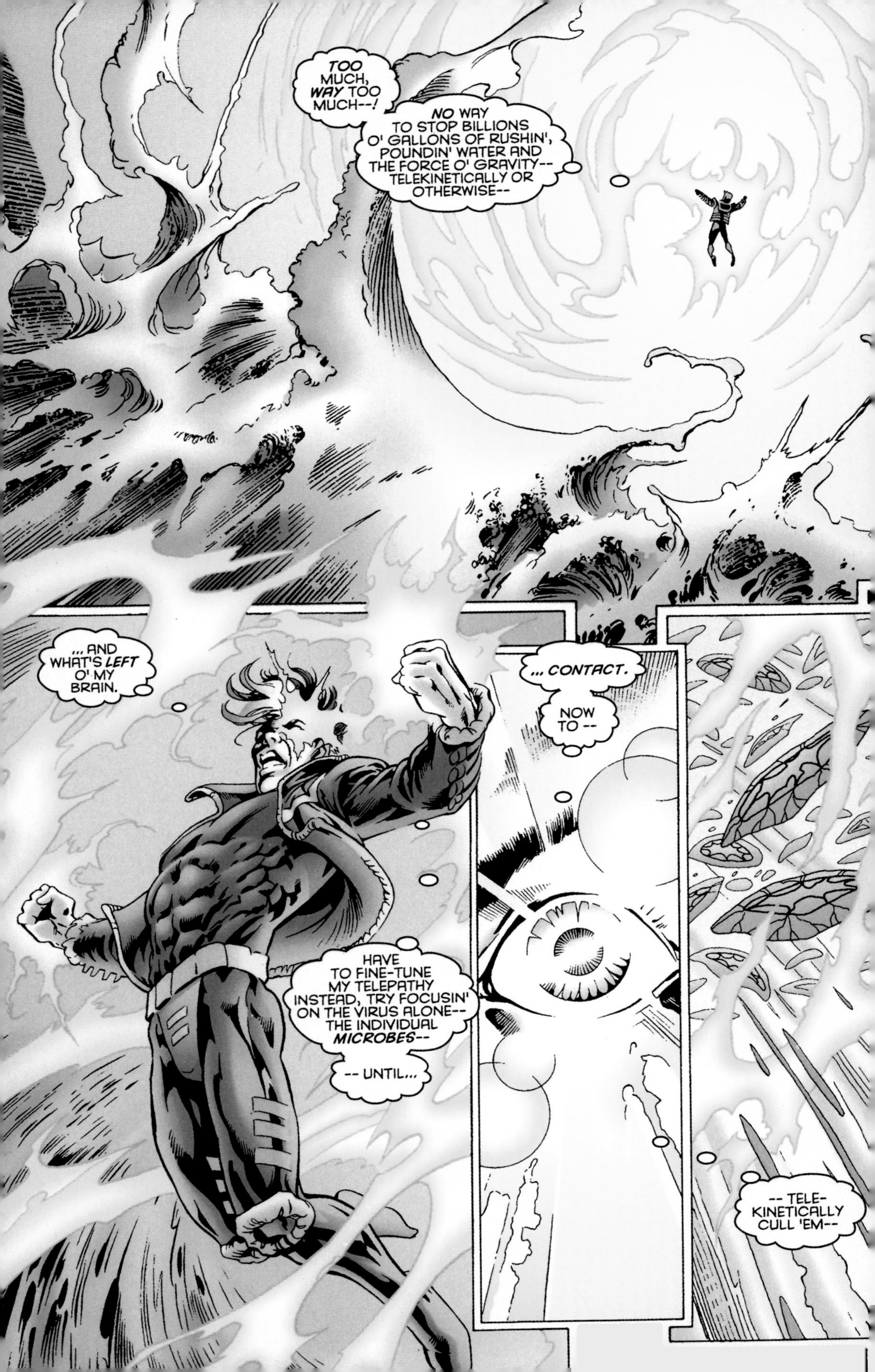
TOO MUCH, WAY TOO MUCH--!
NO WAY TO STOP BILLIONS O' GALLONS OF RUSHIN', POUNDIN' WATER AND THE FORCE O' GRAVITY-- TELEKINETICALLY OR OTHERWISE--
...AND WHAT'S LEFT O' MY BRAIN.
HAVE TO FINE-TUNE MY TELEPATHY INSTEAD, TRY FOCUSIN' ON THE VIRUS ALONE-- THE INDIVIDUAL MICROBES--
-- UNTIL...
...CONTACT.
NOW TO --
-- TELE-KINETICALLY CULL 'EM--

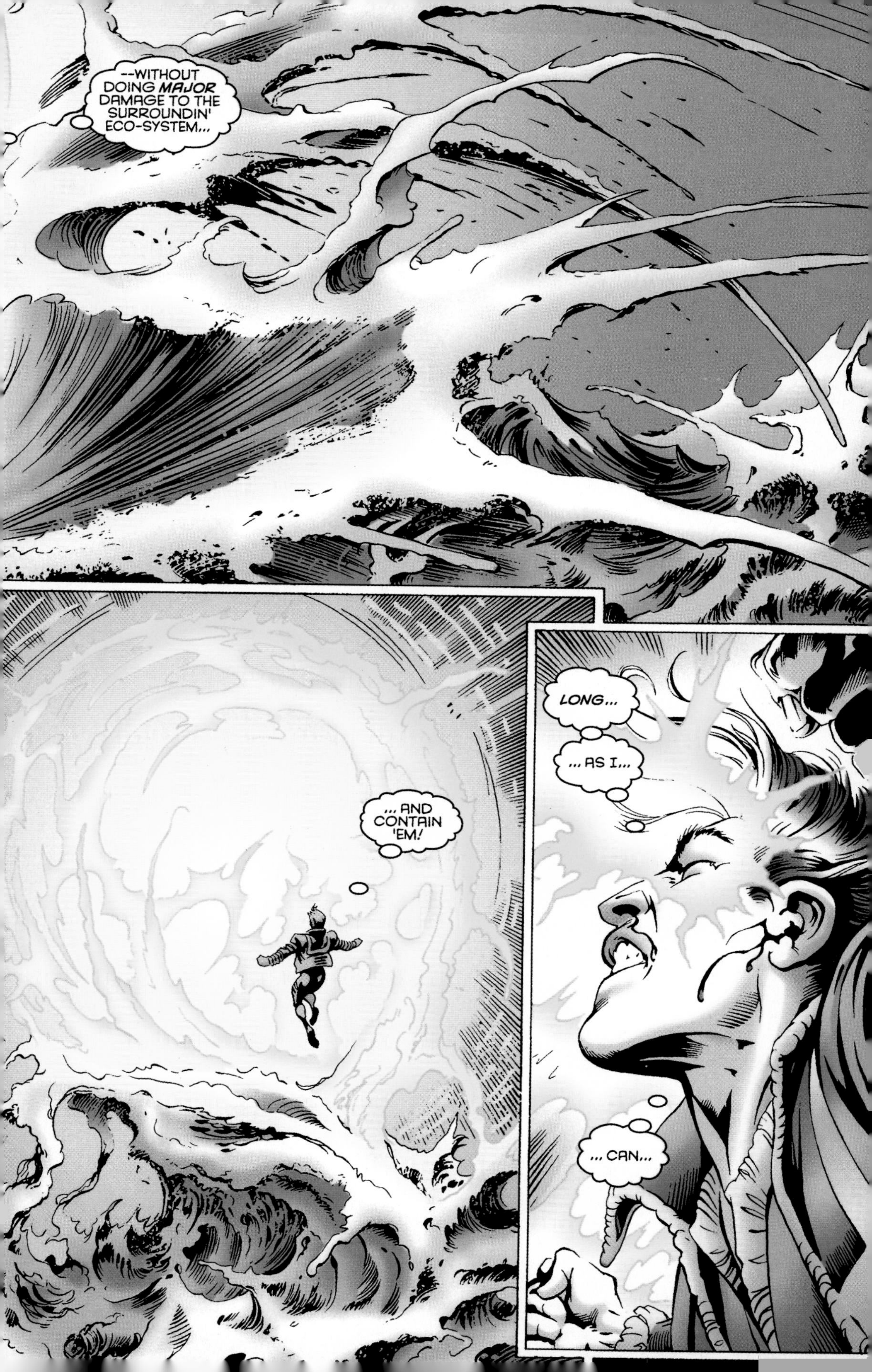
--WITHOUT DOING MAJOR DAMAGE TO THE SURROUNDIN' ECO-SYSTEM...
...AND CONTAIN 'EM!
LONG...
...AS I...
...CAN...

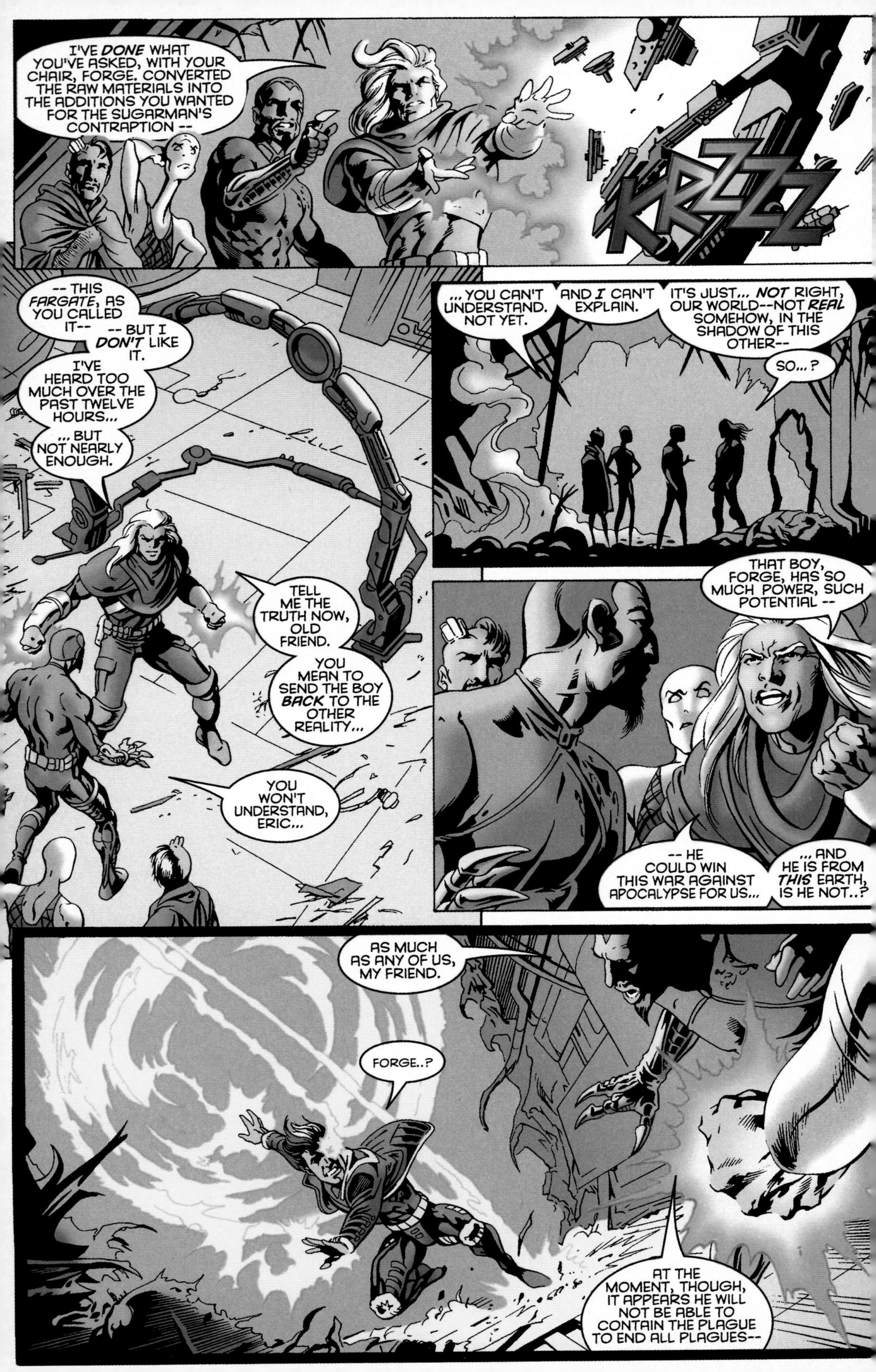
I'VE DONE WHAT YOU'VE ASKED, WITH YOUR CHAIR, FORGE. CONVERTED THE RAW MATERIALS INTO THE ADDITIONS YOU WANTED FOR THE SUGARMAN'S CONTRAPTION --
KRZZZZ
-- THIS FARGATE, AS YOU CALLED IT--
-- BUT I DON'T LIKE IT.
I'VE HEARD TOO MUCH OVER THE PAST TWELVE HOURS...
... BUT NOT NEARLY ENOUGH.
TELL ME THE TRUTH NOW, OLD FRIEND.
YOU MEAN TO SEND THE BOY BACK TO THE OTHER REALITY...
YOU WON'T UNDERSTAND, ERIC...
... YOU CAN'T UNDERSTAND. NOT YET.
AND I CAN'T EXPLAIN.
IT'S JUST... NOT RIGHT, OUR WORLD--NOT REAL SOMEHOW, IN THE SHADOW OF THIS OTHER--
SO...?
THAT BOY, FORGE, HAS SO MUCH POWER, SUCH POTENTIAL --
-- HE COULD WIN THIS WAR AGAINST APOCALYPSE FOR US...
... AND HE IS FROM THIS EARTH, IS HE NOT..?
AS MUCH AS ANY OF US, MY FRIEND.
FORGE..?
AT THE MOMENT, THOUGH, IT APPEARS HE WILL NOT BE ABLE TO CONTAIN THE PLAGUE TO END ALL PLAGUES--

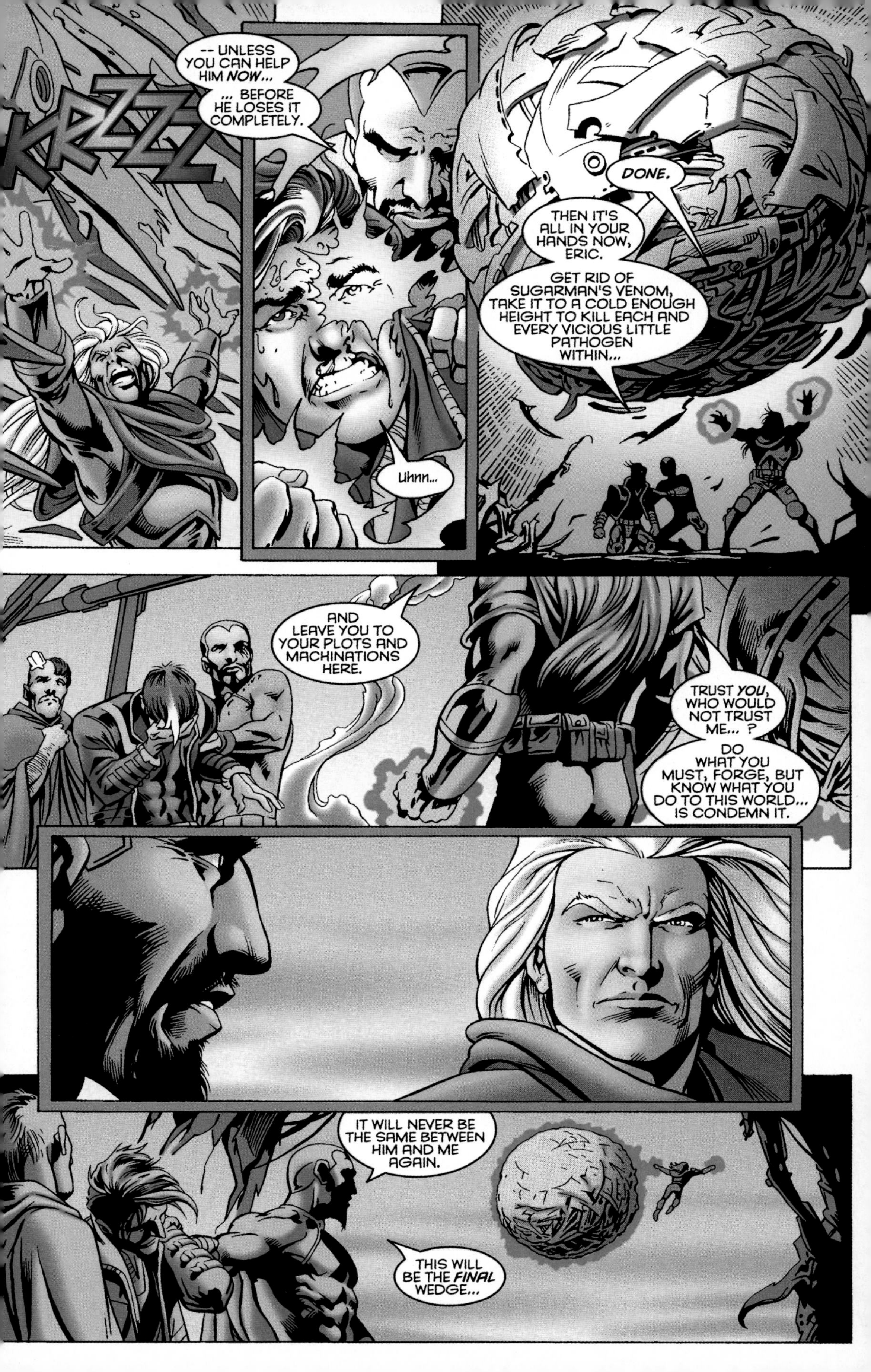
KRZZZ
-- UNLESS YOU CAN HELP HIM *NOW*...
... BEFORE HE LOSES IT COMPLETELY.
Uhnn...
DONE.
THEN IT'S ALL IN YOUR HANDS NOW, ERIC.
GET RID OF SUGARMAN'S VENOM, TAKE IT TO A COLD ENOUGH HEIGHT TO KILL EACH AND EVERY VICIOUS LITTLE PATHOGEN WITHIN...
AND LEAVE YOU TO YOUR PLOTS AND MACHINATIONS HERE.
TRUST *YOU*, WHO WOULD NOT TRUST ME... ?
DO WHAT YOU MUST, FORGE, BUT KNOW WHAT YOU DO TO THIS WORLD... IS CONDEMN IT.
IT WILL NEVER BE THE SAME BETWEEN HIM AND ME AGAIN.
THIS WILL BE THE *FINAL* WEDGE...

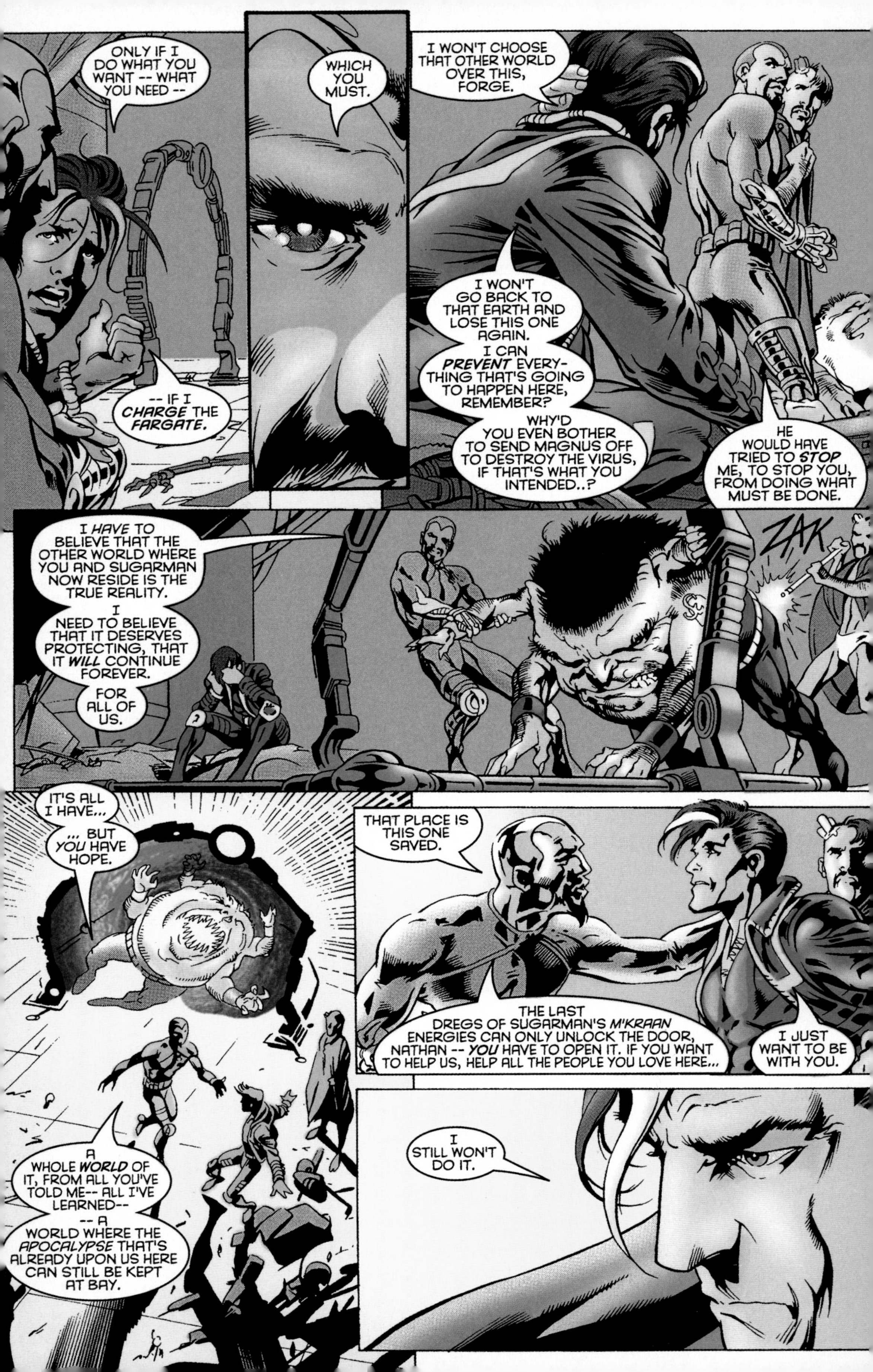

ONLY IF I DO WHAT YOU WANT -- WHAT YOU NEED --
-- IF I *CHARGE* THE *FARGATE.*
WHICH YOU MUST.
I WON'T CHOOSE THAT OTHER WORLD OVER THIS, FORGE.
I WON'T GO BACK TO THAT EARTH AND LOSE THIS ONE AGAIN.
I CAN *PREVENT* EVERYTHING THAT'S GOING TO HAPPEN HERE, REMEMBER?
WHY'D YOU EVEN BOTHER TO SEND MAGNUS OFF TO DESTROY THE VIRUS, IF THAT'S WHAT YOU INTENDED..?
HE WOULD HAVE TRIED TO *STOP* ME, TO STOP YOU, FROM DOING WHAT MUST BE DONE.
I *HAVE* TO BELIEVE THAT THE OTHER WORLD WHERE YOU AND SUGARMAN NOW RESIDE IS THE TRUE REALITY.
I NEED TO BELIEVE THAT IT DESERVES PROTECTING, THAT IT *WILL* CONTINUE FOREVER.
FOR ALL OF US.
ZAK
IT'S ALL I HAVE...
... BUT *YOU* HAVE HOPE.
A WHOLE *WORLD* OF IT, FROM ALL YOU'VE TOLD ME-- ALL I'VE LEARNED--
-- A WORLD WHERE THE *APOCALYPSE* THAT'S ALREADY UPON US HERE CAN STILL BE KEPT AT BAY.
THAT PLACE IS THIS ONE SAVED.
THE LAST DREGS OF SUGARMAN'S *M'KRAAN* ENERGIES CAN ONLY UNLOCK THE DOOR, NATHAN -- *YOU* HAVE TO OPEN IT. IF YOU WANT TO HELP US, HELP ALL THE PEOPLE YOU LOVE HERE...
I JUST WANT TO BE WITH YOU.
I STILL WON'T DO IT.

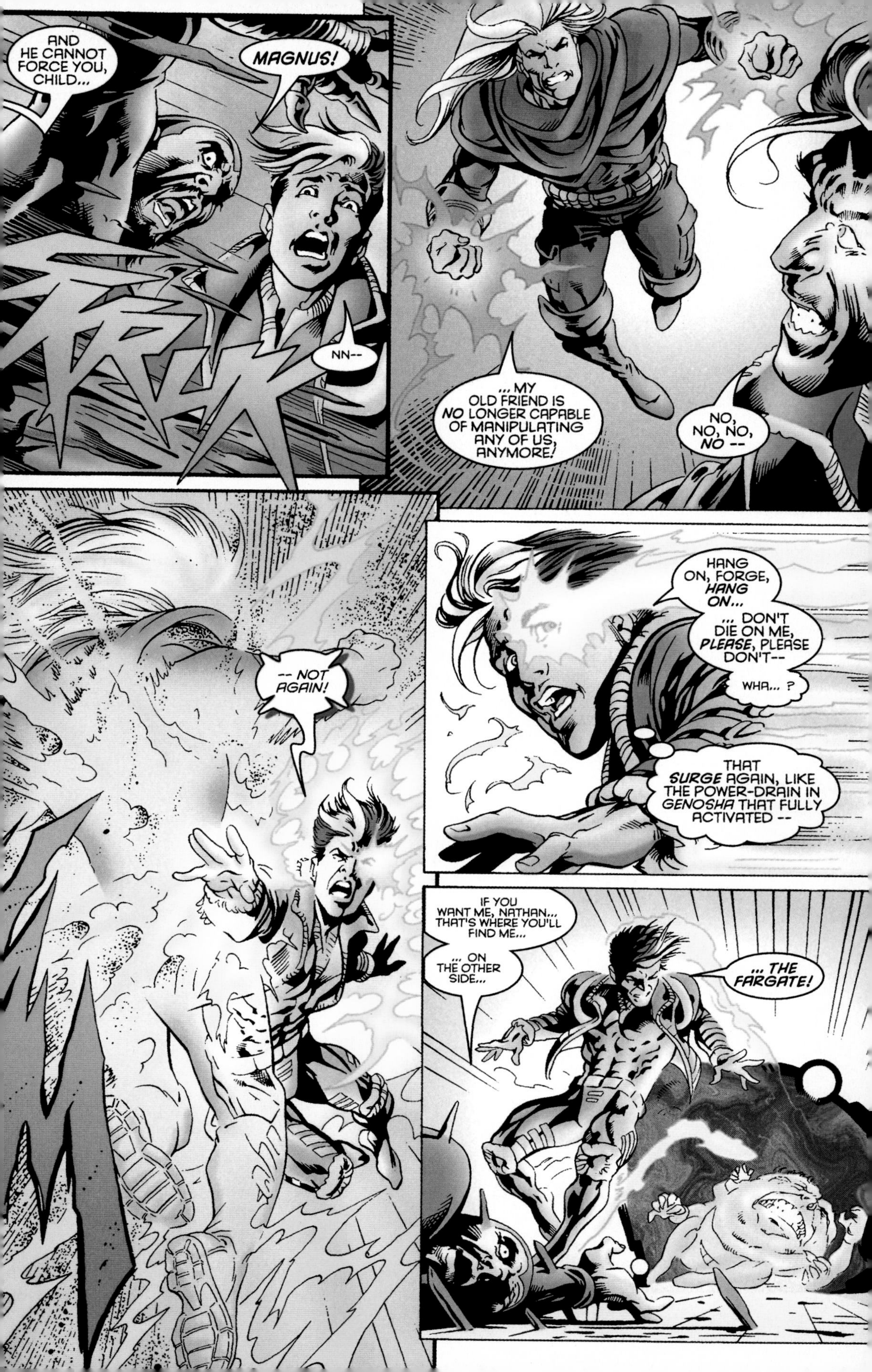
AND HE CANNOT FORCE YOU, CHILD...
MAGNUS!
NN--
... MY OLD FRIEND IS NO LONGER CAPABLE OF MANIPULATING ANY OF US, ANYMORE!
NO, NO, NO, NO --
-- NOT AGAIN!
HANG ON, FORGE, HANG ON...
... DON'T DIE ON ME, PLEASE, PLEASE DON'T--
WHA... ?
THAT SURGE AGAIN, LIKE THE POWER-DRAIN IN GENOSHA THAT FULLY ACTIVATED --
IF YOU WANT ME, NATHAN... THAT'S WHERE YOU'LL FIND ME...
... ON THE OTHER SIDE...
... THE FARGATE!

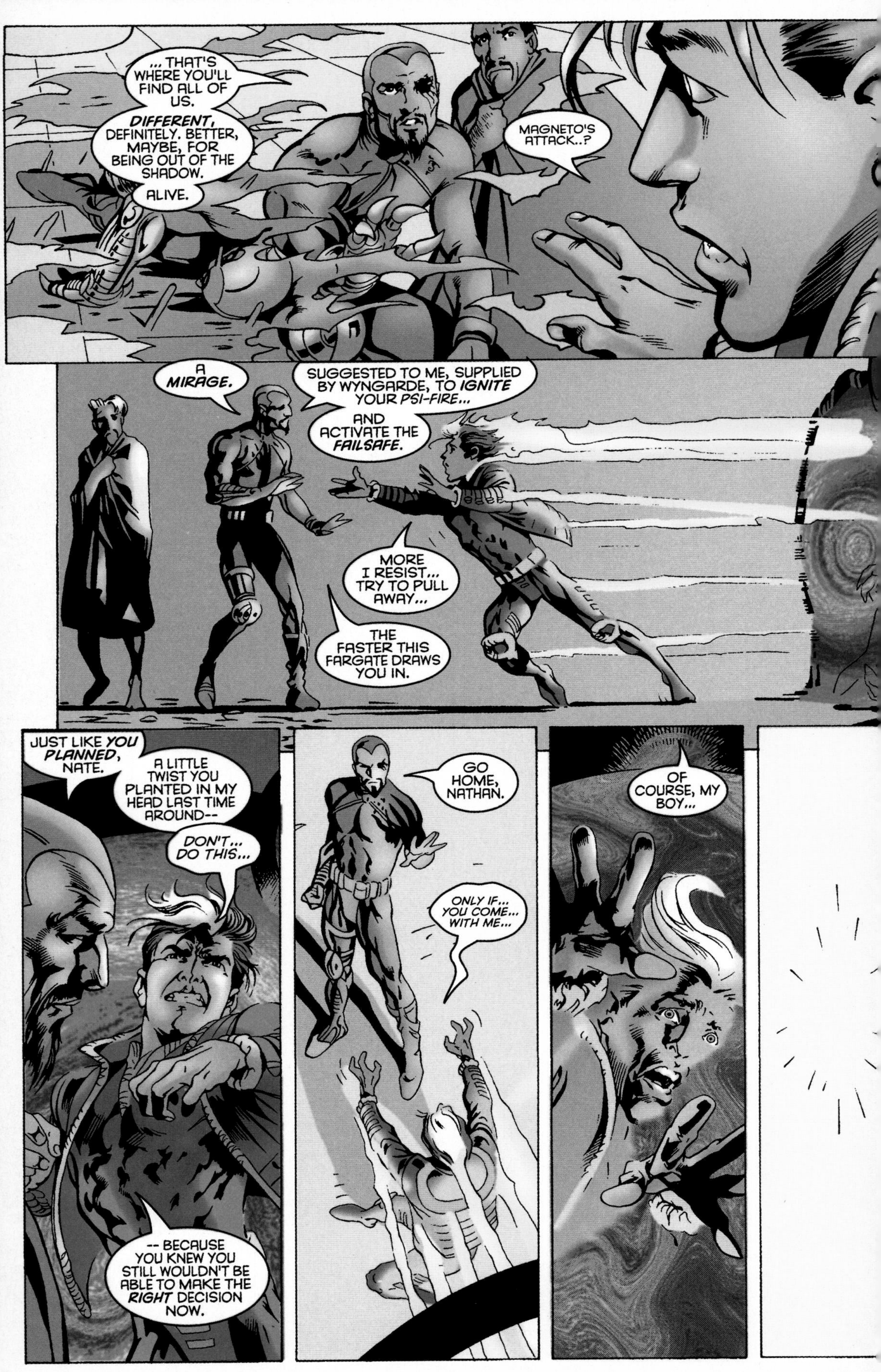

... THAT'S WHERE YOU'LL FIND ALL OF US.
DIFFERENT, DEFINITELY. BETTER, MAYBE, FOR BEING OUT OF THE SHADOW.
ALIVE.
MAGNETO'S ATTACK..?
A MIRAGE.
SUGGESTED TO ME, SUPPLIED BY WYNGARDE, TO IGNITE YOUR PSI-FIRE...
AND ACTIVATE THE FAILSAFE.
MORE I RESIST... TRY TO PULL AWAY...
THE FASTER THIS FARGATE DRAWS YOU IN.
JUST LIKE YOU PLANNED, NATE.
A LITTLE TWIST YOU PLANTED IN MY HEAD LAST TIME AROUND--
DON'T... DO THIS...
-- BECAUSE YOU KNEW YOU STILL WOULDN'T BE ABLE TO MAKE THE RIGHT DECISION NOW.
GO HOME, NATHAN.
ONLY IF... YOU COME... WITH ME...
OF COURSE, MY BOY...

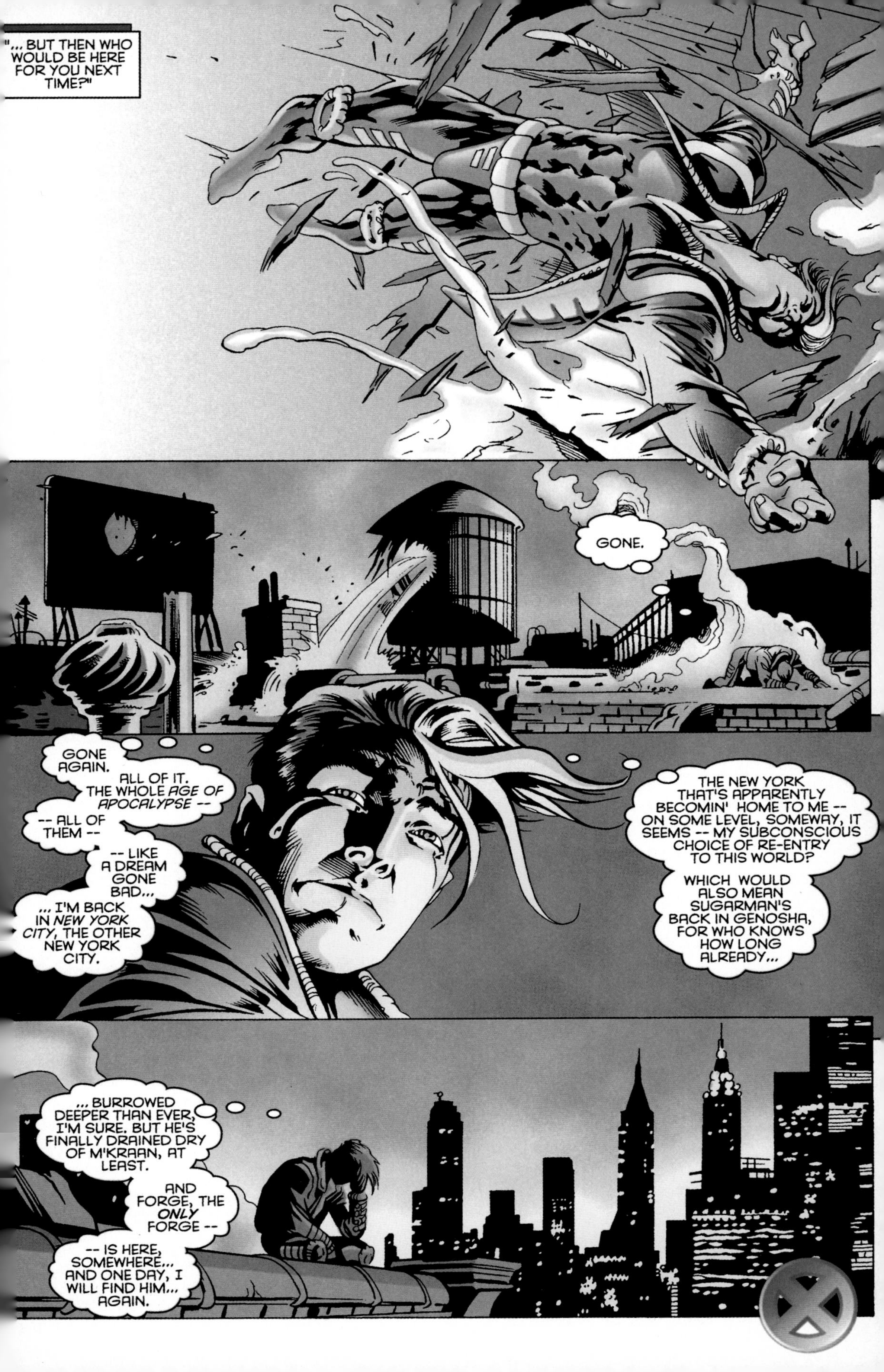
"... BUT THEN WHO WOULD BE HERE FOR YOU NEXT TIME?"
GONE.
GONE AGAIN.
ALL OF IT. THE WHOLE *AGE OF APOCALYPSE* --
-- ALL OF THEM --
-- LIKE A DREAM GONE BAD...
... I'M BACK IN *NEW YORK CITY*, THE OTHER NEW YORK CITY.
THE NEW YORK THAT'S APPARENTLY BECOMIN' HOME TO ME -- ON SOME LEVEL, SOMEWAY, IT SEEMS -- MY SUBCONSCIOUS CHOICE OF RE-ENTRY TO THIS WORLD?
WHICH WOULD ALSO MEAN SUGARMAN'S BACK IN GENOSHA, FOR WHO KNOWS HOW LONG ALREADY...
... BURROWED DEEPER THAN EVER, I'M SURE. BUT HE'S FINALLY DRAINED DRY OF M'KRAAN, AT LEAST.
AND FORGE, THE *ONLY* FORGE --
-- IS HERE, SOMEWHERE... AND ONE DAY, I WILL FIND HIM... AGAIN.

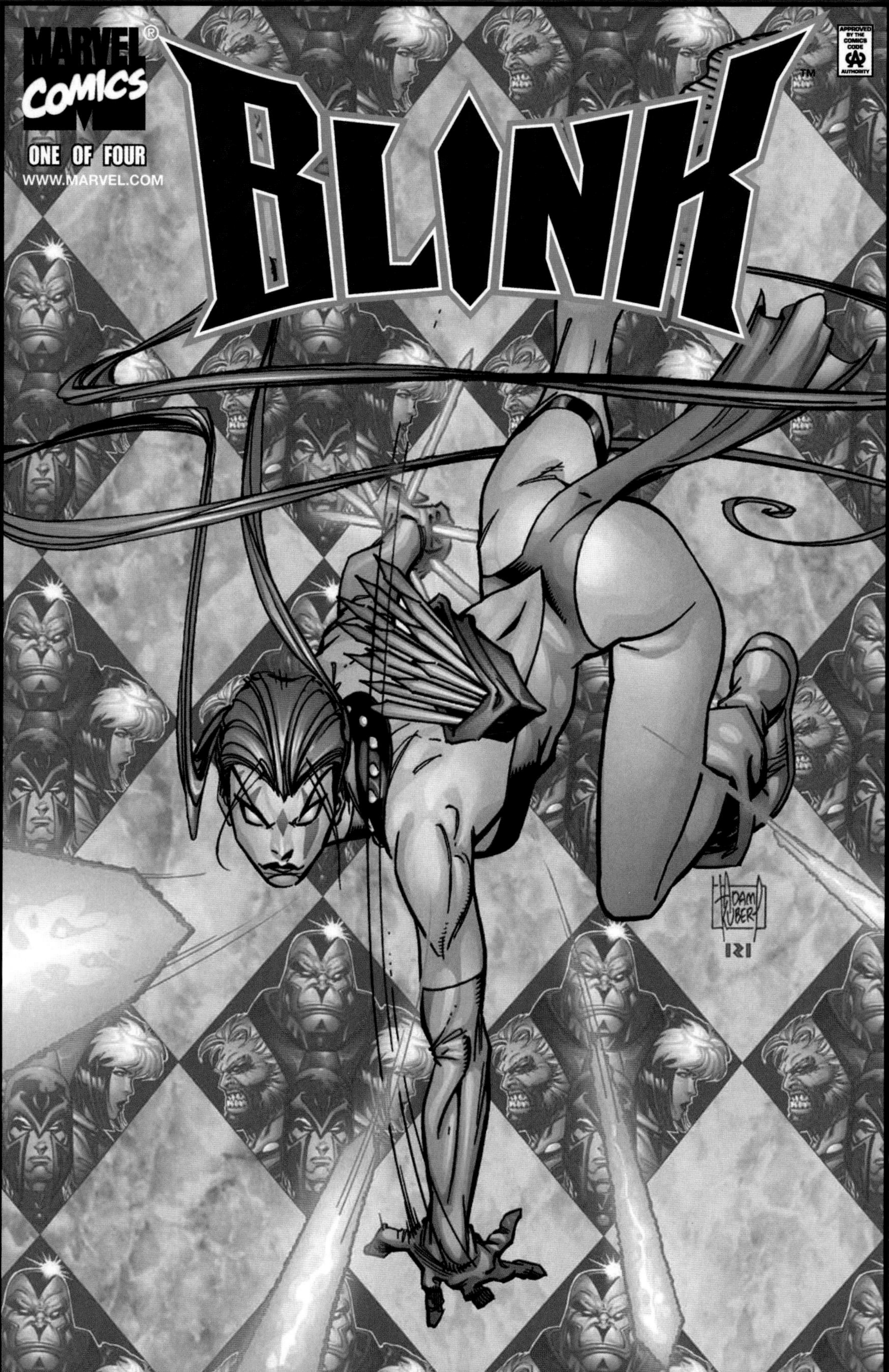
MARVEL COMICS
BLINK
ONE OF FOUR
WWW.MARVEL.COM
APPROVED BY THE COMICS CODE AUTHORITY
ADAM KUBERT

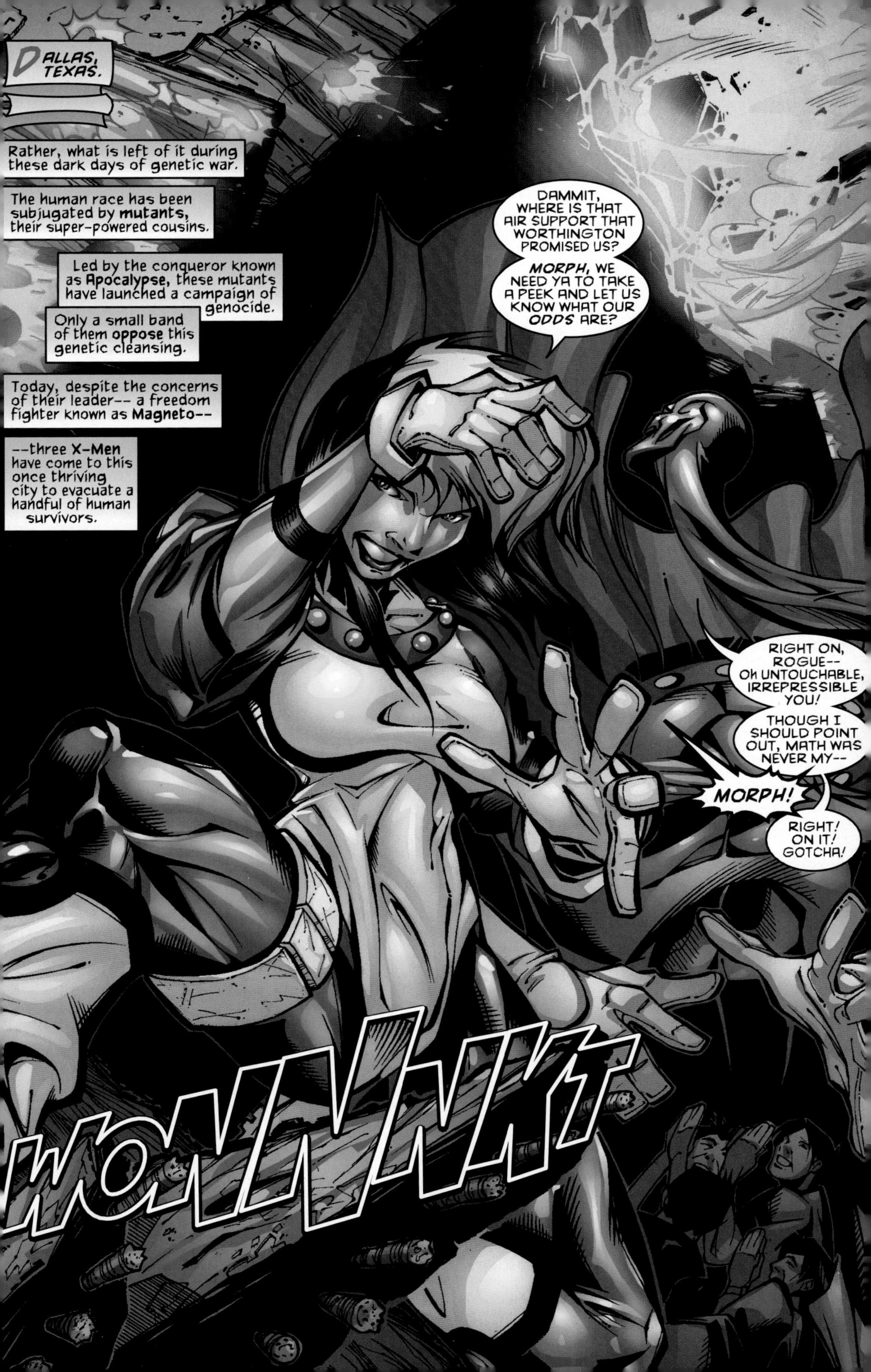
DALLAS, TEXAS.
Rather, what is left of it during these dark days of genetic war.
The human race has been subjugated by mutants, their super-powered cousins.
Led by the conqueror known as Apocalypse, these mutants have launched a campaign of genocide.
Only a small band of them oppose this genetic cleansing.
Today, despite the concerns of their leader-- a freedom fighter known as Magneto--
--three X-Men have come to this once thriving city to evacuate a handful of human survivors.
DAMMIT, WHERE IS THAT AIR SUPPORT THAT WORTHINGTON PROMISED US?
MORPH, WE NEED YA TO TAKE A PEEK AND LET US KNOW WHAT OUR ODDS ARE?
RIGHT ON, ROGUE-- OH UNTOUCHABLE, IRREPRESSIBLE YOU!
THOUGH I SHOULD POINT OUT, MATH WAS NEVER MY--
MORPH!
RIGHT! ON IT! GOTCHA!
WOMMMKT

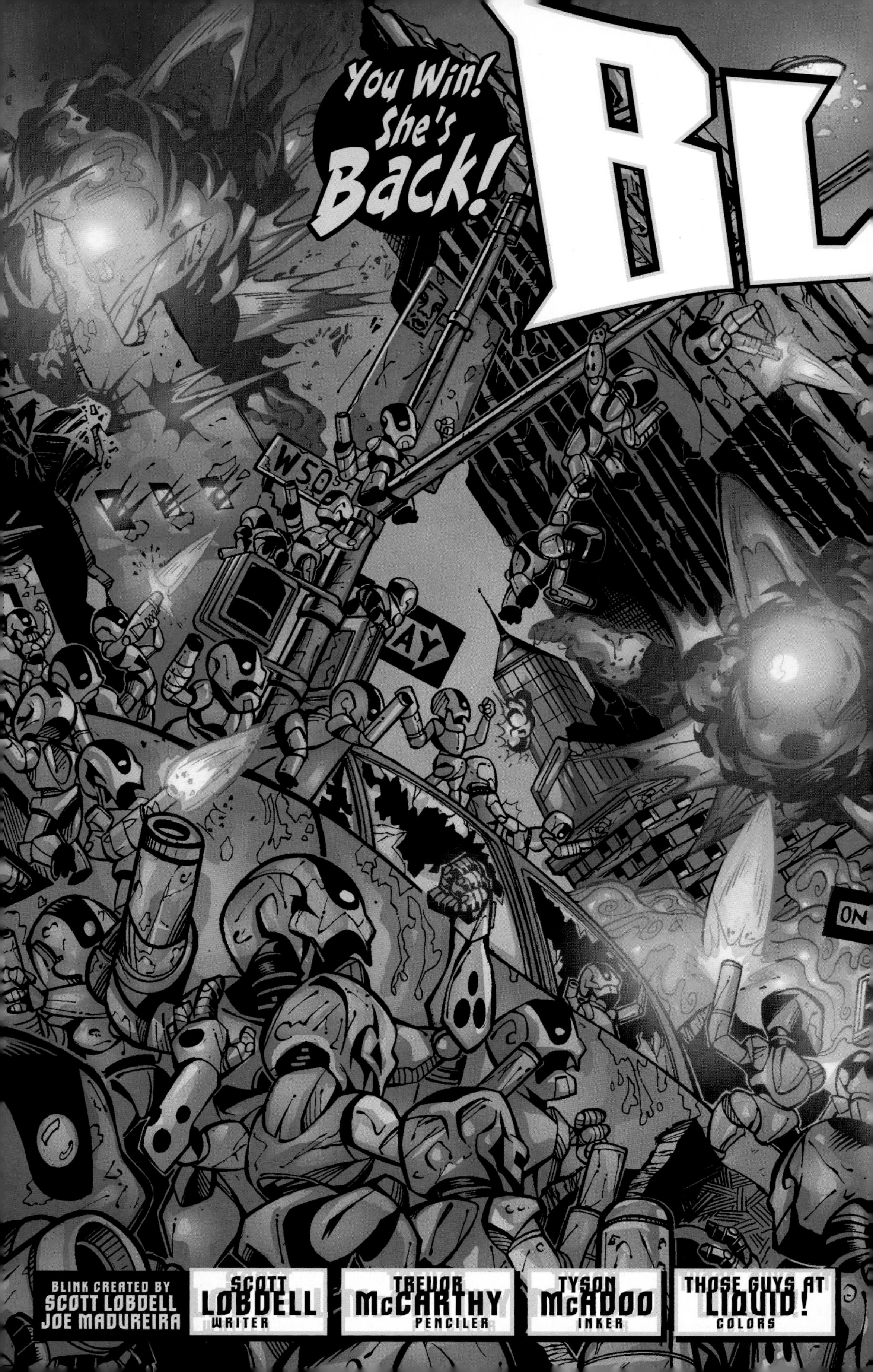
You Win! She's Back!
BL
W50
AY
ON
BLINK CREATED BY SCOTT LOBDELL JOE MADUREIRA
SCOTT LOBDELL WRITER
TREVOR McCARTHY PENCILER
TYSON McADOO INKER
THOSE GUYS AT LIQUID! COLORS

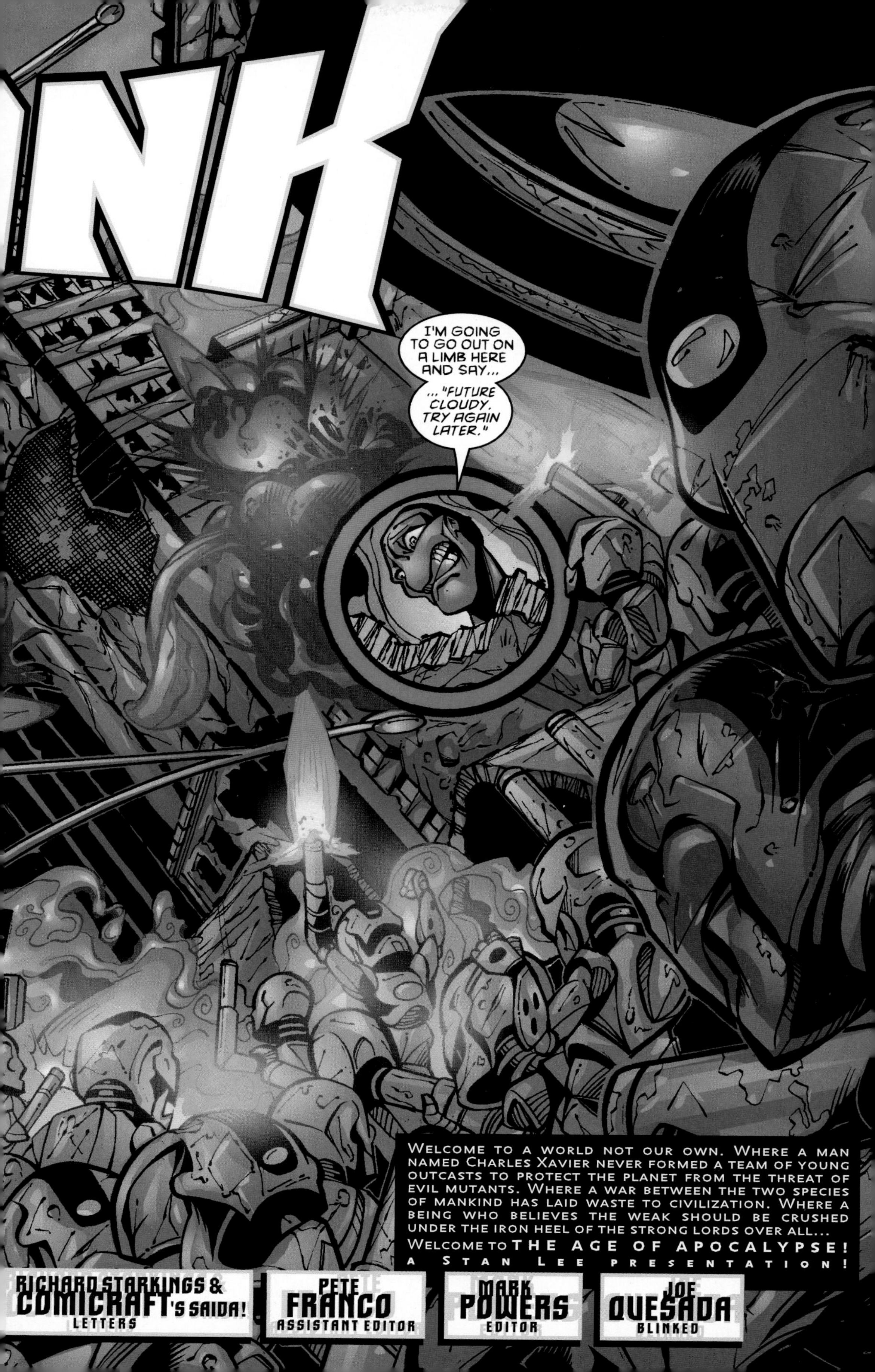
NK
I'M GOING TO GO OUT ON A LIMB HERE AND SAY...
..."FUTURE CLOUDY. TRY AGAIN LATER."
WELCOME TO A WORLD NOT OUR OWN. WHERE A MAN NAMED CHARLES XAVIER NEVER FORMED A TEAM OF YOUNG OUTCASTS TO PROTECT THE PLANET FROM THE THREAT OF EVIL MUTANTS. WHERE A WAR BETWEEN THE TWO SPECIES OF MANKIND HAS LAID WASTE TO CIVILIZATION. WHERE A BEING WHO BELIEVES THE WEAK SHOULD BE CRUSHED UNDER THE IRON HEEL OF THE STRONG LORDS OVER ALL...
WELCOME TO THE AGE OF APOCALYPSE!
A STAN LEE PRESENTATION!
RICHARD STARKINGS & COMICRAFT'S SAIDA! LETTERS
PETE FRANCO ASSISTANT EDITOR
MARK POWERS EDITOR
JOE QUESADA BLINKED

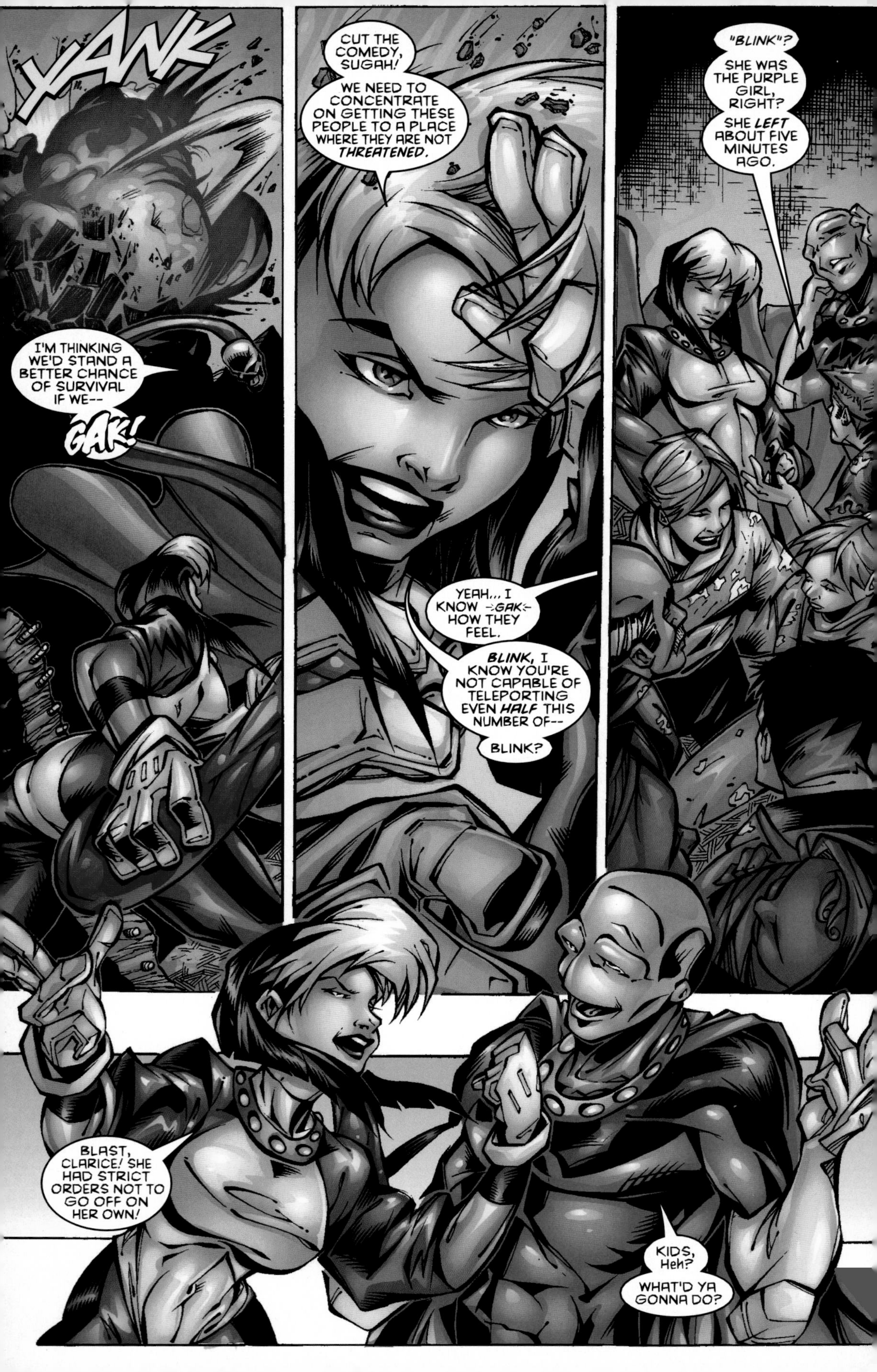
YANK
I'M THINKING WE'D STAND A BETTER CHANCE OF SURVIVAL IF WE--
GAK!
CUT THE COMEDY, SUGAH!
WE NEED TO CONCENTRATE ON GETTING THESE PEOPLE TO A PLACE WHERE THEY ARE NOT THREATENED.
YEAH... I KNOW -GAK- HOW THEY FEEL.
BLINK, I KNOW YOU'RE NOT CAPABLE OF TELEPORTING EVEN HALF THIS NUMBER OF--
BLINK?
"BLINK"?
SHE WAS THE PURPLE GIRL, RIGHT?
SHE LEFT ABOUT FIVE MINUTES AGO.
BLAST, CLARICE! SHE HAD STRICT ORDERS NOT TO GO OFF ON HER OWN!
KIDS, Heh?
WHAT'D YA GONNA DO?

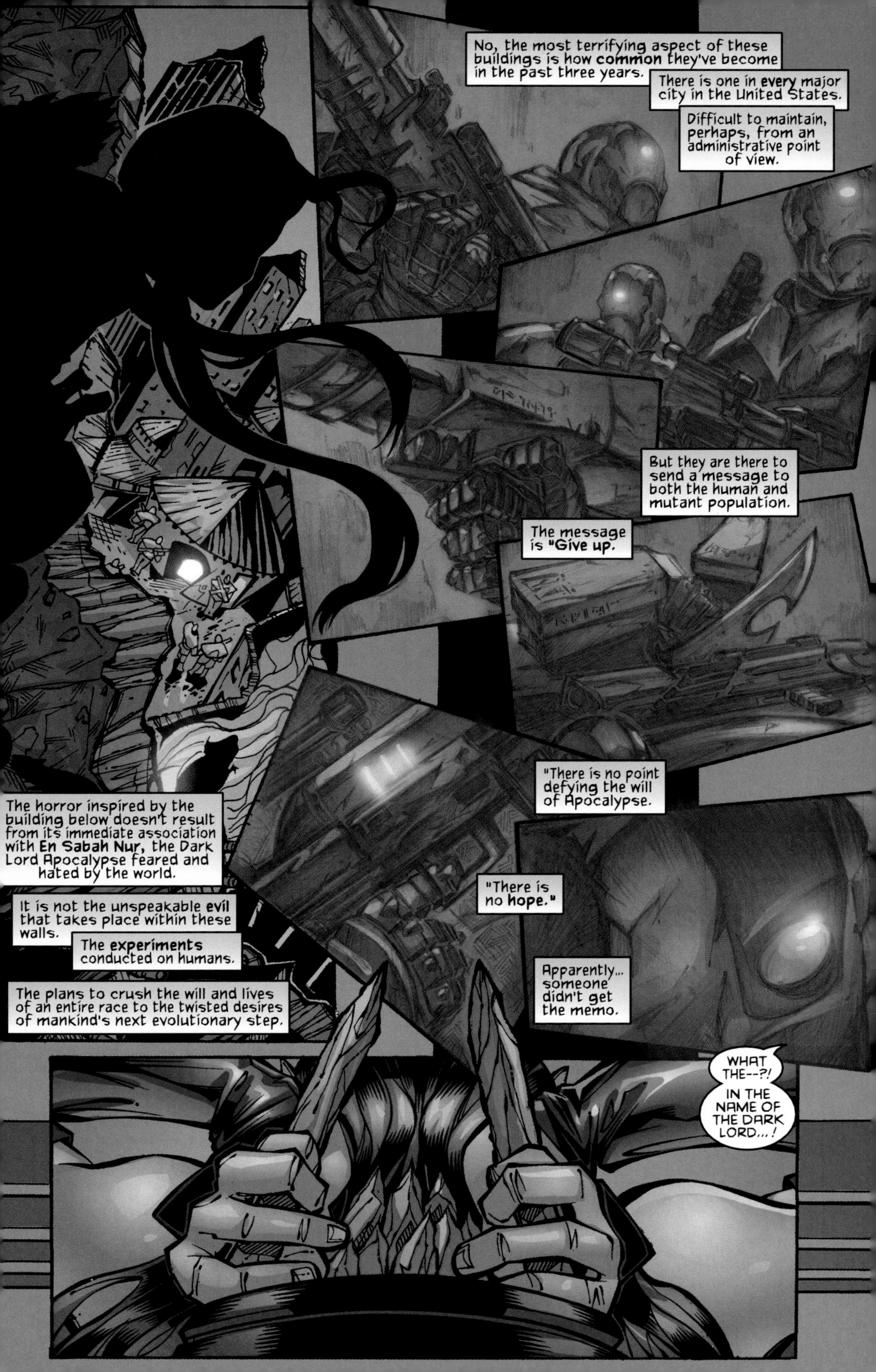
No, the most terrifying aspect of these buildings is how **common** they've become in the past three years.
There is one in **every** major city in the United States.
Difficult to maintain, perhaps, from an administrative point of view.
But they are there to send a **message** to both the human and mutant population.
The message is **"Give up.**
"There is no point defying the will of Apocalypse.
"There is no **hope."**
Apparently... someone didn't get the memo.
The horror inspired by the building below doesn't result from its immediate association with **En Sabah Nur,** the Dark Lord Apocalypse feared and hated by the world.
It is not the unspeakable **evil** that takes place within these walls.
The **experiments** conducted on humans.
The plans to crush the will and lives of an entire race to the twisted desires of mankind's next evolutionary step.
WHAT THE--?! IN THE NAME OF THE DARK LORD...!

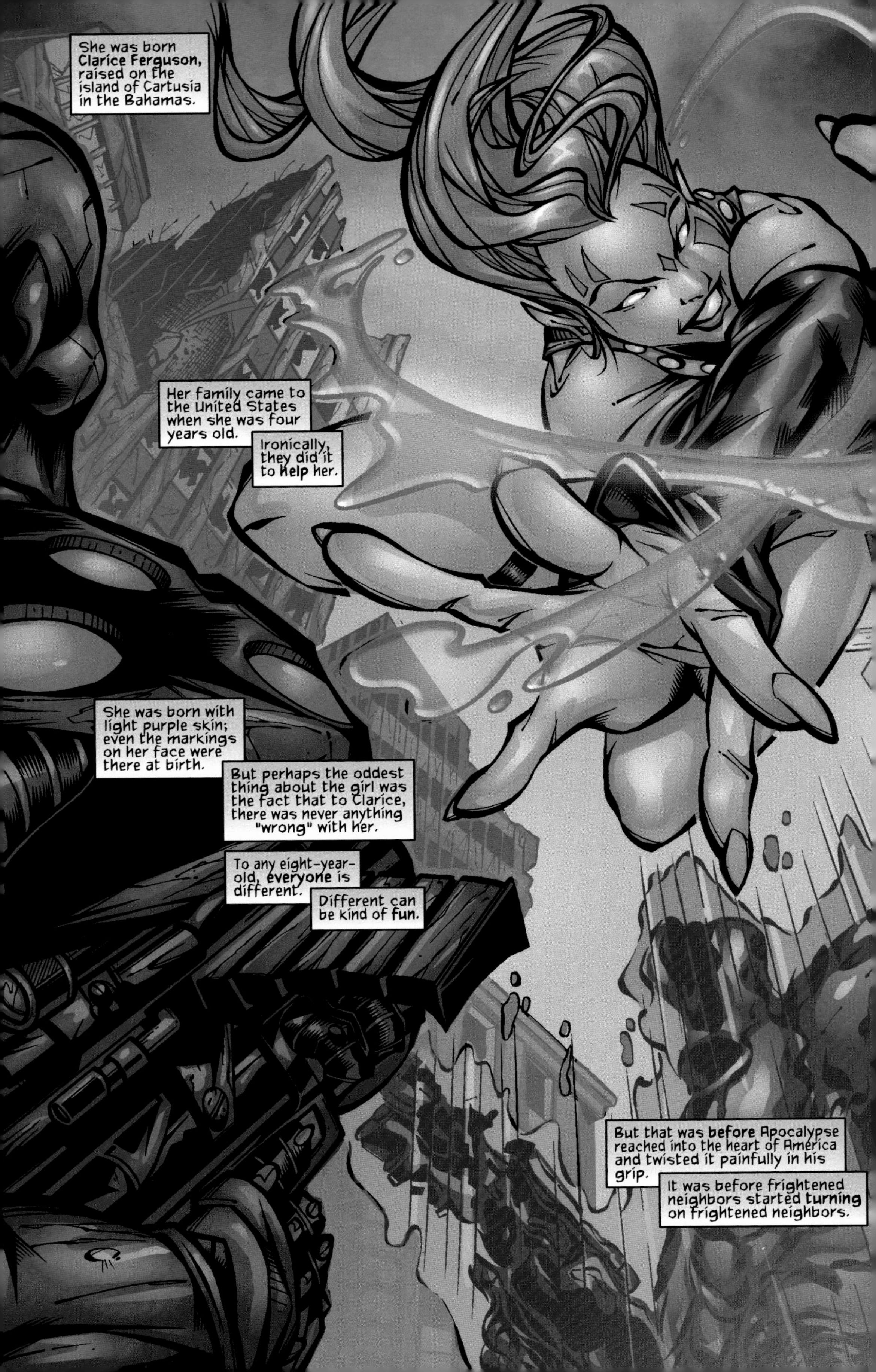
She was born Clarice Ferguson, raised on the island of Cartusia in the Bahamas.
Her family came to the United States when she was four years old.
Ironically, they did it to help her.
She was born with light purple skin; even the markings on her face were there at birth.
But perhaps the oddest thing about the girl was the fact that to Clarice, there was never anything "wrong" with her.
To any eight-year-old, everyone is different.
Different can be kind of fun.
But that was before Apocalypse reached into the heart of America and twisted it painfully in his grip.
It was before frightened neighbors started turning on frightened neighbors.

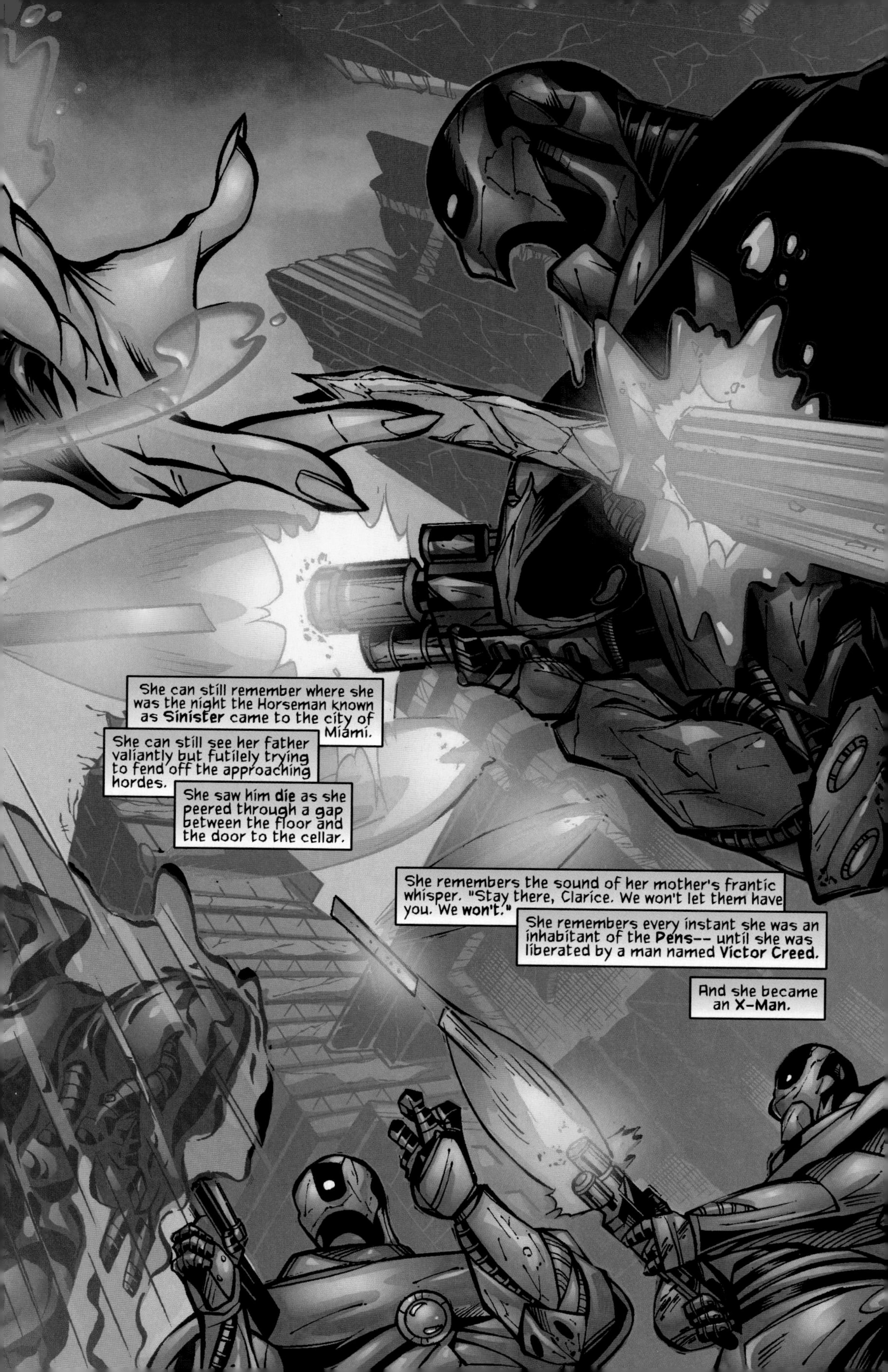

She can still remember where she was the night the Horseman known as Sinister came to the city of Miami.
She can still see her father valiantly but futilely trying to fend off the approaching hordes.
She saw him die as she peered through a gap between the floor and the door to the cellar.
She remembers the sound of her mother's frantic whisper. "Stay there, Clarice. We won't let them have you. We won't."
She remembers every instant she was an inhabitant of the Pens-- until she was liberated by a man named Victor Creed.
And she became an X-Man.

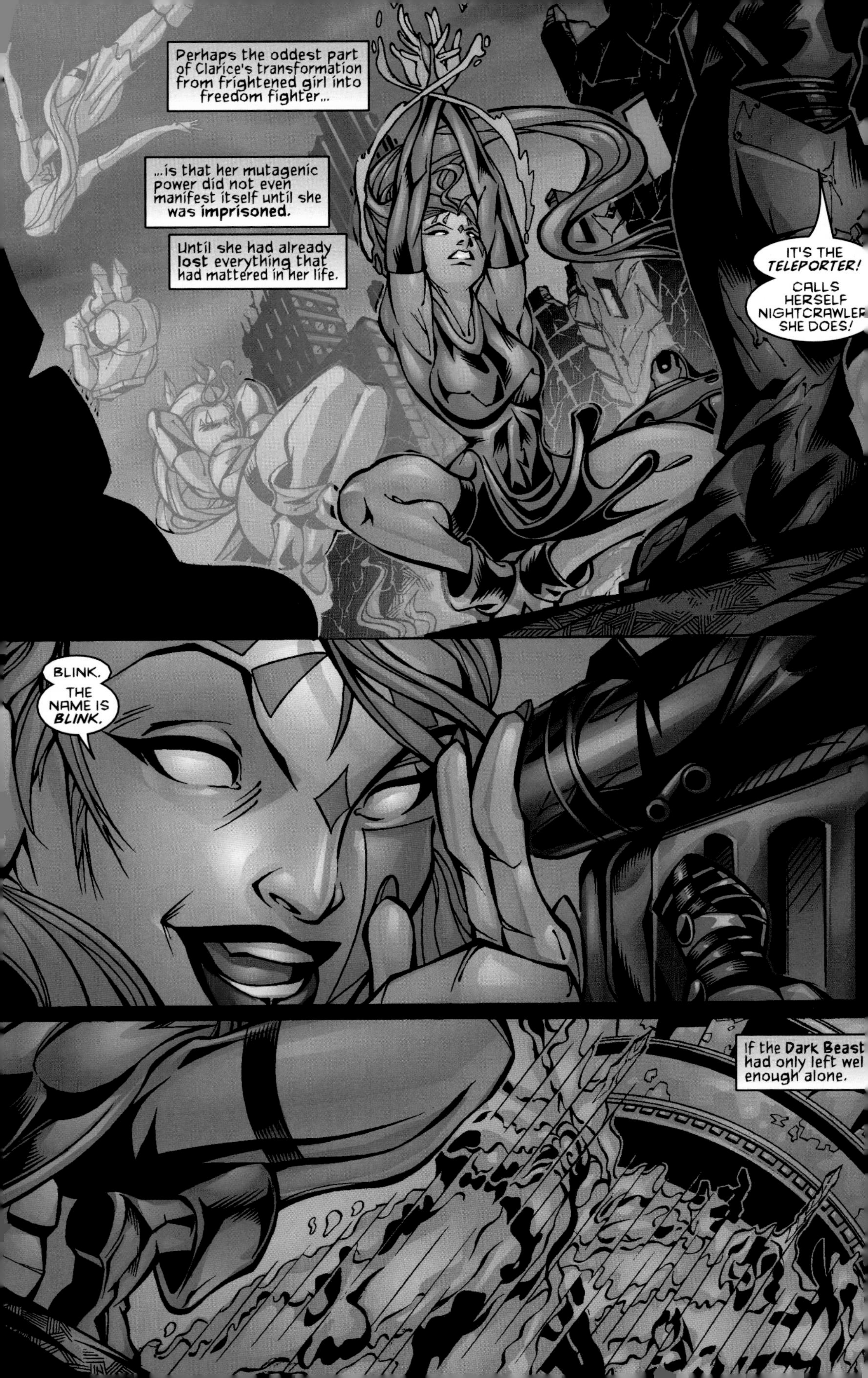
Perhaps the oddest part of Clarice's transformation from frightened girl into freedom fighter...
...is that her mutagenic power did not even manifest itself until she was **imprisoned.**
Until she had already **lost** everything that had mattered in her life.
IT'S THE *TELEPORTER!* CALLS HERSELF NIGHTCRAWLER SHE DOES!
BLINK. THE NAME IS *BLINK.*
If the **Dark Beast** had only left wel enough alone.

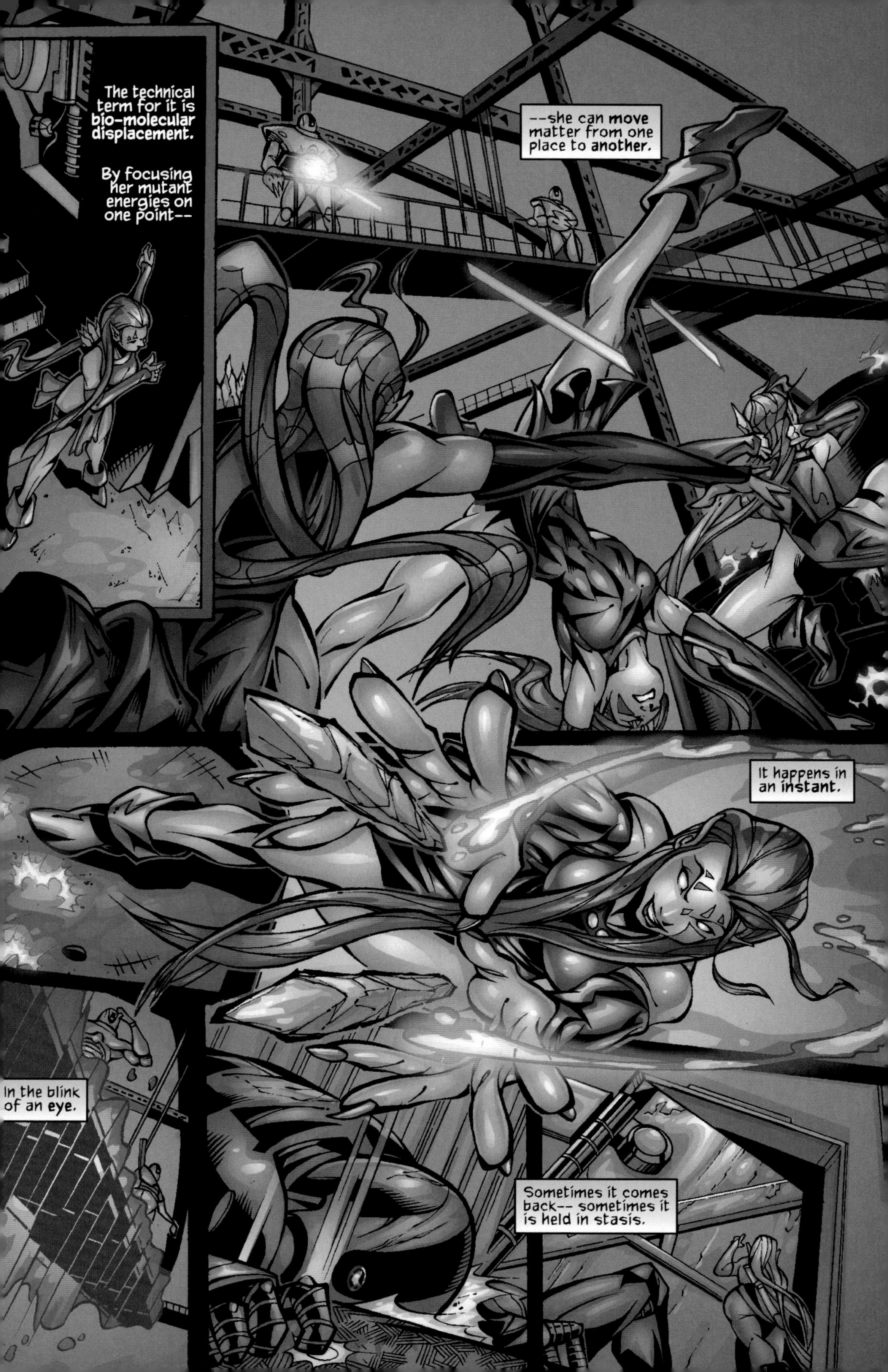
The technical term for it is bio-molecular displacement.
By focusing her mutant energies on one point--
--she can move matter from one place to another.
It happens in an instant.
In the blink of an eye.
Sometimes it comes back-- sometimes it is held in stasis.

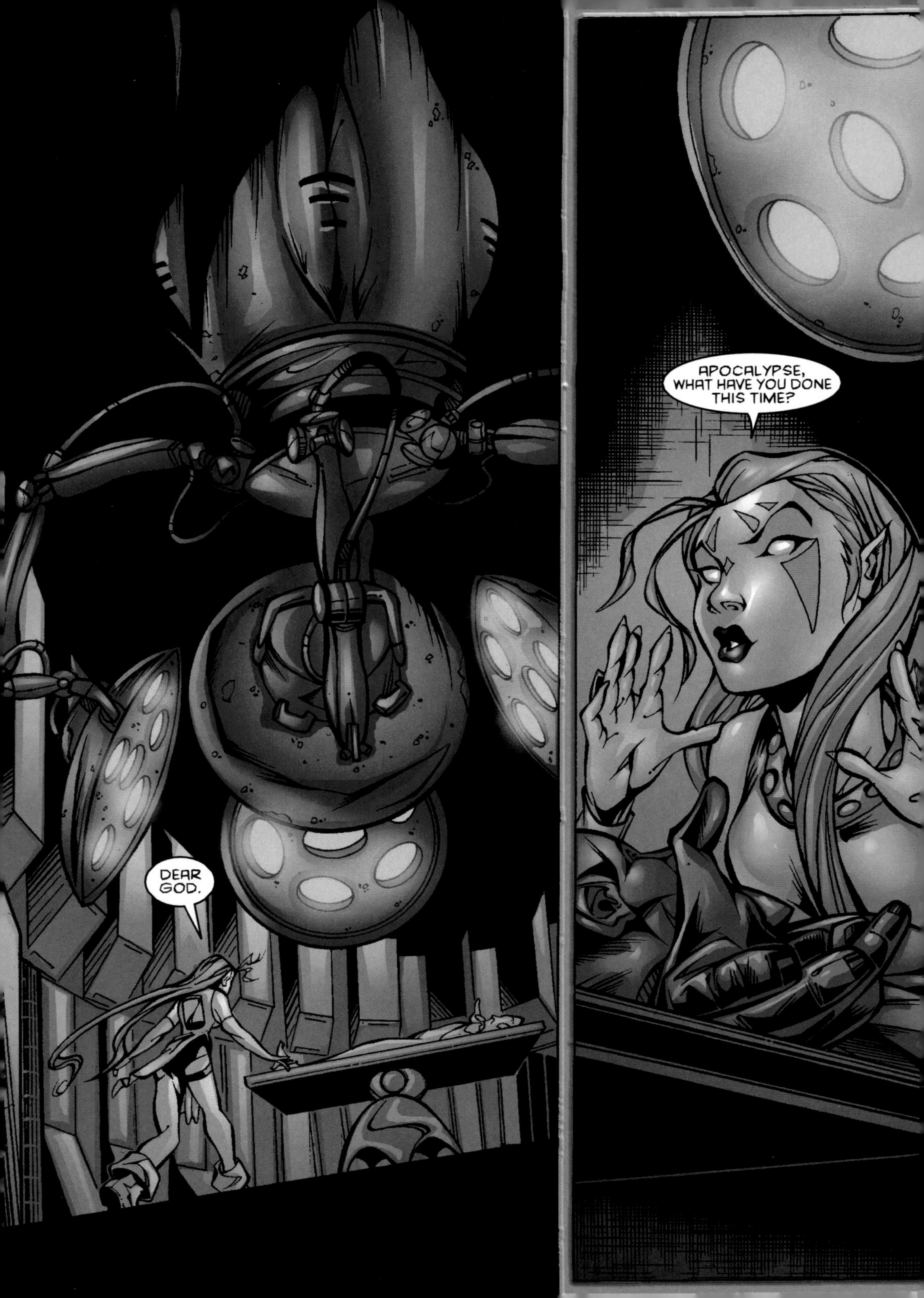
DEAR GOD.
APOCALYPSE, WHAT HAVE YOU DONE THIS TIME?

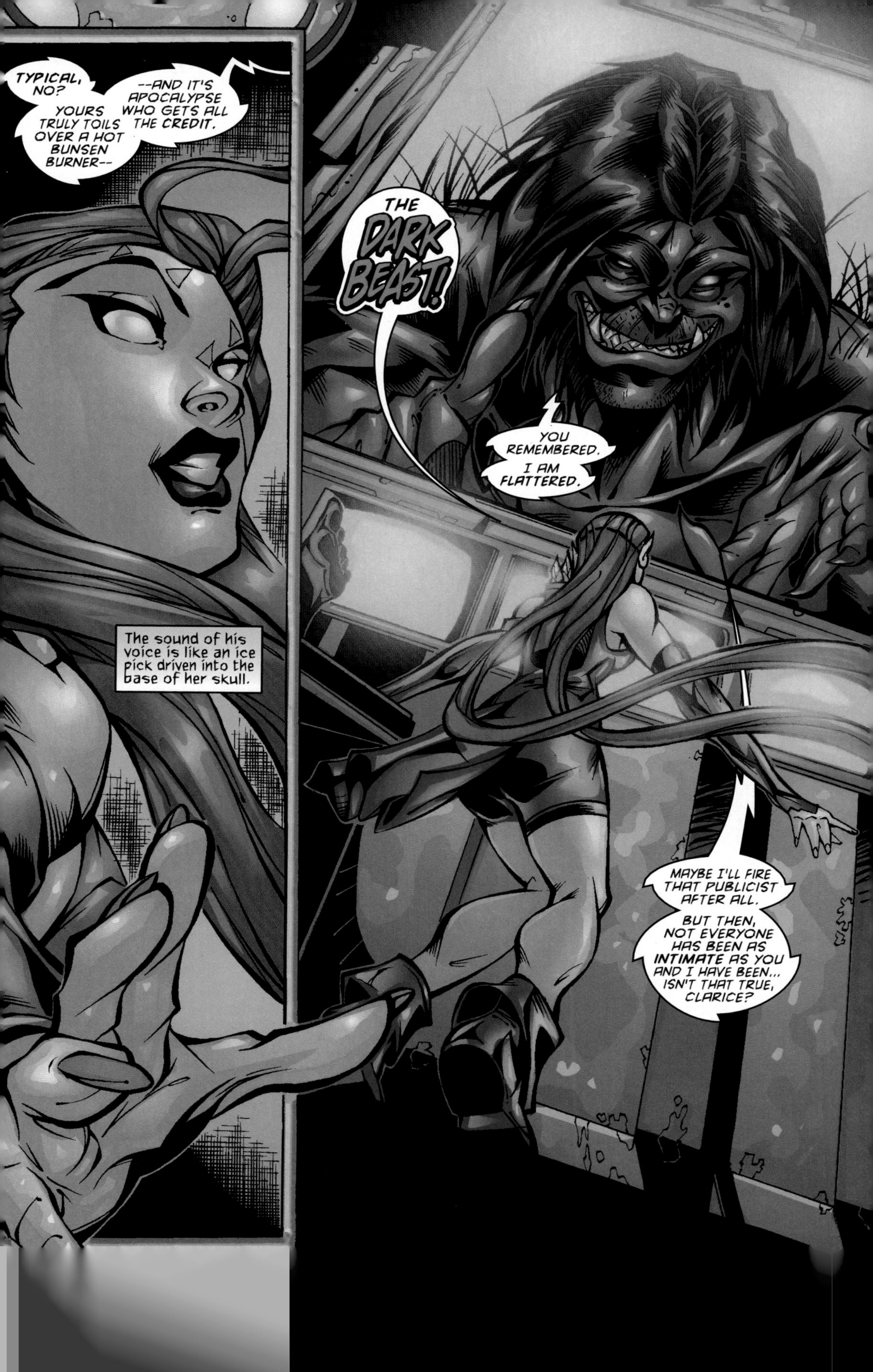
TYPICAL, NO? YOURS TRULY TOILS OVER A HOT BUNSEN BURNER--
--AND IT'S APOCALYPSE WHO GETS ALL THE CREDIT.
The sound of his voice is like an ice pick driven into the base of her skull.
THE DARK BEAST!
YOU REMEMBERED. I AM FLATTERED.
MAYBE I'LL FIRE THAT PUBLICIST AFTER ALL.
BUT THEN, NOT EVERYONE HAS BEEN AS INTIMATE AS YOU AND I HAVE BEEN... ISN'T THAT TRUE, CLARICE?

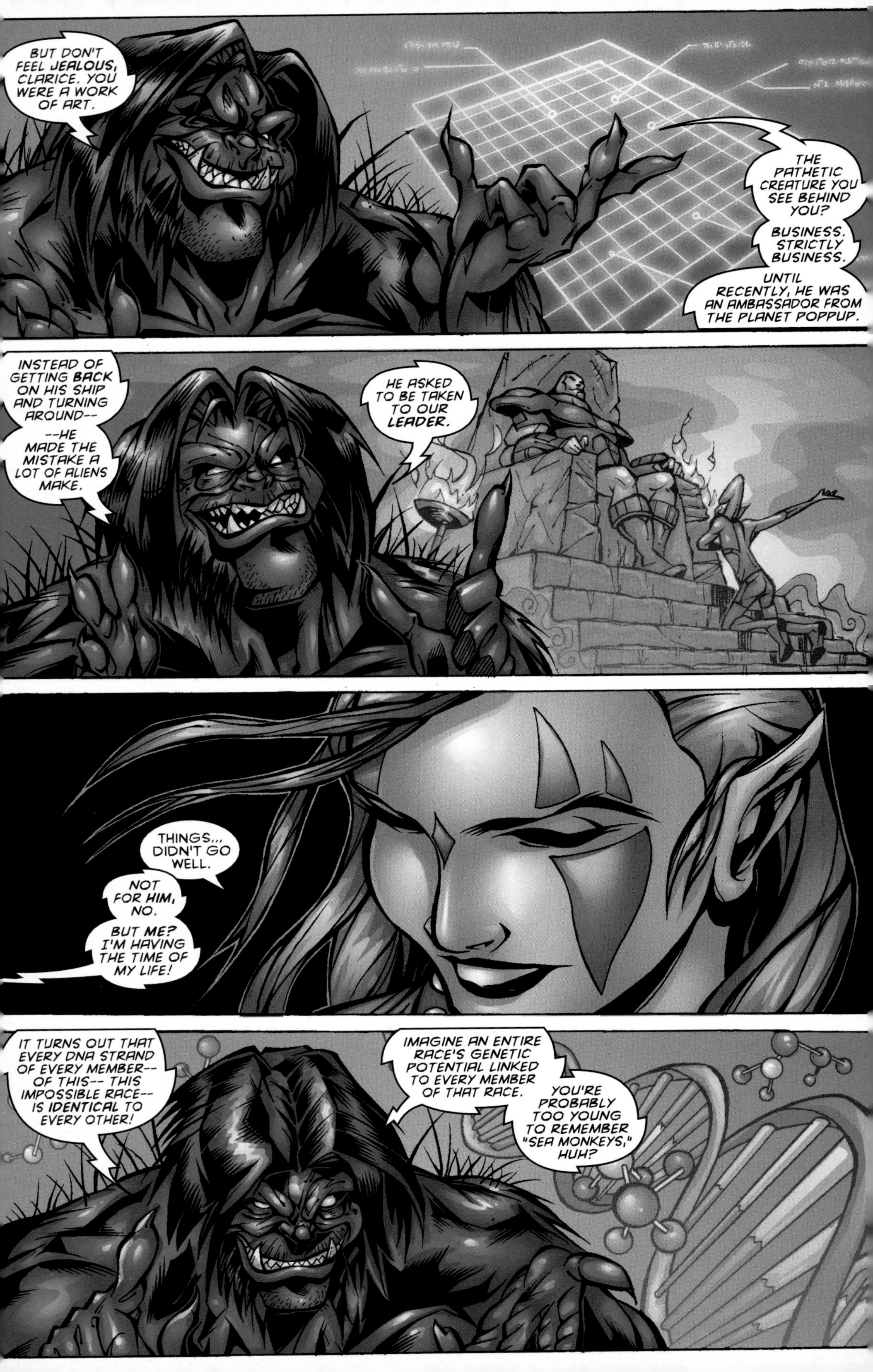
BUT DON'T FEEL JEALOUS, CLARICE. YOU WERE A WORK OF ART.
THE PATHETIC CREATURE YOU SEE BEHIND YOU?
BUSINESS. STRICTLY BUSINESS.
UNTIL RECENTLY, HE WAS AN AMBASSADOR FROM THE PLANET POPPUP.
INSTEAD OF GETTING BACK ON HIS SHIP AND TURNING AROUND--
--HE MADE THE MISTAKE A LOT OF ALIENS MAKE.
HE ASKED TO BE TAKEN TO OUR LEADER.
THINGS... DIDN'T GO WELL.
NOT FOR HIM, NO.
BUT ME? I'M HAVING THE TIME OF MY LIFE!
IT TURNS OUT THAT EVERY DNA STRAND OF EVERY MEMBER-- OF THIS-- THIS IMPOSSIBLE RACE-- IS IDENTICAL TO EVERY OTHER!
IMAGINE AN ENTIRE RACE'S GENETIC POTENTIAL LINKED TO EVERY MEMBER OF THAT RACE.
YOU'RE PROBABLY TOO YOUNG TO REMEMBER "SEA MONKEYS," HUH?

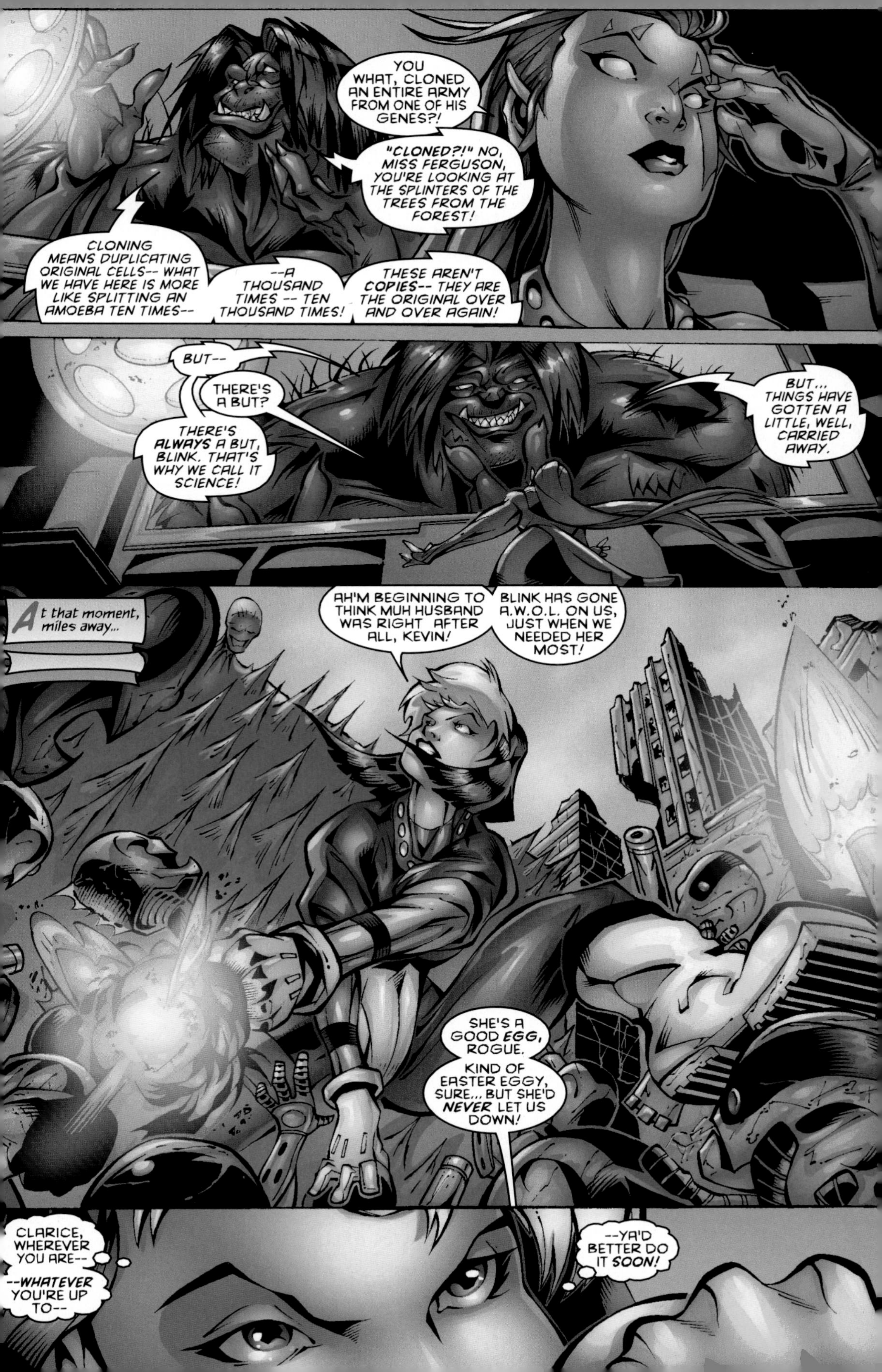
YOU WHAT, CLONED AN ENTIRE ARMY FROM ONE OF HIS GENES?!
"CLONED?!" NO, MISS FERGUSON, YOU'RE LOOKING AT THE SPLINTERS OF THE TREES FROM THE FOREST!
CLONING MEANS DUPLICATING ORIGINAL CELLS-- WHAT WE HAVE HERE IS MORE LIKE SPLITTING AN AMOEBA TEN TIMES--
--A THOUSAND TIMES -- TEN THOUSAND TIMES!
THESE AREN'T COPIES-- THEY ARE THE ORIGINAL OVER AND OVER AGAIN!
BUT--
THERE'S A BUT?
THERE'S ALWAYS A BUT, BLINK. THAT'S WHY WE CALL IT SCIENCE!
BUT... THINGS HAVE GOTTEN A LITTLE, WELL, CARRIED AWAY.
At that moment, miles away...
AH'M BEGINNING TO THINK MUH HUSBAND WAS RIGHT AFTER ALL, KEVIN!
BLINK HAS GONE A.W.O.L. ON US, JUST WHEN WE NEEDED HER MOST!
SHE'S A GOOD EGG, ROGUE.
KIND OF EASTER EGGY, SURE... BUT SHE'D NEVER LET US DOWN!
CLARICE, WHEREVER YOU ARE--
--WHATEVER YOU'RE UP TO--
--YA'D BETTER DO IT SOON!

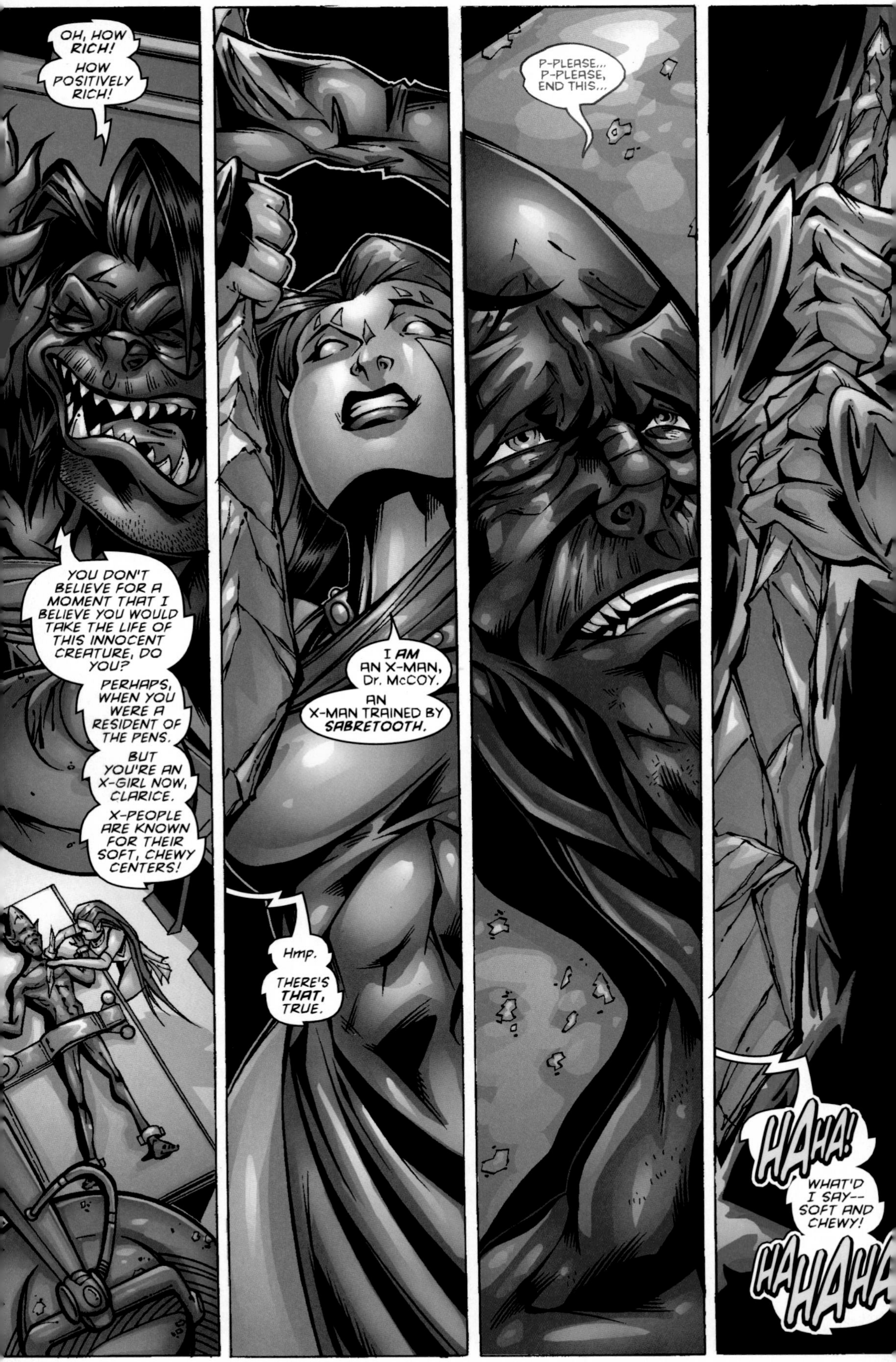
OH, HOW RICH!
HOW POSITIVELY RICH!
YOU DON'T BELIEVE FOR A MOMENT THAT I BELIEVE YOU WOULD TAKE THE LIFE OF THIS INNOCENT CREATURE, DO YOU?
PERHAPS, WHEN YOU WERE A RESIDENT OF THE PENS.
BUT YOU'RE AN X-GIRL NOW, CLARICE.
X-PEOPLE ARE KNOWN FOR THEIR SOFT, CHEWY CENTERS!
I AM AN X-MAN, Dr. McCOY.
AN X-MAN TRAINED BY SABRETOOTH.
Hmp.
THERE'S THAT, TRUE.
P-PLEASE... P-PLEASE, END THIS...
HAHA!
WHAT'D I SAY-- SOFT AND CHEWY!
HAHAHA

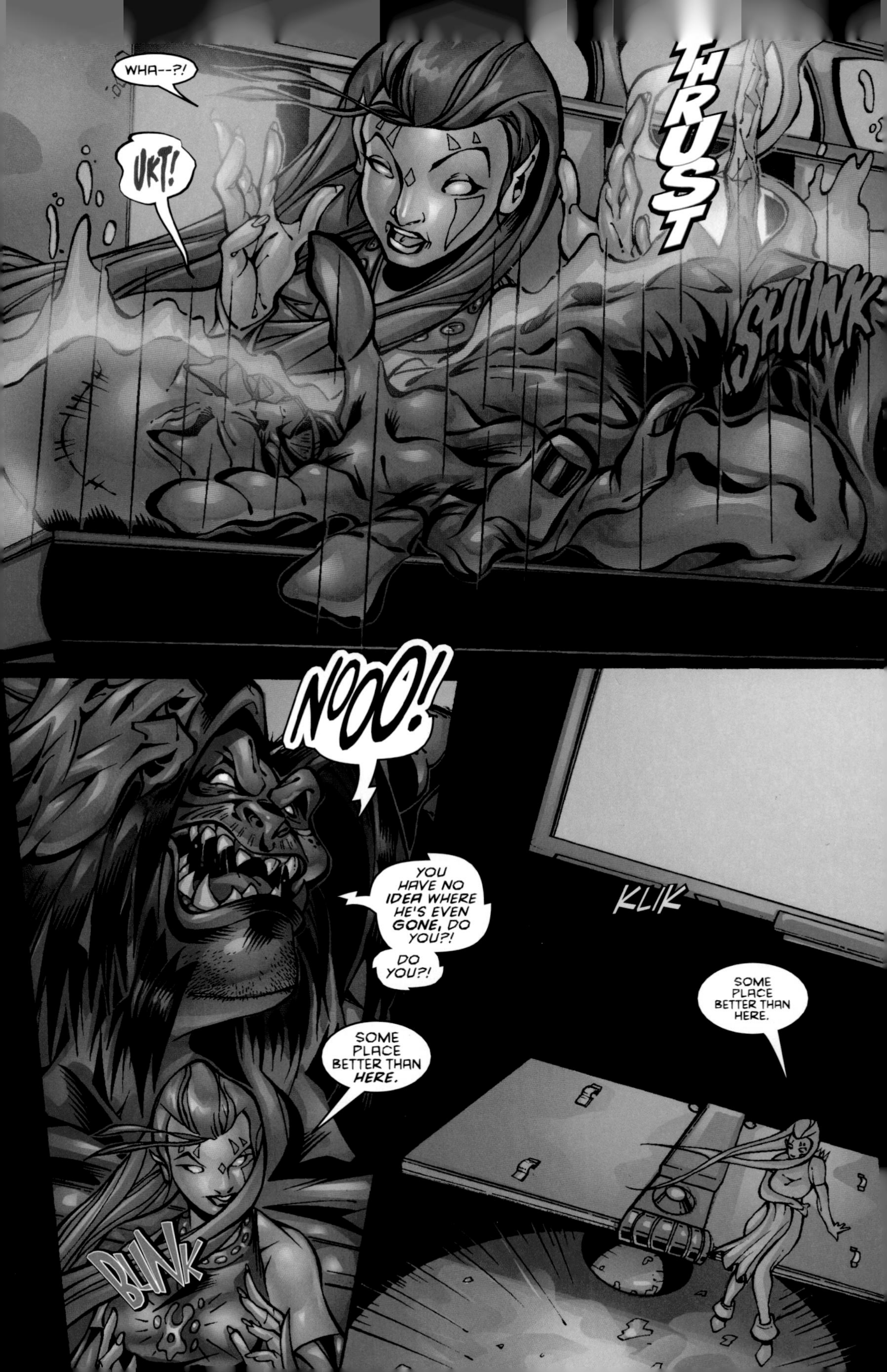
WHA--?!
UKT!
THRUST
SHUNK
NOOO!
YOU HAVE NO IDEA WHERE HE'S EVEN GONE, DO YOU?!
DO YOU?!
SOME PLACE BETTER THAN HERE.
BLINK
KLIK
SOME PLACE BETTER THAN HERE.

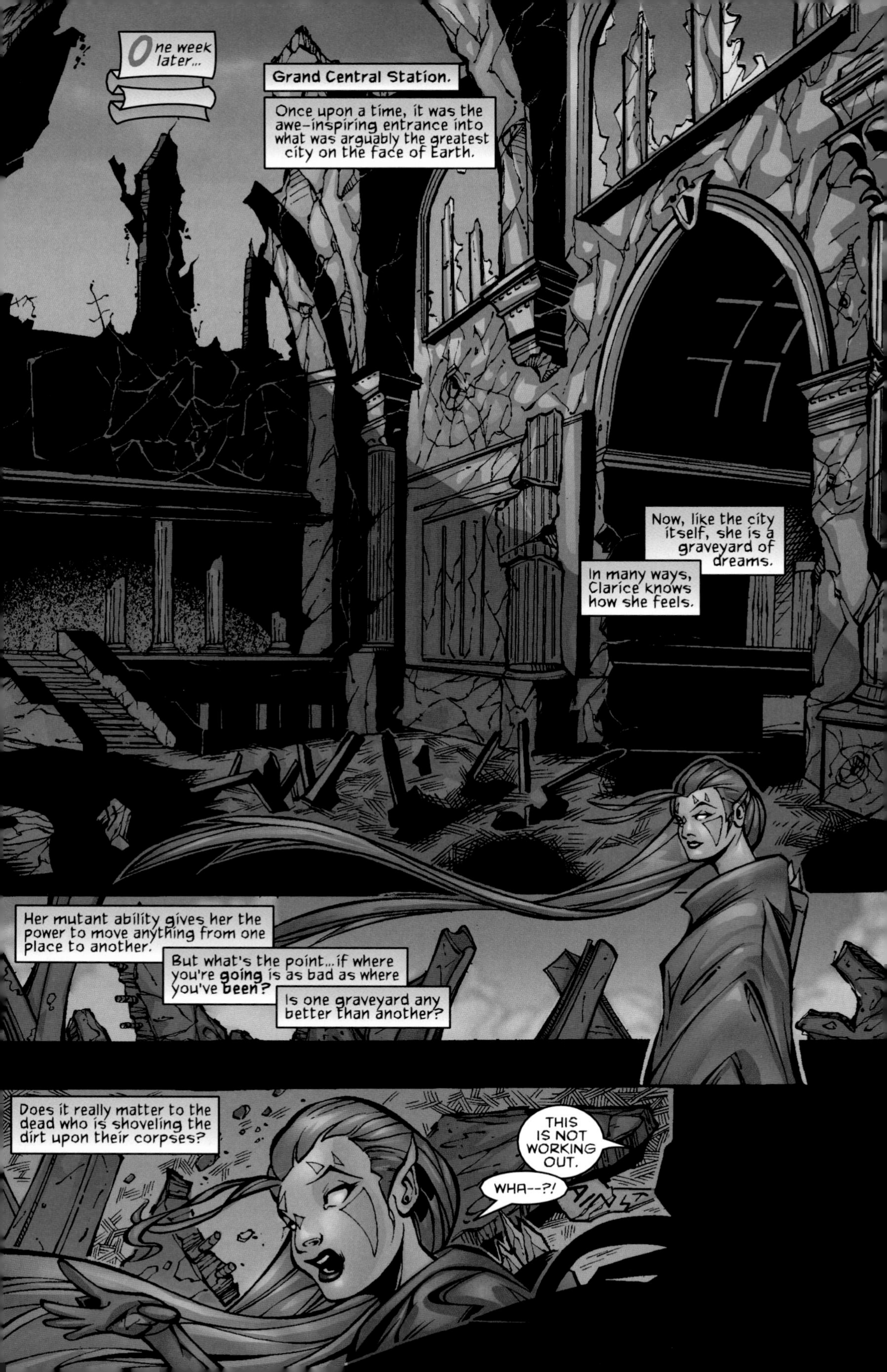
One week later...
Grand Central Station.
Once upon a time, it was the awe-inspiring entrance into what was arguably the greatest city on the face of Earth.
Now, like the city itself, she is a graveyard of dreams.
In many ways, Clarice knows how she feels.
Her mutant ability gives her the power to move anything from one place to another.
But what's the point... if where you're going is as bad as where you've been?
Is one graveyard any better than another?
Does it really matter to the dead who is shoveling the dirt upon their corpses?
THIS IS NOT WORKING OUT.
WHA--?!

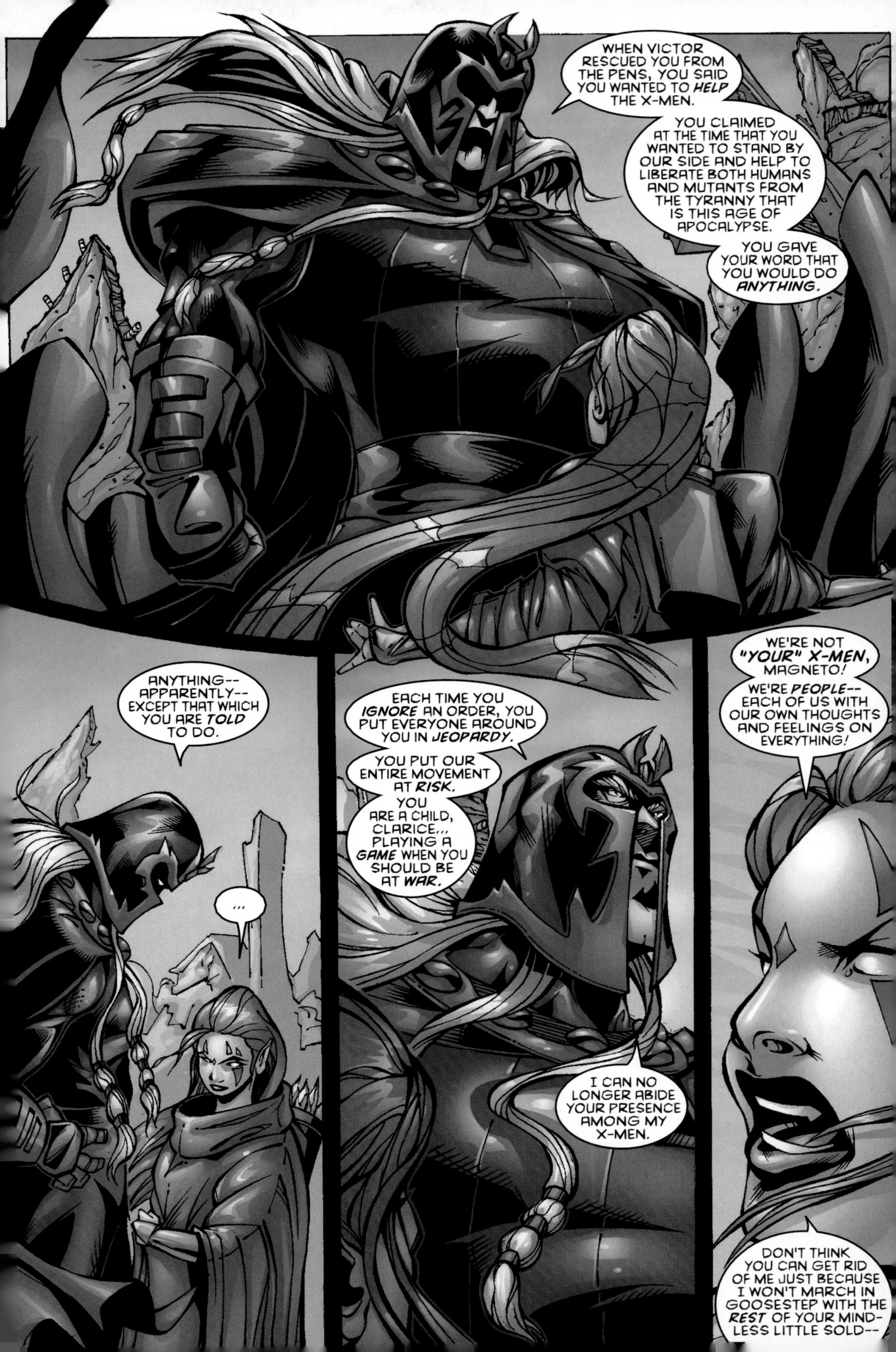

WHEN VICTOR RESCUED YOU FROM THE PENS, YOU SAID YOU WANTED TO *HELP* THE X-MEN.
YOU CLAIMED AT THE TIME THAT YOU WANTED TO STAND BY OUR SIDE AND HELP TO LIBERATE BOTH HUMANS AND MUTANTS FROM THE TYRANNY THAT IS THIS AGE OF APOCALYPSE.
YOU GAVE YOUR WORD THAT YOU WOULD DO ***ANYTHING.***
ANYTHING-- APPARENTLY-- EXCEPT THAT WHICH YOU ARE *TOLD* TO DO.
...
EACH TIME YOU *IGNORE* AN ORDER, YOU PUT EVERYONE AROUND YOU IN *JEOPARDY.*
YOU PUT OUR ENTIRE MOVEMENT AT *RISK.*
YOU ARE A CHILD, CLARICE... PLAYING A *GAME* WHEN YOU SHOULD BE AT *WAR.*
I CAN NO LONGER ABIDE YOUR PRESENCE AMONG MY X-MEN.
WE'RE NOT ***"YOUR" X-MEN,*** MAGNETO!
WE'RE *PEOPLE*-- EACH OF US WITH OUR OWN THOUGHTS AND FEELINGS ON EVERYTHING!
DON'T THINK YOU CAN GET RID OF ME JUST BECAUSE I WON'T MARCH IN GOOSESTEP WITH THE *REST* OF YOUR MIND-LESS LITTLE SOLD--

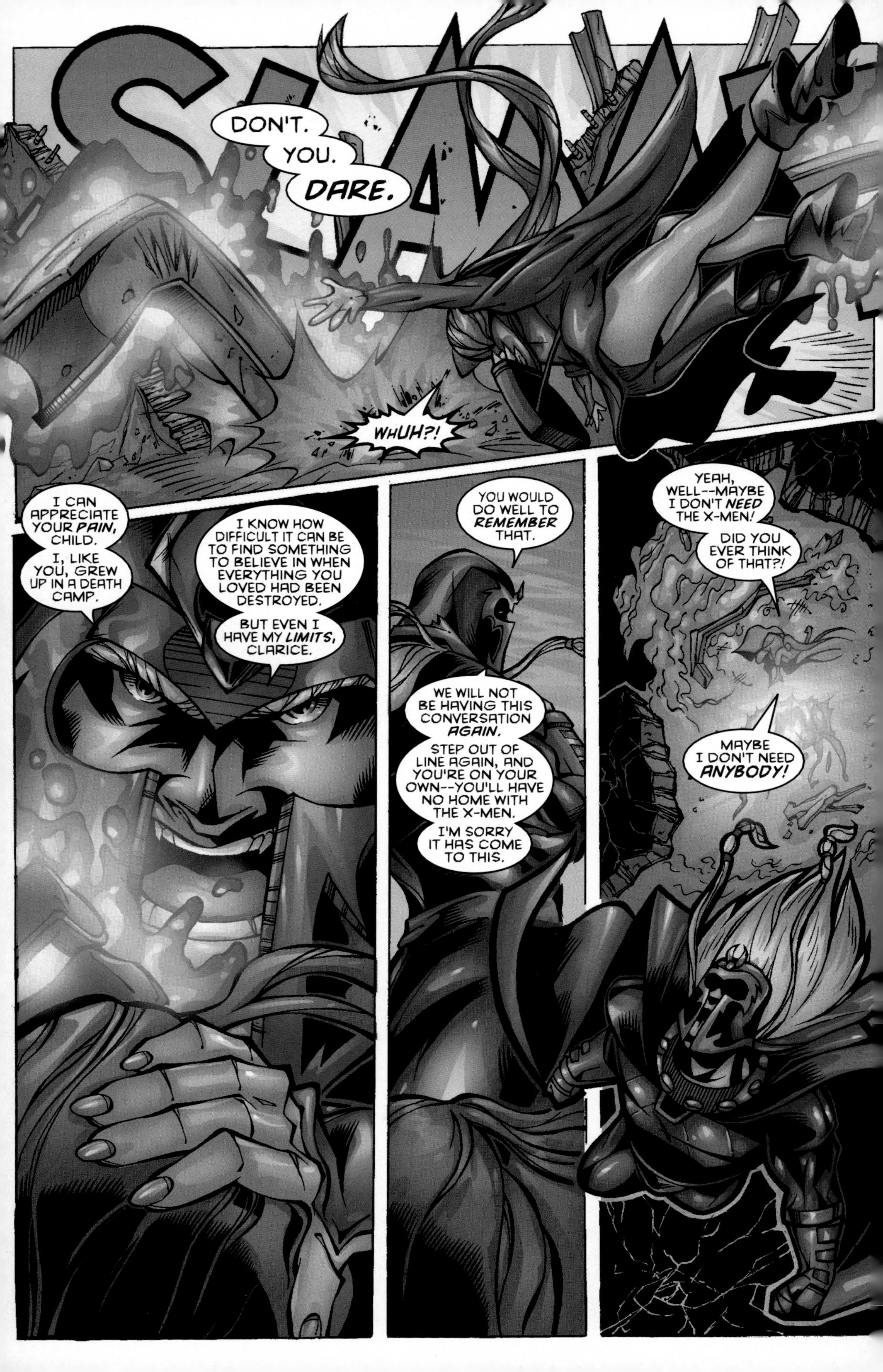

DON'T.
YOU.
DARE.
WHUH?!
I CAN APPRECIATE YOUR PAIN, CHILD.
I, LIKE YOU, GREW UP IN A DEATH CAMP.
I KNOW HOW DIFFICULT IT CAN BE TO FIND SOMETHING TO BELIEVE IN WHEN EVERYTHING YOU LOVED HAD BEEN DESTROYED.
BUT EVEN I HAVE MY LIMITS, CLARICE.
YOU WOULD DO WELL TO REMEMBER THAT.
WE WILL NOT BE HAVING THIS CONVERSATION AGAIN.
STEP OUT OF LINE AGAIN, AND YOU'RE ON YOUR OWN--YOU'LL HAVE NO HOME WITH THE X-MEN.
I'M SORRY IT HAS COME TO THIS.
YEAH, WELL--MAYBE I DON'T NEED THE X-MEN!
DID YOU EVER THINK OF THAT?!
MAYBE I DON'T NEED ANYBODY!

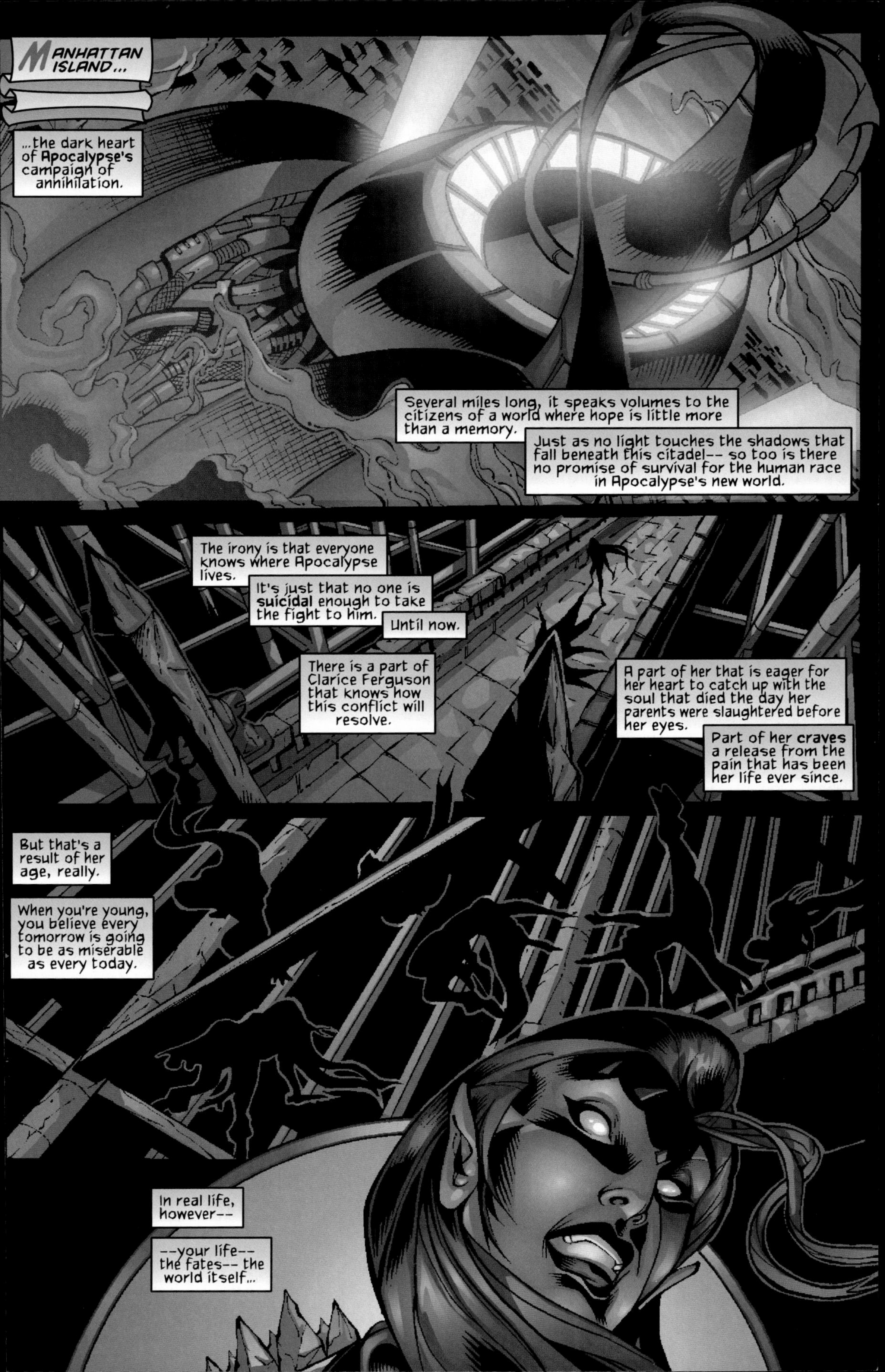
MANHATTAN ISLAND...
...the dark heart of Apocalypse's campaign of annihilation.
Several miles long, it speaks volumes to the citizens of a world where hope is little more than a memory.
Just as no light touches the shadows that fall beneath this citadel-- so too is there no promise of survival for the human race in Apocalypse's new world.
The irony is that everyone knows where Apocalypse lives.
It's just that no one is suicidal enough to take the fight to him.
Until now.
There is a part of Clarice Ferguson that knows how this conflict will resolve.
A part of her that is eager for her heart to catch up with the soul that died the day her parents were slaughtered before her eyes.
Part of her craves a release from the pain that has been her life ever since.
But that's a result of her age, really.
When you're young, you believe every tomorrow is going to be as miserable as every today.
In real life, however--
--your life-- the fates-- the world itself...

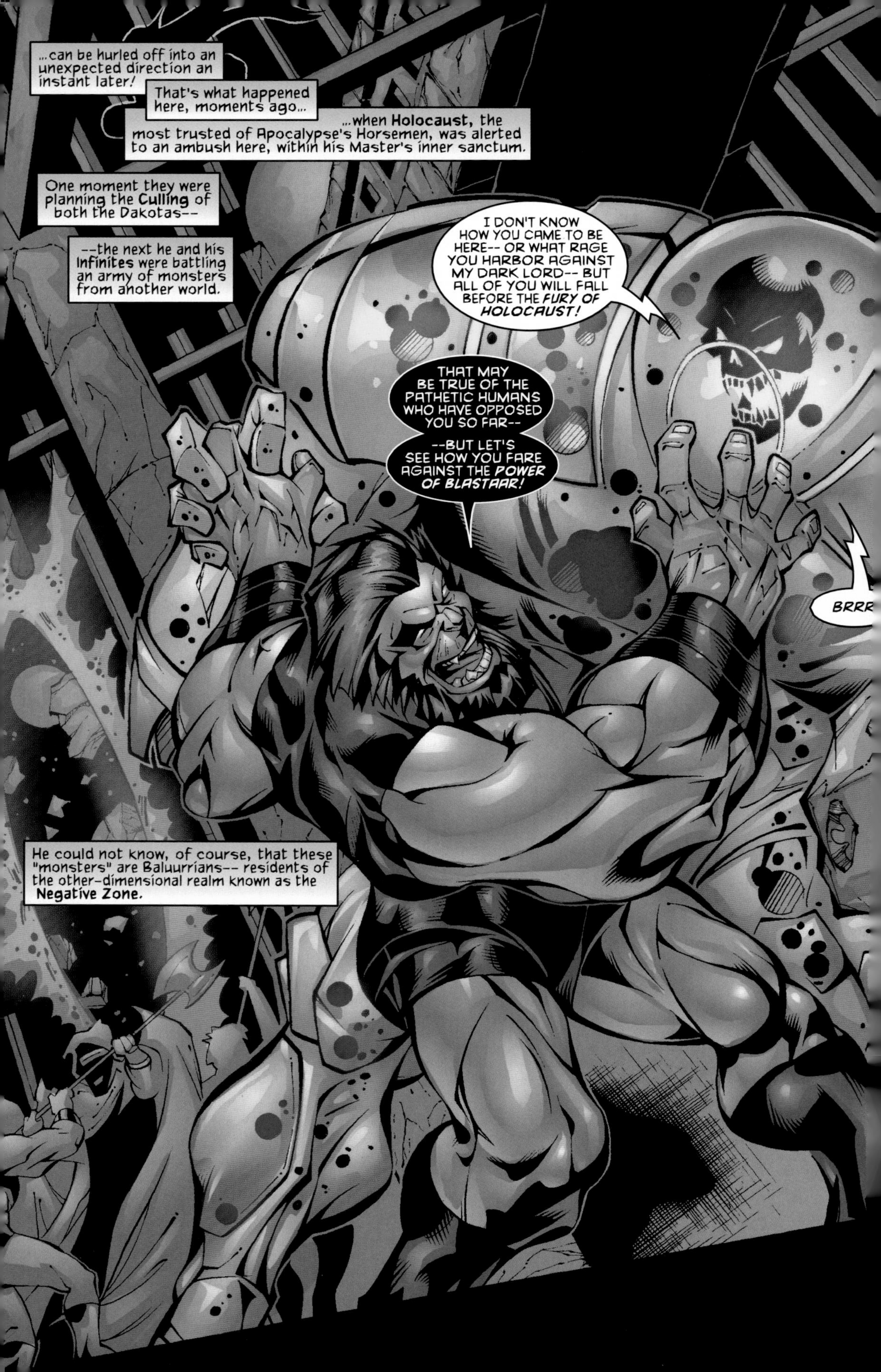
...can be hurled off into an unexpected direction an instant later!
That's what happened here, moments ago...
...when **Holocaust,** the most trusted of Apocalypse's Horsemen, was alerted to an ambush here, within his Master's inner sanctum.
One moment they were planning the **Culling** of both the Dakotas--
--the next he and his **Infinites** were battling an army of monsters from another world.
I DON'T KNOW HOW YOU CAME TO BE HERE-- OR WHAT RAGE YOU HARBOR AGAINST MY DARK LORD-- BUT ALL OF YOU WILL FALL BEFORE THE *FURY OF HOLOCAUST!*
THAT MAY BE TRUE OF THE PATHETIC HUMANS WHO HAVE OPPOSED YOU SO FAR--
--BUT LET'S SEE HOW YOU FARE AGAINST THE *POWER OF BLASTAAR!*
BRRR
He could not know, of course, that these "monsters" are Baluurrians-- residents of the other-dimensional realm known as the **Negative Zone.**

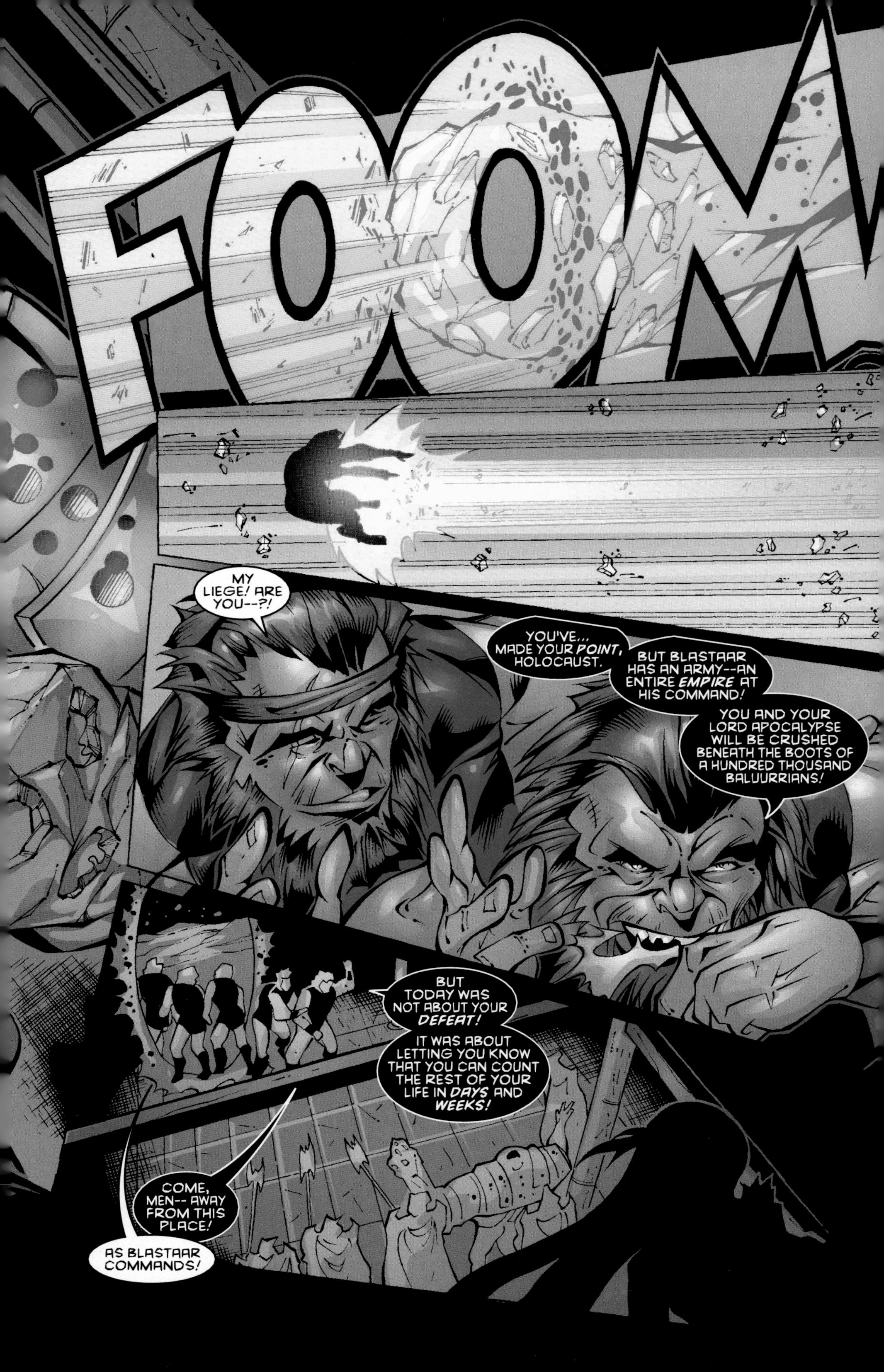
FOOM
MY LIEGE! ARE YOU--?!
YOU'VE... MADE YOUR POINT, HOLOCAUST.
BUT BLASTAAR HAS AN ARMY--AN ENTIRE EMPIRE AT HIS COMMAND!
YOU AND YOUR LORD APOCALYPSE WILL BE CRUSHED BENEATH THE BOOTS OF A HUNDRED THOUSAND BALUURRIANS!
BUT TODAY WAS NOT ABOUT YOUR DEFEAT!
IT WAS ABOUT LETTING YOU KNOW THAT YOU CAN COUNT THE REST OF YOUR LIFE IN DAYS AND WEEKS!
COME, MEN-- AWAY FROM THIS PLACE!
AS BLASTAAR COMMANDS!

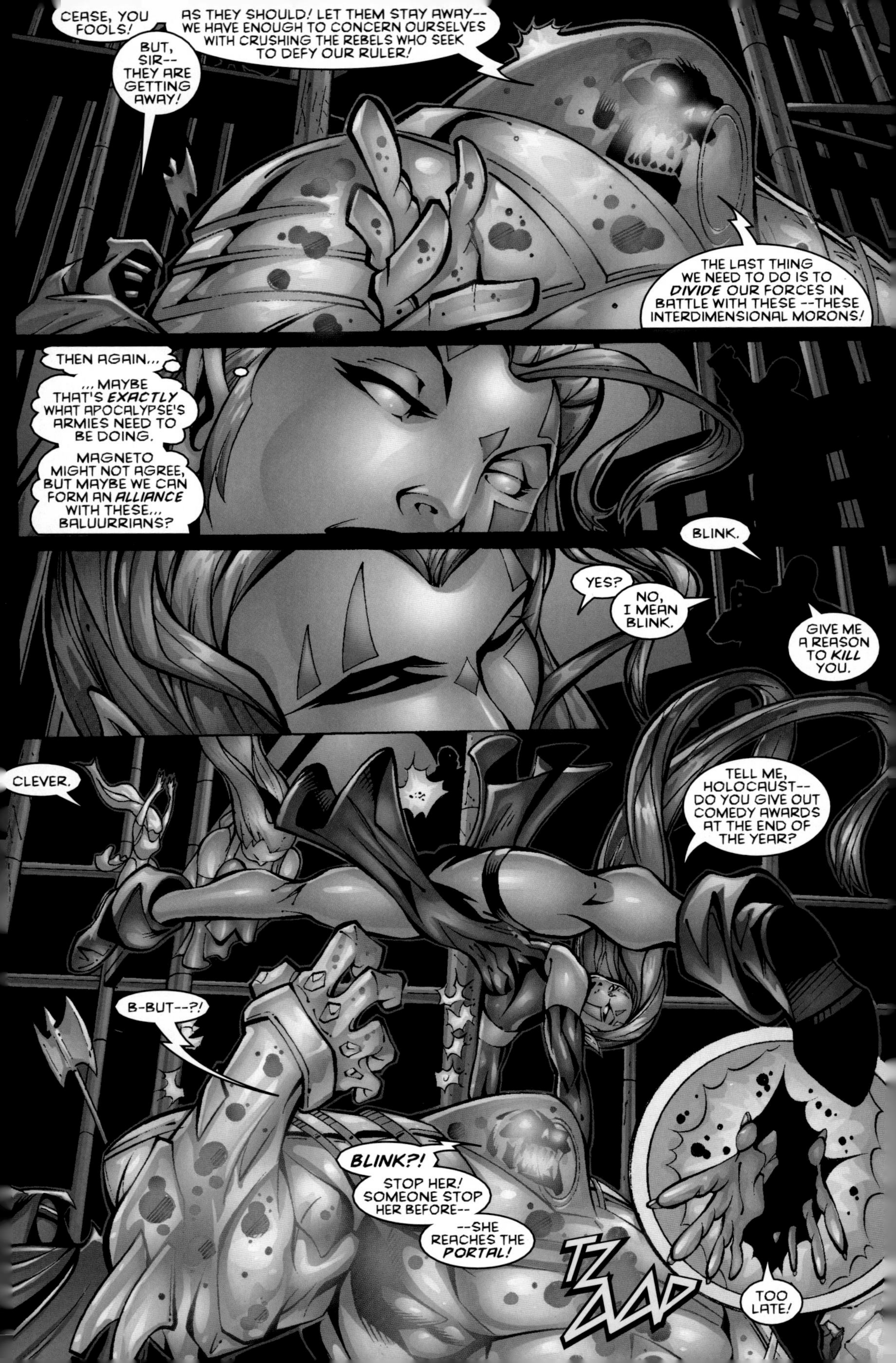

CEASE, YOU FOOLS!
BUT, SIR-- THEY ARE GETTING AWAY!
AS THEY SHOULD! LET THEM STAY AWAY-- WE HAVE ENOUGH TO CONCERN OURSELVES WITH CRUSHING THE REBELS WHO SEEK TO DEFY OUR RULER!
THE LAST THING WE NEED TO DO IS TO *DIVIDE* OUR FORCES IN BATTLE WITH THESE --THESE INTERDIMENSIONAL MORONS!
THEN AGAIN...
...MAYBE THAT'S *EXACTLY* WHAT APOCALYPSE'S ARMIES NEED TO BE DOING.
MAGNETO MIGHT NOT AGREE, BUT MAYBE WE CAN FORM AN *ALLIANCE* WITH THESE... BALUURRIANS?
BLINK.
YES?
NO, I MEAN BLINK.
GIVE ME A REASON TO *KILL* YOU.
CLEVER.
TELL ME, HOLOCAUST-- DO YOU GIVE OUT COMEDY AWARDS AT THE END OF THE YEAR?
B-BUT--?!
BLINK?!
STOP HER! SOMEONE STOP HER BEFORE--
--SHE REACHES THE *PORTAL!*
TZAAP
TOO LATE!

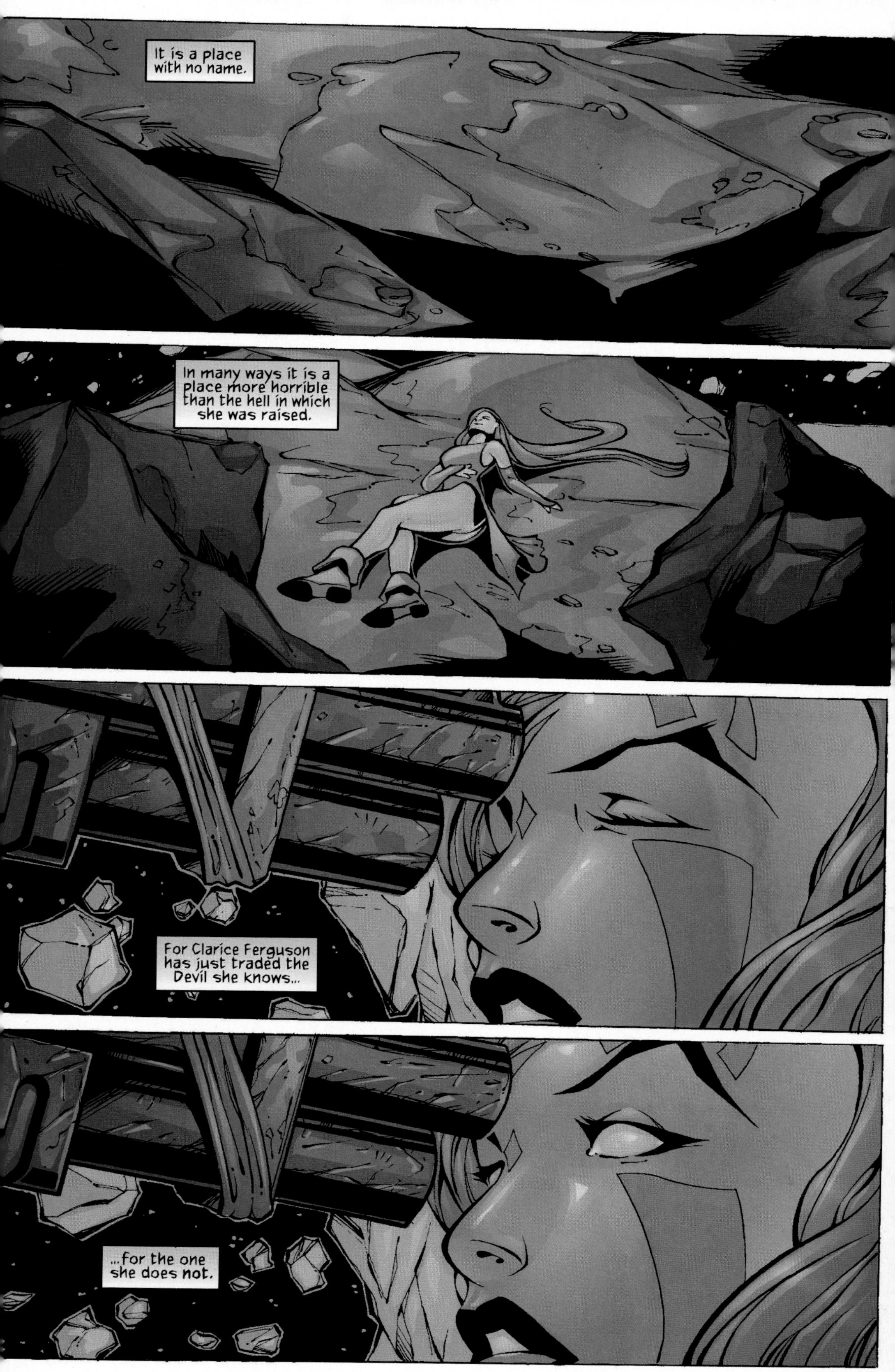
It is a place with no name.
In many ways it is a place more horrible than the hell in which she was raised.
For Clarice Ferguson has just traded the Devil she knows...
...for the one she does not.

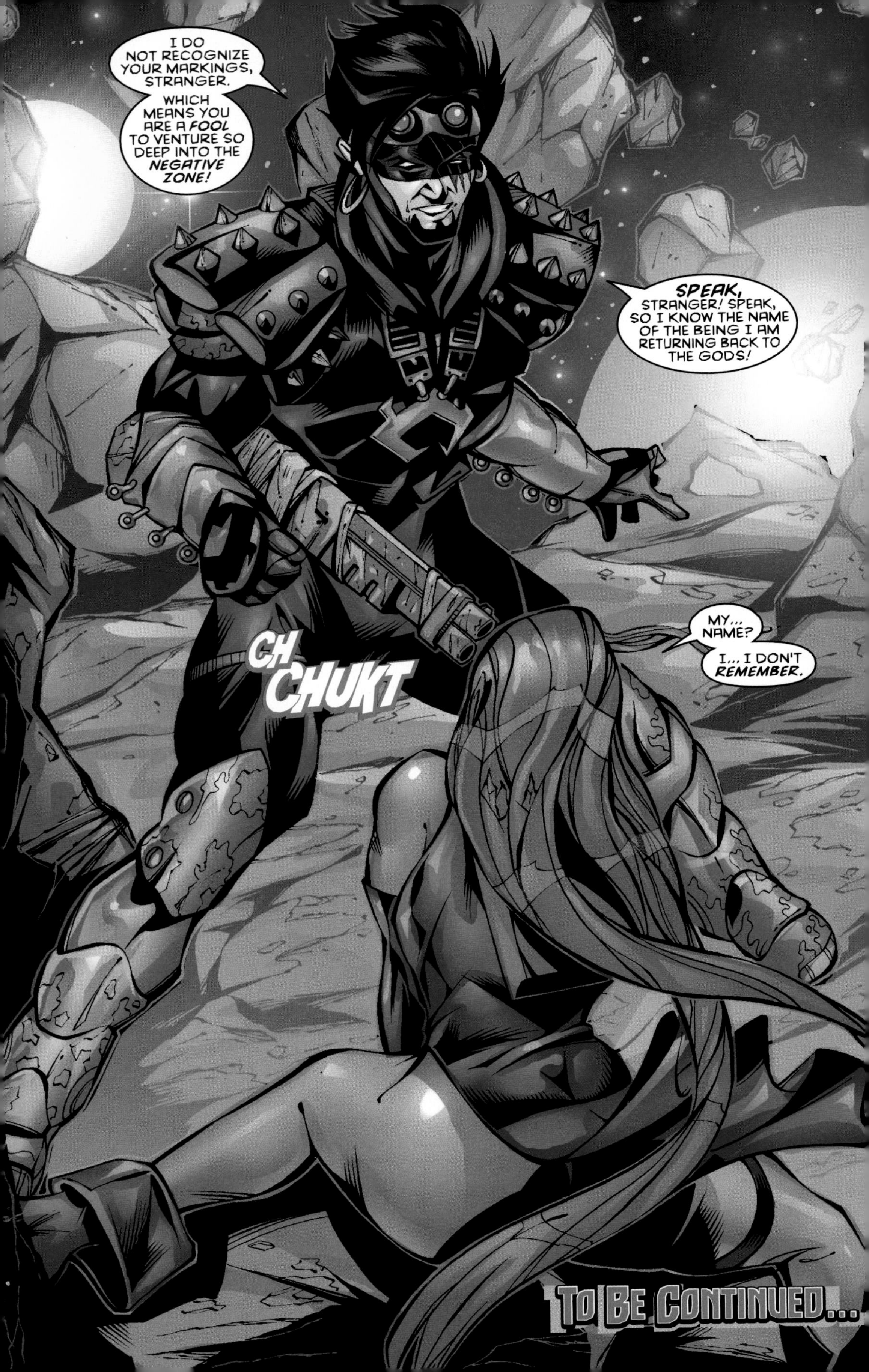
I DO NOT RECOGNIZE YOUR MARKINGS, STRANGER.
WHICH MEANS YOU ARE A *FOOL* TO VENTURE SO DEEP INTO THE *NEGATIVE ZONE!*
SPEAK, STRANGER! SPEAK, SO I KNOW THE NAME OF THE BEING I AM RETURNING BACK TO THE GODS!
CH CHUKT
MY... NAME?
I... I DON'T *REMEMBER.*
TO BE CONTINUED...

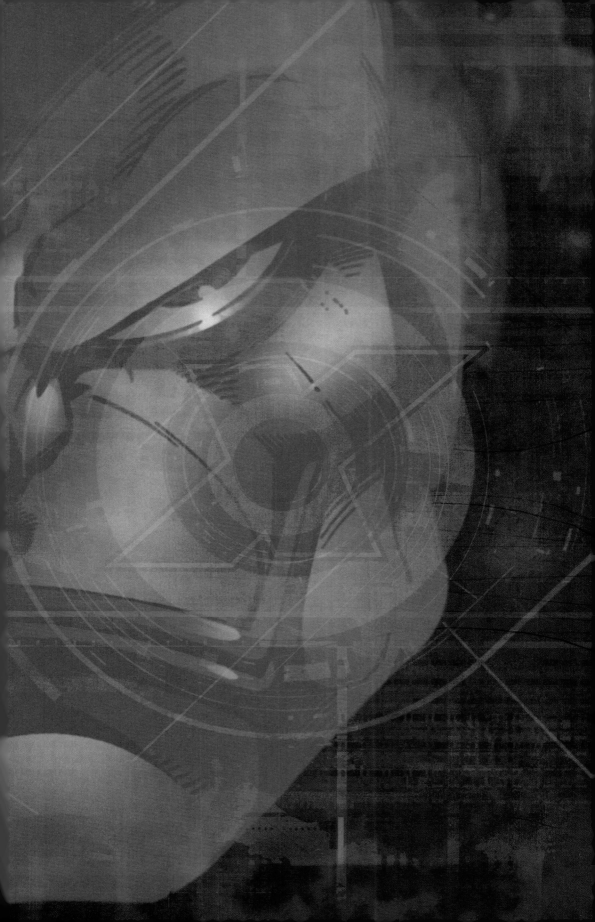

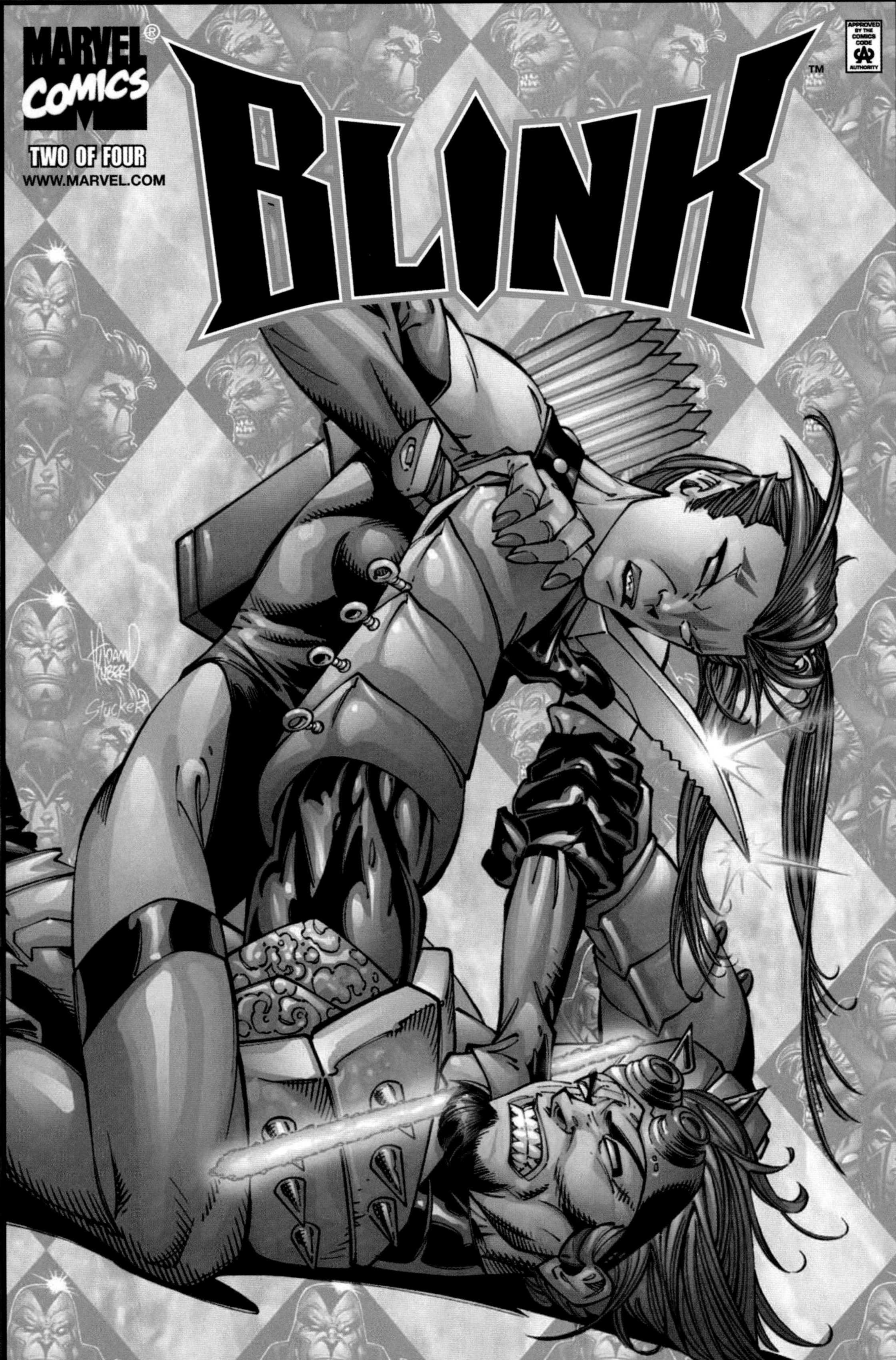
MARVEL COMICS
BLINK
TWO OF FOUR
WWW.MARVEL.COM
APPROVED BY THE COMICS CODE AUTHORITY

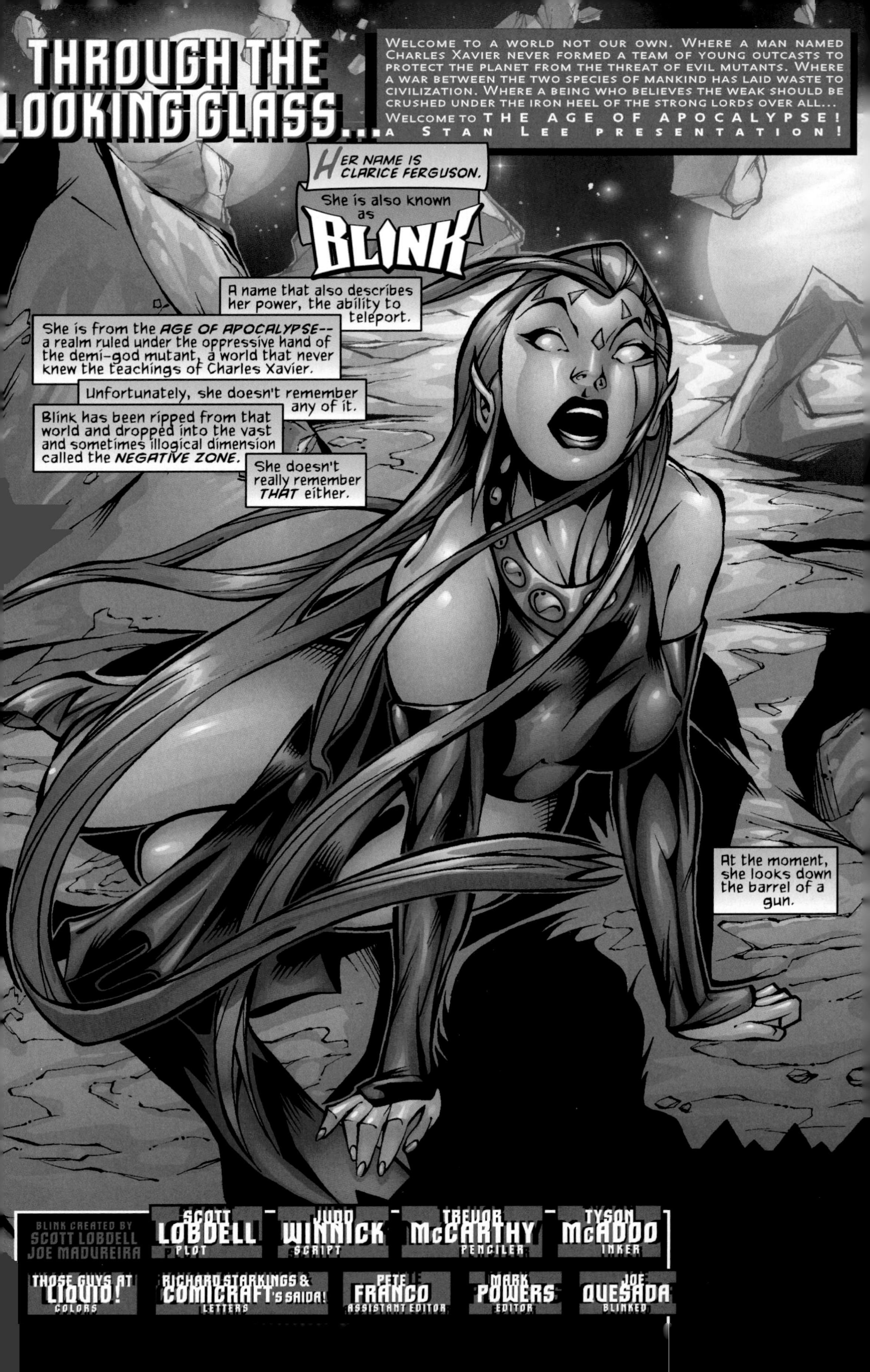
THROUGH THE LOOKING GLASS...
WELCOME TO A WORLD NOT OUR OWN. WHERE A MAN NAMED CHARLES XAVIER NEVER FORMED A TEAM OF YOUNG OUTCASTS TO PROTECT THE PLANET FROM THE THREAT OF EVIL MUTANTS. WHERE A WAR BETWEEN THE TWO SPECIES OF MANKIND HAS LAID WASTE TO CIVILIZATION. WHERE A BEING WHO BELIEVES THE WEAK SHOULD BE CRUSHED UNDER THE IRON HEEL OF THE STRONG LORDS OVER ALL... WELCOME TO THE AGE OF APOCALYPSE! A STAN LEE PRESENTATION!
HER NAME IS CLARICE FERGUSON.
She is also known as BLINK
A name that also describes her power, the ability to teleport.
She is from the AGE OF APOCALYPSE-- a realm ruled under the oppressive hand of the demi-god mutant, a world that never knew the teachings of Charles Xavier.
Unfortunately, she doesn't remember any of it.
Blink has been ripped from that world and dropped into the vast and sometimes illogical dimension called the NEGATIVE ZONE.
She doesn't really remember THAT either.
At the moment, she looks down the barrel of a gun.
BLINK CREATED BY SCOTT LOBDELL JOE MADUREIRA
SCOTT LOBDELL PLOT
JUDD WINNICK SCRIPT
TREVOR McCARTHY PENCILER
TYSON McADOO INKER
THOSE GUYS AT LIQUID! COLORS
RICHARD STARKINGS & COMICRAFT'S SAIDA! LETTERS
PETE FRANCO ASSISTANT EDITOR
MARK POWERS EDITOR
JOE QUESADA BLINKED

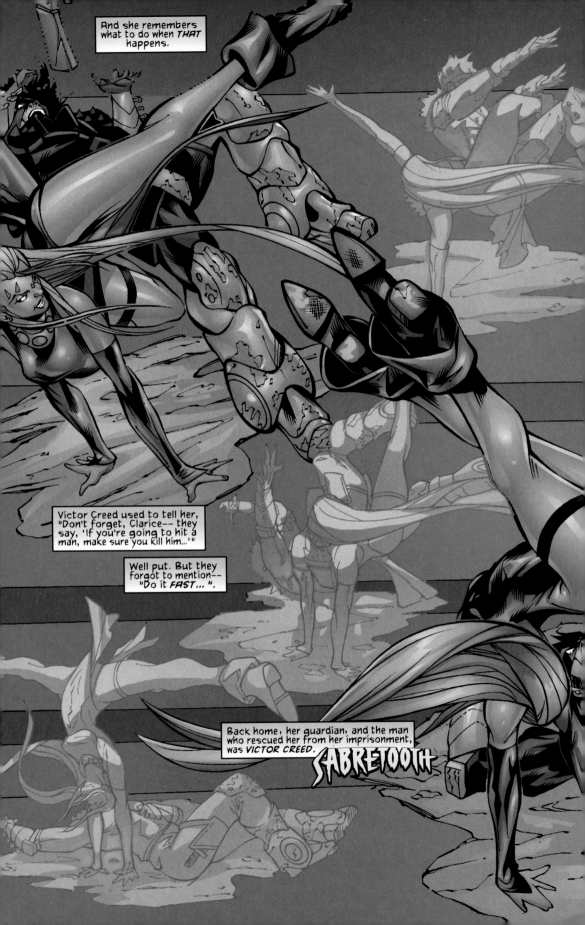

And she remembers what to do when *THAT* happens.

Victor Creed used to tell her, "Don't forget, Clarice-- they say, 'If you're going to hit a man, make sure you kill him...'"

Well put. But they forgot to mention-- "Do it *FAST*...".

Back home, her guardian, and the man who rescued her from her imprisonment, was *VICTOR CREED.* **SABRETOOTH**

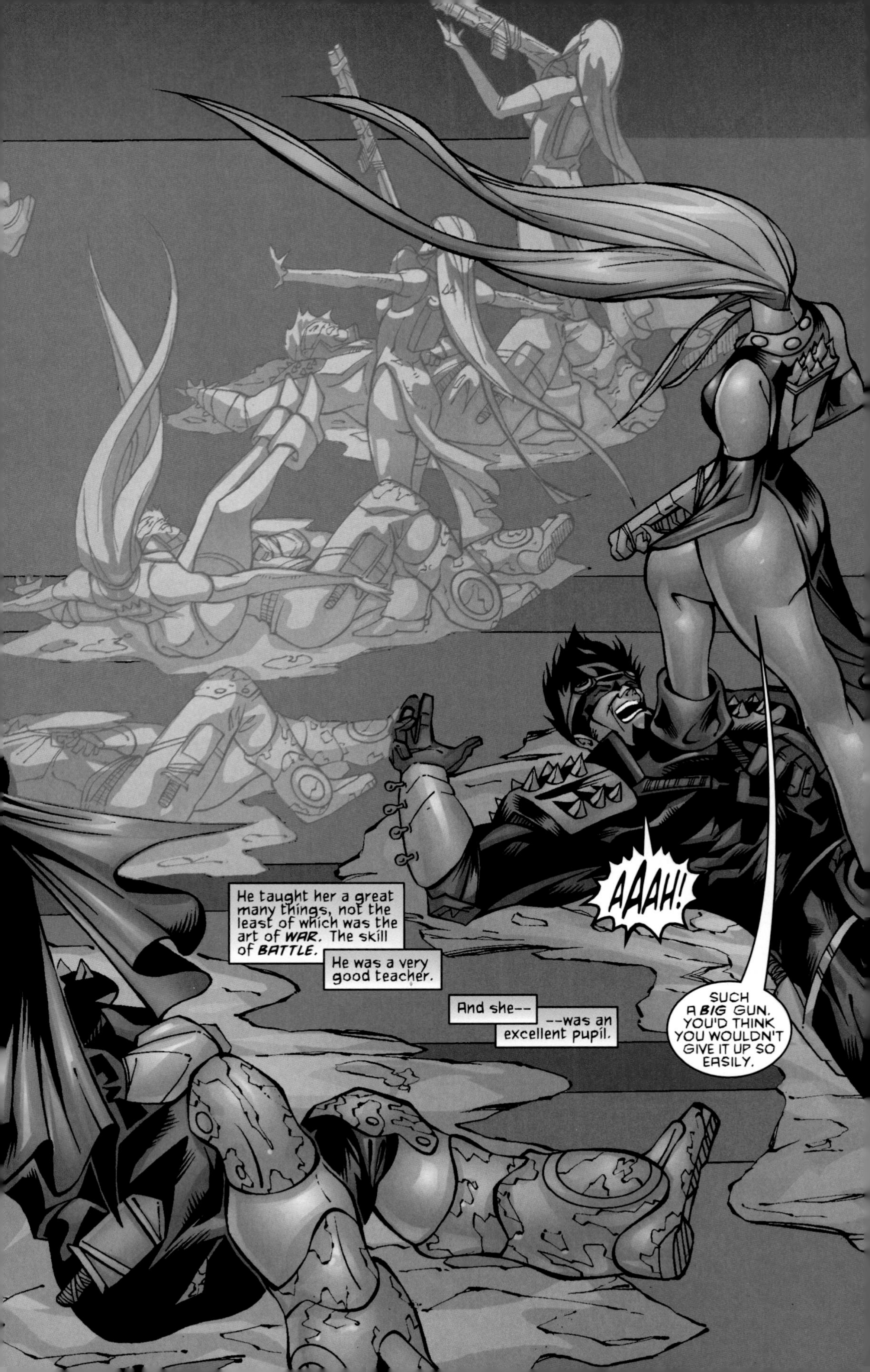

AAAH!
He taught her a great many things, not the least of which was the art of WAR. The skill of BATTLE.
He was a very good teacher.
And she--
--was an excellent pupil.
SUCH A BIG GUN. YOU'D THINK YOU WOULDN'T GIVE IT UP SO EASILY.

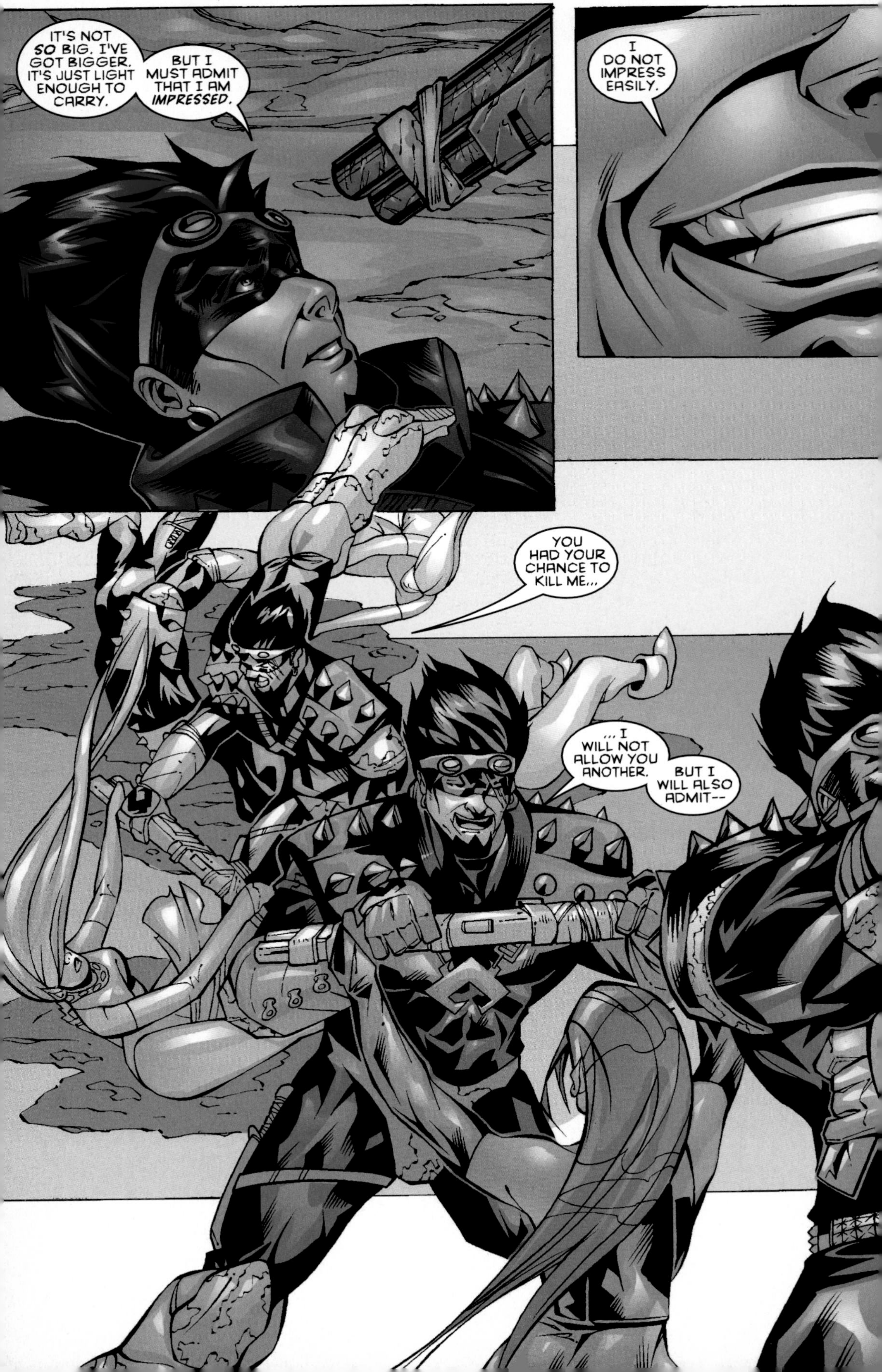
IT'S NOT SO BIG. I'VE GOT BIGGER. IT'S JUST LIGHT ENOUGH TO CARRY.
BUT I MUST ADMIT THAT I AM IMPRESSED.
I DO NOT IMPRESS EASILY.
YOU HAD YOUR CHANCE TO KILL ME...
...I WILL NOT ALLOW YOU ANOTHER.
BUT I WILL ALSO ADMIT--

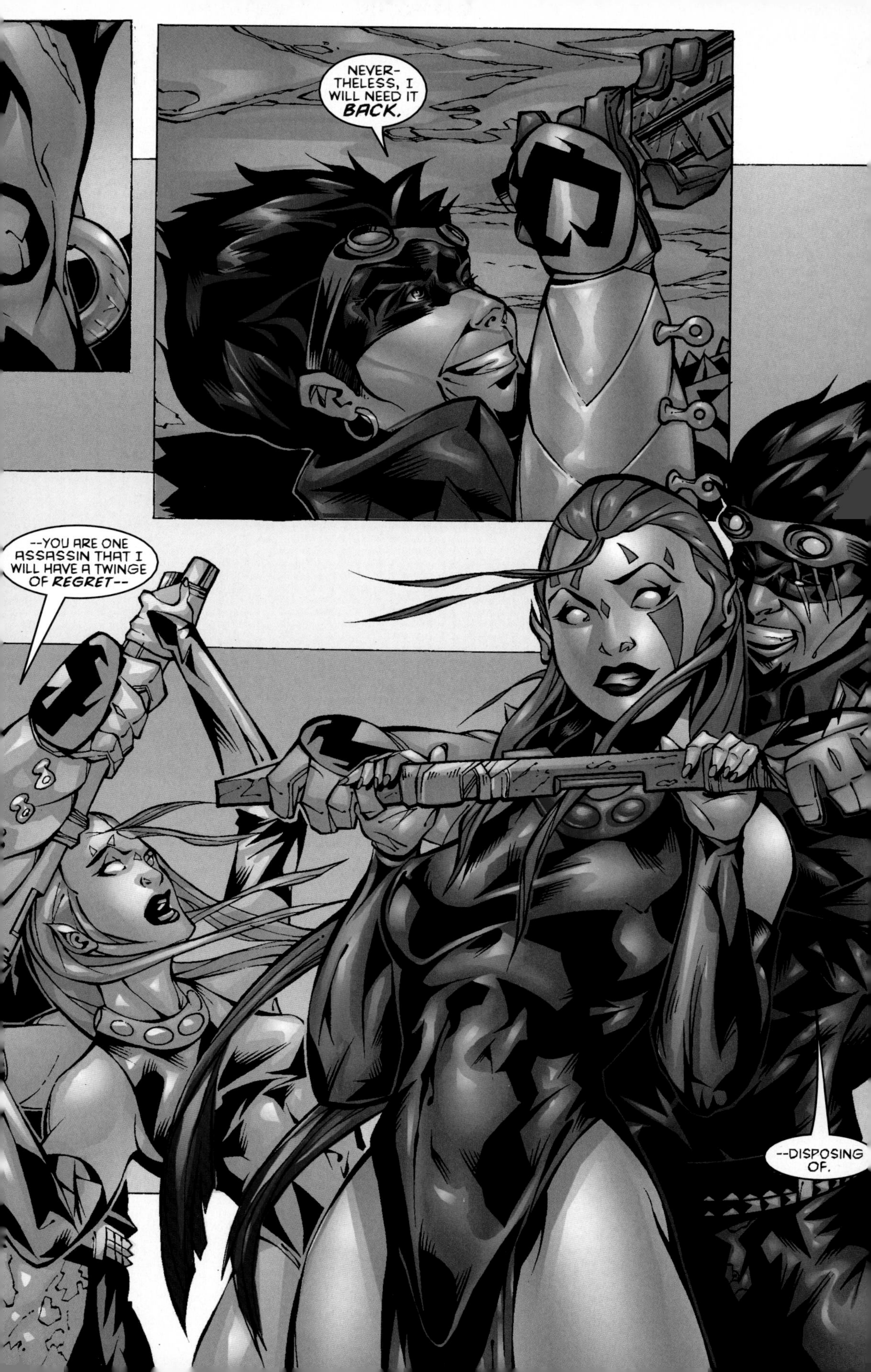
NEVER-THELESS, I WILL NEED IT BACK.
--YOU ARE ONE ASSASSIN THAT I WILL HAVE A TWINGE OF REGRET--
--DISPOSING OF.

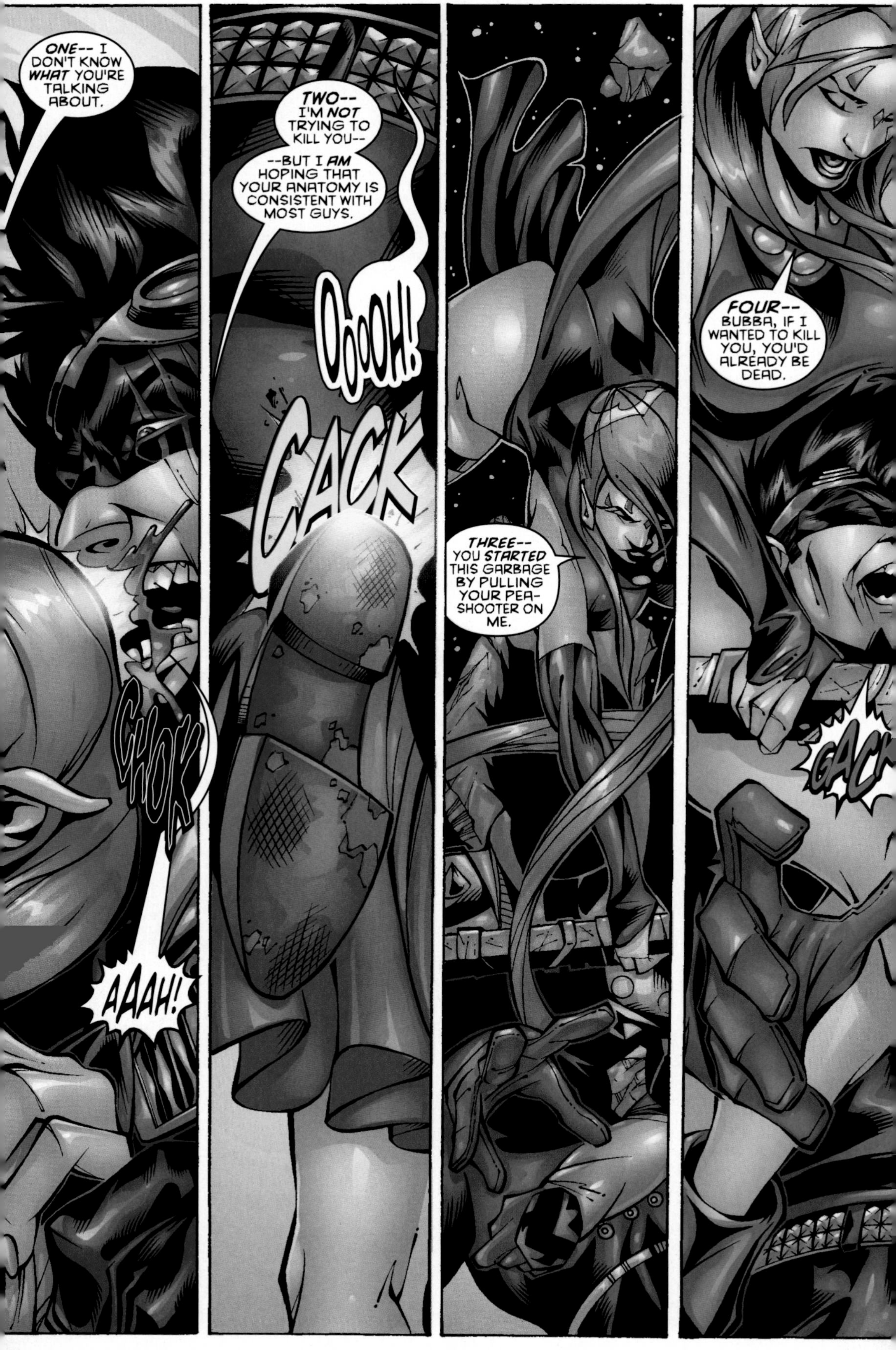
ONE-- I DON'T KNOW WHAT YOU'RE TALKING ABOUT.
CHOK
AAAH!
TWO-- I'M NOT TRYING TO KILL YOU--
--BUT I AM HOPING THAT YOUR ANATOMY IS CONSISTENT WITH MOST GUYS.
OOOOH!
CACK
THREE-- YOU STARTED THIS GARBAGE BY PULLING YOUR PEA-SHOOTER ON ME.
FOUR-- BUBBA, IF I WANTED TO KILL YOU, YOU'D ALREADY BE DEAD.
GACK

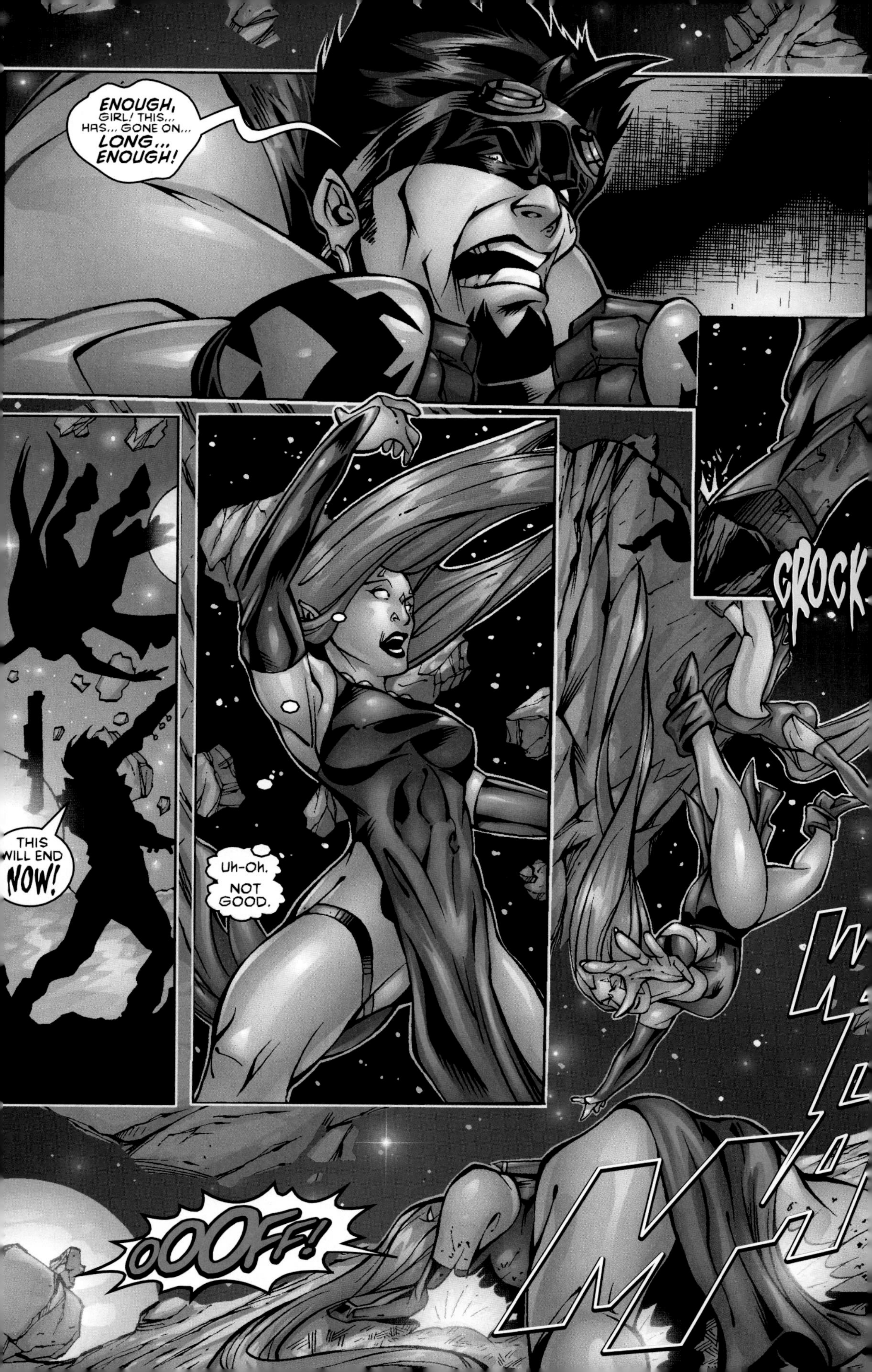
ENOUGH, GIRL! THIS... HAS... GONE ON... LONG... ENOUGH!
CROCK
THIS WILL END NOW!
Uh-Oh. NOT GOOD.
OOOFF!

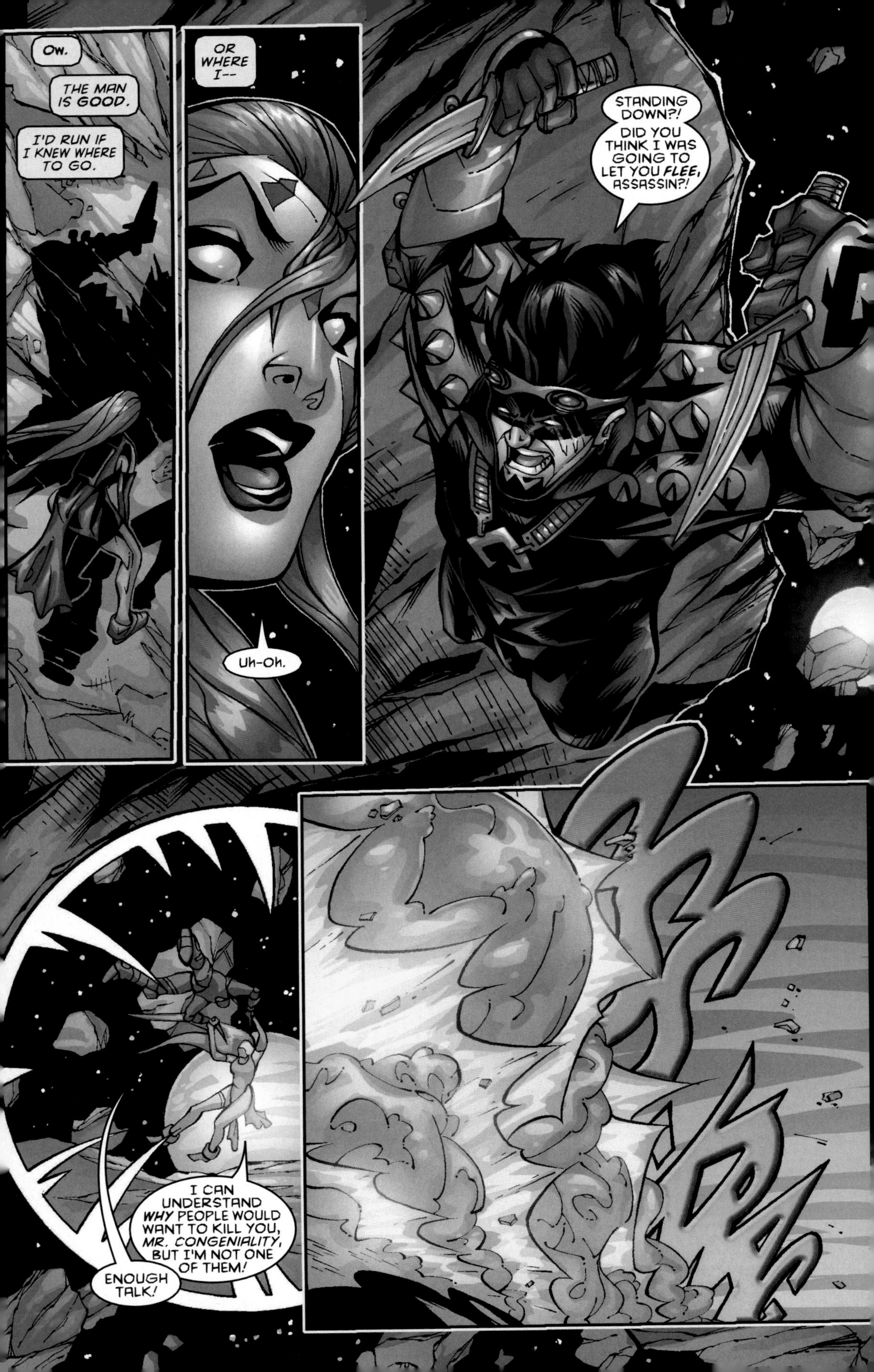
Ow.
THE MAN IS GOOD.
I'D RUN IF I KNEW WHERE TO GO.
OR WHERE I--
Uh-Oh.
STANDING DOWN?! DID YOU THINK I WAS GOING TO LET YOU FLEE, ASSASSIN?!
I CAN UNDERSTAND WHY PEOPLE WOULD WANT TO KILL YOU, MR. CONGENIALITY, BUT I'M NOT ONE OF THEM!
ENOUGH TALK!

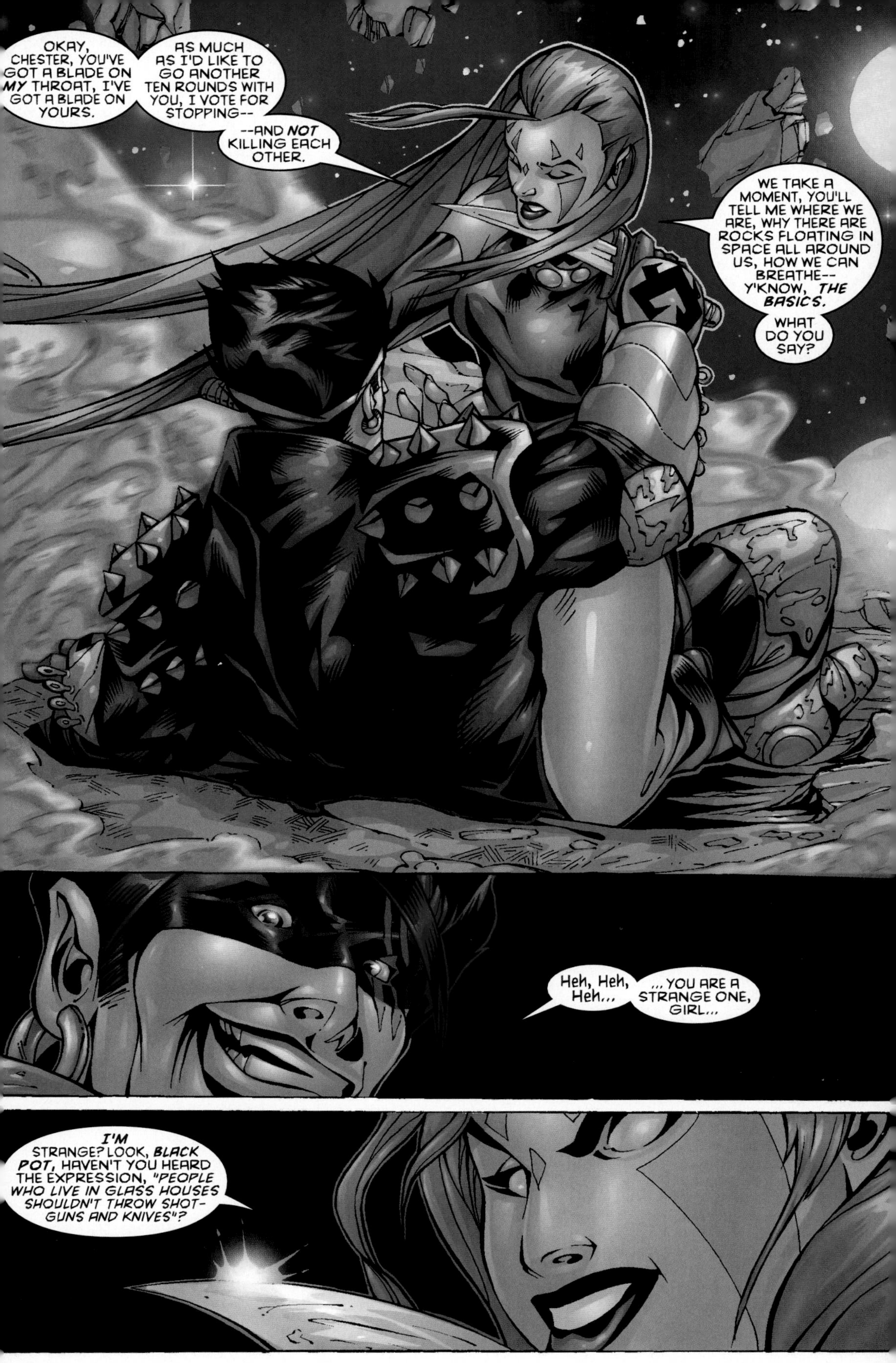
OKAY, CHESTER, YOU'VE GOT A BLADE ON MY THROAT, I'VE GOT A BLADE ON YOURS.
AS MUCH AS I'D LIKE TO GO ANOTHER TEN ROUNDS WITH YOU, I VOTE FOR STOPPING--
--AND NOT KILLING EACH OTHER.
WE TAKE A MOMENT, YOU'LL TELL ME WHERE WE ARE, WHY THERE ARE ROCKS FLOATING IN SPACE ALL AROUND US, HOW WE CAN BREATHE-- Y'KNOW, THE BASICS.
WHAT DO YOU SAY?
Heh, Heh, Heh...
...YOU ARE A STRANGE ONE, GIRL...
I'M STRANGE? LOOK, BLACK POT, HAVEN'T YOU HEARD THE EXPRESSION, "PEOPLE WHO LIVE IN GLASS HOUSES SHOULDN'T THROW SHOT-GUNS AND KNIVES"?

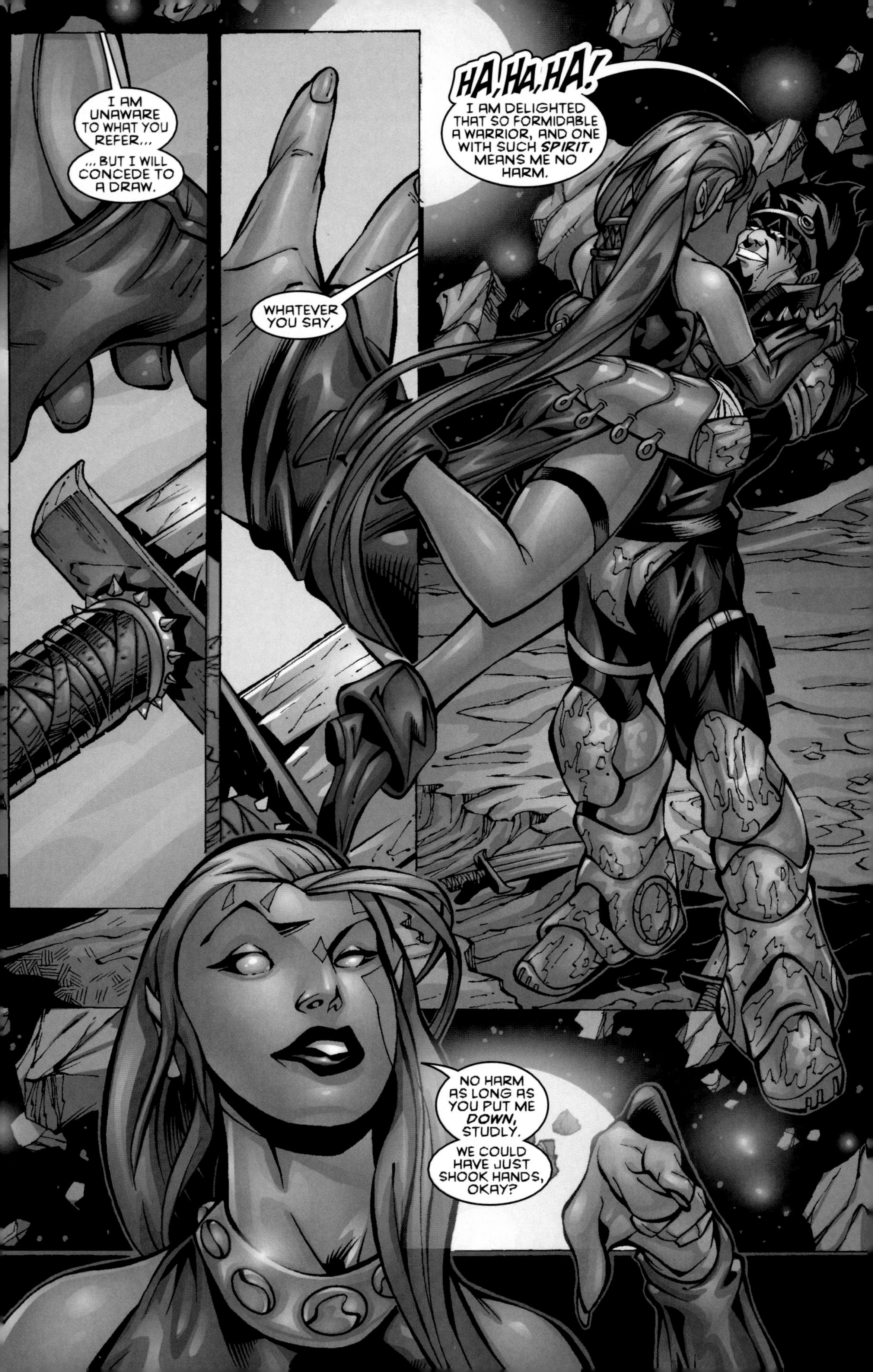
I AM UNAWARE TO WHAT YOU REFER...
...BUT I WILL CONCEDE TO A DRAW.
WHATEVER YOU SAY.
HA,HA,HA!
I AM DELIGHTED THAT SO FORMIDABLE A WARRIOR, AND ONE WITH SUCH SPIRIT, MEANS ME NO HARM.
NO HARM AS LONG AS YOU PUT ME DOWN, STUDLY.
WE COULD HAVE JUST SHOOK HANDS, OKAY?

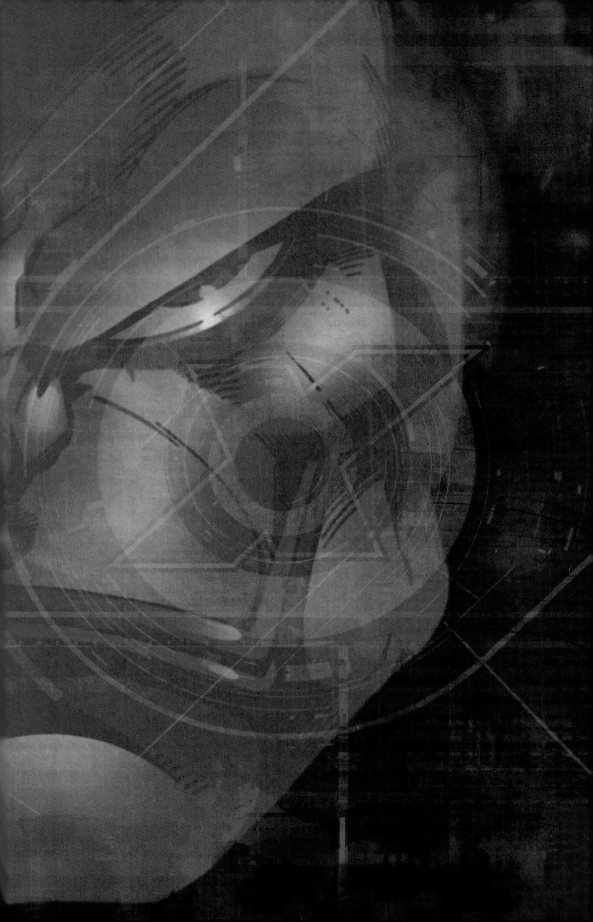

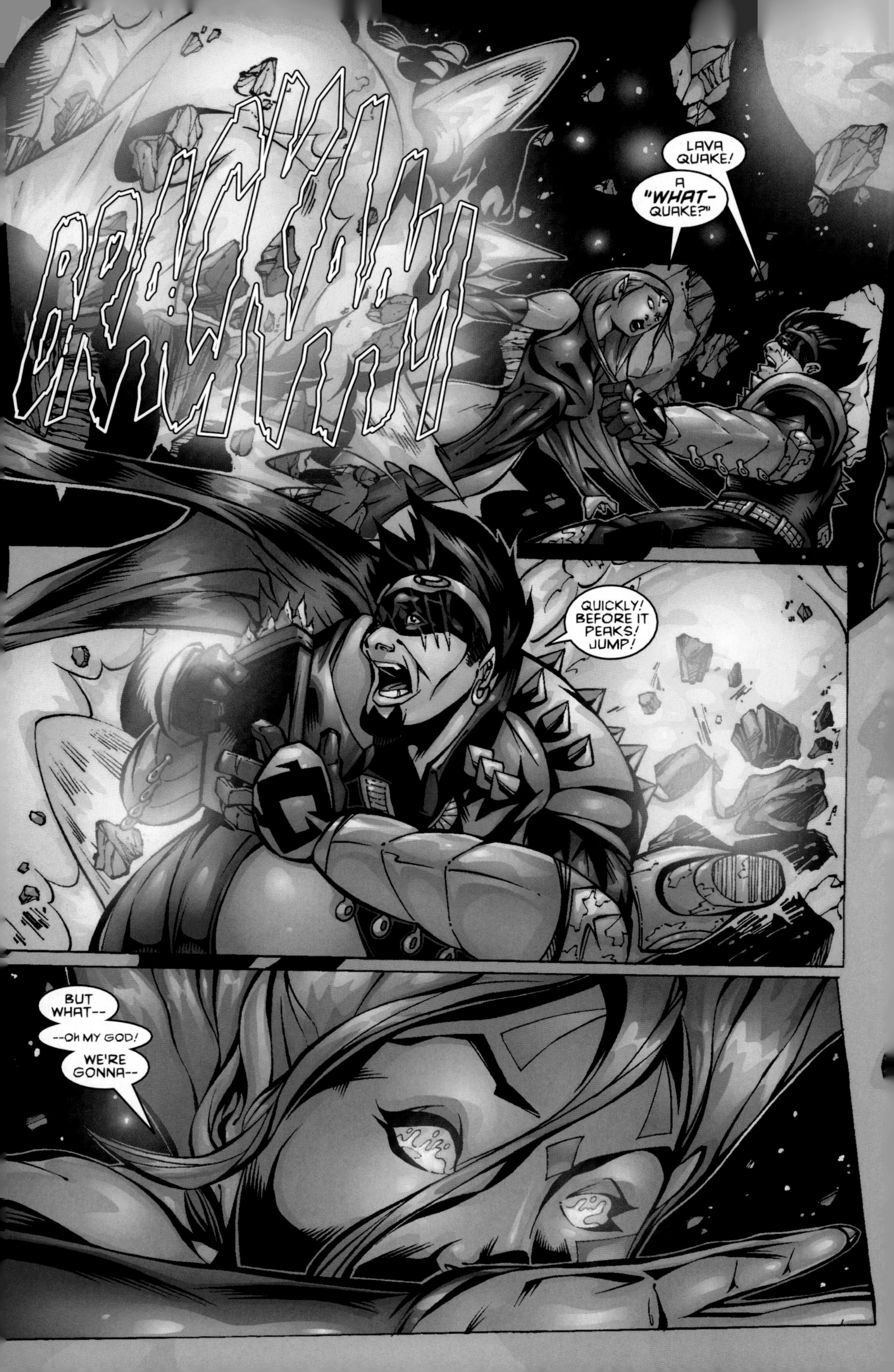
LAVA QUAKE!
A "WHAT-QUAKE?"
QUICKLY! BEFORE IT PEAKS! JUMP!
BUT WHAT--
--Oh MY GOD!
WE'RE GONNA--

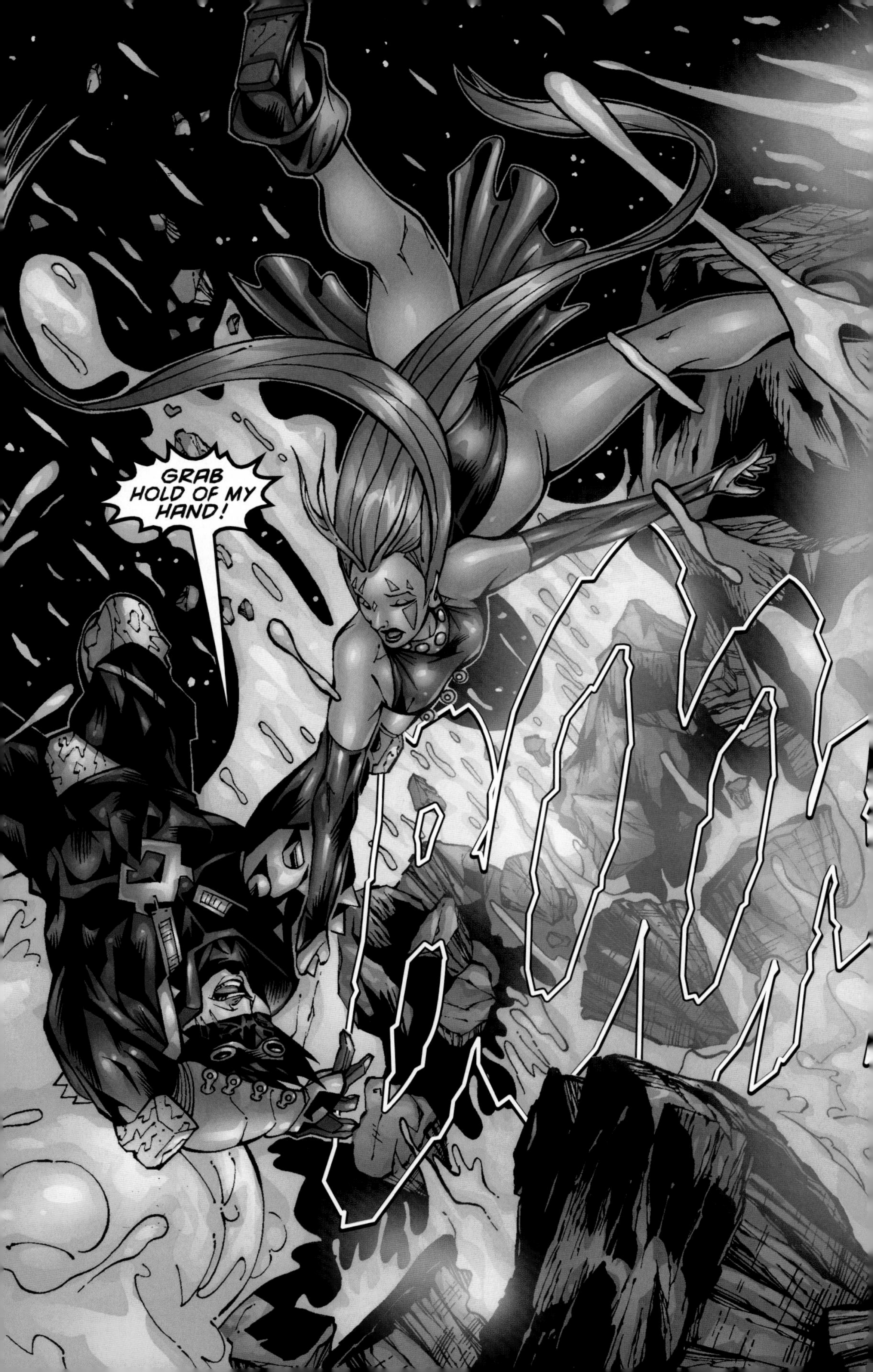
GRAB HOLD OF MY HAND!

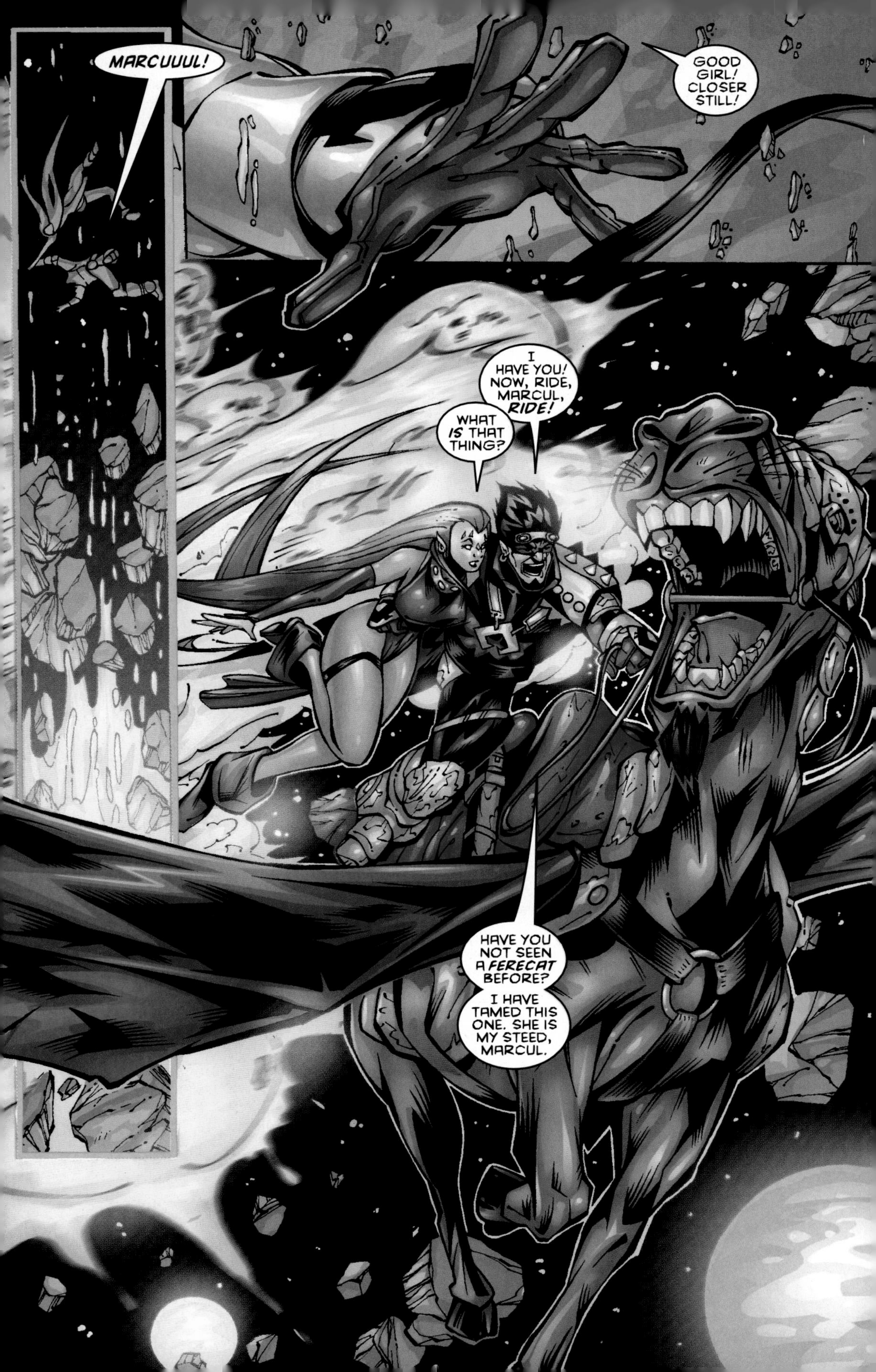
MARCUUUL!
GOOD GIRL! CLOSER STILL!
I HAVE YOU! NOW, RIDE, MARCUL, RIDE!
WHAT IS THAT THING?
HAVE YOU NOT SEEN A FERECAT BEFORE?
I HAVE TAMED THIS ONE. SHE IS MY STEED, MARCUL.

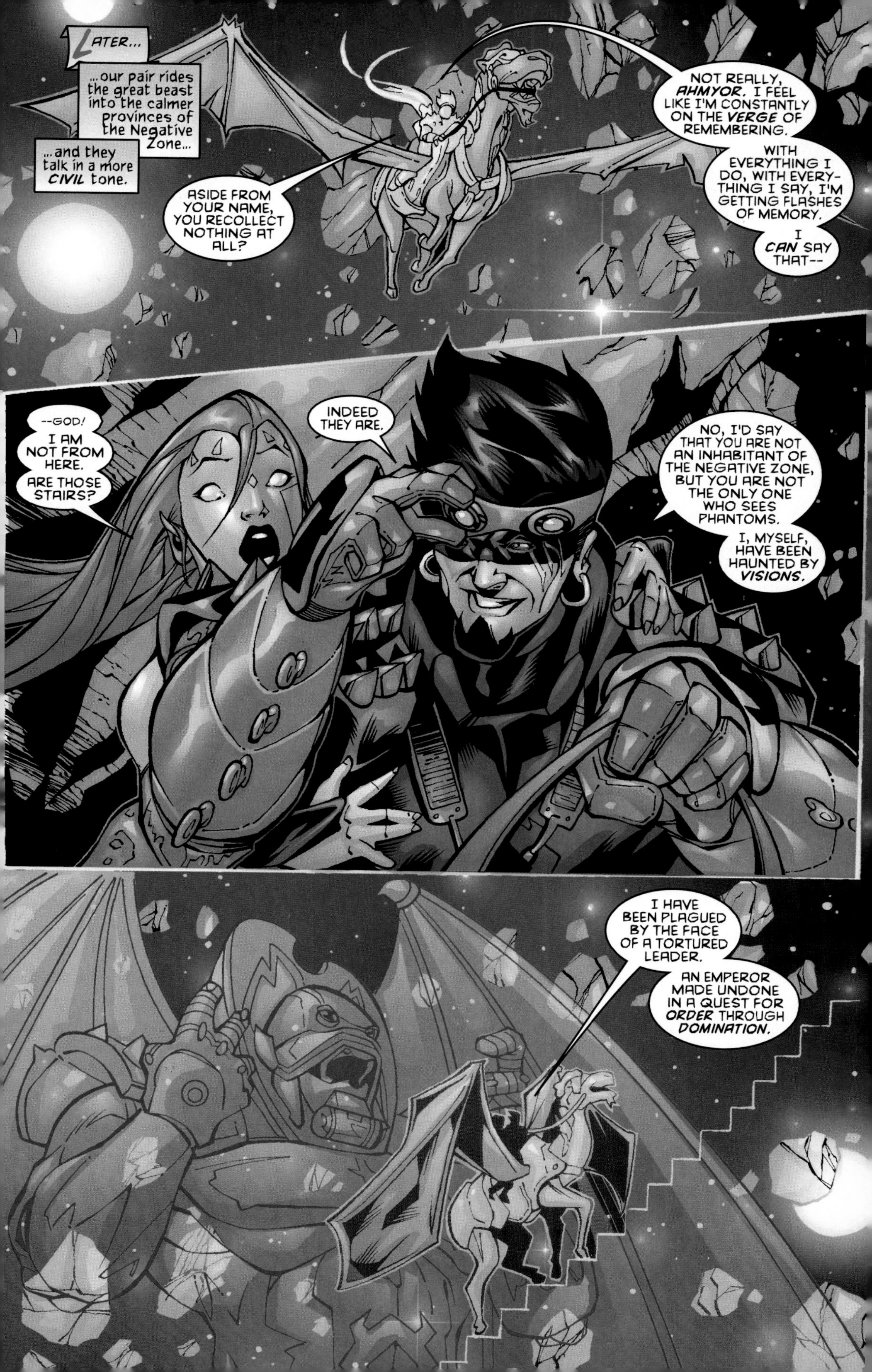
LATER...
...our pair rides the great beast into the calmer provinces of the Negative Zone...
...and they talk in a more CIVIL tone.
ASIDE FROM YOUR NAME, YOU RECOLLECT NOTHING AT ALL?
NOT REALLY, AHMYOR. I FEEL LIKE I'M CONSTANTLY ON THE VERGE OF REMEMBERING.
WITH EVERYTHING I DO, WITH EVERYTHING I SAY, I'M GETTING FLASHES OF MEMORY.
I CAN SAY THAT--
--GOD! I AM NOT FROM HERE.
ARE THOSE STAIRS?
INDEED THEY ARE.
NO, I'D SAY THAT YOU ARE NOT AN INHABITANT OF THE NEGATIVE ZONE, BUT YOU ARE NOT THE ONLY ONE WHO SEES PHANTOMS.
I, MYSELF, HAVE BEEN HAUNTED BY VISIONS.
I HAVE BEEN PLAGUED BY THE FACE OF A TORTURED LEADER.
AN EMPEROR MADE UNDONE IN A QUEST FOR ORDER THROUGH DOMINATION.

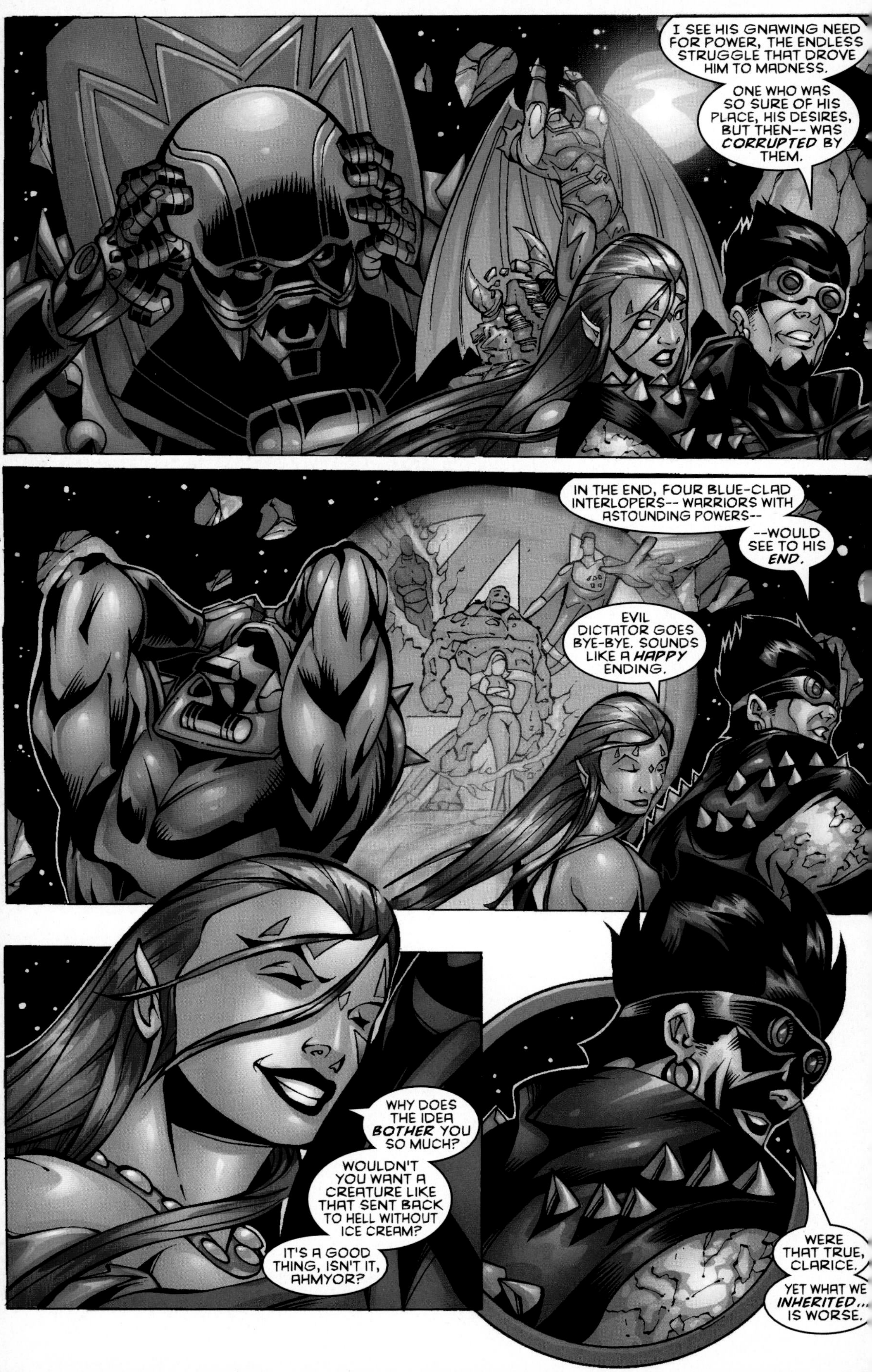

I SEE HIS GNAWING NEED FOR POWER, THE ENDLESS STRUGGLE THAT DROVE HIM TO MADNESS.
ONE WHO WAS SO SURE OF HIS PLACE, HIS DESIRES, BUT THEN-- WAS *CORRUPTED* BY THEM.
IN THE END, FOUR BLUE-CLAD INTERLOPERS-- WARRIORS WITH ASTOUNDING POWERS--
--WOULD SEE TO HIS *END.*
EVIL DICTATOR GOES BYE-BYE. SOUNDS LIKE A *HAPPY* ENDING.
WHY DOES THE IDEA *BOTHER* YOU SO MUCH?
WOULDN'T YOU WANT A CREATURE LIKE THAT SENT BACK TO HELL WITHOUT ICE CREAM?
IT'S A GOOD THING, ISN'T IT, AHMYOR?
WERE THAT TRUE, CLARICE.
YET WHAT WE *INHERITED*... IS WORSE.

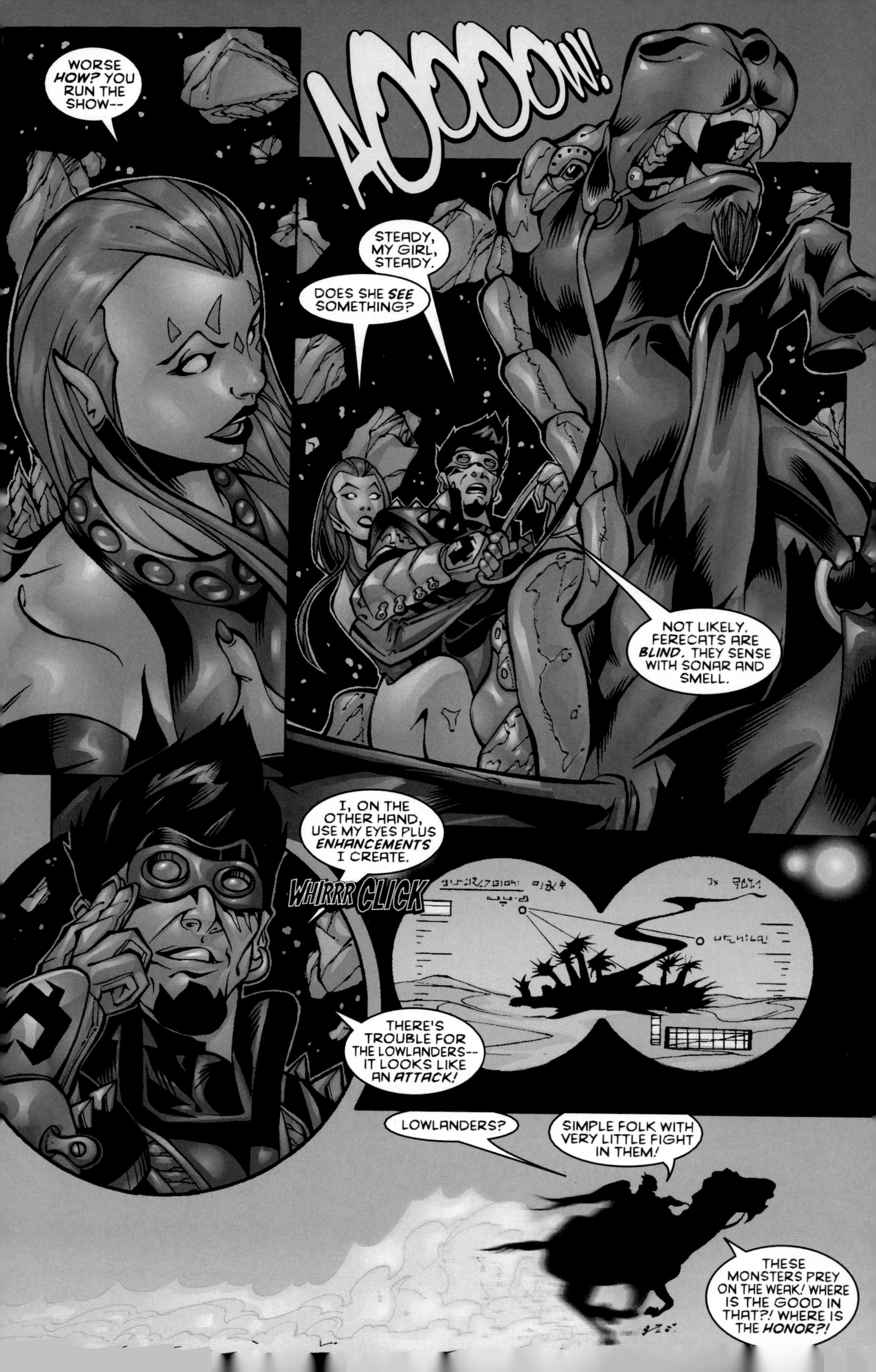
WORSE HOW? YOU RUN THE SHOW--
AOOOOW!
STEADY, MY GIRL, STEADY.
DOES SHE SEE SOMETHING?
NOT LIKELY. FERECATS ARE BLIND. THEY SENSE WITH SONAR AND SMELL.
I, ON THE OTHER HAND, USE MY EYES PLUS ENHANCEMENTS I CREATE.
WHIRRR CLICK
THERE'S TROUBLE FOR THE LOWLANDERS-- IT LOOKS LIKE AN ATTACK!
LOWLANDERS?
SIMPLE FOLK WITH VERY LITTLE FIGHT IN THEM!
THESE MONSTERS PREY ON THE WEAK! WHERE IS THE GOOD IN THAT?! WHERE IS THE HONOR?!

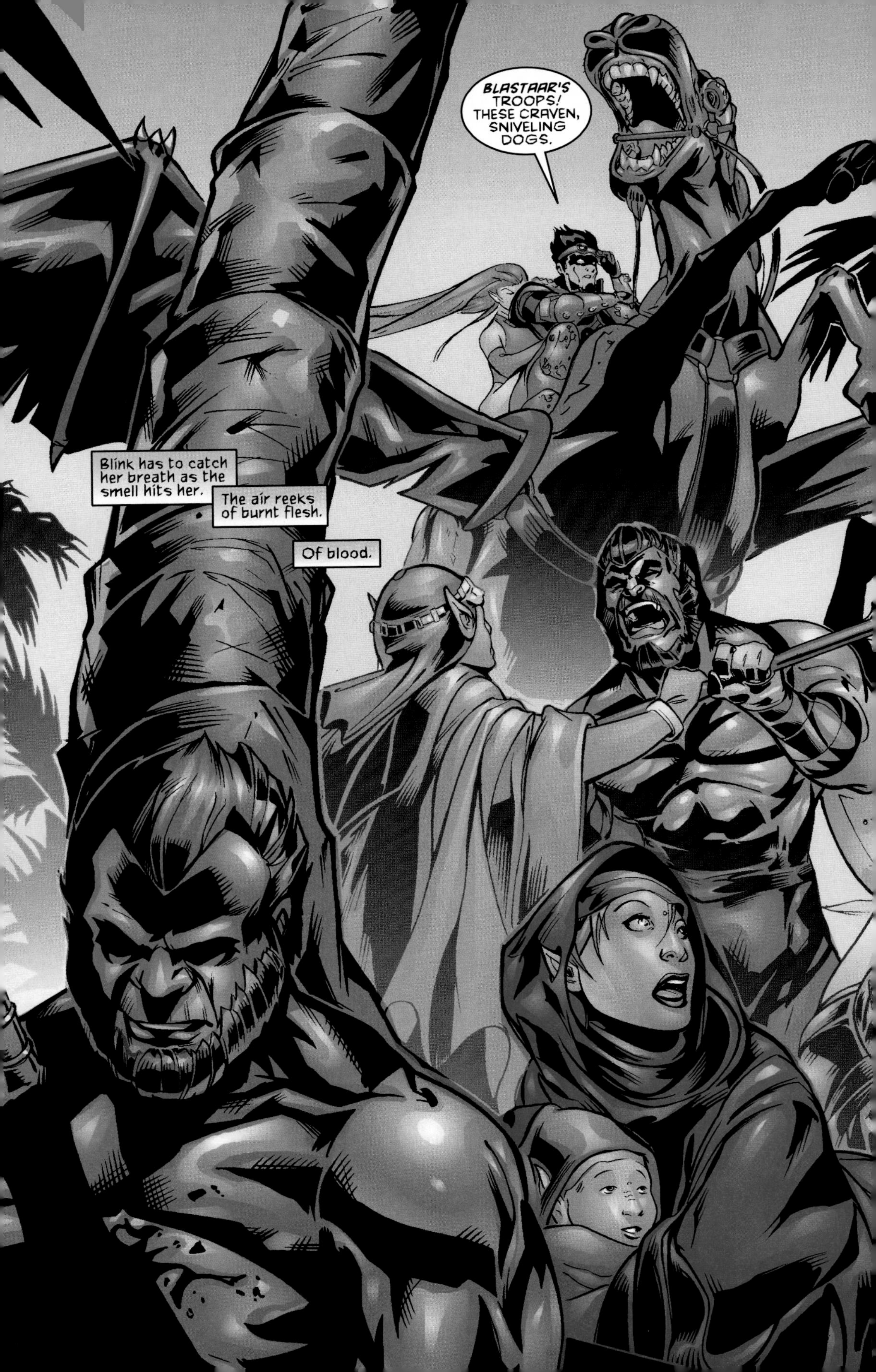

BLASTAAR'S TROOPS! THESE CRAVEN, SNIVELING DOGS.
Blink has to catch her breath as the smell hits her.
The air reeks of burnt flesh.
Of blood.

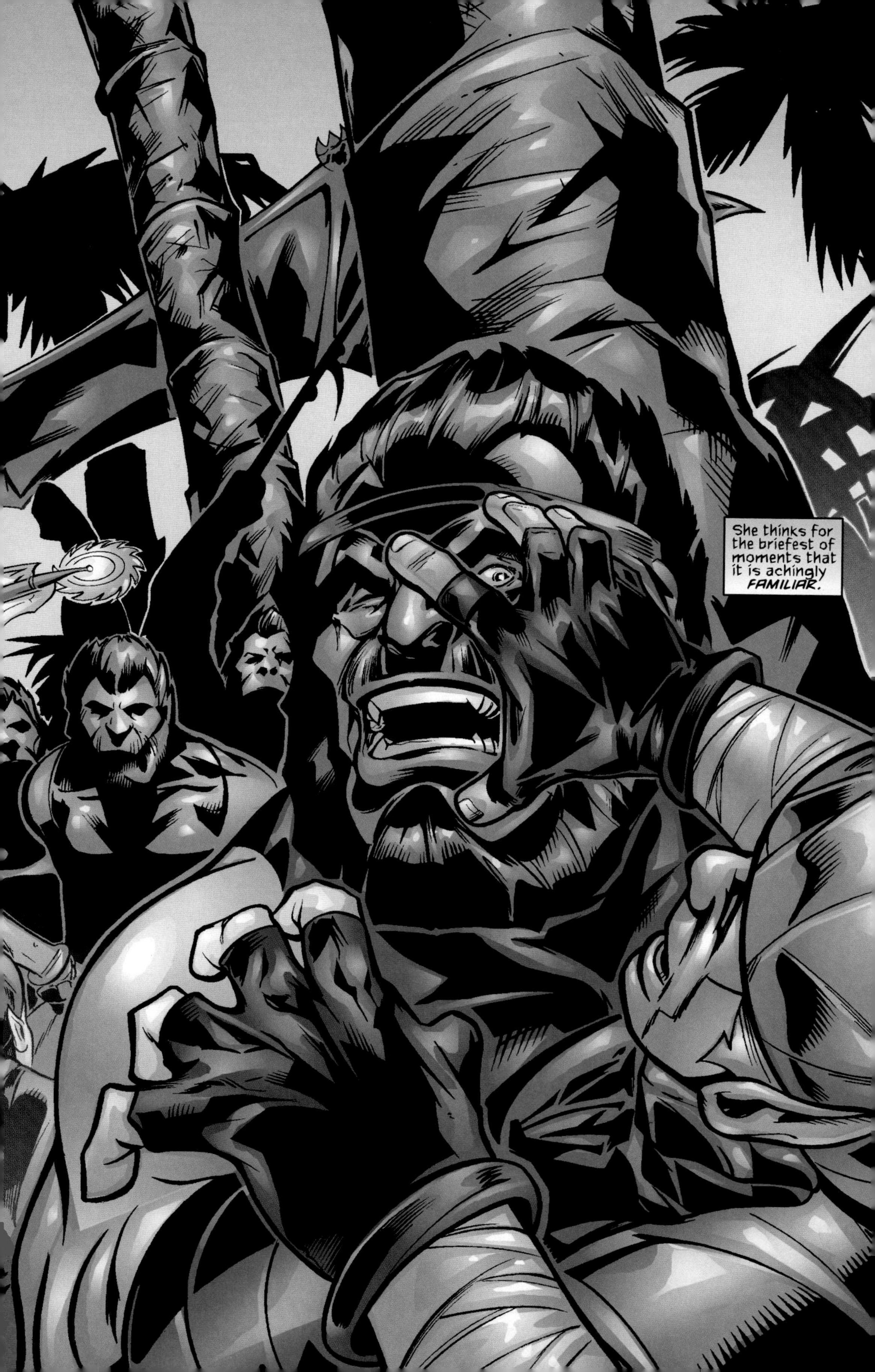
She thinks for the briefest of moments that it is achingly FAMILIAR.

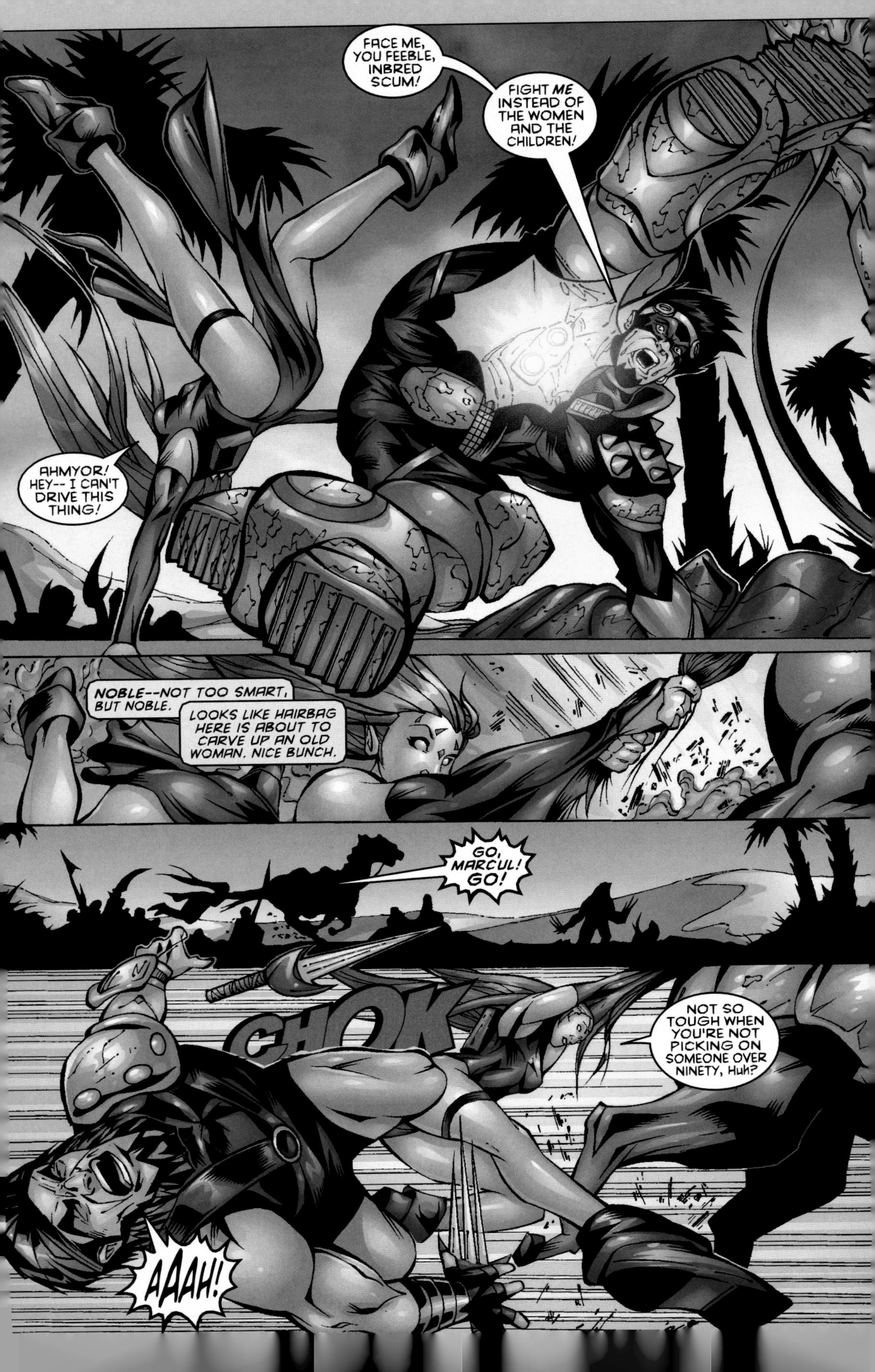
FACE ME, YOU FEEBLE, INBRED SCUM!
FIGHT ME INSTEAD OF THE WOMEN AND THE CHILDREN!
AHMYOR! HEY-- I CAN'T DRIVE THIS THING!
NOBLE--NOT TOO SMART, BUT NOBLE.
LOOKS LIKE HAIRBAG HERE IS ABOUT TO CARVE UP AN OLD WOMAN. NICE BUNCH.
GO, MARCUL! GO!
CHOK
NOT SO TOUGH WHEN YOU'RE NOT PICKING ON SOMEONE OVER NINETY, HUH?
AAAH!

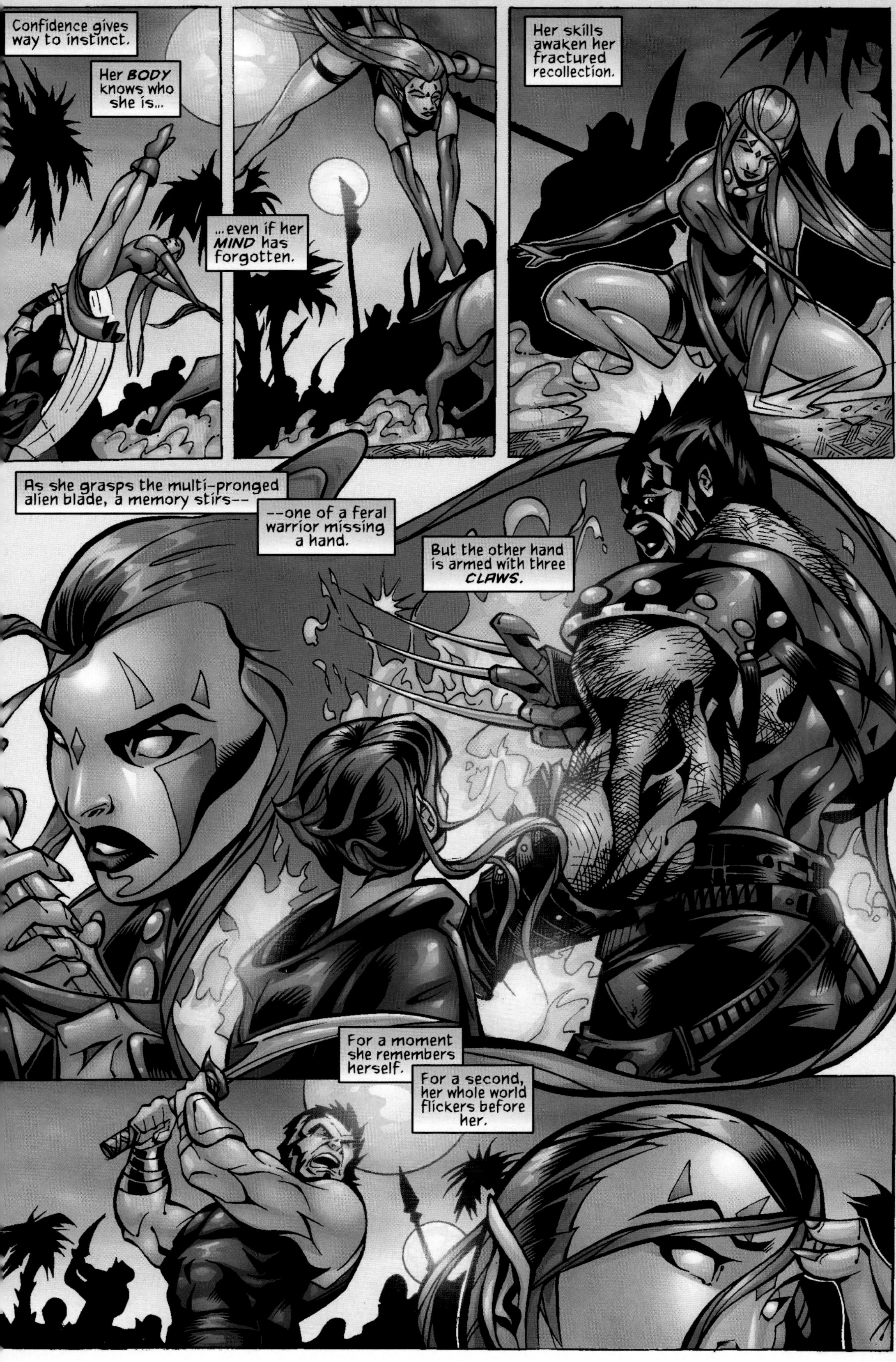

Confidence gives way to instinct.
Her BODY knows who she is...
...even if her MIND has forgotten.
Her skills awaken her fractured recollection.
As she grasps the multi-pronged alien blade, a memory stirs--
--one of a feral warrior missing a hand.
But the other hand is armed with three CLAWS.
For a moment she remembers herself.
For a second, her whole world flickers before her.

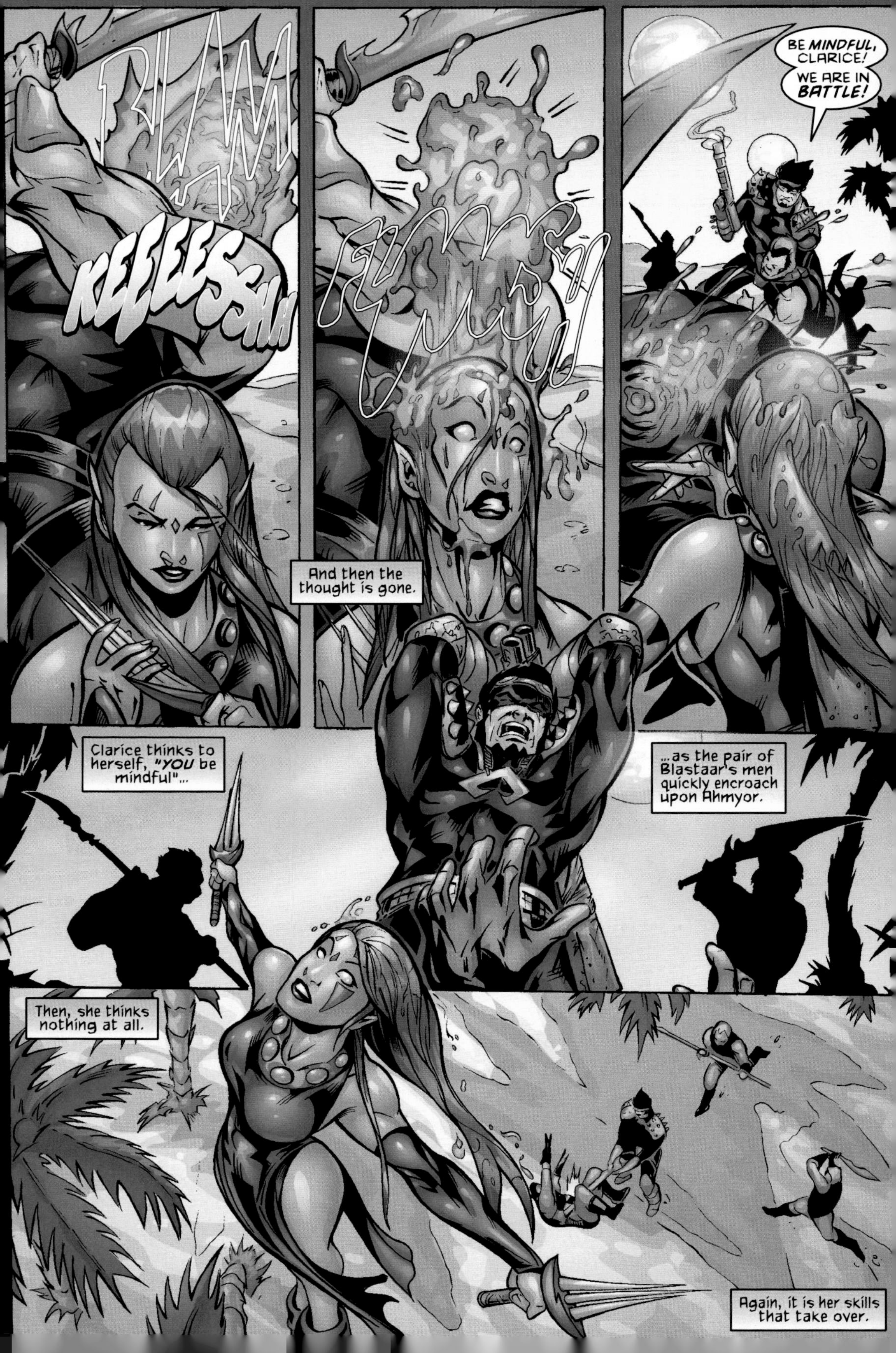

BLAM
KEEEESHH
And then the thought is gone.
BE MINDFUL, CLARICE! WE ARE IN BATTLE!
Clarice thinks to herself, "YOU be mindful"...
...as the pair of Blastaar's men quickly encroach upon Ahmyor.
Then, she thinks nothing at all.
Again, it is her skills that take over.

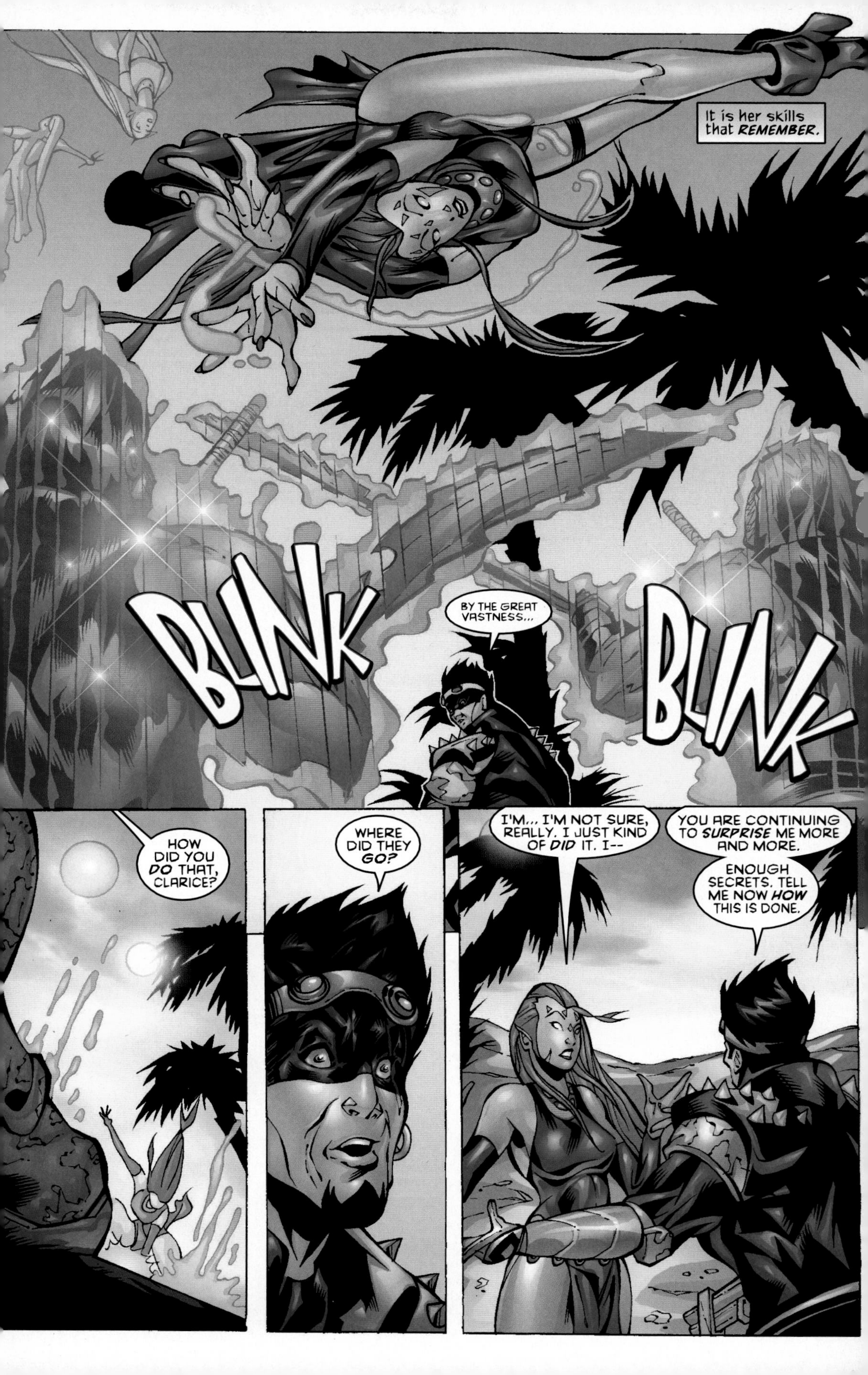
It is her skills that REMEMBER.
BLINK
BY THE GREAT VASTNESS...
BLINK
HOW DID YOU DO THAT, CLARICE?
WHERE DID THEY GO?
I'M... I'M NOT SURE, REALLY. I JUST KIND OF DID IT. I--
YOU ARE CONTINUING TO SURPRISE ME MORE AND MORE.
ENOUGH SECRETS. TELL ME NOW HOW THIS IS DONE.

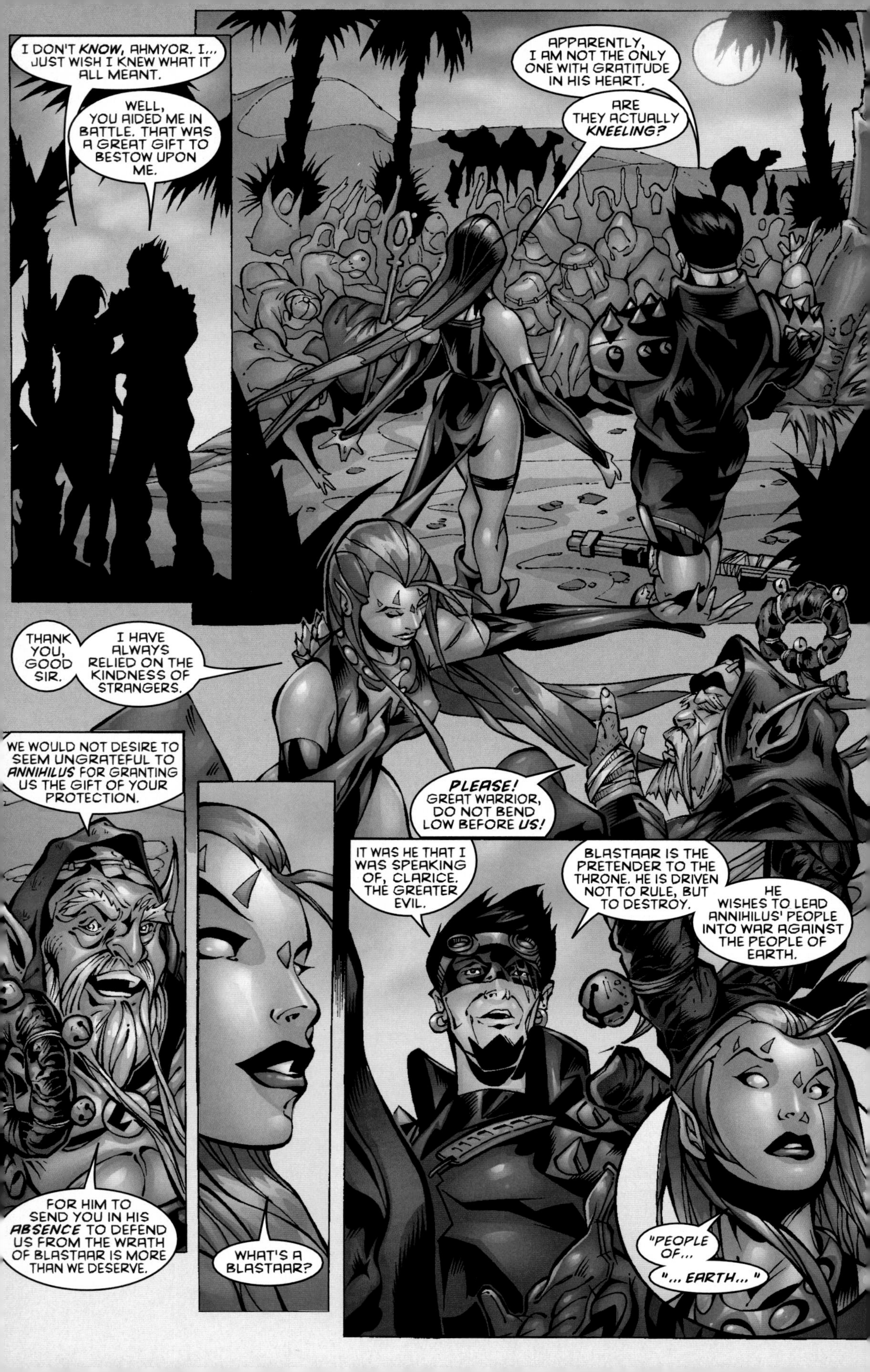

I DON'T *KNOW*, AHMYOR. I... JUST WISH I KNEW WHAT IT ALL MEANT.
WELL, YOU AIDED ME IN BATTLE. THAT WAS A GREAT GIFT TO BESTOW UPON ME.
APPARENTLY, I AM NOT THE ONLY ONE WITH GRATITUDE IN HIS HEART.
ARE THEY ACTUALLY *KNEELING?*
THANK YOU, GOOD SIR.
I HAVE ALWAYS RELIED ON THE KINDNESS OF STRANGERS.
PLEASE! GREAT WARRIOR, DO NOT BEND LOW BEFORE *US!*
WE WOULD NOT DESIRE TO SEEM UNGRATEFUL TO *ANNIHILUS* FOR GRANTING US THE GIFT OF YOUR PROTECTION.
FOR HIM TO SEND YOU IN HIS *ABSENCE* TO DEFEND US FROM THE WRATH OF BLASTAAR IS MORE THAN WE DESERVE.
WHAT'S A BLASTAAR?
IT WAS HE THAT I WAS SPEAKING OF, CLARICE. THE GREATER EVIL.
BLASTAAR IS THE PRETENDER TO THE THRONE. HE IS DRIVEN NOT TO RULE, BUT TO DESTROY.
HE WISHES TO LEAD ANNIHILUS' PEOPLE INTO WAR AGAINST THE PEOPLE OF EARTH.
"PEOPLE OF...
"... *EARTH*..."

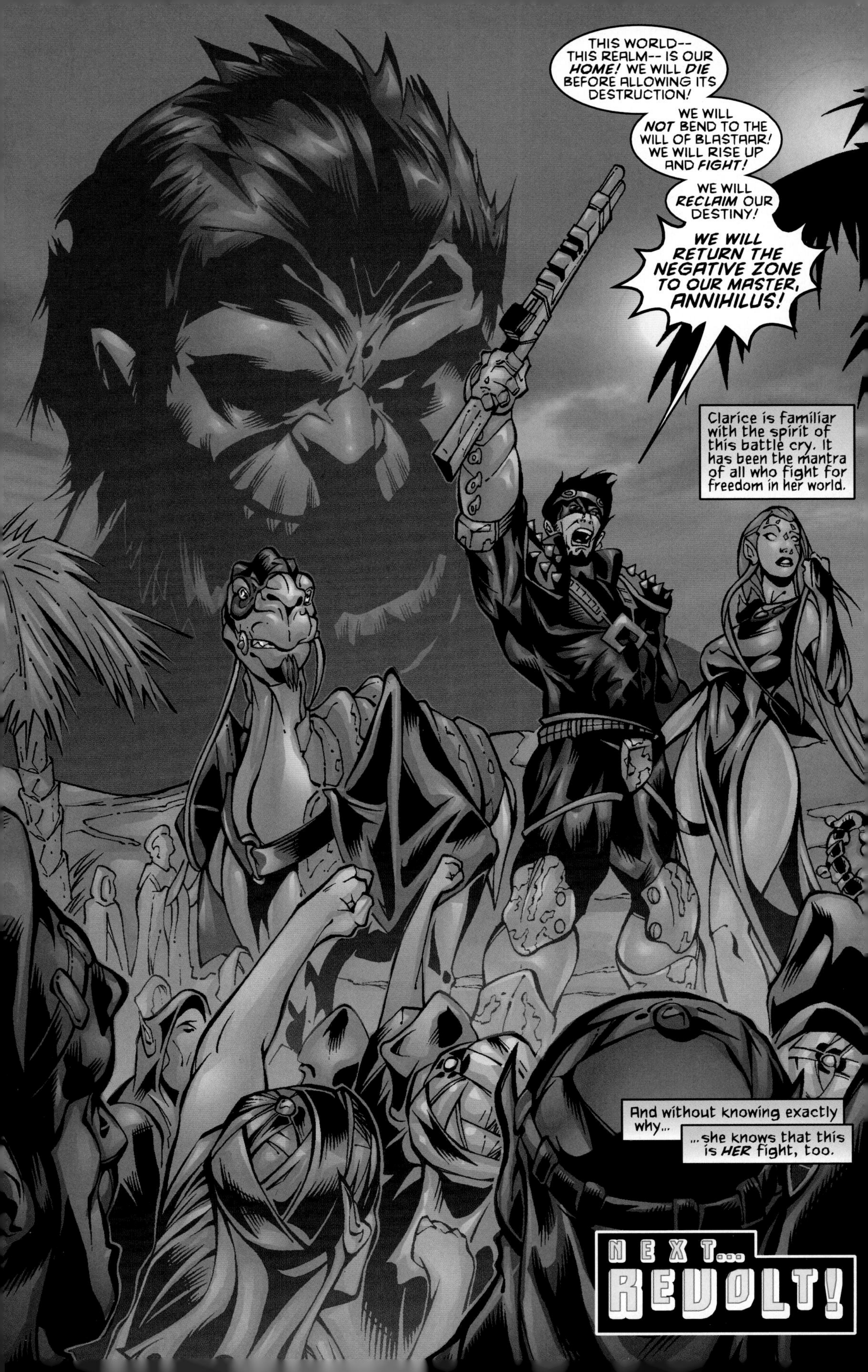
THIS WORLD-- THIS REALM-- IS OUR *HOME!* WE WILL *DIE* BEFORE ALLOWING ITS DESTRUCTION!
WE WILL *NOT* BEND TO THE WILL OF BLASTAAR! WE WILL RISE UP AND *FIGHT!*
WE WILL *RECLAIM* OUR DESTINY!
WE WILL RETURN THE NEGATIVE ZONE TO OUR MASTER, ANNIHILUS!
Clarice is familiar with the spirit of this battle cry. It has been the mantra of all who fight for freedom in her world.
And without knowing exactly why...
...she knows that this is *HER* fight, too.
NEXT... REVOLT!

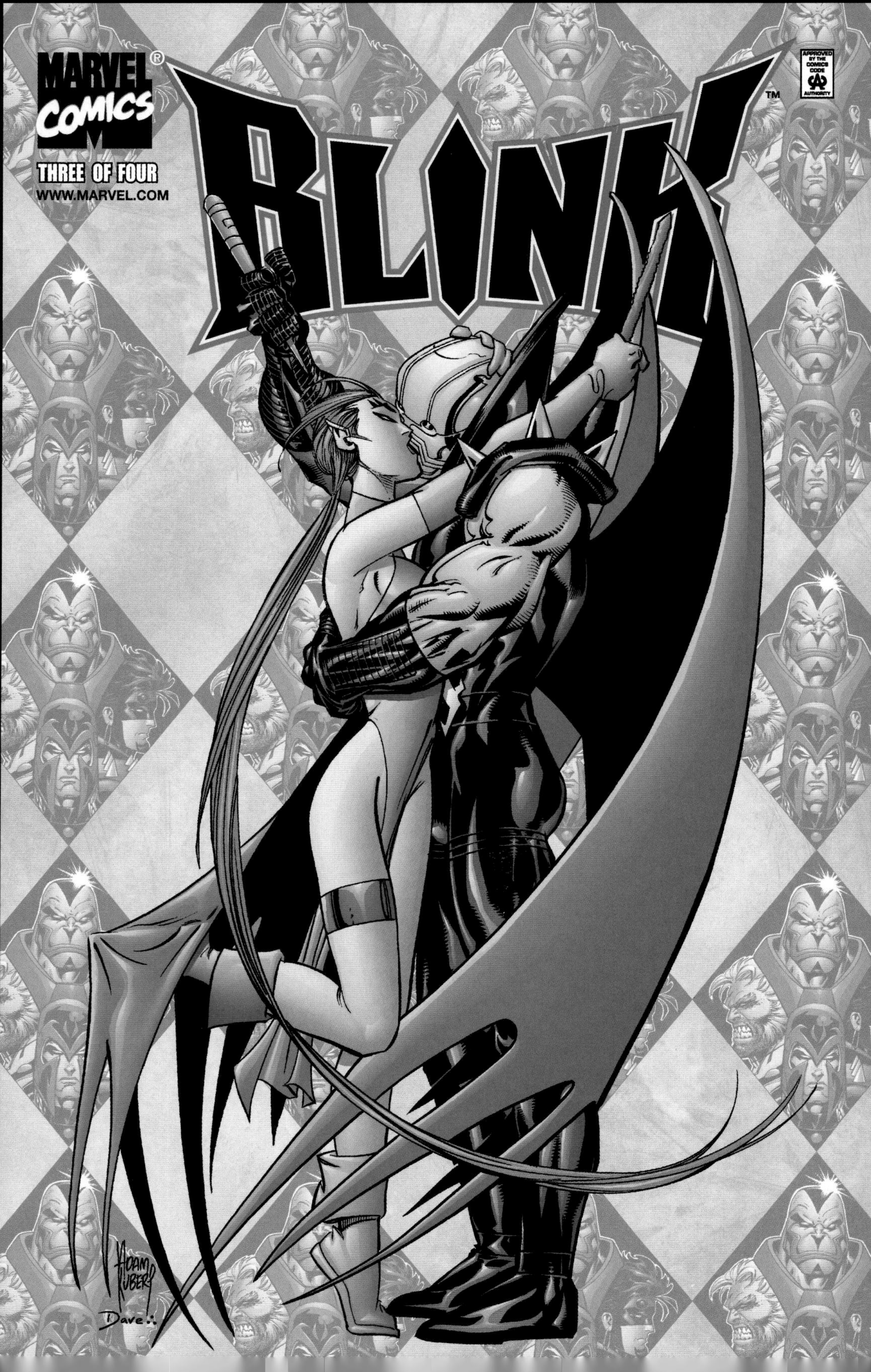
MARVEL COMICS
BLINK
THREE OF FOUR
WWW.MARVEL.COM
APPROVED BY THE COMICS CODE AUTHORITY

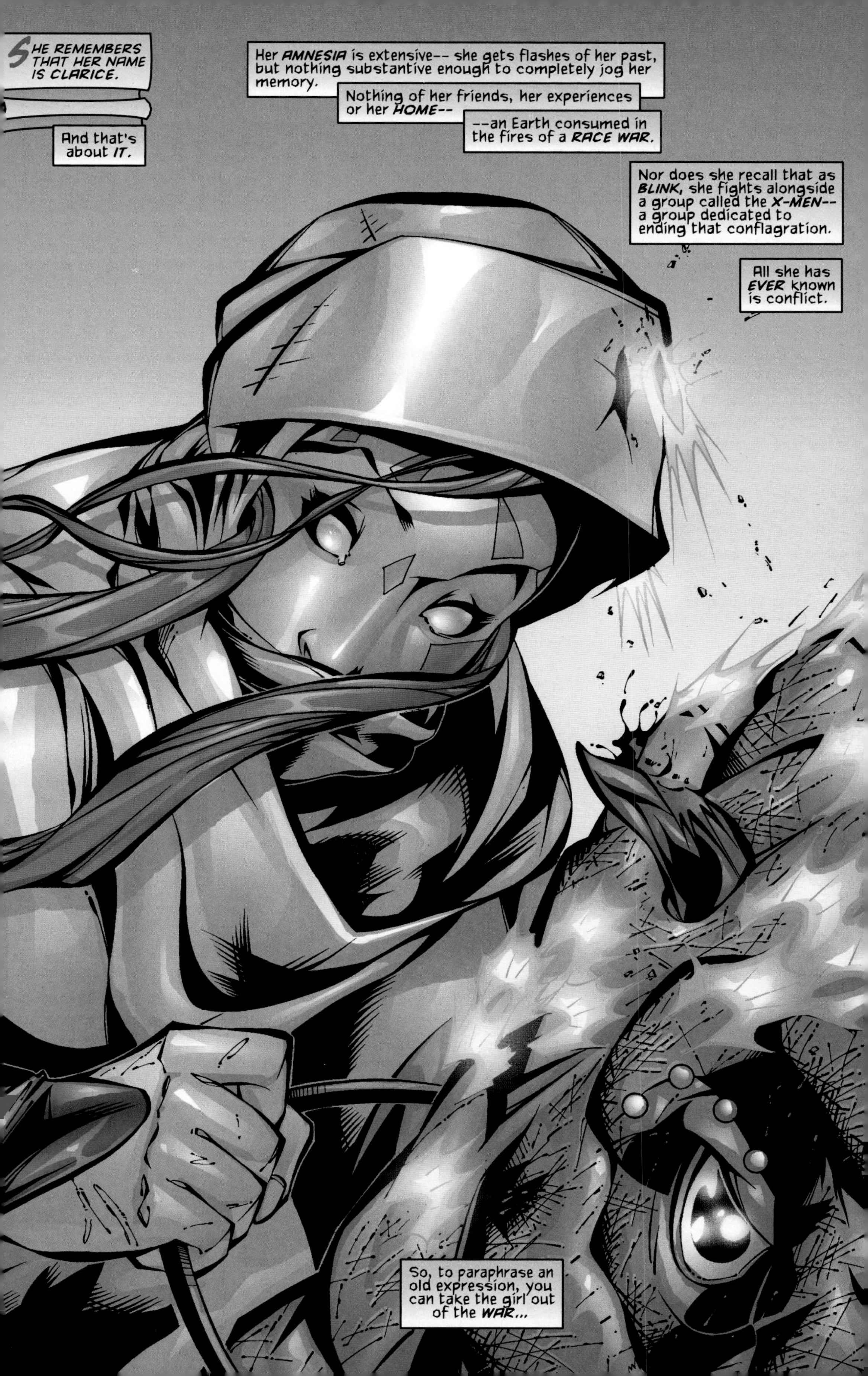
SHE REMEMBERS THAT HER NAME IS CLARICE.
And that's about IT.
Her AMNESIA is extensive-- she gets flashes of her past, but nothing substantive enough to completely jog her memory.
Nothing of her friends, her experiences or her HOME--
--an Earth consumed in the fires of a RACE WAR.
Nor does she recall that as BLINK, she fights alongside a group called the X-MEN-- a group dedicated to ending that conflagration.
All she has EVER known is conflict.
So, to paraphrase an old expression, you can take the girl out of the WAR...

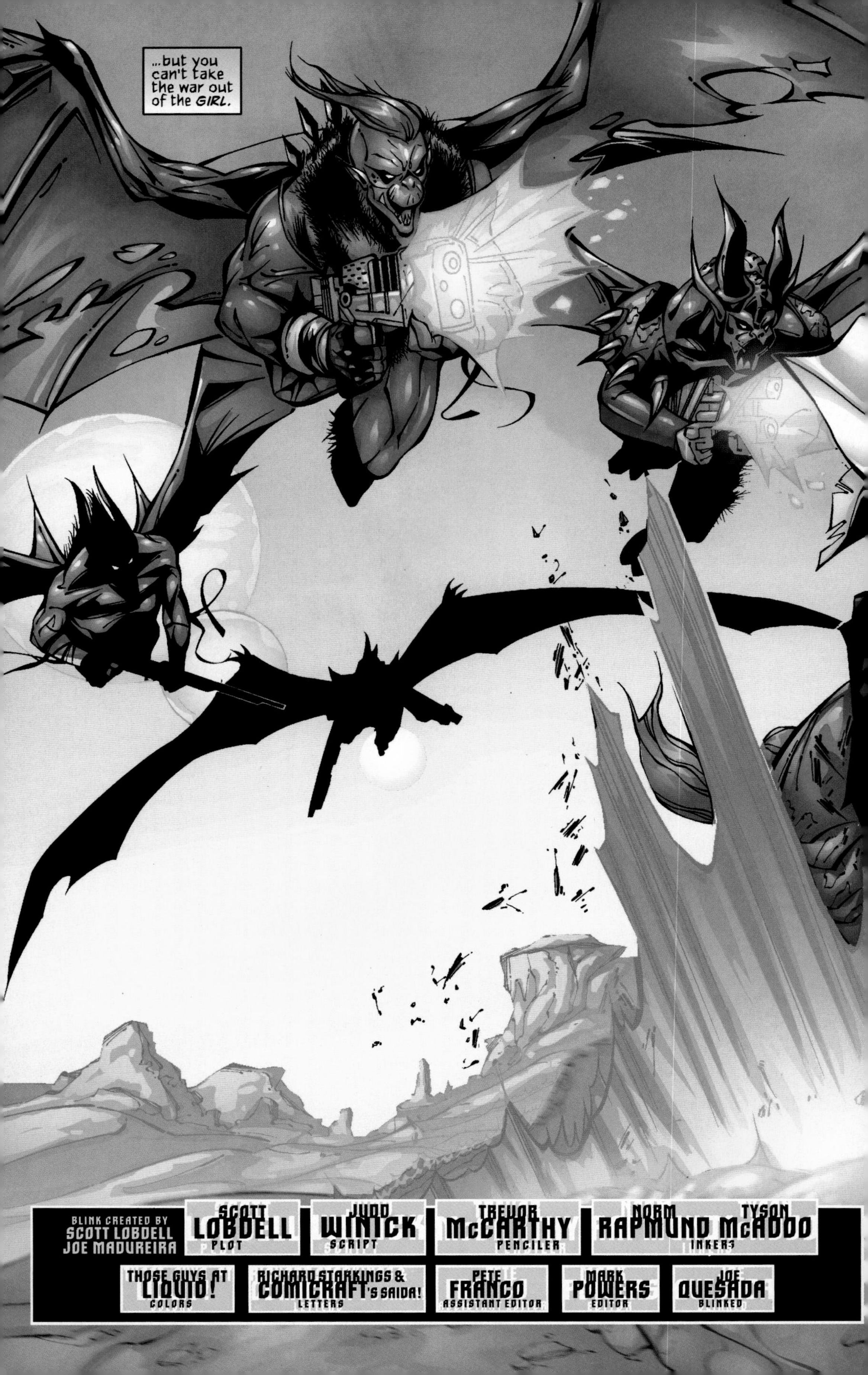

...but you can't take the war out of the GIRL.
BLINK CREATED BY SCOTT LOBDELL JOE MADUREIRA
SCOTT LOBDELL PLOT
JUDD WINICK SCRIPT
TREVOR McCARTHY PENCILER
NORM RAPMUND TYSON McADOO INKERS
THOSE GUYS AT LIQUID! COLORS
RICHARD STARKINGS & COMICRAFT'S SAIDA! LETTERS
PETE FRANCO ASSISTANT EDITOR
MARK POWERS EDITOR
JOE QUESADA BLINKED

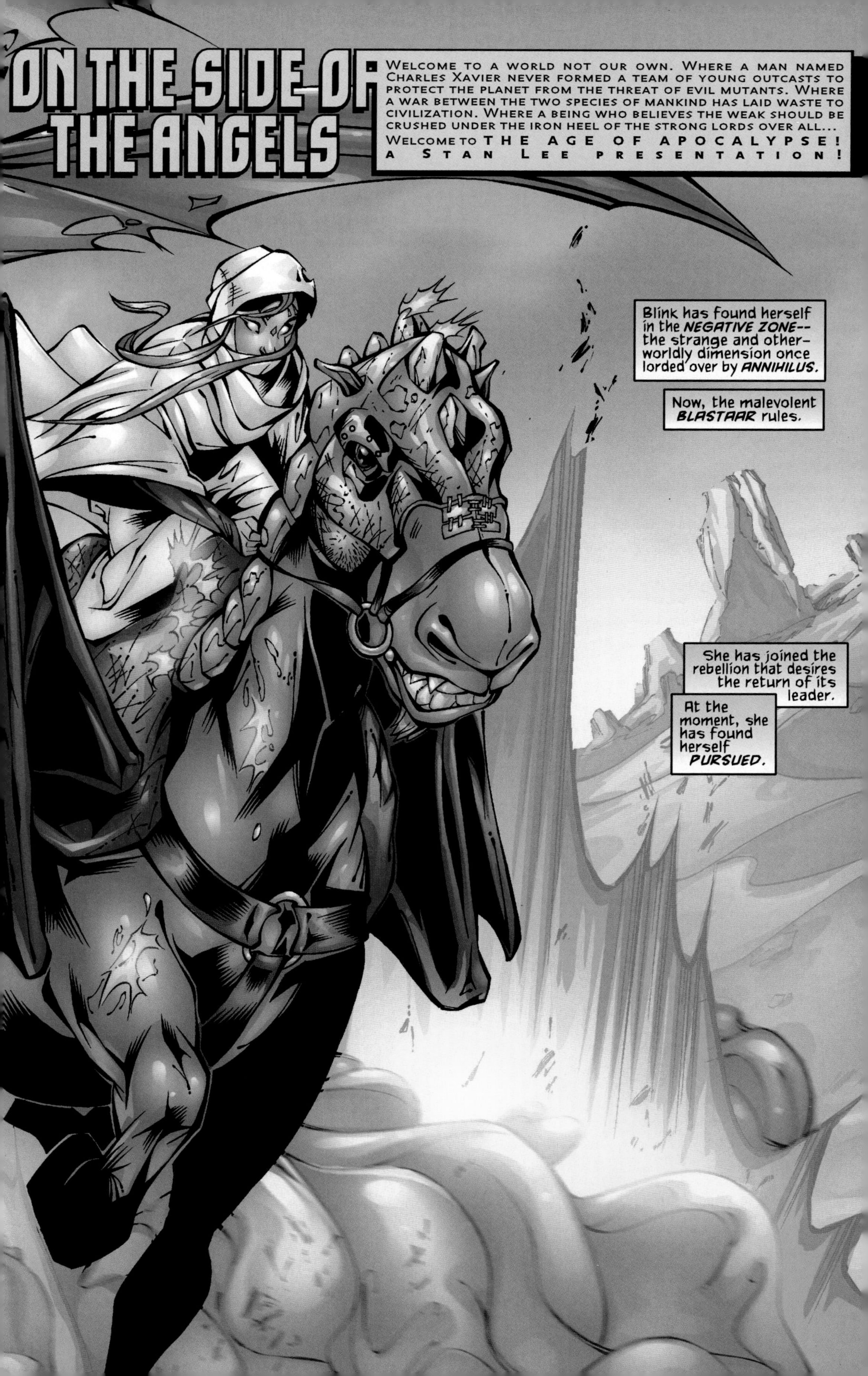
ON THE SIDE OF THE ANGELS
WELCOME TO A WORLD NOT OUR OWN. WHERE A MAN NAMED CHARLES XAVIER NEVER FORMED A TEAM OF YOUNG OUTCASTS TO PROTECT THE PLANET FROM THE THREAT OF EVIL MUTANTS. WHERE A WAR BETWEEN THE TWO SPECIES OF MANKIND HAS LAID WASTE TO CIVILIZATION. WHERE A BEING WHO BELIEVES THE WEAK SHOULD BE CRUSHED UNDER THE IRON HEEL OF THE STRONG LORDS OVER ALL... WELCOME TO THE AGE OF APOCALYPSE! A STAN LEE PRESENTATION!
Blink has found herself in the NEGATIVE ZONE-- the strange and other-worldly dimension once lorded over by ANNIHILUS.
Now, the malevolent BLASTAAR rules.
She has joined the rebellion that desires the return of its leader.
At the moment, she has found herself PURSUED.

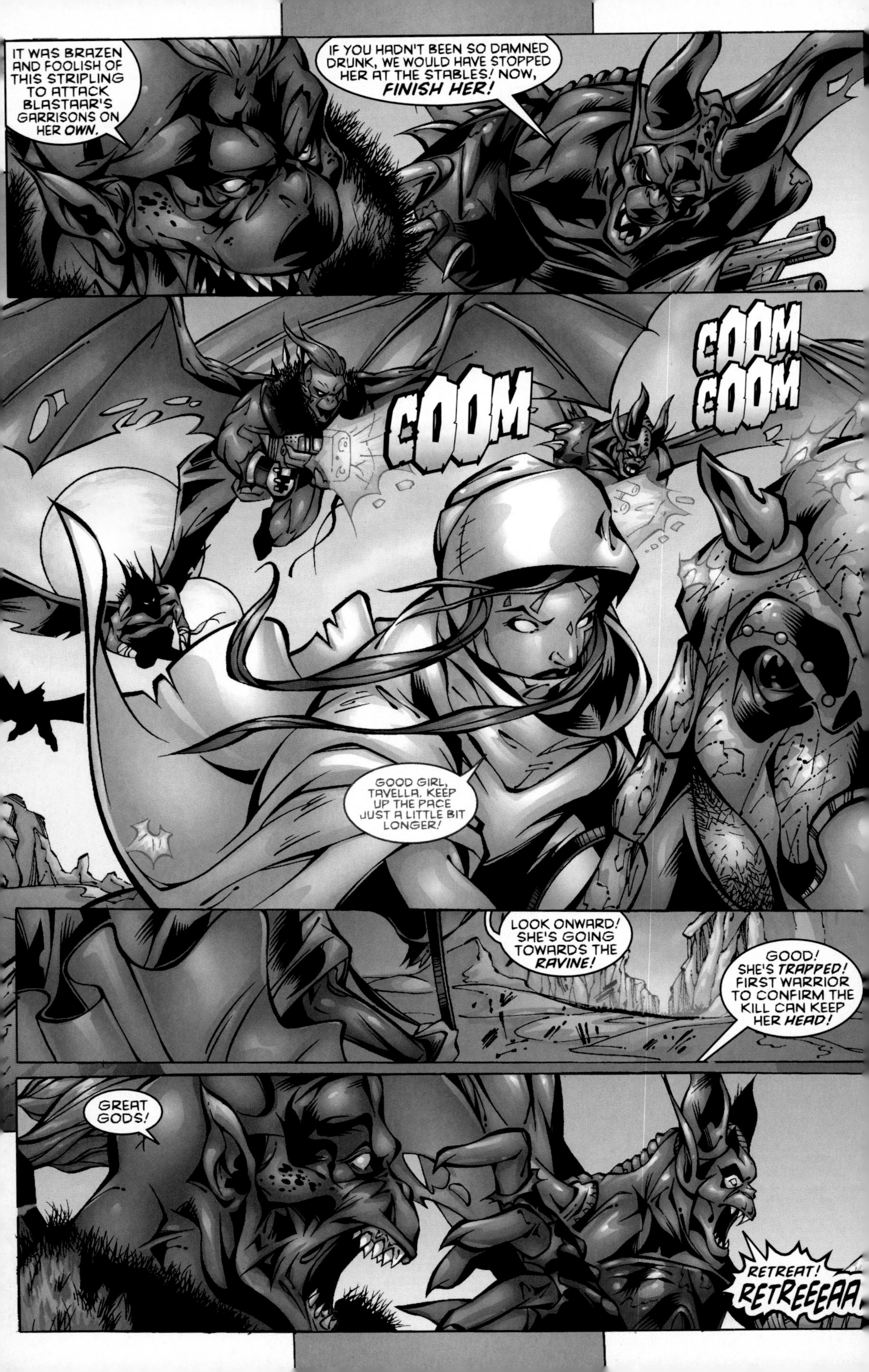
IT WAS BRAZEN AND FOOLISH OF THIS STRIPLING TO ATTACK BLASTAAR'S GARRISONS ON HER OWN.
IF YOU HADN'T BEEN SO DAMNED DRUNK, WE WOULD HAVE STOPPED HER AT THE STABLES! NOW, FINISH HER!
COOM
COOM
COOM
GOOD GIRL, TAVELLA. KEEP UP THE PACE JUST A LITTLE BIT LONGER!
LOOK ONWARD! SHE'S GOING TOWARDS THE RAVINE!
GOOD! SHE'S TRAPPED! FIRST WARRIOR TO CONFIRM THE KILL CAN KEEP HER HEAD!
GREAT GODS!
RETREAT! RETREEEAA

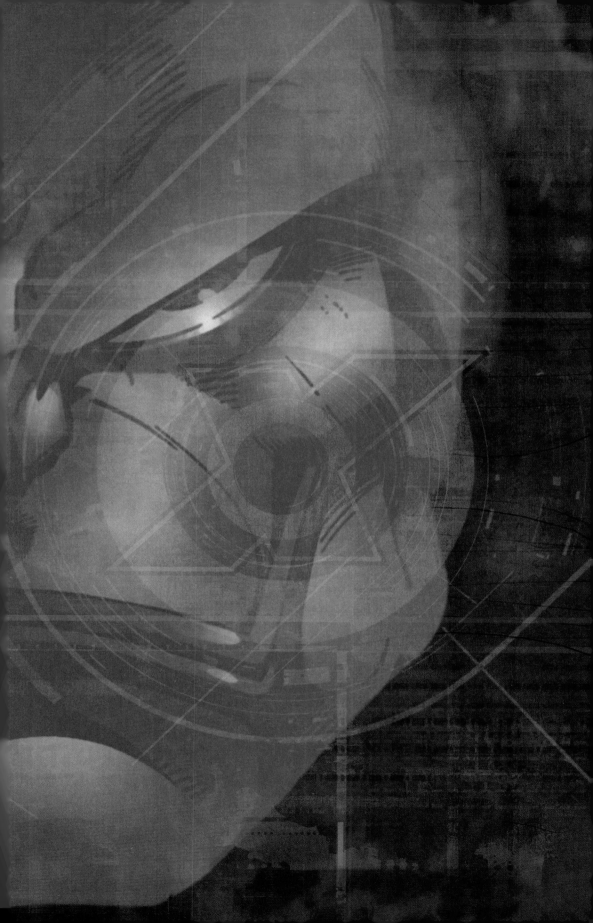

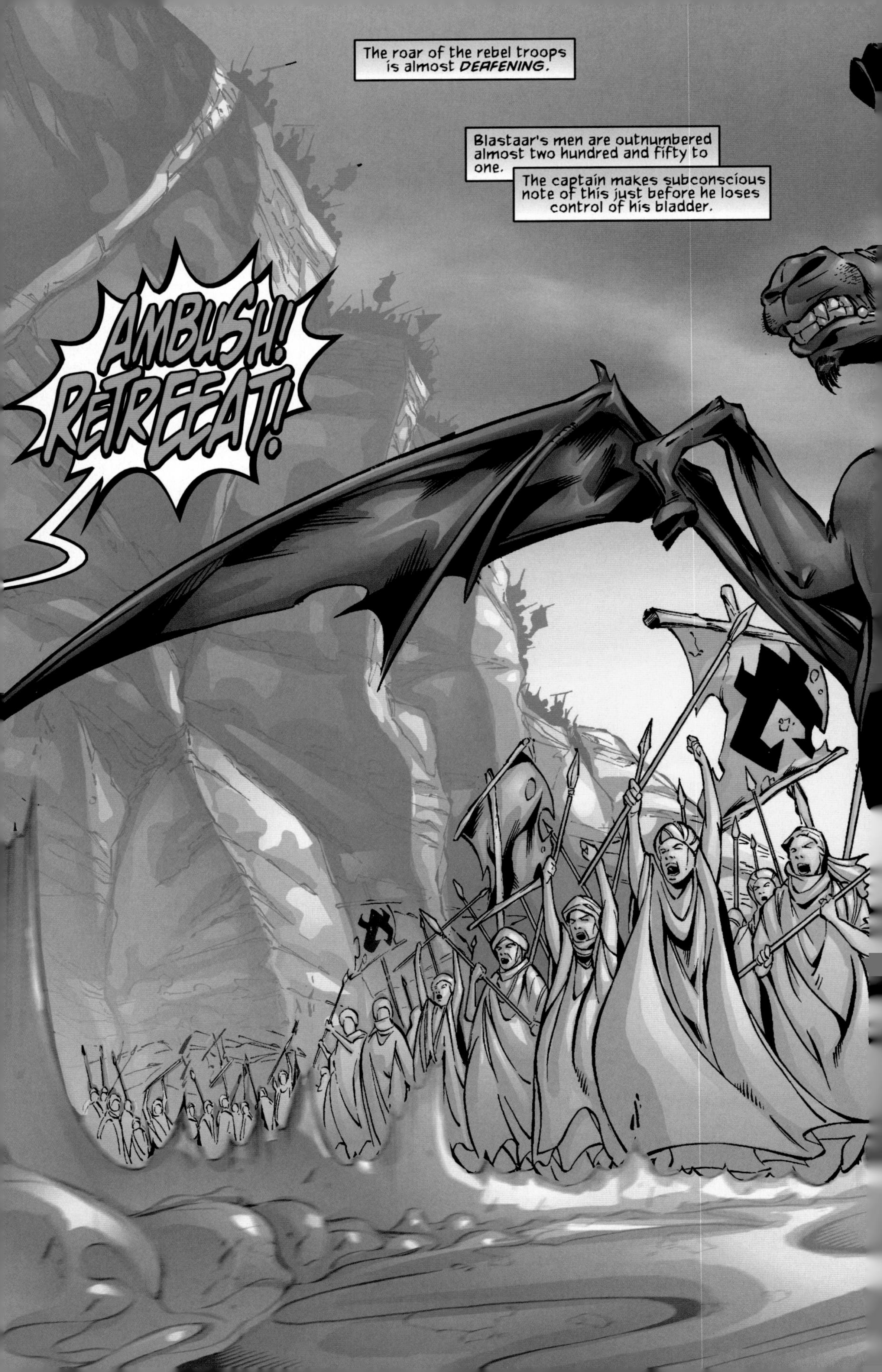
The roar of the rebel troops is almost DEAFENING.
Blastaar's men are outnumbered almost two hundred and fifty to one.
The captain makes subconscious note of this just before he loses control of his bladder.
AMBUSH! RETREEAT!

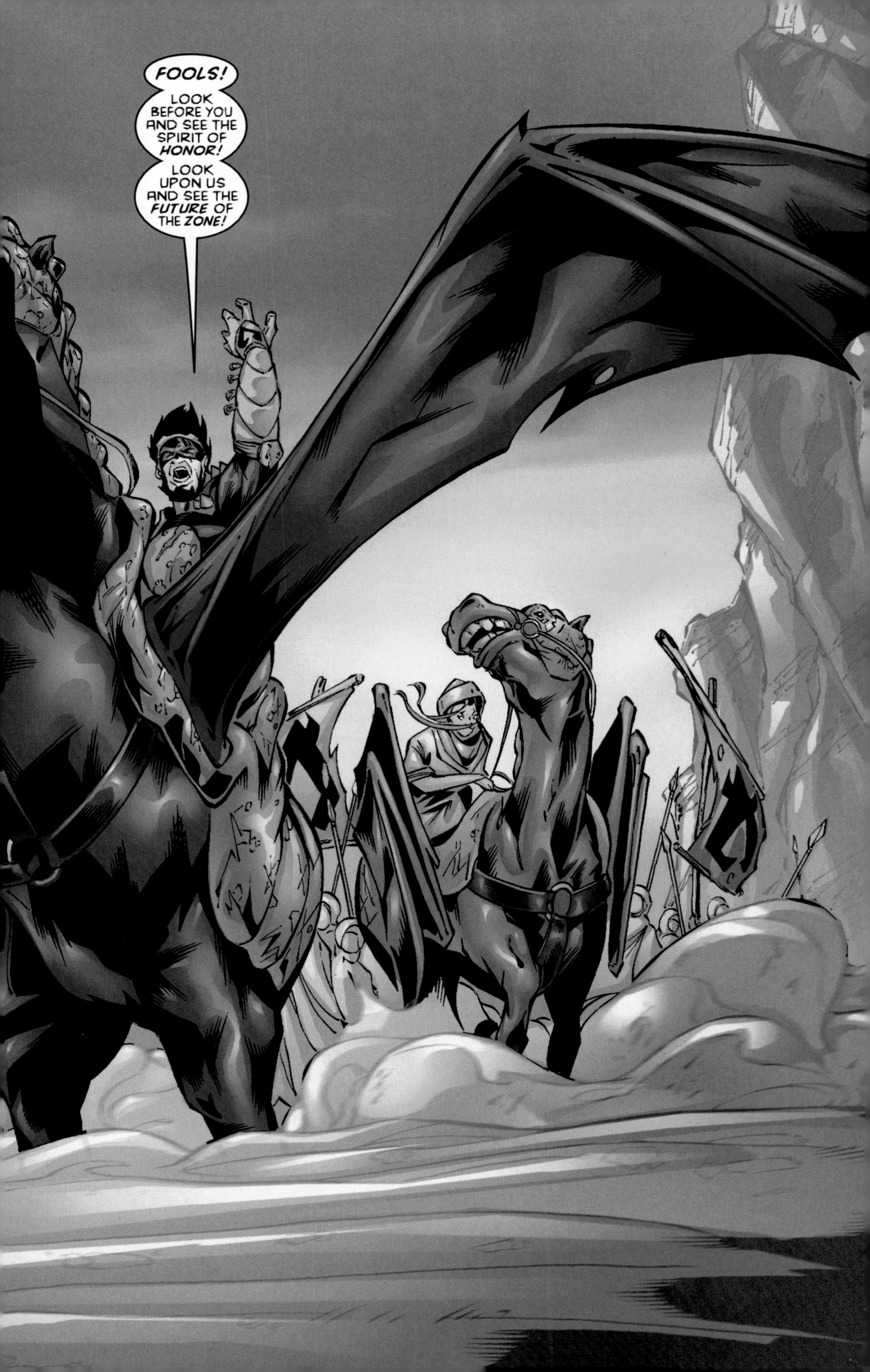
FOOLS!
LOOK BEFORE YOU AND SEE THE SPIRIT OF HONOR!
LOOK UPON US AND SEE THE FUTURE OF THE ZONE!

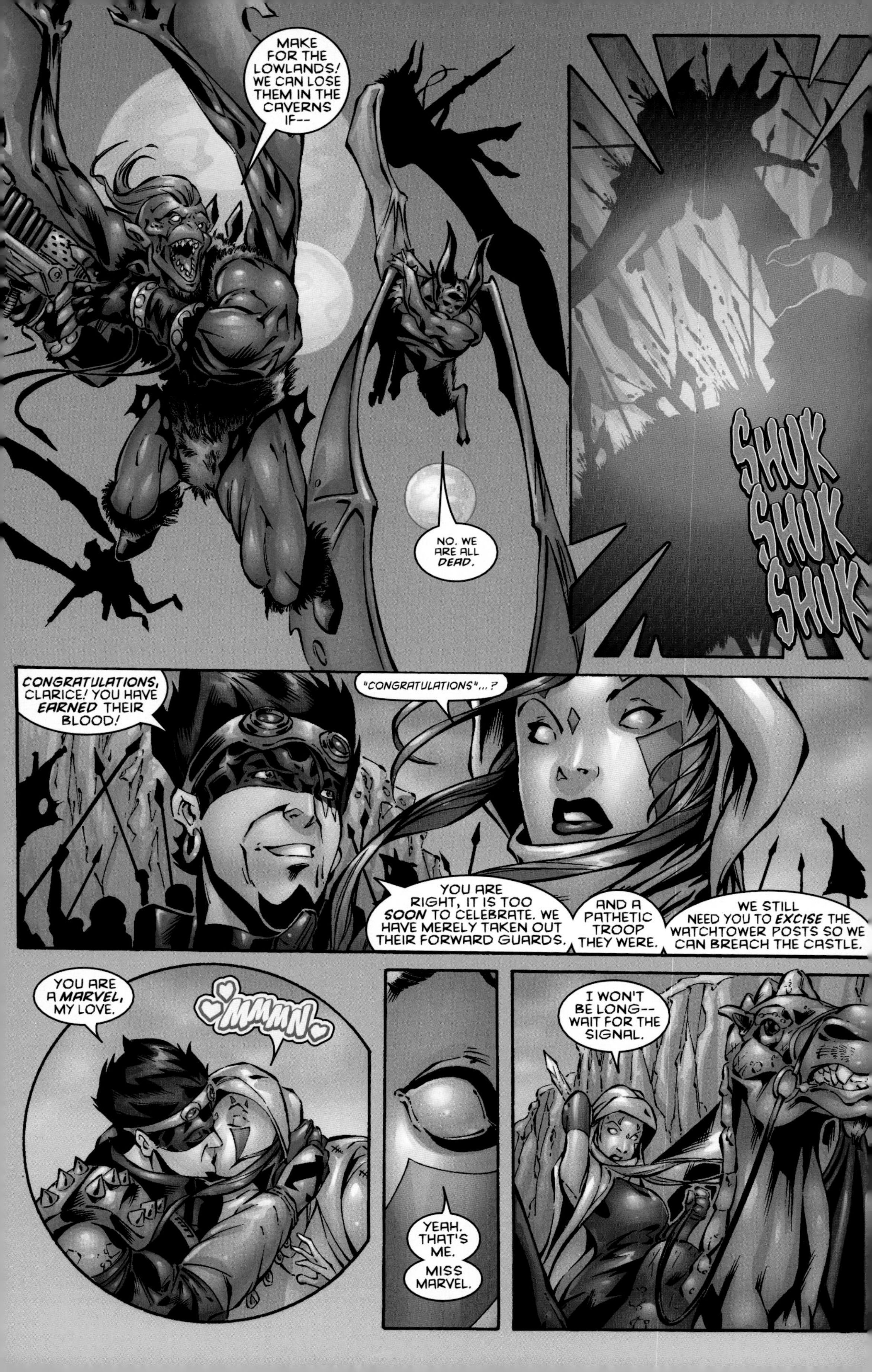
MAKE FOR THE LOWLANDS! WE CAN LOSE THEM IN THE CAVERNS IF--
NO. WE ARE ALL DEAD.
SHUK SHUK SHUK
CONGRATULATIONS, CLARICE! YOU HAVE EARNED THEIR BLOOD!
"CONGRATULATIONS"...?
YOU ARE RIGHT, IT IS TOO SOON TO CELEBRATE. WE HAVE MERELY TAKEN OUT THEIR FORWARD GUARDS.
AND A PATHETIC TROOP THEY WERE.
WE STILL NEED YOU TO EXCISE THE WATCHTOWER POSTS SO WE CAN BREACH THE CASTLE.
YOU ARE A MARVEL, MY LOVE.
MMMN
YEAH. THAT'S ME. MISS MARVEL.
I WON'T BE LONG-- WAIT FOR THE SIGNAL.

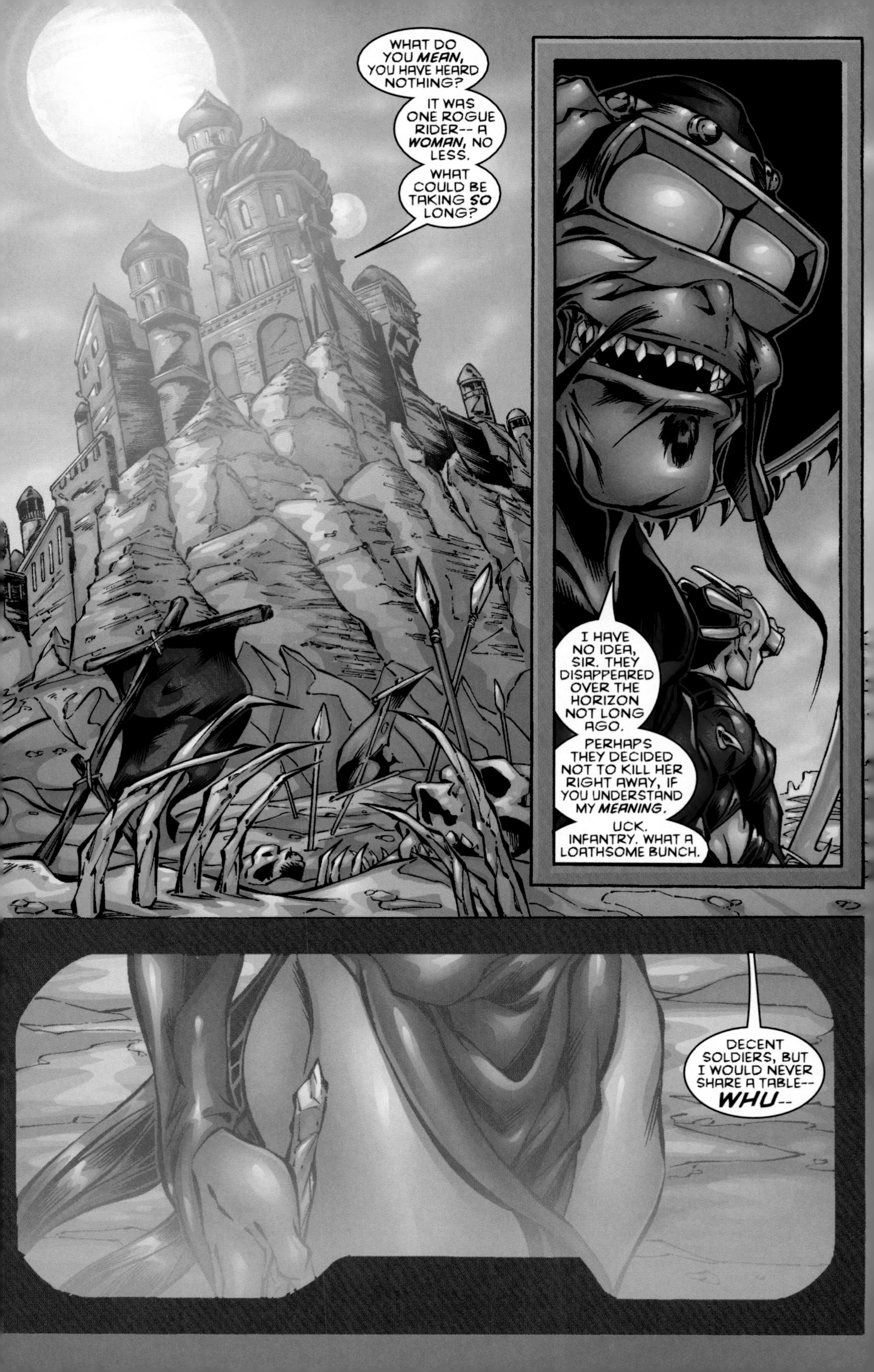
WHAT DO YOU *MEAN*, YOU HAVE HEARD NOTHING?
IT WAS ONE ROGUE RIDER-- A *WOMAN*, NO LESS.
WHAT COULD BE TAKING *SO* LONG?
I HAVE NO IDEA, SIR. THEY DISAPPEARED OVER THE HORIZON NOT LONG AGO.
PERHAPS THEY DECIDED NOT TO KILL HER RIGHT AWAY, IF YOU UNDERSTAND MY *MEANING*.
UCK. INFANTRY. WHAT A LOATHSOME BUNCH.
DECENT SOLDIERS, BUT I WOULD NEVER SHARE A TABLE--
WHU--

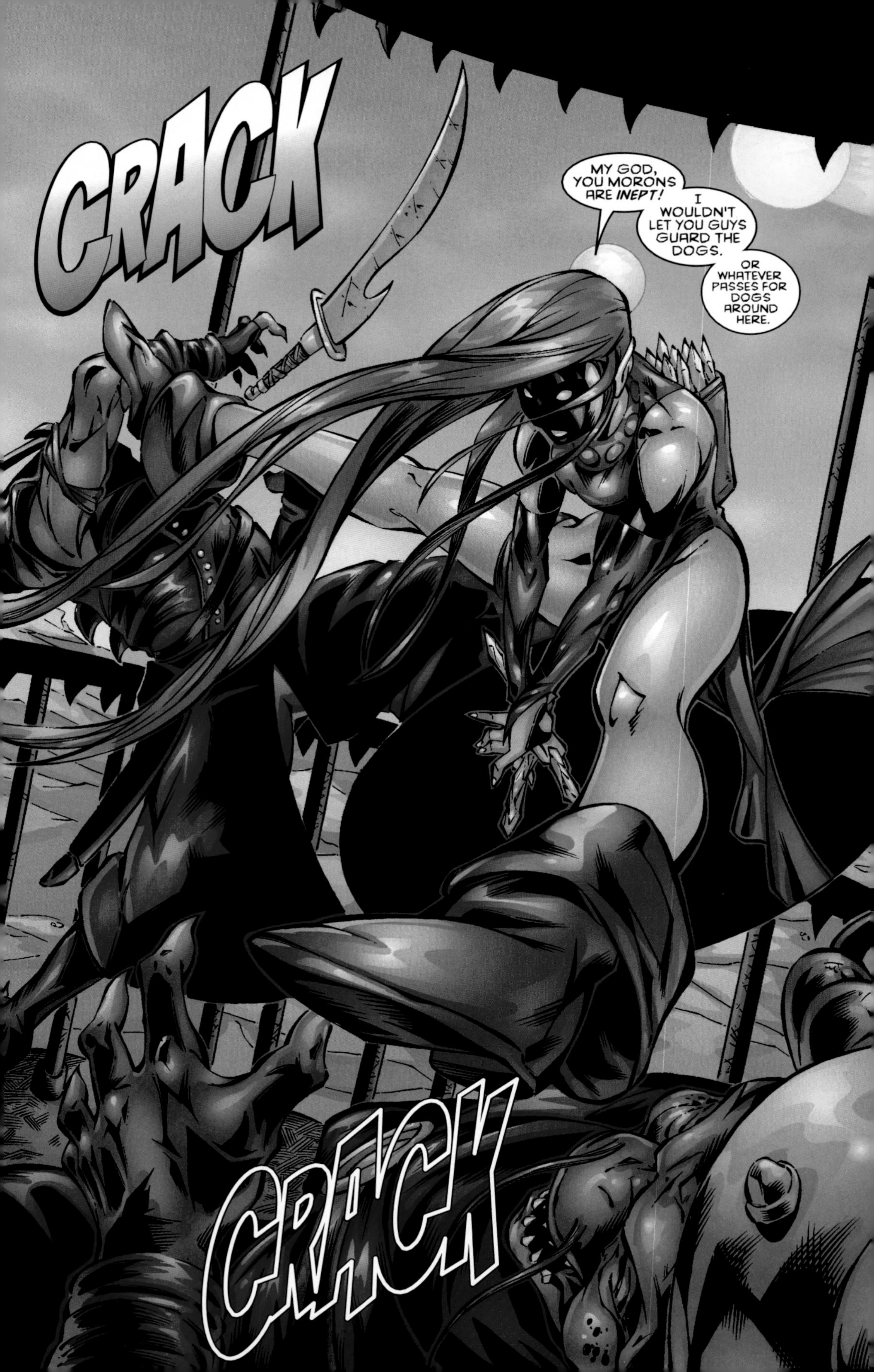
CRACK
MY GOD, YOU MORONS ARE *INEPT!*
I WOULDN'T LET YOU GUYS GUARD THE DOGS.
OR WHATEVER PASSES FOR DOGS AROUND HERE.
CRACK

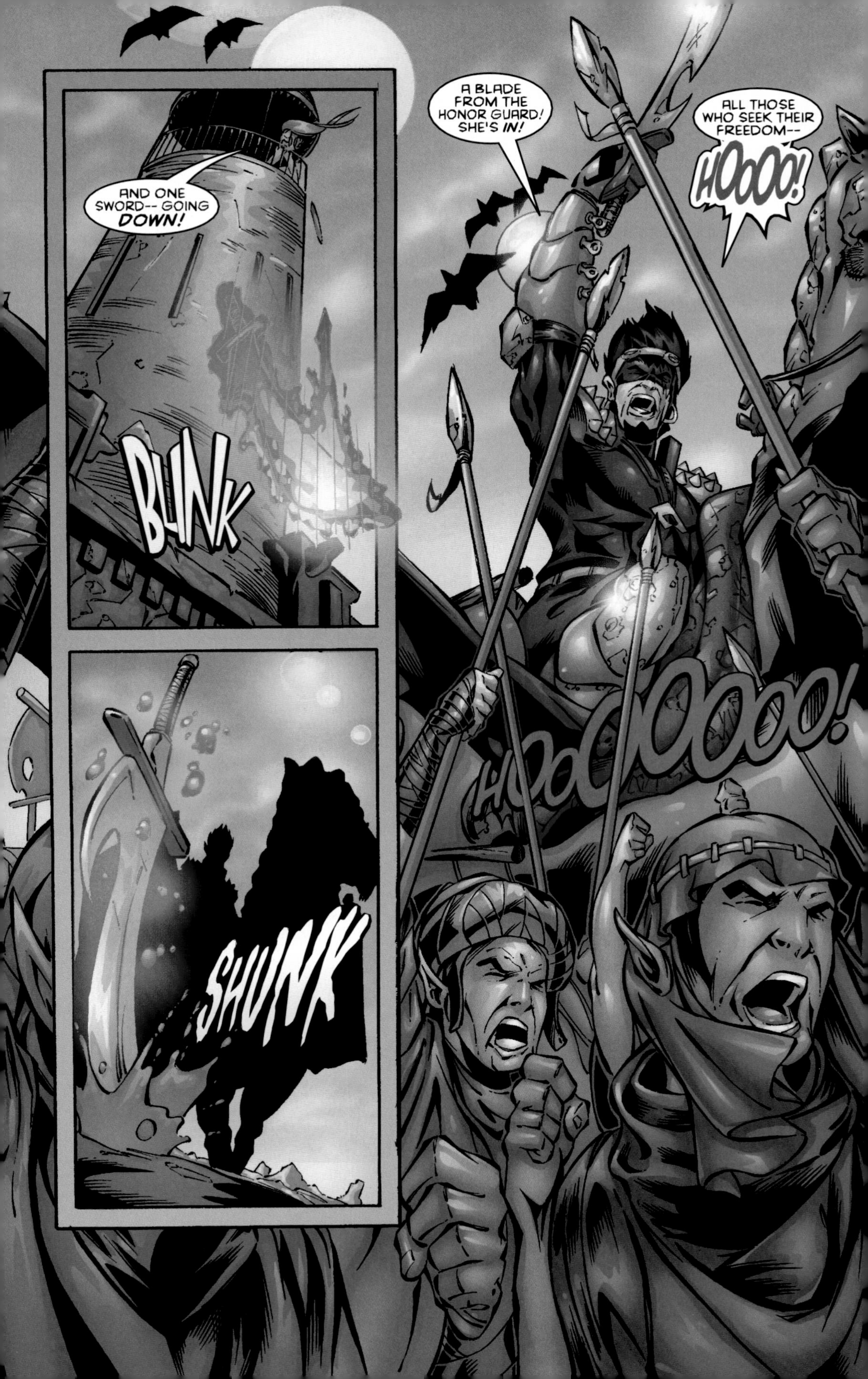
AND ONE SWORD-- GOING *DOWN!*
BLUNK
SHUNK
A BLADE FROM THE HONOR GUARD! SHE'S *IN!*
ALL THOSE WHO SEEK THEIR FREEDOM--
HOOOO!
HOOOOOOOO!

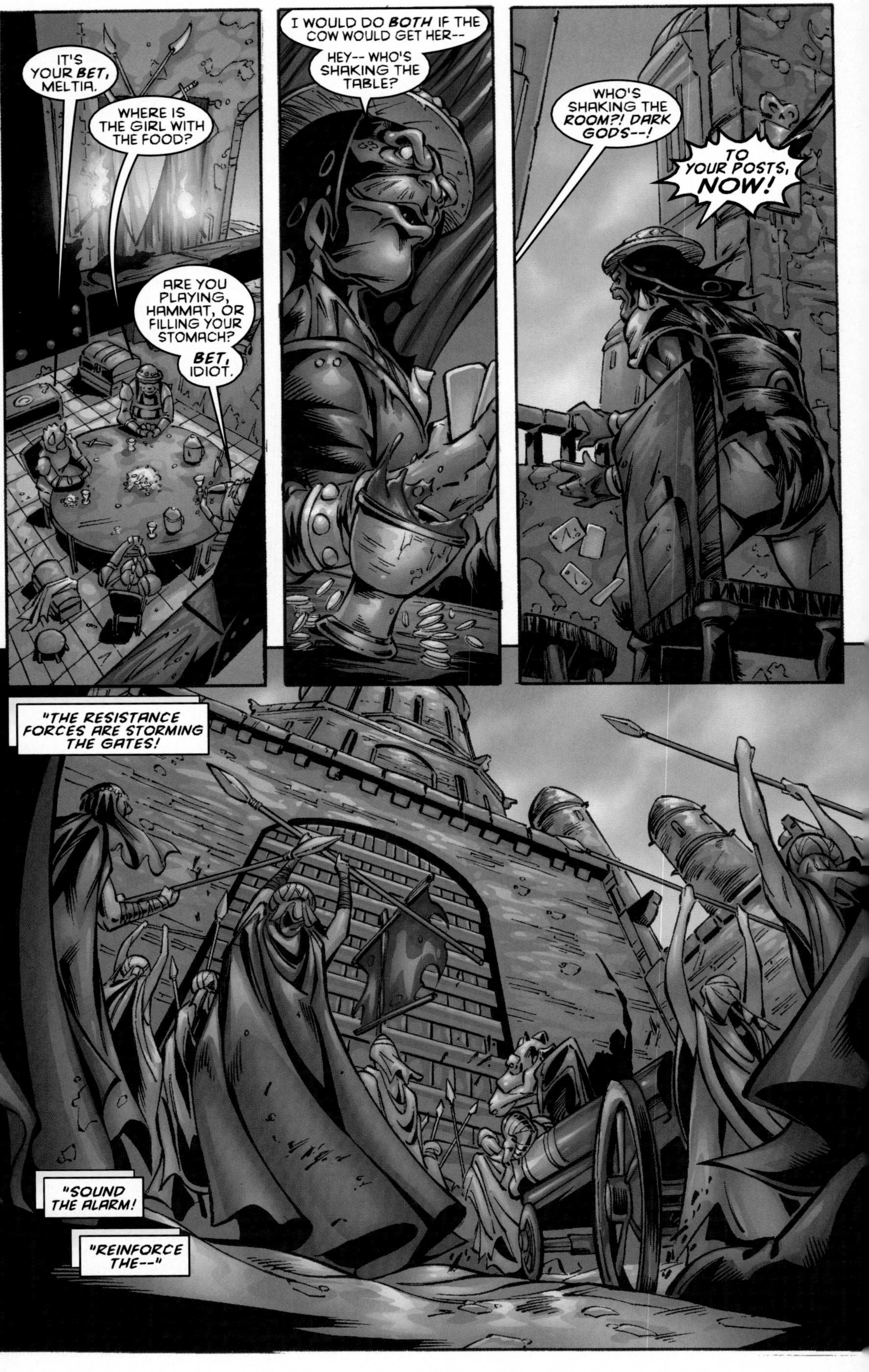
IT'S YOUR BET, MELTIA.
WHERE IS THE GIRL WITH THE FOOD?
ARE YOU PLAYING, HAMMAT, OR FILLING YOUR STOMACH?
BET, IDIOT.
I WOULD DO BOTH IF THE COW WOULD GET HER--
HEY-- WHO'S SHAKING THE TABLE?
WHO'S SHAKING THE ROOM?! DARK GODS--!
TO YOUR POSTS, NOW!
"THE RESISTANCE FORCES ARE STORMING THE GATES!
"SOUND THE ALARM!
"REINFORCE THE--"

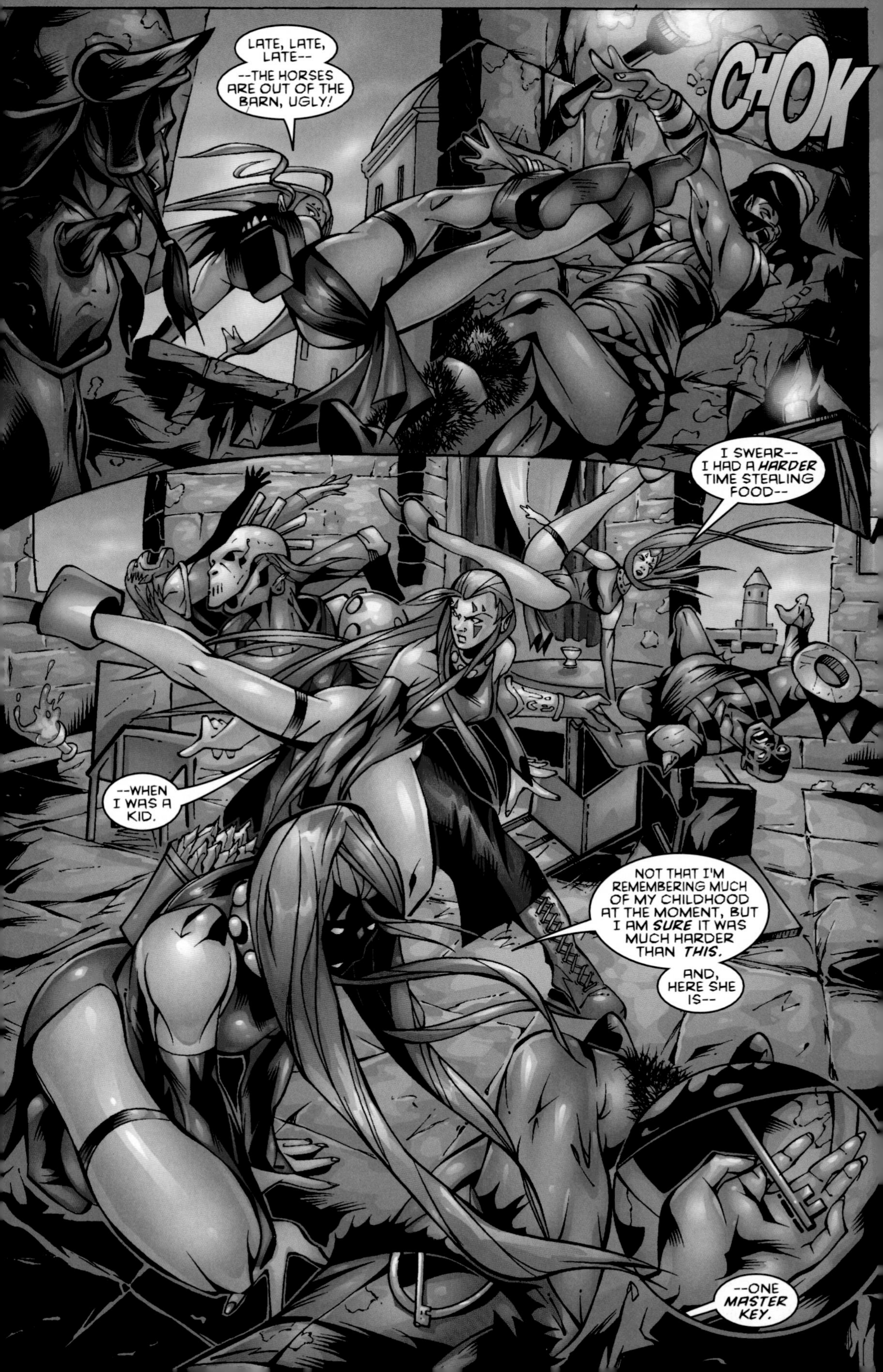
LATE, LATE, LATE--
--THE HORSES ARE OUT OF THE BARN, UGLY!
CHOK
I SWEAR--
I HAD A HARDER TIME STEALING FOOD--
--WHEN I WAS A KID.
NOT THAT I'M REMEMBERING MUCH OF MY CHILDHOOD AT THE MOMENT, BUT I AM SURE IT WAS MUCH HARDER THAN THIS.
AND, HERE SHE IS--
--ONE MASTER KEY.

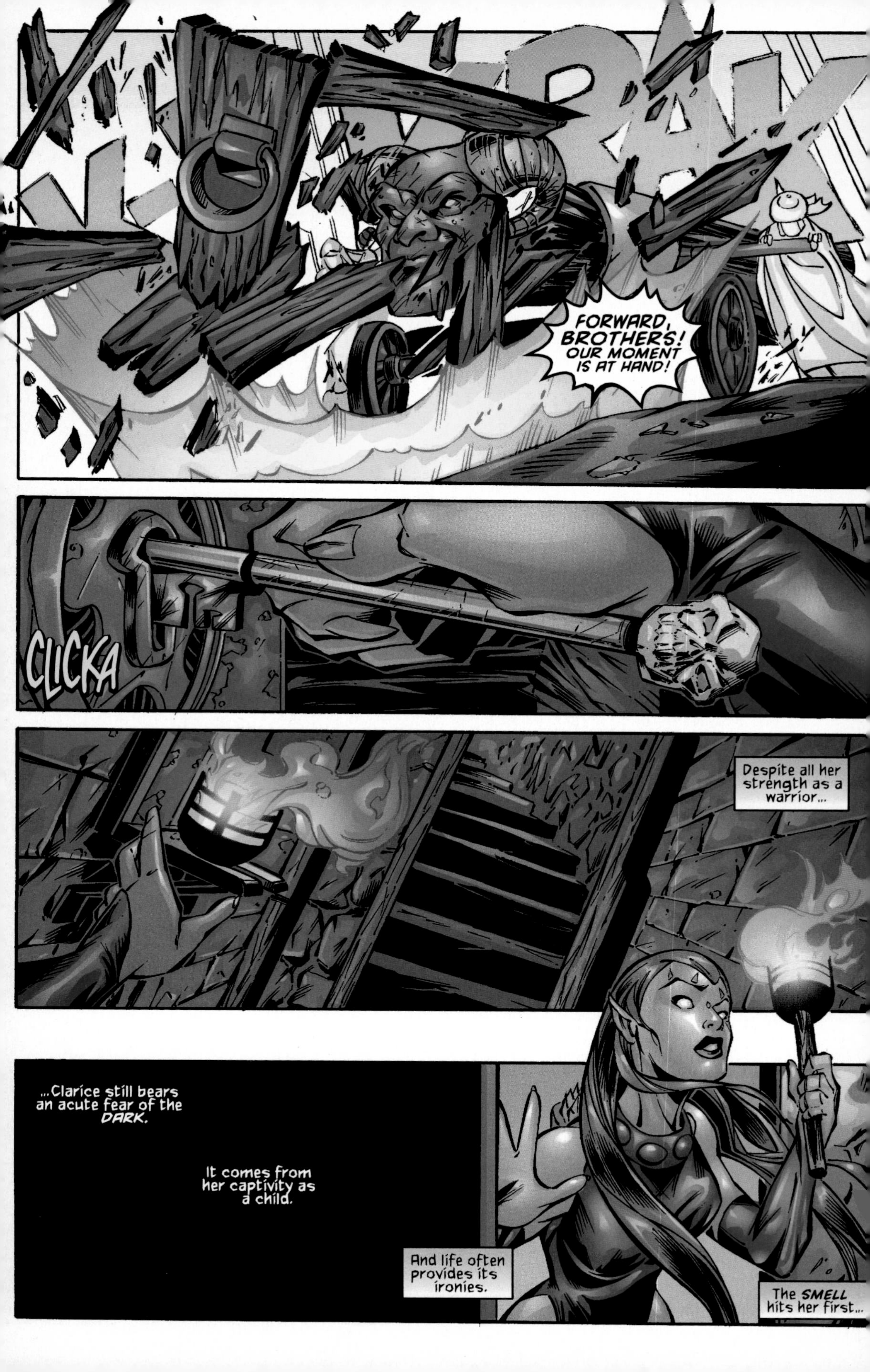

FORWARD, BROTHERS! OUR MOMENT IS AT HAND!
CLICKA
Despite all her strength as a warrior...
...Clarice still bears an acute fear of the DARK.
It comes from her captivity as a child.
And life often provides its ironies.
The SMELL hits her first...

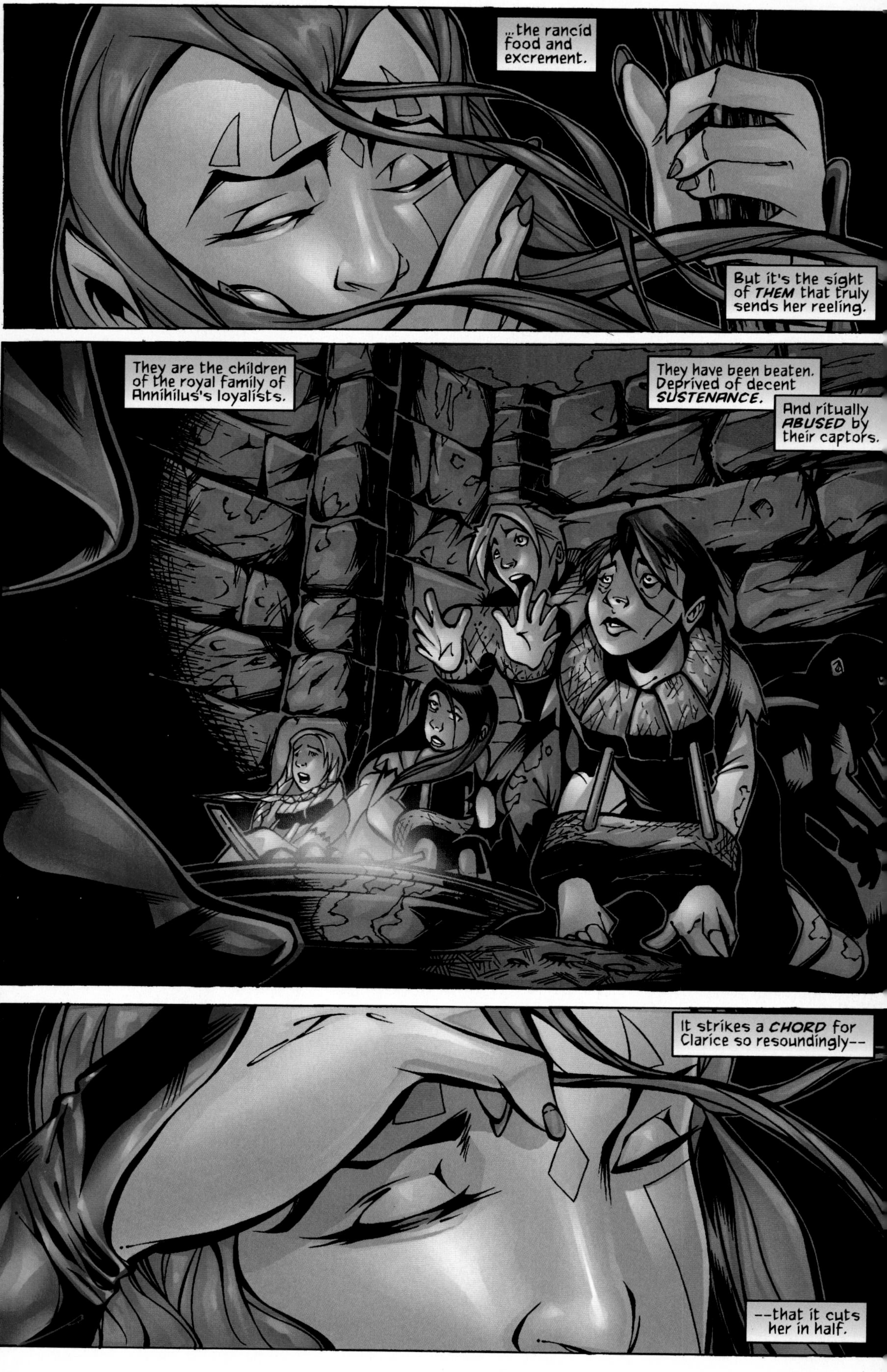
...the rancid food and excrement.
But it's the sight of THEM that truly sends her reeling.
They are the children of the royal family of Annihilus's loyalists.
They have been beaten. Deprived of decent SUSTENANCE.
And ritually ABUSED by their captors.
It strikes a CHORD for Clarice so resoundingly--
--that it cuts her in half.

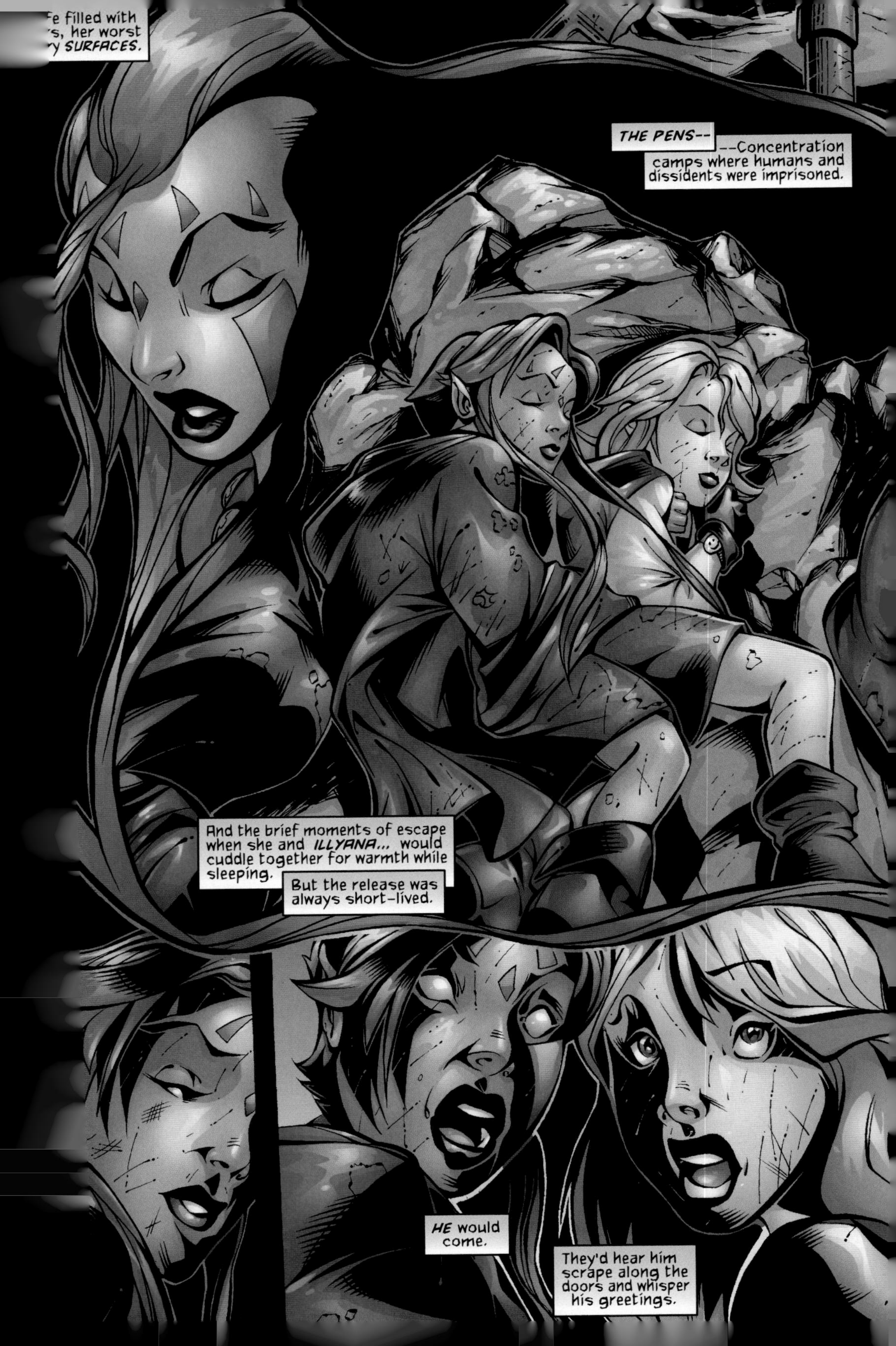

fe filled with
rs, her worst
ry SURFACES.
THE PENS--
--Concentration camps where humans and dissidents were imprisoned.
And the brief moments of escape when she and ILLYANA... would cuddle together for warmth while sleeping.
But the release was always short-lived.
HE would come.
They'd hear him scrape along the doors and whisper his greetings.

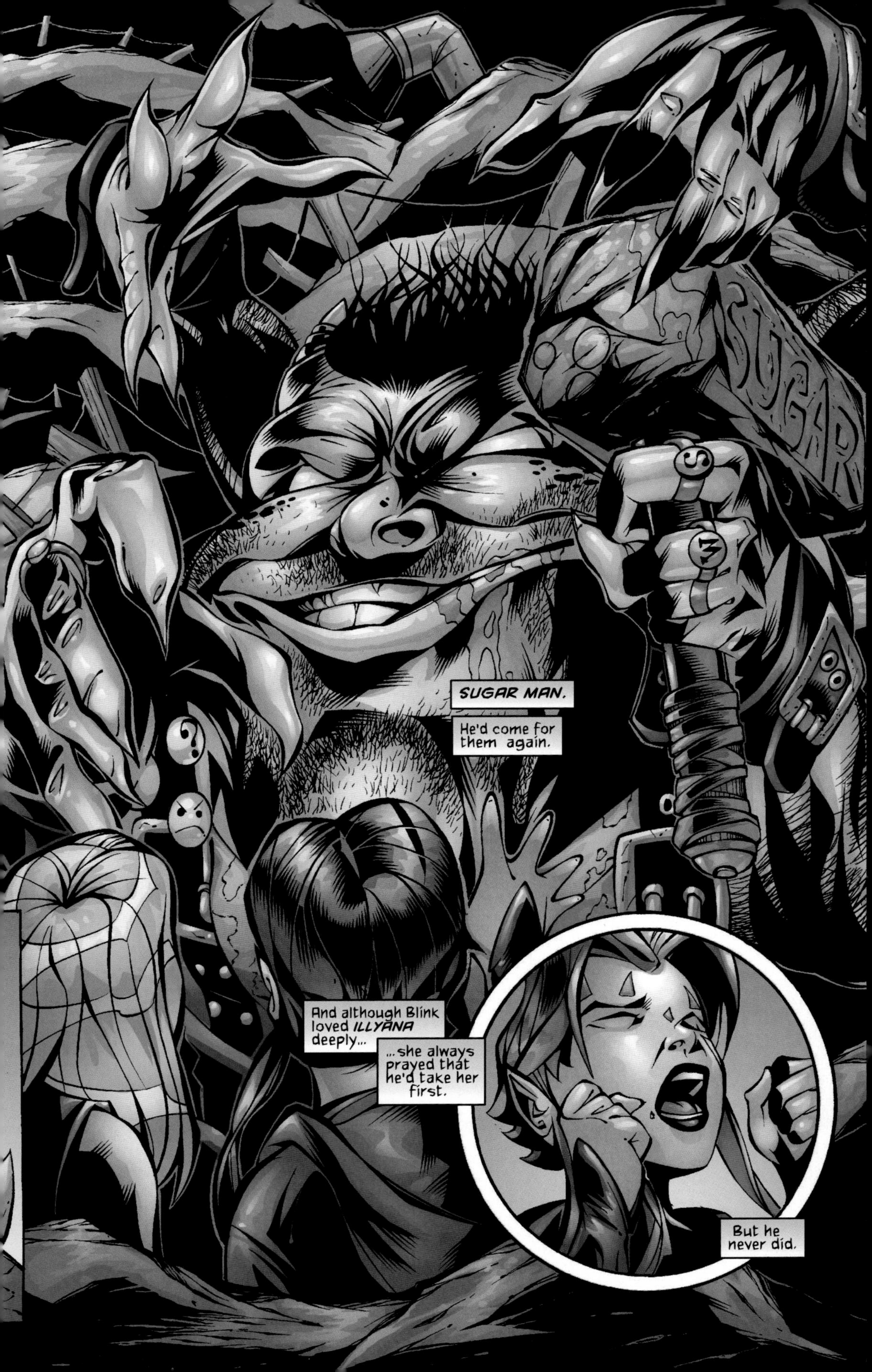
SUGAR MAN.
He'd come for them again.
And although Blink loved ILLYANA deeply...
...she always prayed that he'd take her first.
But he never did.
SUGAR

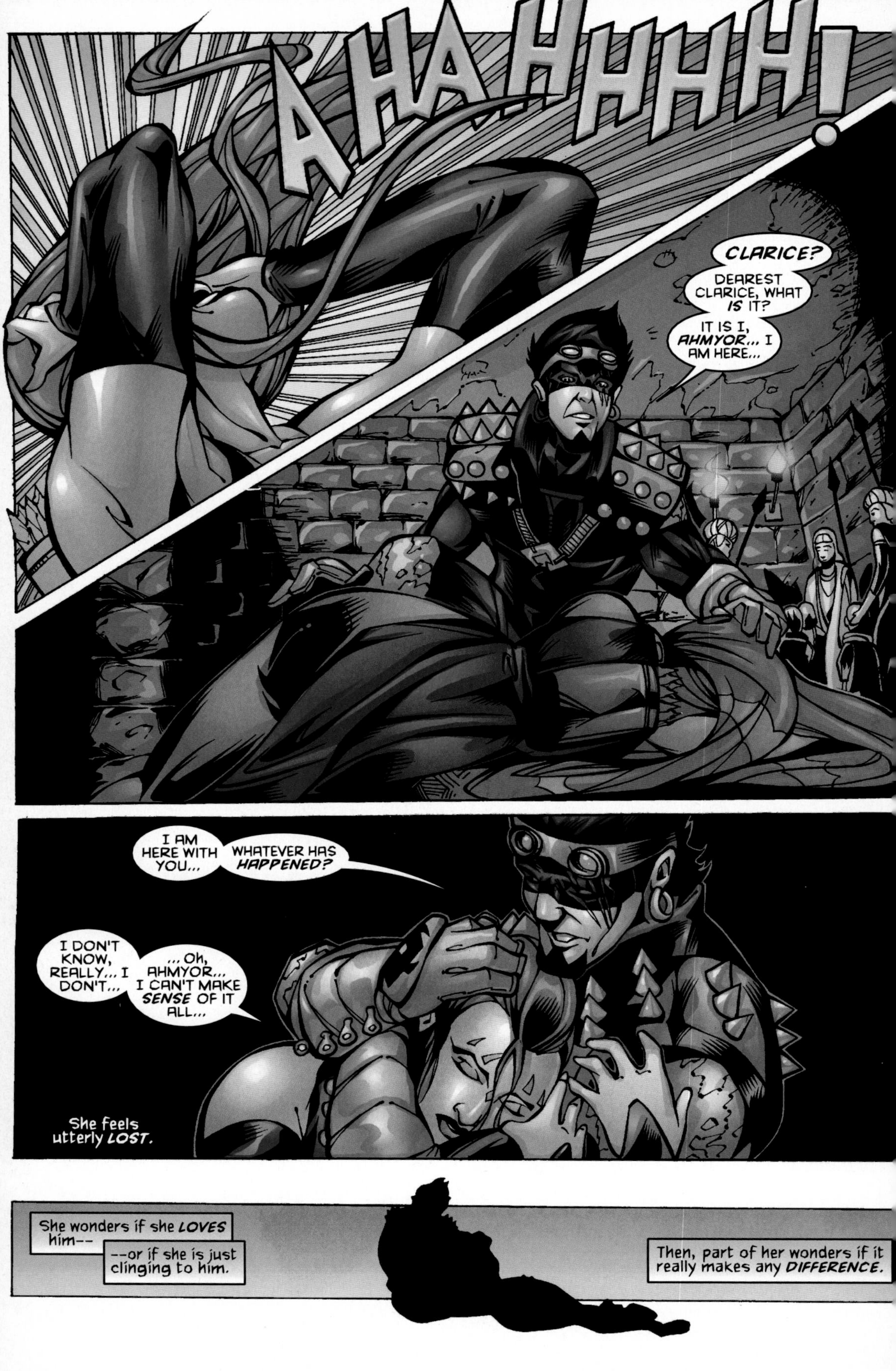
AHAHHHHH!
CLARICE?
DEAREST CLARICE, WHAT IS IT?
IT IS I, AHMYOR... I AM HERE...
I AM HERE WITH YOU...
WHATEVER HAS HAPPENED?
I DON'T KNOW, REALLY... I DON'T...
...OH, AHMYOR... I CAN'T MAKE SENSE OF IT ALL...
She feels utterly LOST.
She wonders if she LOVES him--
--or if she is just clinging to him.
Then, part of her wonders if it really makes any DIFFERENCE.

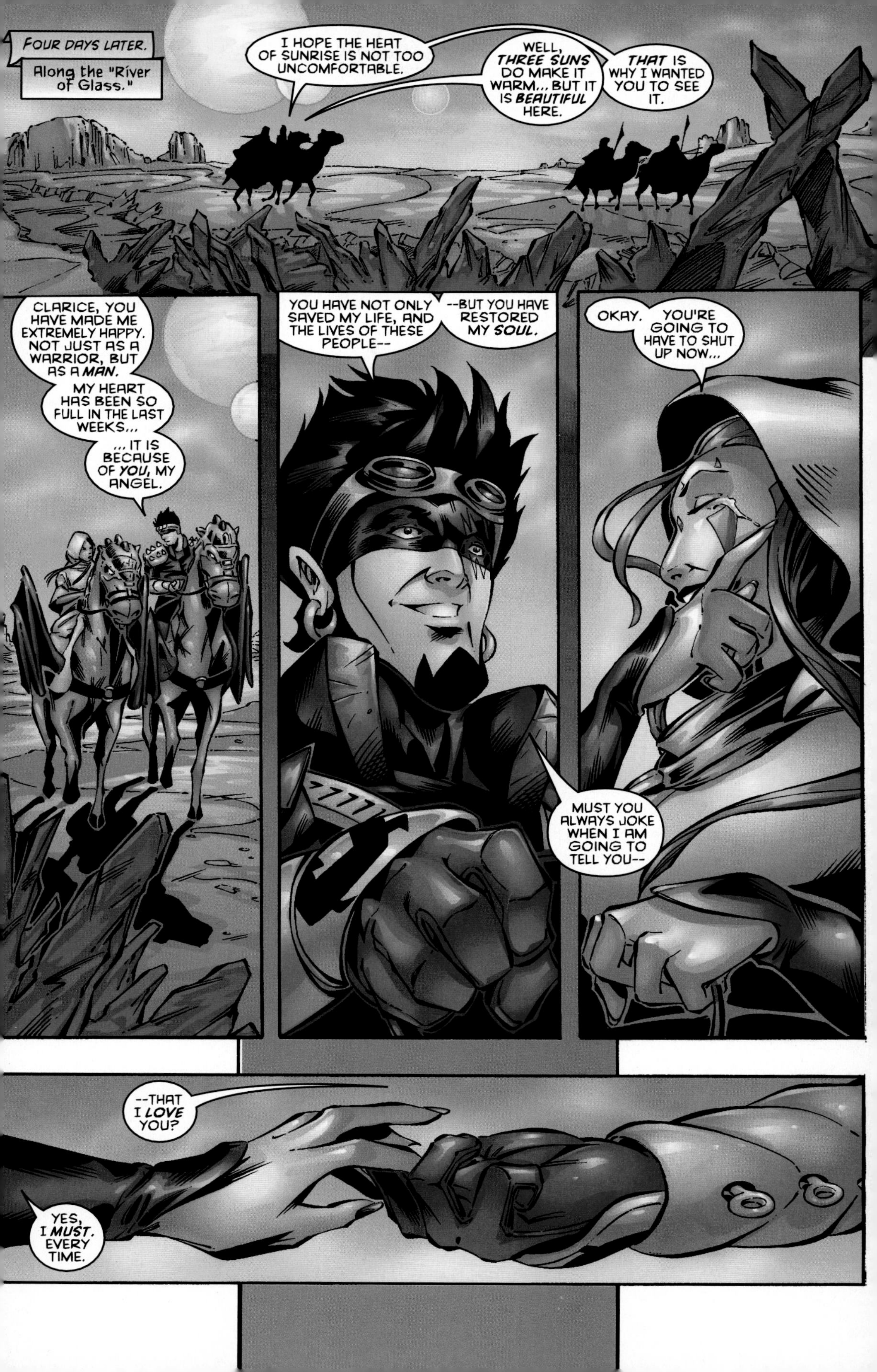
FOUR DAYS LATER.
Along the "River of Glass."
I HOPE THE HEAT OF SUNRISE IS NOT TOO UNCOMFORTABLE.
WELL, THREE SUNS DO MAKE IT WARM... BUT IT IS BEAUTIFUL HERE.
THAT IS WHY I WANTED YOU TO SEE IT.
CLARICE, YOU HAVE MADE ME EXTREMELY HAPPY. NOT JUST AS A WARRIOR, BUT AS A MAN.
MY HEART HAS BEEN SO FULL IN THE LAST WEEKS...
...IT IS BECAUSE OF YOU, MY ANGEL.
YOU HAVE NOT ONLY SAVED MY LIFE, AND THE LIVES OF THESE PEOPLE--
--BUT YOU HAVE RESTORED MY SOUL.
OKAY. YOU'RE GOING TO HAVE TO SHUT UP NOW...
MUST YOU ALWAYS JOKE WHEN I AM GOING TO TELL YOU--
--THAT I LOVE YOU?
YES, I MUST. EVERY TIME.

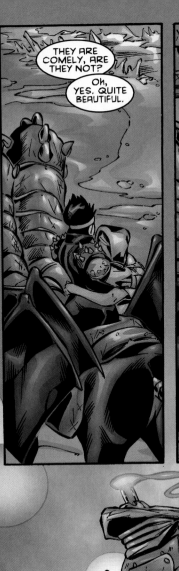

THEY ARE COMELY, ARE THEY NOT?

OH, YES. QUITE BEAUTIFUL.

OH! YOU SHOULD SEE THEM THROUGH THE SCOPE. *RAVISHING.*

OH, I CAN IMAGINE. I ASSUME IT DOES SOMETHING EXQUISITE TO HER HAIR.

BREE

NO!

AND YOU WERE *WORRIED.*

HE'S KILLED MORE SOLDIERS THAN THE TELLAXIAN SYPHILL VIRUS, I WAS WORRIED WITH *REASON.*

HA! WELL, IT'S *OVER* FOR THEM NOW...

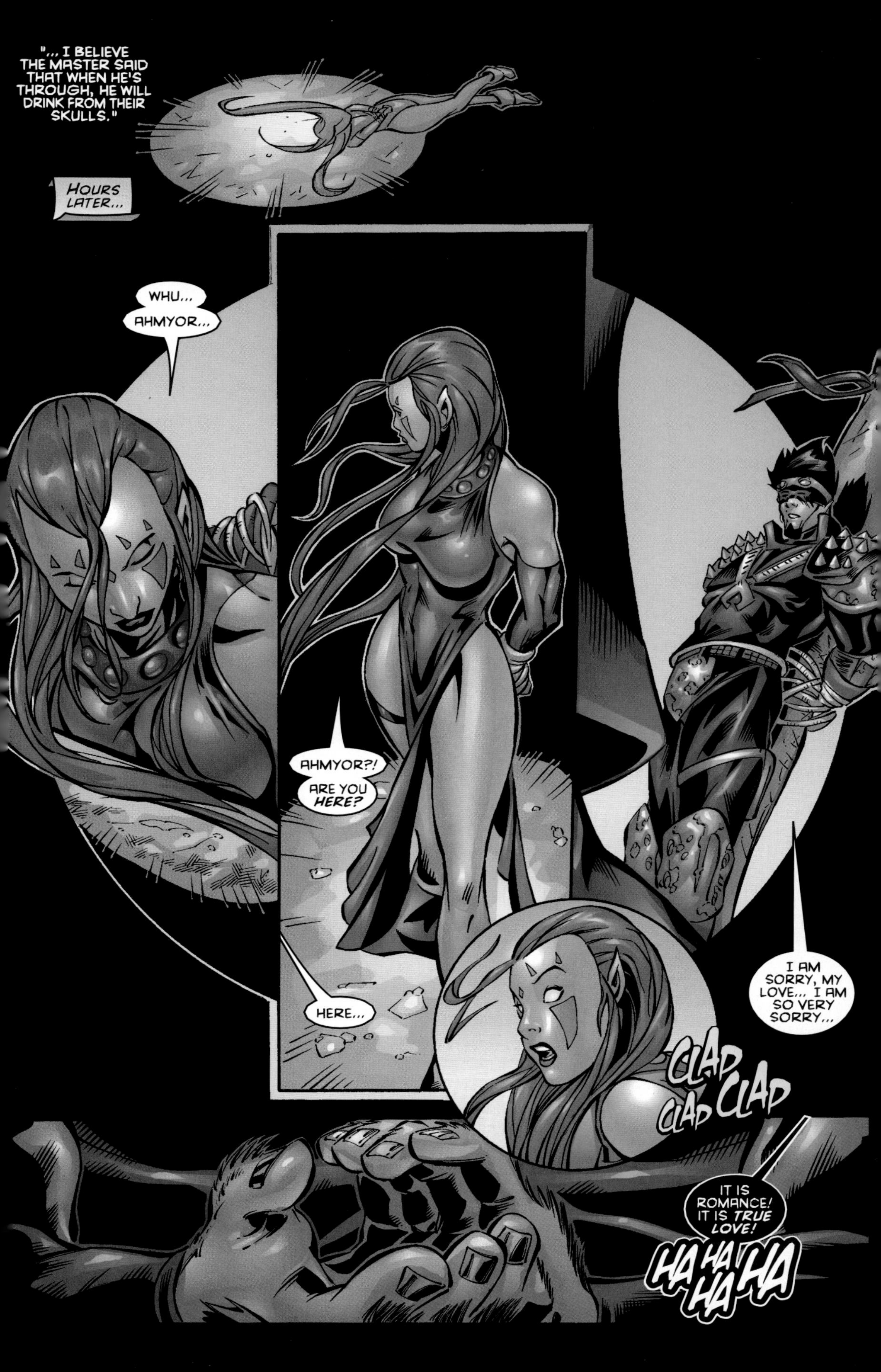
"... I BELIEVE THE MASTER SAID THAT WHEN HE'S THROUGH, HE WILL DRINK FROM THEIR SKULLS."
HOURS LATER...
WHU... AHMYOR...
AHMYOR?! ARE YOU HERE?
HERE...
I AM SORRY, MY LOVE... I AM SO VERY SORRY...
CLAP CLAP CLAP CLAP
IT IS ROMANCE! IT IS TRUE LOVE!
HA HA HA HA

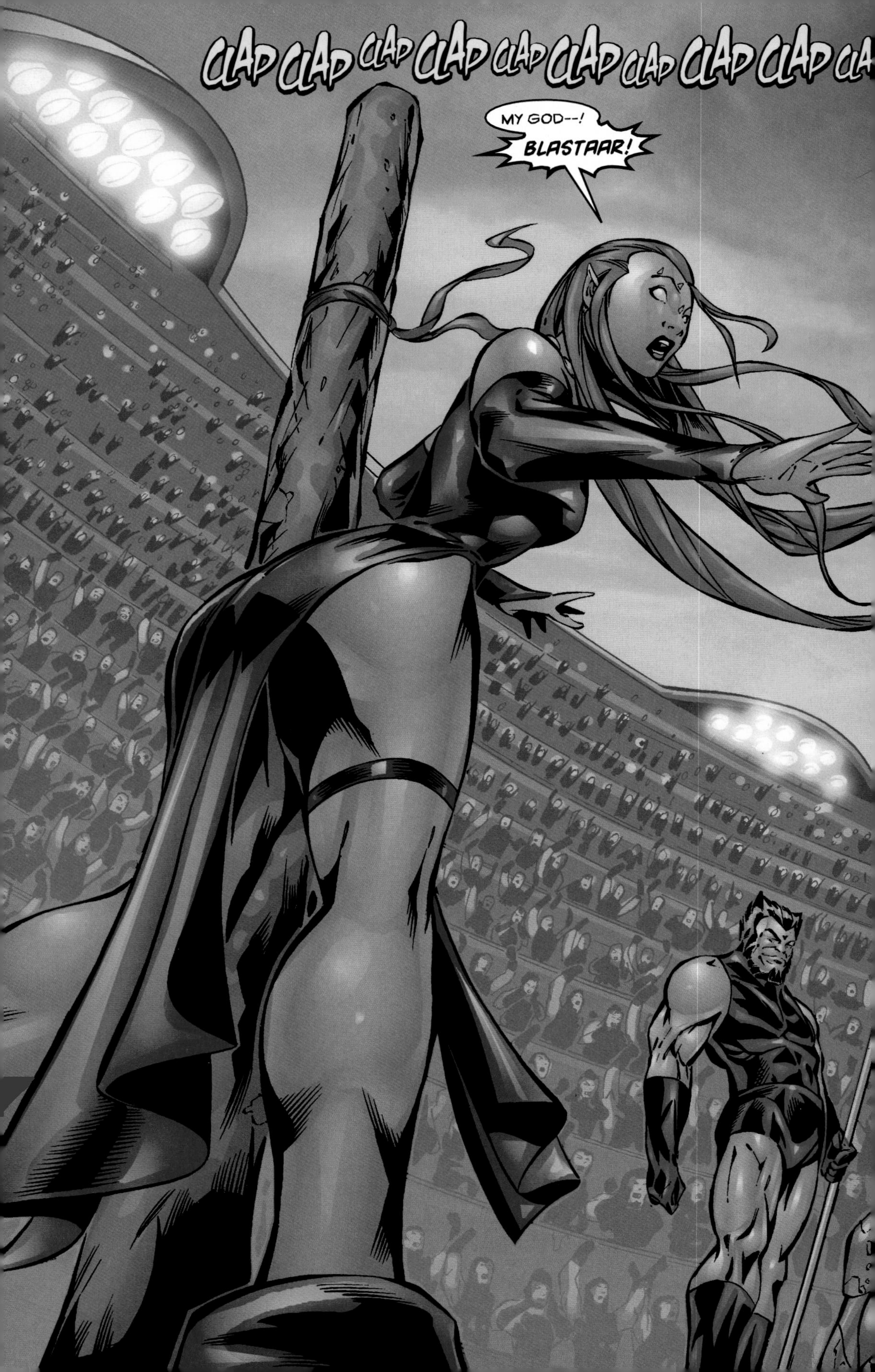
CLAP CLAP CLAP CLAP CLAP CLAP CLAP CLAP CLAP CLA
MY GOD--!
BLASTAAR!

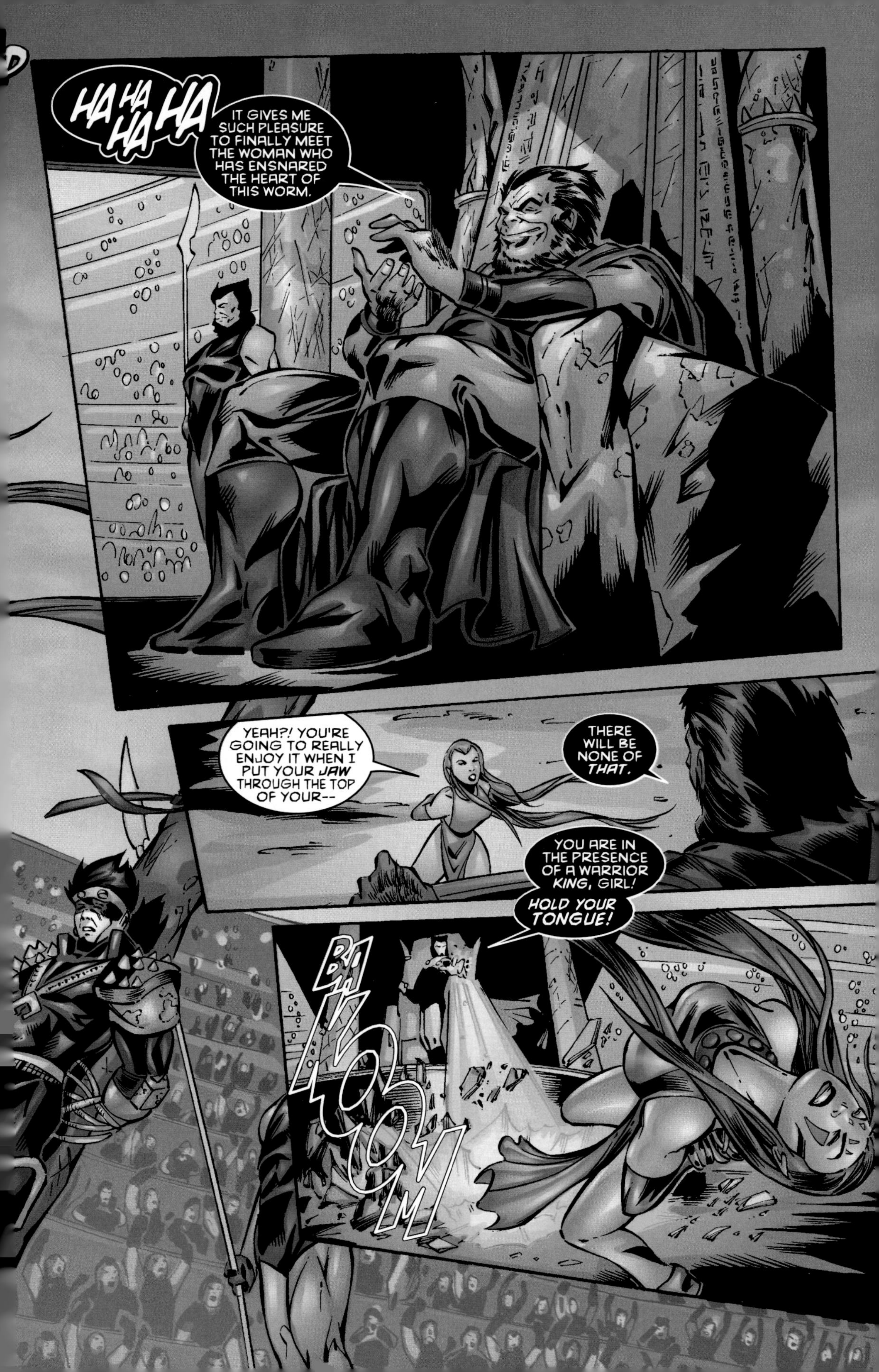
HA HA HA HA
IT GIVES ME SUCH PLEASURE TO FINALLY MEET THE WOMAN WHO HAS ENSNARED THE HEART OF THIS WORM.
YEAH?! YOU'RE GOING TO REALLY ENJOY IT WHEN I PUT YOUR JAW THROUGH THE TOP OF YOUR--
THERE WILL BE NONE OF THAT.
YOU ARE IN THE PRESENCE OF A WARRIOR KING, GIRL!
HOLD YOUR TONGUE!
BABLOOOM

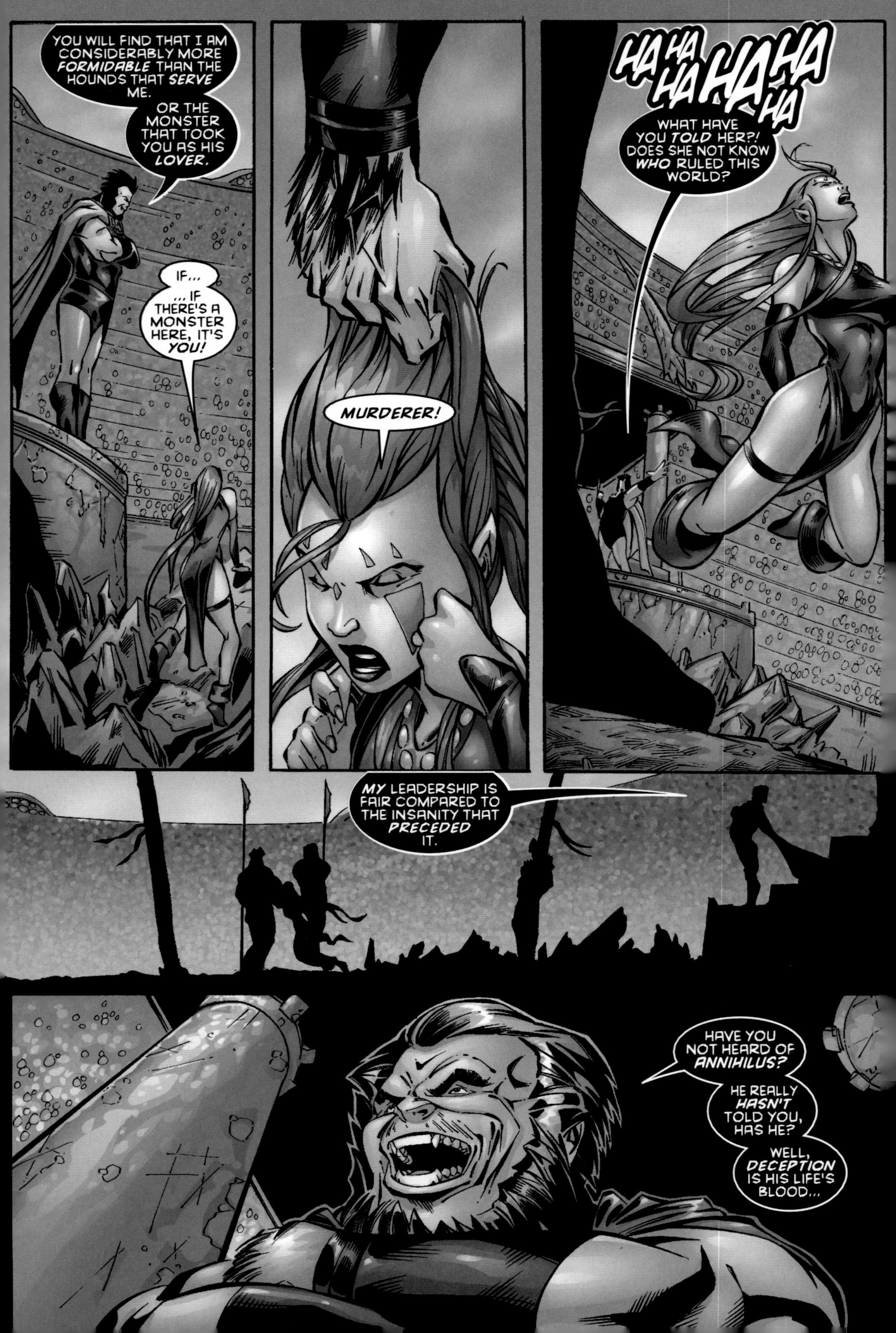
YOU WILL FIND THAT I AM CONSIDERABLY MORE FORMIDABLE THAN THE HOUNDS THAT SERVE ME.
OR THE MONSTER THAT TOOK YOU AS HIS LOVER.
IF...
...IF THERE'S A MONSTER HERE, IT'S YOU!
MURDERER!
HA HA HA HA HA HA HA HA
WHAT HAVE YOU TOLD HER?! DOES SHE NOT KNOW WHO RULED THIS WORLD?
MY LEADERSHIP IS FAIR COMPARED TO THE INSANITY THAT PRECEDED IT.
HAVE YOU NOT HEARD OF ANNIHILUS?
HE REALLY HASN'T TOLD YOU, HAS HE?
WELL, DECEPTION IS HIS LIFE'S BLOOD...

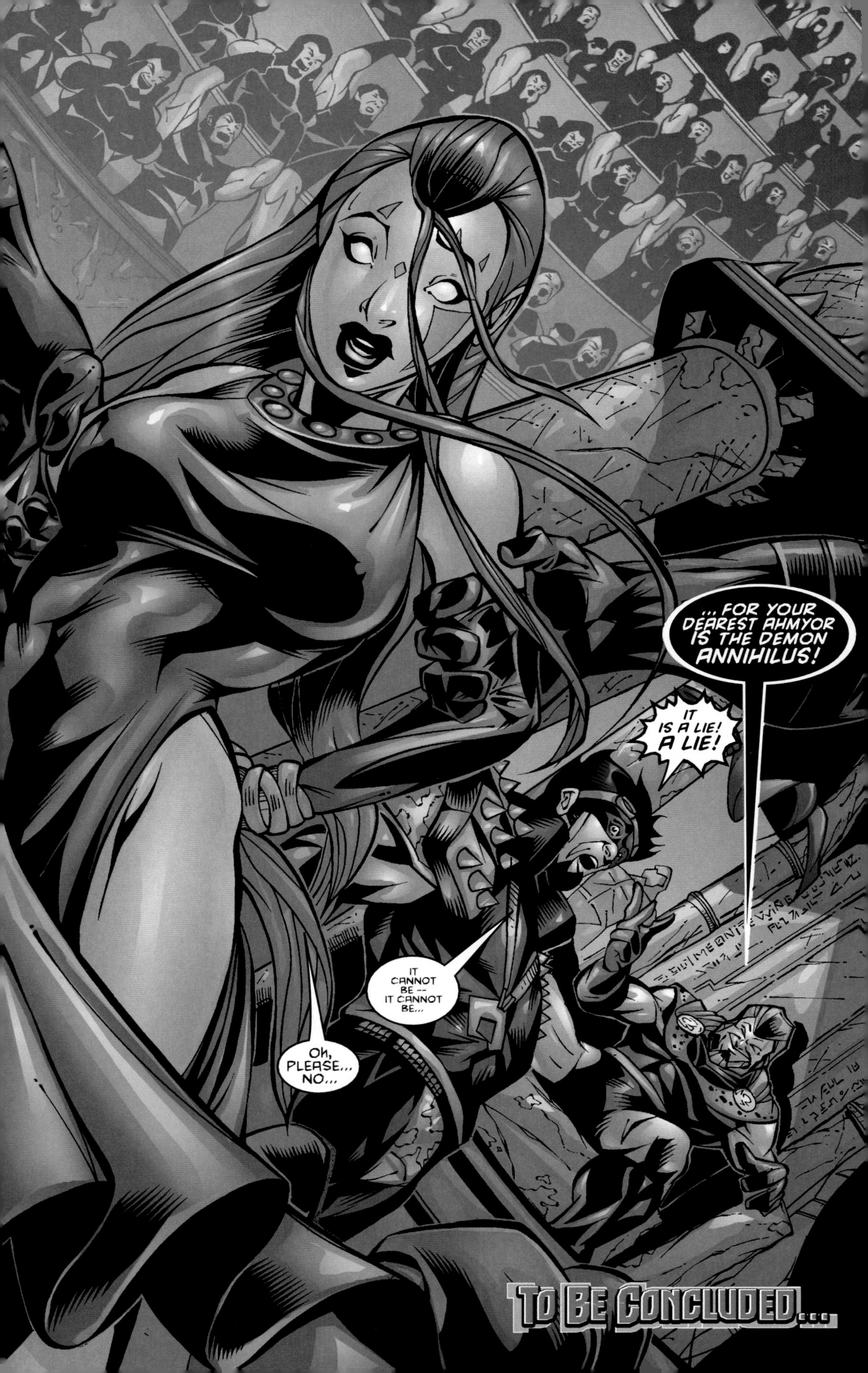
...FOR YOUR DEAREST AHMYOR IS THE DEMON ANNIHILUS!
IT IS A LIE! A LIE!
IT CANNOT BE -- IT CANNOT BE...
Oh, PLEASE... NO...
TO BE CONCLUDED...

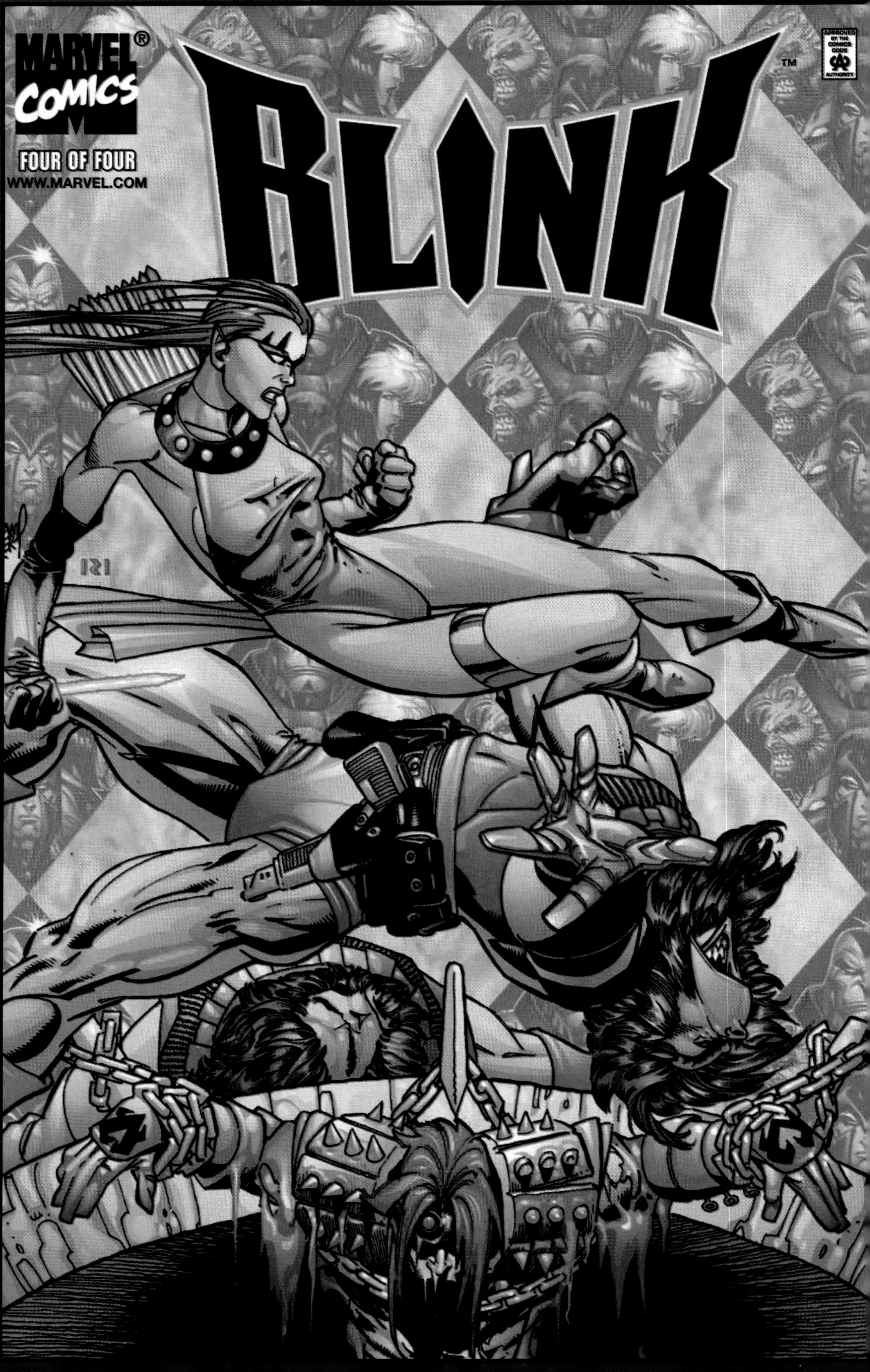
MARVEL® COMICS
BLINK™
FOUR OF FOUR
WWW.MARVEL.COM
APPROVED BY THE COMICS CODE AUTHORITY

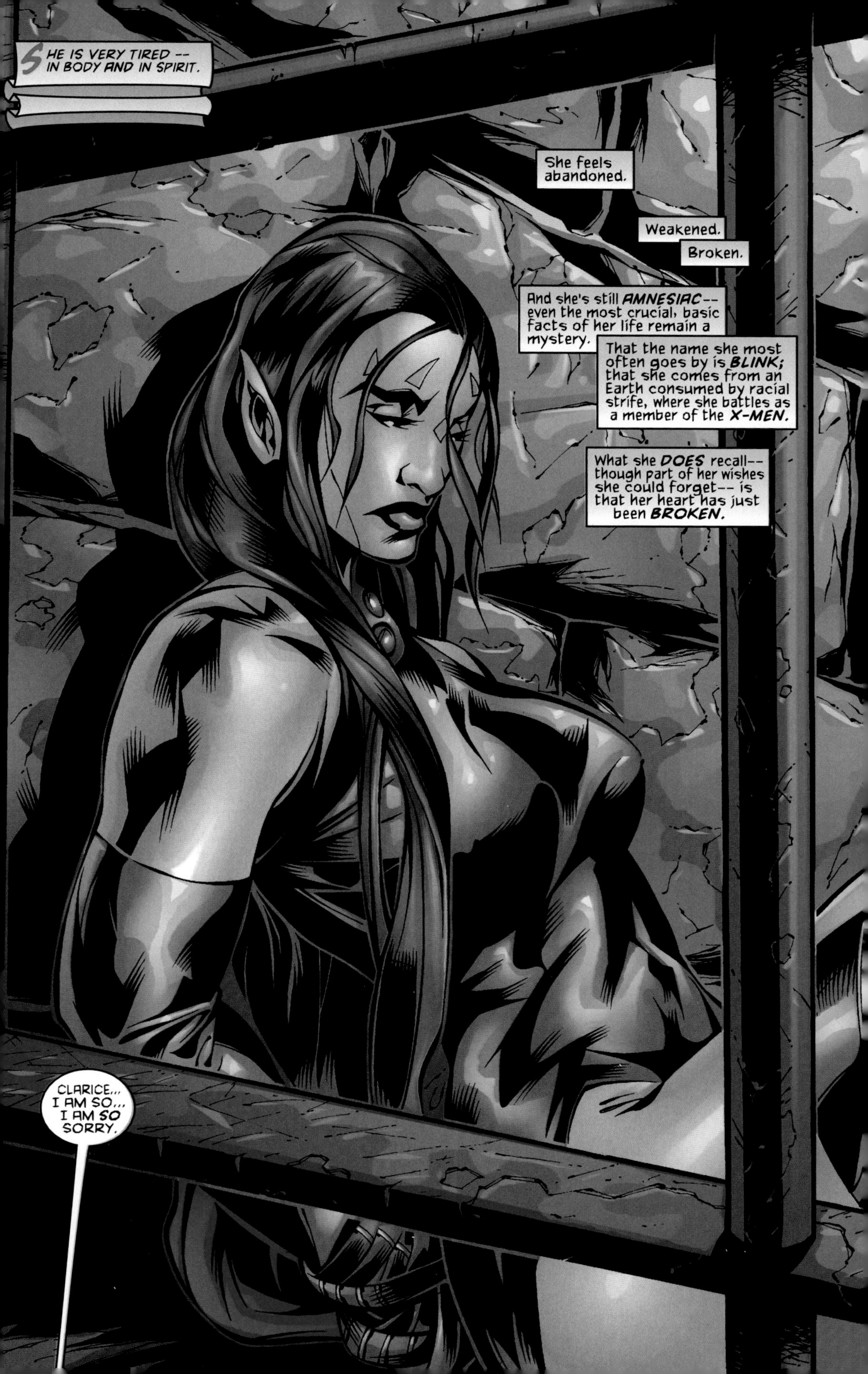
SHE IS VERY TIRED -- IN BODY AND IN SPIRIT.
She feels abandoned.
Weakened.
Broken.
And she's still AMNESIAC-- even the most crucial, basic facts of her life remain a mystery.
That the name she most often goes by is BLINK; that she comes from an Earth consumed by racial strife, where she battles as a member of the X-MEN.
What she DOES recall-- though part of her wishes she could forget-- is that her heart has just been BROKEN.
CLARICE... I AM SO... I AM SO SORRY.

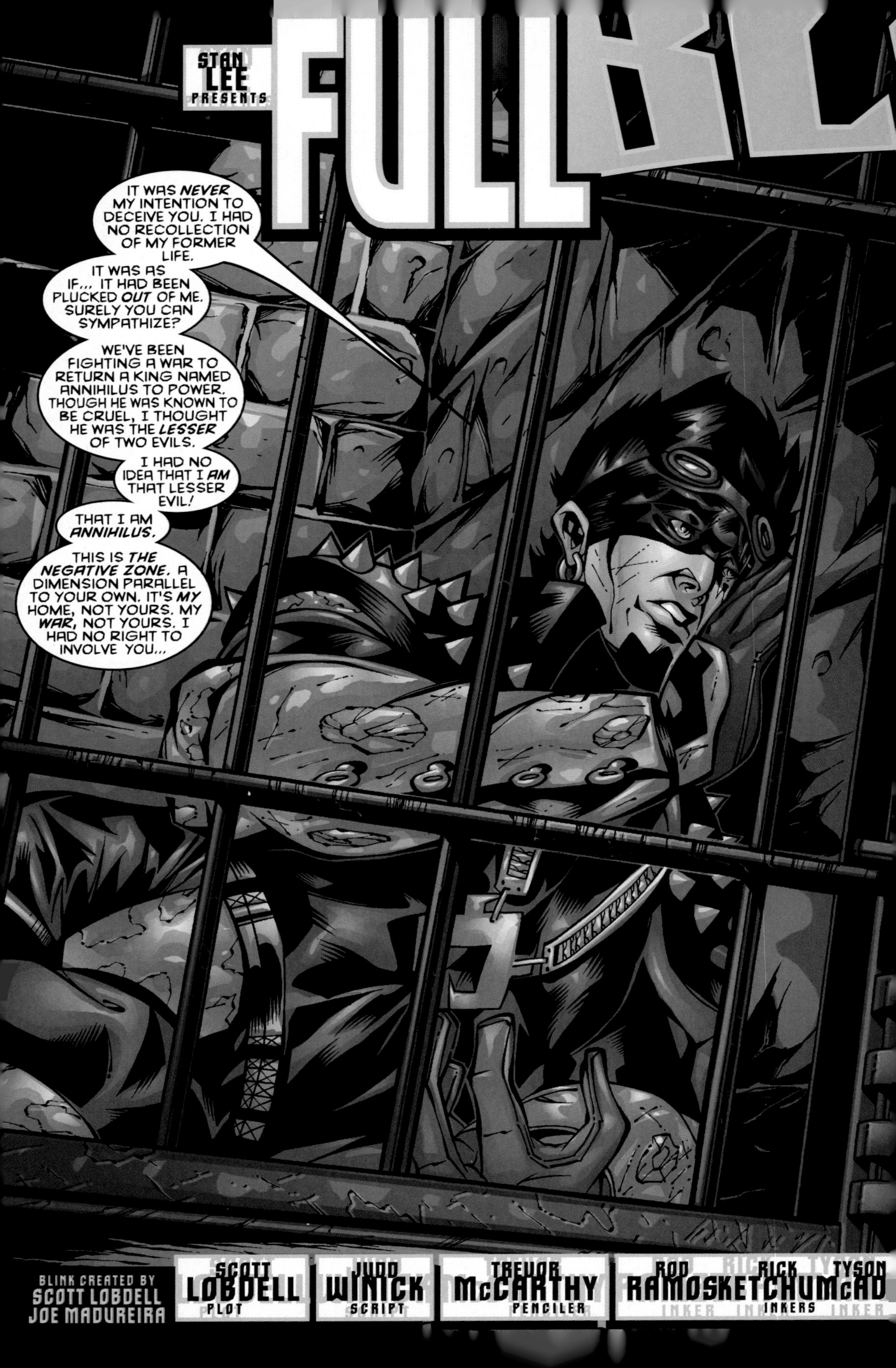
STAN LEE PRESENTS
FULL BL
IT WAS NEVER MY INTENTION TO DECEIVE YOU. I HAD NO RECOLLECTION OF MY FORMER LIFE.
IT WAS AS IF... IT HAD BEEN PLUCKED OUT OF ME. SURELY YOU CAN SYMPATHIZE?
WE'VE BEEN FIGHTING A WAR TO RETURN A KING NAMED ANNIHILUS TO POWER. THOUGH HE WAS KNOWN TO BE CRUEL, I THOUGHT HE WAS THE LESSER OF TWO EVILS.
I HAD NO IDEA THAT I AM THAT LESSER EVIL!
THAT I AM ANNIHILUS.
THIS IS THE NEGATIVE ZONE. A DIMENSION PARALLEL TO YOUR OWN. IT'S MY HOME, NOT YOURS. MY WAR, NOT YOURS. I HAD NO RIGHT TO INVOLVE YOU...
BLINK CREATED BY SCOTT LOBDELL JOE MADUREIRA
SCOTT LOBDELL PLOT
JUDD WINICK SCRIPT
TREVOR McCARTHY PENCILER
ROD RAMOS RICK KETCHUM TYSON McADOO INKERS

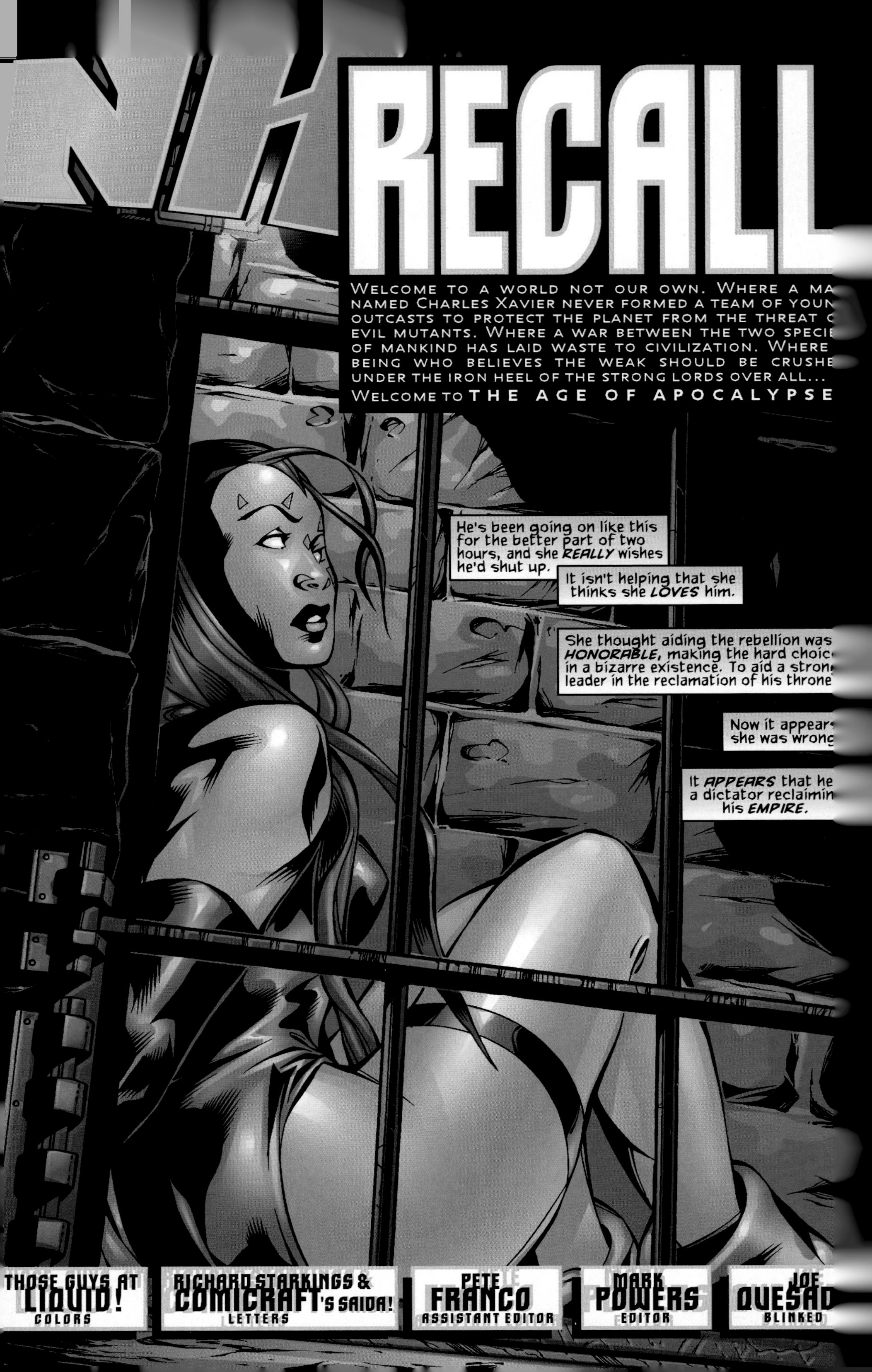
RECALL
Welcome to a world not our own. Where a ma
named Charles Xavier never formed a team of youn
outcasts to protect the planet from the threat o
evil mutants. Where a war between the two specie
of mankind has laid waste to civilization. Where
being who believes the weak should be crushe
under the iron heel of the strong lords over all...
Welcome to THE AGE OF APOCALYPSE
He's been going on like this for the better part of two hours, and she REALLY wishes he'd shut up.
It isn't helping that she thinks she LOVES him.
She thought aiding the rebellion was HONORABLE, making the hard choic in a bizarre existence. To aid a stron leader in the reclamation of his throne
Now it appear she was wrong
It APPEARS that he a dictator reclaimin his EMPIRE.
THOSE GUYS AT LIQUID! COLORS
RICHARD STARKINGS & COMICRAFT'S SAIDA! LETTERS
PETE FRANCO ASSISTANT EDITOR
MARK POWERS EDITOR
JOE QUESAD BLINKED

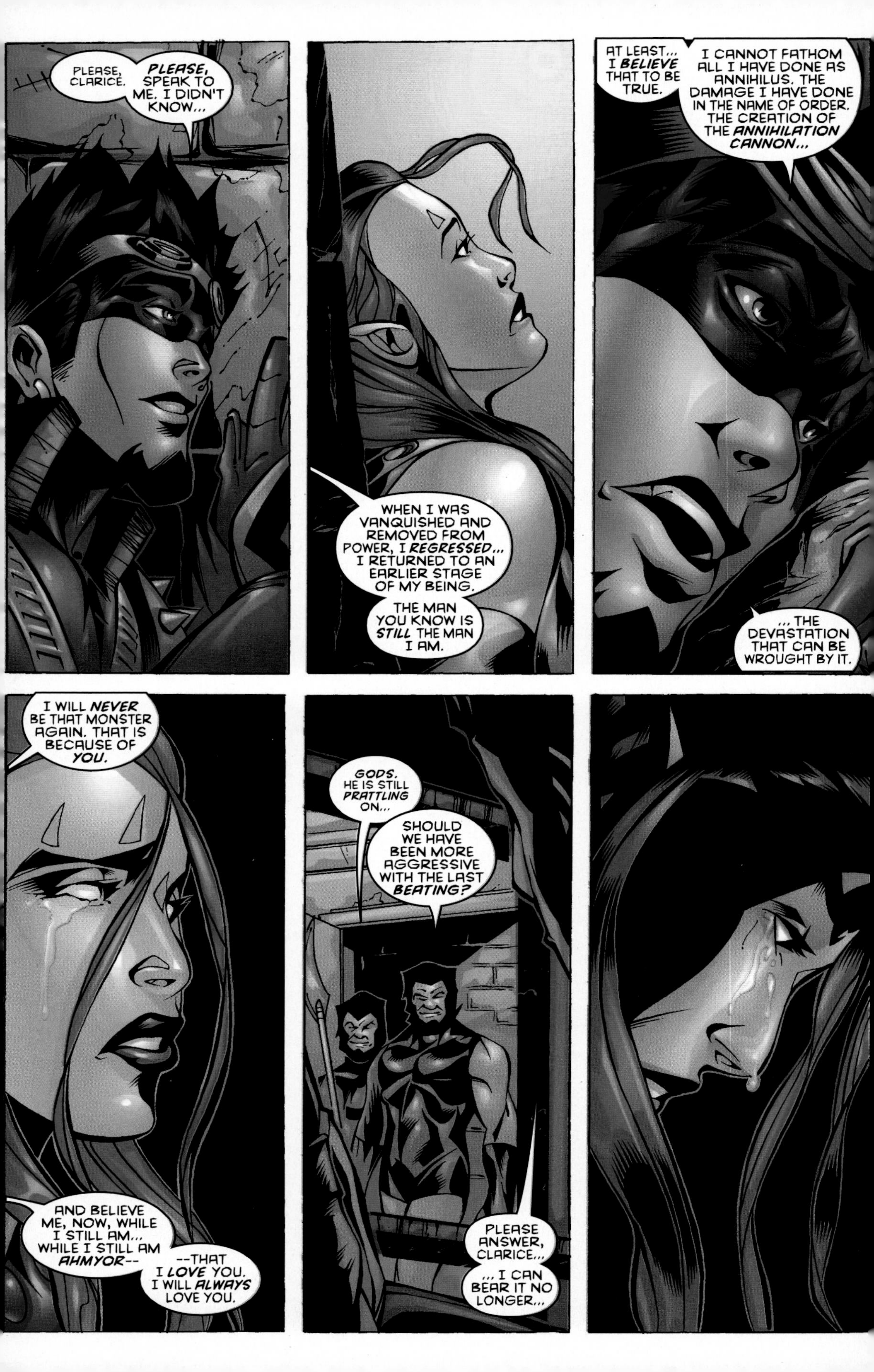
PLEASE, CLARICE.
PLEASE, SPEAK TO ME. I DIDN'T KNOW...
WHEN I WAS VANQUISHED AND REMOVED FROM POWER, I REGRESSED... I RETURNED TO AN EARLIER STAGE OF MY BEING.
THE MAN YOU KNOW IS STILL THE MAN I AM.
AT LEAST... I BELIEVE THAT TO BE TRUE.
I CANNOT FATHOM ALL I HAVE DONE AS ANNIHILUS. THE DAMAGE I HAVE DONE IN THE NAME OF ORDER. THE CREATION OF THE ANNIHILATION CANNON...
...THE DEVASTATION THAT CAN BE WROUGHT BY IT.
I WILL NEVER BE THAT MONSTER AGAIN. THAT IS BECAUSE OF YOU.
AND BELIEVE ME, NOW, WHILE I STILL AM... WHILE I STILL AM AHMYOR--
--THAT I LOVE YOU. I WILL ALWAYS LOVE YOU.
GODS. HE IS STILL PRATTLING ON...
SHOULD WE HAVE BEEN MORE AGGRESSIVE WITH THE LAST BEATING?
PLEASE ANSWER, CLARICE...
...I CAN BEAR IT NO LONGER...

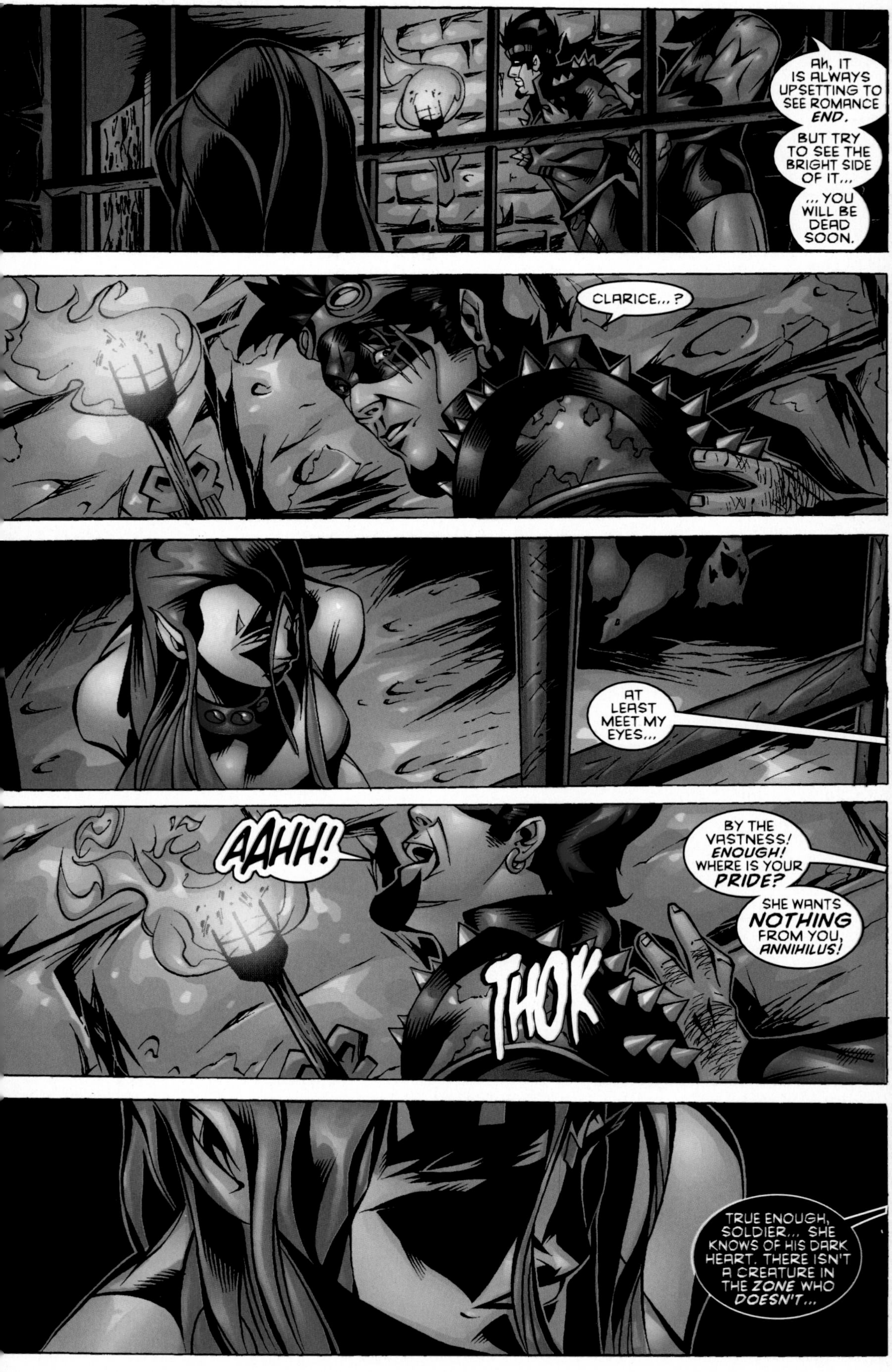
AH, IT IS ALWAYS UPSETTING TO SEE ROMANCE END.
BUT TRY TO SEE THE BRIGHT SIDE OF IT...
...YOU WILL BE DEAD SOON.
CLARICE...?
AT LEAST MEET MY EYES...
AAHH!
BY THE VASTNESS! ENOUGH! WHERE IS YOUR PRIDE?
SHE WANTS NOTHING FROM YOU, ANNIHILUS!
THOK
TRUE ENOUGH, SOLDIER... SHE KNOWS OF HIS DARK HEART. THERE ISN'T A CREATURE IN THE ZONE WHO DOESN'T...

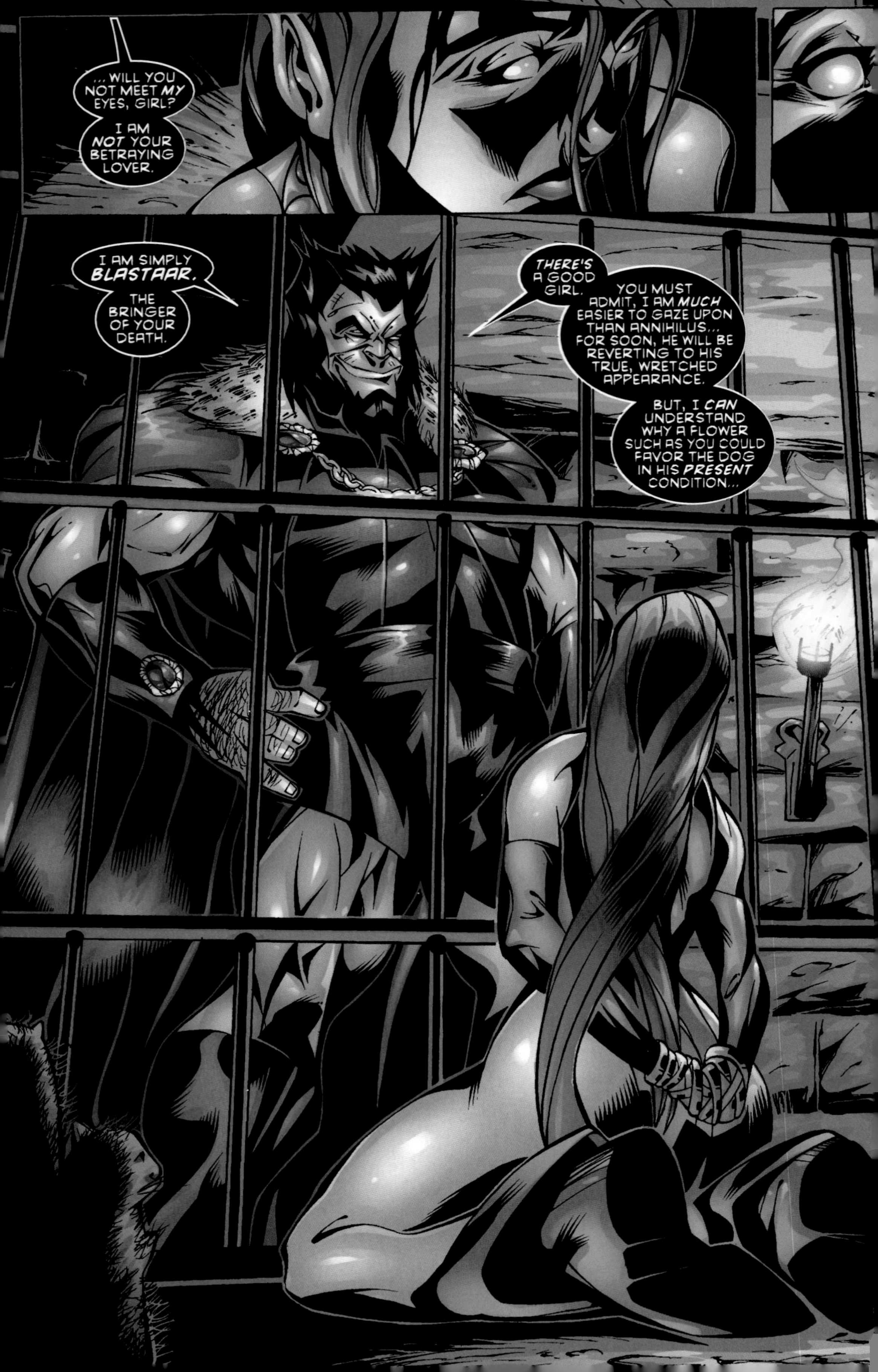

...WILL YOU NOT MEET *MY* EYES, GIRL?
I AM *NOT* YOUR BETRAYING LOVER.
I AM SIMPLY ***BLASTAAR.***
THE BRINGER OF YOUR DEATH.
THERE'S A GOOD GIRL.
YOU MUST ADMIT, I AM *MUCH* EASIER TO GAZE UPON THAN ANNIHILUS... FOR SOON, HE WILL BE REVERTING TO HIS TRUE, WRETCHED APPEARANCE.
BUT, I *CAN* UNDERSTAND WHY A FLOWER SUCH AS YOU COULD FAVOR THE DOG IN HIS ***PRESENT*** CONDITION...

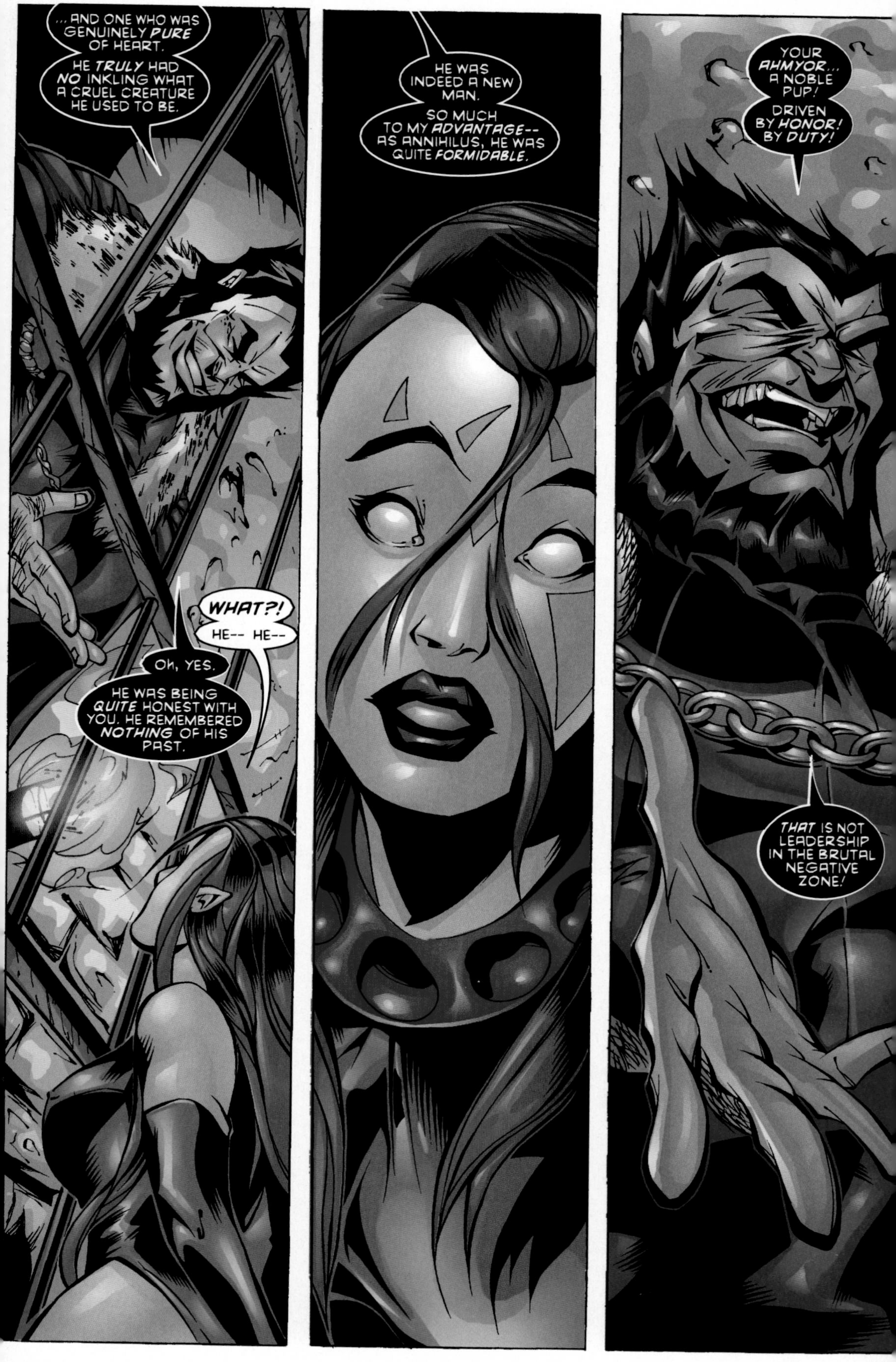
...AND ONE WHO WAS GENUINELY PURE OF HEART.
HE TRULY HAD NO INKLING WHAT A CRUEL CREATURE HE USED TO BE.
WHAT?!
HE-- HE--
Oh, YES.
HE WAS BEING QUITE HONEST WITH YOU. HE REMEMBERED NOTHING OF HIS PAST.
HE WAS INDEED A NEW MAN.
SO MUCH TO MY ADVANTAGE-- AS ANNIHILUS, HE WAS QUITE FORMIDABLE.
YOUR AHMYOR... A NOBLE PUP!
DRIVEN BY HONOR! BY DUTY!
THAT IS NOT LEADERSHIP IN THE BRUTAL NEGATIVE ZONE!

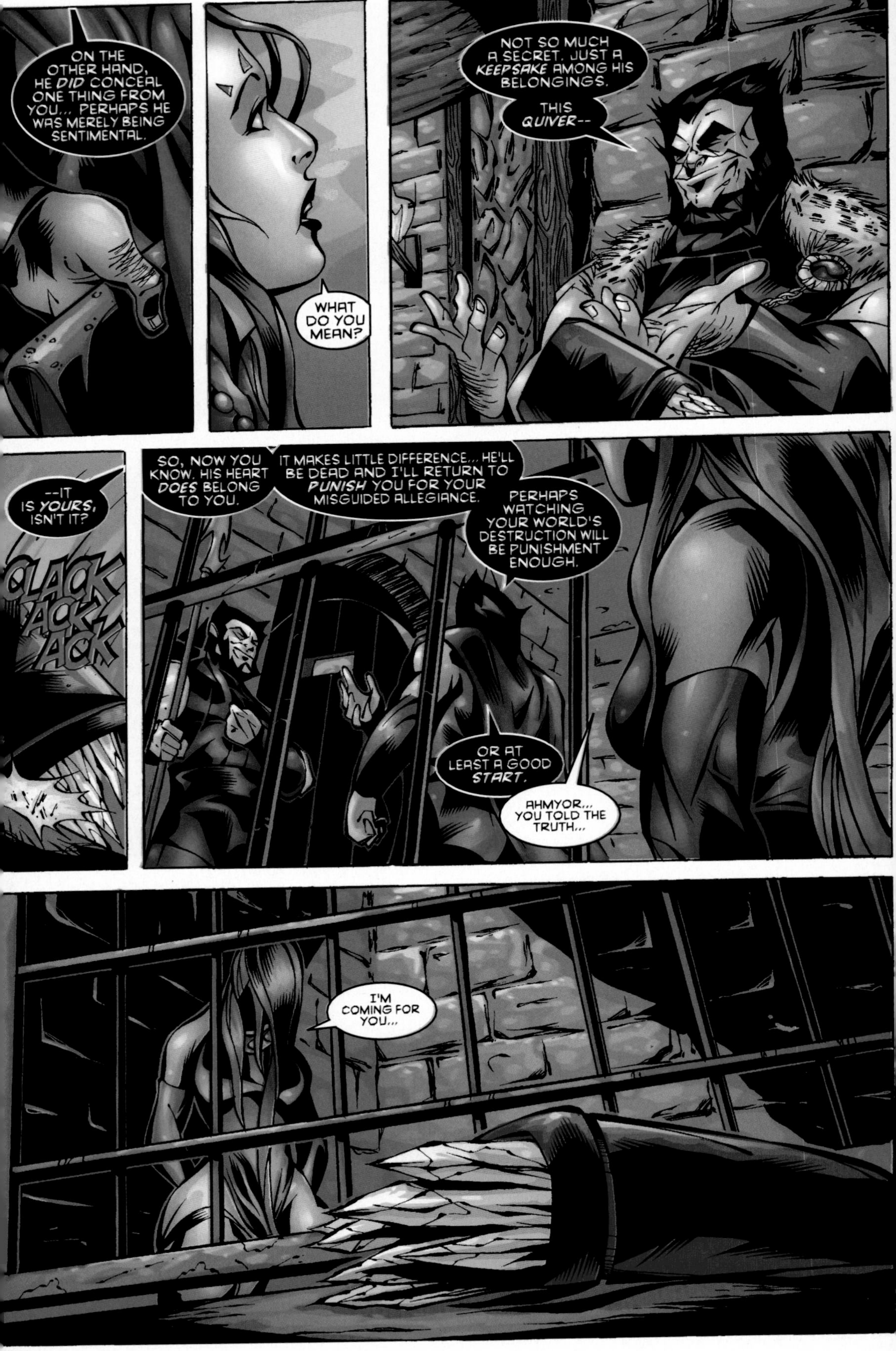
ON THE OTHER HAND, HE DID CONCEAL ONE THING FROM YOU... PERHAPS HE WAS MERELY BEING SENTIMENTAL.
WHAT DO YOU MEAN?
NOT SO MUCH A SECRET. JUST A KEEPSAKE AMONG HIS BELONGINGS.
THIS QUIVER--
--IT IS YOURS, ISN'T IT?
CLACK ACK ACK
SO, NOW YOU KNOW. HIS HEART DOES BELONG TO YOU.
IT MAKES LITTLE DIFFERENCE... HE'LL BE DEAD AND I'LL RETURN TO PUNISH YOU FOR YOUR MISGUIDED ALLEGIANCE.
PERHAPS WATCHING YOUR WORLD'S DESTRUCTION WILL BE PUNISHMENT ENOUGH.
OR AT LEAST A GOOD START.
AHMYOR... YOU TOLD THE TRUTH...
I'M COMING FOR YOU...

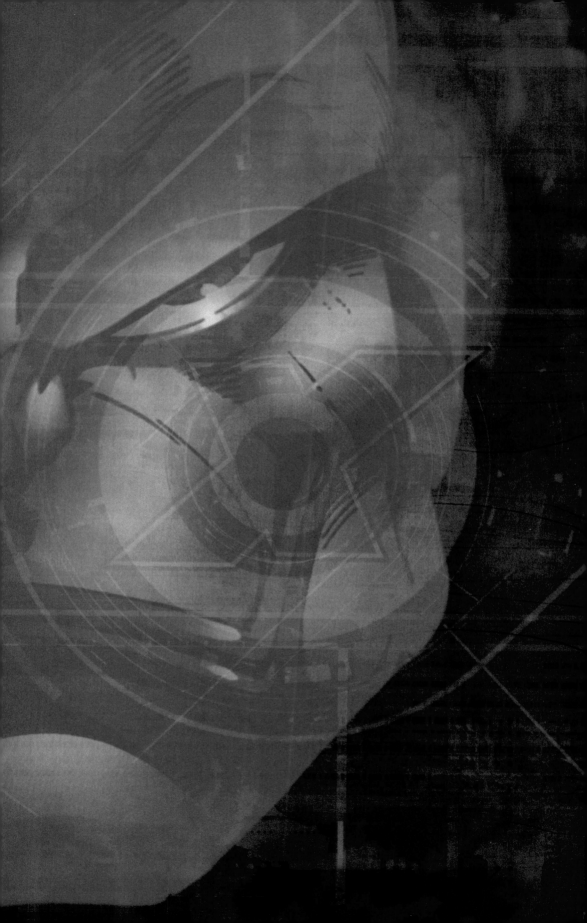

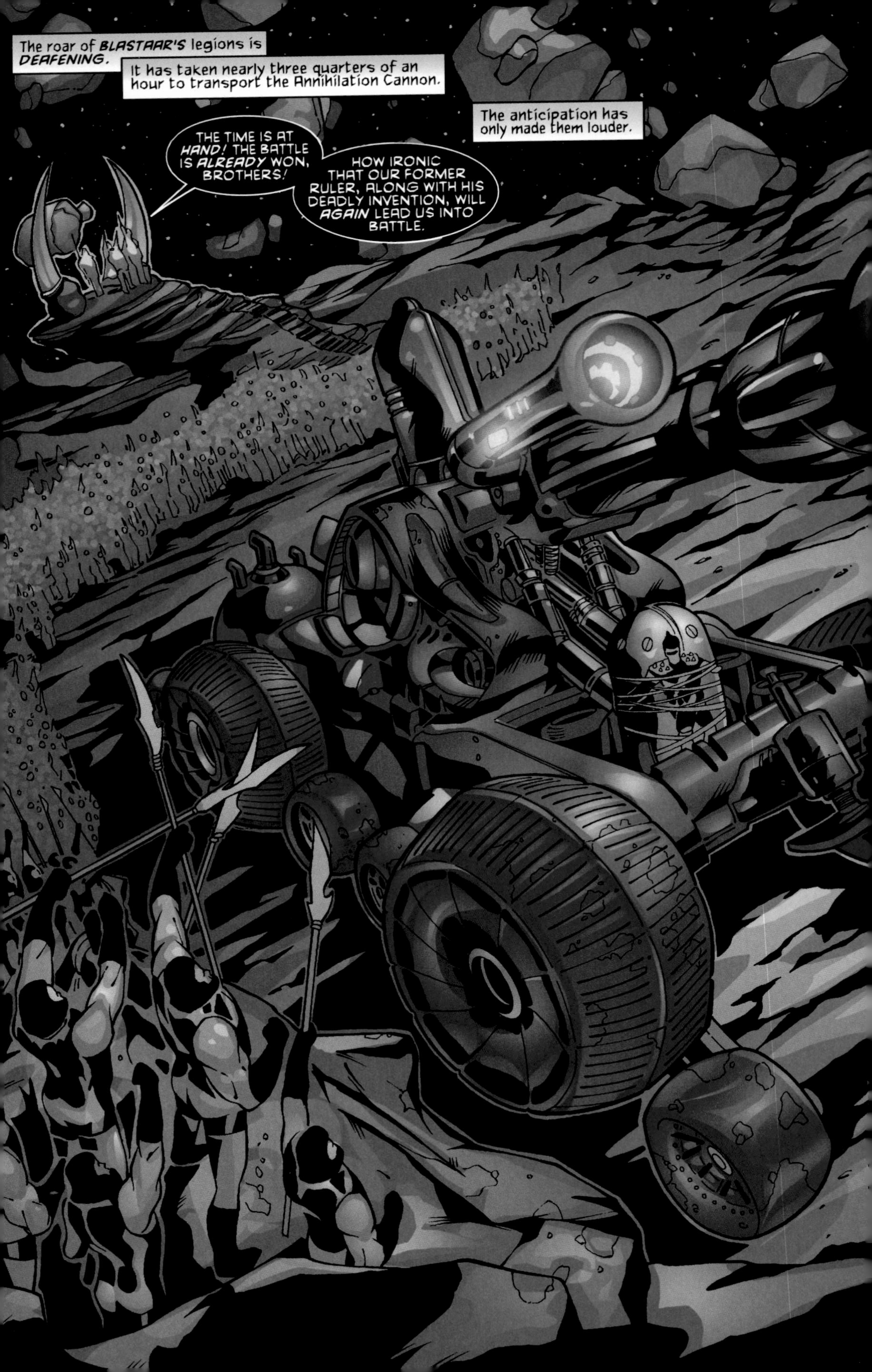
The roar of BLASTAAR'S legions is DEAFENING.
It has taken nearly three quarters of an hour to transport the Annihilation Cannon.
The anticipation has only made them louder.
THE TIME IS AT HAND! THE BATTLE IS ALREADY WON, BROTHERS!
HOW IRONIC THAT OUR FORMER RULER, ALONG WITH HIS DEADLY INVENTION, WILL AGAIN LEAD US INTO BATTLE.

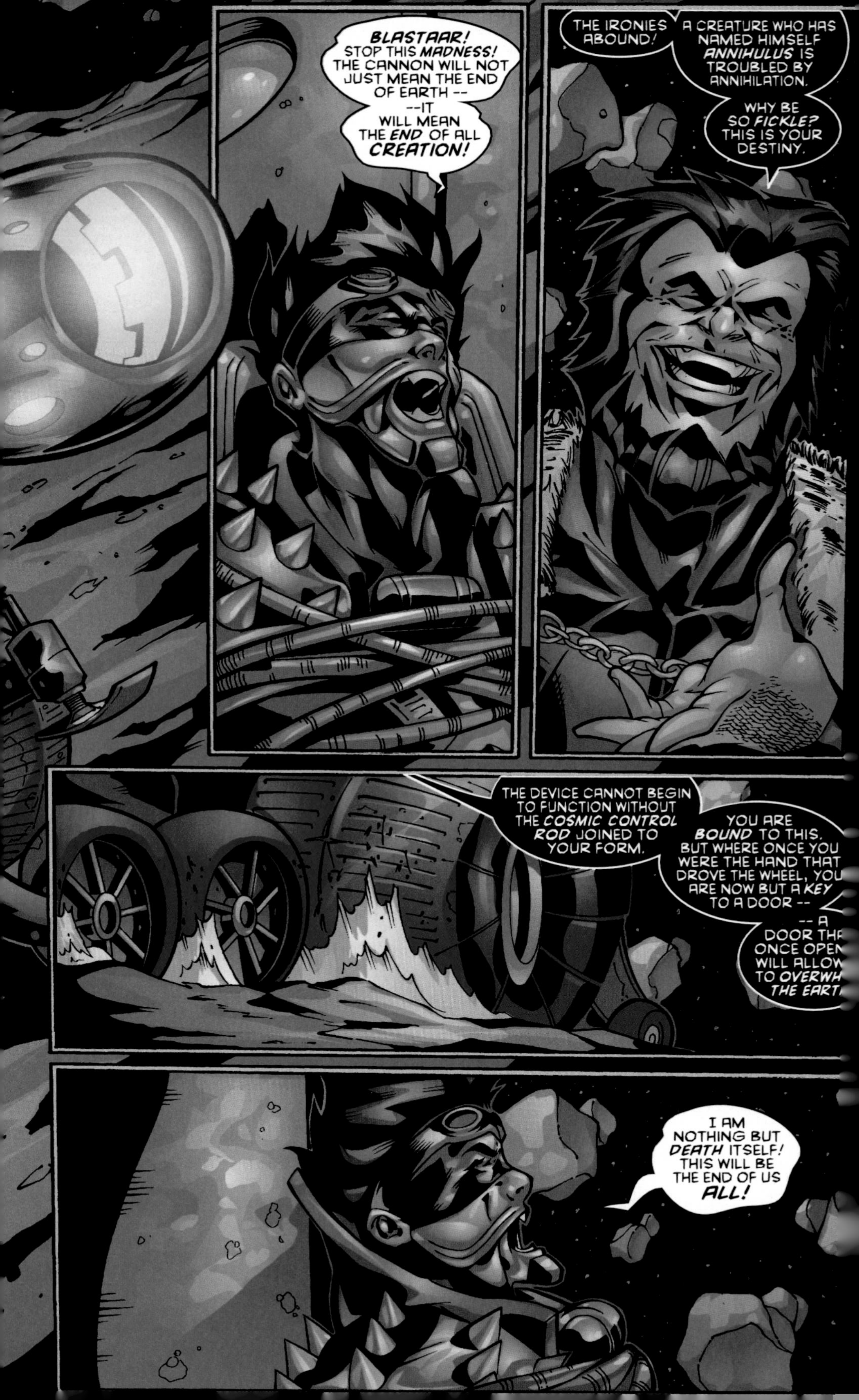
BLASTAAR! STOP THIS MADNESS! THE CANNON WILL NOT JUST MEAN THE END OF EARTH --
--IT WILL MEAN THE END OF ALL CREATION!
THE IRONIES ABOUND!
A CREATURE WHO HAS NAMED HIMSELF ANNIHULUS IS TROUBLED BY ANNIHILATION.
WHY BE SO FICKLE? THIS IS YOUR DESTINY.
THE DEVICE CANNOT BEGIN TO FUNCTION WITHOUT THE COSMIC CONTROL ROD JOINED TO YOUR FORM.
YOU ARE BOUND TO THIS. BUT WHERE ONCE YOU WERE THE HAND THAT DROVE THE WHEEL, YOU ARE NOW BUT A KEY TO A DOOR --
I AM NOTHING BUT DEATH ITSELF! THIS WILL BE THE END OF US ALL!

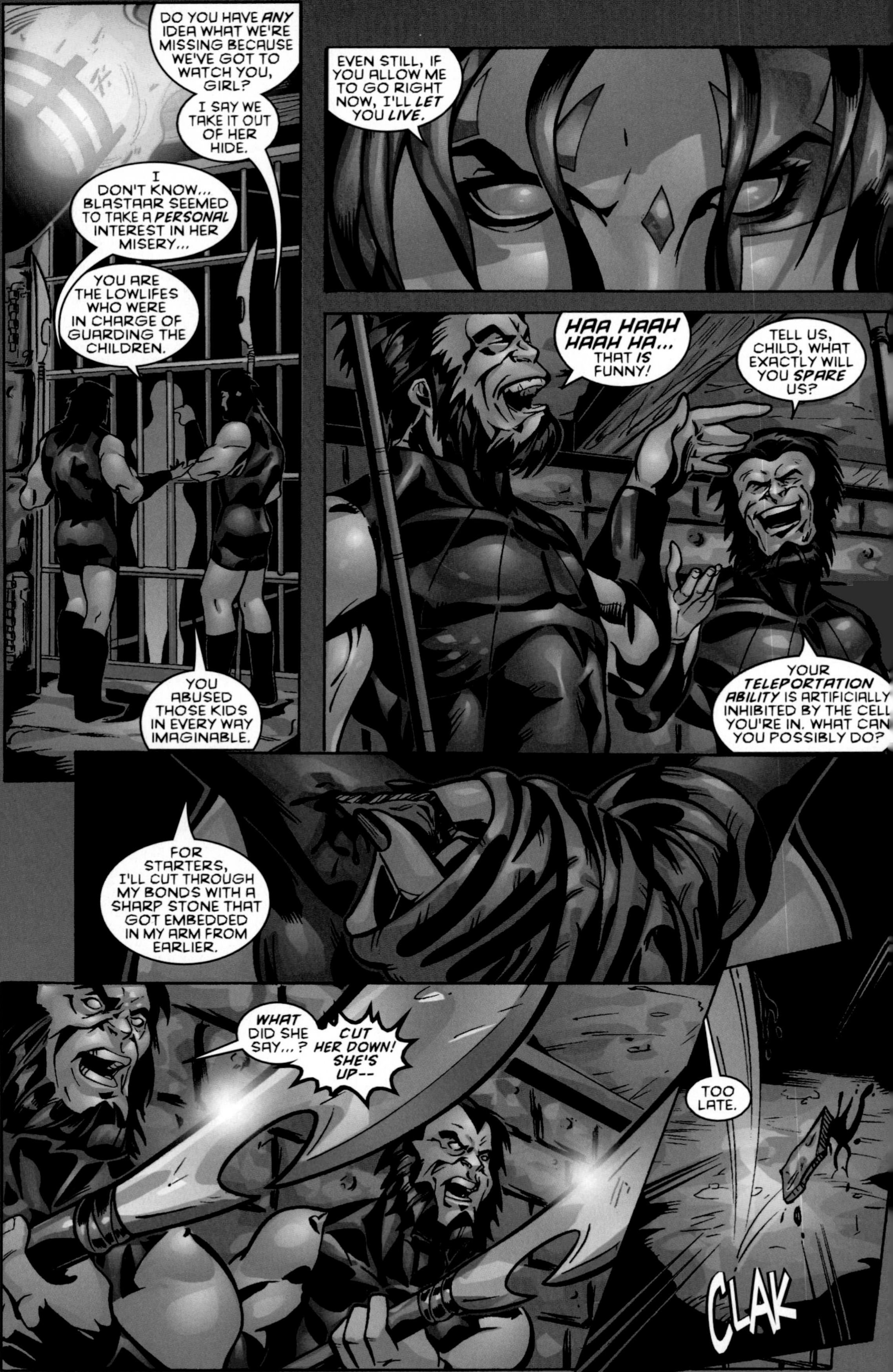

DO YOU HAVE ANY IDEA WHAT WE'RE MISSING BECAUSE WE'VE GOT TO WATCH YOU, GIRL?
I SAY WE TAKE IT OUT OF HER HIDE.
I DON'T KNOW... BLASTAAR SEEMED TO TAKE A PERSONAL INTEREST IN HER MISERY...
YOU ARE THE LOWLIFES WHO WERE IN CHARGE OF GUARDING THE CHILDREN.
YOU ABUSED THOSE KIDS IN EVERY WAY IMAGINABLE.
EVEN STILL, IF YOU ALLOW ME TO GO RIGHT NOW, I'LL LET YOU LIVE.
HAA HAAH HAAH HA... THAT IS FUNNY!
TELL US, CHILD, WHAT EXACTLY WILL YOU SPARE US?
YOUR TELEPORTATION ABILITY IS ARTIFICIALLY INHIBITED BY THE CELL YOU'RE IN. WHAT CAN YOU POSSIBLY DO?
FOR STARTERS, I'LL CUT THROUGH MY BONDS WITH A SHARP STONE THAT GOT EMBEDDED IN MY ARM FROM EARLIER.
WHAT DID SHE SAY...?
CUT HER DOWN! SHE'S UP--
TOO LATE.
CLAK

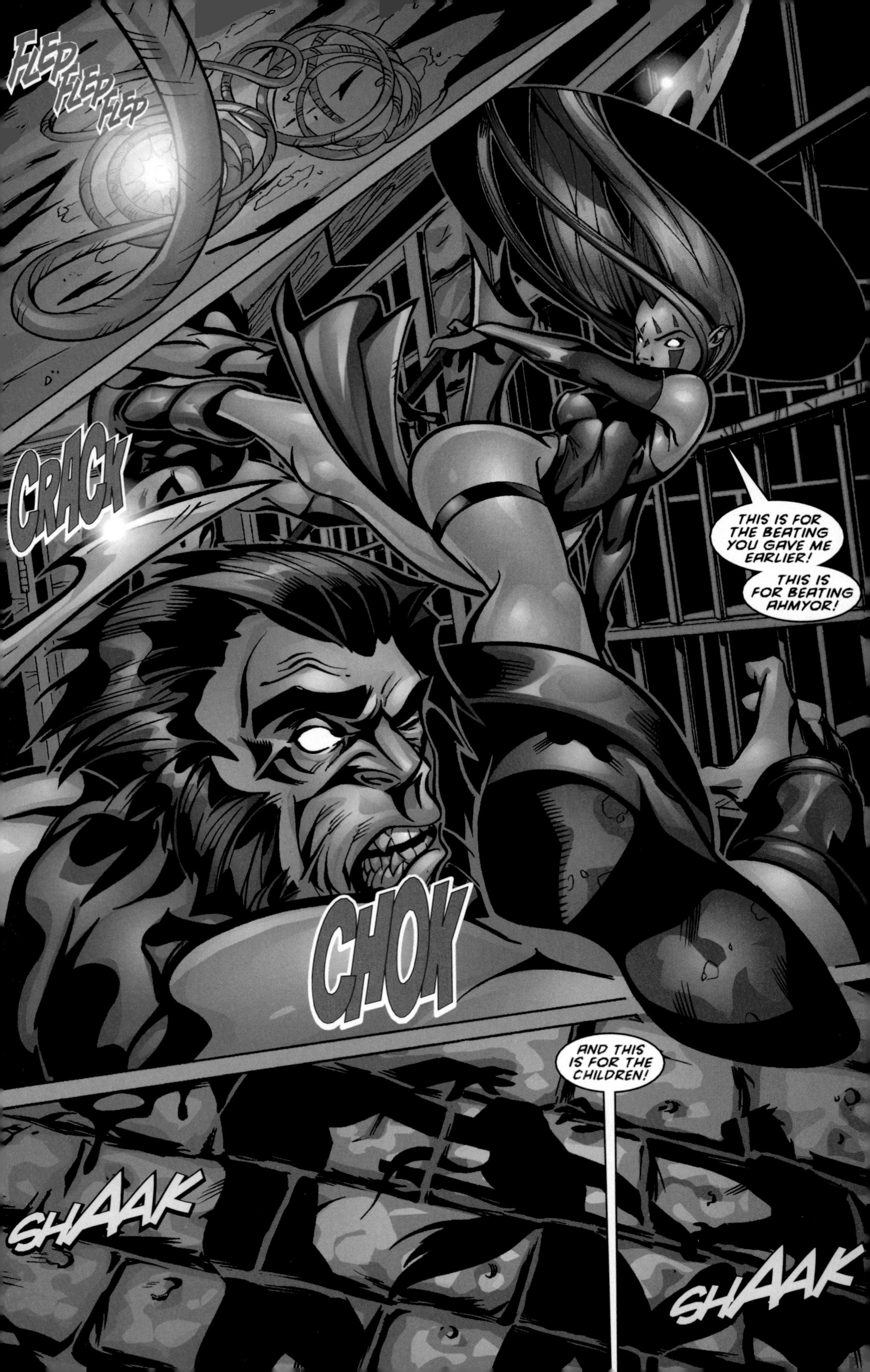
FLEP FLEP FLEP
CRACK
THIS IS FOR THE BEATING YOU GAVE ME EARLIER!
THIS IS FOR BEATING AHMYOR!
CHOK
AND THIS IS FOR THE CHILDREN!
SHAAK
SHAAK

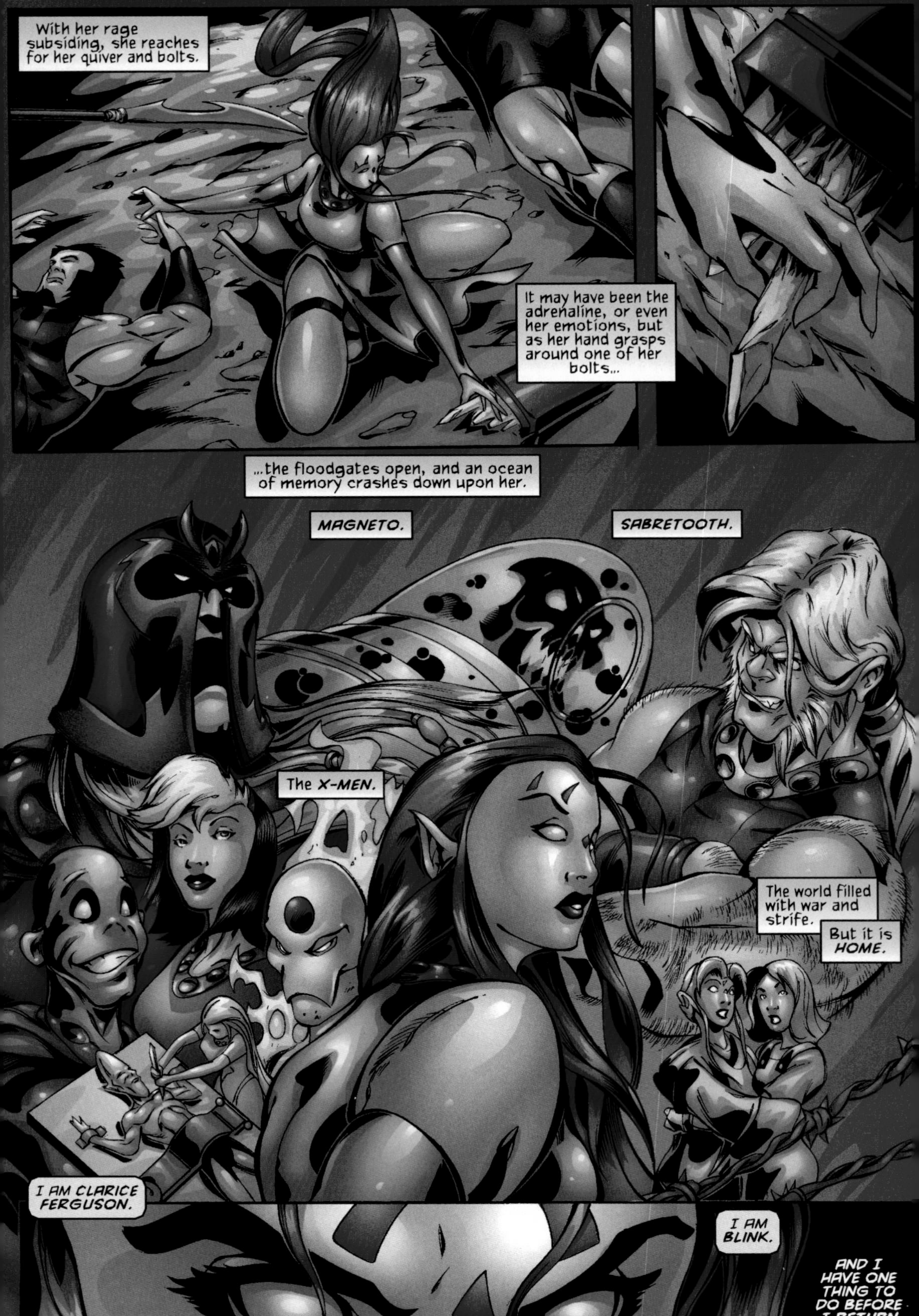
With her rage subsiding, she reaches for her quiver and bolts.
It may have been the adrenaline, or even her emotions, but as her hand grasps around one of her bolts...
...the floodgates open, and an ocean of memory crashes down upon her.
MAGNETO.
SABRETOOTH.
The X-MEN.
The world filled with war and strife.
But it is HOME.
I AM CLARICE FERGUSON.
I AM BLINK.
AND I HAVE ONE THING TO DO BEFORE I RETURN HOME.

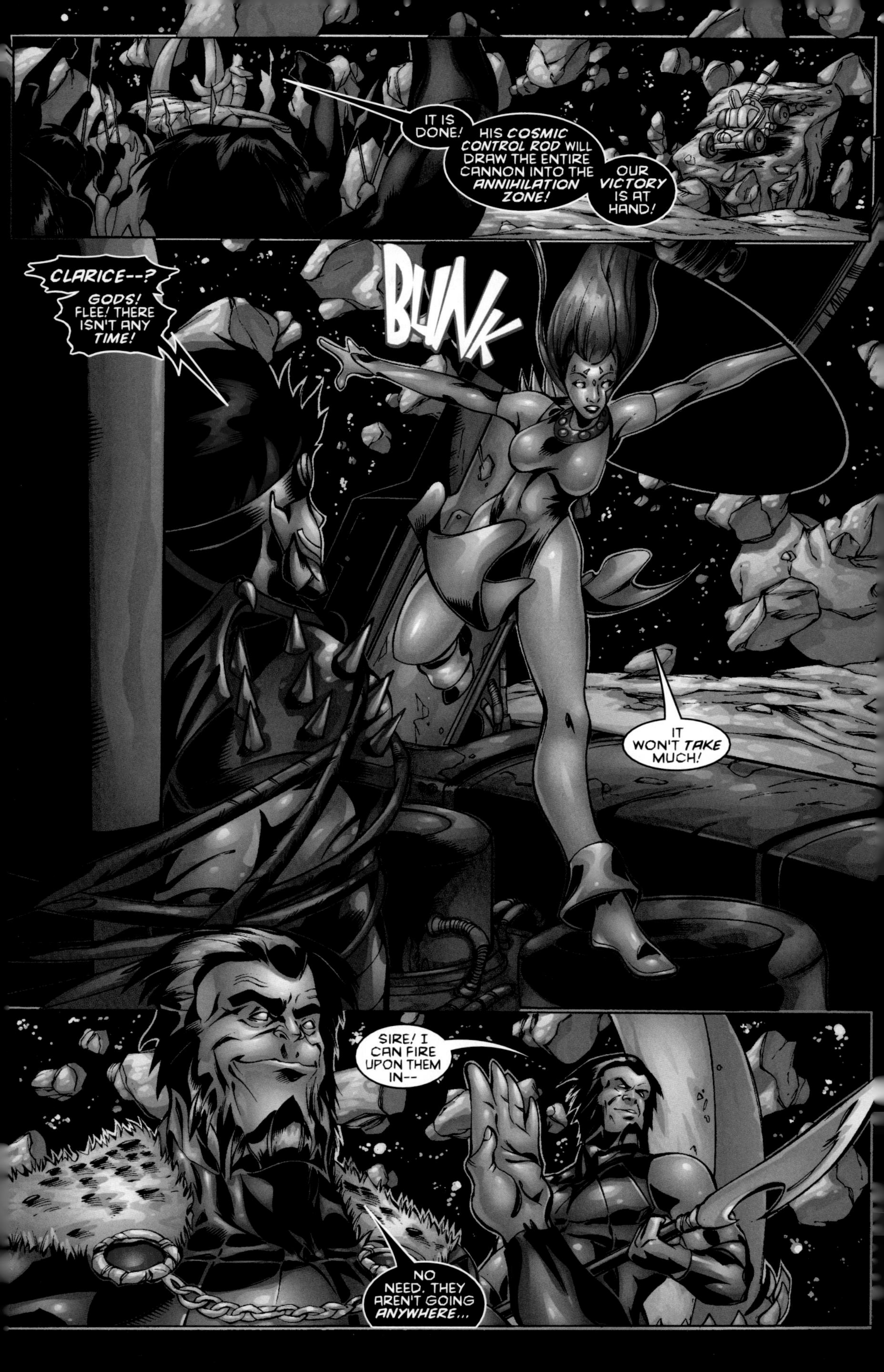

IT IS DONE!
HIS COSMIC CONTROL ROD WILL DRAW THE ENTIRE CANNON INTO THE ANNIHILATION ZONE!
OUR VICTORY IS AT HAND!
BLUNK
CLARICE--?
GODS! FLEE! THERE ISN'T ANY TIME!
IT WON'T TAKE MUCH!
SIRE! I CAN FIRE UPON THEM IN--
NO NEED. THEY AREN'T GOING ANYWHERE...

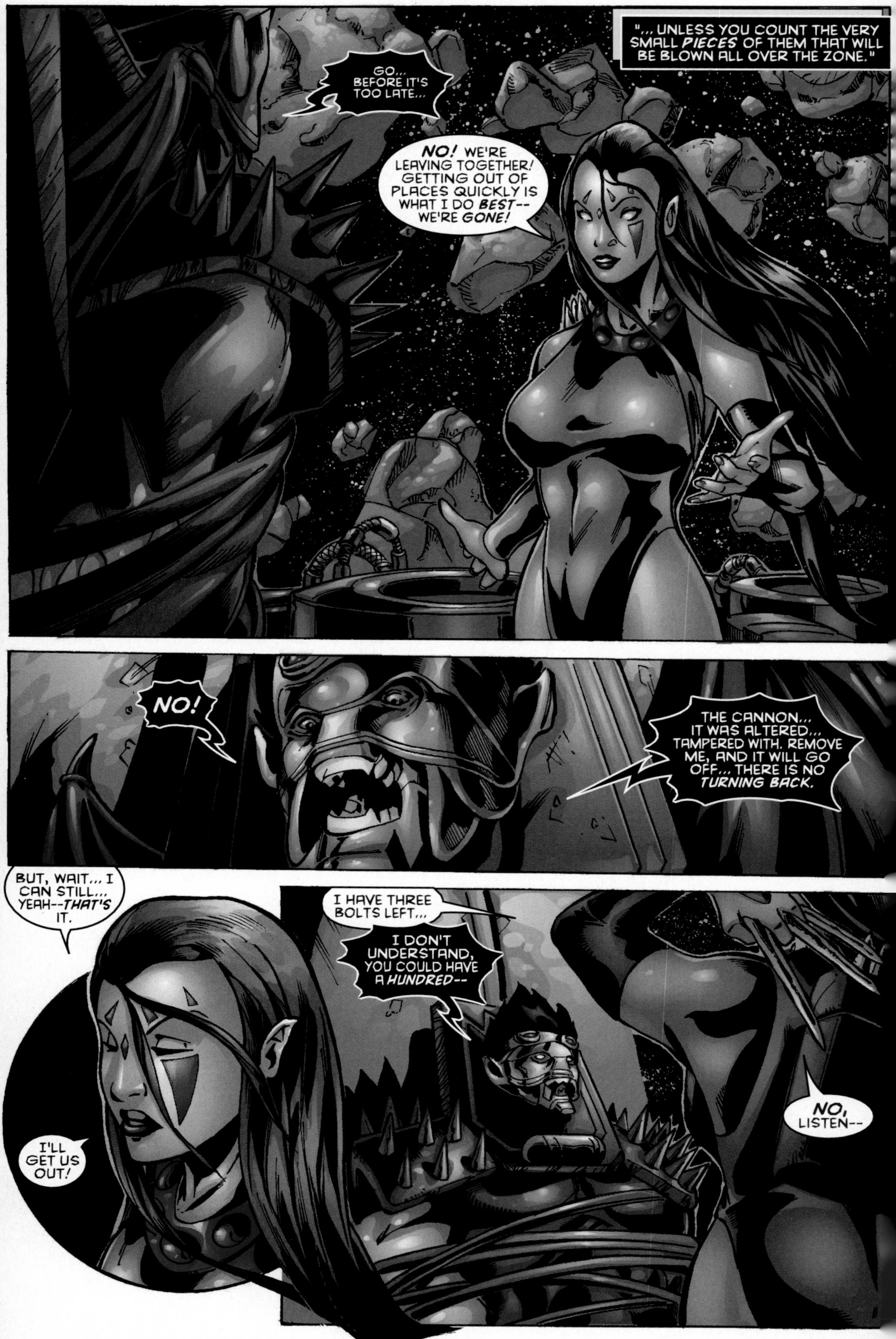
"... UNLESS YOU COUNT THE VERY SMALL PIECES OF THEM THAT WILL BE BLOWN ALL OVER THE ZONE."
GO... BEFORE IT'S TOO LATE...
NO! WE'RE LEAVING TOGETHER! GETTING OUT OF PLACES QUICKLY IS WHAT I DO BEST-- WE'RE GONE!
NO!
THE CANNON... IT WAS ALTERED... TAMPERED WITH. REMOVE ME, AND IT WILL GO OFF... THERE IS NO TURNING BACK.
BUT, WAIT... I CAN STILL... YEAH--THAT'S IT.
I HAVE THREE BOLTS LEFT...
I DON'T UNDERSTAND, YOU COULD HAVE A HUNDRED--
I'LL GET US OUT!
NO, LISTEN--

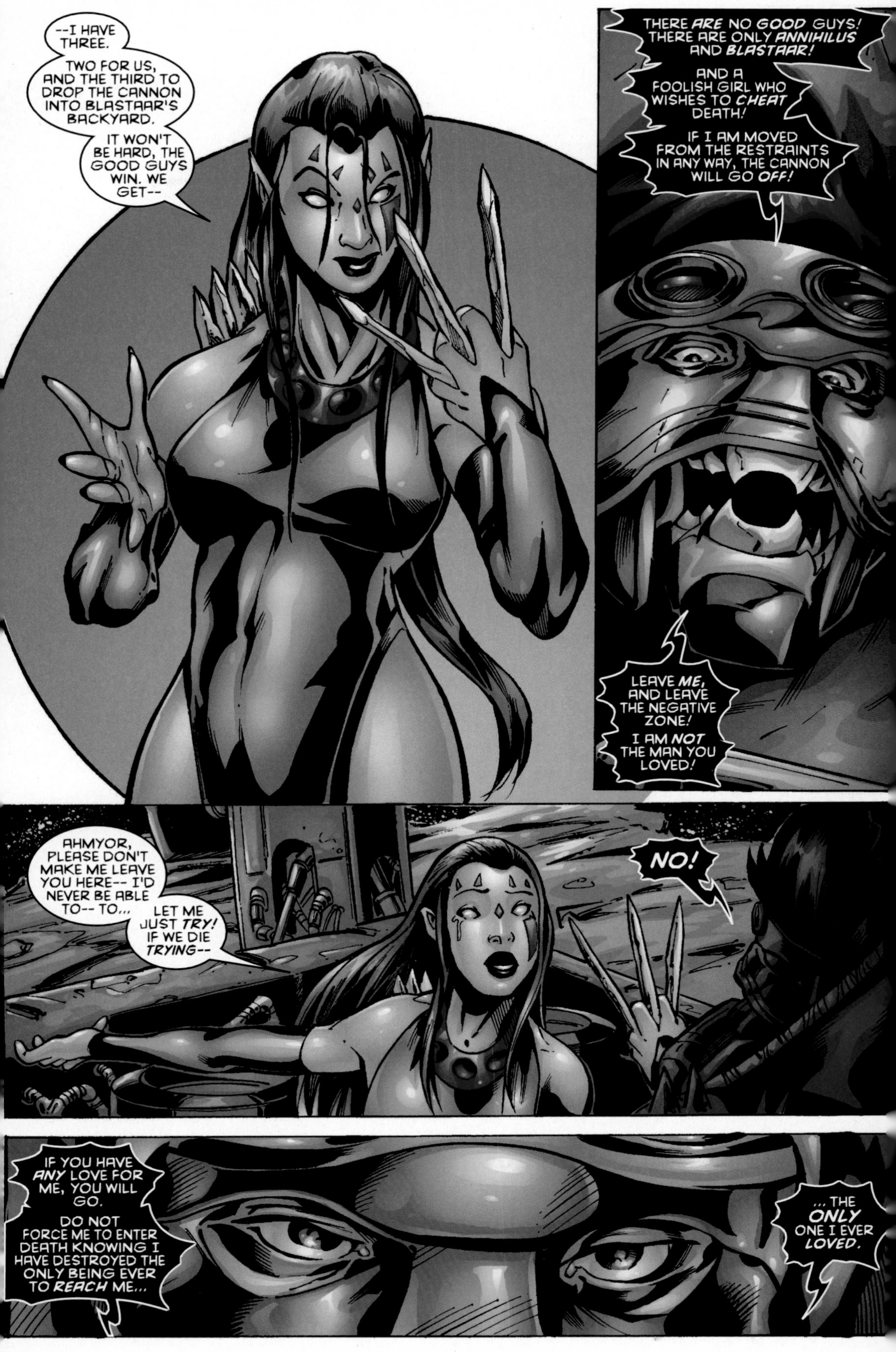
--I HAVE THREE.
TWO FOR US, AND THE THIRD TO DROP THE CANNON INTO BLASTAAR'S BACKYARD.
IT WON'T BE HARD, THE GOOD GUYS WIN. WE GET--
THERE ARE NO GOOD GUYS! THERE ARE ONLY ANNIHILUS AND BLASTAAR!
AND A FOOLISH GIRL WHO WISHES TO CHEAT DEATH!
IF I AM MOVED FROM THE RESTRAINTS IN ANY WAY, THE CANNON WILL GO OFF!
LEAVE ME, AND LEAVE THE NEGATIVE ZONE!
I AM NOT THE MAN YOU LOVED!
AHMYOR, PLEASE DON'T MAKE ME LEAVE YOU HERE-- I'D NEVER BE ABLE TO-- TO...
LET ME JUST TRY! IF WE DIE TRYING--
NO!
IF YOU HAVE ANY LOVE FOR ME, YOU WILL GO.
DO NOT FORCE ME TO ENTER DEATH KNOWING I HAVE DESTROYED THE ONLY BEING EVER TO REACH ME...
...THE ONLY ONE I EVER LOVED.

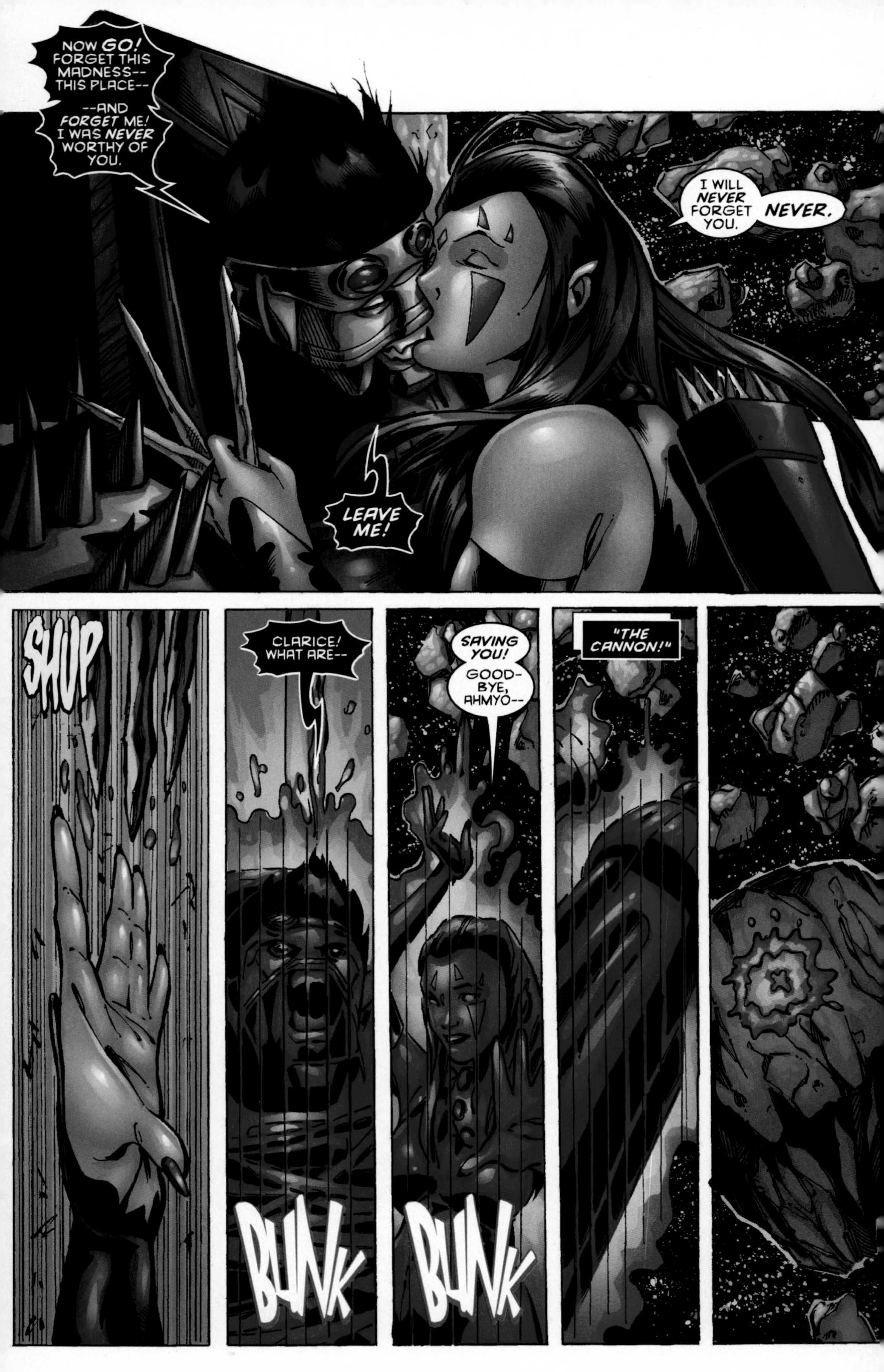
NOW GO! FORGET THIS MADNESS-- THIS PLACE--
--AND FORGET ME! I WAS NEVER WORTHY OF YOU.
I WILL NEVER FORGET YOU.
NEVER.
LEAVE ME!
SHUP
CLARICE! WHAT ARE--
BUNK
SAVING YOU!
GOOD-BYE, AHMYO--
BUNK
"THE CANNON!"

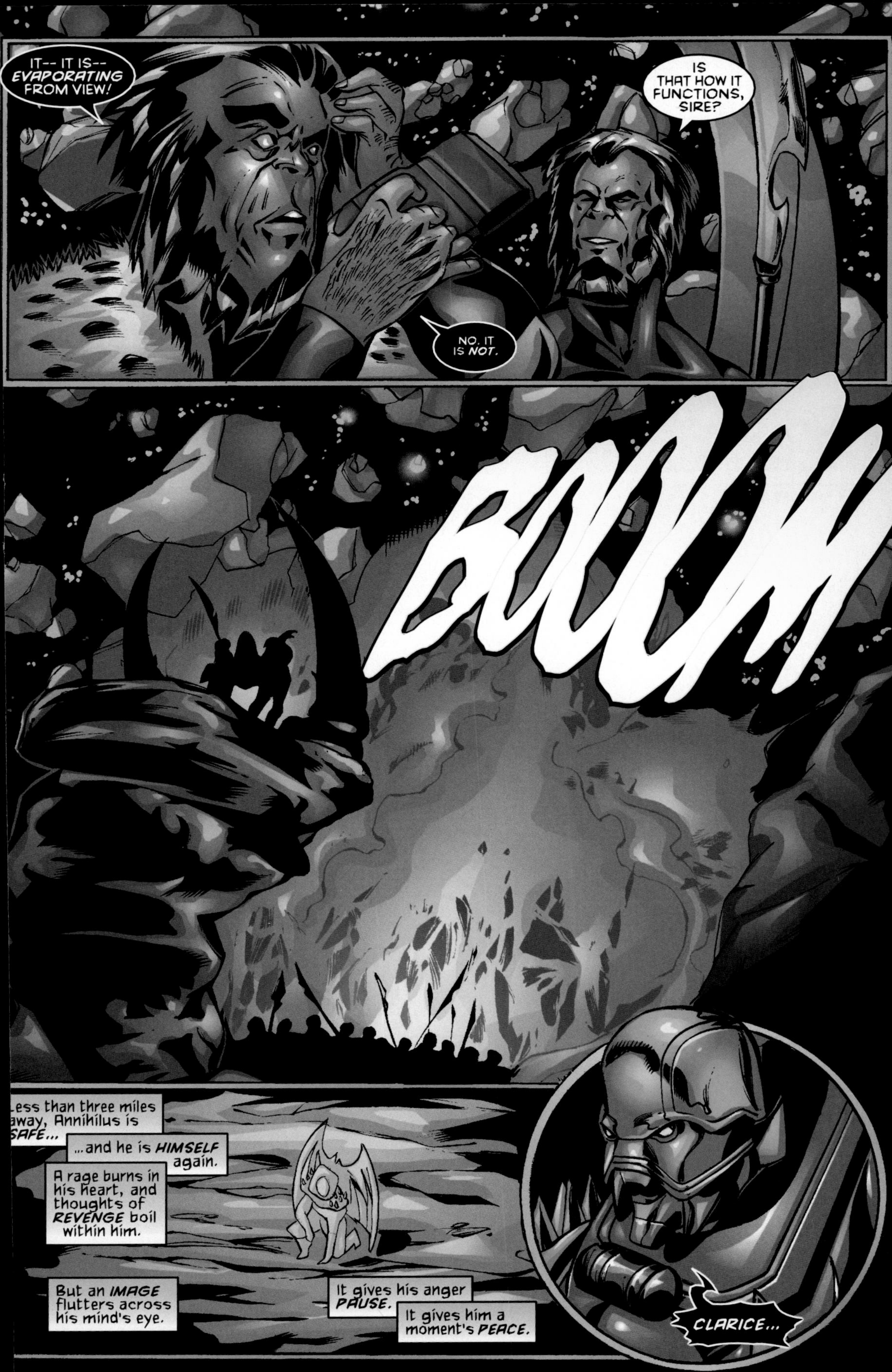
IT-- IT IS-- *EVAPORATING* FROM VIEW!
IS THAT HOW IT FUNCTIONS, SIRE?
NO. IT IS *NOT*.
BOOOM
Less than three miles away, Annihilus is *SAFE*...
...and he is *HIMSELF* again.
A rage burns in his heart, and thoughts of *REVENGE* boil within him.
But an *IMAGE* flutters across his mind's eye.
It gives his anger *PAUSE*.
It gives him a moment's *PEACE*.
CLARICE...

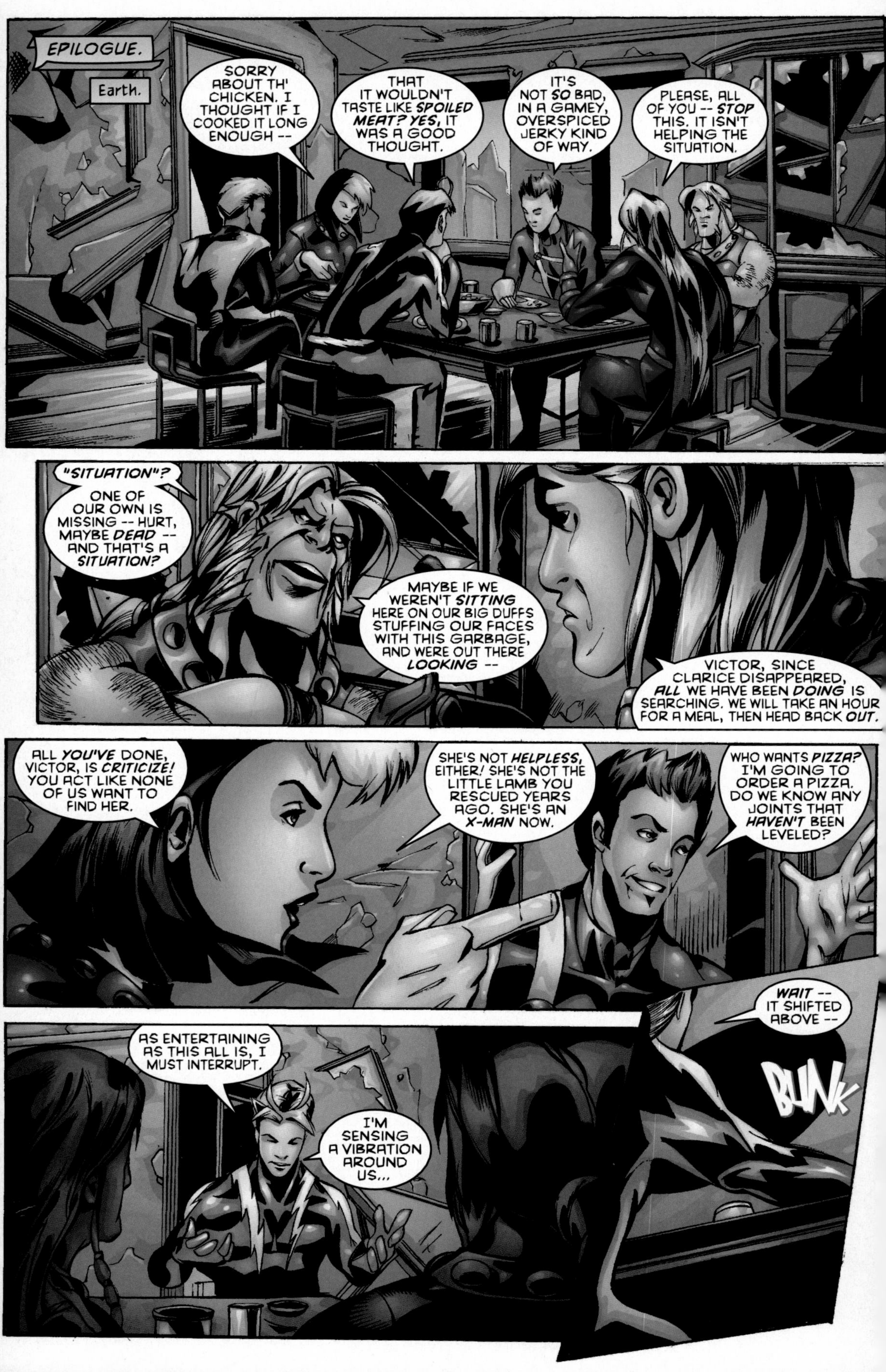
EPILOGUE.
Earth.
SORRY ABOUT TH' CHICKEN. I THOUGHT IF I COOKED IT LONG ENOUGH --
THAT IT WOULDN'T TASTE LIKE SPOILED MEAT? YES, IT WAS A GOOD THOUGHT.
IT'S NOT SO BAD, IN A GAMEY, OVERSPICED JERKY KIND OF WAY.
PLEASE, ALL OF YOU -- STOP THIS. IT ISN'T HELPING THE SITUATION.
"SITUATION"? ONE OF OUR OWN IS MISSING -- HURT, MAYBE DEAD -- AND THAT'S A SITUATION?
MAYBE IF WE WEREN'T SITTING HERE ON OUR BIG DUFFS STUFFING OUR FACES WITH THIS GARBAGE, AND WERE OUT THERE LOOKING --
VICTOR, SINCE CLARICE DISAPPEARED, ALL WE HAVE BEEN DOING IS SEARCHING. WE WILL TAKE AN HOUR FOR A MEAL, THEN HEAD BACK OUT.
ALL YOU'VE DONE, VICTOR, IS CRITICIZE! YOU ACT LIKE NONE OF US WANT TO FIND HER.
SHE'S NOT HELPLESS, EITHER! SHE'S NOT THE LITTLE LAMB YOU RESCUED YEARS AGO. SHE'S AN X-MAN NOW.
WHO WANTS PIZZA? I'M GOING TO ORDER A PIZZA. DO WE KNOW ANY JOINTS THAT HAVEN'T BEEN LEVELED?
AS ENTERTAINING AS THIS ALL IS, I MUST INTERRUPT.
I'M SENSING A VIBRATION AROUND US...
WAIT -- IT SHIFTED ABOVE --
BLUNK

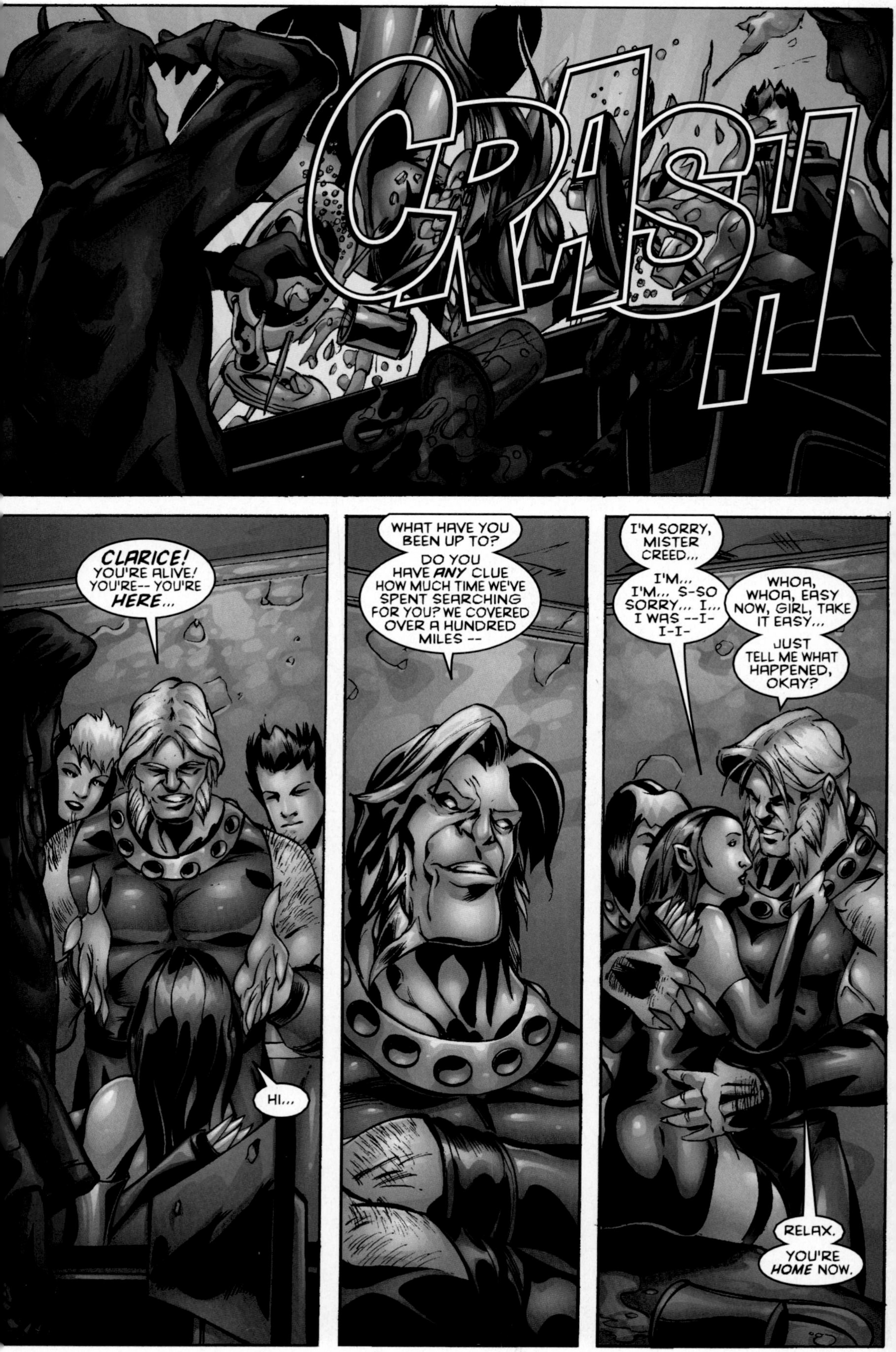
CRASH
CLARICE! YOU'RE ALIVE! YOU'RE-- YOU'RE HERE...
HI...
WHAT HAVE YOU BEEN UP TO?
DO YOU HAVE ANY CLUE HOW MUCH TIME WE'VE SPENT SEARCHING FOR YOU? WE COVERED OVER A HUNDRED MILES --
I'M SORRY, MISTER CREED...
I'M... I'M... S-SO SORRY... I... I WAS --I- I-I-
WHOA, WHOA, GIRL, EASY NOW, GIRL, TAKE IT EASY...
JUST TELL ME WHAT HAPPENED, OKAY?
RELAX.
YOU'RE HOME NOW.

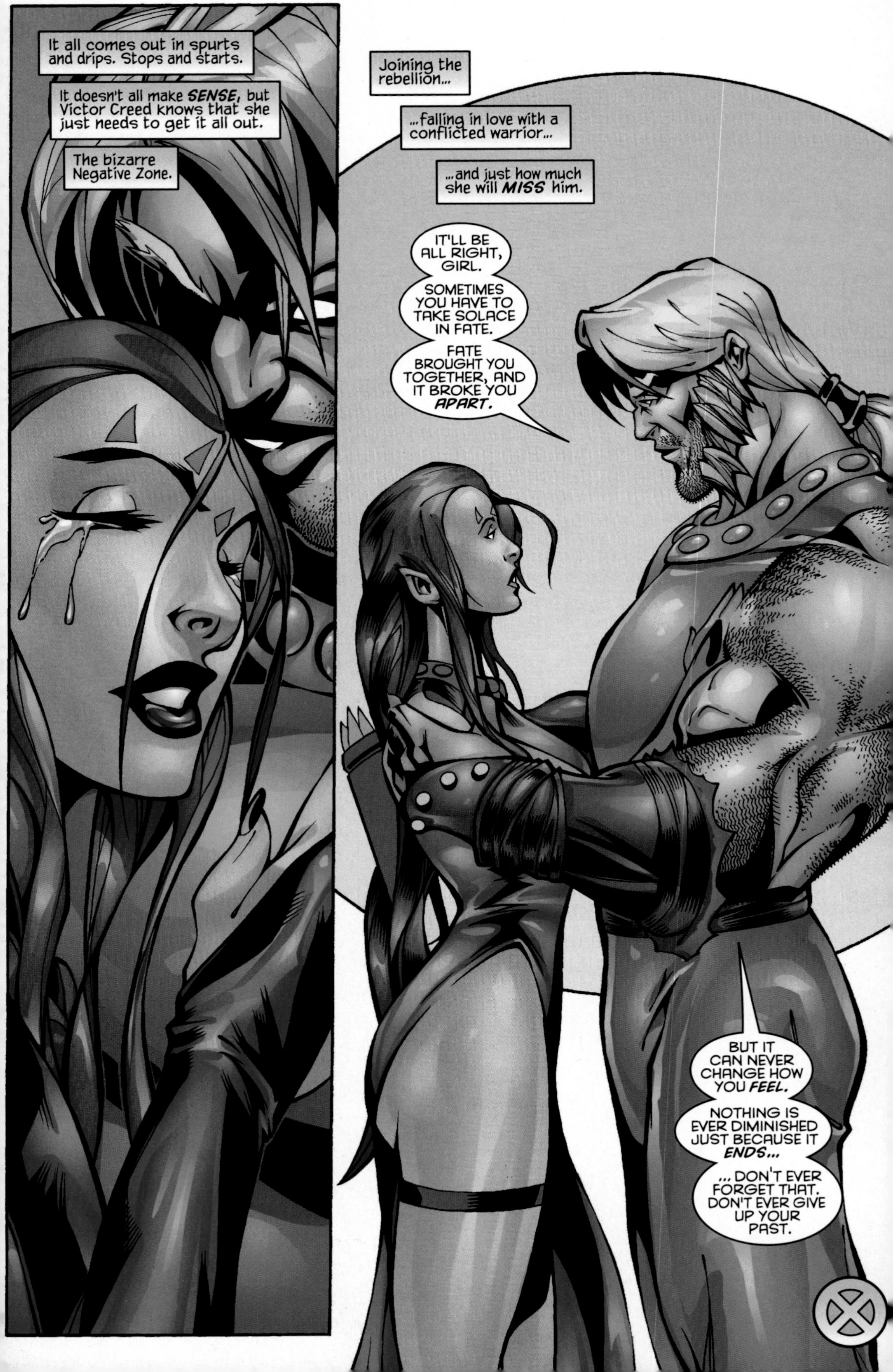
It all comes out in spurts and drips. Stops and starts.
It doesn't all make SENSE, but Victor Creed knows that she just needs to get it all out.
The bizarre Negative Zone.
Joining the rebellion...
...falling in love with a conflicted warrior...
...and just how much she will MISS him.
IT'LL BE ALL RIGHT, GIRL.
SOMETIMES YOU HAVE TO TAKE SOLACE IN FATE.
FATE BROUGHT YOU TOGETHER, AND IT BROKE YOU APART.
BUT IT CAN NEVER CHANGE HOW YOU FEEL.
NOTHING IS EVER DIMINISHED JUST BECAUSE IT ENDS...
... DON'T EVER FORGET THAT. DON'T EVER GIVE UP YOUR PAST.

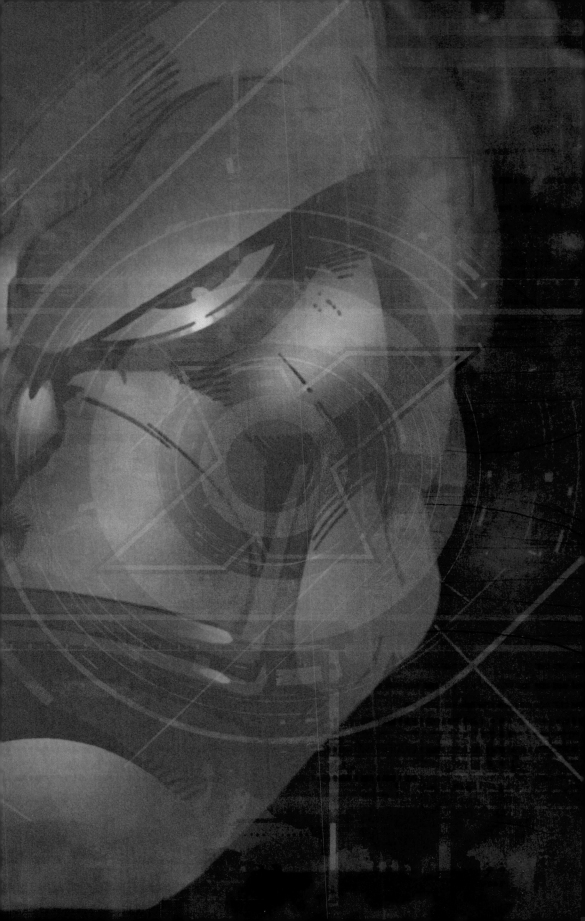

X-FACTS

January 1995

THE DREAM IS OVER...

A man who should never have died is now gone. His passing marks the loss of a world full of promise, a world of hope unfettered, and heralds the coming of a reality rife with the ravages of chaos and confusion, an age of madness and destruction.

ENTER NOW... THE AGE OF APOCALYPSE

...LET THE NIGHTMARE BEGIN!

It all began with a business trip. X-MEN Editor-In-Chief *Bob Harras* was over on the other side of the country, in the middle of a rather important meeting with the producers of FOX's hit Saturday morning X-MEN cartoon, when suddenly, he was visited by a miraculous polemic.

"What would the world be like without Professor X?"

Mulling the idea over and over, Bob finally realized what this ambitious thought meant. It meant that this was a story idea which could potentially have lasting repercussions on the X-Universe like none other. Upon his return to New York, Bob set the wheels which would become the AGE OF APOCALYPSE a'turning.

First order of business to be addressed was...'How to do the deed?' Of all the methods suggested, the one possessed of the greatest sense of urgency involved someone traveling back in time to a crucial moment in X-history that would shake the mutant universe to its very foundations had it never occurred. Thus, a time period was determined. The tragedy would occur during Xavier's days in Israel -- the time just before he set out to found the Xavier School For Gifted Youngsters. After all, if he had never achieved that goal, then there would never have been any X-Men.

Or would there?

Determined to find out, we began our search for the next piece of the puzzle -- *the murderer.*

Which agent of evil would perpetrate this most heinous crime? Villains' names were batted around, but none had the right motivation or capacity to 'pull the trigger' that would assassinate Xavier. Sure, the potential candidates all had their own unique flair for the dramatic, but not a single member of the X-Men's rogue's gallery fit the bill.

Having arrived at an impasse, a new take on the murder was suggested. Why even go after Xavier in the first place? Perhaps it wasn't Charles who had prevented the assassin from achieving his own selfish ends at all, but rather *another* figure whose very

WALL
OF
APOCALYPSE
BADLANDS
SCATTERED HUMAN HIDEOUTS
SAN FRANSISCO
CHICAGO
HOLOCAUST
ABYSS
DALLAS
APOCALYPSE ISLAND
FORMERLY NEW YORK CITY
INFERNAL
GALLOP TO
AVALON
MAIN ROUTE
PERIMETER
SECURITY PLATFORMS
UNCONFIRMED
INFERNAL GALLOP
TO AVALON
MUIR ISLAND
[SENTINEL PROCESSING PLANT ?]
MUIR ISLAND
SECURITY GRID
LONDON
CAPITAL OF HUMAN COUNCIL
SENTINEL PROCESSING PLANTS
IN GERMAN COLONIES
UNCONFIRMED
PROBABLE FLIGHT ROUTES
DESTROYED
HUMAN
SETTLEMENTS
OIL FIELDS
ATROCITY
ZONE
HIGH RAD LEVELS
TO POINT
REDEMPTION
AVALON
RECEIVING
SITES
AVALON
GENOSHA

existence irrevocably shaped this frus-trated character's life?

Like *Magneto*...

Hmnn. That presented an inter-esting twist. There seemed to be a logic to it, but who would have felt that way, and why? One very unique name was suggested, and it was at that very moment that the clock began ticking out the final days of the X-Men.

And that name was...*Legion*.

Being the son of Professor X, Legion was one of the many people whose life's course was determined by forces beyond his control, specifically the ongoing conflict between Xavier and his arch nemesis, Magneto. Had Magneto never gotten in Xavier's way, then perhaps Xavier's dream of a world where humans and mutants co-exist in peace might have come true. Instead, the two men, once the closest of friends, became the most bitter of rivals. Ultimately, neither one's vision was ever fully realized thanks to the other's incessant interference.

Finally realizing the importance of Xavier's goals, and blaming Magneto for the fact that he never got the chance to know his father, Legion would have to figure out a way to get Xavier's attention which had been distracted by his quest for a better world for so long.

And with his delusional mind lucid for the first time in his life, latent aspects of Legion's already formidable mutant powers had reached their full potential. So now he had both the method and the motivation to make thought deed and set things 'right'.

If only he hadn't killed the wrong man...

THE PLOT THICKENS

This past summer, as the techno-organic terror of the PHALANX COVENANT kept the X-teams busy sav-ing the universe, the X-MEN editorial staff conspired to undo all the work our exhausted mutants had accomplished.

Together with writers *Scott Lobdell, Fabian Nicieza, Larry Hama, John Francis Moore, Jeph Loeb, Howard Mackie* and *Mark Waid*, and pencilers *Andy* and *Adam Kubert* and *Joe Madureira*, we stole away from the hustle and bustle of the Big Apple for the serenity of the coun-try. For two steamy, summer days, we bounced around, threw out, accepted and rejected -- and ultimately *accept-ed again* -- thoughts, suggestions, feelings, questions, comments, frus-trations, agreements and dissensions.

Meanwhile, fellow creators *Chris Bachalo, Tony Daniel, Steve Epting, Warren Ellis, Ken Lashley* and *Steve Skroce* -- who couldn't

physically be with us at the conference (y'all were there in spirit, guys) -- were all hard at work in their respective stu-dios, their brains ablaze with activity.

Our collective goal...create a world gone mad, a reality so insane that the unthinkable would become so painfully real that you'd believe that you were in the middle of a Kafka-esque nightmare from which you could never wake up.

But why on earth would such a horrific reality ever exist?

Simple. Because Charles Xavier *never* founded the X-Men. And without his influence to guide the growing mutant community, and no force of good to stem the tide of evil, the time would be ripe for some of the would-be world-beaters to make their move and establish their dominion over the earth.

And that's exactly the kind of situa-tion that *Apocalypse* used to his best advantage. Seeing no opposition to his Darwinist schemes, he tested the mettle of both human and mutant alike. The end result, a world trapped beneath his boot's crushing heel.

Having come to a conclusion as to who would play the role of the heavy in this grim, new world of ours, we needed a group of heroes who would rise to challenge him.

Enter...*this reality's X-Men!*

Of all the people who would have carried the torch of peaceful coexis-tence between Homo Sapiens and Homo Superior, it seemed the most logical that Magneto would take up the mantle that Xavier was so tragically denied. After all, he bore witness to Xavier's murder at a time before the two men ever became adversaries, and since he himself was Legion's *intended* target, it was the last, best way for him to honor their friendship and his late friend's memory.

RADICAL REFLECTIONS

Of course, the next step was figur-ing out who would go where...and why...and what for! If reality were turned on its ear, would heroes *still* be heroes? Heck, we're not dealing with a carbon-copy dimension here, so it's very possible that even the most upstanding of champions in our reality would be a base villain in this new one. Lovers in our world might be mortal enemies here. Characters who have lost their lives may be alive and well...

The list of similarities and differ-ences goes on and on, but no matter what the world may become, there will always be a band of heroes willing to fight for the dream of peaceful coex-istence between humans and mutants.

For in every reality, there remains one constant...*and that's the X-Men*.

The Wish List

ASTONISHING X-MEN #1:

X-MAN #1:

GENERATION NEXT #1:

WEAPON X #1:

X-CALIBRE #1:

AMAZING X-MEN #1:

FACTOR X #1:

GAMBIT & THE X-TERNALS #1:

X-MEN CHRONICLES #1:

X·MEN GALLERY

— VISIONS OF A SHATTERED WORLD —

BEAST JAN CHURCHILL
JAMES PASCOE

MAGNETO / TOM GRUMMETT
ROGUE MATTHEW RYAN

WEAPON-X JAE LEE

FACTOR-X BRYAN HITCH
PAUL NEARY

X-MEN IAN CHURCHILL
TIM TOWNSEND

X-TERNALS TONY DANIEL
KEVIN CONRAD

**GENERATION
NEXT** PAUL SMITH

ANGEL VAL SEMEIKS
BOB McLEOD

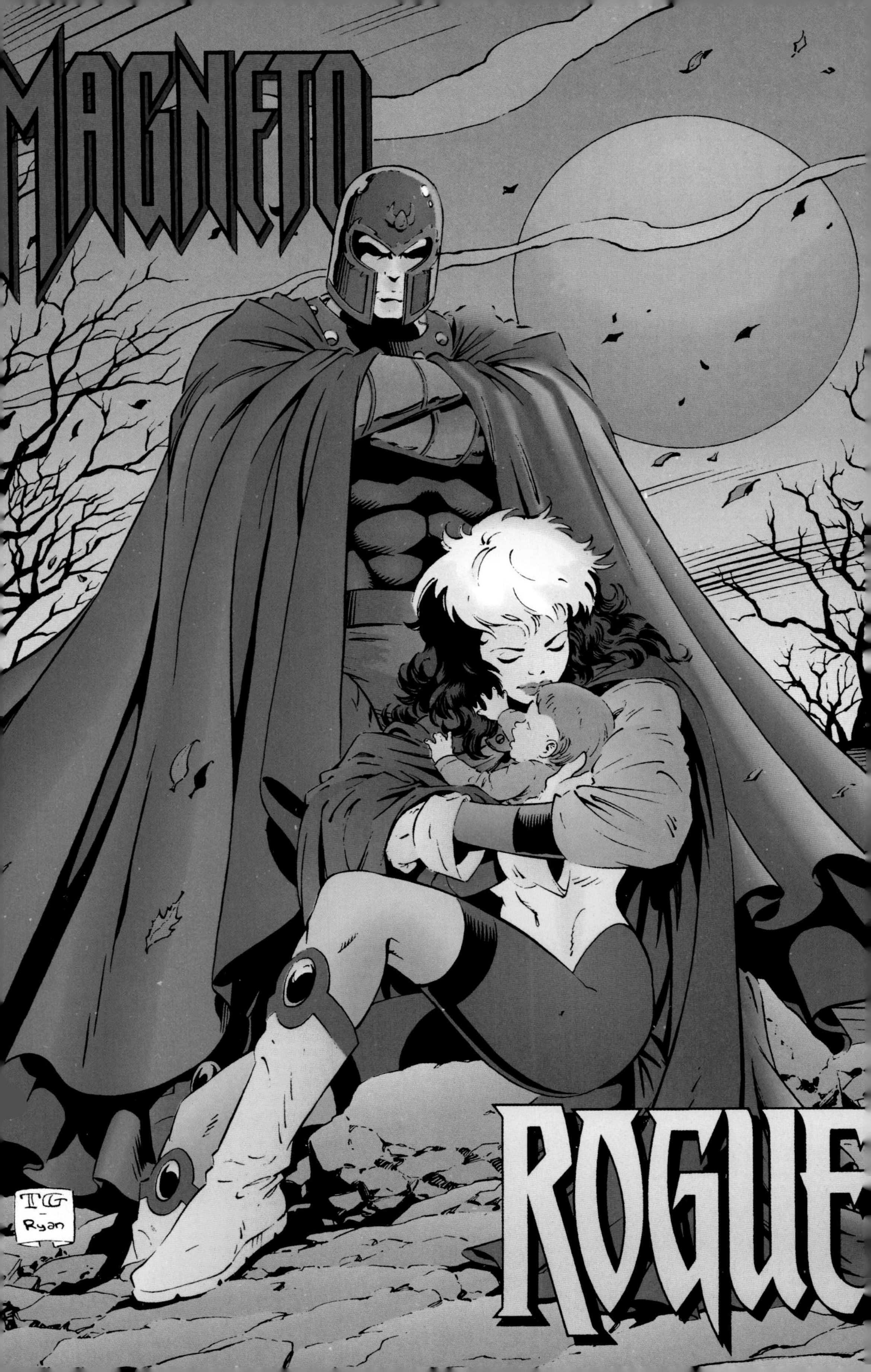
MAGNETO
ROGUE
TG
Ryan

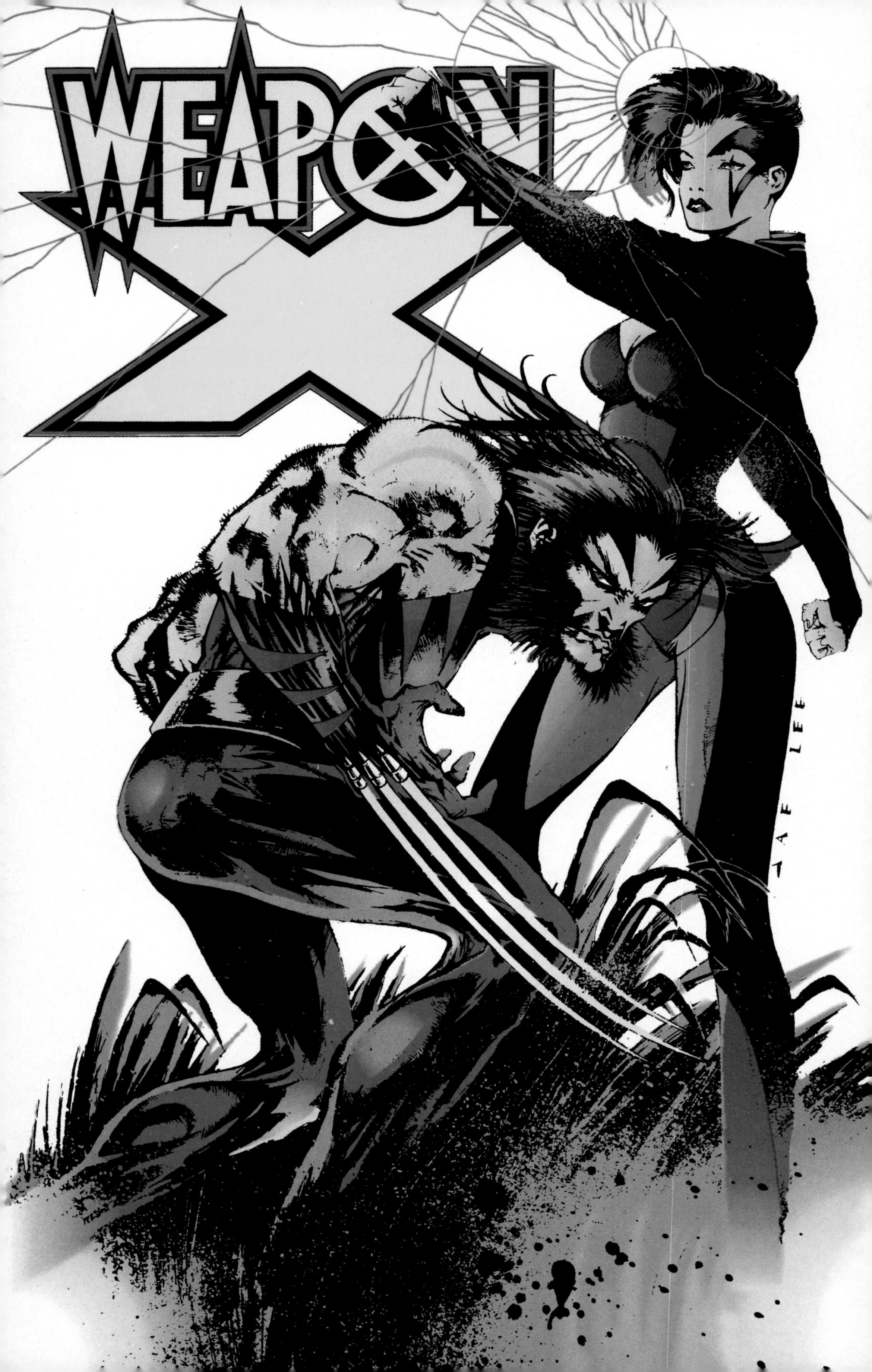
WEAPON X

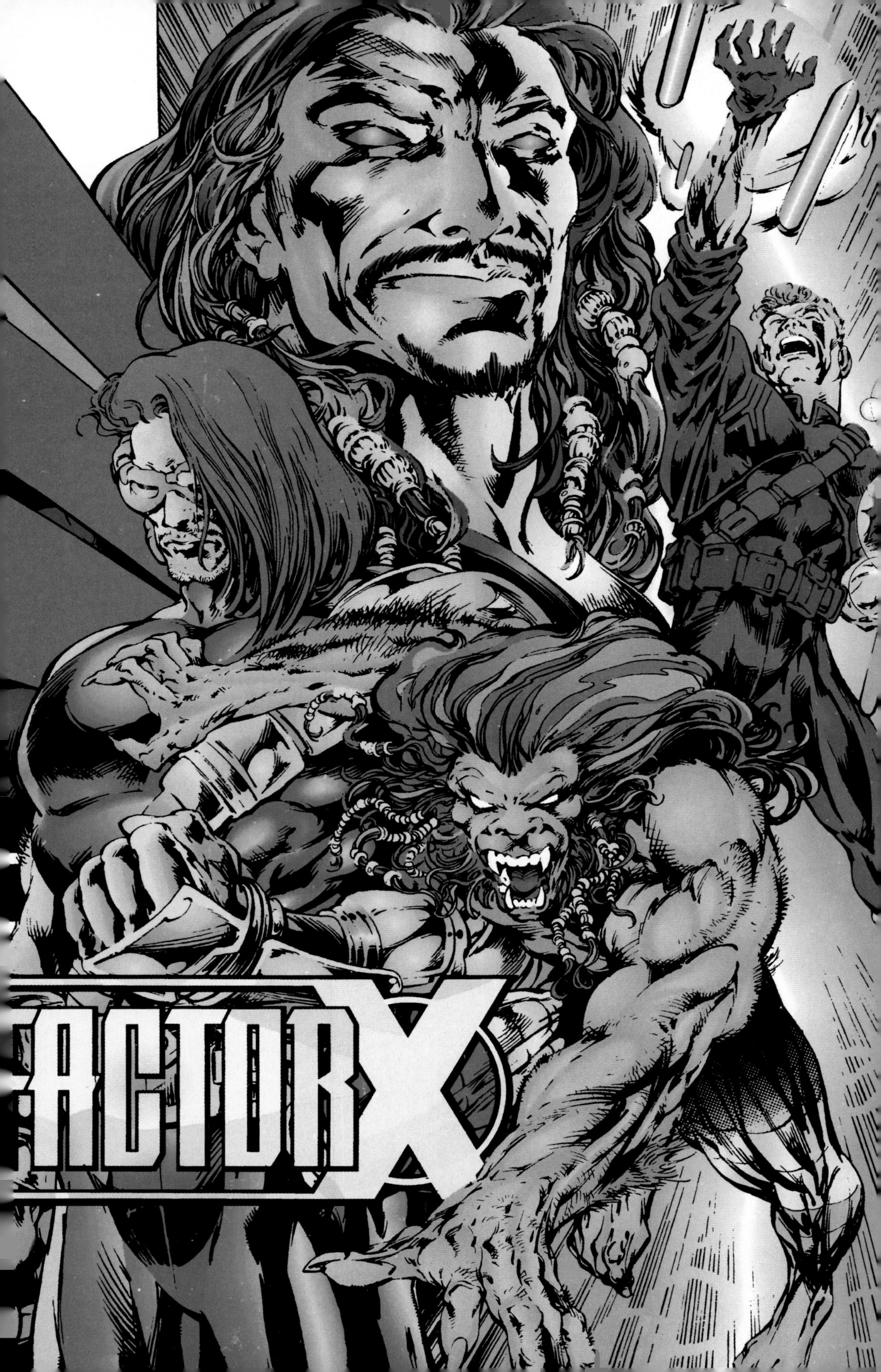
ACTOR X

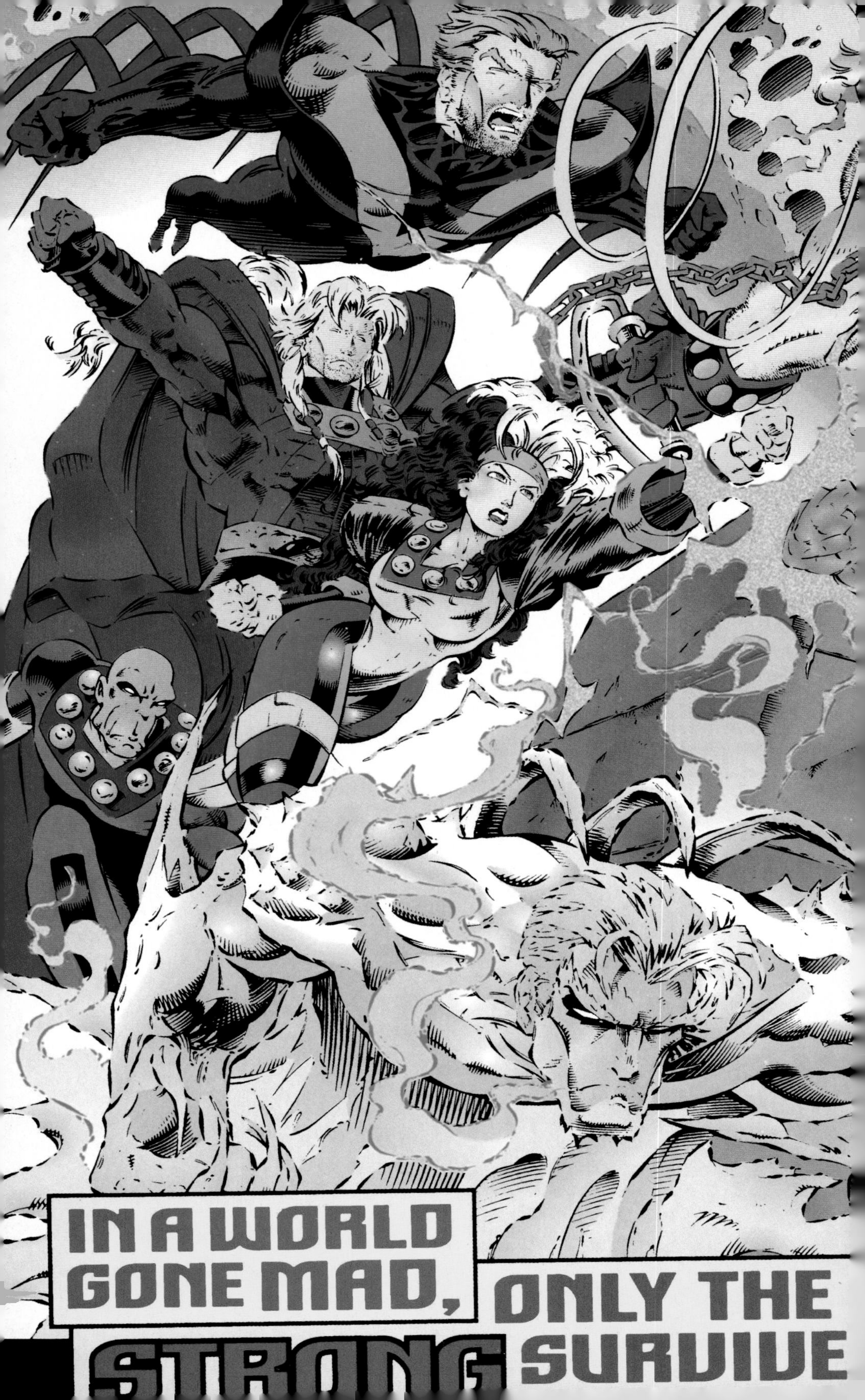
IN A WORLD GONE MAD,
ONLY THE STRONG SURVIVE

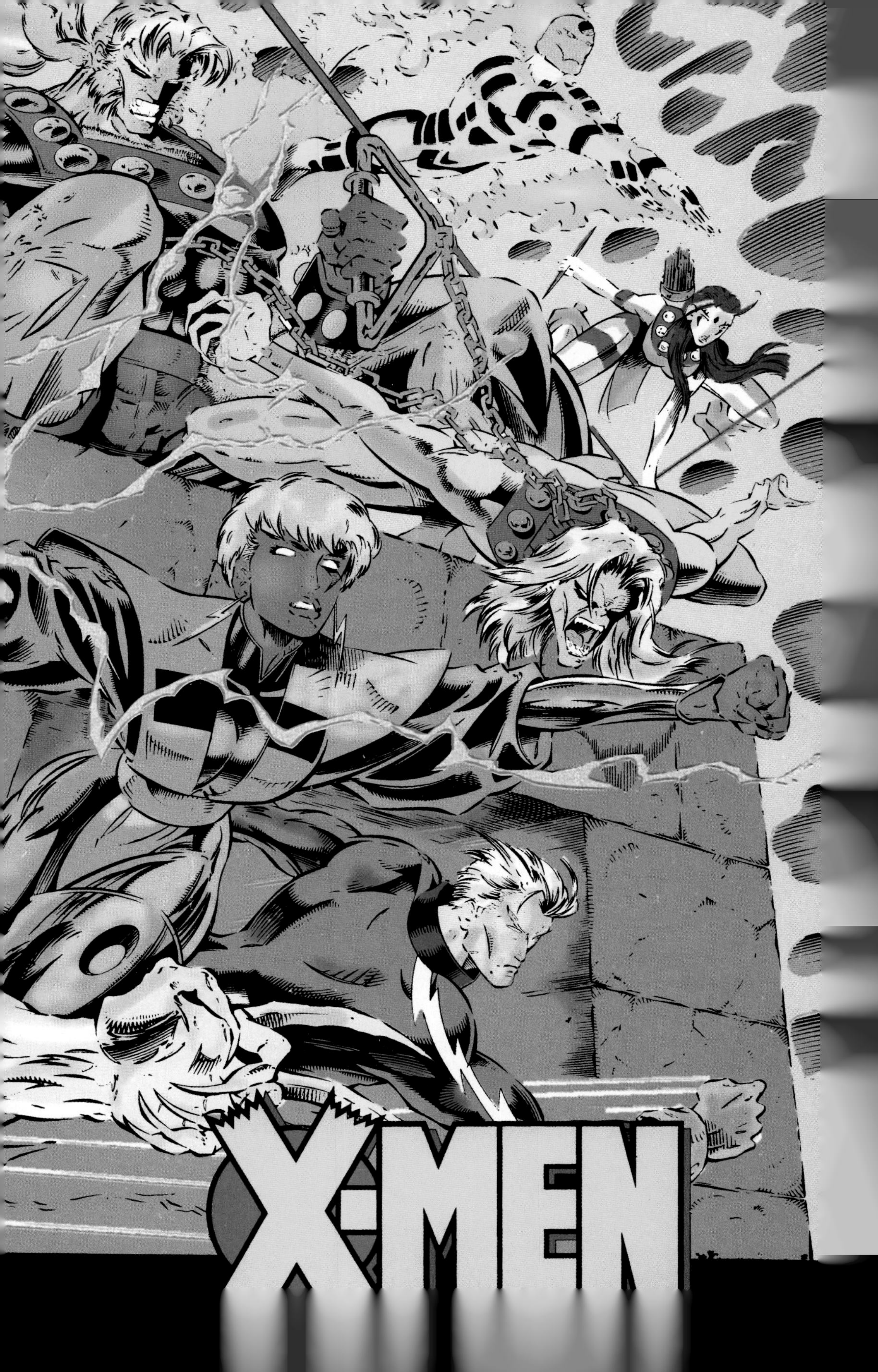
X-MEN

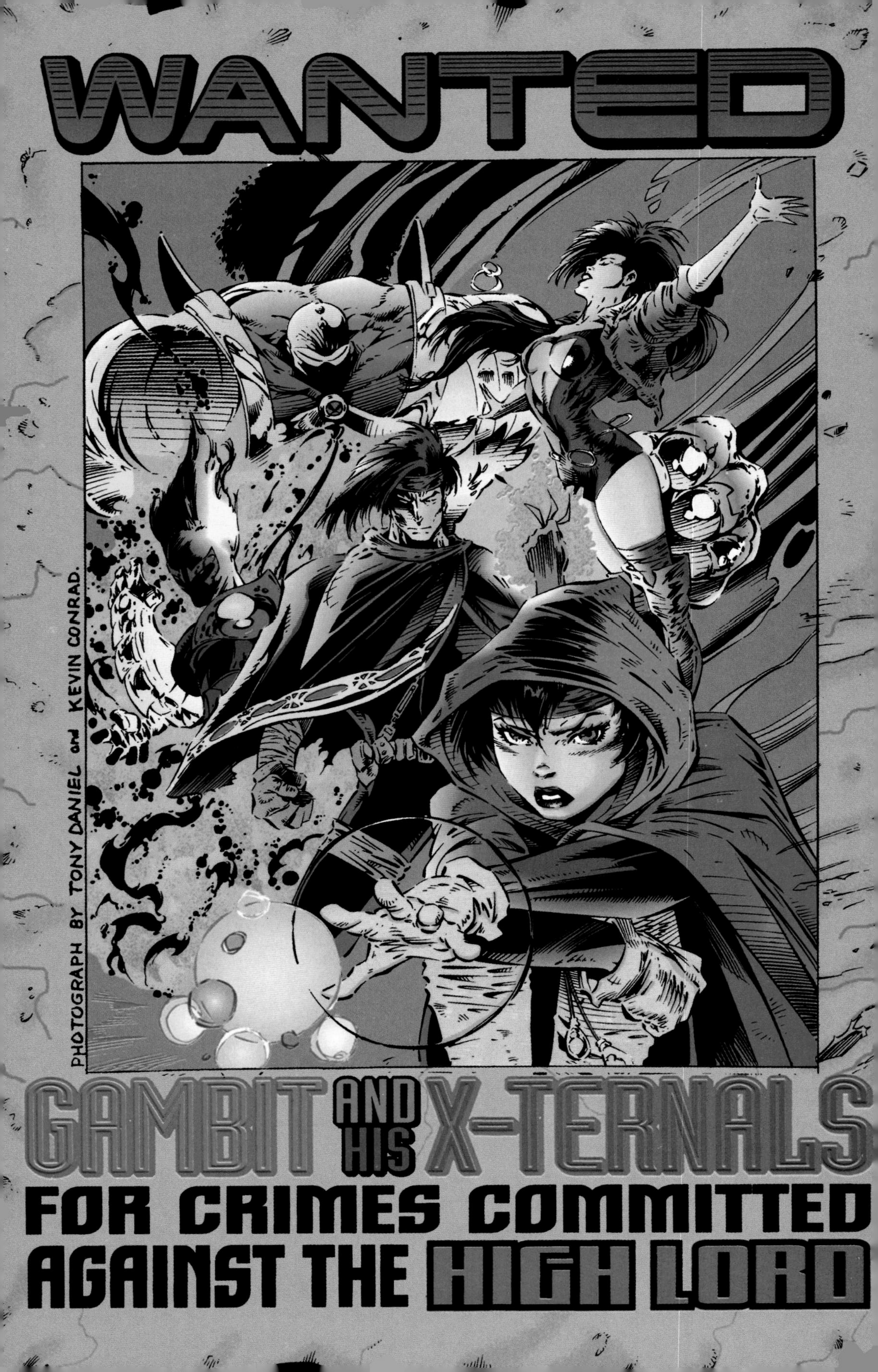
WANTED
PHOTOGRAPH BY TONY DANIEL and KEVIN CONRAD.
GAMBIT AND HIS X-TERNALS
FOR CRIMES COMMITTED
AGAINST THE HIGH LORD

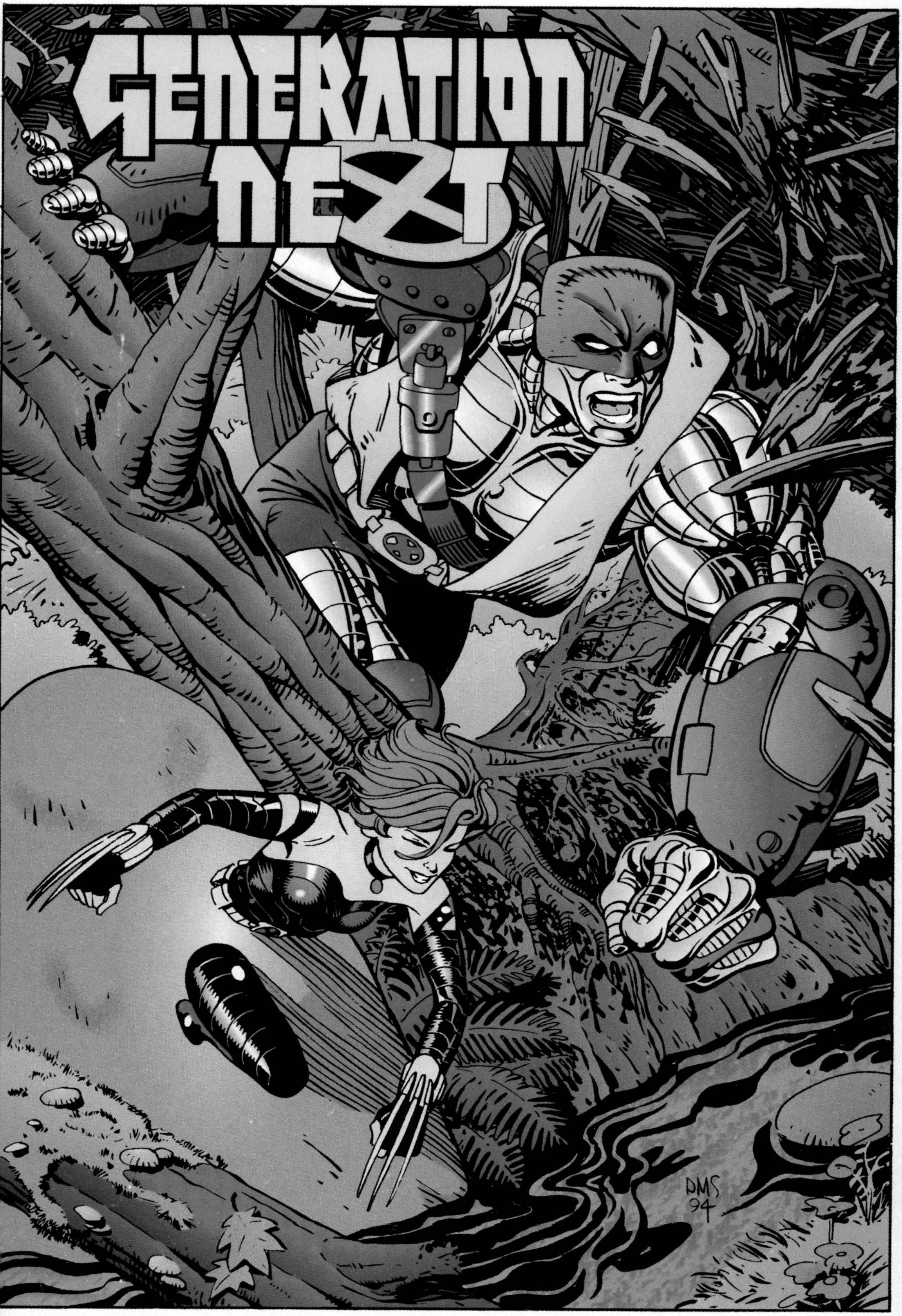
GENERATION NEXT
DMS 94

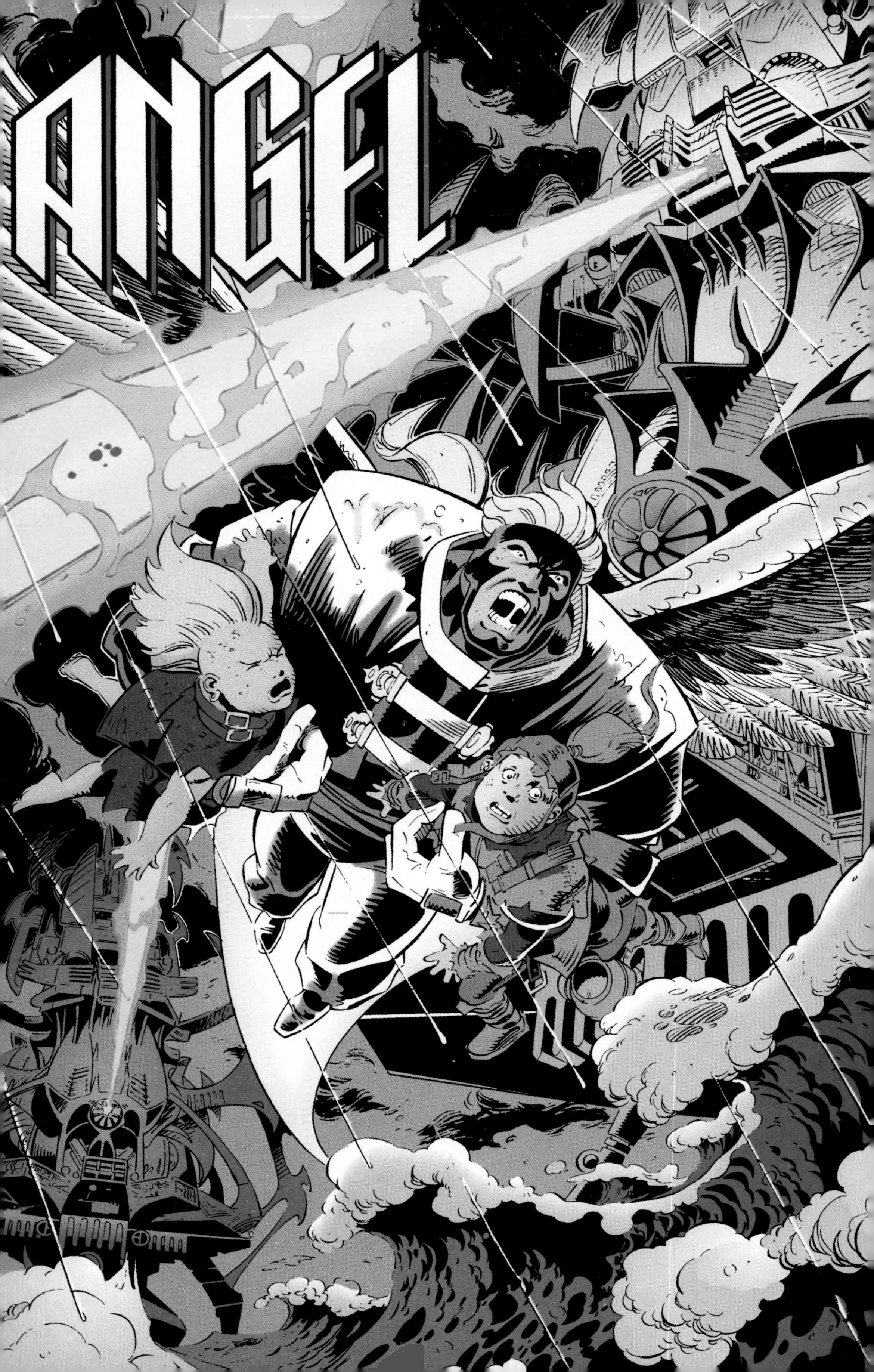
ANGEL

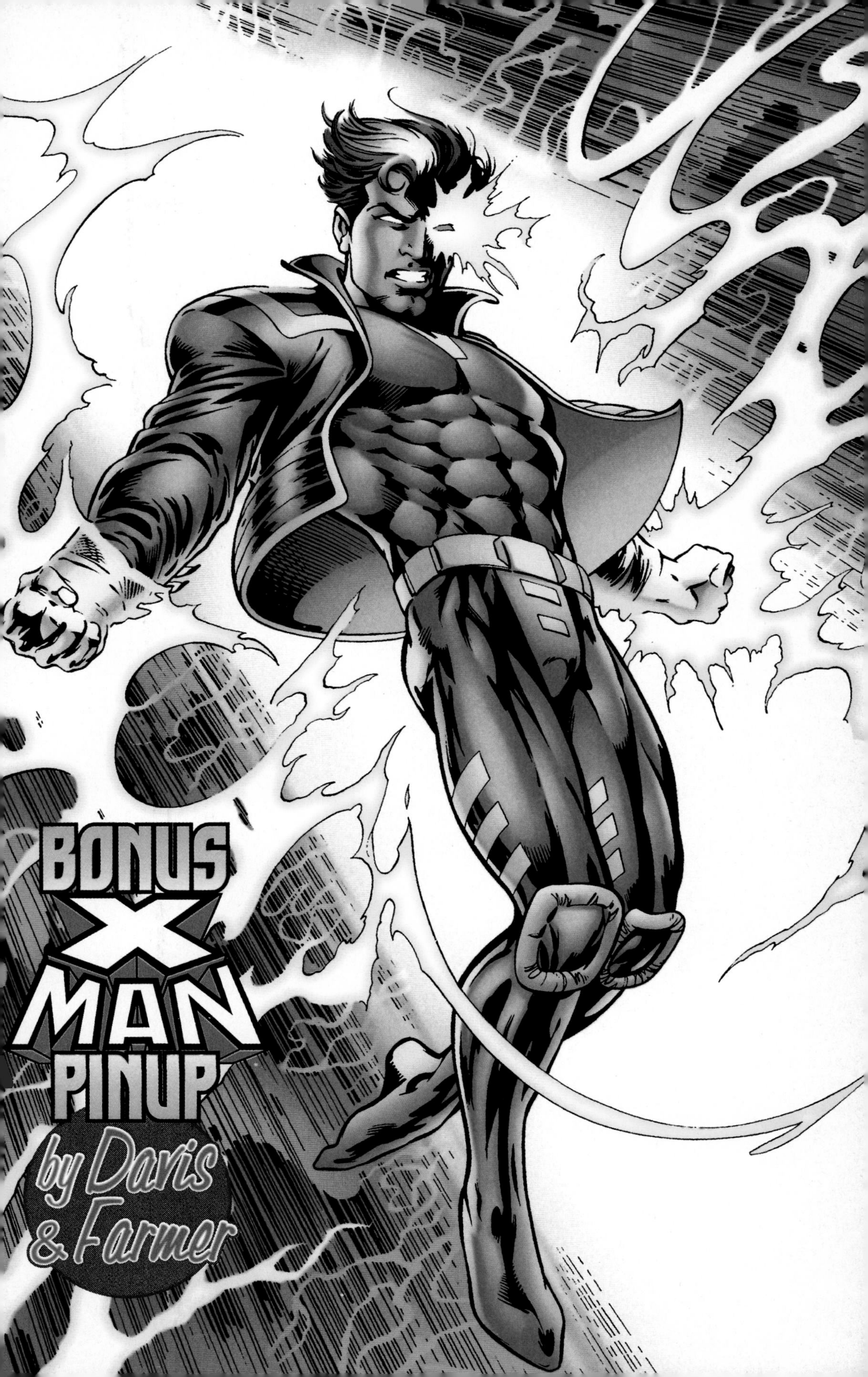
BONUS
X
MAN
PINUP
by Davis
& Farmer

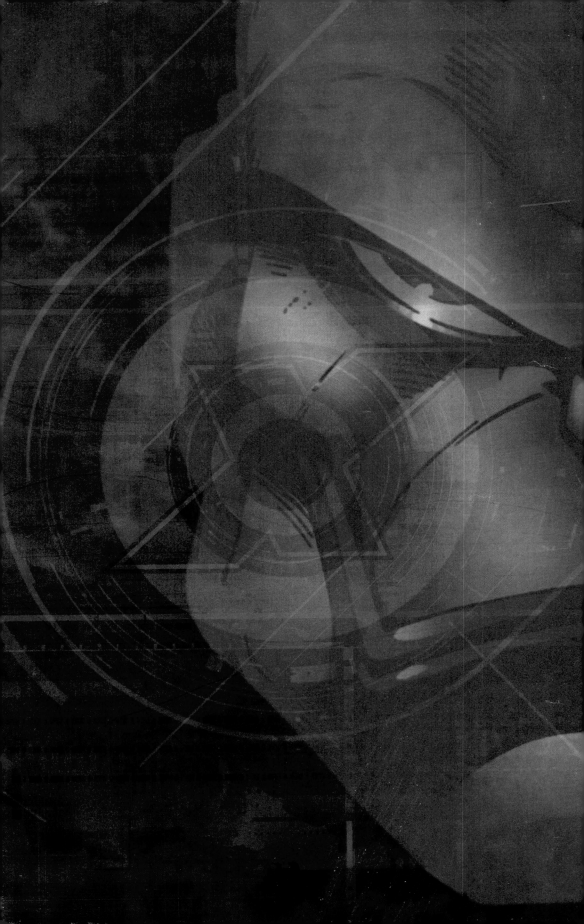